Karen P. Corrigan
Linguistic Communities and Migratory Processes

Topics in English Linguistics

Editors
Susan M. Fitzmaurice
Bernd Kortmann
Elizabeth Closs Traugott

Volume 106

Karen P. Corrigan

Linguistic Communities and Migratory Processes

—

Newcomers Acquiring Sociolinguistic Variation
in Northern Ireland

DE GRUYTER
MOUTON

ISBN 978-3-11-099156-7
e-ISBN (PDF) 978-3-11-061419-0
e-ISBN (EPUB) 978-3-11-061157-1

Library of Congress Control Number: 2020939973

Bibliographic information published by the Deutsche Nationalbibliothek
The Deutsche Nationalbibliothek lists this publication in the Deutsche Nationalbibliografie;
detailed bibliographic data are available on the Internet at http://dnb.dnb.de.

© 2022 Walter de Gruyter GmbH, Berlin/Boston
This volume is text- and page-identical with the hardback published in 2020.
Typesetting: raumfisch.de/sign, Berlin
Printing and binding: CPI books GmbH, Leck

www.degruyter.com

For Frank, who willingly gave up our time for this and with whom I would likely not have had the good fortune to share my life, if he hadn't been a return migrant whose foreign accent intrigued me.

Preface

This book deals with the linguistic consequences of migratory processes from both diachronic and synchronic perspectives. The regional focus is the island of Ireland with particular emphasis on Ulster in the north but diasporic varieties of Irish English are also included. These are captured in historical correspondence corpora documented in Amador-Moreno (2019) and McCafferty & Amador-Moreno (2012a) as well as Fitzpatrick (1994). Historical databases created by the author for previous projects will similarly be put to new uses here. The work also interrogates extensive recordings of contemporary Mid-Ulster English which have been compiled *ab initio* specifically for this purpose from sociolinguistic interviews that the author undertook with local and migrant youngsters in three distinctive locations of Northern Ireland between 2012 and 2014.

Part I takes a novel, inter-disciplinary approach drawing on models and methods first established in historical studies, geography and sociology to offer insights into how population movements impact upon the language ecologies of both sending and receiving countries. It begins with an analysis of the corpora already noted to evaluate key concepts which have been developed in migration theory. That first chapter has two over-arching aims: (i) To determine whether there is robust evidence in the aforementioned diachronic and synchronic corpora of the migration patterns argued for in the scholarly literature; (ii) To provide a new framework for correlating population flows and language ecologies which is then explored in the following chapters. While the analysis pertains particularly to the island of Ireland today and in the distant past, the findings are shown to also resonate in other communities where intensive phases of migration have been intrinsic to their development. I take a chronological approach here beginning with immigration to Ulster during the Mesolithic period and ending with that which characterises more recent times. At the forefront of the discussion in all subsequent chapters of Part I is the interrelationship between migratory movements and their diverse linguistic consequences. Important issues that are addressed is the extent to which the nature of migration has changed over time and whether that, in turn, has impacted upon the degree to which language ecologies can actually be affected.

Part II takes the model a step further by honing in on the specifics of the language contact opportunities afforded by migration for both individuals and societies. Chapter Five therein begins by evaluating and testing on the corpus data already introduced a range of frameworks that have been developed to account for the acquisition of first and second languages as well as language shift scenarios in which the former can attrite when the right social circumstances prevail. Chapter Six details and critiques the data collection methods, protocols and fieldwork techniques associated with the compilation of the contemporary Mid-Ulster English corpus. The latter is then interrogated in Chapters Seven through Nine to uncover the benchmark patterns of variation and change that obtain with respect to features from different modules of the local grammar, i.e. variability with respect to the {-ing} suffix; relative markers and the system of quotation. Although much scholarly attention has been devoted to these variables elsewhere in the English-speaking world, they have never before been examined in this dialect using the comparative sociolinguistic approach advocated here (see Tagliamonte 2004a). Speech samples from matched cohorts of new migrants whose first languages are Lithuanian and Polish, respectively, are then compared so as to assess whether they have acquired similar internal and external constraints on the variation observed. Key research questions explored in Part II would thus include: (i) Do ethnolinguistic minorities maintain their community languages?; (ii) Is the learning of first or second languages different in any respect and how might this be explained?; (iii) What evidence is there of substratal transfer from Lithuanian and Polish and is this factor worth considering more systematically in comparative accounts of how variation is acquired by L2 speakers?; (iv) Can the methods advocated within comparative sociolinguistics be applied to determine not only the extent to which global indigenized varieties do or do not relate to one another but also whether diverse learner Englishes can be explored using the same model?; (v) Are variables from different linguistic modules acquired more or less readily by learners?; (vi) Does it matter whether the dependent variable being learned is stable or not?

Acknowledgements

This volume was only made possible by a Leadership Fellowship grant (reference AH/K008285/1) awarded to the author under the Connected Communities cross-council scheme led by the UK's Arts and Humanities Research Council (AHRC). The programme aimed to improve our understanding of both the changing nature of communities in their historical and cultural contexts as well as their role in sustaining and enhancing our quality of life. The project was entitled *"Múin Béarla do na Leanbháin" ('Teach the Children English'): Migration as a Prism for Viewing Ethnolinguistic Vitality in Northern Ireland* (2014–2016). Its title was inspired by that of Corrigan (1992) which focused on the link between emigration and the loss of the Irish language. The research analysed personal accounts of negative linguistic attitudes captured in responses to a questionnaire on Irish emigration to America. The extract itself and its implications are discussed further in Chapter Three. Gael Linn (GL) and the Mellon Centre for Migration Studies (MCMS) acted as project partners for the AHRC award, providing expertise as well as access to their collections and resources. I am particularly grateful to Réamonn Ó Ciaráin (GL) and staff at MCMS, (especially Johanne Devlin Trew, Ann Duffy, Patrick Fitzgerald, Christine Johnstone, Brian Lambkin and Catherine McCullough). Heartfelt thanks also to Carolina Amador-Moreno, David Fitzpatrick and Kevin McCafferty for permission to undertake new analyses on the historical correspondence corpora they have digitised. The volume has also been greatly enhanced by the original drawing or re-drawing of maps, a task willingly undertaken by Chris Montgomery whose digital cartographic skills proved second to none. Other archival texts, images and resources have been kindly provided by Séan Barden, Armagh County Museum; Rebecca Geddes, Public Record Office of Northern Ireland; Paul Johnson, The National Archives at Kew; Críostóir MacCarthaigh of the Department of Irish Folklore, University College, Dublin; Sinéad Murphy and Raymond Russell, Northern Ireland Assembly; Tom Quinlan, The National Archives of Ireland and Angus Wark, National Library of Scotland.

The AHRC award permitted Adam Mearns and Jennifer Thorburn to not only backfill my post at Newcastle University so I could undertake the fieldwork but also to act as post-doctoral research associates on different aspects of this enterprise. I am deeply indebted to them therefore for their various efforts on my behalf. My employer accommodated the writing-up phase of the volume by providing a sabbatical in Spring 2018 and my head of school (James Annesley) and co-workers have been extremely supportive both practically and intellectually since the project was first conceived. I am indebted, for example, to Mei Lin who helped me grapple with the multilingual text in Chapter Five illustrating translanguaging amongst Chinese Singaporeans.

Considerable thanks are also due to my teams of coders, copy-editors, research assistants, transcribers and translators including: Emily Armstrong, Andrew Boreland, Peter Browning, Mary Carr, Beth Clark, Emma Corteen, Eileen Coughlan, Holly Crudace, Chloé Diskin, Ciara Dowling, Juliet Dunstone, Daniel Jordan, Frank Benno Junghanns, Frances Kane, Olivia Koh, Hannah Leach, John Lonergan, Catherine Mairs, Jennifer Martyn, Sophia McBride, Ewelina Marciniak, Louise Middleton, Shannon Monks, Donald Morrison, Grace Omerod, Liam Owens, Beth Ralston, Laura Richards, Eleanor Robert, Christian Ilbury, Persephone Soulsby, Simon Statham, Terence Szymanski, Nicola Telfer, Lauren Tonge-Ward, John Weston and Sophie Winter.

Special thanks is owed to Ineta Dabašinskienė, Violeta Kalėdaitė, Frances Kane, Laura Kamandulytė-Merfeldiene, Gosia Krzek, Gosia Pociask, Meilutė Ramonienė and Magda Sztencel for fruitful exchanges on the structure of Irish, Lithuanian and Polish.

Aspects of this book have benefited greatly too from stimulating interactions on topics that it explores, i.e. language acquisition, contact, ecology, history, transmission and variation with colleagues and friends in these fields whose own work I greatly admire. They include Dave Britain, Jack Chambers, Jenny Cheshire, Janice Carruthers, Chloé Diskin, Alex D'Arcy, Enda Delaney, the late Terence Dolan, Rob Drummond, Markku Filppula, Sue Fox, Jeff Kallen, Margaret Kelleher, Stephen Levey, Warren Maguire, the late Jim Milroy, Lesley Milroy, Philip McDermott, Gerardine Meaney, Miriam Meyerhoff, Bettina Migge, Dennis Preston, Vera Regan, Erik Schleef, Antonella Sorace, Jeff Siegel, Jen Smith, Sali Tagliamonte, Peter Trudgill and James Walker. I am likewise grateful to Carolina Amador-Moreno, Paul Kerswill and Lesley Jeffries who offered suggestions on draft chapters. Joan Beal volunteered invaluable comments on an early version of the entire manuscript for which I will forever be in her debt. This mammoth task was also undertaken by Bernd Kortmann, my link editor for this series, and both he, alongside Elizabeth Traugott, gave me tremendous support in shaping the volume at proposal stage too. Barbara Karlson, Julie Miess and Anne Rudolph of De Gruyter have been very patient and accommodating editors and thanks in various other practical ways are also due to Ismeta Brdar, Alison Downie, Jane Jamieson and Melanie McAinsh.

I would similarly like to acknowledge the important input from all the educators who discussed the evolution of Northern Ireland's education system with me and the impact upon it of the recent demolinguistic and political changes described in Chapter Four as well as the changing priorities stemming from UK government-imposed austerity measures and the stalemate at Stormont. I would particularly like to mention here Dera Cahalane, Paul Carlin, Dolores Considine (RIP), Noelle Corrigan, Roisin Harbinson, Michael Keenan, Bronagh Mallon, Orla

Grimley, Louise Lynch, Séamus MacDaibhéid, Nan MacKinnon, Deirdre McDonald, Laura McGlone, Catherine McHugh, Niall McParland, Jack and Eithné O'Hare as well as Katrina Thompson.

The can-do attitude of Frances Kane and Kate Mairs has never failed me in our attempts to translate this research into forms that have relevance to the public. This engagement has brought tangible benefits to educators, the heritage sector and society at large which have, in turn, had really positive impacts on changing views about how migrants are perceived across Northern Ireland (see examples in Amador-Moreno, Corrigan, McCafferty & Moreton 2016).

The extensive fieldwork which underpins this research was enabled by the support of my late brother-in-law, my sister-in-law and immediate family in Northern Ireland who not only fed and housed me but shared their contacts (and intuitions) too. Many thanks also go to my husband, Frank, who facilitated my criss-crossing back and forth across the Irish Sea in any way he could.

I am so grateful as well to the administrative/teaching staff, parents and principals at participating schools in Armagh, Belfast and Donaghmore who hosted me for long spells at a time and extended a genuine *céad míle fáilte*. Naturally, I am enormously thankful to all my young participants for sharing not only their voices but also for regaling me with their tales of *barmbrack, bacalhau* and *borscht* when they twigged that I had tired of 'Minecraft' and 'Frozen'.

On a rather more personal note, there are no words to really convey the debt I owe to my parents who themselves experienced the negativity of being Northern Irish migrants in 1950's London while they were training. Despite this, when they returned home to marry they still held the view that *ar scáth a chéile a mhaireann na daoine* 'people live protected under one another's shadow' which they then instilled in me. This volume is first and foremost an intellectual endeavour, of course, but at its heart is a celebration of this 'connected communities' mentality which I hold very dear.

Contents

Preface —— VII

Acknowledgements —— IX

Part I: Migration and language ecologies

1	**Population movements: impetus and process —— 3**	
1.1	Migration theory: an introduction —— 3	
1.2	Typologies of migration and motivating factors —— 4	
1.3	Internal and external migration —— 4	
1.4	Stepwise versus linear migration —— 7	
1.5	Chain migration, pioneers and followers —— 12	
1.6	Voluntary or forced migration? —— 16	
1.7	Synthesis and prospects —— 19	

2 Migration and language ecology: pre-history to Cromwell —— 21
2.1 Language ecologies of prehistoric and early Christian peoples (9000BC–AD1000) —— 21
2.1.1 Settlement during the Mesolithic period and the Bronze Age —— 21
2.1.2 Migration and contact in the Iron Age and early Christian periods —— 21
2.1.2.1 Migration and the formation of new linguistic ecologies in the Christian period —— 23
2.2 Mobility and language in the Medieval and Tudor periods (1177–1602) —— 25
2.2.1 Anglo-Norman and Bruce invasions —— 25
2.2.2 Migration and plantation in the Tudor era —— 28
2.3 The linguistic repercussions of Medieval and Tudor migrants —— 31
2.4 Jacobite colonisation and plantation schemes —— 34
2.4.1 Linguistic repercussions —— 39

3 Migration and language ecology: enlightenment to famine —— 49
3.1 Overview —— 49
3.2 Population distribution and its impact on language ecology during the age of enlightenment —— 50
3.3 Population decline and mobility in the nineteenth century —— 55
3.4 Linguistic repercussions —— 60

4	**Migration and language ecology: partition to globalisation —— 64**	
4.1	Internal and transnational migration in the twentieth century —— 64	
4.1.1	Migration and language ecology in the twentieth century —— 75	
4.2	Immigration and the rise of a superdiverse society in the twenty-first century —— 81	
4.2.1	Migration and language ecology in the twenty-first century —— 90	
4.2.1.1	Language revitalisation planning: the Irish language and Ulster Scots —— 91	
4.2.1.2	Language planning and new speakers of Northern Irish English —— 100	
4.3	The globalisation of Northern Ireland: retrospects and prospects —— 118	

Part II: Migration, acquisition and change

5	**Processes of language contact, shift and acquisition —— 123**	
5.1	Language contact and shift —— 123	
5.1.1	Bilingualism and multilingualism *versus* polylingualism, translanguaging and metrolingualism —— 123	
5.1.2	First language attrition —— 130	
5.1.3	Language contact effects on the second language —— 136	
5.2	Acquiring linguistic and sociolinguistic competence —— 145	
5.2.1	The "Fourth Wave" of analytic practice in variationist linguistics —— 145	
5.2.2	Critical periods in second language acquisition and variationist linguistics —— 159	
5.2.2.1	Early and late acquirers of additional language —— 159	
5.2.2.2	Incrementation and stabilization —— 160	
5.2.3	Acquiring sociolinguistic variation —— 163	
6	**Fieldwork, data collection methods and research tools —— 168**	
6.1	Fieldwork sites —— 168	
6.1.1	History and socio-cultural context of Armagh, Donaghmore and Belfast —— 170	
6.1.1.1	Armagh City —— 173	
6.1.1.2	Donaghmore village —— 176	
6.1.1.3	Belfast City —— 180	
6.1.2	Sociocultural context of participating schools —— 186	
6.1.2.1	Post-primaries: St. Benedict's and St. Celine's, Armagh —— 186	
6.1.2.2	Primaries: St. Agnes's, Belfast and St. Peter's, Donaghmore —— 188	

6.2	The *Múin Béarla* corpus —— 189
6.2.1	Context of the interviews —— 189
6.2.2	Recording and transcription —— 195
6.2.3	Participants —— 198
6.3	Multivariate analysis —— 203

7   Hitt(ING) an Armagh Target —— 210
7.1	Setting the scene —— 210
7.1.1	The origins of (ING) variability in Armagh English —— 210
7.1.2	The origins of (ING) variability in newcomer English —— 215
7.1.3	Language-internal constraints —— 219
7.1.4	Language-external constraints —— 220
7.2	Research questions and methodology —— 226
7.3	Results and discussion —— 229
7.3.1	Frequency distribution of (ING) variants —— 229
7.3.2	Constraints on (ING) —— 232

8   No taming the Armagh vernacular either —— 237
8.1	Setting the scene —— 237
8.1.1	The origins of relative clause variability in Armagh English —— 238
8.1.2	Ancillary strategies in the history of English —— 239
8.1.3	Relative marking strategies in the history of English —— 241
8.2	Relative formation strategies in L1 and L2 English vernaculars —— 244
8.2.1	Relative formation strategies in global Englishes —— 244
8.2.2	Relative formation strategies in Irish English —— 246
8.2.3	The origins of relative clause variability in newcomer English —— 249
8.3	Research questions, methodology and constraints —— 252
8.4	Results and discussion —— 255
8.4.1	Relativizing strategy variants in the *Múin Béarla* corpus —— 255
8.4.2	Distribution of relativizing variants in *Múin Béarla* —— 256
8.4.3	Internal linguistic constraints on Armagh relativizing strategies —— 260
8.4.4	External social constraints on Armagh relativizing strategies —— 265

9   Going global and sounding hyperlocal in Armagh —— 272
9.1	'Blow-ins', relics and the like: How quotation developed in Mid-Ulster English —— 273
9.2	The quotative systems of Mid-Ulster and other vernacular Englishes —— 279
9.2.1	(BE LIKE) *et al.* beyond Armagh —— 279
9.2.2	The quotative systems of Irish English vernaculars —— 283

9.3	Quotative systems and contact —— 288
9.4	Research questions, methodology and constraints —— 293
9.5	Results and discussion —— 296
9.5.1	Quotative introducers in the *Múin Béarla* corpus —— 296
9.5.2	Distribution of quotative introducers —— 298
9.5.2.1	Local English varieties —— 298
9.5.2.2	Newcomer varieties —— 301
9.5.3	Internal linguistic constraints on quotative introducers —— 304
9.5.4	External linguistic constraints on quotative introducers —— 310
10	**Population movements: sociolinguistic consequences —— 315**
10.1	Superdiversity then and now —— 315
10.2	Substrate effects —— 317
10.3	Constraints, complexity and acquisition —— 319
10.4	Language as a social symbol —— 323
10.5	Concluding remarks —— 327

References —— 329

Language index —— 386

Subject index —— 389

Part I: Migration and language ecologies

1 Population movements: impetus and process

"... man hat Arbeitskräfte gerufen, und es kommen Menschen" ['... they have called for a workforce and human beings are arriving'] (Max Frisch in Berwald, Olaf (ed.) 2013. *A Companion to the Works of Max Frisch*, 223. New York: Boydell & Brewer.)

1.1 Migration theory: an introduction

The Swiss playwright and novelist, Max Frisch, made this comment about the appalling treatment in Switzerland's history of economic migrants like those who have flocked to Northern Ireland in their droves during the 2000s. While I agree with Castles (2010: 1567) that population flows fuelled by fiscal inequalities have indeed been a driving force in the promotion of social change from the earliest times to the present day, it is also important to recognize the differences between the transnational migration patterns of today's globalized world and those which characterize earlier periods. Canagarajah (2017: 2), drawing on concepts such as Vertovec's (2007, 2014) notion of "superdiversity", argues that the geopolitical, social and technological advances associated with the twenty-first century have created societies in which temporal and spatial boundaries and the individual relationships contracted within these are more fluid than ever before. Part I of this book thus documents the profound economic, linguistic and sociopolitical transformations which mobility in the context of the North of Ireland have induced. It also highlights the extent to which there are similarities or differences between historical and contemporary population movements regarding the degree to which migration has invoked such change at the individual and societal levels (see Czaika and de Haas 2015: 284). I argue that while migration is far from a new process, its intensity and characteristics in modern times – from a European perspective particularly – has increased the capacity for engendering language contact of novel types because it is grounded in new technology as well as language practices which scholars have variously labelled "metrolingualism" (Pennycook and Otsuji 2015), "plurilingualism" (García 2009) and "translanguaging" (Blackledge and Creese 2017) *inter alia*. These notions will also be discussed further here and in Part II alongside analyses of the linguistic consequences of contact in the twenty-first century between indigenous groups and diverse types of migrant "new speaker" of Northern Irish English (after Ó Murchadha *et al.* 2018: 4 and see also Bermingham 2018).

1.2 Typologies of migration and motivating factors

Various typologies and theories of migration have been developed with an upsurge in scholarly interest in these topics of late (Canagarajah 2017: 2; Castles, de Haas, and Miller 2014: 27; King 2012a: 3). This predilection has arisen predominantly from the large-scale population movements characterising the twenty-first century such that 2.5 million migrants applied for asylum in Europe alone during 2015 and 2016 (Ionesco, Mokhnacheva, and Gemenne 2016).[1] As Czaika and de Haas (2015: 314) contend, twenty-first century Europe has been transformed from being a "global source region of emigrants and settlers" (they are referring here to migratory movements of the nineteenth and twentieth centuries especially) into "a global migration magnet".

Research by Cohen (1996, 2008), King (2002, 2012a, 2012b), King and Skeldon (2010) as well as Manning (with Trimmer) (2013) recognizes four principal binary types of migratory process which will be relevant for subsequent chapters of Part I.[2] Both Fitzgerald and Lambkin (2008) as well as the remarkable Ravenstein (1885, 1889), who first proposed a set of "laws of migration" from which more recent work in migration theory continues to draw, have interpreted these typologies from an Irish historical perspective as this research also does.

1.3 Internal and external migration

The primary distinction argued for in migration theory is that between "internal" and "external", "international" or "transnational" migration (King and Skeldon 2010). The former occurs within a nation or state whereas the latter implies the crossing of a nation-state border, though it is important to recognize the transience of these. Thus, nineteenth century migrants from North County Monaghan in the historical province of Ulster who sought famine relief in their nearest workhouse which happened to be in County Armagh would be

---

[1] Further facts and figures can be obtained from Castles, de Haas, and Miller (2014: 12–13) as well as the European Parliament News at http://www.europarl.europa.eu/news/en/headlines/society/20170629STO78630/eu-migrant-crisis-facts-and-figures (last accessed 4 April 2018).

[2] The term "binary" is used here since typologies within migration theory principally focus on dichotomies, i.e. "internal" *versus* "external", "mobile" *versus* "non-mobile", "step" *versus* "direct" and "forced" *versus* "voluntary". It is also important to note that such "migration binaries, dichotomies or dyads" (Cohen 1996: xi–xiv and King 2002: 90–91; 2012: 8) are far from clear-cut. Where relevant in this context, the blurring of these will be acknowledged but they will serve for present purposes to provide abstract categories for the key mobility processes that are the focus of this research.

considered internal migrants. By contrast, the same move during World War 2 would have entailed the crossing of a nation-state boundary from the Republic of Ireland into Northern Ireland. The latter had remained within the United Kingdom after Partition in 1920 which, in effect, subjected residents of twenty-six of the entire thirty-two county island to a process of 'non-mobile' migration (see also Davies 1997 and Meinhof 2002 for other European examples).

Migration of the international type has two axes that depend on whether the migrant is leaving the nation-state (i.e. emigrating) or arriving/returning (i.e. immigrating/return migrating). Return migrants are those who at one point resided in the nation-state but who emigrated to another for a period of time. As is the case with all migratory moves, residency in the receiving country can become permanent or it can be temporary (for a season or other clearly defined duration associated with a business contract, for instance). The latter type is often associated with international students (Cavanagh and Glennie 2012) as well as seasonal employees such as the twenty-first century immigrants to Northern Ireland who work in the agriculture, construction and tourist sectors (see Chapter Four, §4.2.1.2 as well as King 2012a: 7 and Russell 2011: 20). It is not unusual for immigrant agricultural workers, for example, to return migrate to their sending countries of residence once the labour market shrinks. Others may never return home but their settlement might still be considered temporary in certain respects. This would apply to the youngsters interviewed for this project whose immediate family (or indeed themselves) are engaged periodically at both Monaghan Mushrooms, County Monaghan in the Republic of Ireland in addition to also being employed in Northern Ireland. As such, technically they emigrate for work to the Republic of Ireland and return migrate regularly to their newly established residences in Armagh across the nation-state border without ever returning to the country from which they originated on a permanent basis. An excellent case in point occurs in (1) from one of the *Múin Béarla* interviews with a young woman of Lithuanian heritage who is describing the occupational roles of herself and her older sister in both Northern Ireland and the Republic of Ireland (see Potter and Hamilton 2014).[3]

---

3 Full details of the interview protocol and other aspects of the data collection process that produced this material are described in Part II, Chapter Six. All the interviewees have been assigned pseudonyms appropriate for their expressly preferred genders and ethnolinguistic heritages in order to preserve their anonymity. The schools they attend and in which the interviews took place have also been anonymized for the same reason.

(1) Extract from an interview with 'Anea Manis' re: Monaghan Mushrooms, Armagh, 2014

1	Anea Manis:	Yeah, but my sister's English is really good, she's actually eh an interpreter.
2	KPC:	Oh is that what she ended up doing? So she gave up the Law?
3	Anea Manis:	Well she's doing two … two jobs, she never came back to finish the Law. So she has like two and a half years done.
4	KPC:	Oh!
5	Anea Manis:	But she never went back, but. She got a degree in Translating in here, the first degree they did in Ulster's University.
6	KPC:	Mm-mm.
7	Anea Manis:	So she has like really good qualifications in and she went into ehm … medical translating as well, but she works in Monaghan Mushrooms on the trading desk.
8	KPC:	Oh okay.
9	Anea Manis:	And that's where I work occasionally as well.
10	KPC:	Oh you work there too?
11	Anea Manis:	Yeah, every other weekend. So … <School bell rings>. So she would kind of work the both jobs at the same time.

[NP (F); AM (F); St. Celine's; Armagh, Northern Ireland; 24 Jan. 2014][4]

Both Anea and her sister, whose place of residence is Armagh, Northern Ireland, therefore temporarily migrate back and forth across the very permeable Irish border for their employment. It remains to be seen, of course, whether this continues to be a possibility for them and other migrant workers who are currently also employed in both states and regularly transition between them. The outcome depends on how negotiations between the UK and EU pan out following the former's withdrawal from the EEA on 31st January 2020.

---

[4] This coding refers to an abbreviated version of the speaker name, identifies whether they are female (F) or male (M), which school the interview took place in (St. Agnes's, St. Benedict's, St. Celine's or St. Peter's) and on what date. Further details can be found in § 6.1.2.

1.4 Stepwise versus linear migration

It is also important to bear in mind of course that even transnational migrants who have settled permanently in a host country may have endured periods of a migratory process known as "stepwise" or "transit" migration (King 2012a: 8; Paul 2011: 1842), i.e. a series of temporary moves either internally or externally (Collyer 2007, 2010; Fitzgerald and Lambkin 2008; King 2012a, 2011b; Van Liempt 2011a, 2011b; Paul 2011, 2017; Ravenstein 1885, 1889). This would be the case, for instance, for most migrants from the island of Ireland during the Great Famine of the nineteenth century. Since many of them were rural dwellers, they will often have migrated first to a workhouse in an urban setting in search of famine relief and then had to migrate further internally to a major Irish port town. Subsequently, they will have journeyed to Glasgow or Liverpool as additional internal transit migration points before travelling first to Boston in North America (Miller 1985) and then onward perhaps to the Argentine pampas (Amador-Moreno 2012, 2019; McKenna 1992; Murray 2006) thus migrating both internally and externally several times during their journeys. (2) from the *Corpus of Irish English Correspondence* (CORIECOR) demonstrates a classic example of this stepwise process in a historical Irish context. Edward McNally in this reasonably short extract from his 1851 letter to his brother mentions, in addition to his first internal migratory journey to Liverpool, no fewer than five locations in the United States where he has resided since emigrating from Portaferry, County Down, Northern Ireland:[5]

(2) Extract from William McNally letter, Portaferry, 1851

Title:	Edward McNally, USA to William McNally, Portaferry
Source:	T 1448: Copied by Permission of Mrs. Rose Tomelty, Portaferry, Co. Down
Archive:	The Public Record Office, N. Ireland
Doc. No.:	9002017
Date:	08/06/1851
Doc Type:	EMG
Log:	Document added by JM 25:10:1993

---

[5] At the time of writing, the database includes approximately 5000 texts (c. 3 million words) consisting of 4300 personal letters written to and from Irish emigrants to North America, South America and the Antipodes between the 1700s and the 1940s as well as extraneous materials such as genealogies and the like. For further details as to how the corpus was constructed and its applications for research as well as the generation of wider impacts, see Amador-Moreno (2019); Ávila-Ledesma and Amador-Moreno (2016); Amador-Moreno *et al.* (2016); Bonness (2016); de Rijke (2016); McCafferty & Amador-Moreno (2012a), (2012b). All transcripts from CORIECOR in this book are reproduced exactly from the original digital copies and have not been edited further. They thus retain transcriber's comments (in square brackets) as well as other metadata so that their digital histories are likewise preserved for future reference.

Captain William McNally
Portaferry Co Down
Ireland
Middletown June the 8th 1851

... [we?] Left Liverpool on the 19th of June and arrived in Philadelphia
in the 8 of augest [August?] after a Pleasent [pleasant?] but Rather a
tedieous [tedious?] Passige [passage?]
... when i Landed in that
Citty [City?] i Remained there for the space of 10 days
Constantly looking for work but no chance so i started for the
Citty [City?] of Pitsburg [Pittsburg?] distance three hundred mills [miles?]
from Philadelphia but i had not money enough to carry
over all the way so i began to work on the Centrall [Central?]
Rail road where i remained for some time unto i got a Little
money and then i started for Pitsburg [Pittsburg?] but on my
arivill [arrival?] there the Cholera was bad at that time so i
took the Steam Boat for Cincinnati whitch [which?] is five hundred
mills [miles?] from Pitsburg [Pittsburg?] down the ohio River whitch
[which?] Citty [City?] is the handsomest that i have saw since i
landed in those steates [states?] but there i serched [searched?]
in vain for trade and could not get a single days work and i
found my self without a single Cent in a short time but
thank god i allways [always?] injoyed [enjoyed?] the best of
health so i started for the Rail Road but i had no taste for that
work i could a void [avoid?] it and i fell in with a farmer
and i began to work with him and i no [know?] that you will
Laugh to Learn that became a mower and made surprising Progress
at my new trade but at all events i Pleased my boss Remarkably and
Remained with him unto his work was all done so again i went in
to the City expecting to geat [get?] a shop of some kind but that i
could not find but fell into work with a merchant Discharging
flatt [flat?] boats Laden with fire Brick fire Clay and hee [he?]
took a Likeing [liking?] to mee [me?] and hee [he?] sent mee [me?]
up the river to virgina [Virginia?] where his esstate [estate?] was to
work for the winter but the old Boss hee [he?] had there would not set
mee [me?] to work so then i started for Pitsburg [Pittsburg?] and
could not fall in there and from that to the Centriall [Central?] Rail
Road and on Last Christmass [Christmas?] day i travelled 31 mills
[miles?] and it snowing and blowing through the Drarey [Dreary?] wilds

of this distant Land and i Remained on the Centrall [*Central*?]
into the spring appeared [*opened*?] and then i started for to come east and
i Came into this Little town about a month ago and here
i chanced on a shop for the first since Landed this is a
nice Little Place But it is rather sickly The ague is verry [*very*?]
Prevelent [*prevalent*?] heere [*here*?] as this town is sittuated
[*situated*?] on the Banks of the Susequhana [*Susquehanna*?] River but
thank god since i Landed i never haad [*had*?] better health ...

Edward did not stay long enough in Liverpool for it to have had any impact on his vernacular or indeed on his identity, as Van Liempt (2011a, 2011b) has argued for stepwise Dutch-Somali migrants whose lengthy sojourns prior to their arrival in the UK have actually had important repercussions for their affective responses to citizenship and belonging. Moreover, it would seem that Edward's subsequent migrations upon arriving in North America will probably have prevented him from acquiring either the American Inland Northern, Midland and Mid-Atlantic dialects he was probably exposed to for somewhat longer periods nor the mixed, koiné varieties that were likely used by his fellow railroad workers (Labov, Ash and Boberg 2006; Trudgill 2006). This is because change in the linguistic output of an individual or community of individuals in the cases of large scale language contact scenarios (such as those discussed in Chapter Two regarding the acquisition by native Irish speakers of English and Scots from the Middle Ages onwards) relies upon the frequency of their interactions. Labov, (2001: 19) contends that: "a large part of the problem of explaining the diffusion of linguistic change" is simply the mechanical matter of who speakers most regularly interact with. In a similar vein, Fix (2013: 71) argues that: "Speakers who have meaningful and regularly occurring interactions with those outside of their regional, ethnic, or social groups may come to adopt linguistic features that are distinctive from their native dialects through processes of second dialect acquisition and dialect shift." Edward's itinerant lifestyle means that his chances of acquiring dialectal forms of American English are quite poor since thus far he has not been exposed to new majority variants in any one location for a sufficient period of time.

At the present time, stepwise or transit migration has become associated with the multistage pattern of mobility common amongst contemporary "aspiring" but low capital migrants (Paul 2011) as well as "irregular" migrants (King 2002, 2012a, 2012b; Bogusz 2004), namely, those who enter a nation-state illegally. In addition to the economic issue, which also features prominently in Edward McNally's correspondence where he declares at one point that he was "without a single Cent", stepwise migration is often further exacerbated today by the various legal obstacles to obtaining residency or indeed refugee status, as Collyer (2010: 273) observes. Thus, for a migrant to reach their first preference destination, the move may entail those with little or no capital in developing countries (like the Filipino domestic workers documented in Paul 2011, 2017) having to migrate many times in order to reside in a Western nation-state at the top of their hierarchy of choices. The extract in (3) from another *Múin Béarla* interview containing a conversation with two sisters of Indian heritage whose family migrated to the UK in 2005 shows exactly this pattern. Both siblings were born in Trivandrum in southern India's Kerala state. The oldest sibling, Syiara Sinha, migrated internally over a thousand kilometres away to Mumbai in the state of Maharashtra in the care of an aunt. The youngest one, Shukla, migrated transnationally with their parents even further to Saudi Arabia before the family were eventually reunited in the UK several years later. They moved to their last UK destination in the city of Armagh just over five years before they were interviewed.

(3)   Extract from an interview with 'Siyara' and 'Sukla Sinha', Armagh, 2014

 1   KPC: So, I'm going to first ask you how long have you guys been in Armagh?
 2   Siyara Sinha: In Armagh? Eh about, more than five years.
 3   KPC: Mm-mm.
 4   Siyara Sinha: Yeah, but we've been in eh UK for more than nine years.
 5   KPC: So, so tell me the history, the story of your lives.
 6   Siyara Sinha: Well, she [*her sister Shukla*] was in a different place, I was in a different place, because she was with my parents in Saudi Arabia, well, you [*her sister Shukla*] were in Saudi Arabia from a very young age.
 7   Shukla Sinha: India. Yeah.
 8   KPC: So what age, what age were you, Shukla, when you were in Saudi Arabia?
 9   Siyara Sinha: And I was in ...
10   Shukla Sinha: Eh ...
11   Siyara Sinha: Like since she [*her sister Shukla*] was born. Like two.
12   Shukla Sinha: No like, after I was born, like. Probably one years old.
13   Siyara Sinha: Yeah.
14   KPC: Ok so you emigrated to Saudi when you were one. God isn't she very brave!
15   Shukla Sinha: Yeah.
16   Siyara Sinha: <Laughs>
17   KPC: <Laughs> and so where were you, Siyara, when she was?
18   Shukla Sinha: <Laughs>

19	Siyara Sinha:	I was with, I was with my Dad's sister who was in Bombay.
20	KPC:	Okay.
21	Siyara Sinha:	Mumbai.
22	Shukla Sinha:	Yeah. So we were in two different places.
23	Siyara Sinha:	Yeah, and then we came over here as a family yeah.

[SiSh (F); ShSi (F); St. Celine's; Armagh, Northern Ireland; 22.1.14]

Further on in this interview, it becomes apparent that this stepwise pattern has actually been a migratory process which has characterized the lives of the Sinha family for quite some time, since the girls also mention the fact that their father:

(4) Extract from an interview with 'Siyara' and 'Sukla Sinha', Armagh, 2014

  1 Siyara Sinha: ... he moved from India, like Kerala when he was like eighteen, nineteen. He moved to, he's wen= he went to Germany, London, Saudi. Yeah, he's been most of places.

[SiSh (F); ShSi (F); St. Celine's; Armagh, Northern Ireland; 22.1.14]

Moreover, the eldest daughter Siyara, in connection with an interview question asking whether it was important to develop a Northern Irish accent to integrate locally, made the following statement indicating that she aspires to a stepwise migratory lifestyle similar to her father's:

(5) Extract from an interview with 'Siyara' and 'Sukla Sinha', Armagh, 2014

  1 Siyara Sinha: No, we don't really care because f= I don't think we'll be staying here for the rest of our lives. So, I think we'll be moving to different countries because I don't prefer <*Laughs*>. Like I would rather move to a different country after like qualification like after my uni and everything ...

[SiSh (F); ShSi (F); St. Celine's; Armagh, Northern Ireland; 22.1.14]

The increasing prevalence of mobile lifestyles like these has led to migration theory taking much more cognisance of the fact that migratory processes are not necessarily direct and linear, from Country A straight to Country B, as King (2012a: 8) also argues. From a linguistic perspective, an important outcome of these extensive transit migratory paths is the extent to which the two daughters who relayed the "Sinha" family's migration narratives have become plurilingual.

Unlike Edward McNally whose stepwise migrations likely resulted in no impact at all on the Portaferry variety of English that he left home with, this is not the case for either Syiara or Shukla. While Malayalam is the mother tongue for both young women, their sojourns have resulted in them having been exposed to and achieving some competence in Arabic and Hindi as well as English (both Indian (Pingali 2009) and Northern Irish English (Corrigan 2010) varieties). The "Sinha" sisters are far from unique in this respect and there are many similar scenarios in the *Múin Béarla* interviews as well as in the relevant literature. A good case in point are the Somalians reported on by Van Liempt (2011a, 2011b) whose transit points have included the Netherlands prior to their arrival in the UK as "Dutch Somalians". She argues that they have been enticed there by what they perceive to be different educational and economic advantages from those available to them at earlier stopping off locations on their journeys. The participants in Van Liempt's study all had Somali as a first language and, along with their Dutch passports, had acquired high levels of competence in the language. Hence, she (2011b: 257) reports that: "most interviews were conducted in Dutch as people wanted to practise their language skills and demonstrate their fluency." Van Liempt (2011b) also records the fact that the British involvement in Somalia (as in India) meant that many of the interviewees were strongly oriented to the language and culture of the UK prior to their arrival. Indeed, post-colonial migration patterns are often recognized to follow earlier historical links which is one of the reasons why poorer Irish migrants whose mobility was induced by the Great Famine preferred Britain to Continental Europe (Chapter Three, §3.3; Bakewell and de Haas 2007; Czaika and de Haas 2015: 284). Key aspirations tied to this affiliation with the UK recorded by Van Liempt (2011b) and held by her Dutch-Somali adult participants, were that their children would become highly competent English speakers. They also desired them to obtain degrees from UK Higher Education institutions which is also Siyara Sinha's aspiration, having been interviewed for a place on a nursing degree at Manchester University just prior to interview.

1.5 Chain migration, pioneers and followers

The Dutch-Somalian case analysed in Van Liempt (2011a, 2011b) and the migratory paths of different members of the "Sinha" family illustrate another important distinction recognized within migration scholarship, i.e. the difference between pioneer and chain migrants. The girls' father could be classed as the former being the first of his family to emigrate and this action precipitated a chain that eventually reunited him with his wife and both daughters in Armagh.

Similarly, another significant reason for the Somalians' choice of the UK as being top of their migrant destination hierarchy is the fact that well-established communities from Somalia had already made their homes there, but this was less common in the Netherlands where ethnic Somalian community numbers were very small (Van Liempt 2011a: 263). Hence, the arrival in Britain of new groups via the Netherlands is part of a chain responding to earlier pioneers who now act as what Fitzgerald and Lambkin (2008: 298) term a "bridgehead" facilitating the migration of other individuals from their friendship or kinship networks either in their home countries or in transit locations. Hence, Van Liempt (2011a: 263) concludes that: "The substantial growth of the Somali community in Leicester can be explained by chain migration of Somalis from the Netherlands, influenced by the drive to regroup."

As Van Liempt (2011a: 256) also notes, this migration pattern has resulted in Somali–Dutch bilingual speakers becoming concentrated in just two neighbourhoods in the city. This is often the case in contexts of chain migration and can result in the type of ghettoization of newcomer populations that has important implications for language maintenance, discouraging shift towards the majority language or dialect of the host country in many domains (see Allard and Landry 1994; Clyne 2005; Ehala 2010; Fishman 1991, 2000; Gallois, Cretchley, and Watson 2012; Giles, Bourhis, and Taylor 1977; Harwood, Giles, and Bourhis 1994; Landry and Bourhis 1997; Pauwels 2016; Sanchez-Castro and Gil, 2009; Wölck 2004).

Chain migration via a bridgehead who encourages or indeed financially incentivizes the migration of friends and family is by no means a modern phenomenon, as is very evident from the CORIECOR extracts (6) and (7) below. The first of these was penned in 1765 by John Rea in South Carolina to his brother Matthew in Drumbo, County Antrim.

(6) John Rea letter extract, Drumbo, 1765

Title: John Rea, SC, U.S.A. to Matthew Rea, Drumbo, Co. Antrim
Source: D3561/A/17/2: Transcript presented by Dr. P. R. Green, 15 May, 1965
Archive: The Public Record Office, N. Ireland
Doc. No.: 9901025
Date: 15/05/1765
Doc Type: EMG
Log: Document added by LT, 08:01:99

Letter from John Rea, Esq., thirty-four years settled in South Carolina, to his Brother Matthew Rea of Drumbo.
Rea's Hall, May 15, 1765

In my last letter to you by way of London, I informed you that I had procured a grant from the Governor and Council of Georgia for fifty thousand acres of land in this Province for any of my friends and countrymen that have a mind to come to this country and bring their families here to settle. The land I have pitched upon lies on a fine River called Ogichey, near to which I have my large cow-pens of cattle settled, which will be very convenient for new-comers-in, to be supplied with milk cows. I can also furnish them with Horses and Mares, any number they may want. I am likewise in Hopes of obtaining a Bounty at their arrival; but as this is a young Colony, and of course not rich, they cannot expect so much as Carolina gave to the People who came over with my servants, who are all well and hearty ... Now, Brother, if you think a number of good industrious families will come over here I will do every thing in my Power to assist them; for nothing will give me more satisfaction than to be the means of bringing my friends to this country of Freedom; ... The people that I would advise to come to this country are those that have large families growing up, that they may get land and assist each other. Likewise tradesmen of all sorts, for that will draw a trade amongst them from other settlements, by which they will get money. I would have them bring a clergyman with them, and a school-master that may be [Clerk?], for they are scarce here, and they will have land given them, and what the people can afford with my [Mite?] may procure him a living.

John is a pioneer and bridgehead par excellence given the fact that this letter remonstrates with his brother to assist him in creating a chain migration pattern that includes migrants from Ulster of different social types with a range of skills that will be advantageous to the development of his new Georgian colony. If it were to succeed, and it became in any way similar to powerful estates such as that of the Glass family of the Opequon Settlement, Virginia, where high concentrations of Ulster migrants resided, then there is every chance that features of their original dialect will have been maintained for several generations (Hofstra 2011a: 105–122).[6] Indeed, the region surrounding settlements like Rea's or the Glass's may come to have a long-standing impact on the development of new local varieties of American English, as is thought to be the case in the Appalachians and Ozarks more generally, which were heavily settled by chain migration from Ulster in the early colonial period (see Chapter Three, § 3–3.2 as well as Fischer 1991; Hofstra 2011b; Montgomery 2017; Ridner 2018; Rossiter 2006; Webb 2009; Wolfram and Christian 1976)

The second example (7) is taken from Mary Quin's correspondence sent in 1873 from Barrytown, New York to her sisters in Stewartstown, County Tyrone.

(7) Extract from Mary Quin letter, Barrytown, 1873

Title:	Mary Quin, Barrytown to Her Sister, Ireland
Source:	D 1819/3: Presented by Samuel Park, Esq., The Square, Stewartstown, County Tyrone
Archive:	The Public Record Office, N. Ireland
Doc. No.:	9012059
Date:	01/01/1873
Doc Type:	EMG
Log:	Action By Date Document added by C.R., 10:12:1993

... Ellen is working every day with a gentle man washing and ironen [*ironing*?] clothes she goes at seven in the morning and comes home at seven at night in she has twelve dollars a month and her board and she is very thin and old looking she says she keeps all her earnings to herself that was the way she paid our passages

Although the Quin's situation is markedly different socially from that of John Rea's, the letter makes clear that Mary's sister, Ellen, was the pioneer migrant and

---

6 The extent to which Ulster English of the period diverged from American vernaculars can be intimated from Fischer (1991: 605) who quotes Jonathan Dickinson's 1717 remarks upon witnessing a burgeoning of migration from North Britain to North America. He claims that Philadelphia's streets had filled with: "a swarm of people ... strangers to our laws and Customs, and even to our Language." See also Hickey (2004b) and Kytö (2004).

financial bridgehead for a chain of siblings including Mary, the correspondent, and their brother, Arthur.

1.6 Voluntary or forced migration?

These letters illustrate another important dichotomy of migration theory which relates to the motivation of "new-comers-in" as John Rea describes immigrants in his 1765 correspondence. The binary in this case is that between the type of migration which is termed "voluntary" and that which is "forced". The latter would include slavery (legalized and otherwise), impoverished economic situations as well as threats such as natural disasters. Ethnic, religious and political persecution would fall under this category too taking forms such as mass population displacement or pogroms in a drive to "ethnically cleanse" a nation-state or other bounded territory so as to render it more ethnically homogeneous (Cohen 2008: 2).[7] Prototypical situations in which large-scale compelled dislocation occurs amongst an ethno-religious group are associated with population movements that are termed 'diasporic' in the migratory literature. This notion is most commonly used to refer to the slavery of Africans, the forced displacement or worse of Armenians and Jews at various periods in their histories, the creation of the state of Israel which compelled the Palestinians to disperse as well as the impact of the Great Famine on the Irish in the nineteenth century (Cohen 2008: 2–4).

Diasporic mobility which is forced can have concomitant linguistic effects. On the one hand, it can reduce the extent of diversity within the originating country (or new state in the case of the founding of Israel). On the other, the arrival of the displaced population can increase heterogeneity in the receiving territory since ethnic groups often also have unique languages or dialects associated with them (Fought 2006). In extreme cases, ethnic cleansing can result in the crime

---

[7] The concept "pogrom" was first coined to describe Anti-Jewish persecutions during the Russian Empire period and is relevant for nineteenth and twentieth century immigration by Jews to Ulster, as Chapters Three and Four detail. "Ethnic cleansing" as used here is congruent with that defined by a United Nations Commission of Experts who were mandated to look into violations of international humanitarian law committed in the territory of the former Yugoslavia. In its interim report S/25274, ethnic cleansing is described as "... rendering an area ethnically homogeneous by using force or intimidation to remove persons of given groups from the area." In its final report S/1994/674, the same Commission described the term as "... a purposeful policy designed by one ethnic or religious group to remove by violent and terror-inspiring means the civilian population of another ethnic or religious group from certain geographic areas." See http://www.un.org/en/genocideprevention/ethnic-cleansing.html – last accessed 28 Jan. 2018.

of genocide, a concept first coined by Raphäel Lemkin, a Polish lawyer, to characterize the systematic murder of Jews during the Holocaust. It remains relevant today as a significant driver of migration in the Horn of Africa disputes between Eritrea and Ethiopia which were motivated originally by the 1952 British federation of the two countries, which it controlled at that time. It will be argued in Chapter Two that ethnic cleansing practices were also applied by Commonwealth forces historically on the island of Ireland during various phases of its conquest including the Cromwellian Wars of the 1640s. The forced migrations of the time are still captured in the public imagination by the well-known phrase "To Hell or to Connacht", which features in a CORIECOR text (8) written in 1915 tracing the genealogy of the Moore family of County Antrim (see also the 1641 deposition cited in Chapter Two, §2.4.1).

Cromwell's initiative sought to murder or transport autochthonous Roman Catholic or disloyal dissenter allochthonous populations from the best land for tillage towards the western seaboard (i.e. the less economically viable province of Connacht) where they could be more easily controlled (Lenihan 2007: 135–136). All of these factors (including modern human trafficking) have been implicated in the recent global refugee crisis, already noted (Bauder 2006; Braziel and Mannur 2003; Castles, de Haas, and Miller 2014; de Genova 2017; Ionesco, Mokhnacheva and Gemenne 2017; Pargas 2014; Quirk and Vigneswaran 2012; Wihtol de Wenden 2016). They are relevant also to the situations of John Rea and the Quin family. The former migrated while the Penal Laws, which were instigated in 1695 to delimit the social roles and status of dissenters from the Church of Ireland (mainly Presbyterians, like Rea, and Roman Catholics), were still in force (Adams 1964; Bliss 1991; Corrigan 1999; Fitzgerald 2003; Gillen 2016; Ó Cuív 1991; Ó Duibhín 2007; Schaffer 2000). An important outcome of this legislation will have had a deleterious impact on Rea's freedom of religious expression as well as his ability to have complete control over his affairs socio-economically. He is unlikely to have ever managed to build a Rea's Hall (the address given on his letter) in his homeland of Drumbo, County Antrim or to own "fifty thousand acres of land" there. As will become clear in Chapter Three, John Rea was just one of a number of dissenters who migrated in this period as a means of overcoming these state-controlled inequalities so that his migration could indeed be considered forced in this context. The Quin family, who made the same journey over a hundred years later, were Roman Catholics and while the Penal Laws had been revoked in 1774, their emigration could likewise be perceived as not voluntary but for different reasons. In this case, it was more likely due to the extreme poverty of this social group arising from a natural disaster in the form of successive failures of the staple crop mid-century, in addition to the continuance of Anglicising programmes such as the ethnic cleansing practices introduced previously that persistently undermined the status and socio-economic independence of Roman Catholics (see Chapter Three as well as Whelan 1997).

(8)   Extract from HC Lawlor letter, Ulster, 2015

Title:	H C Lawlor to Mr. Kernoghan, Re Moore and Fleming Families
Source:	D 1897: Presented by Anonymous. #TYPE LET Letter from H.C. Lawlor, Belfast to Mr. Kernoghan concerning Genealogical Research into the Families of Moore, Derrykeighan, Co Antrim and Fleming Aughnacloy Co. Tyrone, 1915
Archive:	The Public Record Office, N. Ireland
Doc. No.:	8909175
Date:	01/01/1915
Doc Type:	EMG
Log:	06:10:1989 LT created 03:10:1990 MC input 08:10:1990 SB checked

No Co. [*County*?] Antrim Moore appeares in the list
of attainted Gentry of King James II's Parliament
nor (I think) in Cromwell's list of protestants
to be deported to Connaght.[8]

As many migration scholars are keen to point out, however, apart from the historical or modern slavery scenarios described in Braziel and Mannur (2003); de Genova (2017); Pargas (2014) and Quirk and Vigneswaran (2012), the dichotomy between forced and voluntary migration is rarely unambiguous (Cohen 2008: 2). It is thus important to step beyond a purely functionalist approach to the process that takes no account of individual agency. Hence, it would, in fact, be relatively straightforward to argue for the opposing view that both John Rea and the Quins voluntarily undertook their migratory journeys in search of better prospects of one type or another in North America. Indeed, the motivators for emigrating are always multiplex and are instigated by a range of so-called "push-pull" factors such as high rates of unemployment in the sending country versus low rates in the receiving country and the like (Fitzgerald and Lambkin 2008: 302; UNESCO 2017).[9] Moreover, some drivers towards mobility are clearly at the "macro-structural" or institutional level and, like the Penal laws and the state mandated

---

[8] "Attainted" is a term that stems from English criminal law and designates those who have been condemned for a serious capital crime entailing the loss not only of the attainted's own life, property and hereditary titles but their heirs also forfeited the right to the latter as well.

[9] Delaney (2016: 499) also argues that the simple push-pull dichotomy relied upon in traditional accounts of migratory movements does not sufficiently "capture the complexities of the human experience." Hence, the following chapters will attempt where possible to go beyond this binary by taking a more holistic approach which also foregrounds the implications of population move-

social engineering of Roman Catholics since the colonisation of Ulster, are largely outside the control of individual members of the polity. By contrast, other factors are micro-structural in the sense that they, as Castles, de Haas, and Miller (2014: 26) argue, "embrace the practices, family ties and beliefs of the migrants themselves". The Quin and Sinha cases of chain migration examined earlier are excellent evidence of such "micro-structural" forces at work despite the vastly different time periods during which these individual agency factors were operating (see also the arguments in e.g. Cohen 1996, 2008; Castles 2010; Castles, de Haas, and Miller 2014; King 2002, 2012a, 2012b; King and Skeldon 2010). Both structural levels are linked to a range of mechanisms that mediate between them often termed "meso-structures" (Castles, de Haas and Miller 2014: 26). These would include the presence in host countries of substantial "immigrant communities", as in the example from Van Liempt (2011a, 2011b) of Somali-Dutch migrants, as well as far-reaching and economically powerful "migrant networks" like the Presbyterian type established by John Rea and the Glass family in early colonial Georgia and Virginia, respectively.

1.7 Synthesis and prospects

Finally, migration theories since their first articulation in early works such as Ravenstein (1885, 1889), have developed frameworks for examining population flows that take account not only of the processes involved but also the motivating forces for migratory movements of diverse kinds. It is now recognized that these are both complex and multi-faceted. There are a range of macro-, micro- and meso-structural factors involved which take cognisance of the fact that the process is governed not just by nation-states but by individual agents and the communities which they leave and in which they choose or are compelled to settle either permanently or temporarily (O'Reilly 2015). The ensuing chapters use migration as a prism for viewing changes in the ethnolinguistic diversity of the North of Ireland since the first settlements to the most contemporary. Chapter Two begins with the immigration of Stone Age peoples during the Mesolithic era and ends with the successful so-called "Plantation" settlements[10] of the Jacobites which altered forever the ethnolinguistic composition of the region, the effects

---

ments on the ethnolinguistic vitality of the island's indigenous and allochthonous languages and dialects.

10 Such schemes are often associated with colonizing efforts and had the intention of planting or settling large numbers of immigrant groups on land formerly owned or worked by an indigenous people so as to maximize the colonizers' profit from it.

of which are still felt to this very day. Chapter Three continues with an external history of Ulster that spans the Age of Enlightenment to the Diaspora of the Great Famine era which witnessed the greatest internal and external dislocations of any period in the region's history and had major consequences for the survival of the island's indigenous language. Part I then closes by examining emigration and immigration processes and motivators in modern times. Chapter Four thus focuses on mobility during the twentieth and twenty-first centuries when Northern Ireland (as the region had then become) was rendered more "superdiverse" (in Vertovec's 2007, 2014 sense) than at any previous point in its history.[11]

---

11 A digest of the linguistic ecology and historical settlement of Ulster articulated in Chapters Two to Four of Part I, can be found in Corrigan (2010: Chapter Five). Given the fact that the earlier work also focuses on the chronology of linguistic contact in Ulster and thus deals with incontrovertible historical facts, some of this material is reproduced here and is used with the permission of Edinburgh University Press. The content has, however, been considerably enlarged and revised to incorporate new research as well as the models of mobility and settlement introduced in this Chapter.

2 Migration and language ecology: pre-history to Cromwell

This chapter traces the impact on Ulster's language ecology of population movements arising from the various drivers argued for in the previous chapter between the Stone Ages and the heyday of the Jacobean plantations.

2.1 Language ecologies of prehistoric and early Christian peoples (9000BC–AD1000)

2.1.1 Settlement during the Mesolithic period and the Bronze Age

The earliest known migration to Ulster can be traced to the hunter-gatherer populations of the Mesolithic age (c. 9000 years ago) who will have predominated in areas such as the northeast with plentiful natural resources and sparse wooded terrain, since the requisite tools to clear forests had not yet been developed (see Fig. 45, p. 177; Herity and Eogan 1996: 17–23; O'Kelly 2005a: 59–64; Stout and Stout 1997: 32–33).

An agrarian economy appeared about 4000 BC with the migration of Neolithic peoples into areas with productive soils such as Lough Neagh. Although prehistoric axe-factories have been uncovered – again in the northeast – their most enduring archaeological legacy is their initiation of the megalithic tomb-building era (see Figure 45, p. 177; Herity and Eogan 1996: 24–34; O'Kelly 2005b: 78–96; Stout and Stout 1997: 34–38).

The Bronze Age brought with it an expansion of settlement, especially in the lowlands where glacial deposits provided an excellent agricultural base and the forests continued to be denuded to make way for livestock and crops.

2.1.2 Migration and contact in the Iron Age and early Christian periods

Of all the prehistoric Iron Age settlements, the arrival of Celtic peoples is key to the development of what is now considered to be the indigenous language and culture of Ireland (MacGiolla Chríost 2005; Morley 2016: 321). This civilisation can be traced to Continental Europe around 450 BC, stretching from the Atlantic to the Black Sea. The first inscriptions of their Lepontic language were found in the *'La Tène'* region on the Swiss-Italian border and date from 600 BC. There were, however, other Celtic varieties as well, including Gaulish used across the Alps in Gaul; Galatian, which is associated with the Anatolian peninsula; and

Celtiberian, once spoken on the Iberian Peninsula. The increasing Romanization of these "Continental" Celtic lands led to the eventual replacement of these varieties by Latin. As such, they can be distinguished from the survival type known as "Insular" Celtic and spoken on the Atlantic Archipelago of which there are two types, namely, "Brythonic" and "Goedelic". Both these daughter languages are associated with inscriptions in the Ogham alphabet, which survive on standing stones dating back to 300 AD (see Figure 28, p. 95; Byrne et al. 2018; Gillen 2016: 321; Russell 2005: 410; Stout and Stout 1997: 44). Modern Welsh and Breton belong to the first category, as did Cornish until it eventually succumbed to English in the eighteenth century (Sayers 2012).[12] Old Irish, which is a member of the Goedelic branch, is much better attested than any of the others in the pre-modern era and it was this variety of the language which flourished amongst the "Insular" Celts of Ireland (MacGiolla Chríost 2005). Moreover, subsequent migration of these peoples eventually created Manx and Scots Gaelic (Byrne et al. 2018: 11; Morley 2016: 321; Russell 1995, 2005; Simms-Williams 1998).

The impact of Insular Celtic culture and language on Ulster emerged c. 400 BC and was initially also felt in the northeast. There is evidence to suggest that this is the first example of contact in this region since the material culture of previous inhabitants appears to have persisted alongside the new one originating in *La Tène* (Herity and Eogan 1996: 222–249; Raftery 2005: 140–146; Stout and Stout 1997: 42–43). There is further archaeological, genetic and other material support for the rise of kingdoms and the division of territory with allied building works such as the creation of fortifications and ceremonial buildings. The most significant royal enclosure of this kind in Ulster was *Emain Macha* erected in 94 BC near what eventually became Armagh City, which is the locus of the sociolinguistic study described in Part II. The name of the modern urban centre is an anglicization of the Irish *Ard Mhacha*, meaning 'height of [the goddess] Macha'. The designation of the Bronze Age earthwork derives from *eo-muin Macha*, which translates as 'neck-pin of Macha' and is supposed to refer to the fact that she marked its dimensions out with her brooch. It is where the pseudo-historical court of Chonchobar Mac Nessa and his warrior elite the "Red Branch Knights" were based and was considered capital of the *Ulaid* tribe, which gave its name to the province as argued in Byrne (2005). Although it declined as a powerbase before the advent of Christian evangelization in Ulster discussed immediately below, the settlement eventually became an important ecclesiastical site lasting up to the present day.

It is important to be aware, of course, that while these Iron Age fortifications promoted the security of the territory of Ulster, there is no suggestion that these

---

[12] In each case, I refer to the original survival languages spoken by native speakers rather than revival or second language varieties associated with twentieth century language movements that sought to reverse language shift (Fishman 1991).

Celtic inhabitants were wholly isolated either from their near neighbours within the British Isles nor from their historic homelands on the Continent. Indeed, the fact that the remains of a Barbary Ape were uncovered during the twentieth century excavations of *Emain Macha* is testament to the persistence of contact between Ulster Celts and regions even further afield (Byrne *et al.* 2018; Stout and Stout 1997: 42). It is hardly surprising, therefore, that closer links with the Roman world in 500 AD would bring about a significant change to the way of life of these people in the form of their introduction to Christianity. This new religion also brought considerable technological advances that improved agricultural practices which, in turn, spurred economic growth and a population rise. Ecclesiastical buildings associated with the Roman Catholic Church are a major feature of the settlement patterns of this era (Doherty 2000: 57–58). They were generally found in the low-lying areas clustering around Lough Neagh and the Fermanagh Loughs, for example, with fewer in the more inhospitable Glens of Antrim or Sperrins (Stout and Stout 1997: 51). The most auspicious of these, like Bangor on the Ards Peninsula, Armagh, as noted earlier, and Derry at the mouth of Lough Foyle, eventually grew into monastic developments by the eighth century. These functioned not just as educational and religious centres but as foci for commerce and minor industries (Hughes 2005a: 313). They were also an important source of influence over other parts of the British Isles as well as Continental Europe. This is because these early Irish Christians set out to establish other monastic settlements like Iona in Scotland and Lindisfarne in Northumbria as well as sites further afield (see Chapter 10: 315–316; Stout and Stout 1997: 52).

2.1.2.1 Migration and the formation of new linguistic ecologies in the Christian period

While Latin was the language of this early European church and it is likely that its Irish brethren had both written and spoken competence in it, they never abandoned Old Irish (Russell 2005: 409).[13] In line with Fasold's (1984: 53) and Fishman's (2003 [1967]: 362–363) interpretation of "extended diglossia", Latin would have been conceived of as the H(igh) language alongside written Old Irish (particularly when the latter became more standardized just prior to the Middle Ages). Spoken Old Irish would have been the L(ow) language and this vernacular remained the sole means of communication for the vast majority of the Irish population (i.e. Ireland at that time was a socio-cultural organization characterised by diglossia without bilingualism) (Kallen 2013: 2; Russell 2005;

---

13 The exact nature of local competence in Latin has recently been subject to considerable scholarly debate, as summarized in Bisagni (2014).

Stout 2000). Evidence for the retention of Old Irish amongst clerics even when they have gone abroad as missionaries comes from glosses in Old Irish to aid the reader that have been found on the Latin text of Pauline letters produced in Würzburg. Indeed, there are many other such glosses on Latin documents created all over the European Church in this era (https://www.uni-due.de/DI/DI_Sources.htm (last accessed 9 May 2018); Bisagni 2014; Kavanagh 2001; McCone 1985; Stam 2017; Ter Horst 2017). There is also support for the view introduced in Kallen (1997: 7) that there was considerable borrowing from Latin into Old Irish, explored in some detail by Ó Cróinín (2005) and Bisagni (2014), which give extensive descriptions of Hiberno-Latin literary texts.

The proto-urban functions of the powerful monastic enclosures that now existed in ninth century Ulster came at a price though, which is recorded in archaeological remains, contemporary genomic analyses (particularly Byrne et al. 2018) and in successive *Annals of Ulster* (McCarthy 2004). Their great riches attracted Viking attention so that in 823 AD, and again the following year, Bangor was sacked. In 832 AD, the *Annals* recall the first terrifying Viking raid on the great monastery at Armagh and much is made in the record for AD 833 when they attempted unsuccessfully to attack Derry. They had considerably more success with destroying the churches on Lough Erne in Fermanagh, demonstrating their ability to penetrate the internal reaches of Ulster by using its extensive system of waterways (Byrne 2005: 610–612; Dudley Edwards (with Hourican) 2005: 31). Nevertheless, the Vikings did not settle in Ulster to the same degree that they did in key areas of what is now the Republic of Ireland, namely, Dublin, Waterford, Wexford, Limerick and Cork (Byrne et al. 2018: 11). In that respect they could be classed as "sojourners" rather than "settlers" in the terms used by Manning (with Trimmer; 2013) to differentiate cross-community migration patterns historically. Although Hughes (2005b: 637) remarks on the devastating toll of the more strategic and concerted Viking wars of 837–873 AD, which included further attacks on Armagh, the fact that no significant Scandinavian powerbases were established anywhere in Ulster meant that long-term Viking impact on its economic, genomic and socio-political structures was considerably weaker (Byrne et al. 2018: 11; Dudley Edwards with Hourican 2005: 31; Hughes 2005b: 639–641). The same is also true of its effect on language in Ulster. The place name evidence cited by Byrne (2005: 31–34) and MacGiolla Easpaig (2009: 81), for instance, is considerably less for this region than for other areas in which the Scandinavians wielded far more influence.[14] By and large, the ecclesiastical houses survived intact

---

14 Byrne (2005: 631–632) cites: (i) "Carlingford" as relating to Old Norse *Kerlingafjǫrðr,* which translates as 'ford of the hags', possibly from the nearby mountain stacks of the Mournes known as the "Three Nuns"; (ii) "Strangford" derived from Old Norse *Strangfjǫrðr* signifying 'rough

and, indeed, grew under the influence of the Anglo-Normans, the next group of migrants to maintain sustained contact with the now very much indigenised Ulster Celts (Hughes 2005b: 639–641).

2.2 Mobility and language in the Medieval and Tudor periods (1177–1602)

2.2.1 Anglo-Norman and Bruce invasions

Prior to the early Middle Ages because of Ulster's geographical position within the British Isles, and on account of the missionary work in Scotland and Northern England discussed earlier, trade and religious links had already been established with the Anglo-Normans. However, at this point there were not yet any significant migratory movements by them to Ulster territory (Hickey 2007: 30; Kallen 1997: 8). There was also continued communication with the Scots in the Medieval and Tudor eras, resulting in an invitation from the Ulster chieftains in the early fourteenth century seeking to rid themselves of the Normans whose settlements were now so powerful that they had begun to de-stabilize the Gaelic chieftains' hold on the country.

The first phase of Anglo-Norman contact occurred from the 1170s until the early thirteenth century, though its impact was largely restricted to Antrim and Down. These counties were initially usurped in a land grab dislocating the indigenous peoples by John de Courcy. He began his march northwards in 1177 from what had already become an "ethnically cleansed" territory within the province of Leinster, in what is now the Republic of Ireland, called "the Pale" (Ellis 2011; Kallen 2013: 17–18; Stout and Stout 1997: 58). Although the extent of what Booker (2018: I) terms these "obedient shires" varied over time in this early Medieval period, as Figure 1 shows, their eastern coastal flank would have stretched from Dalkey, south of Dublin, to the garrison town of Dundalk, County Louth just 22 km south of Newry in Ulster. Inland, the area encompassed Leixlip around the Earldom of Kildare to the west of Dublin and circled north towards Kells.

---

or rapid ford', referring to its strong and unpredictable tides; and (iii) "Ulster" from Old Norse *Ulaðstír*, being an Old Irish genitive of the tribal name mentioned earlier, namely, the Ulaid, along with the Old Norse genitive *s* and the Old Irish word for 'country', that is, *tír*. See also: www.ulsterplacenames.org/maritime_names.htm and MacGhabhann (1997); McKay (2007) and Ó Mainnín (1992). Interestingly, MacGiolla Easpaig (2009: 81) only refers to place names such as "Wicklow", which are in the South of Ireland.

Figure 1 Map of land distribution on the island of Ireland c.1450. (Adapted from http://www.wesleyjohnston.com/users/ireland/maps/historical/map1300.gif – last accessed 8 May 2018).

This was the centre of Anglo-Norman supremacy in Ireland and, indeed, the perception amongst the ruling elite who resided there was that the indigenous inhabitants who lived outside of this territory were both uncivilised and ungovernable: in other words, "Beyond the Pale" (Connolly 2007: 41–42; Hickey 2007: 32). As is often the case in early colonial contexts such as this, De Courcy's attempt to

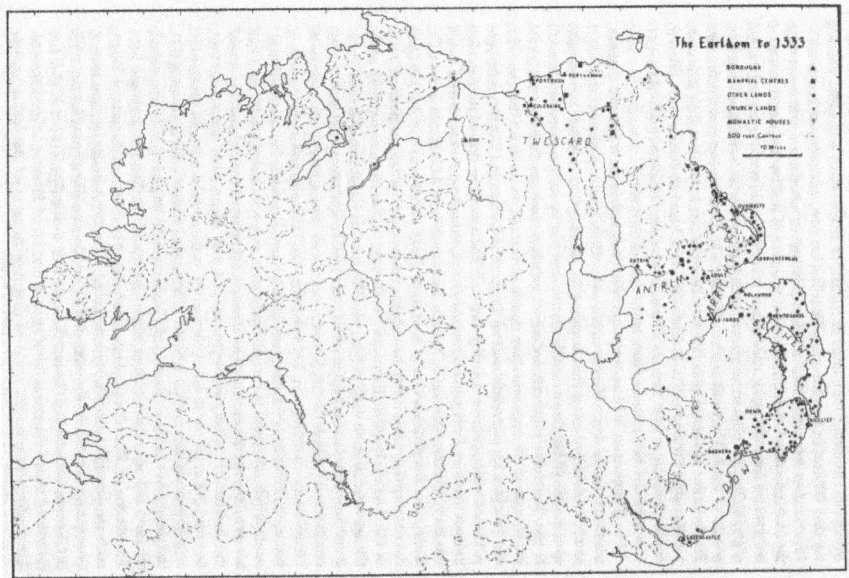

Figure 2 Map of "Pale" type settlement in Medieval Ulster (Image courtesy of T.E. O'Neill (1980: 4) *Anglo-Norman Ulster: The History & Archaeology of an Irish Barony 1177–1400*. Edinburgh: John Donald)[15]

extend Anglo-Norman domination into Ulster established fortified settlements on the most favourable agricultural lowlands of Down and Antrim including Newry, Downpatrick, Dromore, and Carrickfergus (Graham 2000; Jones 2013; Otway-Ruthven 1968: 104 ff.; Smith 2013; Stout and Stout 1997: 53–60; Whelan 1997). The nascent medieval urban spaces, which resulted from this land occupation and grew up around these fortifications (like Carrickfergus Castle in south Antrim), were the first of this "Pale"-like settlement type in Ulster and their extent and principal locations are captured in Figure 2.

This medieval nucleus was then the springboard for the subsequent development of manorial lands and demesnes, which remain an important feature of the landscape of Northern Ireland right up to the present day.[16] By contrast, the Celtic nucleated settlement pattern of the clachán, which also dates back to the medieval period, was quite different (Doherty 2000: 59–62, Evans 1981: 55; Flaherty

---

[15] I am grateful to Angus Wark of the National Library of Scotland for permission to reproduce this digital image from their copy of O'Neill (1980: 4).
[16] Many of these estates are now protected by the National Trust and their history is described in some depth by Reeves-Smyth (1997: 197–205) and Whelan (2000).

2014: 4; Robinson 1991). It persisted alongside the new Anglo-Norman one and indeed, there is considerable archaeological and historiographic evidence to suggest that a Gaelic social and political culture survived both this early medieval phase of colonisation in Ulster, which was Anglo-Norman in character, and the next one which is associated with the Bruce invasions from Scotland during the fourteenth century (Cosgrove 1976; Doherty 2000; Hughes 2005b; Otway-Ruthven 1968; Stout and Stout 1997).

According to Otway-Ruthven, an eminent historian of this period in Ireland, the invasion was probably planned after the Scottish success at the battle of Bannockburn. She also points out that this was clearly a negotiated incursion with the Irish chieftains of Ulster in an attempt to de-stabilize the Anglo-Norman hold over the territory and, of course, to further the Scottish cause against the English (1968: 225).

The key outcome of this alliance between the Scots and the Gaelic leaders reduced the early Anglo-Norman presence in urban Ulster to Newry and Carrickfergus and confined their rural occupation to the eastern coastal fringe (see Figure 2). Edward the Bruce was crowned King of All Ireland as a result of his campaign, which lasted between his first arrival in 1315 near Carrickfergus and his eventual defeat in 1318.

This war is generally accredited with initiating widespread famine on account of the instability that it created since, as Flaherty (2014: 1) argues:

> Human suffering throughout periods of famine is rarely due to lack of food alone. Causes of food insecurity arise not only from inadequacies in food availability and supply channels, but from numerous social factors, such as regional and international trade relations, demographic and agrarian structures, land tenures, political systems and conflicts, and domestic market conditions.

The impact of the Bruce invasion was considerably less deleterious, however, than the food insecurity and allied destabilising factors of the nineteenth century to be discussed in Chapter Three, §3.3. Indeed, the eventual outcome was the resurgence of Gaelic social structures with the result that the third phase of Medieval Ulster (the fifteenth century) is marked by a rather more stable Irish society with the Anglo-Normans retaining their foothold in the east and the two urban centres mentioned above, though internecine struggles continued between the chieftains (see Connolly 2007: 27, 105–106, Graham 1952: 173; Robinson 1994: 4).

2.2.2 Migration and plantation in the Tudor era

The "Reformation Parliament" (1529–1536) of the Tudor era was a key event that also had important repercussions in Ireland (Hickey 2007: 32). Increasingly, the inhabitants of the territory – viewed as they were through the lens of what Palmer (2001: 16) terms "Renaissance anthropology" – are described in *State Papers*, for example, as in need of civilisation and proper government.[17] There is also the suggestion that the Roman Catholic religion that they adhered to and the increasing confrontations previously mentioned between their chieftains and the Anglo-Normans was problematic for Henry VIII who, despite inheriting the title "Earl of Ulster", could not control most of its territory which remained in the possession of its Gaelic chieftains. Indeed, there is evidence that the descendants of the Medieval Anglo-Normans in Ulster (often termed "Old English" to distinguish them from later Jacobite settlers – Booker 2018: 251–253; Connolly 2007: 200; Crowley 2005: 11; Kallen 2013: 17) had acculturated to Gaelic lifestyles and customs. Government edicts imposing the colonists' traditions like the infamous 1366 *Statutes of Kilkenny* had not succeeded in halting this process. Indeed, similar legislation had to be re-enacted in 1537, as the quotation below cited in Ohlmeyer (2016: 27) bears out. The new legal framework attempted once more to Anglicize the Irish and Old English alike by encouraging: "Conformitie, concordance and familiarity in language, tongue, in manners, order and apparel ... betwixt them" and the colonials (see also Booker 2018: 145; Connolly 2007: 34; Crowley 2005: 11–14; Kallen 1997: 10–11, 2013: 15–19). As such, it is clear that the Old English, tied as they were to the same Roman Catholic religion as their Gaelic peers, were also increasingly viewed with suspicion for their unwillingness to participate in Henrician Reformation policies underpinned by Protestantism. Moreover, political unrest in the Pale had spilled into Ulster uniting northern chieftains such as Manus O'Donnell, Earl of Tyrconnell (see Figure 1) with a number of other key Gaelic Houses across much of historical Ulster. These included the O'Neills (whose territory is also located in Figure 1), the Maguires and the O'Cahans, and their collaboration became an important force for the marshalling of Gaelic forces against the King of England and his armies in Ireland (Connolly 2007: 95–107).

While the next phase of Henry's reign in Ireland that is critical to the story of migration and its concomitant promotion of external socio-cultural and linguistic contact had a negligible impact on Ulster at this time, it laid the foundations for a programme of change that would eventually shift the balance of power between allochthonous and autochthonous groups in the region for centuries. The event in question is Henry's so-called "Munster Plantation" (see Kallen 2013: 22). This scheme intended to "plant" or settle loyal British subjects in areas outside of the Pale so as to extend English rule beyond it (Chapter One, §1.6). Although the

---

17 Henry VIII's own negative perspective can be gleaned from: *Letters and Papers, Foreign and Domestic*, Henry VIII: July-December 1536, Volume 11 (1888), pp. 221–257 in: www.british-history.ac.uk/report.aspx. See also Maginn and Ellis (2015).

plantation was not successful in achieving these aims even within the territory of Munster, the idea itself became a cornerstone of English colonial policy in Ireland even after Henry's death (Ohlmeyer 2006). His daughter, Elizabeth I, for example, granted half of County Armagh to a Captain Chatterton (of Wiltshire) who was offered the territories of Orior in the east (near modern Newry, which had always been an Anglo-Norman outpost, as indicated in Figure 2).

Under the terms of his plantation grant, Chatterton was prevented from leasing any land to "mere"[18] Irish or Scots for more than five years. However, in 1576 Chatterton's grant was revoked on account of his failure to make sufficient progress and his endeavours, therefore, had little effect on the distribution of the autochthonous population. Murray (1934) reports that in 1602, Elizabeth I became reconciled to Sir Turlough MacHenry O'Neill, re-granting him the "Orrier" (Orior) lands to the east of this territory (outlined on Bodley's map from the same era in Figure 3) that she had previously awarded to the English captain under a "surrender and regrant" policy.

Figure 3 Map of the Barony of Oneilan in County Armagh by Josias Bodley, 1609[19]

---

18 This does not have the modern meaning, but is closer to the Latin root *mere* meaning 'pure'/'unmixed,' but the intention as a gesture towards social engineering of the ethnic cleansing type is certainly clear.
19 Image courtesy of Paul Johnstone, National Archives at Kew.

2.3 The linguistic repercussions of Medieval and Tudor migrants

This sub-section hones in on the impact of these external, historical events for what Mufwene (2001: 21–24) would term the "language ecology" of the period. In other words, the consequences of language contact for the linguistic environment of individuals which can take the form of cross-dialectal, cross-linguistic and inter-idiolectal variation and can eventually promote change in the entire linguistic system. In this regard, the account also recognises Mufwene's important guiding principle for assigning the causes of variation in such circumstances, namely the so-called "Founder Principle" (2001: 26–27) which entails identifying the specific and often diverse characteristics of the autochthonous and any later allochthonous groups.

It was already noted in §2.1.3 that Latin, as the lingua franca of the Church of Rome, had been in use in Ireland alongside literary and vernacular Old Irish since the introduction of Christianity. The idea that these early Irish Christian institutions had evolved into powerful monasteries in Armagh, Bangor and Derry was also previously discussed. The Anglo-Norman and Tudor eras witnessed even further consolidation and expansion (Stout and Stout 1997: 57). As noted earlier, towards the end of this period, the Old English of Ulster and the Gaelic chieftains were united in their disapproval of the Reformation and indeed the Roman Catholic Church had received considerable wealth from the patronage of both (Stout and Stout 1997: 57).

If we follow the extended diglossia model outlined in §2.1.2.1, Latin was therefore the shared H language of any Anglo-Norman or Gaelic chieftain who had been educated courtesy of the monastic or bardic systems of the time. They each also had H languages that they did not necessarily have in common, namely, literary Gaelic and Norman French, which was the language of the Anglo-Norman legal system subsequent to the colonisation of England in 1066 and, in fact, until 1731 (Kibbee 1991; Rothwell 1998). While literary English was beginning to make an impact on the H domains of Norman French from the 15th century onwards, the spoken English of the servant classes who accompanied the Normans to Ireland would have been perceived as an L language at the time on a par with the Ulster dialect of spoken Gaelic used within this territory (Kallen 1997: 9–10; 2010a: 23; Russell 1995: 69–73). While the Normans were also accompanied by Welsh speakers from Pembrokeshire and Flemish mercenaries, neither of these appear to have had any significant impact on literary Irish or on varieties of Irish English which developed subsequently, which is hardly surprising given their vernacular L status (Hickey 2007: 31).

Of all the potential founder populations of the Medieval and Tudor eras, the Bruce invasion had the least to add to the linguistic heterogeneity of Ulster. This is because of its origins amongst the Gaels of Scotland, coupled with the fact that it was so short-lived. The elites who spearheaded the incursion would also have had access to Latin and to H varieties of Scots Gaelic, itself derived from a previous colonisation of the western seaboard of Scotland c. 500 AD by the Irish *Scoti* tribe from *Dál Riada* (Byrne et al. 2018: 11; Russell 1995: 9–10; Sharpe 2000). The spoken L varieties of the Gaeldom of Scotland used by Bruce's soldiers would, naturally, have developed a certain degree of variation from the Ulster Gaelic L vernaculars at this point, but they must have been mutually intelligible on account of the fact that a dialect continuum that includes shared phonological and morphosyntactic features can be discerned even now (Russell 1995: 61–62; Smith-Christmas and Ó hIfearnáin 2015: 256).

As such, the language ecology amongst the inhabitants of Ulster by the end of the Tudor period was characterised by Latin in the role of H language for elites of both Old English and Gaelic descent alongside the persistence of both Norman French and literary Gaelic as alternative H forms depending on context. English and spoken Gaelic were retained as L forms, though it was clear that the switch from Norman French to English in England, triggered in part by the Hundred Years' War, was beginning to have an impact on the H language preferred in certain circumstances by the Anglo-Normans living in Ireland (Kibbee 1991; Rothwell 1998). Thus, even in the later medieval period, certain governmental and administrative documents, for instance, began to appear in English rather than Norman French (Hickey 1997; Kallen 1997; Lucas 2005). The presence of fifteenth century English manuscripts of Armagh provenance in McIntosh and Samuels (1968: 2), for instance, demonstrates the fact that it already sustained a community of English speakers and writers in this period – most probably on account of its ecclesiastical connections (see Figure 4 and Coote 1804/1984).[20]

As John Swayne declares in the letter to Jamyse Boteler, Fourth Erle of Ormond, contained in the Armagh Diocesan Registry documents and reproduced as Figure 4,

---

20 These texts include four letters from the Armagh Diocesan Registry written between 1428–1441 by Archbishop John Swayne as well as a satirical verse dedicated to female attire included in a Latin document of 1431. The original medieval manuscript requires significant conservation. It is currently in such a poor state of repair that digitising is impossible so I have had to substitute a 17th century transcript of the manuscript. See the original materials in Chart (1935) and their descriptions in Bray (2006: 557–558), which also contains details of a full list of Armagh ecclesiastical manuscripts between 1101 and 1690 as well as Kallen (1994: 164) which focuses on Swayne's contribution. Further elaboration can be obtained from: https://www.nidirect.gov.uk/sites/default/files/publications/armagh-diocesan-registry-archive.pdf (last accessed 9 May 2018). This facsimile is reproduced with the permission of the Deputy Keeper of the Records, the Public Record Office of Northern Ireland and the Registrar of the Diocese of Armagh (PRONI reference number DIO/4/2/4/606/A).

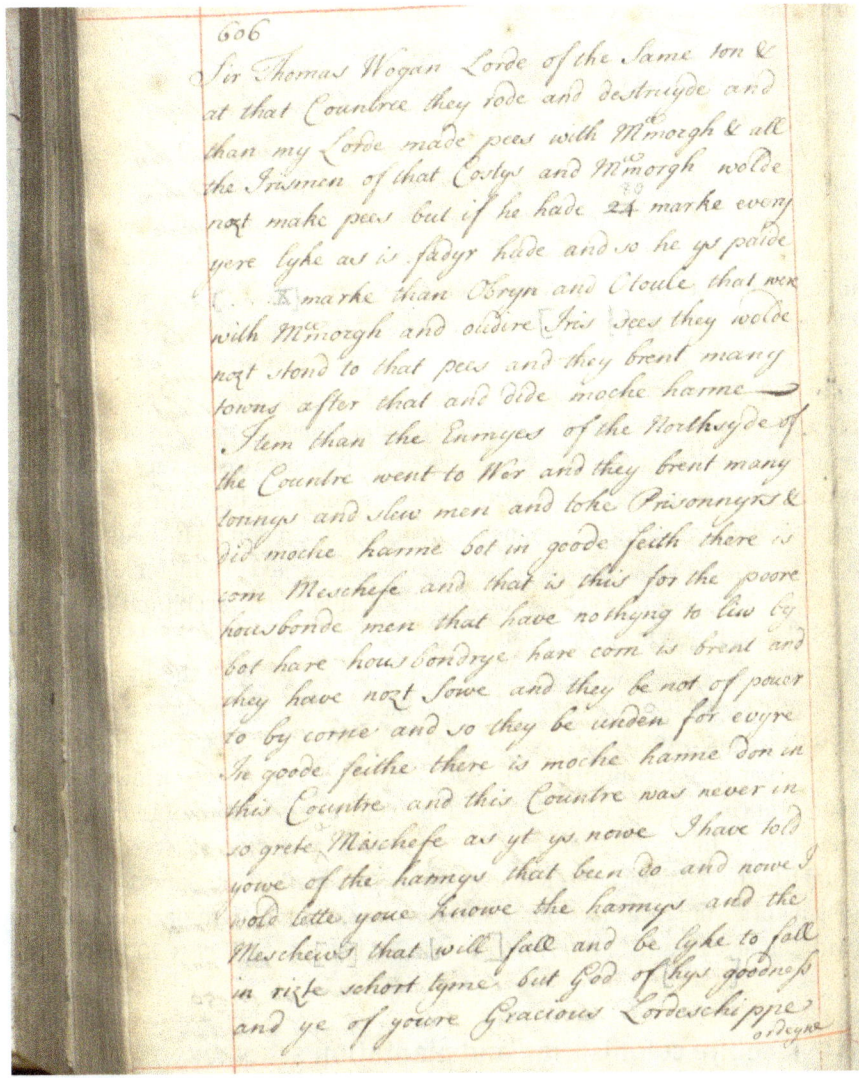

Figure 4 Sample page from a seventeenth century transcript of the original Armagh Diocesan Registry, 1428–1441

there had been considerable unrest in Ireland for much of the medieval period. Indeed, during his own term of office he states that "this Countre was never in so grete Mischiefe as yt ys nowe". He refers, for instance, to "the enmyes of the Northsyde of the Countre" who went to war and "brent many tonnys and slew men and toke Prisonnyrs & did moche harme." It is also important to be aware that the extent to which areas within this factious region were bilingual and which languages inhabitants had competence in depended not only on the origin and social status of the speakers themselves, but also on where they were located. Hence, Anglo-Norman urban settlements there such as Carrickfergus, many of which were redeveloped during Elizabeth I's reign, became commercial and legal centres in which knowledge of both English and Norman French had become essential. This suggests that throughout the sixteenth century, although the rural territories of northern coastal Ulster, for instance, may have owed some allegiance to the Crown, the small numbers of Anglo-Norman settlers who resided in places like this outside of the urban hubs are likely to have further assimilated to the Gaelicised linguistic, legal and socio-political structures that predominated (Barry 2000; Booker 2018: 47 and 52; Connolly 2007: 34; Smyth 2006: 85, 99–100). However, the significance of urban Newry on Strangford Lough for maintaining an open channel of communication between England, its outpost, the Pale and Ulster suggests that its residents will no doubt have increasingly come under the influence of "Englyshe habits", "langage" and "conditions" mentioned in the report on Irish affairs in the *State Papers*[21] offered to Henry VIII in December 1515 (cited in Kallen 1986: 125).

Such reports brought new official declarations that acculturation to the English legal system, lifestyle and language was imperative (such as Henry's decree of 1537). While Conn O'Neill, Earl of Tyrone, is reported shortly afterwards to have declared that his heirs and indeed the people of his earldom more widely would do exactly that, such legislation never really impacted anywhere except in these urban gateways until the Stuart era discussed immediately below. The Nine Years War (1594–1603), in which O'Neill participated against the Tudors, is testament to this, though the defeat of the Gaelic lords – despite assistance from the Roman Catholic Spanish – at Kinsale, County Cork marked the wane of Gaelicised systems of governance that would later be capitalised upon by the Jacobites (Clarke (with Dudley Edwards) 1991: 193; Hayes-McCoy 1996: 51–52; Hickey 2007: 86–87).

2.4 Jacobite colonisation and plantation schemes

James the VI of Scotland (1566–1625) became King of England in 1603 and thus instigated a new era for relations between Ulster and its British neighbours to the south in the Pale and across the sea. Early in his reign he set about reasserting the Henrician Reformation plan. Clarke (with Dudley Edwards 1991: 187), for

---

[21] British History On-line version of Letters and Papers, Foreign and Domestic, Henry VIII: 1515–1518, Volume 2 (1864), pp. 361–375 is available at: www.british-history.ac.uk/report.aspx (last accessed 23 Apr. 2018).

instance, describes his government in relation to Ireland, as "the consolidation of control through deliberate acculturation". This normative approach extended not only to matters of linguistic, religious and socio-political affiliation but also to the terms of land ownership and husbandry. Ulster, which was still heavily Gaelicised and Roman Catholic, was to be the acid test for these Jacobite reforms. A commission was set up to bolster the Tudor "surrender and regrant" legislation so as to introduce Anglicised landholding practices and investigate freehold disputes raised by the Gaelic chieftains and Old English. An important outcome of these machinations was the loss by the newly imprisoned Conn O'Neill of his Clandeboye and Ards estates of north-east Ulster. Sir Arthur Chichester, the Lord Deputy, and two formidable Ayrshire Scots, James Hamilton and Hugh Montgomery, were to be the benefactors. From 1606 onwards, they set about inducing new English and Scottish tenants to migrate to southern Antrim and northern Down, which brought a radical change to the linguistic ecology of the region and initiated the demographic division between the major ethnic groups of contemporary Northern Ireland that will be further elaborated upon in Chapter Four, §4.1. The extent of migration from Lowland Scotland associated with the Hamilton and Montgomery schemes and the origins of the settlers that they attracted, is illustrated in Figure 5.

By comparison to the failed Munster plantation of Henry VIII's reign, these privately funded settlements were a resounding success. While some of the migrants remained in the regions highlighted on Figure 5, it is important to be aware from the perspective of the developing linguistic ecology of the Stuart era that many others eventually travelled further afield (Kallen 2013: 22). Some of these Lowland Scots moved inland settling, for example, in the Fews barony of Armagh also shown on Figure 5, formerly regranted to Sir Turlough MacHenry O'Neill by Elizabeth I (see Oneilan map in §2.2.2). Sites like this were critical to the quest for timber which was in short supply and, therefore, became an important commercial commodity helping the allochthonous population to create new business centres in the barony such as Newtownhamilton and Hamiltonsbawn, named after their Scottish landlord.

More wide-ranging plantations of Ulster during James I's reign were precipitated by the infamous emigration known as "Flight of the Earls" that took place in the early seventeenth century and which can be considered both forced and voluntary in certain respects (Chapter One, §1.5). Though there is not space here to give a full account of the rationale for this event (about which much historical commentary exists, as noted in McCavitt 2005), it refers to the departure without James' permission of leading lights from the Gaelic houses of Ulster to the Continent (Andrews 2000: 153; Clarke with Dudley Edwards 1991: 195–197; Connolly 2007: 274–277; Fitzgerald and Lambkin 2008: 73–75).

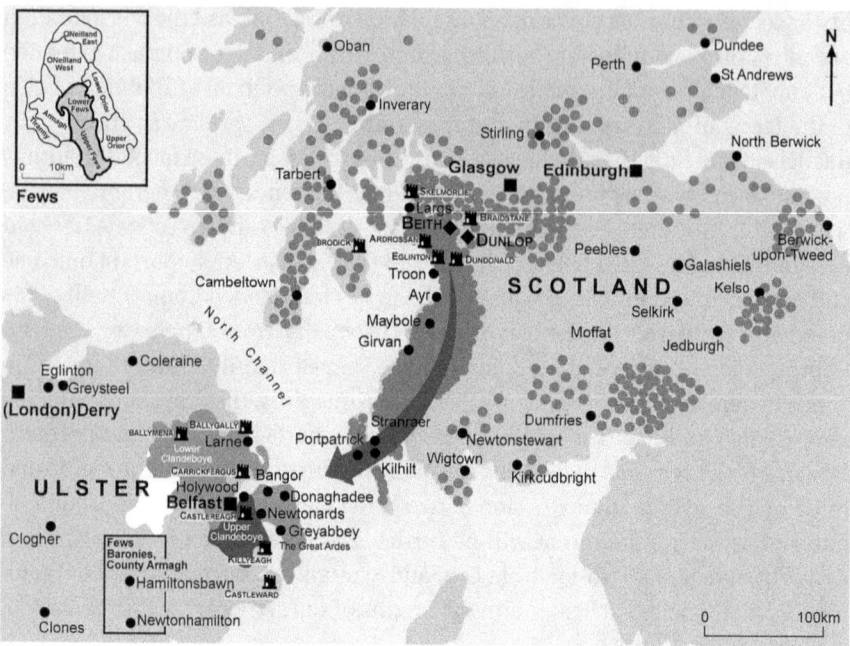

Figure 5 Migratory pathways in Ulster of Lowland Scots settlers under private Hamilton and Montgomery plantation schemes[22]

Particularly crucial to the external linguistic history of Ulster was the fact that on 3rd September 1607 Hugh O'Neill, Earl of Tyrone, left with Rory O'Donnell, Earl of Tyrconnell (both pardoned after the Nine Years' War). This created a vacuum in the prevailing Gaelic power structures, which James rapidly filled by confiscating their vast estates in Armagh, Donegal, Derry, Fermanagh and Tyrone. This allowed him by 1609 to re-constitute the failed plans for the Henrician Munster plantation in Ulster by drawing up the scheme outlined in Figure 6 for re-allocating the O'Neill and O'Donnell lands (Clarke (with Dudley Edwards) 1991: 197–199; Smyth 2006: 85, 99–100).

Ethnic and social groups permitted on the escheated lands, which were not already earmarked for the Church of Ireland or Trinity College Dublin, included "servitors" (royal officials), "undertakers" (wealthy individuals who undertook to transport tenants from their British estates) and "deserving" Irish chieftains thought to be loyal to the Crown. Since servitors often did not have enough private

---

[22] I am grateful to Edinburgh University Press for permission to reproduce this image from Corrigan (2010: 116).

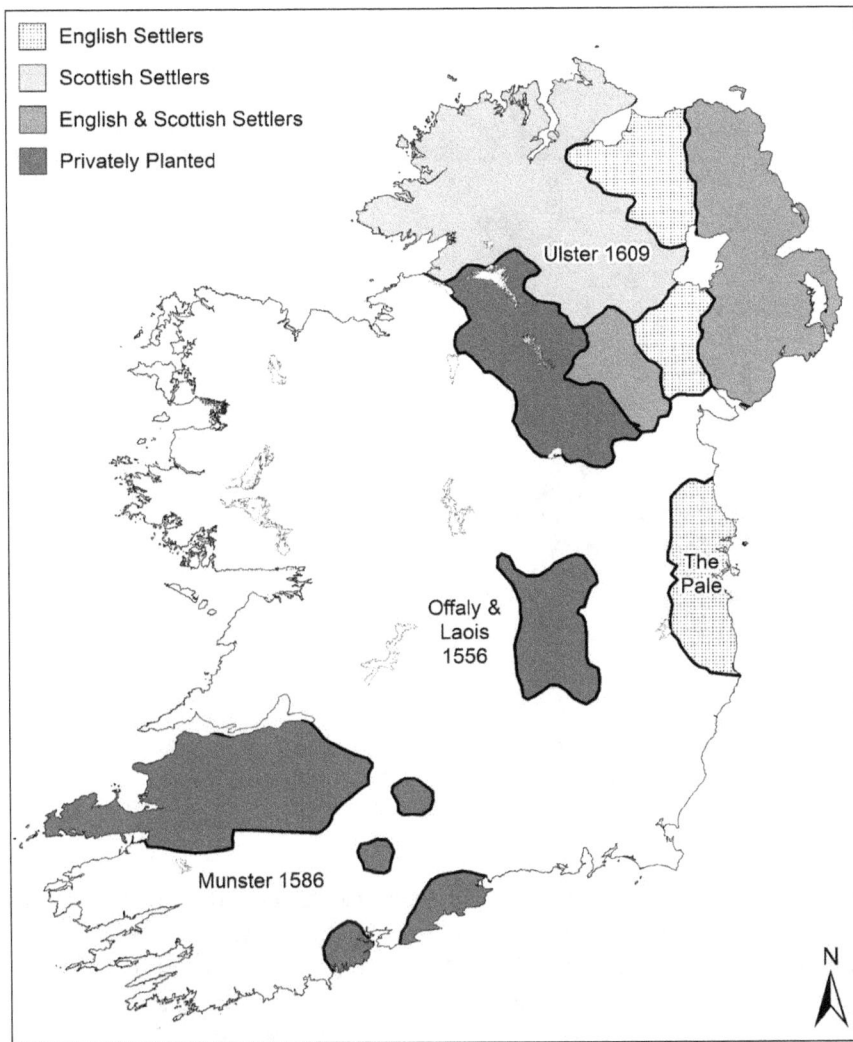

Figure 6 Map of the Irish Plantation schemes, 1550–1610. (After http://www.wesleyjohnston.com/users/ireland/maps/historical/map1609.gif – last accessed on 15 May 2018.)

capital to fund their colonisation activities, their estates were subsidised by the City of London. In recognition, James I granted the town of (London)Derry and lands around Lough Foyle to the City (Braidwood 1964: 21–22; Canny 2001: 200; Clarke with Dudley Edwards 1991: 197–205; Hickey 2007: 89; Robinson 1994: 79–86).

Given the origins of these new British planter populations in the Scottish Lowlands and English north and north Midlands as well as further afield, their arrival would bring new possibilities for language/dialect contact and mixing in Ulster that would be on a scale beyond anything that the region had witnessed in its earlier history (Adams 1958, 1967; Corrigan 1999).

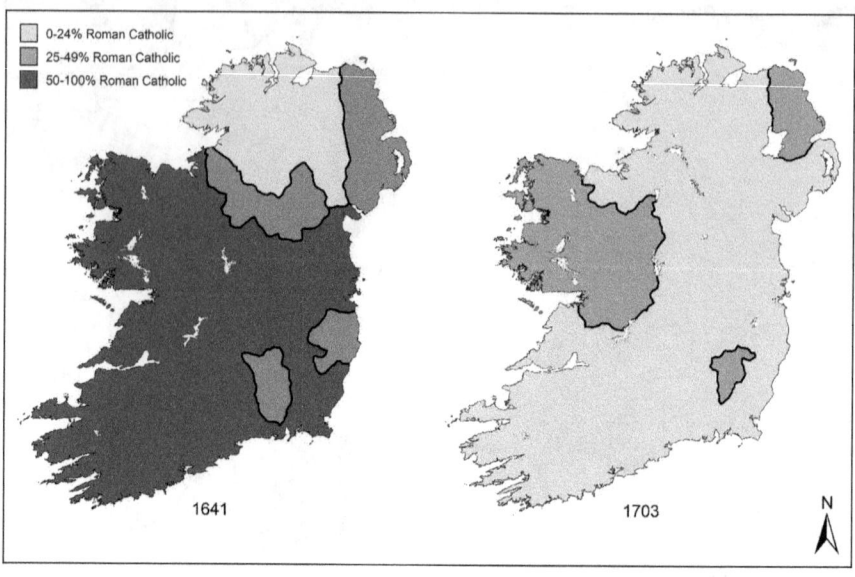

Figure 7 Maps indicating the effect of Cromwell's campaigns on land ownership across the island of Ireland between 1641 and 1703. (After http://www.wesleyjohnston.com/users/ireland/maps/historical/mapcromw.gif – last accessed 17 May 2018.)

The Jacobite plan was largely shaped by the critical lesson learned from the failure of the Munster plantation, namely, to ensure that the Ulster settlement would be secured from future rebellion. Thus, land grants to chieftains were generally restricted to lasting no longer than their lifetimes or that of their spouses, and former Irish tenants on the O'Neill territories were to be relocated to less profitable land. This was an ethnic cleansing policy of sorts (see Chapter One, §1.5) which Garner and Gilligan (2015: 507) assert to be the English State taking on the "role of organising the process of Plantation, and aiming to alter the demographic and social balance of the country" resorting to tactics that "dehumanised the Irish in the eyes of the settlers" (2015: 508). This tactic made the scorched earth policy of the Stuart era as well as later clearances under Cromwell in the 1640s, for instance (which are clear from the contrasts between the 1641 and 1703 maps in Figure 7) justifiable to the planter populations (see Gillen 2016: 49–51). These displacements included forced migrations of the autochthonous population to indentured servitude in far-flung places such as the Caribbean (Delaney 2016: 498).

The overarching aim was to concentrate the British planters around new towns or garrisons, which they were to establish, and they were banned from either taking Irish tenants or from selling land to members of the Gaelic houses. Figure 8 below illustrates the allocation plan for what is now Northern Ireland (omitting Antrim and Down since their colonisation was already established, as noted previously).

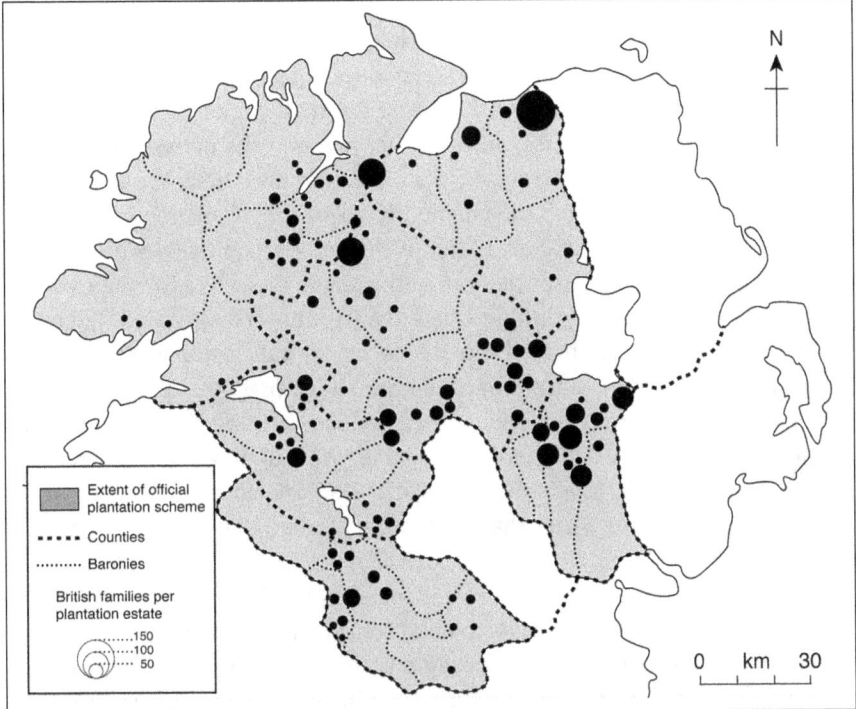

Figure 8 British plantation settlement in Ulster based on the plantation surveys of 1622[23]

2.4.1 Linguistic repercussions

This new phase of plantation settlement across the regions of Ulster had local successes as well as failures and these largely depended on the numbers of British tenants the new landlords could attract as well as the amount of capital the land itself generated to subsidise the rather optimistic agrarian and urbanising

---

[23] I am grateful to Edinburgh University Press for permission to reproduce this image from Corrigan (2010: 118).

demands of the original scheme (Clarke with Dudley Edwards 1991: 223–224). Moreover, Braidwood (1964: 25) notes disagreements over the respective roles of the servitors and undertakers, suggesting that in certain counties they "were at odds" with each other (often because they were unable to secure sufficient British tenants who might arrive under one undertaker's scheme and then transfer their tenancy to another's). As a result, by 1628, legislation was eventually enacted in order to permit Irish tenancies (though the grants were reissued at higher rents to dissuade the practice). While even the most successful plantations succumbed to permitting these, there does not appear to have been much scope in the early plantation phase at least for linguistic or cultural assimilation outside the urban centres, since the act required the natives "to live and build together, and not be dispersed" (Cal. S.P. Ire., 1625–1632, 351 in Robinson 1994: 102). This suggests that Irish monolingualism and a "distinctive identity" persisted even in those rural areas that were densely populated with the new British, and that this was especially so in the poorer areas like the slopes of the Glens, Sperrins and Slieve Gullion where the Irish now congregated (Robinson 1994: 187; and Figure 8). Indeed, the displacement policy which created these isolated pockets of resistance to Jacobite normative practices of urbanisation, land use and inheritance is often credited – along with the Crown's continued suppression of Roman Catholicism, of course – for fuelling the 1641 rebellion led by Phelim O'Neill, involving the seizure of Charlemont Fort in Co. Tyrone and other garrisons in Ulster that precipitated Cromwell's entanglement with Ireland, introduced in § 1.5 of the previous chapter (Clark with Dudley Edwards 1991; Canny 2001: 570; Lenihan 2007; Wheeler 1999). A contemporary description of the events which likely precipitated considerable ethnolinguistic change in this era is captured in a 1641 deposition (9) from Margaret Bromley, a Protestant refugee, formerly residing in affluent Tandragee ('Tonoragge') north County Armagh and expelled from there by the actions of O'Neill and his followers:

(9) Extract from a 1641 deposition from Margaret Bromley, Tandragee
411
Margret Bromley of Ballymore alias Tonoragge in the County of Ardmagh widowe sworne and examined deposeth and sayth That since about the begining of the present Rebellion she this deponent was forceibly at Ballimore aforesaid expelled from deprived robbd or otherwise dispoyled of her goo meanes goodes and Chattells of the value and to her present losse of hereafter mencioned vizt of howshold goods Cattle Corne apparell and money amounting to three hundreth Powndes And that dennis mc Connikin Phelim <a> Mc Gennis Phelomy ô Hanlon and Eveline Hanlone all of the parish of Tondregee are a whoe are all actors in the presente Rebellion

are and stand indebted to her this deponent in seuerall somes amounting in all to lxxvij li. ster. ..... the said Phelomy mc Gennis and Glasny ô Hanlon Nice mc Murphy Callogh ô Hanlon and Laghlin o Rorke, hanged her husband James Bromley and one Richard Wigson murthered william Tod his wife and child, and alsoe they murthered George Copeland and his wiffe John Tost and his wife & 3 children John mc Leglan and his wiffe, and twoe children and drowned John Hartley & Ann watkins And they alsoe murthered Ann Cooke and her twoe Children and one Adam an English yowth all putt to death on May <c> Eve last, And further saith that Aughie ô Hanlon Turlogh ô Hanlon and Henry o Hanlon Edmund ô Neile and shane o Neale murthered John [*draiten*?] this deponents father, and hanged Charles Perkins, although they had first receved three prisoners from Lisnegarvy in exchang for him which were prisoners there And this deponent further saith that the part i e sevenscore and tenn protestants men women and <1.> children were all drowned at Portadowne at one tyme by Toole mc Cann of Portadowne and his Companions and the <2.> Rebells gathered out of seuerall parishes within the County of Ardmaghe

[TCD, 1641 Depositions Project, online transcript January 1970 (http://1641.tcd.ie/deposition.php?depID<?php echo 836040r021?> – last accessed 9 May 2018)]

Interestingly, from our perspective, the settlement patterns stemming from the population movements of the Jacobite era, though they were not always strictly adhered to in reality, are nevertheless key to an understanding of the subsequent development of the contemporary isoglosses that bisect the region, illustrated in Figure 9.

The three major dialect zones of Ulster identified here have traditionally been drawn largely on the basis of phonological criteria, particularly vowel quantity, namely, the duration or length of the vowel segment (Harris 1984; Hickey 2007; McCafferty 2007). South Ulster English (SUE) spoken in border regions of Northern Ireland and the Republic of Ireland, for instance, can be distinguished from Ulster Scots (US) on the basis that, unlike the latter, SUE maintains the historical phonemic vowel length system of West Germanic, as do all varieties in southern Ireland (Kallen 2013). Thus, SUE has two sets of stressed vowel phonemes, one long in duration and one short. Speakers of US varieties, by contrast, have inherited the disrupted system of vowel length transported to Ulster by the Lowland Scottish tenants of Chichester, Hamilton and Montgomery whose speech incorporated an innovation to the West Germanic system which had become established in the Older Scots period (fifteenth to sixteenth century). This new structural property entailed that the length of a vowel was not intrinsic but was determined by the phonetic characteristics of the segment that followed it.

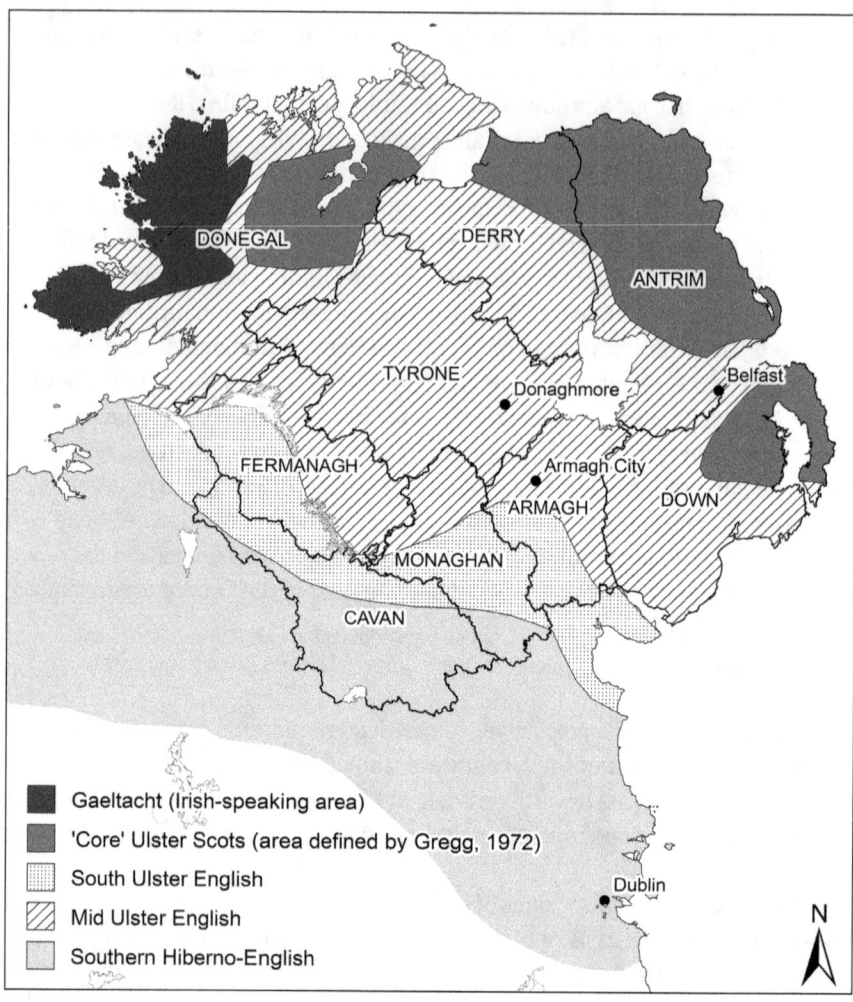

Figure 9 Spatial distribution of language and dialect zones in the original nine counties of Ulster

There are a number of factors which predict vowel quantity and since the phenomenon affects all Scots-influenced dialects it is therefore generally known either as the *Scottish Vowel Length Rule (SVLR)* or *Aitken's Law* in honour of the linguist who first highlighted this important difference between West Germanic-type vowel length and the innovative Scots system (Aitken 1981; McColl Millar 2007). It is important to bear in mind that speakers in the Mid-Ulster English (MUE) zone, being contiguous to both the US- and SUE- speaking regions, will likely have been transitional with respect to vowel quantity as they remain today in settlements to the south, east and west of this zone such as Armagh City, Belfast and Donaghmore, indicated on the map. Thus, some speakers from this dialect zone will have had a system that was closer to West Germanic, while others incorporated the SVLR. As Figure 9 illustrates, this is the predominant dialect region of Ulster stretching as it does south and west along the Lagan Valley from Belfast Lough towards north Armagh and Fermanagh. It also incorporates the whole of County Tyrone as well as the southern reaches of Derry and the North Eastern coastal tip of County Antrim, including Torr Head and Rathlin Island, which were not part of the plantation schemes of this region described earlier given their isolation and low economic value from a colonist's perspective. As such, the MUE zone covered vast tracts of the region's rural landscape, as well as its key urban centres like Newry established from the Medieval period onwards and allocated to the English and Scottish servitors and undertakers. The mixed nature of this variety at all structural levels is reinforced by the interview reproduced in (10) with a SUE speaker from a corpus for Corrigan (1997: Appendix) who notes the similarity in lexis between Counties Armagh (MUE) and Antrim (US).[24]

(10)   Extract from an interview with Jonathan Rogers, Dromintee, 1945

Manuscript: 976
Date: February 1945
Informant: Mr. Jonathan Rogers
Location: Dromintee, County Armagh
Topic: Names

U2200/L3259–3261
What would you say there if you were drivin' the cow out from the byre into the street?

U2201/L3261–3262
Sure what else only "drive the cow out to the Kassie."

U2202/L3262–3263
What else could you put on street in Irish?

U2203/L3263
That's what they always sayed.

U2204/L3263–3264
An' I heard it in County Antrim, that Antrim people call the street the Kassie. [*Own phonetics*]

---

24 The data was compiled from folklore narratives collected by a local fieldworker, Michael J. Murphy, when employed by the Irish Folklore Commission between 1942 and 1974. The original manuscripts are contained in the archives of *Roinn Bhéaloideas Éireann* ('The Irish National Folklore Collection') at University College, Dublin and the material is used with permission.

U2205/L3265-3266
An' there's a lot of other names we have that the Antrim people have.

U2206/L3266
A sort of Scotch.

Population censuses along modern principles in this region did not begin until 1851 and, as such, the success of the private and Jacobite plantation schemes with respect to the introduction of Early Modern English and Older Scots varieties needs to be assessed via different means. Figure 10 gives approximate demographic distributions of different British groups in 1630 according to surnames on the muster rolls. This demonstrates the fact that by 1622 distinctive "preferred areas of settlement" (Robinson 1994: 94) were emerging that were constantly replenished by the internal and external chain migration of similar ethnolinguistic groups. The migratory pattern is not at all dissimilar to the eighteenth century Presbyterian American plantations established by John Rea and the Glass family described in Chapter One, §1.5 nor indeed to the re-grouping of Dutch-Somalis in contemporary research on Leicester conducted by Van Liempt (2011a, 2011b). Fertile and strategic areas like north Armagh, north Derry and the Fermanagh Loughs supported both English and Scots settlers, as Figure 10 (based on research by Robinson 2006a: 7) confirms.

Figure 10 also reveals that migrants of Scottish heritage predominated in Coleraine in northeast Derry as well as the coastal fringes of northeast Antrim and the Ardglass Peninsula. Places with more marginal land like mid-Ulster, Rathlin Island and the adjacent mountains of northeast Antrim as well as the extreme south of Fermanagh and the *Oirghialla* district of south Armagh and Down, by contrast, must have had concentrated clusters of native Irish inhabitants on account of the low numbers of British surnames on the rolls. In addition, there is considerable personal name and genealogical evidence that supports the persistence of indigenous groups in this region (Smith 1995: 30–31). Unsurprisingly, therefore, south Armagh especially was a hotbed of insurrection for centuries leading it to be dubbed during the so-called "Troubles" of the later twentieth century as "Bandit Country" by Merlyn Rees, the then Secretary of State (see Chapter Three, §3.2, §3.4 and Chapter Four, §4.1; Russell 2015: 10–12; and Figure 12). Hence, there is evidence that even as early as the seventeenth century the SUE dialect zone illustrated in Figure 9 was already becoming established, and that the north eastern corner of Antrim, where a modern dialect isogloss separates the US-speaking regions from an isolated pocket of MUE, was already immune from the considerable Scots influence in their hinterlands. Evidence for the persistence of these demographic settlement patterns and their reflection in contemporary dialect differences across Northern Ireland, as argued in

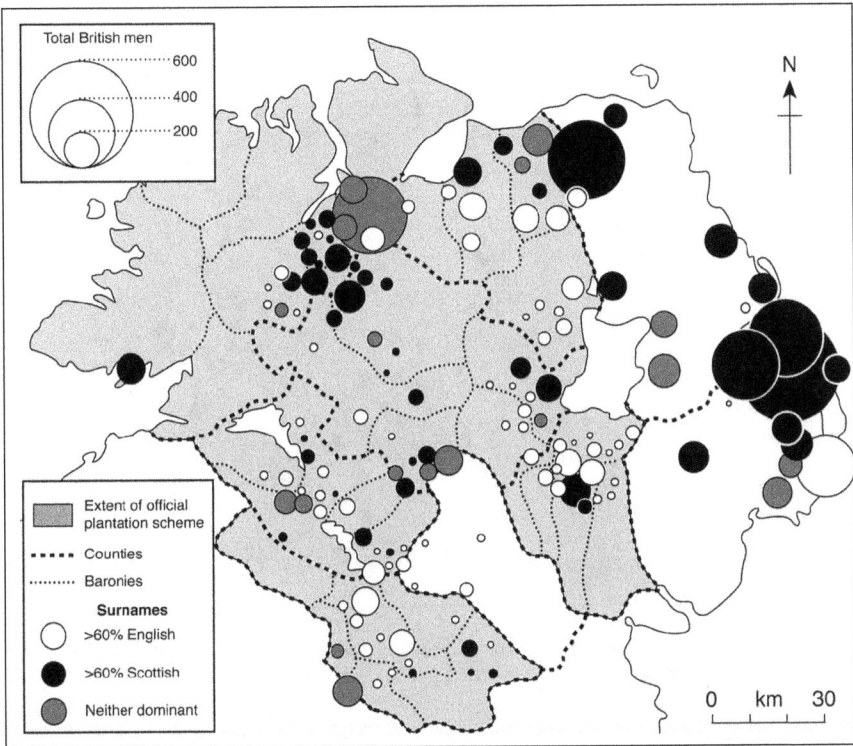

Figure 10 Map showing the demographic distributions of different British groups in 1630 according to surnames on the muster rolls[25]

Corrigan (2010), is clear from Figures 11 and 12 based on new data captured from responses to the Northern Ireland 2011 Census. The US dialect zone transpires centuries beyond the initial plantation schemes to remain closely affiliated with those regions where at least 75% of the population declared themselves in 2011 to have a Protestant background (i.e. of ethnically Scots or English extraction) (see Russell 2015: 10–12; and Figure 11).

In the same vein, Table 1 below, which is adapted from Corrigan (2010: 120) and Robinson (1994: 105), gives the demographic proportions of ethnically Irish as well as inhabitants of British (English and Scottish) heritage per county on the basis of an early "Census" compiled by Sir William Petty between 1655 and 1659. Although the Scots and English are not separated in this Table and there are

---

[25] I am grateful to Edinburgh University Press for permission to reproduce this image from Corrigan (2010: 119).

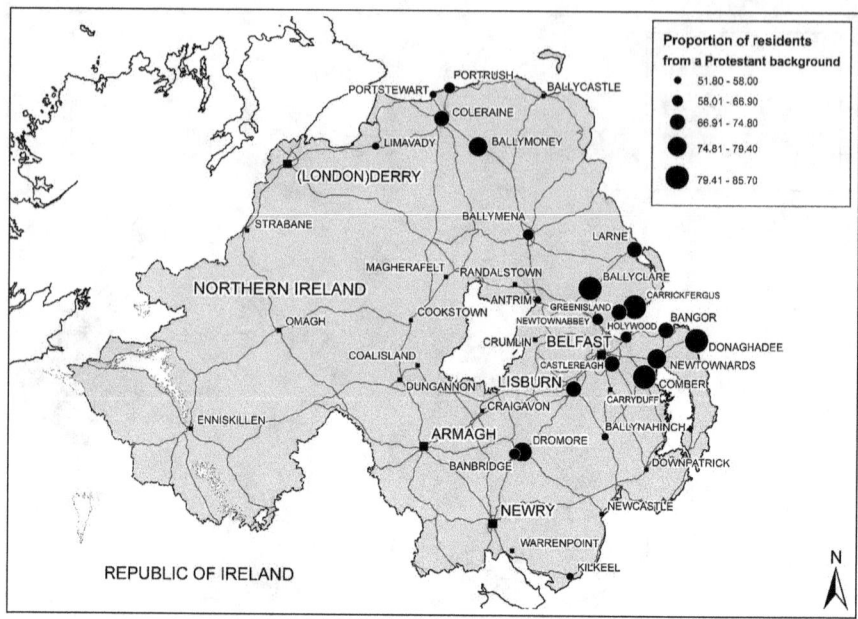

Figure 11 Settlements in Bands A-E where the proportion of residents from a Protestant community background exceeded 50 % in the 2011 Census of Northern Ireland[26]

Table 1 Demographic proportions of ethnically distinctive inhabitants of 5 Ulster Counties[27]

County	British	Irish
Antrim	45 %	55 %
Armagh	35 %	65 %
Derry	45 %	55 %
Down	43 %	57 %
Fermanagh	11 %	89 %
Total	**37 %**	**63 %**

---

26 Adapted from Russell (2015: 11).
27 The poll-tax lists for Tyrone have, unfortunately, not survived (Robinson 1994: 105) but would most likely have included Irish surnames in areas of marginal land like the Sperrins which, as we shall see in subsequent chapters, supported a *Gaeltacht* ('Irish-speaking district') community well into the twentieth century.

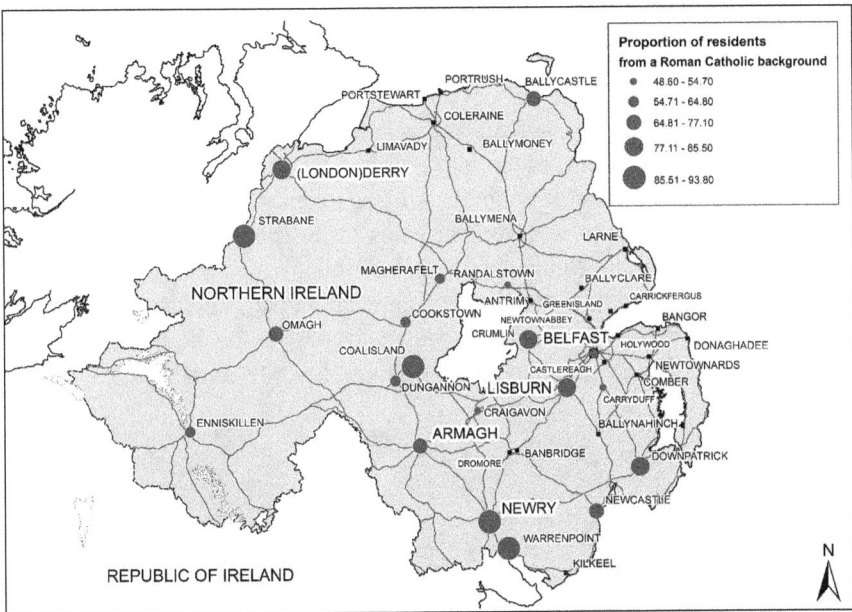

Figure 12 Settlements in Bands A-E where the proportion of residents from a Roman Catholic community background exceeded 45% in the 2011 Census of Northern Ireland[28]

aspects of the source itself that are problematic,[29] it is useful from the perspective of further demonstrating the predominance of native Irish in Armagh and Fermanagh at this time.

Interestingly, the preponderance for higher concentrations of autochthonous groups to remain in the poorer regions of counties that extend into the SUE dialect zone such as Armagh, Down and Fermanagh is echoed in the demographic data presented in Figure 12. It was supplied by respondents to the most recent 2011 Census claiming to have been raised within the Roman Catholic religion (i.e. between 45% to 94% in these counties, as detailed in Russell 2015: 10–12).

As far as the effects on language and dialect use of the population distributions illustrated in Figures 10–12 and Table 1 are concerned, then, the overall pattern for the native Irish at the close of the Stuart era appears to be one of maintaining Gaelic rather than shifting to varieties of English or Scots. This will have been especially true for areas like Rathlin Island, the Glens of Antrim and remoter parts of *Oirghialla* and Fermanagh as well as the more inhospitable reaches of

---

28 Adapted from Russell (2015: 10).
29 Andrews (2000) and Smyth (2000) provide critiques.

mid-Ulster such as the Sperrins in west Tyrone. Nevertheless, specific areas can be conjectured in which: (i) stable Irish-English bilingualism prevails (rural areas near centres of influence like the new market towns established by the British, for instance) and (ii) unstable bilingualism with Gaelic increasingly recessive (particularly amongst urbanites in more established towns and villages). As for the British populations, there is evidence of dialect contact throughout the region that is roughly contiguous with contemporary MUE. The Scots settlers in Antrim and northeast Down, by comparison, will have maintained their original varieties more readily since they had less communication with English settlers – not least because of their resistance as dissenters to adapt to the requirements of the Established Church, already detailed in Chapter One, §1.5 and discussed further in the next.

3 Migration and language ecology: enlightenment to famine

3.1 Overview

The period from the dramatic internal and external migrations of the Stuart era discussed in the previous Chapter to modern times is marked particularly by four principal cultural and social changes. In the first place, there is evidence of increased contact between diverse ethnolinguistic groups because of improved communication links both internally and externally. In addition, there were far-reaching economic, political and societal changes that also had an impact on the language ecology of the region. These included the instigation of the Catholic Relief Act of 1792 which provided new opportunities for educated members of the autochthonous population who could now seek work in professional contexts such as the law, from which they had previously been barred (Gillen 2016: 48, 64). Alongside measures such as these which were intended to ameliorate the position of Roman Catholics, there was also further ethnic cleansing affecting the autochthonous groups in the form of Roman Catholic expulsions during the 1790s. Whelan (1996: 123) cites the expulsions of 1795 and 1796 as recalled by one of their victims, a John Lennon who was forced to flee from County Armagh into Drogheda (now in the Republic of Ireland):

(11)   John Lennon's personal recollection of the 1790s Catholic expulsions

I cannot forget when six hundred families were banished from their homes, in the county of Armagh, in one year; every Catholic house was closed at night, and all their windows built up with stone and mortar, unless weavers' windows, which were filled up at night with bog oak blocks, lest the inmates be shot at their work, as many were. Every magistrate in Ulster, but one or two, was an Orangeman, and no justice could be obtained either in courts of law, or elsewhere.

In the south of the County, the Forkhill disturbances placed the native Irish at a further psychological distance from loyalists who popularly came to view the region as a "fount of discord" (Miller 1983: 178) where they could not "stem the unrest ... on the part of Catholics enraged by physical and cultural encroachments of an improvement scheme" (Miller 1983: 179).

Unsurprisingly, therefore, this period also witnessed accelerated migration streams to North America. First to leave in the early eighteenth century were

Ulster Presbyterians such as John Rea and the Glass family, who already featured in Chapter One, §1.5 (see Hickey 2004b: 102–104). More significant was the diasporic forced migrations and mortality rates (particularly amongst Roman Catholics) associated with agrarian disasters of the 1840s and 1850s (Chapter One, §1.4 and 1.5 and see Hickey 2004b: 104–106).

3.2 Population distribution and its impact on language ecology during the age of enlightenment

The eighteenth century, often termed the "Age of Enlightenment" can also be considered an era of improvement in Ulster. Killen (1997), Smyth (2000) and Whelan (1997) all confirm that the period was pivotal for upgrading communications both within Ireland and to Britain, facilitating internal and external migration as well as linking what Chambers and Trudgill (1998: 183) in their gravity model of diffusion refer to as "central" places with outlying districts, especially the once "peripheral" rural areas.

Agrarian improvements and the demands of the burgeoning linen industry required significant development of the region's infrastructure, particularly the creation of new turnpike roads linking Dublin with much of the north east coast as well as Armagh, which remained the ecclesiastical capital (Gillen 2016: 60–61; Killen 1997: 209). Moreover, McCutcheon (1965: 11) also cites the opening of the eighteenth century as the period when "the concept of inland navigation along artificial cuts emerged as an essential factor in the growth of industry and commerce already beginning to gather momentum."

In fact, linen production here became the first industry in Ulster to have a truly global reach so that many former villages that were well situated geographically near these communication networks became heavily industrialised with bleaching greens, beetling mills, weavers' cottages and new merchants' villas all in close proximity (Cohen 1997; Harris 1998; Rankin 2002). While these were especially prevalent in Antrim and Down, they existed right across the region (Flaherty 2014: 4; Whelan 1997: 77). Whelan (1997: 192) defines such settlements as "Irish outliers of the British industrial village tradition, encompassing company towns like Sion Mills and Bessbrook". Their presence and the strong mobility links they created between the rural population and industrialists in larger urban centres who took on responsibility for manufacturing and selling the raw materials which these villagers produced was critical to the future industrialisation of the east coast of Ulster in particular (Whelan 1997, 2000; McCutcheon 1984; MacRaild 2011; Rankin 2002; Warden 2013).

The switch in the eighteenth century from local cottage industry to commercial manufacture and international trade led to increased affluence amongst the immigrant British planter populations of Ulster. This economic boom could not be matched either by Roman Catholics living in the territories reserved for them by colonial edicts where they had become ghettoized as a result of forced migrations, or indeed by their peers in isolated rural enclaves where Gaelic identity was strongest. Both types of autochthonous group for much of the eighteenth century, in fact, persisted with a traditional agrarian economy. Towards the end of the century, however, Roman Catholics had entered into the linen industry – though as the less lucrative weaver class, as noted in Whelan (1996). Manufacturers, however, seem to have been drawn largely from the new British settler population such as those like Ogilvy Graham mentioned in Chapter Four §4.1, who successfully ran the York Street Flax Spinning and Weaving Company in Belfast and Lurgan – the largest of its kind in the world at the time. They were joined in the later nineteenth and early twentieth centuries by groups of German (Jewish) merchants who migrated to Ulster and became key players there on the back of the wealth and status they also accrued as linen and shipbuilding barons (see Chapter Four to follow as well as Gibbon 1975; Rankin 2002 and Warden 2013).

An important consequence of the abandonment in the eighteenth century of agriculture in favour of linen production, with respect to the language ecology of the region, was the subdivision of farm holdings and greater concentrations of unsegregated religious populations within the linen heartlands. There was thus renewed competition for livelihoods between the autochthonous and allochthonous groups as well as what Flaherty (2014: 3) terms diverse "socio-ecological regimes". A flavour of the socio-economics and mobility of the period is captured in this correspondence extract (12) from Fitzpatrick's *Oceans of Consolation* corpus (1994: 375), which discusses the success of *waving* ('weaving').[30] It was written from Killicomane (near contemporary Portadown, County Armagh) in 1844 to Joseph Hammond who had recently emigrated to Melbourne, Australia.[31]

---

30 For analysis of the MEAT/MATE apparent merger that results in such pronunciations in Irish English historically, see Harris (1985); Maguire, Clark and Watson (2013) and Milroy and Harris (1980). See also Hickey (2004b: 109–110) as well as Corrigan (2010: 34–35) who discusses its persistence in the casual speech styles of contemporary speakers.
31 I am grateful to David Fitzpatrick for sharing all his original *Oceans* corpus data with me for this purpose. See also Corrigan (2020) who uses these and similar materials to assess the extent of Irish migrant settlement in Australia during the Gold Rush era and its impact on the subsequent development of Australian English.

(12)   Letter to Joseph Hammond, Melbourne Australia, 1844

> Killicomane
> 14th May 1844
>
> Dear Son
> The waving Buisness is doing well in this Country at present and provisions on a reasonable Scale. William Murry has took to drapering these last few years and is in a fair way of makeing a fortune, and we think that Coloney will Be a poor place in the course of a few years by reason of so much Emigration to it yearly, and but bad Encouragment when there for the working Classes. And we further hope that what we have Said on the Subject will make a deep Impression on Your mind to fulfill the same if God permit.
>
> Mary Develine
> John and Mary ann Hammond
> Danl Develine

Other socio-political changes in the period likewise had an impact – particularly the repeal of previous colonial legal sanctions such as the Penal Laws outlined in Chapter One, §1.5, which included the granting of the right to bear arms to assimilated Roman Catholic and other converts to the Church of Ireland. These changes are captured in the text below from CORIECOR indicating the socio-economic advances of the Moore family from County Antrim referred to already in Chapter One, §1.5. Interestingly, the right to bear arms for this clan was apparently not granted until well into the nineteenth century, as (13) indicates.

(13)   HC Lawlor letter extract, Ulster, 1915

Title:	H C Lawlor to Mr Kernoghan, Re Moore and Fleming Families
Source:	D 1897: Presented by Anonymous. #TYPE LET Letter from H.C. Lawlor, Belfast to Mr Kernoghan concerning Genealogical Research into the Families of Moore, Derrykeighan, Co Antrim and Fleming Aughnacloy Co. Tyrone, 1915.
Archive:	The Public Record Office, N. Ireland
Doc. No.:	89009175
Date:	01/01/1915
Doc Type:	LET
Log:	06:10:1989 LT created 03:10:1990 MC input 08:10:1990 SB checked

It seems only to have been from about 1700 any of the Co [*County?*] Antrim Moores became men of some inportance, and if I am

> not mistaken the [*Ballydivity?*] Moores
> had no money to secure a perpetuity lease
> from the 5th Earl of Antrim about 1740 –
> This may I think be regarded as the
> foundation of the Family – I think the
> Moore Lodge & Moorefort families date
> from about the same time as their lands
> seem to be parts of the Forfeited lands of
> Sir James McDonald ... **no Moore of County
> Antrim was entitled to bear arms up to at
> least 1840** ...

Important also with respect to the social advancement of hitherto repressed ethnic groups during the Enlightenment era was the disbanding of the radical (Jacobin) Protestant Volunteers and their replacement with a largely Roman Catholic militia after the outbreak of war with France in 1793 (Miller 1990; Whelan 1996). These concessions, coupled with the fact that Roman Catholics had gained a foothold in Ulster's economic power via the linen industry, gave them membership of the polity that, since Jacobean times, had been the preserve of the allochthonous groups. Secret societies like the "Defenders" who hoped to reassert a Gaelic way of life began to surface. As they emerged, so too did the Protestant "Peep o' Day Boys" and eventually the "Orange Order" (formed in north Armagh in 1795) in direct opposition to any democratisation of autochthonous or allochthonous dissenter groups (Parkinson and Phoenix 2010: 40; Whelan 1996: 39–40, 115–116). Curiously, from the perspective of the contemporary sectarian politics of this region, which will become an important focal point of Chapter Four, the Scots dissenter population, who themselves had their own share of exclusions from the body politic to contend with – on account of their Presbyterianism – sided with the Defenders to form the "United Irishmen" (Gillen 2016: 55; Whelan 1996: 101). The two groups challenged, though failed to overcome, the British Protestant ascendancy in the 1798 rebellion (precipitated largely by the mass expulsions of Roman Catholics in south Ulster in 1795 and 1796, as noted in Miller 1990 and Whelan 1996). The evictions themselves – akin to the Highland Clearances of the same era in Scotland (Devine 2006; Smith-Christmas and Ó hIfearnáin 2015) – as well as the rebellion and its aftermath – undermined traditional kinship network structures in the most heavily Gaelicised regions, and this had important consequences for the stability of the autochthonous population and their mother tongue, which will be explored further in §3.4.

Events like the forced migrations and unsuccessful rebellions – alongside the eventual collapse of the linen industry, which could not compete with slave cotton – also encouraged many affluent Presbyterians like John Rea, mentioned earlier, from the core US areas (Antrim, Derry, Down and Donegal) to emigrate to North America as "Scotch-Irish" (Fischer 1991; Hofstra 2011b; Montgomery 2017; Ridner 2018; Rossiter 2006; Webb 2009). The mood of the times amongst this dissenter group is testified to in this CORIECOR letter extract (14) printed in the June edition of the *Belfast Newsletter* in the same year as the 1774 Irish Oath of Allegiance was passed (referred to here as 'the late act' and designed to ameliorate the position of Roman Catholics, as articulated in Morley 2009):

(14) Extract from a letter printed in a 1774 edition of the Belfast Newsletter

Title:	Extract of a Letter From Derry, June 14, 1774
Source:	The Belfast News-letter, Tuesday 21 to Friday 24 June, 1774
Archive:	The Central Library, Belfast
Doc. No.:	1200322
Date:	21/06/1774
Doc Type:	LET
Log:	Document added by LT, 19:12:00

… You cannot conceive the ferment the Presbyterians are in on acccount of the late act. **Multitudes *are daily arriving here to go to America.** There are 5 large ships in this port ready to sail, each of whom will take at least 500 passengers, which will amount to 2500 souls of the most industrious people of this kingdom. We are apprehensive that the spirit of emigration will soon depopulate this country, if some method is not speedily taken to put a stop to it …

The arrival of the Scotch-Irish helped to fuel the Anglophobia that was a precursor to the War of Independence (1775–1782) and the creation of the new Republic out of another British colony. (Daniels 1991; Fischer 1991; Fitzgerald and Lambkin 2008; Harrison Taylor 2017; Hofstra 2011b; Jones 1960; Leyburn 1989; Montgomery 2017; Ridner 2018; Rossiter 2006; Spencer and Wilson 2006; Webb 2009). Likewise, events across the Atlantic involving dissenting Ulster Presbyterians no doubt precipitated the passing of the Act of Union in 1801 – a legislative manoeuvre that the British government hoped would finally quell Irish nationalism and insurrection.

3.3 Population decline and mobility in the nineteenth century

The employment opportunities which manufacturing as well as the new shipbuilding and other heavy industries of the nineteenth and later centuries created in and around Belfast (now surpassing Newry in importance) became an important pull factor encouraging the further growth of the urban settlements of the east coast and the Lagan valley (Geary and Johnson 1989; Fitzgerald and Lambkin 2008). This was especially so after linen production became uneconomic, and, naturally, the food insecurity (Flaherty 2014) associated with the onset of the large scale potato blight which began in the late 1840's also encouraged population displacement, arising from both internal migration to urban areas in search of famine relief in the burgeoning Victorian poor houses, as well as external migration of the type referred to in the Hammond letter outlined in (12), §3.2 (Cousens 1960; Davis 1992; Duffy 2000; Fitzgerald and Lambkin 2008; Flaherty 2014; Harris 1998; Kennedy *et al.* 1999; Kinealy and MacAtasney 2000; Kinealy 1995; Kinealy and Parkhill 2014; McCutcheon 1984; MacRaild 2011; Miller 1985; Neal 1998; Ó Gráda 2000; Ó Riagáin 1997; Thomas 2005). Thus, as noted in NISRA (2005: 29), "in 1821, 2% of the population lived in towns over 10,000 in population (in effect, in Belfast). By 1901, the proportion was 28% spread over a greater number of settlements, and by 1926, it was 36%."

Other wide-ranging socio-economic changes were already taking place in Ulster prior to the 1840s, including a reduction in the fertility rate and the introduction of new family structures as well as agricultural and industrial practices (Duffy 2000; MacRaild 2011; Whelan 1997). As Whelan (1997: 89) notes, therefore, an important outcome of the successive potato blights of the mid nineteenth century was the acceleration of these changes to enhance "agrarian Anglicisation" and promote a "social engineering" programme that would allow the Protestant Ascendancy to remove from their estates "a pauper [Catholic] tenantry whose tenacious grip on the land was providentially loosened by the blight". Reasonably reliable estimates of population decline suggest that between 1846 and 1851 almost one million people across the whole of the island died of starvation and the epidemics that followed. Moreover, two million emigrated over a very contracted time-span (1845–1855), as the declines in population figures for these years in particular, in Figure 13, illustrates.

While these figures and contemporary reports generally indicate that Ulster fared comparatively better and recovered quicker from these events than either Munster or Connacht, for instance, it did not go unscathed and the southern counties like Armagh, Cavan, Fermanagh and Monaghan were particularly affected (MacRaild 2011; Kinealy and Parkhill 2014).

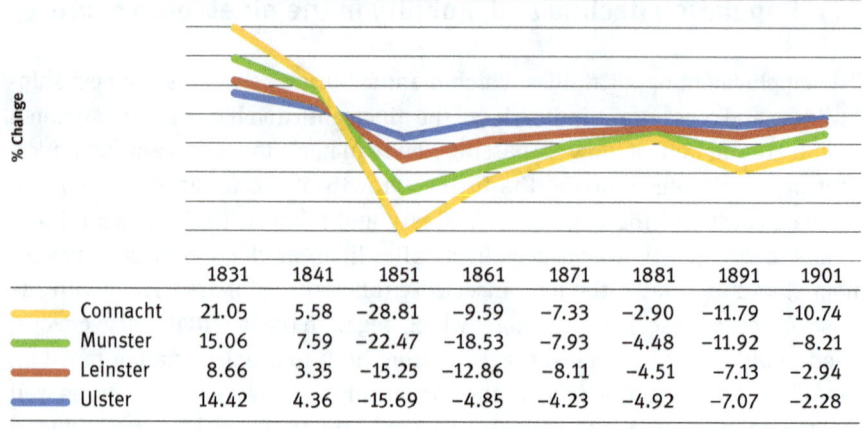

Figure 13 Percentage change in population by province, 1831–1901 (After Vaughan and Fitzpatrick 1978: 15–16)

Insight into the impact of these successive failures of the potato crop can be gained from the suggestion by socio-economic historians like Ó Gráda (2000: 232) and others that the global scale of destruction that accompanied this agricultural disaster was proportionately higher than that of any other famine in either modern or current times (see also Boylan 2016). The CORIECOR letters for the 1840s are replete with commentary on the impact locally, such as that in this 1846 letter in (15), written by a member of the Lawless family and sent from Callystown, County Louth to a relation in Wisconsin, in the United States of America (USA). These are also testament to the devastating results of the successive blights affecting the staple crop feeding South Ulster's population during what rightly became known as the Great Famine.

(15)   1846 Letter from Lawless Family, County Louth to Wisconsin, USA

Title: Lawless, Callystown, Louth, To John Lawless, Wisconsin
Source: T.2345/2: Copied by Permission of Dr E R Green, Dept of History, Manchester Univ. Manchester, G.B. #TYPE LET [?] Lawless, Callystown, Co. Louth, To His Brother, John Lawless, Patch Grove Post Office, Wisconsin Territory, Upper Mississippi, America. 30th July 1846
Archive: Public Record Office Northern Ireland
Doc. No.: 8809134
Date: 30/07/1846
Doc Type: LET
Log: 21:09:1988 GC created 12:12:1988 ET input 24:01:1989 PG checked

> Callystown
> 30 July 1846
>
> The potato crop has failed
> in this country this years as it did in 1845 with
> the difference that the distemper or infection set in this
> year about the end of June before the late crop
> planted in May had time to form – the early ones
> are very much infected in places but the disease
> is progressing & we all consider that there will not
> be a potato to put in in November. We have also
> have great rains & secure gales of wind which it is
> [?] has injured the corn crops so that you see
> there is a poor look-out for the ensuring [*ensuing?*] spring &
> summer should the potato crop fail as is anticipated
> my business falls to the ground

In a similar vein, Froggatt (1989: 143–144) describes the impact on the local Board of Health in Belfast established in 1847 directly in response to the famine conditions just described. 15,630 epidemic cases were admitted to all the Belfast hospitals (as well as temporary accommodation) and 2,500 of these patients subsequently died. When weighed against the general population of Belfast by this time (c. 100,000), this figure accounts for the death of one in six of its inhabitants. Of course, this does not include the hundreds who undoubtedly also died outwith the health board institutions at home, as Delaney (2012: 144–145) recounts, or in workhouses and the like. These would include the 95 who Kinealy and Parkhill (2014) report to have succumbed in just one week of February 1847 also in Lurgan, County Armagh – the epicentre of "prosperous and industrious" Ulster (Delaney 2012: 41) (Delaney 2014; Craig 1974; Kinealy and MacAtasney 2000; Kinealy and Parkhill 2014; MacRaild 2011; Whelan 1997: 89).

The reasons for this major famine event in world terms are neatly summarized by Boylan (2016: 419) who argues that it:

> took place in a very severe and unforgiving ideological climate that ultimately, because of a fervent adherence to the 'natural laws' of God and the market and a determination to force modernization on a recalcitrant nation, meant that relief measures were inadequate to the task facing them.

It is not difficult to understand therefore why forced migration was a typical response. Moreover, as far as Famine emigration from Ulster to the United States is concerned, Akenson (1992: 105) estimates that after Munster, the inhabitants of northern counties were most likely to emigrate, and this view is echoed by

Garner and Gilligan (2015: 512) as well as Miller (1985: 293) who argues for a chain migration scenario, i.e. that: "the potato blight merely confirmed the already-established patterns of pre-Famine emigration" and migrants from south Ulster were especially mobile (see Figure 14).

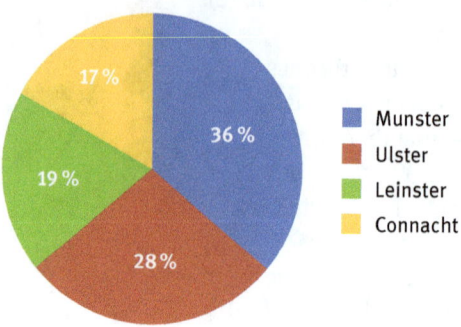

Figure 14 Source of Irish emigrants by province (1851–1900)

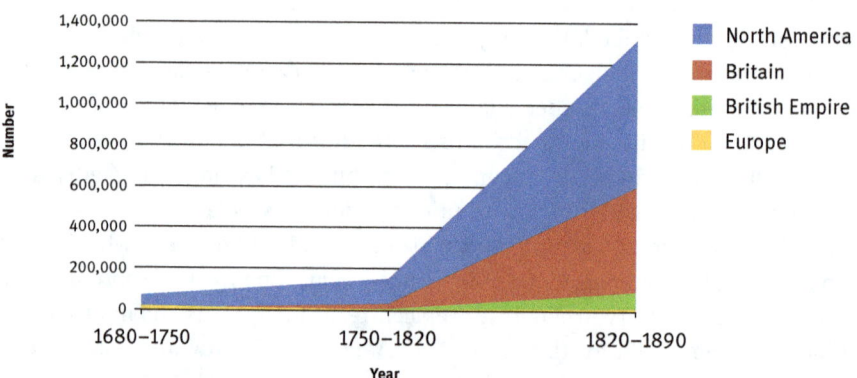

Figure 15 Principal destinations of Ulster emigrants (1680–1890)

This was likely due to the fact that Scotch-Irish mobility links between Ulster and North America via bridgeheads had already been established in the eighteenth century, as already noted in this Chapter and elsewhere. The consequences of this chain migration process are clearly evident from Figure 15, which roughly estimates the emigration destination patterns between the late seventeenth and nineteenth centuries (based on figures cited in Fitzgerald 2006, Fitzgerald and Lambkin 2008 and Devlin Trew 2013) in which North America is the most prominent destination for much of the period.

While this era also included migration to what became the British Empire (particularly Australia from the 1750s onwards, as documented in Fitzpatrick 1994 and Corrigan 2020) as well as Continental Europe (Lyons and O'Connor 2008), poorer migrants during the Famine exodus preferred Britain to North America (Cousens 1960; Swift 1992). They settled especially in those Victorian cities in Figure 16 that were driving the Industrial Revolution such as Glasgow, Liverpool, London, Newcastle and Manchester (Akenson 1992; Beal and Corrigan 2009; Corrigan 1992, 1999; Crowley 2012; Delaney 2014; Devlin Trew 2013; Fitzpatrick 1994; Fitzgerald 2006; Fitzgerald and Lambkin 2008; Grant 1990; Kerswill 2018; MacRaild 2006, 2011; Neal 1997, 1998, 1999; Ó Gráda 2000: 31, 33, 42, 88, 110; Kinealy and Parkhill 2014; Swift 1992; Whelan 1997: 92).

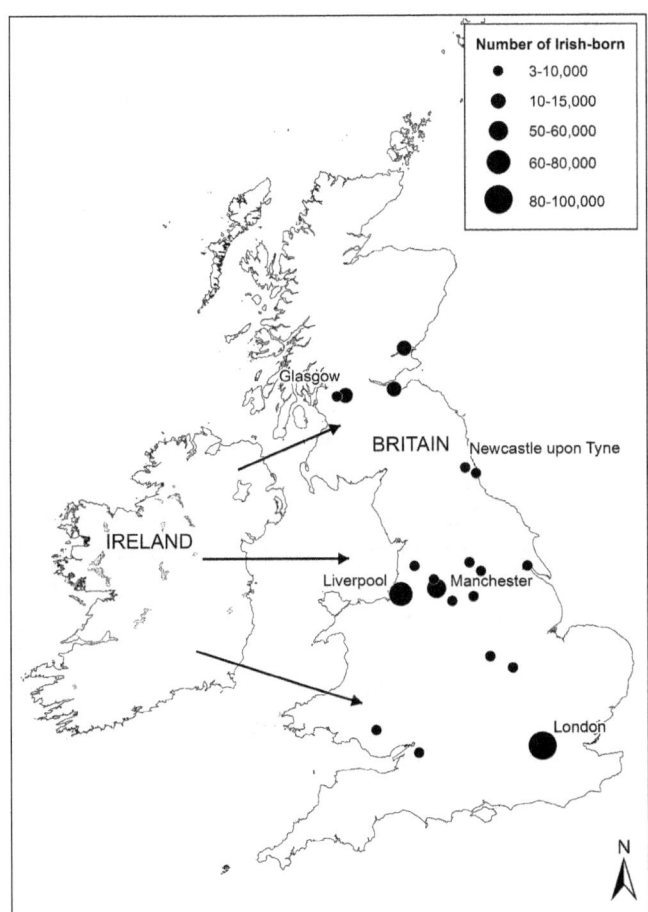

Figure 16 Irish settlement in Britain in 1851

3.4 Linguistic repercussions

The eighteenth and nineteenth centuries in Ulster, therefore, can be characterised as a period in which enhanced communication networks between central places brought about wider language contacts, since they afforded its rural and urban populations greater internal and external geographical mobility. The expanding linen economy increased population densities along Ulster's major communication networks, promoting interaction between the indigenous Irish population and the British planters who, by the end of the century, were engaged in the same occupation. As Gillen (2016: 61) argues: "commercialization encouraged bilingualism." The political climate in these areas which enforced allochthonous customs was such that there were tangible incentives for urban and rural Roman Catholic alike to conform and assimilate to the socio-cultural and linguistic norms of the linen capitals. The most isolated reaches of south Ulster remained staunchly disinclined to do so, and its Roman Catholic inhabitants had demonstrated in the rebellion of 1798, alongside the Presbyterians, that they would resort to violence in order not only to maintain the *status quo* but also to redress the issue of Stuart dispossession detailed in Chapter Two. Radical changes to the extent of linguistic diversity within these southern enclaves during the Age of Enlightenment, which were brought about by these socio-political and economic transformations, are captured in Figure 17 (adapted from Fitzgerald 1984: 134 and Corrigan 2003a: 215). It illustrates the loss of Irish in sub-regions of Southern County Armagh between 1771, just prior to the expulsions, and 1801. The Tiranny barony is closest to the County capital, Armagh city where the "cultural", "economic" and "social" "capital" (Bourdieu 1986) of ethnolinguistically allochthonous groups would have been at a peak. Upper Orior (formerly granted to Chichester and then MacHenry O'Neill) is more peripheral from such values than even the Upper Fews, which has Newtownhamilton on its doorstep (granted to Montgomery and Hamilton in 1606, as noted in Chapter Two, §2.4, and thus also dominated to some degree by British linguistic and socio-cultural values).

From a linguistic perspective, these external events are likely to have favoured the diffusion of English and Scots across the zone defined as MUE in Chapter Two, §2.4.1. However, in what is the SUE zone (including Upper Fews and Upper Orior) as well as in other peripheral and high risk social-ecological (Flaherty 2014) areas like Rathlin, County Antrim and the Sperrins (spanning Counties Derry and Tyrone), while we might project a number of Irish-dominant bilinguals amongst weavers for commercial reasons, the majority are more likely to have continued to be Irish monoglots. It is very likely, in fact, that these regions will have remained *Gaeltachtaí* ('Irish-speaking districts') for considerably longer,

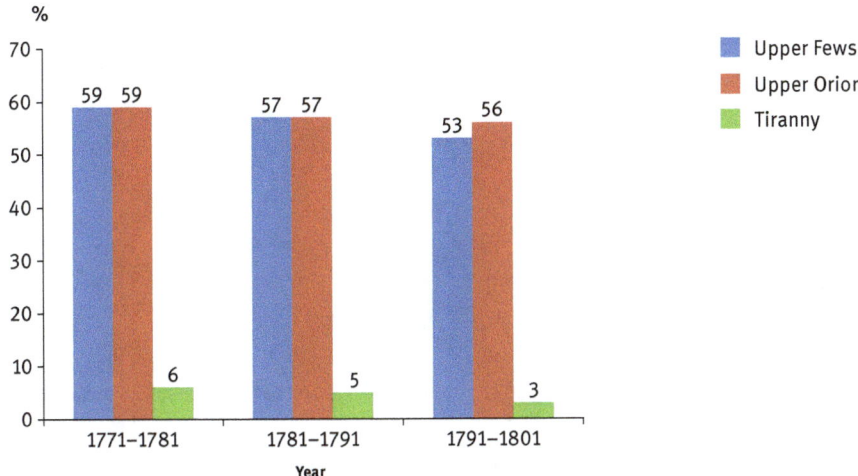

Figure 17 Estimates of minimum level of Irish-speaking amongst successive decennial age cohorts in Upper Fews, Upper Orior and Tiranny, South Armagh, Northern Ireland, 1771–1801 (after Fitzgerald 1984: 134 and Corrigan 2003a: 215)

as will be argued in the following Chapter (see also Adams 1979: 116; Fitzgerald 1984; Ó Duibhín 2007; Sweeney 1988; Wagner 1958: xix). The Dissenters' defeat and their subsequent emigration as Scotch-Irish in large numbers, coupled with the proto-industrialisation of the US-speaking northeast urban centres which had established a new relationship with Belfast on account of their economic importance to the linen trade, will have also provided ideal opportunities for a certain amount of English to diffuse into the US zone, though the impact of these events on language ecology did not fully penetrate this region until the twentieth century, as the next Chapter will argue.

The radical population decline and displacement through internal and external migration of the Famine years in Ulster were absolutely crucial in promoting linguistic destabilisation. This is particularly so when considered in the light of the contention by Fishman (1991, 2000), already noted in Chapter One, §1.5, that survival is more likely when threatened language groups are spatially concentrated (see Allard and Landry 1994; Beal and Corrigan 2009; Corrigan 1992, 2020; Clyne 2005; Ehala 2010; Gallois, Cretchley and Watson 2012; Giles, Bourhis and Taylor 1977; Harwood, Giles and Bourhis 1994; Landry and Bourhis 1997; Pauwels 2016; Sanchez Castro and Gil, 2009; Wölck 2004). Hence, the fate of Ulster Irish and the diffusion of SUE particularly in former *Gaeltachtaí* like Upper Fews and Upper Orior, County Armagh, can clearly be seen in the stark changes recorded in Figure 18, which now captures estimates for Irish speakers in these regions

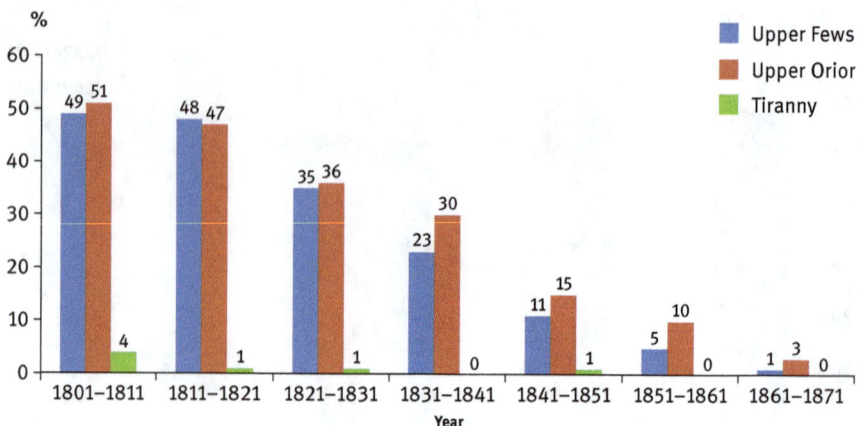

Figure 18 Estimates of minimum level of Irish-speaking amongst successive decennial age cohorts in Upper Fews, Upper Orior and Tiranny, South Armagh, Northern Ireland, 1801–1871 (after Fitzgerald 1984: 134)

between 1801 and 1871. The "tipping point" (Dorian 1989) of the years 1841–1851 for Irish in this region in favour of the diffusion of SUE clearly reflects the population losses in South Ulster arising from the Great Famine, argued for by Kinealy and Parkhill (2014) as well as MacRaild (2011) *inter alia*. The extent to which this decline through increased mortality as well as emigration rates impacted upon language shift towards monoglottism in English is addressed in Corrigan (1992) and (2003 a,b) *inter alia*.

On a personal level, the facsimile extract in Figure 19 taken from an account by Séan Ó Dubhda, a respondent to the Irish Folklore Commission's 1955 Emigration Questionnaire draws the same conclusions:[32]

---

[32] As noted in the acknowledgements, this response was the inspiration behind the choice of title for the AHRC grant (reference AH/K008285/1) which funded the project reported on here. The full translation of Ó Dubhda's extract is 'Teach the children English and they won't be blind like the assess who are emigrating now.' The metaphor of Irish monoglots being akin to asses (an animal commonly associated with stupidity and other pejorative traits since representations of it as such in Ancient Greek literature) is in itself telling of the extent to which the language was viewed negatively on both sides of the Atlantic (see also Corrigan 1992, Ihde 1994 and Nolan 2014 and, in preparation). National Folklore Collection, University College, Dublin, Ireland, reproduced with the permission of Críostóir Mac Carthaigh, Archivist.

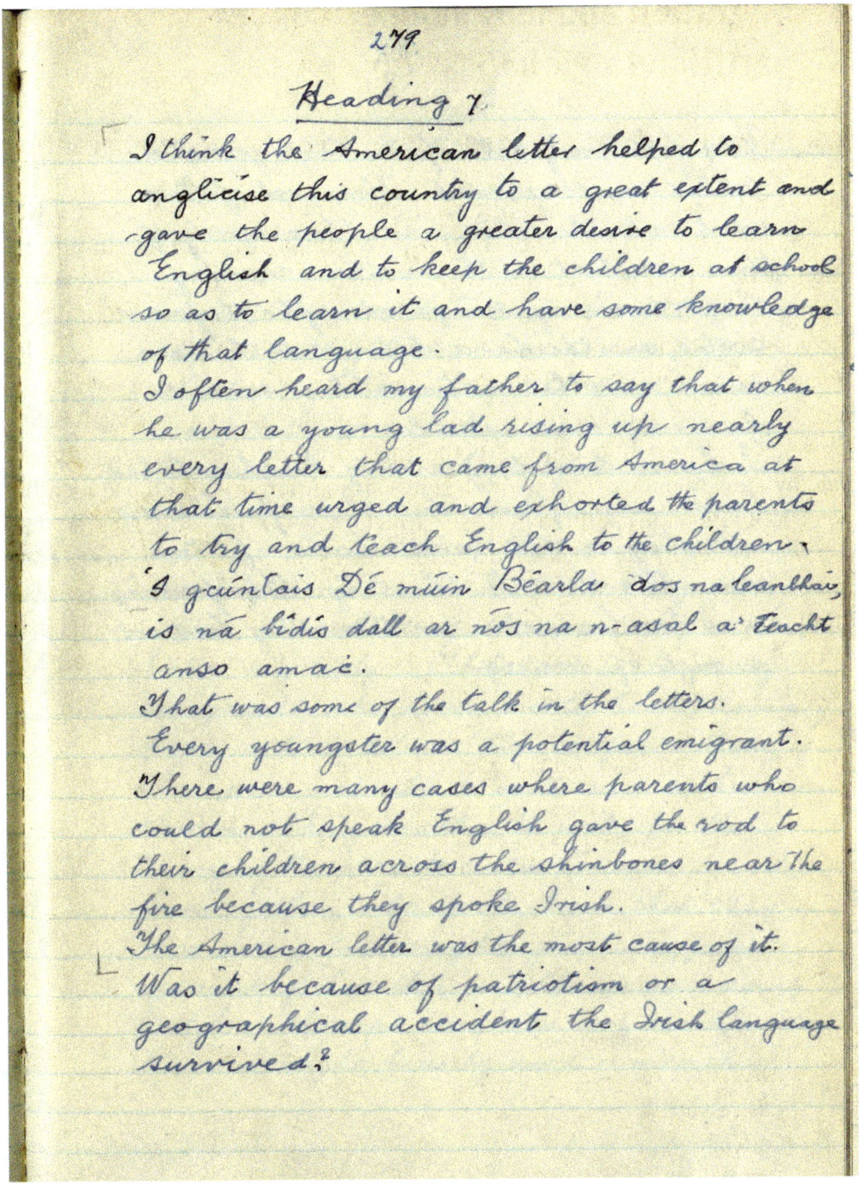

279

Heading 7.

I think the American letter helped to anglicise this country to a great extent and gave the people a greater desire to learn English and to keep the children at school so as to learn it and have some knowledge of that language.

I often heard my father to say that when he was a young lad rising up nearly every letter that came from America at that time urged and exhorted the parents to try and teach English to the children. 'I gcuntais Dé múin Béarla dos na leanbhaí, is ná bídís dall ar nós na n-asal a' teacht anso amac.'

That was some of the talk in the letters.

Every youngster was a potential emigrant. There were many cases where parents who could not speak English gave the rod to their children across the shinbones near the fire because they spoke Irish.

The American letter was the most cause of it.

Was it because of patriotism or a geographical accident the Irish language survived?

Figure 19 Extract from the Irish Folklore Commission's 1955 Emigration Questionnaire

4 Migration and language ecology: partition to globalisation

4.1 Internal and transnational migration in the twentieth century

One of the most pivotal socio-historical events of the twentieth century was undoubtedly the partitioning of the island of Ireland. This resulted in the creation of the Irish Free State in 1922 and stemmed from further political and violent agitations for autonomy from the British Empire (Coakley 2004). These included the 1916 Easter Rising, which manifested the Roman Catholic desire for Home Rule, as well as a Civil War between factions who were for or against the proposed treaty to partition the land mass in response to this drive for autonomy (Foster 2015). The political climate of the times and the persistent negative views held by allochthonous elites on both sides of the Atlantic about the autochthonous population are captured in these extracts from CORIECOR. The earlier text (16) was penned by Ida Blackwood and received by Mr. Smyth, an Irish emigrant now living permanently in Toronto, who had recently returned from a visit to family and friends in Ulster (including Ida). It was sent from County Monaghan in the South of the province, which, as was argued in previous Chapters, had persistently been the scene of much unrest.

(16) Extract from Ida Blackwood letter to Mr Smyth, Toronto, 1912

Title: Ida Blackwood, Ireland to "My dear Mr Smyth"
Source: Corpus of Irish-English Correspondence
Archive: Mr & Mrs J Smyth, Castledamph, Plumbridge
Doc. No.: 0511090
Date: 12/09/1912
Doc Type: LET
Log: Document added by LT, 28:10:2004

Ballinarea [*Ballynarea?*]
Altnamackan
Castleblaney
Co Monaghan
12th Sep : 12

My dear Mr Smyth,
... I thought I would wait until you
landed before writing ... Since your return I suppose
you have done nothing but go around and see

all your old friends, and renew
acquaintances ... I am sure you are glad to
get back to Canada, the people in Ireland
are so slow, that is one of their greatest
faults in my eyes ... Most of the people here are of
Scotch descent but at the present day are perfect types
of bigoted Irish Protestants. They are very
few Roman Catholics in the district and
these are owing to their isolated position,
harmless and inoffensive beings. In the town land of
Ballinarea [*Ballynarea?*] in which my father lives,
we are the only Protestant family. On one side all are
Protestants and on the other all R. C's.
We get on well with the latter folks as all our fore fathers did ...
All our work is done by R.C. [*Roman Catholic?*]
hands ... they were never any thing only uncommonly
decent and obliging with us and yet I am
quite convinced that should we get Home
Rule, which will be inevitably [*inevitable?*],
Rome rule that we shall see a great change in
our former good neighbours. The Hibernian
association laws too must be obeyed, and in the
last year or two about home this assoc: or
order has has increased alarmingly, In the
parish of Cully hanna [*Cullyhanna?*] it consists
largely of the working class of men, the majority
of these are totally uneducated, you would
be suprised how many can neither read
nor write, although in Cully hanna [*Cullyhanna?*]
there are two splendid National schools.[33]

---

33 During the period of the Penal Laws detailed in previous Chapters, the autochthonous population were prevented from becoming educated as part of the scheme (though there is good evidence that a "Hedge School" tradition persisted during this time in contravention of the legislation (Daly and Dickson 1990: 6–8; 53–54, 155; Dowling 1935; O'Donaghue 2000)). The "National School" system was founded in 1831 in response to the repeals noted in the previous Chapter. Much scholarship has argued that they were an important factor for promoting the shift towards English amongst the indigenous population outlined in Chapter Three, § 3.4 (Akenson 1970, 1989 and Hindley 1990). They were even declared to be "murder machines" by Padraig Pearse who himself ran a school in Dublin and was a key player in the Easter Rising of 1916. Corrigan (1996) and (2003a) provide alternative viewpoints based on triangulated data not used in previous research.

The second extract (17) is drawn from the correspondence of F.C.T. O'Hara, the Deputy Minister for Trade and Commerce in the Canadian government, who wrote the letter in Ottawa on September 3rd 1921 less than two months from the date when a ceasefire was declared that would eventually end the Irish War of Independence and seal the fate for Partition. The correspondence was sent to Colonel Ogilvy Graham, whose family made their fortune in the linen trade (Chapter Three, §3.2). He inherited Larchfield Estate on the Clandeboye lands once owned by the autochthonous O'Neill clan (Chapter Two, §2.3). The main living quarters are surrounded by a wall built during the Great Famine (a common relief practice to provide work for destitute Roman Catholics, as argued in Harzallah 2009). During the insurrections of the 1770s a group known as the "Hearts of Steel" with similar leanings to those of the Peep O' Day Boys, whose activities were described in the previous Chapter, assembled to burn it to the ground, but were apparently dissuaded (Donnelly 1981).

(17)   Extract from F.C.T. O'Hara letter to Colonel Ogilvy Graham, Belfast, 1921

Title: F. C. T. O'Hara, Ottawa, Canada to Ogilvy Graham, Belfast
Source: D.1754/32: Presented by J. A. Gamble, Esq., Coleraine
Archive: The Public Record Office, Northern Ireland
Doc. No.: 9503046
Date: 30/09/1921
Doc Type: EMG
Log: Document added by LT, 14:03:1995

Department of Trade and Commerce
Canada

Office of
The Deputy Minister
F. C. T. O'HARA
OTTAWA, September 3rd., 1921.
PERSONAL

Dear Mr. Graham,
Much water has flowed under London Bridge
since I had the pleasure of meeting you in Belfast in
1908, but the memory of my visit to the good city of
Belfast and to Larchfield remains a very happy one.
I have noticed in the press of late that your
establishment has been the centre of street fighting. I
presume you are still connected with those famous
mills. We are now awaiting with great interest the

outcome of the correspondence between Lloyd George and de Valera. I have been wondering whether conditions in Ireland are exaggerated in the press. Much of the news we get comes through New York and is doubtless doctored to please the Irish Americans in that city. We are hoping that the troubles of Ireland will soon be over, though, without being pessimistic, I rather fear that peace will not come in our generation.

The object of this letter is to ask if you would be good enough to complete a few details in the enclosed sketch of my grandmother's family tree. You will note the information I have is very limited. I shall be glad if you could add the dates wherever possible.

My mother, I am happy to say, is still in the land of the living, enjoying excellent health; but I suppose you seldom hear from any of the Dobbs family, especially since the death of Aunt Meat some years ago. She, I believe, always kept up an active correspondence with our Irish relatives.

I have been in England twice since I saw you in Belfast; once in 1911, and again in 1913; but my trips were very hurried and I could not get beyond London. I am always hoping against hope that I shall get over there again, and if so I shall be delighted to renew our too brief acquaintanceship of years ago.
Encl. [*Enclosed?*]
With kindest regards, believe me

Yours faithfully,
F. C. T. O'Hara

Oglivy Graham, Esq.,
York Street Spinning Co. Ltd.,
Belfast, Ireland.

The decline in emigration to North America in the twentieth century, in particular (as evidenced in Figure 20, based on data from Fitzgerald 2006, Fitzgerald and Lambkin 2008 and Devlin Trew 2013), was due in no small part to the impact of both the War of Independence and the Great War. Absolutely key to the deceleration though was the 1929 Wall Street Crash and the resulting worldwide Great Depression, which made North America much less attractive (Devlin Trew 2013: 40). Its impact can be seen in the letter in (18) composed a year later by D. M. Eagle, principal of an English-French Teacher Training School in Sandwich, Ontario, sent home to County Tyrone. The extract in (19) written in 1930s Philadelphia paints an even grimmer picture of the financial instability of Irish migrants in their new host country.

(18) Extract from D.M. Eagle letter to James A. Smyth, Co. Tyrone, 1930

   Title: D.M. Eagle, Sandwich to James A Smyth, [Castledamph?]
   Source: Corpus of Irish-English Correspondence
   Archive: Mr & Mrs J Smyth, Castledamph, Plumbridge
   Doc. No.: 0612002
   Date: 23/05/1930
   Doc Type: EMG
   Log: Missing from archive

   English-French Teachers Training School
   Principal D.M. Eagle
   Sandwich, Ont. [Ontario?]

   May 23 1930

   Dear Jim:
   Hearty congratulations old boy on your trying your hand in Irish politics. I would like to hear that you are successful. You do not say who your supporters were but gave rather a formidable list of opponents, Unionists Clergy and Orange Order ... your privations are numerous ... Was elected Reeve of Sandwich by acclamation in Dec. last. I am also Secretary of Essex County Old Age Pension Board which is a new appointment since you left. It was a County Council appointment and brings in a little extra dough which we need in these hard times. Things are not as brisk here as a couple of years ago but I think it is only temporary. Unemployment is felt here as in the mother countries.

(19) Extract from McClean letter to Mr Ruttedge, Philadelphia, 1930

   Title: George McClean, Philadelphia to Mr. Ruttedge, Philadelphia
   Source: Corpus of Irish-English Correspondence
   Archive: Dr. J. S. Garvin
   Doc. No.: 0207083
   Date: 19/09/1930
   Doc Type: EMG
   Log: Document added by LT, 06:09:2002

19th Sept"30
1854. E. [*East?*] Wishart St
Kensington Ave,
Philadelphia . P.a. 2o/
U S A
Mr Ruttedge

Dear Sir
We never intended being so long as this without getting you paid but we cannot help it

Just a few lines in answer to your letter and acounts [*accounts?*] received yesturday [*yesterday?*]. Well we are very sorry for keeping you so long without getting you paid but we cannot posible [*possibly?*] help it as times are so. bad out here and every. thing is so very expensive. To tell you the truth sometimes we cannot hardly make out at all. It takes us pretty busy and there are hundreds out of work and the rents are so very high, we are paying £ 6 pounds per month for a house. and the food is so high in price not mentoning [*mentioning?*] clothes its very hard to make out a living at all especally [*especially?*] with a large family these hard times with the cost of living being so high. There was a great many families had to go back to Scotland and Derry again. They were not able to make a living out here at all. This country is not as good as the people over there think it is. We tried our best to get back to Ireland last year but we could not get the money gathered up to take us so we had to remain on here. If some of our boys was joined work it would always be a help but having so many to provide for its pretty hard. If we only had a knew [*of known?*] times was [*were?*] going to turn out like this we would never been out here at all. So Mr Rutledge you will have to excuse us for some time yet as we could not send you any money for some time until times improve, we have had lots of sickeness [*sickness?*] since we came out here. and with the expense of the hospital and every thing we could not possible [*possibly?*] send you any just now But you rest assured we will pay you as soon as ever we can see our way to do so. So you need not be afraid of not getting it for we will certainly pay you as soon as ever we can and we never had any other intention but to do so. The

climate does not agree with us very well out here. If we only
could see our way of getting back there again we would not
be long out here times are so hard some times we hardly know.
what to do to make out for the best. so you rest content
you will get paid by us Sure. and as soon as ever we can, If
you. dont belive [*believe?*] us. about times being so hard and bad,
write to some body else out here. and they will can (sic) tell you
all about it as people dosent [*don't?*]. know any thing about it over
there. its awful out here. at present. so we are really
sorry we cannot send you any at present. but will as Soon as
we ever are able to do so. We remain. yours faithfully.
George. and Annie McLean.

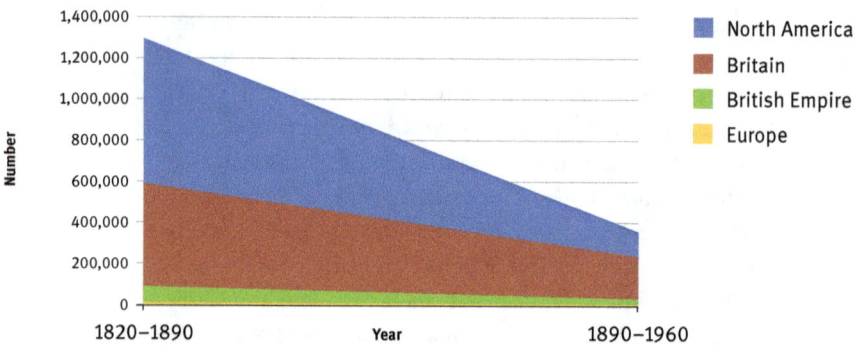

Figure 20 Principal destinations of Ulster emigrants (1820–1960)

This fall in emigrant numbers is especially interesting given the fact that the new Northern Ireland Government enacted legislation which continued to reinforce Protestant (in this case Unionist) traditional values which were diametrically opposed to the ideologies of Roman Catholic nationalists (Garner and Gilligan 2015: 515; McKittrick and McVea 2012: 7–16).

Ulster was not immune to immigration during this period either in the form of return migrants, a possibility mentioned in (19) for the McLean family as well as allochthonous groups. The latter were often skilled Scottish and English workers who came to take advantage of the burgeoning labour market, which the shipyards and linen factories of urban Belfast, Derry and Lurgan offered (many of which were established by earlier inflows of wealthy German Jewish migrant families like the Wollfs and Jaffes (Appleton *et al.* 2014)). Skilled artisans from Italy were also attracted by the employment prospects created by luxury liners, such as the ill-fated Titanic, as well as a rise in the number of Roman Catholic Churches, like St. Patrick's Cathedral, Armagh (built between 1840 and 1904), which was painted by Oreste Amici and contains sculptures created by the distinguished Roman sculptor, Cesare Aureli (Dietz 2011: 20).

There was an increase too in forced migrants from further afield like the Jews from Russia and Eastern Europe (especially Lithuania and Poland) who sought asylum from the religious persecution meted out to them there (Appleton et al. 2014; Russell 2011: 9–10; Warm 1998). Hence, the Census returns for 1901 indicated that there were 708 Jews residing in Belfast, like the seven members of the Genn family of Russian origin living at 34 Alloa Street, whose lives are captured there on Census day (Figure 21).

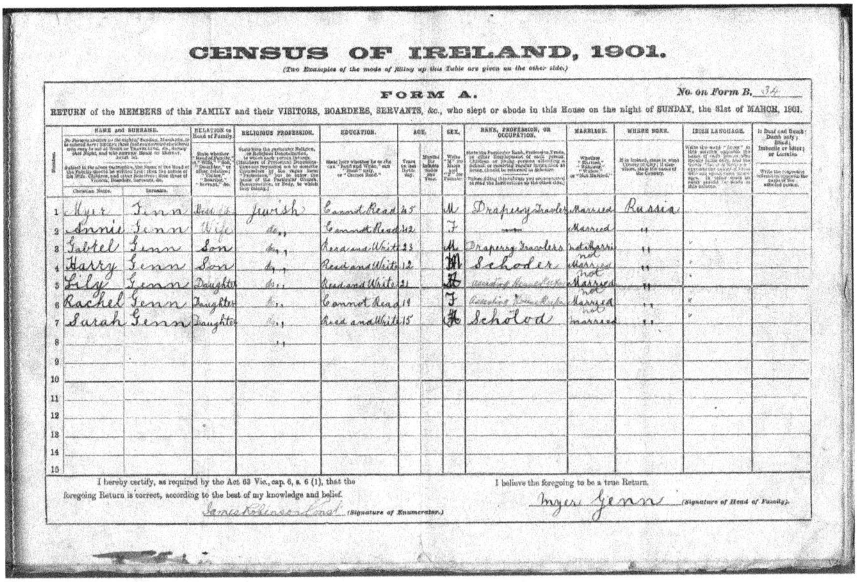

Figure 21 Census of Ireland, 1901, Clifton, County Antrim, Belfast, 34 Alloa Street; Form A Household Return for Genn Family (The National Archives of Ireland)[34]

The early twentieth century also witnessed the in-migration of Commonwealth peoples from the South-Asian Subcontinent (Bangladesh, India and Pakistan especially – though at different time periods and in response to diverse socio-political conditions in their homelands). The in-flow began as a trickle during the Depression years and then increased substantially post-1940 with many newcomers

---

[34] Reproduced with permission of the Director of the National Archives, Dublin, Ireland.

having already resided elsewhere in the UK prior to their arrival (the exact stepwise path of the later twenty-first century Sinha migrant family mentioned in Chapter One, §1.4). It may have been this ready familiarity with western culture (partly also of course on account of the so-called "Irish Raj", coined by Kapur 1997 and detailed also in Lennon 2004) that has led to their being considered the most integrated minority in the commercial, cultural and social life of twentieth century Northern Ireland (Irwin and Dunn 1997: 76; Kapur 1997; McDermott 2011: 86–87).

Ulster had not seen any significant diverse linguistic or cultural contact of this kind in many centuries, so the presence of these new ethnic minority immigrants who had been attracted there is notable, despite their relatively modest numbers for most of the twentieth century (Hainsworth 1998; Irwin and Dunn 1997).

There were some small increases in the Jewish population (around 10,000) on account of asylum seekers from Nazi Germany during the Second World War, 300 of whom were accommodated at Millisle Refugee Farm, County Down (Appleton *et al.* 2014; Gross 2016; Holfter 2014, 2016; Russell 2011: 10; Warm 1998). However, the outflow of migrants from Northern Ireland was exacerbated by the hostilities, including the internment and subsequent transportation of members of the Italian community (Barton 1995; Dietz 2011). In many respects though, Northern Ireland fared better than many other regions of the UK (Barton 2010). Belfast Lough was not only strategic to the war effort (particularly as the southern English ports were often besieged), but the city's famous Harland and Wolff and Short Brothers companies produced ships and other vital military hardware. They relied heavily on the textiles now mass-produced in Belfast's linen factories earning the city the name "Linenopolis". This economic boom was largely partisan, though, in that a majority of employees in all of these industries were Protestant males (Garner and Gilligan 2015: 515; McKittrick and McVea 2012: 11). As a consequence, it is believed that Roman Catholics were much more predisposed to migrate during the period (Devlin Trew 2013: 94–96; Elliott 2000: 383–394; Ó Dochartaigh 2016: 146). This is likely to have been a forced migration stream on account of the socio-cultural and religious discrimination evident at community level, as Liza Smyth's letter from CORIECOR reveals in (20).

(20)   Extract from Liza Smyth letter to James A. Smyth, Ontario, 1921

Title: Liza Smyth, Castledamph to James A. Smyth, Ontario
Source: Corpus of Irish-English Correspondence
Archive: Mr & Mrs J Smyth
Doc. No.:   0604122
Date: 17/01/1921
Doc Type: LET
Log: Missing from archive

Castledamph
January 17th 1921

Dear Bro

I think since I wrote last we have got two letters from you ... I had intended to write regarding Andy Ballantines land it was only set for this year or rather Willies farm they dont intend to sell till next year at present Andy is two weeks in Belfast Hospital with his eyes & will remain a week yet we have not heard how he is doing now to go back to the land Tom got the hill & two fields before the Auction started at £ 18 its quite cheap but they didn't want a Catholic to get it and the sale of both farms will be the same Tom would get the first chance so they told him that day well there will be another year to think over it now & perhaps land will be like all else going down in price ...

Roman Catholic repression was also embodied in Northern Ireland Government edicts dominated by Unionism (Hughes 2014: 254; Ó Dochartaigh 2016: 142–143). Moreover, they also had high levels of economic deprivation to contend with arising from their being prevented from accessing work to the extent that unemployment rates for this ethnic group was nearly three times that of their Protestant peers (McKittrick and McVea 2012: 11; The Portland Trust 2007: 7).

Another important push factor generating an outflow of migrants (both ethnic minorities and locals) in the twentieth century was the onset of the so-called "Troubles" in the late 1960s (Devlin Trew 2013: 51–52; Ó Dochartaigh 2016: 141–142). It began with a civil rights movement to ameliorate the socio-cultural and economic position of Roman Catholics and escalated into a guerrilla war that lasted for decades (Garner and Gilligan 2015; McKittrick and McVea 2012). The population of Belfast was particularly affected. Thus, Darby and Morris (1974: summary page C) as well as Hughes (2014: 254) report that between 6.6 % and 11.8 % of its population (estimated to be nearly 60,000 people) moved elsewhere as a result of intimidation of the ethnic cleansing type already discussed in earlier Chapters, in addition to the escalating violence (Boal 1999; Callame and Charlesworth 2009; Darby and Morris 1974; Hughes 2014; Garner and Gilligan 2015; Jarman 2005). Darby and Morris (1974) also document internal migratory movements – albeit smaller in scale – in other towns and cities across Northern Ireland including County Armagh, where from March 1972 to March 1973 "between 700–750 families" were coerced out of their homes. It is hardly surprising, therefore, that at the height of the Troubles (1971–1981) emigration numbers for the whole of that decade in Northern Ireland rose to –111,423, according to the Registrar General, much of which could be classed as the forced type, detailed in

Chapter One, § 1.5 (Devlin Trew 2013: 95; Russell 2011: 4). One of the adult participants in the *Múin Béarla* project, a member of the dwindling Jewish community in Belfast, describes this period in Northern Ireland's history as pivotal for the sharp decline in their numbers between the twentieth and twenty-first centuries, and there is considerable support for this view in the literature as well as in local media and Hebrew congregation databases (Appleton *et al.* 2014; Warm 1998).[35]

(21)   Extract of interview with 'Menachem Bialystok', Belfast, August 2015

1	Menachem Bialystok:	Well the I think it's g=yes, it [*the Jewish population of Northern Ireland*] it it peaked round about the nineteen=sixties and there would have been about fifteen hundred members of the community, and there were other people who weren't members but would still be Jewish. We now have eighty members of the community
2	FK:	Small.
3	Menachem Bialystok:	Ehm, so eh it's it's gone past the tipping point, we've no young kids or, you know, even teenagers.
4	FK:	Mm-mm.
5	Menachem Bialystok:	When I say 'no', we had our first Bar Mitzvah in the Synagogue in seven years.
6	Menachem Bialystok:	So it's eh from a from a from eh and the Troubles didn't help.

[MB (M); Belfast, Northern Ireland; 6 Aug. 2015]

There was, however, one noteworthy source of in-migration during this period in the form of the so-called "Vietnamese Boat People" (who were actually ethnically Chinese in origin, as Russell 2011: 10 notes). They were escaping the aftermath

---

35 See for instance http://www.bbc.co.uk/news/uk-northern-ireland-31003098 and https://www.belfasttelegraph.co.uk/life/features/lost-tribe-of-belfast-34407866.html as well as the documentary film entitled *The Last Minyan*, which aired on 7th August 2014 as part of BBC Northern Ireland's True North series (https://www.bbc.co.uk/programmes/b03xq462, last accessed 20 May 2018). Similarly, the Hebrew Congregation database records a population of 1200 in 1934 but just 130 in 2004 (see: https://www.jewishgen.org/jcr-uk/Community/Belfast/index.htm#Hebrew%20Congregation, last accessed 20 May 2018). Table QS201NI from NISRA's (2012) report of the 2011 Census gives a figure of just 26 respondents across the whole of Northern Ireland who declared "Jewish" to be the ethnic group to which they belonged. Thanks to one of my research associates, Dr Frances Kane, who undertook the Menachem Bialystok interview.

of the Vietnam War and by 1980, 141 refugees had been given asylum by the UK government (Blee 2011; Delargy 2007). The Boat People were sent principally to Craigavon in County Armagh, a new town constructed in the late 1960s, itself causing considerable controversy on account of the number of local families who were forced to internally migrate in order to build it.

This period also saw the arrival of migrants direct from China itself (Hong Kong and the poorer cantons of the mainland) whose home languages were Cantonese or Hakka (Russell 2011: 10–11). There is a degree of heterogeneity within this community – particularly with respect to newcomers who originally hailed from Hong Kong versus those from the Chinese Mainland, as noted in Feng-Bing (2006). Nevertheless, there is a view that these early Chinese migrants especially did not become particularly proficient in English nor were they well integrated in Northern Irish society – largely on account of their lifestyles and principal occupations (Delargy 2007; McDermott 2012). Second and third generation Chinese migrants, however, are considerably more assimilated and this is largely due to the fact that they are no longer tied principally to occupations within the catering industry (Russell 2011: 11).

4.1.1 Migration and language ecology in the twentieth century

According to data from the 1911 Census (the last to be conducted between Partition and 1991 that contained a language question) as well as research by Adams (1964, 1975, 1976, 1979); Corrigan (2003a); Fitzgerald (2003); Hickey (2007); Holmer (1940); Ó Dochartaigh (1987); Ó Searcaigh (1925); Sommerfelt (1929); Sweeney (1988) and Wagner (1958), four relict Irish-speaking regions within post-1922 Northern Ireland are apparent. There were over 2,000 native-speakers of South Armagh Irish recorded (mainly in the baronies of Upper Orior and Upper Fews highlighted in Chapter Three, §3.4). These figures meant that as far as absolute numbers are concerned, it now ranked between other areas in which monoglottism was projected in the eighteenth century, namely, the Corgary *Gaeltacht* of west Tyrone and the Mid-Ulster *Gaeltacht* of the Sperrins (north Tyrone and south Derry), with the largest number of speakers remaining situated in the isolated Glens of Antrim and Rathlin island *Gaeltachtaí* of the northeast.

Sweeney (1988: 4) remarks that "it is likely that the decline of Irish speaking continued after that time [1911] even in those areas where a relatively high level of Irish speaking had been registered". There is evidence, however, from various sources including Wagner (1958), which suggests that small numbers of Irish speakers in these regions persisted even beyond 1945. Thus, Wagner (1958: 15) states that although "Irish had almost disappeared from East Ulster by the time we began our scheme... Twenty years ago, we would have got excellent subjects in South Armagh". Indeed, Ní Bhaoill (2010: 318–333) has published materials from the 1931 Doegen collection that includes prayers and songs from Mary Harvessy (1856–1947) born in Clonalig, County Armagh who was a native speaker. Moreover, the corpus developed for Corrigan (1997: Appendix) referred to in Chapter Two, §2.4.1, includes participants from the same region who report in the later twentieth century that they too grew up as bilinguals.[36] In addition, they recall other individuals (such as those cited in (22) to (24) below) who were predominantly Irish monolinguals or were Irish dominant bilinguals, as well as those who had competence in the language of the four different types recognised within endangered language studies, i.e. "rememberers", "passive (receptive) bilinguals", "semi-speakers" and "terminal speakers" (Craig & Bert 2011).

(22) Extract from interview with Oliver Maguire, South Armagh, 1973

Manuscript: 1810
Date: July 1973
Informant: Mr. Oliver Maguire
Location: South Armagh
Topic: Gaelic Speakers

U142/L222–223
They spoke nothin' but Irish, couldn't hardly speak a word of English at all.

U143/L223–224
I heard my father talk of them and he told this yarn, and of course he would put it in Irish and explain it to you.

U144/L224–225
I mind it well.

(23) Extract from interview with Francis Callan, Forkhill, Armagh, 1974

Manuscript: 1861
Date: February 1974
Informant: Mr. Francis Callan
Location: Forkhill
Topic: Cleaver

U36/L58–59
She was a one they called Aíne Proinsias Ruagh; that was 'Red Frank'.

---

36 This material is reproduced courtesy of the National Folklore Collection, University College, Dublin, Ireland where the Michael J. Murphy manuscripts, which is the original source, is housed. At their request, the actual personal names of the individuals referred to in the narratives have been substituted for pseudonyms.

U37/L59-60
She had great old Irish sayings, and Irish herself.

U38/L61-62
Róise Hollywood of Carriffe – she was Róise Preckon [*Phonetic*]: 'Rosie of the Bushes'.

U39/L62
There was a rock beside her and it was all whin bushes.

U40/L63-64
Padraig Bowen of Carrive, he had Irish too, he used to say "Janey, a vick, I'll put a wisp to Boney's Castle."

(24) Extract from interview with Francis Callan, Forkhill, Armagh, 1972

Manuscript: 1803
Date: May/March 1972
Topic: Francis Callan's Father

U381/L588
My father had Irish; he had.

U382/L588-589
My uncle ... or he's uncle ... was an Irish teacher.

Leaving aside the Anglicising influences of the urban centres and port towns described by Adams (1976: 77) as "freakish compared with the surrounding countryside", the rural pattern of concentration appears to be internally consistent across the baronies of different *Gaeltacht* regions like the South Armagh one, where this material comes from, and across time. As one would expect on the basis of the diffusion model articulated in Chambers and Trudgill (1998), for instance, there existed graduated buffer zones where balanced bilingualism predominated, intervening between areas of complete loss and those in which Irish monoglottism and Irish-dominant bilingualism persisted (Ó Duibhín 2007). Nonetheless, *Gaeltacht* regions within Ulster were now completely isolated from one another and both MUE and SUE were increasingly restricting their geographical extent (Figure 22). The former was diffusing into the Sperrins, Rathlin and the Glens as well as the *Oirghialla* region of South Down while SUE from the former Pale region was increasingly becoming a second language in South Armagh. Adams (1979: 120) describes the spread of English in this era as a "pincer movement" of southward expanding Ulster English and northward expanding Leinster English, a process which intensified with the coming of the railways (see Corrigan 2010: 5–12 and Morley 2016: 334–336).

Adams (1964) makes an important distinction between three specific types of Irish-speaking community in 1911 that there is not space here to explore (see Corrigan 2010; Fitzgerald 1984, 2003; Ní Bhaoill 2010). To summarise, the numeric data quoted previously and upon which the map in Figure 22 is drawn, refer to what Adams (1964) terms "relict" zones, which are co-terminus with what he refers to as "survival Irish". *Gaeltachtaí* are recorded here as regions where over 30% of the population are Irish-speaking in the 1911 Census. However, the most isolated parts of counties such as Armagh, as already noted, continued to support Irish speakers. Thus the 1911 Census (1913: 291) records the fact that 2.3% of the county population as a whole declared knowledge of the language. Moreover, Fitzgerald (1984, 2003) and Ní Bhaoill (2010) cite Census 1911 figures for South Armagh amongst the over 60's population as being between 3% and 50% Irish-speaking depending on their location. Adams (1964) and Ní Bhaoill (2010: 11) also include discussion of "immigration Irish", which one would expect to find in the urban and port centres like Belfast and Newry, for instance, on account of the World Wars and other push factors that further promoted the trend towards urbanisation in Ulster described previously and further articulated in Morris (2013). This may be why Belfast County Borough is reported as having just 0.4% of its population who declared themselves to have knowledge of Irish in the 1891 Census, while the numbers grew by 1.6% only two decades later (Census of Ireland 1913: 291). "Revival Irish", by comparison to either of these two, is the learning of the language as an L2, motivated by the various reasons articulated in Crowley (2005: 192–198) including educational, leisure, nationalistic and so on (see also McCoy 2001; Morley 2016: 336–339; O'Reilly 1999: 1–17; Zwickl 2002). This has led to the establishment in the later twentieth century of *Gaeltachtaí* populated by new speakers of the minority language (in the sense of Ó Murchadha *et al.* 2018: 4) in areas of Northern Ireland like Belfast where survival Irish had not been spoken for some considerable time (Antonini, Corrigan and Wei 2002; Antonini 2012). The *Gaeltacht* of *Pobal Feirste* ('People of the Farset') in west Belfast, which was initiated during the Troubles, successfully managed to fund a *Bunscoil* ('primary school'). Eventually (after much wrangling with the Department of Education, according to O'Reilly 1999: 129–132) a *Meánscoil* ('secondary school'), which taught all subjects through the medium of Irish, was also funded. The latter was partly achieved by availing of leverage gained by government declarations connected with the Peace Process.

It has already been argued with regard to new migration inflows how important this phase of Northern Ireland's history has been for improving the attractiveness of the region as an immigrant destination. There were other dividends too from a linguistic perspective that could be argued to have had some influence on halting the diminution of Irish in the later twentieth century. Direct Rule from Westminster was invoked at the start of the Troubles in 1972 until the devolved settlement that

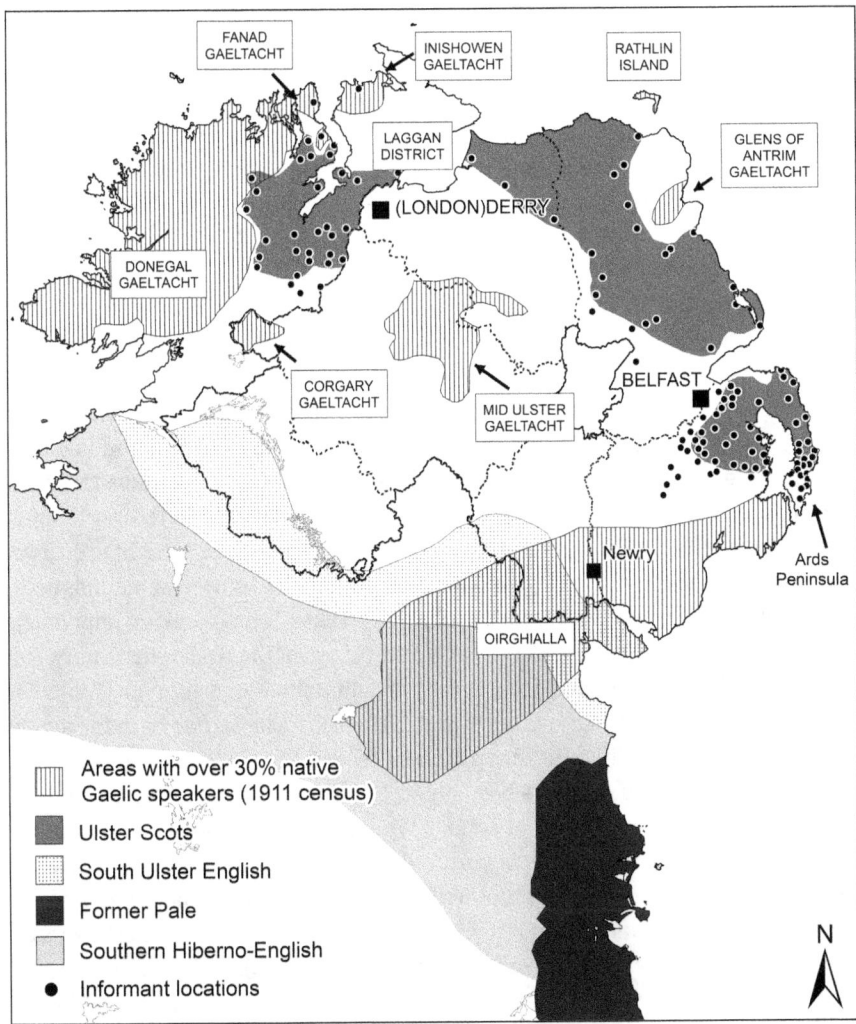

Figure 22 Northern 'survival' *Gaeltacht* regions in the 1911 Census in the context of intruding South Ulster English, Mid-Ulster English and Ulster Scots (adapted from Robinson 2006a: 3)

was introduced in 1999, following the Belfast/Good Friday Agreement (Besley and Mueller 2009; Darby and MacGinty 2000; Hughes 2014; McKittrick and McVea 2012; O'Hearn 2000; Rusciano 2016). In addition to establishing a plan for devolution, decommissioning of arms and reforming criminal justice and policing to democratise Northern Irish society, the Agreement has led to the creation of new intergovernmental institutions as well as Equality and Human Rights Commissions. As part of this package of reforms, the UK government on 27th March 2001 ratified the European Charter for Regional or Minority Languages with respect to both Irish and Ulster Scots in Northern Ireland.[37] Moreover, the Agreement itself provided specifically for improving the status of both. This move recognised for the first time in this context the symbolic importance of Irish and Ulster Scots to the identity and culture of the autochthonous, Roman Catholic and allochthonous, Protestant communities respectively (Crowley 2005: 198–200, 2006).[38]

While this entailed, for example, the compilation of translation leaflets to accompany the 2001 Census form, written in both Irish and Ulster Scots, the language question in the document was restricted to seeking information on ability in Irish (see Figure 32 below; McCoy 2001: 215).[39] The returns indicate that 167,490 respondents claimed competence in Irish. This is markedly different to the return of 142,003 for 1991 (the first year in which a language question was restored to the NI Census since 1911 – largely for political reasons on account of the perceived association between the Irish language and nationalism, as argued in various contributions to Mac Póilin 1997). Although Dunbar (2002/2003: 102) may well be right to suggest that the number who claimed Irish fluency is likely to be an overestimation, there was no official source whatever for the size of the Ulster Scots-speaking population until the 2011 Census (see §4.2.1.1 below). At the close of the twentieth century, the Ulster-Scots Language Society (one of many community-based support groups for this variety) in a 1994 article entitled "What is Ullans?" claimed it to be in the region of 100,000 speakers. While Hickey (2007: 98–99) and Görlach (2000: 20) note that this figure may or may not have been an accurate reflection of actual numbers it does function as a comparator of sorts.[40] What is likely, of course, is that native Ulster Scots speakers had greater opportunities for being exposed to MUE as a result of expanding employment opportunities in Second Word War Belfast alongside the improved communications and rise of the knowledge economy that characterise the twentieth century (Garicano and Rossi-Hansberg 2006). Such external factors may well be the source for Kingsmore's (1995) findings that in Coleraine, originally a US heartland, different generations of speakers and males *versus* females exhib-

---

[37] Last accessed 9 April 2019.
[38] That is not to say of course that these divisions are exclusive, as Blaney (1996), McCoy (1997), Ó Snodaigh (1995) and Carruthers and Ó Mainín (2017) highlight in their work touching on Protestants and Presbyterians engaged with the Irish language in some respect or other.
[39] A copy of the leaflets produced in various languages, including Ulster Scots, can be obtained from: https://www.nisra.gov.uk/publications/2001-census-community-liaison-materials (Last accessed 16 March 2018).
[40] See Ó Riagáin (2003), Crowley (2005: 201–206) and McMonagle and McDermott (2014) for accounts of the legal position of both majority ethnic and minority ethnic languages in early twenty-first century Northern Ireland.

ited varying amounts of typical Ulster Scots features with MUE variants intruding amongst certain social groups. (Boal and Royle 2006; Williams 2006.)

Although there were small increases in the numbers of ethnic minority migrants during the twentieth century, there is good evidence to suggest that they had little influence on local language ecologies. This was due to their overall modest numbers (less than 1% of the population); their occupational preferences (largely as lower tier workers in the catering and other trades with little status); as well as their preference for urban areas and the eastern counties, which kept them relatively isolated from the major ethnic groups (especially Roman Catholics, who predominated in the south and west of the state including the former *Gaeltachtaí*, Figures 12 and 22). The fact that the ethnic minority languages which they spoke were not included alongside Irish and Ulster Scots in the UK's ratification of the European Charter for Regional or Minority Languages reflects the fact that their linguistic cultural capital in Bourdieu's (1986) sense was as low as that pertaining to their economic and social capital.

4.2 Immigration and the rise of a superdiverse society in the twenty-first century

The 2001 census, which was the first to include a question on ethnic identification, indicated that the vast majority of Northern Ireland's population remained "White" (99.15%). In the light of the population movements from South East Asia just discussed, it is unsurprising that of the remaining <1%, "Chinese" was returned as the largest ethnic minority group (0.25%) (NISRA 2008).[41] Hainsworth (1998) and Irwin and Dunn (1997) provide systematic demographic data for the most numerous ethnic groups beyond the "White" category – including Chinese citizens but also Jews, the indigenous White Irish Traveller population and chain migrants from the Indian Sub-Continent/South-East Asia who

---

[41] The language and ethnic identification data arising from modern censuses like these undertaken using systematic and principled methods are considerably more reliable than those which typify Irish historical censuses such as that conducted in 1851 when a language question was first asked unambiguously (albeit relegated to a footnote until 1881 when the responses become rather more reliable as a result – see: Adams 1979; Corrigan 2003a; Kallen 2013; Ó Riagáin 1997). Nevertheless, the phrasing of the questions and other factors even in contemporary censuses can be problematic (Busch 2016). McDermott (2008: 6–7) raises this issue for the 2001 census in Northern Ireland and similar concerns have been noted for the language question in the 2011 censuses in England, Scotland and Wales by Bak and Mehmedbegovic (2017); Gopal and Matras (2013); Matras and Robertson (2015); Matras, Robertson and Jones (2016); Mehmedbegovic and Bak (2017); Sebba (2018; 2019).

followed in the wake of bridgeheads who had already established themselves during earlier waves of migration (see Chapter 1, §§ 1.4, 1.5).

Although ethnic minority migrants in Northern Ireland at this time predominately resided in urban centres (McDermott 2012: 190–191), Indian migrants were the most geographically dispersed, while the Chinese population, in contrast, had largely settled in eastern regions and in Belfast. 7 % of the Pakistani community lived in western Northern Ireland and while a significant number also resided in Northern Ireland's capital, a majority of these settlers likewise lived and worked in eastern counties. A small proportion of Travellers were also recorded there but they predominated in the west and, to a lesser extent, Belfast, though, naturally, as a nomadic people, their geographical mobility is wider than any other ethnic minority group. Although this native minority is small in number (only 1,301 "Irish Traveller" respondents are recorded in the most recent 2011 Census (QS201NI)), their culture, distribution, language and status have traditionally received considerably more attention than other ethnic minorities in the region (see Hickey 2002: 399–404; Kirk and Ó Baoill 2002).[42] Nevertheless, small-scale studies have provided some further insights into the nature and experiences of the latter using demographic and socio-economic data from the late twentieth century, including Bangladeshis (Holder 2001), the Black African community (Connolly and Keenan 2000), the Jewish population (Appleton *et al.* 2014; Warm 1998), Latin Americans (Holder and Lanao 2001) and the Portuguese (Soares 2002).

The rather modest numbers of non-indigenous ethnic minorities recorded in the 2001 census (just 12,569 when the White population stood at 1,670,988) changes dramatically when compared with the figures for ethnic identification documented in the most recent 2011 iteration and elsewhere.[43] Between 2000 and 2015, approximately 188,000 long-term international migrants came to Northern Ireland and while only a net total of 35,000 settled permanently, the number of allochthonous ethnic minorities has more than doubled in this reasonably short time (Russell 2017: 3). Thus, while the 2011 Census records "White" to still be the ethnic identifier for a majority of respondents (98.21 %), other significant ethnic

---

[42] The "Irish Traveller" population has thus shown a decrease of just less than 25 % from the previous Census a decade earlier (see NISRA, Table KS06). The 'Other Ethnic Group' categories include respondents of "Bangladeshi", "Chinese", "Indian", "Other Asian" and "Pakistani" heritages.

[43] In addition to the information arising from the 2011 census, Northern Ireland Statistics Research Agency (NISRA) figures cited here are triangulated with data from Medical Card registrations/de-registrations and applications for National Insurance numbers as well as data from the School Census, Health and Social Care Trusts, the Northern Ireland Housing Executive and birth registrations, which NISRA deem to be reliable methods (Devlin Trew 2013: 55–59; Russell 2017: 8). Such triangulation is important on account of the issues noted previously regarding census data *sensu stricto*.

minority groups have gained some ground so that the "Chinese" category constitutes a majority (0.35 %) with "Indian" not far behind (0.34 %) followed by "Other Asians" (0.28 %) while "Black Africans" now account for 0.13 % of the population (NISRA 2012, Table KS201NI).[44]

In-migration stems from three primary sources: (i) The dividends of the Peace Process culminating in the Belfast/Good Friday Agreement of 2nd December 1999, which ameliorated the region socio-economically (Besley and Mueller 2009; Darby and MacGinty 2000; Hughes 2014; McKittrick and McVea 2000; O'Hearn 2000; Rusciano 2016; The Portland Trust 2007; White 2013); (ii) The influx of forced migrants in the form of refugees and asylum seekers generated by the migrant crisis affecting the whole of Europe (De Genova 2017; Devlin Trew 2013: 61; Grigonis 2016; Malischewski 2013; McNulty 2014, 2017; McVeigh 2002; Potter 2014; Refugee Action Group 2007; Tennant 2000); and (iii) Changes to the structure of the European Union (EU). In May 2004, eight Central and Eastern European countries ("A8") gained entry to the EU via a new accession treaty. Legislation was enacted to enhance mobility between new and old member states and both the United Kingdom (UK) and the Republic of Ireland were among the EU15 states that agreed to immediately open their labour markets to the A8 group (Bauere et al. 2007; Kempny 2010, 2013; McNulty 2014, 2017; Okólski and Salt 2014; Russell 2011, 2012, 2016, 2017; Svašek 2009). Two further nations ("A2") were permitted to join the EU in 2007 (Bulgaria and Romania) though their employment access, by contrast, was "severely limited" by the UK government (Russell 2011: 4) until 2014 when A2 nationals were given the same rights as those which citizens from the A8 and other EU member states enjoyed. This step resulted in significant rises in the economic migration of Bulgarians and particularly Romanians to Northern Ireland in 2014 and 2015 (Russell 2017: 11–12).

Increased immigration figures arising directly from the Peace Process are hard to approximate but Fitzgerald and Lambkin (2010: 229) suggest that new migratory patterns are discernible in the 1990s when Northern Ireland became a more attractive destination (hence the 1994–1995 ceasefire peak in Figure 25 below). Devlin Trew (2013: 211) singles out indigenous immigrants who had emigrated at the height of the Troubles returning to the region in the period as another important trend. Prior to 2001, this figure was 54,980 and between 2001 and the 2011 census it was 50,670 usual residents who were born in NI but who had settled elsewhere and then returned (NISRA, Census 2011, Table 4.16).

---

44 It is important to be aware that the "White" category is not entirely contiguous with autochthonous groups since many EU migrants also fall into this category. In fact, as will be discussed further below, respondents of Polish heritage now outnumber those claiming Chinese to be the ethnic minority they are affiliated with.

Exact population sizes for asylum seekers are notoriously difficult to validate (Correa-Velez and Gifford 2007; Hanna 2019). There is a particular issue with the statistics for Northern Ireland on account of the fact that the UK does not publish separate demographics for each of its devolved regions (Potter 2014: 9 and 12). Estimates based on applications for asylum within Northern Ireland specifically as well as numbers in dispersed accommodation or seeking subsistence there put the figure at about 400 new cases per year (the Home Office processed about 200 applications in 2015 (McNulty 2017) when the refugee crisis in Europe was at its peak). These migrants hail largely from China, Iran, Nigeria, Somalia, Sudan and Zimbabwe though countries of origin naturally vary over time in response to local conflicts such as Syria's civil war, which began in 2011 and will have boosted Northern Ireland's refugee numbers by approximately 2000 people over five years from 2015 (McNulty 2014: 42–43, 2017: 12–13; McVeigh 2002; Potter 2014: 9; Tennant 2000).

EU migrants, on the other hand, are more likely to act as respondents to official population censuses with the result that data from the 2011 iteration in Table 2 alongside other authorized sources clearly indicates a reversal in the fortunes of Chinese heritage migrants who are now no longer the dominant allochthonous group, which is, in fact, newcomers from Poland, 19,658 of whom were recorded as present in the 2011 census (NISRA 2013a). Although there was a dip in their numbers and indeed in immigration more broadly with a concomitant rise in emigration due to the effects of the 2008 global recession (Devlin Trew 2013: 54; Russell 2012: 4), the strong impact of EU migration continues to be felt since 1,872 Poles were recorded as registering for new medical cards in 2015 while 1,367 Romanians did so in the same year (Russell 2017: 12 and 13).

While medical card registration data captures adult migration patterns, the inflow of younger people is more prominent in annual Department of Education for Northern Ireland (DENI) school census data where they are termed "newcomers". This notion is defined as a pupil "who has enrolled in a school but who does not have the satisfactory language skills to participate fully in the school curriculum, and does not have a language in common with the teacher, whether that is English or Irish" (Russell 2017: 17). Figure 23 provides longitudinal data recording the presence of newcomers in local schools across Northern Ireland. It indicates exponential increases as a result of new migrant inflows of populations for whom English is not their main language. Thus, between 2009/10 and 2018/19, the number of newcomers rose by over 50% (from 7,899 to 16,238). They now constitute 4.7% of the school-going population overall with a majority of newcomers (80%) being in early years and primary school education (Russell 2017: 17–18 and DENI 2017a, 2019a/b).[45]

---

[45] The data naturally relies on schools recording this data accurately and there is an issue too with the fact that only one newcomer language per pupil is notified to DENI. Twice during

Table 2 Top 10 international migrant countries of origin, Census 2011

Country of Origin	Numbers
Poland	19,658
Lithuania	7,341
India	4,796
USA	4,251
Germany	3,908
Philippines	2,947
Slovakia	2,681
Canada	2,323
Latvia	2,297
China	2,223

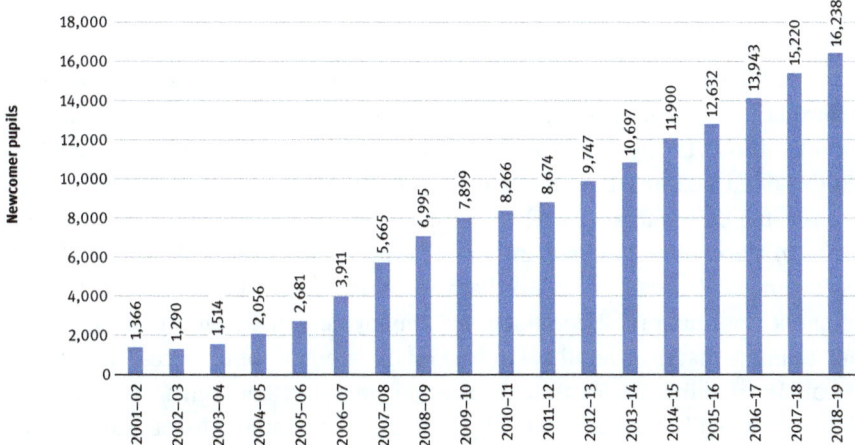

Figure 23 Numbers of Newcomer Pupils in NI Schools from 2001–2019[46]

---

fieldwork for the *Múin Béarla* project, it became apparent that two different schools had no knowledge of what transpired to actually be the main language of their pupils. One of them (Nauris Dokis, attending St. Benedict's) was recorded as Latvian-speaking when, in fact, he was bilingual in both Latvian and Russian with the latter being dominant. Another (Raka Marar at St. Agnes's) was described as speaking Malayalam when Telugu was actually her preferred language and the school had no record of her ability in it (see Part II, Chapter 6).

46 I am grateful to statisticians Rachel Grumley, Paul Matthews and Leonie Robinson of DENI who provided this data.

With the exception of the asylum seekers and refugees already discussed, adult inflow migration to Northern Ireland amongst other ethnic minorities is without doubt economically driven. It derives principally from differences in the buoyancy of the labour market and economic growth between the UK and other nations. The pattern in question is not dissimilar to the situation with respect to the Irish diaspora *vis à vis* their emigration destinations in earlier periods, as noted in previous Chapters. This is especially significant for the A8/A2 countries, which acceded to the EU from 2004 onwards. Of course, it also pertains to other economically deprived EU states such as Portugal[47] (Dustmann and Frattini 2013; Eaton 2007; Okólski and Salt 2004; Montague and Shirlow 2014). However, as Burrell (2010), Luthra, Platt and Salamońska (2014) and Okólski and Salt (2004: 25) also note, pull/push factors invariably include: "a concurrence of political circumstances, socio-demographic forces... and a pent-up demand in the UK for low-skilled labour." There is excellent evidence that migrants to Northern Ireland are often highly skilled too though – they are higher tier employees in the health sector, for example, as argued in Montague and Shirlow (2014: 17) as well as Russell (2015: 23) and, as we will see, this can have an important impact on the extent to which they are multilingual. That said, migrants often undertake roles in the host country that are not commensurate with their education, skills or experience (Bauder 2006; DEL 2009: 2, 42–43; Kobiałka 2014; Pietka, Clark and Canton 2013; Trevena 2013, 2014; Visintin, Tijdens and van Klaveren 2015). Both skilled and unskilled migrant employees make important fiscal contributions to the UK economy as a whole (estimated at 25 billion pounds between 2000 and 2013, according to Dustmann and Frattini 2013, as well as Luthra, Platt and Salamońska 2014). As far as Northern Ireland in particular is concerned, 2008 numeric data from the Department for Employment and Learning (DEL) (2009: 42) estimate that the overall net impact on the economy of EU accession workers created an additional 37–40,000 jobs and produced between £1.06 and £1.2 billion of what is termed Gross Value Added (i.e. a common fiscal rating for the value of economic output, principally consisting of salaries and profits) (see also Russell 2015: 24 and Montague and Shirlow 2014: 9 and 13). The DEL report also established the fact that A8 migrants especially had taken up employment in

---

47 As far as this specific migrant population is concerned, it also included small numbers of individuals (10%) who are likewise Portuguese-speaking but who did not originate within the EU and are often involved in stepwise migration processes prior to arrival of the kind described in Chapter One, §1.4. Instead, they hail from third countries in which Portugal had some prior colonial involvement such as Angola, Brazil, Mozambique and East Timor in particular – a sizeable proportion of whom have settled in Dungannon and Portadown (Eaton 2007: 176–178; Eaton 2010: 14; McDermott 2011: 98; O'Sullivan *et al.* 2014: 5 and 27).

nearly all economic sectors with the most intense area being the manufacture of food and beverages (18% post-2004, DEL 2009: 36 and Lynn 2013: 54). An important consequence of this preference is the density of migrants in rural, semi-rural and market town locations across the region in which such economic activities are concentrated. In fact, residents from the top five migration inflow states indicated in Table 2 (Poland, Lithuania, India, the USA and Germany) are not evenly dispersed geographically, with the Lithuanian-born group being the most concentrated in certain locations (Krausova and Vargas-Silva 2014: 10), which was a key factor in the choice of fieldwork sites for the *Múin Béarla* project discussed further in Chapter Six. For instance, although the residents of Belfast amount to 15.5% of the population of Northern Ireland as a whole, its residents whose country of birth was Lithuania represent 37% of the entire Lithuanian population of Northern Ireland. Belfast's Indian-born and Polish-born inhabitants accounted for 31% and 4%, respectively, of all those born in these nations prior to taking up residency in Northern Ireland. German migrants, by comparison, are distributed in a pattern that matches the overall population distribution of Northern Ireland reasonably well. Moreover, Poles and Lithuanians dominate in market towns like Armagh, Craigavon and Dungannon, which are as central to the manufacturing of food in the twenty-first century as they once were to Northern Ireland's linen industry referred to in previous Chapters (see Figure 34 below as well as DEL 2009; Lynn 2013: 3; NISRA 2011, Table QS208NI and Krausova and Vargas-Silva 2014: 5–10). The ideal locations of these A8 migrants particularly therefore diverge in certain key respects from the settlement patterns of ethnic minorities in the twentieth century who were more attracted to eastern counties, as previously noted. Between 2004 and 2014, new migrants resided at greater intensities in the Local Government Districts of the west and southwest – particularly Armagh City, Banbridge and Craigavon (9,200), Mid Ulster (9,100) and Newry, Mourne and Down (5,900) (see Figure 35 below as well as Eaton 2007: 172, 2010: 15; Lynn 2013: 26 and 38; McDermott 2011: 98; Russell 2017: 3). This trend is also evident in Medical Card Registration data and translation requests as well as the DENI annual schools census (see Tables 3/4 and Figures 24/39 below as well as Montague and Shirlow 2013: 19–20; Russell 2011, 2012, 2015). The 2006–2007 *Annual Report* from the Northern Ireland Council for Ethnic Minorities (NICEM) provides an analysis of requests it received for translating and interpreting services. These also demonstrate the significance of recent migration from A8 countries like Lithuania (almost 600 requests) and Poland (over 500) by comparison to those languages like Cantonese (about 50) and Hindi (fewer than 10) spoken by historically earlier migrant groups. In the same vein, Table 3 below, which displays data from the five Health and Social Care (HSC) Trusts across Northern Ireland indicating the top twenty languages for which interpreting and translation requests had been made in 2004–2005, the year of the first EU accession treaty noted earlier – by comparison to 2016–2017 (Table 3), highlight the diversity of heritage language backgrounds of newcomers to Northern Ireland over time.[48]

Table 3 Top 20 languages for which interpreting and translating requests had been made to HSC Trusts in the financial years 2004–2005, and 2016–2017

2004–2005		2016–2017	
Languages	**Number of Requests**	**Languages**	**Number of Requests**
Portuguese	1,034	Polish	31,220
Chinese (Cantonese)	171	Lithuanian	15,866
Polish	152	Romanian	8,975
Chinese (Mandarin)	113	Portuguese	8,323
Russian	104	Arabic	6,203
Lithuanian	100	Slovak	5,356
French	30	Tetum	5,319
Arabic	28	Chinese (Mandarin)	5,103
Ukrainian	19	Bulgarian	3,421
Slovak	16	Hungarian	3,387
Tetum	14	Chinese (Cantonese)	2,858
Spanish	13	Russian	2,541
Romanian	10	Latvian	2,042
Thai	9	Somali	1,151
Urdu	6	Czech	855
Latvian	5	Chinese (Haka)	748
Hindi	5	Spanish	589
Bengali	3	Farsi	515
Bulgarian	3	Bengali	369
Albanian	3	Urdu	297

---

48 I am grateful to Peter Shepherd of the HSC Interpreting Service who located the data and to the HSC Business Services Organisation for use of their statistics under a freedom of information request.

Further evidence for the spatial settlement preferences of allochthonous groups can be found in the DENI School Census for 2012/13, which reported that newcomer intakes were highest in Education and Library Boards associated with migrant intense employment sectors such as Presentation Primary, Craigavon (69%), St. Patrick's Primary, Dungannon (58%), St. Patrick's College, Dungannon (30%) and Drumcree College, Portadown (30%) (Montague and Shirlow 2014: 19–20). These migrant-dense locations are discernible in Figure 24 from Russell (2017: 18) based on numeric data from NISRA (2016a) showing the regional distribution of newcomer pupils in diverse Local Government Districts in the school year 2015/16. While that of the capital, Belfast, has the highest number (2,680), both Armagh City, Banbridge and Craigavon as well as Mid Ulster councils with 2,605 and 2,265, respectively, are not far behind. By contrast, regions such as Ards and North Down, which were favoured by ethnic minorities in the twentieth century, have considerably fewer newcomers (just 310) (see also Krausova and Vargas-Silva 2014: 10 and O'Sullivan et al. 2014, which compares Dungannon (Mid Ulster) and Larne (Ards), reaching similar conclusions).

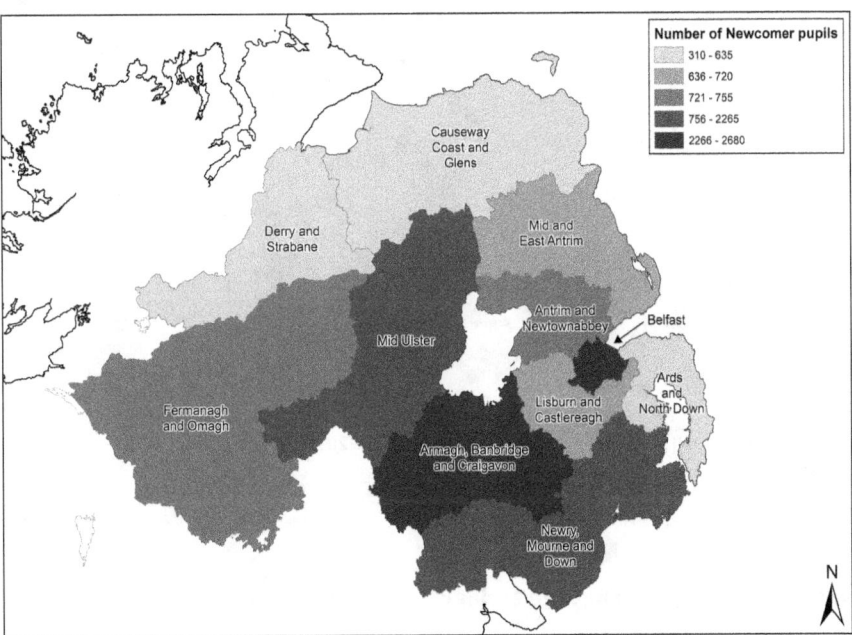

Figure 24 The spatial distribution of newcomer pupils in diverse local government districts in the school year 2015/16

NISRA's (2016b) mid-year estimates for Northern Ireland's inhabitants gives the size of the resident population as 1.862 million people and attributes the rise to more births than deaths coupled with net inward migration of 1,500 residents (up by 1.0 %). These levels do not match the highest observed population increase in the state's history in the period 2005–2007, due mainly to the birth rate outstripping the death rate and in-migration rising faster than out-migration. Thus, from 2006–2007, there were 23,800 births and only 14,700 deaths and while 22,500 people emigrated, 32,300 immigrated. This increase is obvious in Figure 25 summarising the causes of the peaks and troughs of population movement in twentieth and early twenty-first century Northern Ireland already discussed here and in §4.1.

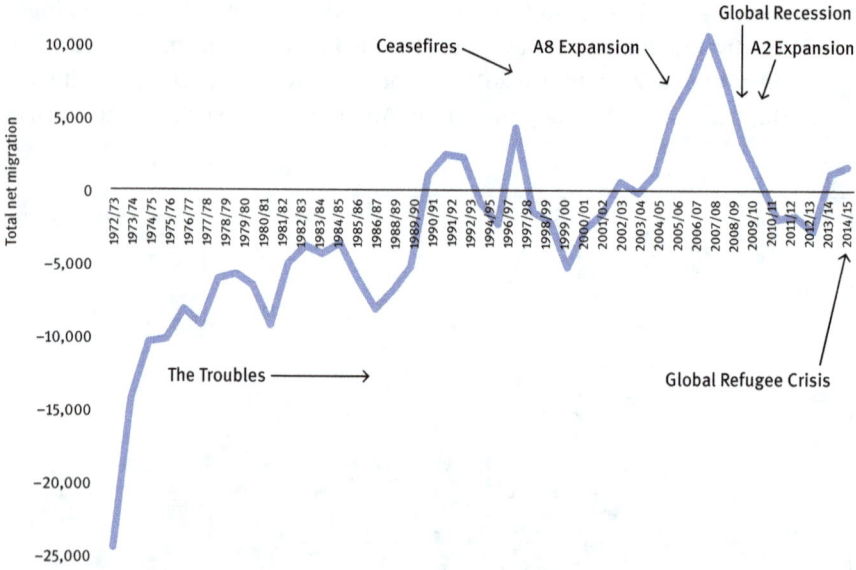

Figure 25 Trends in Annual Total Net Migration, 1972–2015 (Adapted from NISRA 2016b and Russell 2012: 9)

4.2.1 Migration and language ecology in the twenty-first century

The language ecology of twenty-first century Northern Ireland has changed in two significant respects. One of them revolves around language revitalisation movements that have received further impetus from the new rights afforded to both Irish and Ulster Scots by the implementation of the Belfast/Good Friday

Agreement, outlined in §4.1. The second reflects the migration inflows that have forged Northern Ireland into the type of state that meets Vertovec's (2007, 2014) criteria for being termed "superdiverse", which Russell (2017: 1) describes as a "remarkable demographic change."

4.2.1.1 Language revitalisation planning: the Irish language and Ulster Scots

As Carruthers and Ó Mainnín (2017: 160) observe, revival Irish has gone from strength to strength in the twenty-first century. For instance, Northern Irish educational institutions supporting the language as a means of instruction are no longer confined to urban Belfast since the terms of the Belfast/Good Friday Agreement obliged the Department for Education to facilitate Irish-Medium Education (Carruthers and Ó Mainnín 2017; Moriarty 2015). According to DENI (2019a: 15), this sector now caters for more than 6,500 pupils in dedicated schools or Irish-Medium Units attached to English-Medium schools that are now spread across all 6 counties of Northern Ireland (see Matthews 2016), and this is also reflected in the areal distribution of Irish speaking claimed by respondents to the 2011 Censuses in Northern Ireland and the Republic of Ireland who were over the age of three, as depicted in Figure 26.[49] With respect to youngsters in particular, the most recent DENI Schools Census (2018/19) recorded the fact that 28 newcomers (predominantly speakers whose L1 was Polish) were now also enrolled in schools within the Irish-Medium Sector, which is a completely new phenomenon worth tracking longer-term.

Grassroots support for the revival of the language in daily use by autochthonous and newcomer, allochthonous parents enrolling their children in Irish-Medium schools is bolstered by recent political and legal transformations which have seen the development of North-South bodies responsible for Irish. For example, *Foras na Gaeilge,* founded in 1999, entails the Government of Northern Ireland promoting and funding Irish revitalization efforts in ways that could never have been predicted even in the later twentieth century. Particularly noteworthy are the concessions that have transformed the linguistic landscape of Northern Ireland in the sense of Landry and Bourhis (1997: 23) i.e. "the visibility and salience of languages on public and commercial signs in a given territory or region" (Figures 27 and 28). These normalize and demarginalize Irish by incorporating it in monuments and street signage – as has been the long-standing

---

[49] The most recent figures for Irish-Medium Enrolments published on 29th April 2019 give a grand total of 6,519 for all school categories from nursery to post-primary – see https://www.education-ni.gov.uk/publications/school-enrolments-northern-ireland-summary-data (last accessed 3 July 2019).

practice in the Republic of Ireland (Kallen 2010a, 2010b) – despite what Mac an Bhreithiún and Burke (2014: 86) argue are the "collateral political and cultural implications" of doing so. These can be so divisive that public bodies as well as the Northern Ireland Assembly (the devolved legislature of Northern Ireland) have been found to be in breach of the terms of the 1998 Belfast/Good Friday Agreement with respect to their failure to implement policies towards Irish. An excellent example is the recent High Court ruling (March 2017) in a case taken by *Conradh na Gaeilge* (a social and cultural organisation for promoting the Irish language) against the Executive Committee of the Assembly, which was found to have "failed, in breach of its statutory duty under 28D (1) of the Northern Ireland Act 1998, to adopt a strategy setting out how it proposes to enhance and protect the development of the Irish language." In the same vein, Belfast City Council were subsequently advised that they too could potentially be subject to "judicial review in relation to allegations of the Council's non-compliance" with international and domestic legal obligations and standards with respect to the language (Belfast City Council 2017: 3). This is especially problematic given the fact that in the 2011 Census, 13.45 % of the Belfast population (aged 3+) have some ability in Irish, compared with 10.65 % of the population of Northern Ireland as a whole. Moreover over 16,000 people in Belfast speak, read, write and understand Irish and nearly 3,000 pupils (i.e. a majority of enrollments in that sector) receive education through the medium of Irish there (Matthews 2014: 15; NISRA, Table QS212NI).[50]

In this regard, at the time of writing, there is indeed considerable political and public discussion about the implementation of a core tenet of the St. Andrews Agreement[51] signed by all parties in 2006 which stated that:

> The Government will introduce an Irish Language Act reflecting on the experience of Wales and Ireland and work with the incoming Executive to enhance and protect the development of the Irish language.

---

[50] Details of the High Court's ruling can be found at: https://www.judiciary-ni.gov.uk/judicial-decisions/2017-niqb-27 (last accessed 14 March 2018). Belfast City Council in recognition of their non-compliance launched a Language Strategy (2018–2023) on May 14th 2018 which can be downloaded from: http://www.belfastcity.gov.uk/council/Languagestrategy/Language-strategy.aspx (last accessed 18 May 2018).

[51] See also Carruthers and Ó Mainnín (2017); McMonagle (2010), McMonagle and McDermott (2014), Moriarty (2015) and https://www.gov.uk/government/uploads/system/uploads/attachment_data/file/136651/st_andrews_agreement-2.pdf (last accessed 12 March 2018).

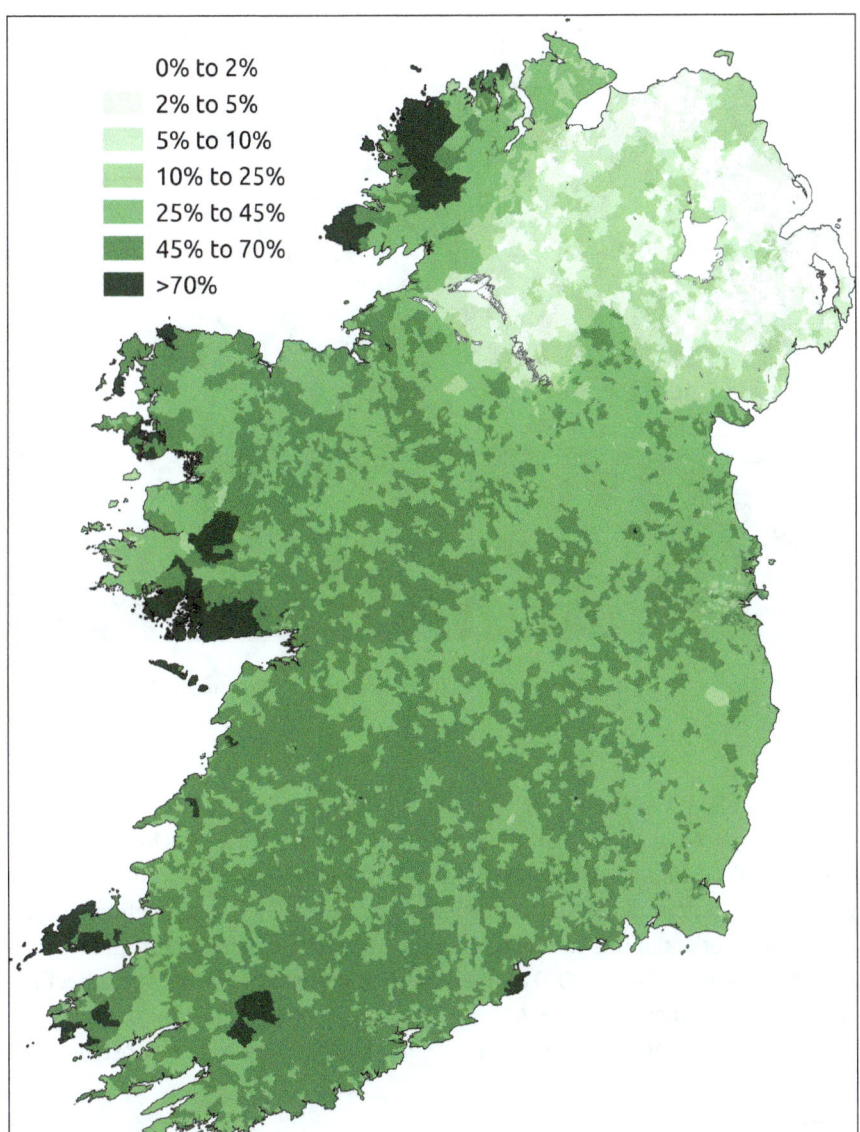

Figure 26 The proportion and spatial distribution of respondents in the 2011 Censuses in Northern Ireland and the Republic of Ireland aged 3+ who stated that they can speak Irish (after Tier 2014a). See https://commons.wikimedia.org/wiki/File:Irish_speakers_in_2011.png (last accessed 17 April 2019)

Figure 27 Photo of bilingual signage on Irish Street, Armagh City, 27th June 2019[52]

Northern Ireland's Culture Minister, Carál Ní Chuilín revealed draft proposals for such an Act in early 2015 which were met with parody and derision by members of the Democratic Unionist Party (DUP) (representing descendants of the colonising planter populations discussed in previous Chapters), which is staunchly opposed to it.[53] Whether or not this Act is ever implemented (the Assembly was, in fact, suspended between 2017 and 2020 as the Executive wrangled over this and other divisive issues, as McKendry (2017: 144) also notes), it is certainly the case that the position of the Irish language in Northern Ireland has changed radically between the

---

52 Image commissioned from and supplied by Órlaith Cullinane (www.orlaithcullinane.com).
53 The exchange between Gregory Campbell (DUP) and Ní Chuilín and its consequences can be found at: https://www.youtube.com/watch?v=fxmypnzhzgw and https://www.youtube.com/watch?v=Pf8m6JOZdSY (last accessed 13 March 2018). A summary of the political and cultural ramifications of the attempt to enact an Irish Language Act is nicely summarized here: http://www.bbc.co.uk/news/uk-northern-ireland-38601181 (last accessed 14 March 2018). This news item published by the *Belfast Telegraph* newspaper captures the currency of the debate: https://www.belfasttelegraph.co.uk/news/northern-ireland/storm-over-qub-refusal-to-put-up-signs-in-irish-36698738.html (last accessed 14 March 2018).

Figure 28 Photo of 'Welcome' monument in Ulster Scots (left), Ogham (middle) and Irish (right), Dunloy, County Antrim erected in 2004[54]

early twentieth century – when a question on ability in the language was dropped after partition, until 1991, when it was reinstated – and the twenty-first century – when the number of residents claiming knowledge of the language on the census is on an upward trajectory. That is, from 2.3% in 1991 to 10.65% in 2011, as noted in Census 2011, NISRA, Table QS217NI, Moriarty (2015) and Russell (2014: 15).

Another dividend of the Peace Process as regards increased recognition for linguistic diversity in contemporary Northern Ireland can be seen in Figures 29 and 30, which demonstrate further changes to what McDermott (2011) defines as the "public space", this time with respect to the other national minority variety, namely, Ulster Scots.

---

54 The original image is courtesy of Mark Thompson, former chair of the Ulster-Scots Agency/ *Boord o Ulstèr-Scotch* (*Foras na Gaeilge's* counterpart but responsible for Ulster Scots) and the monument is discussed in Mac an Bhreithiún and Burke (2014: 121–122). An insight into the local interest surrounding its installation is captured in a 2004 BBC Northern Ireland radio programme called "A Kist o Wurds" and available at: http://www.bbc.co.uk/programmes/p00b0dv1 (last accessed 13 March 2018) as well as in a more recent 2010 TV programme called "Stanes" and available at: http://www.bbc.co.uk/programmes/p00bpknq (last accessed 13 March 2018).

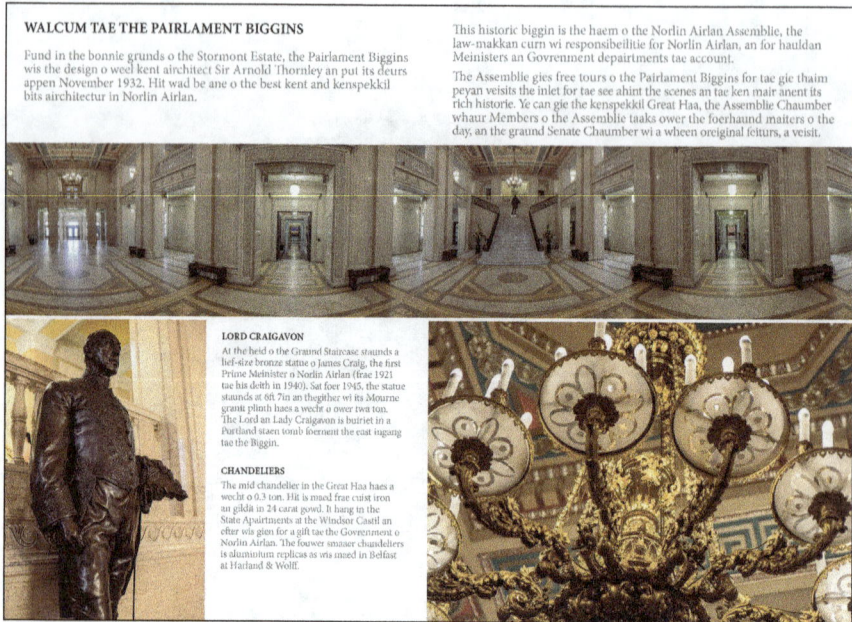

Figure 29 Ulster Scots Leaflet advertising tours of the Norlin Airlan Assemblie ('The Northern Ireland Assembly')[55]

As McMonagle and McDermott (2014: 247) have also argued, while Ulster Scots is not apolitical by any means, it features much less in public and governmental discourse on language policy than Irish does.[56] This may partly be a reflection of its uncertain status *qua* language or dialect (Carruthers and Ó Mainnín 2017: 167; Corrigan 2010: 16–17; McDermott 2018; NicCraith 2001), coupled with the fact that its meteoric rise is less recognisable as the direct outcome of grassroots movements for revitalization (McDermott 2018: 6). This is because its recent success has occurred in the main as a by-product of changes in the position of Irish within Northern Ireland. One important consequence is that the High Court ruling discussed previously makes it clear that the judgement also applies to Ulster Scots.

---

[55] I am grateful to Sinéad Murphy, Deputy Communications Officer for the Northern Ireland Assembly, for supplying this image. Parliamentary copyright images are reproduced with the permission of Northern Ireland Assembly Commission.

[56] For instance, Mid-Ulster District Council produced a policy document for the Irish language before they introduced one for Ulster Scots: https://www.midulstercouncil.org/getmedia/5e400ab9-6795-48f1-8263-55efcc06de6e/Irish-Language-Policy-Mid-Ulster-Council-English-Version.pdf?ext=.pdf and https://www.midulstercouncil.org/getmedia/8d5c6d56-cc51-4343-847f-e5d9f10a08c1/Ulster-Scots-Policy-2017.pdf?ext=.pdf (last accessed 15 March 2018).

It is fair to say that policy changes with respect to Irish have been viewed as precipitating the appropriation of Ulster Scots by devotees of the Unionist traditions, introduced earlier, in the hope that it could secure leverage for them in language policy debates of the kind already noted (Gardner 2016). There is evidence too, however, that its status as a language that can clearly be demarcated from English, in the respects that Irish can, has been controversial even amongst Unionists, which has muddied the waters somewhat (Carruthers and Ó Mainnín 2017: 167; Crowley 2005: 198–200, 2006; McDermott 2018: 5; McMonagle and McDermott 2014: 246).

Figure 30 Photo of road sign in Ballywalter, County Down in English and Ulster Scots[57]

Corrigan (2010: 130) suggested that one of several issues hampering the revitalisation of Ulster Scots was the fact that: "strictly monolectal speakers have been confined to rural areas for some time." Proponents of the revival movement were, however, principally urban dwellers who were often bidialectal in Ulster Scots and the regional standard, and whose headquarters were in Belfast. As such, there was a dissonance between the heartlands of native speakers in eastern enclaves and their ability to influence public and governmental opinion in the urban hubs (Fenton 2006a: iv, vii-ix; 2006b: 43; McDermott 2018: 8). The geographical dispersal of Ulster Scots speakers captured in the 2011 Census (which, as already noted, was the first to include a question on competence in the vernacular) bears this view out, as Figure 31 illustrates.

---

57 The term *lang syne* translates as 'formerly', as indicated, and *auld loanen* simply means 'old track.' I am grateful to Kate Mairs for permission to use this image taken in March 2018 in a village on the Ards Peninsula in County Down.

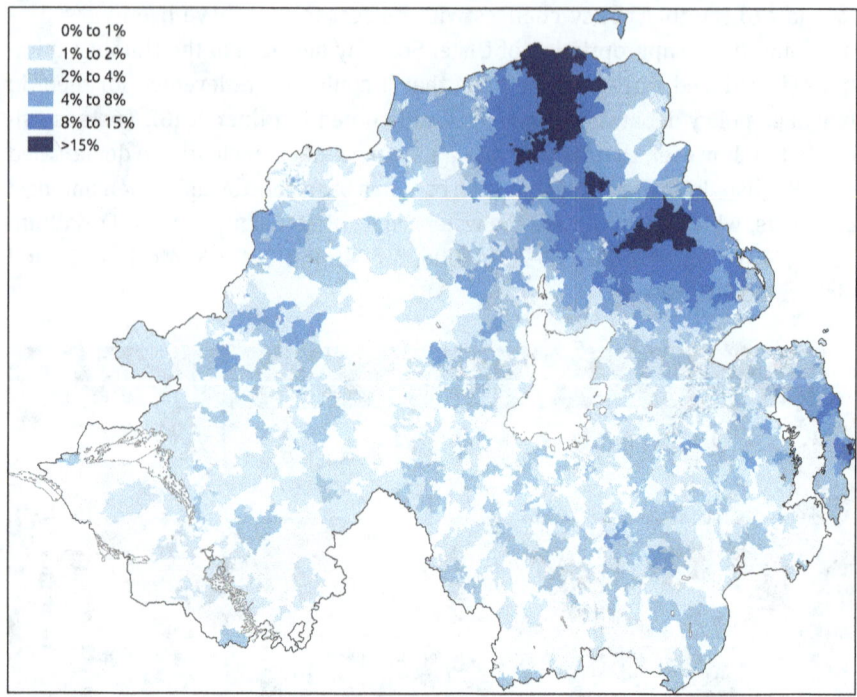

Figure 31 The proportion and spatial distribution of respondents in the 2011 Census aged 3+ who stated that they can speak Ulster Scots (After Tier 2014b). (https://upload.wikimedia.org/wikipedia/commons/archive/d/de/20160228183144%21Ulster-Scots_speakers_in_the_2011_census_in_Northern_Ireland.png – last accessed 15 March 2018)

Leaving geographical distribution aside, in Northern Ireland as a whole, just 8% of respondents to the 2011 Census declared themselves to be speakers of Ulster Scots, i.e. nearly 3% fewer than those who recorded their competence in Irish and there were only a hundred people who noted that Ulster Scots was their "main language" (Sebba 2019, and NISRA, Table KS210NI). Of interest too, was the fact that the figure for those who claimed to have an ability to "understand" the vernacular was three times greater (13%) than those who responded that they could "speak" Ulster Scots (just 4%) (NISRA 2012: 17).[58] These outcomes are especially

---

58 Further relevant data can be obtained from: https://www.nisra.gov.uk/statistics/people-places-and-culture/heritage-and-languages; https://www.communities-ni.gov.uk/publications/knowledge-and-use-irish-and-ulster-scots-northern-ireland-201516; https://www.communities-ni.gov.uk/articles/development-and-use-ulster-scots; https://www.communities-ni.gov.uk/topics/statistics-and-research/culture-and-heritage-statistics (last accessed 15 March 2018).

interesting when the overwhelming similarities between Ulster Scots and English are taken into account, as is evident from the document in Figure 29 above. It is also worth mentioning the fact, captured in Figure 32, that there are important contrasts between the number of Northern Ireland residents who can speak, read, write and understand Irish (3.7%) and those who declare the same abilities in Ulster Scots (only 0.9%).

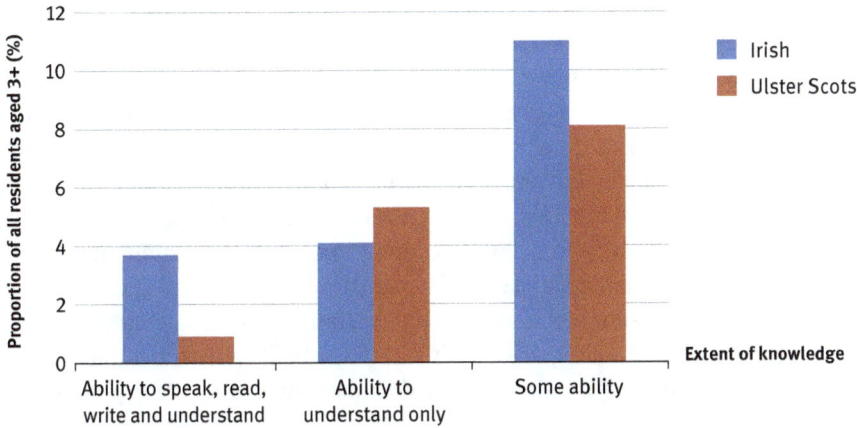

Figure 32 Knowledge of Irish and Ulster Scots by Assembly Area (age 3+), Census 2011 (after NISRA 2012: 17 and Russell 2013: 17)

This differential between respondents is likely due to the fact that the primary literary tradition associated with Ulster Scots significantly pre-dates the twenty-first century (Ferguson 2008). After all, it was only five years prior to the Census that a "spelling standardisation committee" was established (constituted as a Committee of the Ulster-Scots Academy Implementation Group (USAIG)) in response to the new requirements for written Ulster Scots arising from the socio-political and legislative changes described earlier (see Herbison, Robinson and Smyth 2012 and McDermott 2018). Such language planning strategies have also entailed USAIG becoming responsible for inventing new Ulster Scots lexis in registers with which native speakers from the heartland areas have never had to be acquainted. Thus, new terms have been coined such as *laa* 'legislation', *outrax* 'outreach', *resydentèrs* 'residents', *unnèr-docht* 'minority', *wabsteid* 'website', *wittens* 'data' and the complex *thaimwilangtholedbadness* meaning 'someone with a disability'.[59]

---

[59] These are found in the following online governmental and district council resources in Ulster Scots: https://www.midulstercouncil.org/getmedia/8d5c6d56-cc51-4343-847f-e5d9f10a08c1/

The latter is based on the Old English root *ðolian* meaning to 'endure' or 'suffer' and *lang*, a variant of 'long' combined with *thaim* for 'them', *wi* for 'with' and the noun *badness,* all of which are much more recognisable as derivable from English. There is little evidence that these lexical items are in common parlance, however. Certainly, all of them would need to be learned *ab initio* in written form as they are not intuitive except to those with specialist knowledge. As such, it's not surprising that even speakers of Ulster Scots from the core areas are reluctant to declare reading/writing abilities in the vernacular since they may well struggle to read policy documents and the like (even when they are ostensibly designed to accommodate this readership).

Mac an Bhreithiún and Burke (2014: 122) remark that the trilingual sign which features in Figure 28 is a "rare but hopeful local example of a perhaps increasing appreciation" of collective ethnolinguistic resources pertaining to the national minority groups. The evidence presented here clearly demonstrates that the management of Northern Ireland's linguistic landscape has taken a different tack in the twenty-first century and, as a consequence, the cultural capital of Ulster Scots has indeed been ameliorated alongside that pertaining to Irish, so that they are both represented in public spaces (both within the built environment, in bodies established for their promotion and in documentation and literary works of various types).

4.2.1.2 Language planning and new speakers of Northern Irish English

The cultural capital of the heritage languages spoken by new speakers of Northern Irish English has not improved to the same degree in this era, however, despite significant increases in their numbers from the early 2000s. As McDermott (2011: 2) remarks in a wider European context, this is largely a result of the inability of migrant communities to claim indigeneity, which is usually tantamount to any requests made to nation states for linguistic and other sociocultural support falling on deaf ears.

Returning to Vertovec's (2007, 2014) criteria for what constitutes a "superdiverse" society, it will become apparent that Northern Ireland now squarely fits the model and so there should be a strong case for the recognition of heritage languages alongside the national minority vernaculars.[60] Not only does social life

---

Ulster-Scots-Policy-2017.pdf?ext=.pdf and http://www.niassembly.gov.uk/about-the-assembly/general-information/information-leaflets/ulster-scots/; https://www.nisra.gov.uk/sites/nisra.gov.uk/files/publications/2001-census-translation-leaflet-ulster-scots.pdf (last accessed 15 March 2018).

60 It remains to be seen whether equality of opportunity policies such as that recently adopted by Belfast City Council, already noted, will have any positive impact. It certainly has the potential to, given that it declares a specific focus on "new communities' languages" in addition to the

in Northern Ireland encompass increased mobility, a more extensive number of ethnic minorities and diversity with respect to their countries of origin but, as Figure 33, demonstrates, there is now a considerably wider range of foreign languages spoken within the region, exactly as Vertovec's criteria demand.

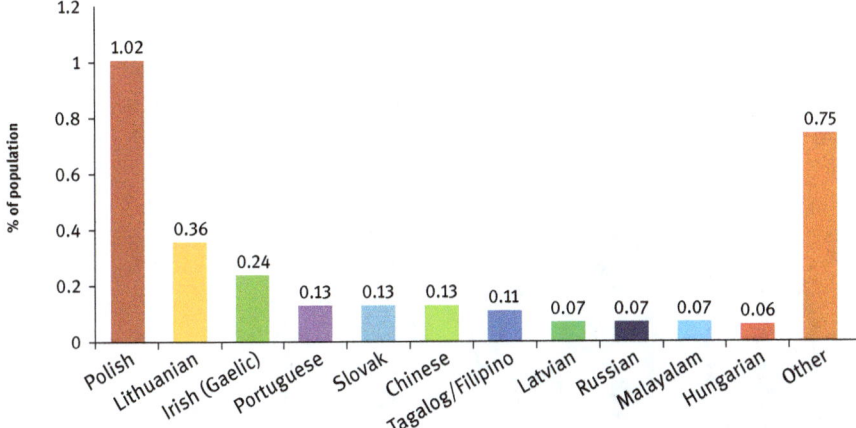

Figure 33 Percentage of the population (aged 3+) whose Main Language is not English[61]

---

ethnic majority varieties as well as British Sign Language/Irish Sign Language and languages and communications for disabled people. At the time of writing, other Local Government Districts such as Mid Ulster are developing translation and interpreting policies that may also have similar effects on the status of community languages. Councils, like Armagh, Banbridge and Craigavon, by contrast, have not yet managed to attain enough local government support for such language empowerment initiatives (not even for Irish or Ulster Scots), so impacts with respect to autochthonous languages would seem to be piecemeal for the short term at least as far as the wider region is concerned.

[61] The A8 countries here include: The Czech Republic, Estonia, Hungary, Latvia, Lithuania, Poland, Slovakia and Slovenia while the rest are not spoken in the wider European Economic Area. Figures are from: NISRA, Census 2011 Key Statistics for Northern Ireland (2012), Table KS207NI and indicate major languages spoken by 1000 or more residents. The next Northern Ireland census in 2021 may reveal new trends here since the most common languages after English recorded in the more recent Department of Education for Northern Ireland (DENI) School Census were actually Polish, Lithuanian and Romanian (DENI 2019b). Similarly, NISRA's (2016a) Mid-Year Population Estimates note that two of the most common countries of previous residence were Poland and Romania (NISRA 2017, 2019 and also see Russell 2016). These demolinguistic changes reflect new legislation dating from 2014 that allowed Romanians and Bulgarians the same rights as other European nationals to live and work in the UK, as detailed in § 4.2.

Vertovec's (2007: 1025) concept likewise entails that in order to qualify as "superdiverse", such states must also be characterised as having migrant residents with:

> differential immigration statuses ... divergent labour market experiences, discrete gender and age profiles, patterns of spatial distribution ...

The presence in contemporary Northern Ireland of refugees and asylum seekers which had largely been unknown there since the arrival of small numbers of Jews as a result of nineteenth century pogroms in Eastern Europe and during the Second World War means that it does indeed have residents of differing immigration statuses when these are compared with A8/A2 populations, for instance.

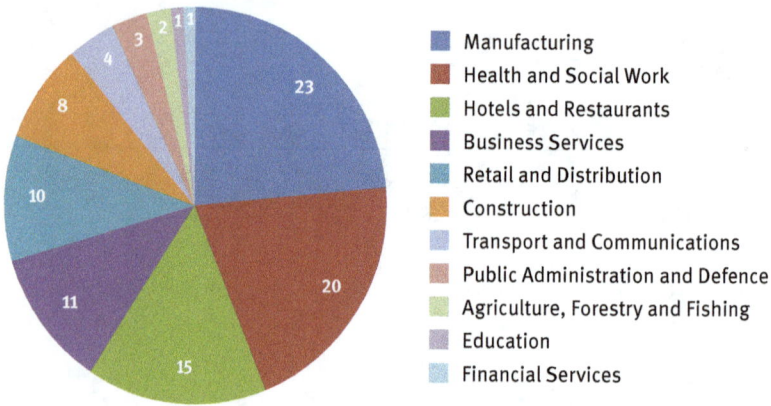

Figure 34 Percentage of Non-UK and ROI foreign-born employees by sector (2008) (After DEL 2009: 64)

The latter groups, in particular, can easily be argued to have diverse experiences as employees since they occupy a wide range of labour market sectors, as Figure 34 indicates.

The 2011 Census demonstrates that the age and gender profiles of new residents to NI born outside the UK or its closest neighbour, the Republic of Ireland, also contribute to Northern Ireland meeting Vertovec's "superdiverse" criteria.

Hence, Krausova and Vargas-Silva (2014: 4) report that new ethnic minorities are younger (i.e. aged 16–34) than migrants born within the British Isles. Moreover, gender balance amongst the latter group is 51.1% female, whereas those born further away had a slightly lower female-male ratio (49.7%). Moreover, the gender profiles of new ethnic minorities were age-group dependent. Slightly higher numbers of males belonged to the age cohorts 0–15 and 35–64 while 58% of females were in the over 65 age-bracket.

It was already noted that some regions of Northern Ireland are more migrant dense than others for economic as well as social reasons connected to chain migration patterns, as Table 4, which is based on new medical card registrations indicates:

Table 4 Northern Ireland Medical Card Registrations from Non-UK Nationals by top three countries of last residence by Local Government District (January to December 2015) (NISRA 2016c)

Area[62]	First country (number)	Second country (number)	Third country (number)
Antrim and Newtonabbey	Poland (100)	Romania (100)	Lithuania (100)
Ards and North Down	Lithuania (<50)	Romania (<50)	Poland (<50)
Armagh City, Banbridge and Craigavon	Poland (400)	Lithuania (300)	Portugal (300)
Belfast	Romania (400)	China (400)	Republic of Ireland (400)
Causeway Coast and Glens	Poland (100)	Republic of Ireland (100)	Germany (<50)
Derry City and Strabane	Republic of Ireland (200)	Poland (<50)	USA (<50)
Fermanagh and Omagh	Republic of Ireland (200)	Poland (100)	Hungary (100)
Lisburn and Castlereagh	Poland (100)	Republic of Ireland (100)	Romania (<50)
Mid and East Antrim	Romania (400)	Poland (200)	Czech Republic (100)
Mid-Ulster	East Timor[63] (300)	Poland (200)	Lithuania (200)
Newry, Mourne and Down	Republic of Ireland	Poland (200)	Bulgaria (100)
Northern Ireland	**Poland (1,900)**	**Republic of Ireland (1,500)**	**Romania (1,400)**

---

[62] Figure 24 maps the spatial distribution across Northern Ireland of all the Local Government Districts cited here.

[63] The territory is now officially known as the Democratic Republic of Timor-Leste (Timor-Leste) and this nomenclature will be used passim unless, as here, it refers to statistics or other materials compiled by the Northern Ireland Statistics and Research Agency or its ilk which persist with the former name of the state.

In a similar vein, Figure 35, which is based on the foreign languages (i.e. not English or Irish) declared by speakers aged 3+ in the 2011 Census, visualizes the spatial distribution patterns of these non-indigenous residents lending further support to this view. In keeping with Vertovec's (2007) definition, regions shown as having residents who speak foreign languages at a rate greater than 10 % coincide with the case made earlier regarding the density of migrants, principally in the Local Government Districts of Armagh City, Banbridge, Craigavon and Mid-Ulster to the south and west of Lough Neagh as well as Belfast, capital of the East.

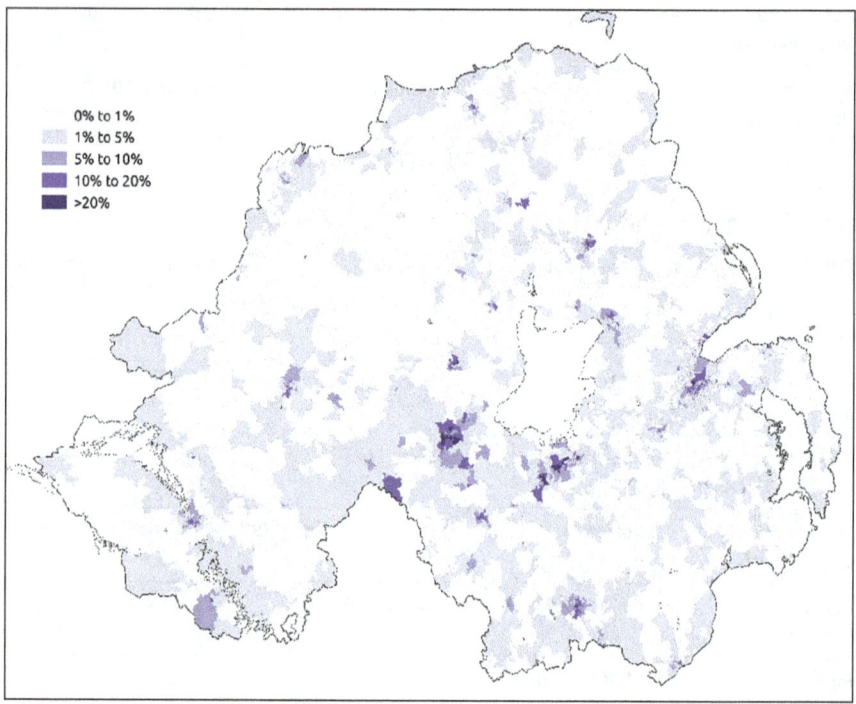

Figure 35 Map showing the percentage of people aged 3+ whose main language was other than English or Irish in the 2011 census (after Tier 2014c). (http://commons.wikimedia.org/wiki/Category:2011_United_Kingdom_census#mediaviewer/File:Foreign_languages_in_northern_ireland.png – last accessed 13 March 2018)

The geographic concentration of specific migrant groups in certain locations across Northern Ireland such as the Portuguese/Timor-Leste in Portadown (Eaton 2007; Doyle & McAreavey 2016) has important consequences both for the maintenance of the mother tongue in spite of the inter-ethnic situation as well as the ability to acquire English as an L2, which will be explored further in the next and subsequent Chapters. Isolation of a minority ethnic group in a majority language context also delimits their opportunity to shift away from the mother tongue in daily interactions and curtails the predisposition of adults, in particular, to do so (Allard and Landry 1994; Corrigan 2020; Ehala 2010; Fishman 2000; Gallois, Cretchley and Watson 2012; Giles, Bourhis and Taylor 1977; Harwood, Giles and Borhis 1994; Landry and Bourhis 1997; Pauwels 2016; Wölck 2004).

As noted previously in connection with first generation Chinese immigrants in twentieth century Northern Ireland, the types of employment undertaken by these groups can also have a distancing effect on inter-ethnic communication, promoting mother tongue maintenance (see also Pauwels 2016: 97). There is excellent evidence of what is known as "occupational segregation" (DEL 2009: 3) as regards migrant and indigenous workers in contemporary Northern Ireland. The former predominate in sectors and positions which locals have eschewed requiring low skills and generating minimal earnings (Eaton 2010: 15; Gilmartin 2015: 774; Potter and Hamilton 2014: 394). A good case in point is the food processing industries of Moy Park, Craigavon (Northern Ireland's largest private sector employer, which has nearly 10,000 employees and a turnover in excess of one billion pounds) as well as Dunbia, Dungannon (employing nearly 4000 and having a £900 million turnover), both of which are heavily reliant on migrant labour for the lowest-status roles.[64] Thus, Lynn (2013: 54) records the fact that 60% of Dunbia's employees at operative level belong to ethnic minority groups.

At first blush, migrant-dense employment sectors in which a range of minority ethnic groups are occupied might seem like ideal conditions for the transmission of Northern Irish English as a lingua franca for inter-ethnic communication, as Kingsley (2013) argues in relation to her research on international banking in multilingual Luxembourg.[65] Moreover, according to McDermott (2011: Ch. 6), there is abundant evidence that adult immigrants to Northern Ireland are actively trying to improve their language skills in English. However, as articulated in Chapter Five, this is a complex process that is much harder after the critical period and requires considerable motivation as well as aptitude and opportunity. In addition, the contexts in which the transnational workers in Kingsley's (2013) research find themselves are markedly different to the present case. Thus, Potter

---

[64] This numeric data was obtained from: http://www.top1000.ie/industries/food-and-beverage (last accessed 20 March 2018).
[65] Lithuanian, Polish and Portuguese/Timor-Leste minorities are in the majority in Dunbia, for instance, as noted in: http://www.migrantworkersni.com/media/3fd0852501ff4fb3825f89b200d 60b0aLR%20A5%20migrant%20worker%20brochure.pdf (last accessed 21 March 2018). The dominance of only a small number of ethnolinguistic groups may be helpful in this regard, as Goldstein (1997) argues in relation to the persistence of Portuguese rather than English amongst migrant factory workers in Canada.

and Hamilton (2014) highlight the social isolation of migrant workers in Northern Ireland's mushroom industry where (as already noted in Chapter One, §1.3) many of the parents and wider adult personal ties of youngsters interviewed in the *Múin Béarla* project are engaged, as (25) demonstrates:

(25) Extract from interview with 'Gabija Zalins', Armagh, 2014

> 1 KPC: What does your mummy and what does your daddy do? So, he drives as well, drives lorries and things?
> 2 Gabija Zalins: Um no he doesn't drive lorries he like, washes like the ...
> 3 KPC: Walls? Windows!
> 4 Gabija Zalins: No the thingy called like the inside there's like mushrooms in it and then.
> 5 Nadežda Smetona: A co...ehm
> 6 KPC: Oh I know what you mean the wee kind of yeah, he keeps everything er, we would call that irrigated.
> 7 Gabija Zalins: Yeah. My whole family nearly works in mushrooms ... I mean every, m= all my family works in mushrooms, none of them work up in factories.

[NS (F); GZ (F); St. Celine's; Armagh, Northern Ireland, 20 Oct. 2014]

Such workers are employed as small teams drawn from ethnolinguistically diverse groups in unpredictable shift rotations and are largely confined to rural farm locations (see McAreavey 2010). Moreover, the employees are generally supervised by other migrants who themselves share neither the language nor the nationality of those who they manage. This scenario is demonstrated in a discussion from the *Múin Béarla* corpus (26) on the degree of plurilingualism often associated with employment in this sector:

(26) Extract from interview with 'Sofia Kovak', Armagh, 2014

> 1 KPC: And, so I guess your mum must've learned Russian as a child when Russia and Lithuania were joined.
> 2 Sofiya Kovak: Yeah. Yeah. She has. Eh, and then she learned Polish, and then she came to Ireland, then she was
> 3 KPC: How come?
> 4 Sofiya Kovak: <Laughter> eh she <Laughter> was work eh she came to Ireland to work in a mushroom factory, eh with all these different, eh, people as well and she learned Polish there, basically. Yes ... And so she, so she still carries on

5	KPC:	since. Yeah, and she learned better Russian in there as well, like. Oh, so it kind of improved her Russian? Good, that's great.
6	Sofiya Kovak:	Yeah.
7	KPC:	And would most of those mushroom factory workers be international?
8	Sofiya Kovak:	Yeah, yeah. A lot of people come, like, and they don't know the language so you wouldn't get a job with customers where you have to speak in English, like, if they don't know the ... the language. So you would go working in some factory first, unless, and then if you do learn and improve your English you get to work with different customers ...

[SK (F); St. Celine's, Armagh, Northern Ireland, 21 Oct. 2014]

In addition, even different circumstances – like working on a regular basis as an operative on a mechanised factory floor where there are high levels of noise, making communication difficult in any language – are not conducive to the acquisition of a common language either (de Neve 2005: 202). Moreover, one suspects that during social periods of the working day, migrants who are ethnolinguistically similar are more likely to seek each other out for conversation than those who are dissimilar (see Gilmartin and Migge 2015: 290–291). Indeed, this is exactly the practice I often observed during meal and other social periods amongst newcomer versus indigenous pupils enrolled in the schools participating in this project. There is ample evidence for the self-isolating dynamics of homogeneous ethnolinguistic groups reported by newcomer participants in the *Múin Béarla* corpus with respect to themselves (27) and their parents (28). Autochthonous dyads who were interviewed also record that they have witnessed similar social practices amongst allochthonous groups at school as well as outside of this domain (29).

(27) Extract from an interview with 'Nikolay Danshov', Armagh, 2013

1	KPC:	And what about ... do you find that the in the school that the Latvians kind of stick together, the Lithuanians kind of stick together, the Poles stick together or not really?
2	Nikolay Danshov:	Well yeah actually they're very Polish, there's a lot of them so there's actually they're always walk together.

3   KPC: Mm-hm.
4   Nikolay Danshov: And Lithuania maybe sometimes too.

[ND (M); St. Benedict's; Armagh, Northern Ireland; 11 Oct. 2013]

(28)   Extract from an interview with 'Patros Stain', Armagh, 2013

1   KPC: And what about things like um do you think your mum might benefit from having friends who were Irish and try to draw her out in terms of getting her to speak English?
2   Patros Stain: Well yeah it's better to have Polish and Irish than only Polish.
3   KPC: But does she tend not to have any Irish friends at all, she only has Polish friends because she can't speak English?
4   Patros Stain: Well yeah she doesn't have Irish because she can't speak English yeah.

[PS (M); St. Benedict's; Armagh, Northern Ireland; 11 Oct. 2013]

(29)   Extract from an interview with 'Katherine Gormley' and 'Michelle Maguire', Armagh, 2013

1   KPC: And do you think that the kids who are Polish and Lithuanian or Chinese kind of have problems with that and they would be better off in a unit of their own?
2   Katherine Gormley: I think it'd be very hard for them just to come like from another country in here [*the Irish Medium Unit*] where they haven't the best English and they just sort of stick together right enough they always just seem to stick together.
3   Michelle Maguire: Mm they always do stick together
4   Katherine Gormley: And talk their own language and ...
5   KPC: Uh-huh and do you think that that makes people feel kind of more prejudiced towards them because they kind of they're segregating themselves almost?
6   Katherine Gormley: Yeah not in all not always.
7   Michelle Maguire: Mm.
8   KPC: Mm.

9	Katherine Gormley:	Because you would get the one in our year like would just sit and talk to anyone which I think's better like just mixing with everyone like instead of making a divide.
10	KPC:	Mm-hm so and in general would they be like that would they would they generally not mix do you think?
11	Katherine Gormley:	Yeah.
12	Michelle Maguire:	Yeah.

[KG (F); MM (F); St. Celine's; Armagh, Northern Ireland; 7 Aug. 2013]

In the same vein, the interviews also document the fact that many of the first generation migrants continue to struggle with acquiring Northern Irish English in a range of domains as well as fully comprehending conversations with autochthonous dialect speakers even after many years of residing in Northern Ireland. Extracts on just this topic from one of the *Múin Béarla* interviews with two young Lithuanian women in (30) illustrates their parents' issues with English competence and the language brokering role which each of the youngsters then has to play in interactions with native speakers, often in confidential contexts such as medical examinations where this is hardly appropriate, as also noted in Antonini (2016) and Russell, Morales and Ravert (2015) (see also Gilmartin 2015: 83; Gilmartin and Migge 2015: 293; Migge 2012: 316–317; Nestor and Regan 2011: 44).

(30) Extract from an interview with 'Roxy Bite' and 'Iera Simonis', Armagh, 2014

1	Iera Simonis:	... my dad he's just like "yeah you're my translator, let's go and find me a work".
2	KPC:	Mm-mm.
3	Iera Simonis:	And I'm like "pay me first!"
4	Roxy Bite:	That's same as mine.
5	KPC:	So your dad's the same, is he? He makes you translate everything?
6	Roxy Bite:	Yeah, everywhere like if his car needs like some part or new tyres he just takes me everywhere.
7	Iera Simonis:	Yeah, even if you go to the doctor's.
8	Roxy Bite:	So I know like half of the people who are engineers and stuff.
9	KPC:	His built-in translator. He just shoves you in the passenger seat.
10	Roxy Bite:	He's like "we're going there like. Ok."

11	KPC:	And do you find that when he talks that kind of specialised vocabulary to you about the problems with his car, do you ever not understand what he's talking about?
12	Roxy Bite:	In Lithuanian, no not really, but he's like kind of really good explaining things even if he doesn't know the language so he just takes the person explaining it to the, so um yeah, it's quite easy.
13	KPC:	Mm-mm. And do your mum and dad have an English accent that is really strongly marked by Lithuanian, you know, does it sound very Lithuanian which you know so when you hear them speak English you think…
14	Roxy Bite:	Yes. My mum.
15	Iera Simonis:	It's like they pronounce the R really, really badly.
16	KPC:	So what do they say, what do they say?
17	Iera Simonis:	So, it's i= it's usually my mum saying … She ju= she pitches her voice up sometimes. I'm like "why are you pitching your voice up?" And she just doesn't answer me she continues talking in pitched up voice. I'm like "Oh my God stop doing that" and then she just goes "Hello, how are you doing?" [*mimicking her mother's voice*] I'm like, she p…her voice is so pitched up I sometimes don't understand what she's saying and it's kind of embarrassing so I just go over in a corner and stand away from her like "She's not my mom, I don't know her".
18	KPC:	So tell me what she does with her Rs? What does she say?
19	Iera Simonis:	She pronounces them okay but sometimes when an R comes like say "right" she goes "Right, okay. Ok, ok, right, right, right" [*pronounced with initial alveolar trill [r]*]. I'm like "what is going on?"
20	KPC:	And what about your mummy?
21	Roxy Bite:	It's exactly the same. She studied English in eh Lithuanian so it's like really different things. No, it's like the same but in different ways like you would say: "I went to the shop yesterday", she would be like "I go to the shop yesterday and stuff." So it's kind of weird and she has a different accent.
22	KPC:	So she doesn't use like the kind of right verbs and things so she sort of gets it right because it's 'go' and it's kind of 'go' but she … That sort of thing?

23 Roxy Bite: Yeah, like different kind of things.
24 Iera Simonis: If she tells, she tells me what to say if we are going to the doctor she tells me what's wrong with her. But then I ask her repeat it about ten times because I don't understand what she's saying ... Yeah, no like in Lithuanian. She tells me one thing, I'm like "what does that mean?" And she's like "just tell the doctor" I'm like "but what does that mean? I don't know what it means." And then when I try to go to tell the doctor she's just like "right tell her what I said." I'm like "right, ok, em, eh I don't really know what she said, I don't know what's wrong with her because she won't explain me the word." So I just sit there staring at the wall!

[IS (F); RB (F); St. Celine's; Armagh, Northern Ireland; 27 Jan. 2014]

Additional evidence for language abilities across Northern Ireland as a whole is provided in Question (20) on the 2011 Census form which asked "How well do you know English", providing a range of possible responses from "very well" to "not at all". There were 54,540 individuals aged 3+ who self-declared that their main language was not English (including 4,164 Irish speakers as well as the 100 Ulster Scots noted previously and who similarly declared). There were slightly fewer females (26,533) than males (28,007) who claimed that their main language was not English. Amongst the proportion who ticked either "cannot speak English" or "cannot speak English well", the proportion was equal between both genders (26.5%). When the figures are broken down according to the HSC Trusts where these individuals reside, over a third of respondents in the Southern Trust (where Moy Park is situated) indicated that they had serious issues with English (HSC 2014: 24). This is corroborated by the fact that this Trust made by far the greatest number of requests for translating and interpreting services of all five HSC Trusts across Northern Ireland in the same financial year 2010–2011 as the Census (26,279 versus 25,455 for all the rest – its closest rival being the Belfast Trust, which made more than 50% fewer requests).[66] Of interest in this regard too is the fact that very high proportions of usual residents over the age of 3 whose main language was declared to be either Tagalog or Malayalam assessed their ability to

---

[66] This trend continued in subsequent years such that 50,291 requests were made in 2016–2017 by the Southern Trust with its closest rival, Belfast, supporting just 31,852. I am grateful to Peter Shepherd of the HSC Interpreting Service who located the data and to the HSC Business Services Organisation for use of their statistics under a freedom of information request.

speak English as being "well" or "very well" (99 per cent and 92 per cent, respectively, NISRA 2013b: 4). This is likely to be correlated to the concentrations of ethnically Filipino and Malay residents in professional occupations often linked to health care (as nurses and doctors e.g.) where proficiency in English is mandatory (NISRA 2013b: 2). By contrast, fewer of those residents belonging to ethnic groups engaged in routine occupations, such as those associated with the food processing industries already mentioned, professed to be able to speak English "well" or "very well" (i.e. Hungarians 68%, Latvians 71%, Lithuanians 62%, Polish 66%, Portuguese 73%, Russians 66% and Slovakians 64%). Moreover, 41% of respondents aged over three who claimed not to speak any English at all had a main language which was instead Polish. 14% spoke Lithuanian primarily, 6.4% used Chinese as their main language, while 4.6% of such respondents used Slovak and 4.5% were principally Portuguese-speaking (NISRA 2013b: 4).

The long-standing nature of ethnically Chinese populations in Northern Ireland documented in Blee (2011), Delargy (2007), Feng-Bing (2006) and Hainsworth (1998) *inter alia* has resulted in important changes to the linguistic landscape of Northern Ireland, as Figure 36 below illustrates. The images in Figure 37 and 38 capture the fact that the arrival of new ethnolinguistic groups in the twenty-first century has also begun to have an impact on public space in the sense of McDermott (2011).

However, there is a key difference between the officially sanctioned "top-down" signage generated by the domestic and international agreements referred to earlier with respect to Irish and Ulster Scots and the type of "bottom-up" landscapes associated with commerce, private cultural organisations and the like (Gorter 2006: 3; Kallen 2010b). Language policy initiatives in Northern Ireland at the present time do not readily extend to new ethnolinguistic minorities even though Section 75 of the Northern Ireland Act (enacted as a result of the Belfast/Good Friday Agreement) explicitly prohibits all types of racial and ethnic discrimination. The legislation has, however, largely been interpreted in top-down contexts as being limited to eradicating the types of inequity associated with the traditional socio-political and economic divisions amongst the autochthonous ethnic majority groups (McMonagle and McDermott 2014: 247–248). Consequently, changes to the public space illustrated by Figures 36–38 are not the result of pluralist official policies generated by the "civic authorities" in Kallen's (2010b) sense, so they lack prestige and are thus often considerably more ephemeral in nature (Blommaert 2010: 9–10; Gilmartin 2015: 84; Kallen 2010b; Sebba 2010). They do, however, serve to some extent at least to legitimize the more extensive linguistic diversity which now characterizes Northern Ireland's cityscapes especially.

Immigration and the rise of a superdiverse society in the twenty-first century — 113

Figure 36 Photo of Chinese figures, based on the terracotta Warriors of Xi'an, in the grounds of Belfast City Hall (taken on 16th August 2013), by Albert Bridge and licensed under CC-BY-SA 2.0 (https://www.geograph.ie/photo/3603604 – last accessed 17 April 2019)

Figure 37 Photo of bilingual signage at a Polish delicatessen, Armagh Northern Ireland (24th June 2016)

Figure 38 Photo of multilingual graffiti in Dungannon, Co. Tyrone (18th March 2015)[67]

There is some supporting evidence too for the extent to which social practices like these in addition to the deployment of authochthonous and allochthonous groups in segregated occupations and locations noted earlier foster heritage language maintenance and discourage the acquisition of local English dialects within new migrant communities. This is especially true amongst adults, as recorded in figures supplied by the Northern Ireland Health and Social Care Interpreting Service which indicate that between the financial years 2004–2005 to 2016–2017, there were 722,363 such requests for interpreters (see also Russell 2017: 3). These longitudinal changes demonstrating exponential increases in translating services since the instantiation of EU accession legislation in 2004 (detailed in §4.2) are obvious in Figure 39:

---

[67] *Bem Vindo* is Portuguese for 'welcome' while *Sveiki* is used in Latvian and Lithuanian to mean 'hello'. Both *Witajcie* and *Haksolok mai* also mean 'welcome' in Polish and the Tetum language of East Timor, respectively.

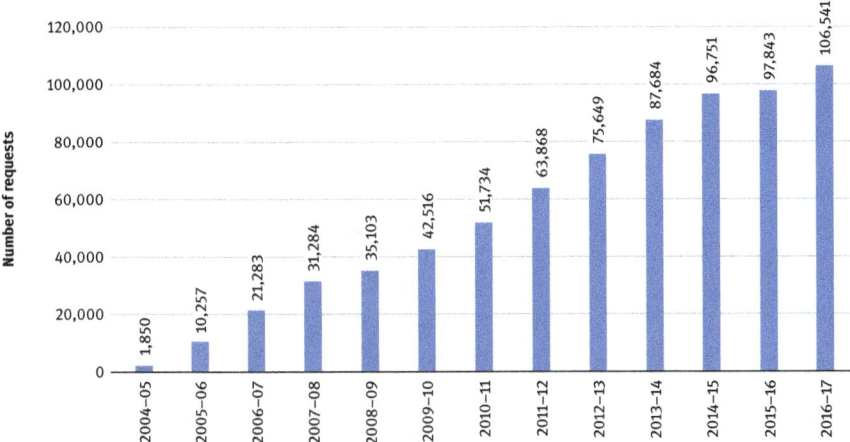

Figure 39 Northern Ireland Health and Social Care (HSC) Interpreting Service Yearly Statistics for the financial years 2004–2005 to 2016–2017[68]

The extent to which younger first generation migrants persist with their heritage languages is harder to determine since interpreter requests to assist minors, for example, will never explicitly be recorded as having been prompted by them but instead will have been instigated by educators, medical teams, parents or guardians, social workers and the like. However, there is certainly evidence of the establishment across Northern Ireland of supplementary school networks in migrant heritage languages, which is a litmus test of sorts in this regard (see also McDermott 2012: 197, and McKendry 2017: 154). Their function is to maintain and improve skills amongst youngsters in particular, many whom will have lost the chance to acquire reading and writing competencies in these languages prior to arrival since they migrated before starting any formal schooling abroad. For example, a network of eleven Polish Language Schools operate across Northern Ireland, some of which are located in or near the fieldwork sites for the *Múin Béarla* project. Indeed, as extracts (31) and (32) from these interviews indicate, there is good evidence that some of the participants at least attended such supplementary Saturday schools.

---

[68] I am grateful to Peter Shepherd of the HSC Interpreting Service who located the data and to the HSC Business Services Organisation for use of their statistics under a freedom of information request.

(31)   Extract from an interview with 'Erelis Norkus', Armagh, 2013

1	Erelis Norkus:	But then when I was here I went to this Lithuanian school, Saturday school ...
2	KPC:	And how long did you go to the Lithuanian school for on a Saturday?
3	Erelis Norkus:	You know, I went for like three years or more.
4	KPC:	Very good.
5	KPC:	And did you find that lots of other Lithuanians went and stayed for a long time or not?
6	Erelis Norkus:	Yeah. Especially those who started from like the first you know year that they started off.
7	KPC:	Yes.
8	Erelis Norkus:	Usually most of them stayed to the end.
9	KPC:	Mm-mm. So you can only stay for about three years.
10	Erelis Norkus:	No, you could stay for longer but, I don't know why but it closed down I think.
11	KPC:	Oh!
12	Erelis Norkus:	And there's like 'cause for wee children it's very good, there's a like a wee children Lithuanian Saturday school.
13	KPC:	Oh is there? Where is that?
14	Erelis Norkus:	Yeah, so it's the [*Names local Catholic Maintained post-primary school for boys*].
15	Erelis Norkus:	You know so yeah.
16	KPC:	Oh, ok.
17	Erelis Norkus:	And it's for little ones, it's like you know it's very useful, and for us big ones we go to school from Monday to Friday and then there's Saturday full day and it's like 'No, <@> hum I had enough'.

[EN (F); St. Celine's; Armagh, Northern Ireland; 18 Dec. 2013]

(32)   Extract from an interview with 'Amelia' and 'Mariana Olavo', Armagh, 2014

1	KPC:	You guys use Portuguese to sort of chat to each other in class maybe, especially you two?
2	Amelia Olavo:	No.
3	Mariana Olavo:	No but I use to to her loads of times. [*Laughter*]
4	KPC:	So you would use it like if you met each other in the corridor, you wouldn't speak in English?

5	Amelia Olavo:	No.
6	Mariana Olavo:	No.
7	KPC:	And what about at home, would you ever speak in English at home, you two?
8	Amelia Olavo:	No we're not allowed to [*Laughter*].
9	KPC:	Oh you're not allowed to?
10	Amelia Olavo:	No because my mum wants us to not forget Portuguese, our language and we go to Saturday school which is Portuguese school, so.
11	Mariana Olavo:	School.
12	KPC:	Mm-mm. So that must be how your reading and writing is very good in Portuguese then, I noticed that on the CEFR form.
13	Amelia Olavo:	Yeah

[AO (F); MO (F); JF (F); St Celine's; Armagh, Northern Ireland; 27 Jan. 2014]

Moreover, the most recent enrolment data for the Polish school in Belfast declares that they have 180 weekly attendees who would eventually be awarded language certificates recognised in Poland. This accomplishment will be an important advantage should the pupils ever become return migrants and there is certainly substantiation in the *Múin Béarla* interviews that this is indeed a key objective for some individuals, as the exchange with a young Polish woman reproduced in (33) indicates.[69]

(33)   Extract from an interview with 'Polly Wiczorek', Armagh, 2013

1	KPC:	And how did she find it when she [*Polly Wiczorek's older sister*] first came? It must have been very hard for her.
2	Polly Wiczorek:	Oh, she was, she was depressed 'cause she had all her friends back in Poland. She was twelve.
3	KPC:	That's a hard age to move isn't it really when they're – you're on the cusp of being a teenager and your friends have become so important to you.
4	Polly Wiczorek:	Yeah, so she didn't like it. But she does … she doesn't like it still. She wants to go back.

[PW (F); St. Celine's; Armagh, Northern Ireland; 5 Aug. 2013]

---

69 See: http://peca-ni.org/polish-schools-ni/pss-belfast/ (last accessed 16 April 2018).

Other support for schemes that would facilitate return migration through the promotion of language maintenance amongst this group especially is available from diverse sources. These would include, for instance, testimonials from post-primary principals engaged in Continuing Professional Development programmes that highlight the importance of maintaining the cultural and social capital of newcomer pupils for identity purposes as well as to enhance their range of skills for the global job market. Thus, following one such event, the principal of St. Patrick's College, Dungannon, (which, as noted in §4.2, currently has a newcomer school population which is one in four of their entire student cohort):

> appointed a member of staff to coordinate and foster cultural diversity, had made inclusivity a top priority in her school development plan … had also set targets to enable students to take GCSEs in their own language or in a cognate language such as Spanish for the Portuguese students (p.c.).

The success of initiatives such as these as well as the efforts of the supplementary schools to maintain the first language amongst sufficient numbers of minority ethnic youngsters remains to be seen, however. This is particularly so in the light of the official DENI position which allocates funds only to assist newcomer pupils "in their acquisition of the language of instruction, whether it be English or Irish, in an inclusive manner, to enable them to access the curriculum in particular and partake in every aspect of school life" (DENI 2009: 1–2).

4.3 The globalisation of Northern Ireland: retrospects and prospects

The title of McLaughlin (1994: 3) declares Ireland to be an "emigrant nursery." His intention in this monograph is to take a revisionist approach to understanding Irish diasporic movements of former times as well as "new wave" emigration processes characterising the mobility of the autochthonous population in the twentieth century, detailed in §4.1. An important objective is to demonstrate that the factors precipitating emigration are multiple and complex, going beyond the mere identification of push-pull motivators of one type or another. McLaughlin (1994) argues that the complexity cannot be understood without viewing Ireland – a peripheral region both geographically as well as with respect to world systems of economics and socio-political processes – in global terms. This orientation has also influenced the account presented in Chapters One to Four of population changes in Ulster from pre-historic times to the present day. The discussion has taken McLaughlin's approach one step further by extending it beyond the twentieth century into the twenty-first when the region, on account of various domestic and international agreements as well as forced and economic migrations of one kind or another, has been transformed from an emigration nursery into what might be termed an "immigration kindergarten". O'Reilly (2015: 25) observes that such migration (especially that which is international in nature):

> has the potential to change individuals and societies in diverse and interesting ways, the potential to exploit, to enrich, to bring about competition, and to engender change. It raises questions about identity, belonging, location, resources, social cohesion and social divisiveness.

Part I has demonstrated that migration in the context of the North of the island of Ireland has indeed engendered socio-cultural change of these types. It also highlighted the fact that internal and external mobility have brought about concomitant and no less radical changes to the language ecologies of the region. Looming on the horizon of course is the important question: What impact on migratory trends and linguistic diversity in Northern Ireland will the UK's triggering of Article 50 to initiate their withdrawal from the EU have? As Hogan-Brun (2018: 50) rightly argues, Brexit potentially entails the UK being forced to locate from within its own resources enough highly skilled bilinguals to negotiate not only the market value of goods and services with individual partners within the EU, but also with states internationally with whom the UK also needs to trade. Although there will not be another official Census in Northern Ireland until 2021, evidence is emerging already from other sources that further socio-cultural change and a reduction in linguistic diversity is underway because the possibility of recruiting workers from the EU has fallen so dramatically since the Brexit vote. A recent survey entitled "Harvesting Tomorrow's Skills", undertaken by the Northern Ireland Drinks and Food Association (which was shown in §4.2 to be a key employer of immigrant (especially EU) labour across Northern Ireland), records that firms in the sector reported an 80% drop in recruitment compared to levels prior to the vote.[70] Naturally, this reduction in immigrant numbers (if it persists) will generate further changes to the demolinguistics of Northern Ireland. While a majority of voters there chose the "remain" option in the Brexit vote, its five hundred mile border with the Republic of Ireland has made it once more a focal space for socio-political and economic agendas at the very heart of transnational migration's "cohesion" and "divisiveness" spectrum to which O'Reilly (2015: 25) refers.

Part II will hone in on migration from two principal orientations: (i) language variation and change studies (Chambers and Schilling 2013) and (ii) scholarship

---

[70] See: https://www.thedetail.tv/articles/agrifood-firms-struggling-to-recruit-eu-workers-since-brexit-vote (last accessed 1 Aug. 2018).

in the sociolinguistics of globalisation (Blommaert 2010). Firstly, it examines the processes involved in the acquisition of Northern Irish English from various theoretical perspectives (Chapter Five). Chapter Six explores and evaluates the data collection methods, protocols and fieldwork techniques underpinning the *Múin Béarla* corpus. Chapters Seven through Nine undertake sociolinguistic quantitative analyses of Northern Irish English features from different levels of the grammar, querying the extent to which they have or have not been acquired by newcomer migrants and hypothesising what the findings might entail for explaining the dynamics of language contact and change more broadly. In addition to furthering our understanding of the internal factors that govern variability in Northern Irish English dialects from a comparative sociolinguistic perspective (Tagliamonte 2004a), these Chapters also address social questions such as the extent to which males or females are more successful at acquiring autochthonous features or at exploiting them for the indexing of ethnic or other affiliations. Part II then closes with Chapter Ten, which scrutinizes O'Reilly's (2015: 25) assertions more closely and takes a "Fourth Wave" approach to the sociolinguistics of migration research (Eckert 2008 and Silverstein 2003; §5.2.1 of Chapter Five). It focuses on aspects of the personal narratives of experience captured in CORIECOR as well as in the *Múin Béarla* corpus, so as to articulate and evaluate the processes whereby migrants either assimilate to their host communities or remain staunchly opposed to doing so. Chapter Ten also explores allochthonous groups' capacities and desires to "cross" in the sense of Rampton (2005) between their heritage ethnolinguistic identities and those they have assumed upon settling in their host countries, i.e. their pluridialectal or plurilingal "social lives in language" (Meyerhoff and Nagy 2008 and also see Sankoff 1980b).

Part II: **Migration, acquisition and change**

5 Processes of language contact, shift and acquisition

5.1 Language contact and shift

Prolonged inter-cultural contact between speakers of different languages, through migratory processes or in colonizing contexts when it occurs in the absence of *lingua francae*, inevitably results in some degree of bilingualism. Chapters Two and Three, in particular, have demonstrated how the external history of Ulster has led to just such a scenario where English was acquired as a Second Language (L2) on a massive scale by autochthonous groups whose First Language (L1) was one of the historical major dialects of Irish, depending on their geographical location (Ulster, Munster or Connacht). Evidence was also provided for the proposal that there were spatial and temporal differences with respect to the rate of L2 acquisition. Hence, more isolated communities became monoglot English speaking considerably later than those situated closer to commercial hubs where, as early as the 1700s, becoming bilingual was necessary for individuals to gain access to the polity and for the speech community as a whole to function as a viable economic and socio-political unit (see Bratt Paulston 1994). Similarly, in immigrant scenarios where the L1 speaker is removed from what Py (1986: 165) refers to as the "lectal chain" i.e. close physical contact with speakers from the sending country, in addition to their separation from the linguistic norms of their home communities, they can readily become bilinguals. In addition, if they do not sustain personal networks of communication with speakers of their heritage language either in the sending or receiving countries, they can prove vulnerable to monolingualism in the most extreme cases and to various degrees of what is termed "first language attrition" in others as the L2 increasingly dominates their daily lives (see §5.1.2 for further discussion of this process).

5.1.1 Bilingualism and multilingualism *versus* polylingualism, translanguaging and metrolingualism

Various types and degree of bilingualism are recognized within the literature (Auer and Wei 2007; Baker 2006; Bhatia and Ritchie 2008; Blackledge and Creese 2017; Dorian 1981; García 2009; Grosjean 1982; Pennycook and Otsuji 2015; Romaine 1989, 1995; Spolsky 1988; Wei 2018; Weinreich 1953 *inter alia*). They include "incipient" bilingualism, which refers to the type of language emerging shortly after the first sustained contacts with L2 speakers begin. This category is recognizable in the Medieval Ulster contexts detailed in Chapter Two in which the acquisition of English and Scots dialects by elites of the Gaelic population starts to be viewed as an advantage. "Coordinate" bilingualism is that in which the learning contexts are clearly separate and the languages are independent, and thus tallies with the linguistic practices of the monasteries with respect to Irish and Latin in the Old Irish period, also outlined in Chapter Two. The two languages of the "compound" bilingual, on the other hand, are interdependent, and this would apply to the youngest speakers in the *Múin Béarla* sample who were born in Northern Ireland and so have grown up being exposed to Northern Irish English as well as a community or heritage language (see Chapter Six for details). Such individuals can be viewed as "double monolinguals" since their languages are acquired in the same environment. "Sub-coordinate" bilingualism describes speakers for whom their competence in one of the languages is clearly more dominant than their linguistic skills in the other. As noted in §4.2.1.1 of the previous Chapter, this category is an excellent descriptor for the low English proficiency levels of some allochthonous parents of the youngsters in the *Múin Béarla* database, for whom they are occasioned to act as language brokers. The term "semi-lingual" bilingualism could also be described as incipient monolingualism, in that it refers to the abilities of those individuals for whom the weaker native language has shifted to such a degree that they retain only partial or limited competence in it and have, in fact, instigated the first language attrition process already introduced. As the interview extracts in (40)–(42) (also in §5.1.2 below) demonstrate, there are some participants in the *Múin Béarla* project whose L1 competence is moving in this direction.

Once skills in the L1 have diminished to this extent, then it is possible for speakers to become one of the four different types of bilingual recognised within endangered language studies (including the "terminal" type, as noted in §4.1.1). The latter category aptly describes the vast majority of Northern Ireland's population in the nineteenth century, notwithstanding their descent historically from ethnically Irish or Old English lineage (Chapter Two, §2.2.2), on account of the wide range of economic, political and socio-psychological forces between the Middle Ages and the Twentieth Century that favoured the acquisition of English.

As early as 1976, however, Fishman argued that the measures (usually the speed of response and automaticity in translation tasks) which had been used in previous research to test the type of bilingualism acquired by speakers (balanced/X-dominant/Y-dominant) were being replaced by less normative definitions which were "socio-functionally contextualized" (1976: 62). In the same vein, Clyne (1997: 302) suggested that "the choice of language among multilinguals is determined according to social variables." Hence, in bilingual communities there is often a socially pertinent nexus between language and interlocutor. In this regard, Gal (1979) reports that speakers were addressed in Hungarian or German in her study of language shift in Oberwart, Austria depending on their age and the social role relationships of the interactants. Similarly, stable bilingual communities in which diglossia obtains (like the monastic settings of Medieval Ulster described in Chapter Two), reserve one language for private functions (topics and venues) and the other for public affairs. Consequently, proficiency in language X or Y will depend on the degree to which it is embedded in particular social situations, so it is difficult to conceive of any bilingual having strictly equal competence in both of their languages. Moreover, should the right social conditions for language shift prevail, as previous Chapters have demonstrated, we might conceive of the process as encroachment of the socially dominant language into the domains of the language which has lower status. Invariably, in language shift situations, the bilingual phase is essentially a transitional one as L1 speakers become increasingly competent in L2 to the point that the mother tongue's functionality decreases in inverse proportion to that of the second language. During this process, and upon reaching the semi-lingual/monolingual state, the non-pathological attrition of the first and acquisition of the second language induces a variety of well-documented internal linguistic effects, which can be related to the manner in which the new language has been acquired (in naturalistic (Hellerman and Vergun 2007; Sankoff et al. 1997) or in formal classroom settings (Cook 2009; Doughty and Long 2006; Kasper and Kellerman 1997) for instance) as well as a range of other factors (§5.1.2). With respect to long-term migrants such as those who are the focus of this study, the path to acquisition incorporates factors such as age of arrival, the length of time between migrating and settling in the host country as well as the number of L1 ties they have contracted within their personal networks of communication (de Bot, Gommans and Rossing 1991; Ehrensberger-Dow and Ricketts 2010; Flege 2009; Flege, Yeni-Komshian and Liu 1999; Milroy 1980; Saito and Brajot 2013; Sharma 2014; Skaaden 2005). Other less obvious impacts have also been proposed on the basis of evidence such as that of Schmid (2002) who explored the L1 competence in German of Jewish World War Two refugees such as those discussed in the previous Chapter who likewise settled in Anglophone L2 contexts, though in this case it was either in England or the United States of America. Her findings indicated that attrition with respect to their morphosyntactic competence in their L1 actually correlated most conclusively with the extent to which they had been persecuted prior to arrival. As such, attrition is clearly a multifactorial process.

I have already argued in §1.1 of Chapter One that the novel nature of migration at the present time in terms of its scale and the demolinguistics of the diverse mobile populations participating has generated language contact opportunities that were much rarer historically (Wihtol de Wenden 2016). One reason for the divergent language practices which result is the arrival of and ready access to new media technology and computer-mediated systems of communication, stemming from the creation of the Unicode standard in 1991 which then permitted alphabets such as Arabic, Chinese, Cyrillic and Thai to be utilised that were unavailable prior to the 1990s, because the original SMS systems were developed only with European languages in mind (Androutsopoulos 2006a: 428; Gillam 2003: 48). As a result, even refugees nowadays are in a position to stay connected with the kinds of friendship and kinship networks that support mother tongue maintenance and indeed such practices can lead to the establishment of so-called "virtual ghettos" (Bates and Komito 2012: 107) isolating the migrant from the host community and their linguistic and cultural norms to a large extent (Androutsopoulos 2006b; Hepp, Bozdag and Suna 2012; Collin, Karsenti and Calonne 2015; Komito and Bates 2009, 2011; Komito 2011; Latonero, Poole and Berens 2018; Maurais 2003; UNHCR 2016; Wright 2004; Yang 2003). In addition, social and broadcast media from the homeland is regularly accessed by what have been termed "mediatized migrants" (Androutsopoulos 2006b; Hepp, Bozdag and Suna 2012) which would include those participating in the *Múin Béarla* project as the interview extracts in (34)–(36) confirm (Appadurai 1996; Fortunati, Pertierra and Vincent 2012). There is also good evidence globally for diasporic initiatives run from the host country that revolve around developing websites in the heritage language in order to foster multilingualism or revitalisation efforts (Androutsopoulos 2006b; Debski 2012; Ivković and Lotherington 2009; Jones 2014; Ouakrime 2001; Warschauer 2002).

(34) Extract from an interview with 'Polly Wiczorek', Armagh, 2013

1	KPC:		And eh you have Polish radio, Polish TV?
2	Polly Wiczorek:		Yeah, yeah.
3	KPC:		Polish internet I suppose?
4	Polly Wiczorek:		No it's no it's just normal internet it's just websites you go.
5	KPC:		Normal internet.
6	KPC:		But would you tend to go on Polish websites?
7	KPC:		Or English ones?
8	Polly Wiczorek:		No. Yeah like watch soaps and all yeah.
9	KPC:		Yeah would you?
10	Polly Wiczorek:		Yeah.
11	KPC:		So you can keep up with things yeah.
12	Polly Wiczorek:		Yeah, I listen to Polish radio yeah. Yeah, I actually listen to both.

| | 13 | KPC: | Yeah. |
| | 14 | Polly Wiczorek: | In like Cool FM and Polish Radio everything mixed. |

[PW (F); St. Celine's, Armagh, Northern Ireland; 05 Aug. 2013]

(35) Extract from an interview with 'Erelis Norkus', Armagh, 2013

	1	KPC:	And what about the radio? Do you listen to the, to Lithuanian radio?
	2	Erelis Norkus:	I do ... Well it's when I'm at, like at home and I just put, you know the internet is on so I just put on, you know, also the you know internet [*Laughter*]. You can listen to everything, I do listen because it's also, I used it more, so.
	3	KPC:	Mm-mm.
	4	KPC:	And what about your friends, do they also watch Lithuanian TV programmes and listen to Lithuanian radio?
	5	Erelis Norkus:	Most of them.

[EN (F); St. Celine's; Armagh, Northern Ireland; 18 Dec. 2013]

(36) Extract from an interview with 'Bolek Folta' and 'Makary Mruk', Armagh, 2014

	1	KPC:	Uh-huh and when you watch TV, do you ever watch Polish television?
	2	Bolek Folta:	I have Polish television.
	3	Makary Mruk:	Yeah, we have Polish TV.
	4	KPC:	And would you prefer to watch Polish television or English television.
	5	Bolek Folta:	I think it's Polish because it's better to understand English.
	6	Makary Mruk:	Polish because it's
	7	KPC:	Yeah?
	8	Makary Mruk:	Yeah.
	9	Bolek Folta:	'Cause I don't know few words in English ...
	10	KPC:	And eh do your mum and dad always watch Polish TV or do they watch English TV?
	11	Bolek Folta:	Polish TV.
	12	Makary Mruk:	Yeah, my mum and dad only Polish TV.

[MM (M); BF (M); St. Benedict's; Armagh, Northern Ireland; 30 Jan. 2014]

New technology has also been implicated as crucial in promoting better outcomes for the learning of second or other languages since it has expanded the range of tools available (Chapelle 2003; Comas-Quinn and Mardomingo 2009; Golonka et al. 2014; Kessler and Bikowski 2010; Lan, Sung and Chang 2007; Laufer and Levitsky-Aviad 2006; Salaberry 2001; Seedhouse 2017; Taylor 2009). Hand-held devices and other computer-mediated communication systems have been harnessed, for instance, in the context of even highly mobile populations such as refugees in order to provide novel opportunities to improve their linguistic and literacy skills which had not been possible historically, as documented in research by UNESCO (2018). These technological innovations, coupled with politically motivated language policies imposed, for instance, on Russified regions where several of the youngsters in the *Múin Béarla* project emigrated from, such as Latvia, Lithuania and Poland, result in high levels of multilinguality amongst these ethnolinguistic groups even prior to entering the UK as A8 or A12 migrants (Grenoble 2003; Kamusella 2009). In addition, stepwise migration patterns of the type described in Chapter One, §1.4, which is a process that many migrant families in this study engaged in, as already mentioned, likewise engender knowledge of "Lingua Franca English" (in Canagarajah's 2007: 291 terms) and other languages as well as their associated cultures. In the context of these and further factors articulated in Chapter Four, therefore, it is not unreasonable to contend that the linguistic practices of certain newcomers to Northern Ireland will conform to notions invoked earlier such as "metrolingualism" (Pennycook and Otsuji 2015), "plurilingualism" (García 2009) and "translanguaging" (Blackledge and Creese 2017, 2019; Wei 2018). In essence, these terms capture patterns of linguistic behaviour that go even further than Fishman's (1976) sociofunctional approach to understanding bilingualism or indeed multilingualism (what Wei 2018: 26 defines as "Post-Multilingualism practices of the Twenty-First century"). Pennycook and Otsuji (2015: 251) assert the:

> need to escape the predefinition of a language user by geographical location, ethnicity or other ascribed identities, and to move instead towards an understanding of local language practices.

The intention is to view plurilingualism as a resource which speakers can draw on in diverse ways during daily social interactions to conduct creative and novel conversations in which languages, styles, registers and variants are used dynamically to convey a multiplexity of meanings and mutable personae specially selected for that occasion (Blackledge and Creese 2017, 2019). In this regard, the orientation is not dissimilar to ideas invoked in Third Wave approaches to language variation and change (Eckert 2016) as well as acquisition, including the notions of "crossing" associated with the adolescent language experimentation studies of

Rampton (1995, 2001, 2006) in addition to Piller's examination of "passing" in her 2002 publication on identity and L2 acquisition (see also Bucholtz 1995, 1999; Bucholtz and Hall 2004, 2005; Cutler 1999; Gnevsheva 2015; Lo 1999; Rampton 2013, 2016, 2018). As García (2009: 140) remarks:

> translanguaging is the act performed by bilinguals of accessing different linguistic features or various modes of what are described as autonomous languages, in order to maximize communicative potential.

In an interview with the English as an Additional Language Coordinator at St. Celine's, she confirmed that both inside and outside the classroom she has witnessed these practices on a regular basis amongst the young women of migrant backgrounds at the school, many of whom participated in the *Múin Béarla* project.[71] In the same vein, Wei (2018: 13) reports on the conversation below between Chinese Singaporeans who translanguage between no fewer than seven languages or varieties in this short exchange (English and Singlish (in plain font and italics, respectively); Hokkien in bold; Teochew in angled brackets < >; Mandarin which is underlined as well as Malay indicated by double quotation marks, while Cantonese is in single).

Seetoh: *Aiyoh* (discourse particle), we are all <ka ki nang> (自己人 = own people, meaning 'friends', **bian khe khi** (免客气 = don't mention it). <u>Ren lai jiu hao</u> (人来就好 = good of you to come), why bring so many 'barang barang' ('things'). **Paiseh** (歹劳 = I'm embarrassed). 'Nei chan hai yau sum' (你真有心 = you are so considerate).

Jamie: *Don't say until like that.* Now, you make me malu ('shame') only. You look after my daughter for so many years, **mei you going lao ye you ku lao** (没有功劳也有苦劳 = you have done hard work even if you don't want a prize). I feel so bad that I could not come earlier. 'Mm hou yi si' (不好意思 = I'm embarrassed). I was so shocked to hear about Seetoh, **tsou lang ham ham** (做人 ham ham – meaning life is unpredictable), <u>jie ai shun bian.</u> (节哀顺变 = hope you will restrain your grief and go along with the changes).

Seetoh: <u>ta lin zou de shi hou hai zai gua nian</u> (他临走的时候还在挂念 = he was thinking of Natalie before he passed away) Natalie (Jamie's daughter). Of all your children, he 'saying' ('love') her the most.

---

71 A similar scenario is sketched in the post to the EAL journal captured here: https://ealjournal.org/2016/07/26/what-is-translanguaging/ (last accessed 24 June 2019).

5.1.2 First language attrition

Theoretical interpretations of L1 attrition from a linguistic rather than a social orientation include that of Flynn (1989); Håkansson (1995); Montrul (2009); Sharwood Smith and van Buren (1991) as well as Seliger and Vago (1991), all of which are grounded in versions of Chomsky's Universal Grammar (UG) and Parameter Setting framework.[72] The path to attrition in the Seliger and Vago (1991: 5) scheme is modelled in Table 5 below:

Table 5 Stages in the language attrition process

STAGE 1 Compound I Bilingualism	STAGE 2 Coordinate Bilingualism	STAGE 3 Compound II Bilingualism
L1 → L2	L1 → L2	L2 → L1
UG → L2	L2 → L2	L2 → L2
	UG → L2	L1 → L2
		UG → L2?
		UG → L1

At the stage of "Compound I" bilingualism, the language user is beginning to acquire the socially dominant language or the language of their new L2 immigrant environment and relies upon both their knowledge of L1 and innate UG principles in constructing for themselves the grammar of L2 which is marked by transfer errors and the like (see §§ 5.1.3 and 5.2). At the "Coordinate" stage, the grammars of L1 and L2 gradually separate and the bilingualism is of the type that the speaker has a full social and linguistic competence in both, as the learner builds up a set of L2 rules that do not depend exclusively on those of the first language (although there is still evidence of a role for L1 transfer and UG principles). In the third and final phase ("Compound II") which is most clearly associated with the semi-speaker of Dorian (1977, 1981), increasing fluency in L2 begins to affect the domains of L1, and the direction of transfer is reversed. As far as UG is concerned, Seliger and Vago (1991) point out that at this stage, it is not clear

---

[72] There are, in fact, four main theoretical models that have been developed in the literature since the topic became focal in the 1980s though they are not mutually exclusive such that certain phenomena can be explained using one or all of the frameworks. Thus, for present purposes, the Chomskyan paradigm adopted here will suffice. Schmid and de Bot (2008) present an overview and critiques of the main types.

whether UG continues to impact upon L2 and may indeed impact on L1 as their diagram suggests.[73]

Clearly, the appearance of L2 elements in L1 at Stage One is not necessarily indicative of attrition, since the phenomenon could equally represent stable bilingualism in which code-switching is practised. The latter refers to stretches of discourse in which two languages are used simultaneously both inter- and intra-sententially. There appear to be language-specific and universal constraints which govern code-switching at the structural level and it is normally socially controlled (expressing, for instance, power or solidarity) (Green and Wei 2016; Jake and Myers-Scotton 2017; Muysken 2000; Myers-Scotton 1997, 2009; Wei 2013). In stable bilingual settings, both language grammars retain relative autonomy, and speakers are able to control their switching from language to language as appropriate in a predictable manner, as in the examples below from (37) Swahili English (Myers-Scotton (1997: 221) and (38) Irish English (Stenson 1990: 169) bilingual contexts [74]:

(37) *hata siku hizi   ni-me-*DECIDE   *kwanza ku-tumia   sabuni y-a mi-ti*
     even days these 1S-PERFECT- decide first   INFIN-use soap   of sticks
     'Even nowadays, I first decide to use stick soap'

(38) Speaker A   *An bhfuil Eoghan imithe a   chodhladh?*
                 Q   BE   Eoghan gone PRT sleep-VN
                 'Has Eoghan gone to sleep?'

     Speaker B   Doubtful.   *Sa m*bathroom, I'd say
                              in-the
                 'Doubtful. I'd say in the bathroom'

However, Compound I bilingualism leading to attrition may be inferred where speakers fail to have a full command of the structural and social correlates normally associated with code-switching in their bilingual community (Myers-

---

[73] A concrete example of a similar process in a contact setting is offered in de Haan (2017) whose study of middle field orders in corpora representing the writing of L1 Dutch speakers with extremely high levels of bilingual competence in English as an L2 has occasioned their use of English word orders in their Dutch writing practices. The suggestion is that while Dutch is clearly not attriting amongst this group in the normal sense, the study does provide evidence that Dutch middle phenomena may be becoming more inflexible over time, which is not unlike certain erosion procedures identified in first language attrition contexts.

[74] A more nuanced analysis from a plurilingual, twenty-first century perspective is offered by Wei (2018).

Scotton 1997: 225). This is especially so with respect to production skills in the L1 while the loss of perceptual competence arguably takes longer (Skaaden 2005: 438). There is also some evidence that bilinguals are themselves unconscious of innovations such as these from which attrition can be inferred. Thus, Seliger (1989: 176) in a study of an English-Hebrew setting concludes that:

> the bilingual may lose a sense of what is grammatical for one or both of the languages and not be able to control the mixing of the two. That is, the bilingual may not be aware of the transfer and mixing of elements from one language to another and the creation of new forms in the "host" language.

There is also a concomitant reduction in the number of L1 registers available eventually leading to what Dressler (1988) and Dressler and Wodak-Leodolter (1977) term "monostylism". In effect, this process leads to the ability to control a repertoire of styles becoming so reduced that only one style remains. This is normally the most informal or "casual" type in a Labovian (2001: 97–98) sense, as in the East Sutherland Gaelic scenario articulated in Dorian (1981, 1989) as well as the Breton case which Dressler and Wodak-Leodolter (1977) consider. Occasionally, however, it is formal styles which remain as in the "Latinate pattern" (Campbell and Muntzel 1989: 185) associated with the survival of Latin in Roman Catholic liturgical services prior to Vatican II or to Hebrew, for example, before its revival period.[75]

As speakers move through the three stages of the Seliger and Vago (1991) model, the structural changes to the grammar of L1 reported in the literature are generally simplificatory in nature (rule generalizations, calqueing, meaning extensions and so on) (Schmid and de Bot 2008).

As far as lexis is concerned, when the language contact is sustained and widespread bilingualism has occurred, as in the scenario for Ulster outlined in previous Chapters, the indiscriminate attrition of the native lexicon induces a process that Hill and Hill (1977) first described in this context as "relexification" (i.e. the L1 vocabulary is replaced by that of L2). Craig (1997: 262–263); Campbell and Muntzel (1989) and Dorian (1981) *inter alia* report that research into attrition at the phonological level suggests the following attendant features: (i) fewer phonological distinctions are available; (ii) simplification does not occur when L1 and L2 converge, so that these phonological distinctions are preserved; (iii) distinctions with a low functional load are lost. Campbell and Muntzel (1989: 187)

---

[75] While the suggestion that L1 attrition induces monostylism does indeed appear to be a well-supported generalisation, the practice can also be individuated as Sánchez-Muñoz (2007) argues in the context of Spanish as a heritage language amongst bilingual Spanish-English communities in the United States.

note that speakers of Chiltiupan Pipil, which is obsolescing to Spanish, have lost contrastive vowel length by merging the long and short series because the contrast is marked in L1 and unavailable in the dominant language. Most investigations of community language shift have focused on the type of paradigmatic levelling caused by allomorphic reductions (see Vago 1991). Hence, Schmidt (1985), in an account of attritioning Dyirbal, reports that it has replaced its rather complex noun classification system with a simple natural gender system based on animacy and sex. Similarly, Schmid (2002: 319) in her study of Jewish refugees noted earlier argues that deviance with respect to verb phrase morphology especially is impacted upon by a protracted "period of non-use". In another non-migrant context, the inflectional system of East Sutherland Gaelic observed over many years by Nancy Dorian has also been levelled to a considerable degree by L1 attrition. Dorian (1977), for example, states that although speakers of the southern Sutherland dialect, who could be described as semi-lingual, had conserved the morphological distinctions associated with the perfect, they were hesitant about the suffixes of both the future tense and conditional mood. L1 attrition at the syntactic level normally involves reductions in the frequency of usage of particular patterns rather than the loss of the constructions themselves. Craig (1997: 264) reports that the most common syntactic change recorded in the literature is the loss of "morphological tense/aspect or voice forms (such as future or passive) in favor of periphrastic ones, which become overused". In this regard, Campbell and Muntzel (1989: 192–193) note that current Pipil speakers consistently replace the future suffixes recorded in early texts with such periphrastics. Moreover, Maher (1991: 74) in a cross-linguistic account of language contact and attrition states that: "this factoring process or decomposition of complex structures ... is the most striking feature" of the obsolescing languages found in the immigrant enclave communities which are the focus of her investigation. Complex constructions, in general (particularly those associated with subordination), tend to become disfavoured in these settings being replaced by coordinate expressions and simple juxtaposition. The same syntactic changes have been argued for with respect to L1 attrition in the indigenous enclave communities investigated by Hill (1973) and Schmidt (1985). The language contact situations to which they refer are themselves quite distinctive (English and aboriginal languages in southern California (Hill 1973) and Australia (Schmidt 1985)) Nevertheless, both researchers observe that users of the obsolescing languages exhibit comparatively low frequencies of subordinating strategies, often relying solely on contextual cues to convey the matrix-embedded relationship so that there appear to be universal processes controlling L1 attrition at least to some extent.

As is generally true for bilinguals (even those who are at the incipient stage) the participants in the *Múin Béarla* project possess high degrees of metalinguistic awareness that allow them to precisely identify what aspects of their heritage languages are attriting (Ben-Zeev 1977; Bialystok 1993; Bialystok, Peets and Moreno 2014; Cummins 1978; Galambos and Goldin-Meadow 1990; Yelland, Pollard and Mercuri 1993). The extracts in (39)–(41) confirm that the process is indeed underway for some speakers. Two young siblings (Gracja and Zosia Wolak) whose L1 was Polish, discuss their difficulties with lexical retrieval along with their mother's computer-mediated communication strategy for helping to overcome the deficit in (39), which has been identified as a common technique for supporting lexical retrieval amongst migrant populations by Demmans Epp (2017). During the interview from which (40) is derived, Eva Kava, who declares that they speak Lithuanian at home, nevertheless remarks on how her older sister has to assist her too on occasion to finish her sentences and make herself understood. The attrition in this case also appears to relate to vocabulary items but there are other aspects of her competence that likewise seem impaired such that Eva is forced to code-switch between English and Lithuanian, though in her case by necessity rather than by choice. The very fact that Eva is aware that her practice is deliberate also lends support to the view that her heritage language competence is attriting since it is generally accepted within the literature that skilled bilinguals are characterized by their "seeming unawareness of the alternation between languages" (Poplack 1980: 601). Example (41) draws on a conversation in which Emília Michalíková, a young Slovakian participant, has noticed how her system of inflectional morphology with respect to the verbal paradigm does not match that of her parents, who attempt to correct her Slovak (though one suspects that this may well have little impact on how "wobbly" her L1 might become longer term (Ammerlaan 1996)).

(39)   Extract from an interview with 'Gracja' and 'Zosia Wolak', Donaghmore, 2014

1	KPC:		So, do you find ever that when you're talking Polish that you sometimes forget the Polish word?
2	Gracja Wolak:		Yeah, I don't really know how to say a lot of words.
3	Zosia Wolak:		Yeah.
4	KPC:		Do you not?
5	Gracja Wolak:		Yeah.
6	KPC:		And what about you, do you also forget some Polish words?
7	Zosia Wolak:		Yeah, sometimes I forget them, and then I ask my mummy, and then she doesn't understand. So, she writes it in a thing.
8	KPC:		In Polish?
9	Zosia Wolak:		Internet. Yeah.

	10	KPC:	Oh, I know what you mean. So, she tries on the internet, and she uses the internet to try and translate for you?
	11	Zosia Wolak:	Yes. Yeah.

[GW (F); ZW (F); St. Peter's; Donaghmore, Northern Ireland; 29 April 2014]

(40) Extract from an interview with 'Eva Kava', Armagh, 2014

	1	Eva Kava:	'Cause like I'm starting to forget the whole language and it's really hard so it is.
	2	KPC:	Mm-mm.
	3	Eva Kava:	So, my sister just fills out fills it out.
	4	KPC:	Uh-huh so does that mean then that you don't speak Lithuanian at home?
	5	Eva Kava:	Oh, I do speak Lithuanian at home but it I get like confused in some of the words.
	6	KPC:	Mm.
	7	Eva Kava:	Because and like I speak mainly English.
	8	KPC:	Okay.
	9	Eva Kava:	And I only speak Lithuanian at home so.
	10	KPC:	Uh-huh.
	11	Eva Kava:	Like I forget most of the words or I have to like say the words in English for them to like understand.

[EK (F); St. Celine's; Armagh, Northern Ireland; 23 Jan. 2014]

(41) Extract from an interview with 'Emília Michalíková', Armagh, 2014

	1	Emília Michalíková:	But even if I speak, I sometimes say words differently.
	2	KPC:	So tell me about that. So what do you do?
	3	Emília Michalíková:	Sometimes ehm for a [*school bell rings*]. I have to go.
	4	KPC:	Bell, I hate that bell, it's horrible, it's really intrusive. I know you do, sweetheart. So, tell me about your verbs first and then go.
	5	Emília Michalíková:	Ehm like there's a there's a word but it has like different endings.
	6	KPC:	Mm-mm.
	7	Emília Michalíková:	But sometimes I use a different ending than I should have. And my parents are like, "No that's not how you say it. Say it differently."

8	KPC:	So are they kind of correcting you as you go along?
9	Emília Michalíková:	Yeah.

[EM (F); HS (F); St. Celine's; Armagh, Northern Ireland; 21 Jan. 2014]

Such contemporaneous evidence when combined with the scholarly literature lends considerable support to the likelihood that similar phenomena were also concomitant with what Chapter Three identified as the key period for language shift in Ireland. Excellent evidence in this regard stems from Stenson's (1982) contribution examining the decline of genitive case marking and changes in the verbal paradigm of Irish dialect speakers between 1832, when the vast majority of the population were still Irish-speaking, and 1945, when English dominated practically everywhere.

As Schmid, de Bot and Köpke (2013) observe, L1 attrition is not a straightforward process and it is multifaceted with respect to causality. Moreover, its development is non-linear both at the level of the individual (Schmid 2013: 120) and also with regard to cases like historical Ulster where whole communities collectively engage in the process as they shift to an L2 (though some enclave groups proceed along the path to attrition at a slower rate) (Corrigan 1996; Filppula 1999; Stenson 1982). The next section will focus not on the attrition of the L1 but on its impact upon the acquisition of the L2 during the transitional bilingualism phase that can also generate profound and enduring change at different levels of the grammar.

5.1.3 Language contact effects on the second language

As regards such innovations to English as a second language in Ulster, brought about during the bilingualism phases of the eighteenth to twentieth centuries described in Chapters Three and Four, the Seliger and Vago (1991) scheme follows most research in this field by recognising the effects which the lexical, phonological, morphosyntactic and discourse-pragmatic systems of the native language have on the recently acquired socially dominant language (i.e. L1→L2 in Table 5, §5.1.2). As Romaine (1989) argues, the influence of the native language in this regard has been variously described as "interference" (after Weinreich 1953: 1) and the more neutral "transference" (originally Clyne 1967) and "crosslinguistic influence" (Sharwood Smith and Kellerman 1986). Weinreich's (1953) definition of "interference" encompasses all distinctions existing between the L1-dominant bilingual and monolingual versions of Language X that cannot be attributed to either borrowing or simple transfer. The use of "transference" by Clyne (1967) was an adaptation of a term used in psychology and psychiatry to refer to the extension of previous knowledge to novel contexts. Both it and "cross-linguistic influence" are defined rather more broadly as the adoption of any L1 characteristic in the target language (or as Sharwood Smith (1989: 185) puts it: "the influence on the learner which one language system which he or she possesses may have on another language system"). Indeed, unlike Clyne's interpretation of "transfer", cross-linguistic influence is even less narrow in that it additionally refers to borrowing transfers and influence in both directions between L1 and the target. More recently, research in the fields of language contact and L2 acquisition tend to differentiate between "interference" and "transfer" (the terms "reallocation" "reassignment" or "reanalysis" are also used). The former is conceived of as an effect on the speaker's L2 that is beyond their control whereas they can exercise some command over the latter and it involves active reinterpretation of a feature from the L1 often for some social purpose such as marking an ethnolinguistic distinction (Benor 2010, 2012; Dubois and Horvath 1998; Newlin-Łuckowicz 2013; Sankoff 2001; Thomason 2003). Moreover, as Thomason and Kaufmann (1988), Newlin-Łuckowicz (2014), Tóth (2007) as well as van Coetsem (1988) and others propose, in cases of language shift at the individual or community level such as those considered here, interference affects the first generation of new speakers to the greatest degree but becomes diluted over time. Innovations that are a result of transfers, by contrast, are retained by subsequent generations of bilinguals and are thought to be governed to some degree by the "markedness" of the feature in question, i.e. How easy is the feature to learn? or How commonly does it occur cross-linguistically? The more cognitively challenging that the feature change involving transfer is and the rarity of that characteristic as a type across the world's languages, the less likely it is thought to be that the feature would become a candidate for reallocation in a language, dialect or ethnolect shift scenario (Britain 2002, 2004; Britain and Trudgill 2005; Sharma and Sankaran 2011; Thomason 2001, 2003, 2010; Trudgill 1974, 2006; Wolfram 2013). Hence, one might argue that the presence in diverse dialects of Irish English of a form of TH-stopping in contexts where dental fricatives would be expected is due to markedness. In other words, the transfer from Irish (which has no dental fricatives within its phonemic inventory) occurred and has persisted as a shibboleth to the present day because /θ/, /ð/ present greater complexities for acquisition than the source language's /t/, /d/ do, coupled with the relative rarity of these sounds cross-linguistically (Corrigan 2010: 41; Kallen 2013: 50–52).[76]

---

[76] Dubois and Horvath (1998, 2000) come to a similar conclusion with respect to their investigations of TH-stopping phenomena in Cajun English, which originates from contact with French. Also see Lombardi (2003) which examines a wide range of L2 interference phenomena with respect to English interdentals and the constraints on its operation. Flege (1995) and Major (2008)

Clyne (1997: 311) argued that the effects of transfer also occur "above and beyond phonology" (Sankoff 1980a) and indeed that they are "are manifested at all levels of language" (see also Odlin 1989). It is for this reason that Chapters Seven to Nine will be dedicated to analyses of their effects on the phonology, grammar and discourse-pragmatics of new speakers of Irish English drawn from interviews in the *Múin Béarla* corpus. Two distinct types of transfer or cross-linguistic influence are recognized: namely, positive and negative, though it is the latter which has received most attention in the language contact literature. Positive transfer describes those occasions when forms in L1 and L2 coincide so that native speaker competence facilitates second language learning. Where the two languages diverge, then previous knowledge of the L1 interferes with the acquisition process and negative transfer occurs. In settings where the transitional phase is prolonged as it must have been in Ireland, L1 interference according to Romaine (1989) causes imperfect learning on a community-wide scale so that:

> during language shift the target language has innovations forced upon it by the shifting speakers ... these features persist in the speech of monolinguals long after a period of active bilingualism has disappeared from the community. This happens especially where there is a homogeneous subgroup living in relative geographic isolation.

Weinreich (1953: 14–28) provides a detailed treatment of the principal effects of these types of L1 transfer on the phonological systems of the target language, namely, substitution, re-interpretation, under-differentiation and over-differentiation.[77] The first of these is documented in Baetens-Beardsmore (1982: 72) for Dutch-English bilinguals who substitute English [g] for Dutch [ɣ], which shares the place of articulation with the English phoneme but neither its manner of articulation nor its voice quality. Reinterpretation applies to the application of L1 phonological distinctions that are irrelevant in L2 which Romaine (1989) exemplifies by Italian-English renderings of <patty> as [patti]. Over-differentiation occurs when phonological distinctions in L1 are maintained in L2 despite being no longer relevant. Ó Baoill (1991) argues that the palatalization/velarization rule (often associated with medial two consonant clusters in Irish such as [st]/[rs], as

---

present critiques of such transfer studies that focus on phonological change (see also Flege and Eefting 1987; Newlin-Łukowicz 2014).

77 There is evidence too that phonological interference can occur in the opposite direction amongst bilinguals with high levels of competence in both languages. Thus, Nagy and Kochetov (2013) investigated the performance of bilinguals from three diverse heritage backgrounds (Italian, Russian and Ukrainian) in the Anglophone context of Toronto. Their observations led them to conclude that the Voice Onset Time (VOT) for applying voicing to obstruents in English, which has a longer duration to that of either Russian or Ukrainian, was likewise causing interference of a similar type in the heritage language.

noted in Ní Chiosáin 1999 *inter alia*) was applied to the L2 English of transitional bilinguals during the period of language shift in Ireland documented in previous Chapters. The phonotactics of this regular variation in Irish entail that consonants are palatalized or velarized depending on the environment in which they occur and this includes consonant clusters, which are thus rendered identical in velar or palatal quality. Hence, when /s/ occurs in a labial environment, [ʃ] is its realization on account of over-differentiation in the L2. Ó Baoill's (1991) evidence for the transfer in Irish English includes eye dialect spellings such as <shoul> for 'soul' and <counshillor> for 'councillor'. This interference phenomenon can, in fact, be dated back to the earliest forms of Irish English recorded and feature in many of the texts documented in Bliss (1979) which have spellings that include <horsh> replacing 'horse' and <ash> instead of 'as' in *The Pretender's Exercise* from 1727 (p. 160). They also occur prominently in Thomas Shadwell's *The Lancashire Witches* from 1681/1682, which has the lines "Shome things! Phaat dosht dou talk of shome things? By my shoule I vill not see a better Church in a Shommers day" (p. 121).[78] This issue will be returned to in Chapter Seven, § 7.1.2 in connection with the realization by Lithuanian and Polish *Múin Béarla* participants of word final (ING) as [ɪŋk]/[ɪŋg] on account of the influence on their L2 English of transfer from their first languages.

This type of interference has also been identified at the subsegmental level, particularly with respect to differences between L1 and L2 speakers regarding the manner in which VOT is realized, as already noted with respect to the research by Nagy and Kochetov (2013). Newlin-Łukowicz (2014: 360) for instance, finds that in reading tasks, first generation Polish-Americans who grew up in Poland "exhibit a general pattern of VOT interference" which does not comply with the processes associated with native speakers such as those identified in Docherty (1992), Flege and Brown (1982) and Flege and Eefting (1987). Under-differentiation, as one might expect, refers to the opposite process whereby phonological distinctions are not applied in the target language because they do not occur in the L1, which Odlin (1989) exemplifies with reference to the absence of the [r]/[l] distinction in the L2 English of L1 Chinese, Japanese and Korean speakers (see also Brown 1998; Flege 2007; Gut, Fuchs and Wunder 2015).

The key areas of syntax in which positive/negative target language transfers have been argued for have been: (i) negation (Cancino, Rosansky and Schumann 1978; Eubank 1987; Hyltenstam 1977; Gil, Marsden and Whong 2017; Odlin 1989,

---

[78] As Joan Beal p.c. points out in this regard, literary uses of this kind may well have led to Thomas Sheridan's 1780 prescriptive pronouncing dictionary being questioned by his contemporaries on account of spellings such as <na-tshur> and <tart-tshur> for 'nature'/'torture' since he himself was Irish.

§§ 6.2 and 6.3; and Wode 1977, 1980, 1981) and (ii) word order/relativization strategies (Bates and MacWhinney 1989; Biberauer and Roberts 2017; Clahsen 1984; Clahsen and Muysken 1986; de Haan 2017; Eckman 2004; Flynn 1987, 1989; Gass 1979; Ioup and Kruse 1977; Los and de Haan 2017; Mede 2011; Meisel, Clahsen and Pienemann 1981; Odlin 1989; Pienemann 1989; Phoocharoensil and Simargool 2010; Scontras, Fuchs and Polinsky 2015; Singler 1988; Tarallo and Myhill 1983; van Vuuren and de Vries 2017). The research of Wode (1977, 1980, 1981), for example, examines the acquisition of negation by four German-speaking and four English-speaking children in a naturalistic setting and compares their performance with thirty-four L1 German children learning English in a classroom. In Wode (1981: 91) he states that his aim was to "characterize the nature of naturalistic L2 acquisition within an integrated theory of language acquisition" by comparing the negation strategies used by these groups so as to derive a universal sequence of acquisition for L1-/L2-learners and for German and English. His findings suggest that language transfer does not fully account for the development of the five stages of acquisition that were isolated. This is because the evolution of the sequences was the same for both L1 and L2 learners suggesting that they are due to universal negation strategies which "are part of man's basic devices to acquire language" (Wode 1980: 294). These findings are supported by the research of Cancino, Rosansky and Schumann (1978) who examined the acquisition of English by Spanish children and Hyltenstam's (1977) investigation of Swedish negation. Both were able to isolate developmental stages which are roughly equivalent to those of Wode's (1981), despite the typological differences between English, German, Spanish and Swedish. These collated findings suggest that in the early stages of acquisition at least, sequencing is paramount over the negating strategies of both native and target adult languages. That is not to say, of course, that first languages do not influence production, which is the reason given by Wode (1981) for the low frequencies of postverbal negation amongst English L1 learners and the rather higher frequencies of these constructions amongst the German children. There is also some evidence from Eubank (1987) that the context in which L2 learning occurs can have a bearing on the developmental sequences that result.[79] An important typological difference between English and German is the fact that negation with full verbs follows object NPs and certain adverbials (Holmberg 2015). This predilection is a consequence of German's verb-second ordering exemplified in (42), adapted from Betz (2011: 417), which examined a conversational corpus of L1 German speakers who had migrated to Romania and settled there.

---

79 This issue will be touched upon in Chapter Six, §6.2.1 when the learning experiences of the migrant participants and setting of the interviews that generated the *Múin Béarla* corpus are considered further.

(42) **Speaker K** dieses   briecht det Ina Nichen
           this kind needs   the Ina not
           {O}   {V}   {S}
           'This kind Ina does not need'

Two stages of acquisition [Neg+ X] and [Internal Neg] found by Eubank (1987) match those of Cancino, Rosansky and Schumann (1978) and Wode (1981) in naturalistic settings. However, he also uncovered a third which he terms [S+ Neg] since it takes the ungrammatical form: *ihr harr ist schwartz nicht. Eubank argues that the structure is evoked by the classroom setting in which students are often coerced into speaking full sentences of L2 (see also Sankoff et al. 1997).

While the study of L2 negation has uncovered controlling factors that include developmental sequence, transfer and setting, research into the acquisition of word order strategies has additionally suggested that "an important influence of language universals seems to be the effect that discourse has on the arrangement of basic clause constituents" (Odlin 1989: 110). Investigations of word order amongst L2 speakers has focused primarily on directionality and rigidity. The first of these encompasses three subdivisions: namely, canonical word order; intra-clausal word order and branching direction, which distinguishes whether or not recursive devices (subordinate clauses and so on) are pre-posing (to the left of the phrasal head/left-branching) or post-posing (to the right of the phrasal head/right branching). A majority of the world's languages exhibit the three basic word orders viz. SVO, VSO and SOV. It is also thought that there appear to be language-particular preferences for a single canonical order and the rigidity with which this order is enforced (Lambrecht 1987; Newmeyer 2003). Thus, Odlin (1989: 86) remarks that while both English and Russian prefer the SVO order as a basic pattern, the latter is more flexible in its use of the other three as a probable consequence of its morphological properties.[80] It has been argued that both of these properties are transferable during second language learning. Thus, Meisel, Clahsen and Pienemann (1981) in a study of L1 Italian, Spanish and Turkish guest workers in Germany conclude that SVO orders have been transferred into their L2 German in that subordinate clauses which they produced were frequently not SOV. This is particularly significant in that other research by Clahsen (1984), for instance, suggests that the L1 acquisition of German never proceeds through such a stage.

---

80 An obvious parallel here would be the link between inflection and word order variability in earlier stages of English, as argued in Biberauer and Roberts (2017); Corrigan (1997); Fischer, van Kemenade, Koopman and van der Wurff (2001); Hinterhölzl (2017); Hinterhölzl and van Kemenade (2012); Hudson (1997); van Kemenade (2012); Lightfoot (1991); Pintzuk (1993, 1996); Roberts (1985, 1993, 1995); Taylor and Pintzuk (2012) and Warner (1993).

Thus, the adults begin with an SVO order in both main clauses and subordinate clauses and eventually learn to use SOV in the latter. German-speaking children, however, begin with SOV orders for both main and subordinate clauses adapting SVO orders for the former in the final stages of acquisition (see also Clahsen and Muysken 1986). Research into both L2 production and comprehension tasks has demonstrated that the degree of flexibility permitted by native languages is also a transferable syntactic property. Odlin (1989: 87), for example, reports that L2 learners of English (which has a relatively inflexible SVO canonical order, as noted) are prone to make more word order errors if their L1 is flexible (Finnish/French) than if it is not (Swedish). There also appears to be a universal tendency for L2 learners in the early stages of acquisition to prefer topic (information-focus) + comment (information-elaboration) orders in their discourse as an aid to communicative efficacy. In languages like English in which this order normally corresponds to subject-predicate (hence SVO), this strategy is highly appropriate. However, in a language like Irish in which VSO order is the norm and which has a propensity for narrative fronting devices (Duffield 1995; Filppula 1986, 1999; McCloskey 1996; Ó Siadhail 1989), the use of topic+comment structures by learners would, by contrast, be suggestive of non-native competence. In a similar vein, van Vuuren and de Vries (2017) present evidence for L1 (Dutch) transfer with respect to this area of the grammar in their examination of written texts produced by highly proficient Dutch-English bilinguals. They demonstrate that despite their competence in L2 English, word order differences between the two languages (V2/SOV in the case of Dutch and SVO for English, as previously mentioned) still generate L1 interference with respect to the manner in which even highly proficient bilinguals handle information structure in their writing. The evidence for or against syntactic transfer is somewhat more ambivalent with regard to the ordering of elements within clauses as Odlin (1989: 96) reports, though there is confirmation presented in Selinker (1992) that a majority of the errors in the placement of adverbials in the English produced by L1 Hebrew speakers is of this type. Flynn (1987) and (1989) summarize her research on cross-linguistic evidence for transfer of native right-branching or left-branching properties into L2 English. Comparisons of the performance of L1 Spanish and L1 Chinese/Japanese learners of different levels of ability showed that successful production in each case was linked to transfer. Thus, the advanced Spanish learners scored 57 % as a result of positive transfer from the L1 which, like English, favours postpositions, whereas the same level of Japanese learner scored only 24 % because of negative transfer from their L1 which is preposing typologically. Flynn (1989: 128), therefore, concludes that:

> We have basically three sets of learners at the same level of English ability yet two distinct patterns of acquisition emerge ... Where there is a match ... for head-direction between the L1 and the L2, acquisition is facilitated ... [this] demonstrates the role of the L1 experience.

There has also been a considerable amount of L2 research into whether or not the so-called *Case Accessibility Hierarchy* (CAH) proposed in various publications by Keenan (1972, 1975, 1985, 1987) governs the acquisition of relative clauses and their marking strategies, which will be the focus of Chapter Eight. To date, this issue has been examined primarily from the perspective of the acquisition of English as an L2 (Corrigan 2009; Eckman, Bell and Nelson 1988; Eckman 2007; Ioup and Kruse 1977; Gass 1979; Gass and Lee 2007 *inter alia*). There has also been further research extending the model to other L2 contexts such as Xu's (2014) investigation of the manner in which second language learners of Chinese handle the differing complexities of Chinese relative clauses (see also Chen *et al.* 2008; Hawkins 1989 (L2 French); Jeon and Hae-Young 2007 (L2 Korean); and Ozeki and Shirai 2007 (L2 Japanese)). The CAH is thought to predict the degree of difficulty associated with relativising Case positions from subject through to genitive, the latter being more complex than the former. Certain languages, therefore, have evolved rather different strategies for relativising NPs in complex and non-complex positions. The main division is between those languages which mark the more difficult Cases (indirect object and genitive) using a resumptive rather than a relative pronoun and it is this feature which Gass (1979) and Singler (1988) report to be readily transferable in the context of second language acquisition.[81] This hypothesis is tested in Filppula (1999) which analyses four corpora of Irish English from diverse regions in which contact with Irish could be adduced at different periods of time (i.e. the participants who generated the urban Dublin corpus are further removed from a period of community wide Irish-English bilingualism than those in rural, west Clare – where, according to Stack (2015), the last native speaker, the *seanchaí* Paddy Pharaic Mhichil Shannon of Fisherstreet, Doolin, died only in the early 1990s). Employing a resumptive pronoun (RP) relative strategy to mark determiner phrase (DP) positions low on the CAH (such as genitive), is a well-documented process of modern and historical Irish as in (43) (Duffield 1995; Goodluck, Guilfoyle and Harrington 2006; McCloskey 1985, 1990, 2001, 2002, 2017; Neilson 1808/1990; Ó Siadhail 1984, 1989; Scott 2003).

(43) An   bhean   a   bhfuil   a [RP]   páistí   díolta
      the   woman   whose   are   her [RP] children   sold
      'The woman whose children are sold'

---

[81] Eckman (2004) makes an interesting case for the presence of a resumptive pronoun type in the relative clause marking strategies of L2 speakers which is an innovation rather than a transfer effect from any native language that is also worth mentioning in this context.

It has been argued that the prevalence in all dialects of Irish English of RP strategies for relative clause formation, as typified in examples (44)–(47), is thus a case of interference from the L1. Indeed, Filppula (1999: 191) goes so far as to argue that the mechanism "indicates a definite role for the Irish substratum."

(44) <u>This man</u> **he** lived over there where this woman was reared
      (Corrigan 2009: 142, South Armagh English)

(45) <u>This girl</u> that I was actually travelling with **her mother** is in hospital
      (Policansky 1982: 45, Belfast English)

(46) They jumped <u>banks</u> that time on the race course ... that they wouldn't hunt over **them** today
      (Filppula 1999: 185, Wicklow English)

(47) <u>A herb</u> that the **root o' it** was boiled
      (Henry 1957: 210, Roscommon English)

Although the infrequency of examples such as these in his regional corpora led Filppula (1999: 191) to conclude that "the use of resumptive pronouns must be considered a rather rare feature, which is most probably on the wane even in the Western [Irish English] dialects", their incidence in the latter remains nearly four times higher than the rates for dialects in the East at the heart of what would originally have been the Pale, defined in Chapter Two (§ 2.2.1) (Filppula 1999: 191).

Given the arguments just presented, there is the possibility therefore that transfer will also have an impact on the migrant participants' output regarding their acquisition of Northern Irish English relative clause marking strategies just as it does on the inter-learner effects associated with their production of word final (ING), already noted. Polish, for example, has recourse to a resumptive pronoun relativising strategy of a similar type to that discussed by Filppula (1999), as Szczegielniak (2005) argues. This endowment may make the *Múin Béarla* participants of this heritage more inclined to use these structures (also preserved via L1 interference in the modern descendant dialect grammars of the English speakers who provide their input variety). This variant was, however, coded for in the protocol used to conduct the variationist analysis of relative clause marking amongst Armagh teenagers in Chapter Eight, and proved to be similarly rare in the speech of both the allochthonous as well as autochthonous groups. Nevertheless, it is important to remain mindful of the "mysteries of the substrate", as Labov (2008) conceives of linguistic influence in this context, and so it will be considered where possible in the variationist analyses which feature in Chapters Seven to Nine.[82]

Moreover, when the period of loss (i.e. the time taken for a community to shift from Seliger and Vago's (1991) Stage One to Stage Three) extends across several generations as it did in the historical Irish scenario, the resultant transitional bilingualism permits ample opportunity for cross-linguistic influence effects from the L1 to become embedded in the emergent English varieties and to persist amongst monolinguals. Furthermore, the research reviewed thus far suggests that in addition to the presence of positive and negative interference, we would expect the learning of an L2 to be universally constrained (adhering to particular developmental sequences, for instance, as well as limitations associated with the critical period articulated further in the next section), which will also be important to consider when choosing the L2 participants for the variationist analyses which follow. In addition, as far as historical language shift across the island of Ireland is concerned, the process of learning English was naturalistic in that acquisition was *via* immersion rather than schooling (Sankoff *et al.* 1997). This factor may also have an impact on the L2 variety that results and this will be borne in mind in subsequent Chapters exploring transfer and related phenomena in the English of newcomers to Northern Ireland who are learning the language both formally and in their immediate environment (amongst their peer group especially given the emic or "age-related place in society" which they hold (Eckert 1997a: 155)).[83]

5.2 Acquiring linguistic and sociolinguistic competence

5.2.1 The "Fourth Wave" of analytic practice in variationist linguistics

As Howard, Mougeon and Dewaele (2013: 340) have noted, studies examining the acquisition of sociolinguistic competence in a naturalistic environment where one can expect considerable face-to-face exposure have not been as numerous as one might expect since early publications such as Preston (1989).

---

[82] The remit of the current project precludes more than a brief discussion of this important issue here but I intend to return to the topic in future research that will more fully exploit the *Múin Béarla* corpus for this purpose, since this remains an important gap in knowledge within the field of sociolinguistic acquisition, as Corrigan (2016), Davydova (2015), Davydova and Buchstaller (2015) and Labov (2008) all contend.
[83] See Odlin (1994) and also Chapter Four, §4.1, which discusses the ineffectiveness of formal education for the transmission of English historically.

In the last decade or so, however, research in this vein might be conceived of as a "Fourth Wave"[84] of analytic practice within variationist linguistics.[85] This is because its focus is on multilingual rather than monolingual communities yet, as is true of "Third Wave" research on the latter, "Fourth Wave" studies like these also examine variation in terms of its being what Eckert (2012: 87) defines as a "robust social semiotic system, potentially expressing the full range of social concerns" within multilingual communities. Likewise, it takes account of stylistic routines (potentially influenced by the L1) as well as addressing the idea that variation "constructs social change" and is thus not a mere reflection of it (Eckert 2012: 87). The most significant outcomes of "Fourth Wave" variationist analyses within multilingual contexts are outlined in (i)–(xi) below.[86]

(i) Informal and vernacular sociolinguistic variants are underused when compared to native speaker frequencies even by advanced learners (Buysse 2010; Davydova 2015; Davydova and Buchstaller 2015; Mougeon, Rehner and Nadasdi 2004, 2010; Müller 2005; Neary-Sundquist 2014; Regan 1996). Recent research

---

84 As argued in Eckert (2012), the history of variationist research can be divided into three phases (or "Waves" in her terms). The first examined the extent to which social categories like socioeconomic class or sex correlated with a range of linguistic variables. "Second Wave" variationists instead preferred a bottom-up, ethnographic approach that focused on micro-societal, local manifestations of these macro-societal categories. "Third Wave" approaches contend that "patterns of variation do not simply unfold from the speaker's structural position in a system of production, but are part of the active–stylistic production of social differentiation" (Eckert 2012: 98) such that in everyday interactions, a speaker's expression of their linguistic identity is not entirely bound by the broad social categories to which they ostensibly belong. See also Tagliamonte (2016a) who provides a compelling history of variationist sociolinguistics in which scholars in the discipline describe the "virtual revolution" it has undergone in the 50 years since its foundation (Tagliamonte 2016a: viii).
85 Although the following is not a definitive list by any means, typical studies within this paradigm on the acquisition of sociolinguistic competence by non-native speakers of English and other languages across the globe include: Adamson (1989); Adamson and Regan (1991); Aaron and Hernández (2007); Bayley (2004, 2005); Bayley and Regan (2004); Beebe (1980); Blondeau and Nagy (2008); Buysse (2010); Davydova and Buchstaller (2015); Diskin (2017); Diskin and Levey (2019); Drummond (2011); Howard, Lemée and Regan (2006); Howley (2015); Leung and Young-Scholten (2013); Mar-Molinero and Paffey (2018); Meyerhoff and Schleef (2014); Migge (2015); Mougeon, Rehner and Nadasdi (2004); Nestor, Ní Chasaide and Regan (2012); Newlin-Łukowicz (2014); Otheguy, Zentella and Livert (2007); Rampton (2013, 2016, 2018); Regan (1996); Ryan (2018); Sankoff, *et al.* (1997); Schleef (2017); Schleef, Meyerhoff and Clark (2011); Sharma (2014); Tarone (2007); Verma, Corrigan and Firth (1992); Wolf (2012) and Young (1991), *inter alia*.
86 There is not space here to develop a definitive account of the major findings within this field, so I will focus on those that are either most frequently cited in the scholarly literature or are pertinent in some respect to the analyses discussed in subsequent Chapters. Howard, Mougeon and Dewaele (2013) provide a more comprehensive overview.

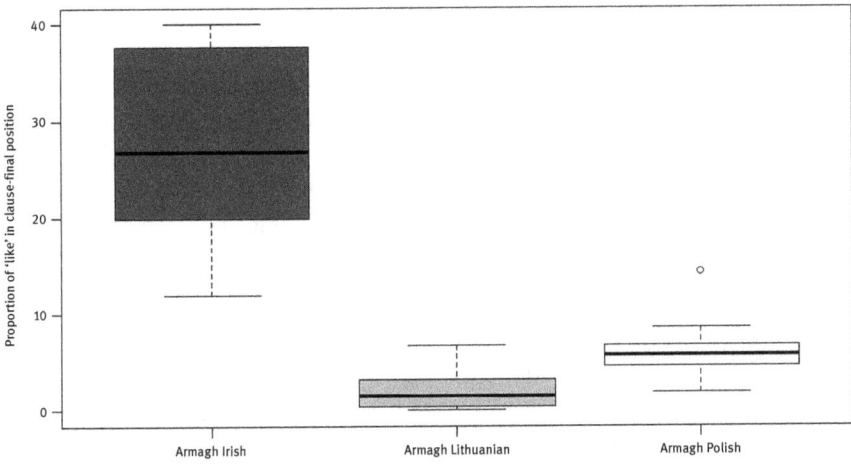

Figure 40 Proportion of clause-final *like* by nationality in Armagh

by Corrigan and Diskin (2020) on preferences for *like* as a discourse pragmatic marker (DPM) amongst diverse ethnolinguistic groups drawn from the Armagh teenage sub-corpus of the *Múin Béarla* project supports this argument in interesting ways. While their findings with respect to overall frequencies amongst native and non-native speakers show that the heritage language groups have actually adopted the overall frequency of *like* usage typical of the community norm (see Figure 40), this is not so with respect to their propensity to use this DPM in clause-final position. Thus, as Figure 40 indicates, those youngsters with Lithuanian and Polish backgrounds are not nearly so inclined to avail of this very typical local Northern Irish English feature as their native speaking peers are (see also Corrigan 2010, 2015). This variant might be considered to be, or to have become, indexical of "Irishness" (D'Arcy 2017: 13; Corrigan and Diskin 2020: 23; Nestor, Ní Chasaide and Regan 2012; Nestor 2013) and, as such, there may well be mileage in the argument put forward by Corrigan and Diskin (2020: 24) that because it belongs to a "local ethnographic category" (Bucholtz and Hall 2005: 587), non-native speakers avoid clause-final *like* on the grounds that its use would somehow be perceived as disingenuous (Bucholtz and Hall 2005: 585). Using the variant may also not comply with how they wish to identify themselves as "global" rather than "local" with futures as long-term step-wise migrants in the Anglophone world, just as Siyara Sinha declares herself to be in extract (5) of Chapter One, § 1.4.

(ii)   In order to become more proficient, L2 learners must progressively master the correct relationship between form and function so as to fully acquire the probabilistic constraints governing the use of informal and vernacular variants by native speakers. This is a really complex task which, as the research detailed in §5.1.3 demonstrates, is made rather more complicated on account of the potential for negative transfer from the first language. As one might expect, given the arguments and evidence rehearsed above, L2 sociolinguistic variants that have a formally similar counterpart in the L1 can result in positive transfer, while negative transfer can occur when there is a mismatch between the first and second languages (Bayley and Regan 2004; Davydova and Buchstaller 2015; Howard, Mougeon and Dewaele 2013: 340; Meyerhoff and Schleef 2014; Regan 2004, 2005; Tarone 2007).

(iii) Moreover, in order to sound native-like, L2 acquirers must advance not only to master what Howard, Mougeon and Dewaele (2013: 340) define as "Type I Variation" but also "Type II Variation". The former consists of alternation between L2 variants (including non-native forms). The latter refers instead to the successful acquisition of native-like patterns of sociolinguistic variation which includes knowledge of which social context would favour the standard imperative *read that/you read that* and which circumstances would permit instead local, NIE variants such as *read **you** that,* which has an alternative order in which verbs can raise in the imperative to produce inverted verb-subject orders (Henry 1995: 45). Indeed "Type II Variation" can consist of even more subtle contrasts like that governing the final unstressed (ING) variable, already noted, which fits the brief of "vernacular root" argued in Chambers (2003: 265).[87] The two variants of this variable ([ɪn] and [ɪŋ]) are known to be governed by an impressive range of internal and external linguistic constraints that will feature prominently in Chapter Seven.

(iv) Successfully acquiring native-like patterns of variability does seem to be variant-specific, as has already been indicated with respect to the earlier discussion of clause-final *like* amongst the Lithuanian and Polish migrants in Armagh, whose competent acquisition of other variables will be examined in further detail in this regard in Chapters Seven to Nine, so as to ascertain the extent to which this finding holds true with respect to other discourse-pragmatic as well as morphophonological and morphosyntactic variables. Davydova and Buchstaller (2015), Howard, Mougeon and Dewaele (2013), Leung and Young-Scholten (2013) as well as Meyerhoff and Schleef (2014) document cases in which only partial or no acquisition ever occurs. Moreover, intralinguistic constraints are more likely to be partially reconstructed and extralinguistic factors, if acquired at all, are often reorganized. These processes are described by Meyerhoff (2003, 2009: 313) as

---

[87] Other terms that have been used for the select few phonological and grammatical processes that constitute vernacular universals of this type are described in some detail in Kortmann and Szmrecsanyi (2004, 2009).

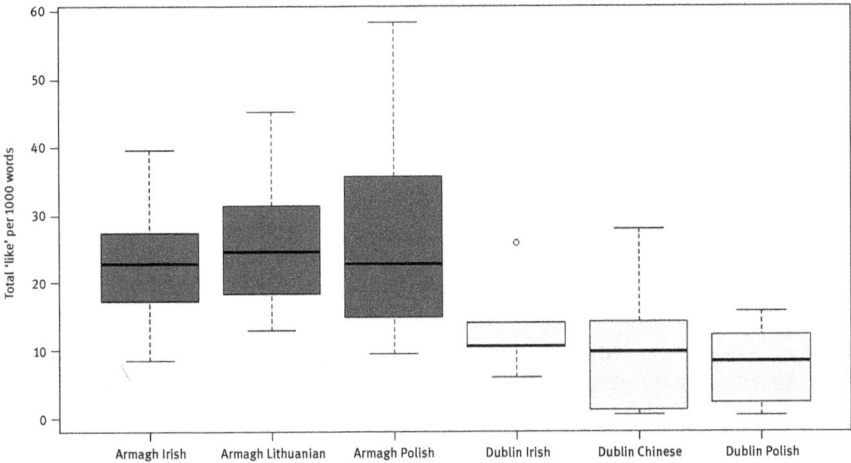

Figure 41 Frequency of *like* by nationality in Armagh and Dublin

"transformation under transfer" which is similar to Britain and Trudgill's (1999) notion of "reallocation", i.e. while the variants are constant, the constraints which operate on them are transformed or their ranking may be re-ordered (or even reversed).

(v) Curiously too, some L2 learners "go rogue" and end up displaying idiosyncratic constraints that have no parallels in native speech at all, in a manner which is akin to what Dorian (1973, 1980, 1994, 2010) terms "personal-patterned variation" arising in language attriting scenarios like those described in §5.1.1.[88] Mougeon and Rehner (2001) address the phenomenon in second language acquisition contexts. Johnstone (1996) also argues for a "linguistics of the individual speaker" but in broader terms and with respect to monoglots (see also Britain 2003; Chambers 2003; Guy 1980 and Macaulay 1978 who all identify individuation of one type or other with respect to conforming to the patterns of variation typical of local community norms in L1 contexts). It may indeed be for similar reasons that an interesting conclusion drawn by Meyerhoff and Schleef (2014: 111) from their research on bilingual migrant teenagers in Edinburgh was that, although their participants do use vernacular variants relatively frequently, there are a number of "differences between individual learners." Figure 41 is reproduced from Corrigan and Diskin's (2020: 12) analysis introduced earlier that

---

[88] See also Smith and Durham (2019) which report on similar individuation with respect to the acquisition of first languages by children.

focused on the use of *like* as a DPM by native and non-native speakers from different heritage backgrounds in Armagh, NI and also Dublin in the Irish Republic. They draw the same conclusion with respect to the overall frequencies of usage for the variable across all the cohorts, as can be seen in the box plots above. These indicate visible individual variation, particularly among the Armagh Poles, and this issue will likewise be returned to in subsequent Chapters with respect to the acquisition of other variables by L2 participants in the *Múin Béarla* project.

(vi) Accounts within this framework have also demonstrated the diverse effects on successful acquisition triggered by exogenous factors such as numbers and types of contact with native speakers. The higher the levels of such interactions and the more integrated within the local community the learner appears to be, the more native like their sociolinguistic choices become (Davydova and Buchstaller 2015; Hellermann and Vergun 2007; Howard, Mougeon and Dewaele 2013: 344; Regan 2005; Sankoff 1997). In this regard, a range of second language learning environments have been explored in Davydova and Buchstaller (2015), Major (2004), Meyerhoff and Schleef (2012, 2014) as well as Regan (2010). All of these provide excellent evidence to suggest that it is only L2 learners with the widest range of native speaker contacts who can become fully sensitized to the internal and external constraints that govern native speaker systems.

(vii) There is clear collinearity of course in this regard with respect to other factors tied to increased contacts, such as length of residence (LoR), which has received considerable attention in the Second Language Acquisition literature (Best and Tyler 2007; Flege 1995, 2009; Saito and Brajot 2013). It also features prominently in research on the acquisition of sociolinguistic variation but (as will become even more apparent in subsequent Chapters), what one might consider to be an obvious connection between residency/increased native speaker input does not necessarily prove to be significant. Hence, Meyerhoff and Schleef (2014: 109), in an investigation similar to that reported here but focusing on teenagers in Edinburgh, comment that "number of months living in Scotland ... almost invariably failed to be chosen as significant in our analyses". Similarly, Corrigan and Diskin (2020) find no influence for this extralinguistic variable on the frequency of DPM *like* usage amongst non-native speakers who had spent different periods of time in the two regions of Ireland already referred to in Figure 41. As with residency, age of arrival (AoA) takes centre stage in the Second Language Acquisition literature (Saito and Brajot 2013) alongside age of acquisition (discussed at length in § 5.2.2). It is likewise a major focus in research with a more sociolinguistic orientation, such as Aaron and Hernández (2007) as well as Otheguy, Zentella and Livert (2007), which both examine this external factor with respect to immigrant varieties of Spanish in the United States. This issue is returned to briefly in (ix) below in connection with the linguistic choices made by two speakers in the *Múin Béarla* pre-adolescent sample. They are the same age but can be contrasted by their LoR/AoA in Northern Ireland. Interestingly, their output is contrary to what one might have predicted, indicating that there may well be other forces at work of a more sociopsychological nature that are also worth exploring and which are dealt with in (ix)–(xi) below as well as in Chapters Seven and Ten.

(viii) In a similar vein, successful acquisition of a second language is also often linked to the role which the mother tongue plays in conducting daily interactions and maintaining local as well as translocal relationships with friends and family (Flege, Frieda and Nozawa 1997). The greater the degree of "entrenchment", in the sense of MacWhinney (2017),[89] the more likely competent L1 learners are to persist with substrate inter-learner effects and the less motivated they are to acquire the L2, since social routines are primarily conducted in the mother tongue. A good case in point is that of the first-generation Chinese migrants to Northern Ireland, whose lack of proficiency was noted in §4.1 of the previous Chapter.[90]

(ix) In more general terms then, personal ties, social networks and "communities of practice" (Eckert 2000) have all been cited as instrumental in predicting the degree to which learners do or do not become proficient in a second language. In the transition from L1 to L2, there is likely to be an element of identity reconstruction that accompanies the language learning process (Block 2007; Norton and McKinney 2011). For some L2 speakers, their ethnic, gender and other identities that they normally index are intimately tied to their mother tongue, which they regularly use for daily interactions as well as maintaining long distance relationships. As such, they may well be reluctant to invest the time it takes to acquire the complex system of L1 "indicators", "markers" and "stereotypes" (Labov 2001: 196) which need to be drawn upon to index new L2 identities incorporating these. Second and Third Wave approaches to sociolinguistics in monolingual contexts have characterised the manner in which individuals establish social networks based on the nature of their personal ties, and on how they participate in

---

[89] That is, as L1 proficiency improves, the representations of the first language become progressively fixed such that the task of acquiring second language representations becomes ever more intractable.

[90] It is important to bear in mind that this is not always the outcome. An investigation of proficiency levels amongst L1 Spanish-L2 Swedish bilinguals described in Bylund, Abrahamsson and Hyltenstam (2012) has demonstrated that L2 attainment is not necessarily hindered by maintenance of the mother tongue. Moreover, the evidence presented below demonstrates that persisting with such effects in the L2 may primarily serve identificatory purposes for those who actually have quite a weak link to their first language.

multiple communities of practice which they dip into and out of in the course of joint endeavours during their lifetimes (as typified by the findings presented in Barrett 1997; Bucholtz 1995, 1999; Butler 1990; Browder 1999; Eckert 1997b, 2000, 2008, 2016; Fought 2002, 2006; Hall 1995; Holland 1988; Milroy 1987a,b; Milroy and Gordon 2003; Milroy and Milroy 1977, *inter alia*). This propensity to "cross" between identities and the diversity of personal network ties amongst multilingual newcomers demonstrated in §4.2.1.2 is likewise epitomised in certain other ethnographic aspects of the *Múin Béarla* interviews to be explored more fully in Chapter Ten. Just such a scenario is captured in the exchange below (48) between the interviewer and a native speaker who describes her observations of the linguistic behaviours often associated with highly proficient L2 newcomer learners (described as "passing" by Piller 2002, and also see Bucholtz 1995, 1999; Bucholtz and Hall 2004, 2005; Cutler 1999; Lo 1999; Rampton 1995, 1999a/b, 2001, 2013, 2016, 2018).

(48)   Extract from an interview with 'Elizabeth Siocháin', Armagh, 2013

   1 Elizabeth Siocháin: ... when his mum would ring and he wouldn't answer 'cause he didn't want us to hear him speaking Lithuanian.
   2 KPC: So, he's almost ashamed of it then, huh?
   3 Elizabeth Siocháin: Yeah, which is a shame that someone would be ashamed of you know where they come from and but I suppose people do get a lot of grief over here. Like, I tend to find that majority of them *[newcomer teenagers]* don't like being identified as not from here, specifically the boys. That's what my feeling is. Any of the boys that I know that aren't from here they don't like people knowing they're not from here like they're not proud of the fact that they're not from here.

   [ES (F); St. Celine's; Armagh, Northern Ireland; 17 Dec. 2013]

Piller's (2002) concept applies to the routines of several project participants which they divulged during the ethnographic phases of the interview, since their language choices are often clearly temporary and are tied to their interlocutors, the context of speaking and the medium in which the interaction takes place. Hence, while certain newcomers, such as the individual overheard by Elizabeth Siocháin, reported in (48), may wish to dissociate from their heritage language in the company of native speakers, many such individuals simultaneously declare that they readily communicate with family in their L1 and attend the type of L1 after school classes described in §4.2.1.2 and in (55) below (often at their parents' behest). Some of the participants also produce telling narratives about other social practices which are relevant here, such as playing soccer or games associated with the autochthonous population like Gaelic football, hurling and camogie which can have important consequences for a newcomer's ability to embed themselves within diverse local communities of practice. Successful entry to the latter is not, of course, guaranteed as the contrast between the narratives on access to the Gaelic football team of one of the participating schools (St. Benedict's) in (49) and (50) illustrate. Patros Stain, a Polish teenager who had lived in Armagh for five years at the time of interview has clearly not succeeded in his "adequation" tactics, as Bucholtz and Hall (2004: 383) would define his attempt at pursuing socially recognised similarity with local peers.

(49) Extract from an interview with 'Patros Stain', Armagh, 2013

   1 KPC: And what's the best thing you like about living in Ireland?
   2 Patros Stain: Well there's more sports because you get soccer here and Gaelic and hurling so yeah. There's more sports.
   3 KPC: And do you play all three?
   4 Patros Stain: Well I used to play Gaelic but then I moved to soccer ...
   5 KPC: Why did you give up Gaelic football?
   6 Patros Stain: Well, I was the only Polish one people-person playing Gaelic so I didn't feel really happy about it. They bullied me ... in school and at Gaelic ...
   7 KPC: So, they bullied you then. Do you think that was because you were Polish?
   8 Patros Stain: Well yeah they was t- telling me to go- go to your own- go to your own country ... and they were pushing me around ...

   [PS (M); St.Benedict's; Armagh, Northern Ireland; 11 Oct. 2013]

At the other end of the scale, Melchor Nogoy (50) has likely to make even greater efforts to erase "distinction" (in the sense of Bucholtz and Hall 2004: 384) so as to access autochthonous communities of practice than even Polish newcomers like Patros do, since his family migrated from the Philippines and are of Austronesian descent. As such, he is clearly marked out by the colour of his skin and other ethnic Filipino characteristics. Interestingly, Melchor shows similar reticence to that identified in (49) with respect to his retention of Tagalog, for instance. This is partly on account of his admission that: "when I try to speak Tagalog I can't really like I'm missing like the like words and all like that there ... I kind of like mix it with English" (see §5.1.2), but also because Melchor declares himself to be reluctant to do so in the company of his Gaelic football-playing peer group, reserving its use for "when I'm just with my mum and dad". The scenario presented in (50) whereby Melchor demonstrates his adherence to the norms of the community of practice associated with his school's Gaelic football team is thus an excellent example of successful "adequation". By affirming that he carries on after injury and doesn't dive when playing, this young Filipino teen is attempting to overcome his "potentially salient differences ... in favour of perceived or asserted similarities that are taken to be more situationally relevant" (Bucholtz and Hall 2004: 383).[91]

(50)　Extract from an interview with 'Melchor Nogoy', Armagh, 2014

1	KPC:	And do you play soccer or Gaelic?
2	Melchor Nogoy:	Yeah. Uh Gaelic.
3	KPC:	Gaelic? And are you any good?
4	Melchor Nogoy:	I hope so anyways ...
5	KPC:	And what about have you even been to see a County match?
6	Melchor Nogoy:	Yeah we [*him and his Filipino father*] usually watch the Armagh matches ...
7	KPC:	I know but it feels like the smallest little knock and they're [*soccer players as opposed to Gaelic players*] "ah ah ah ah".
8	Melchor Nogoy:	It's the wee dives you get that they're sent off or booked or like that there.
9	KPC:	And why do you think Gaelic isn't like that? Are we Irish made of sterner stuff?
10	Melchor Nogoy:	Yeah [*laughter*] that's it [*laughter*] yeah [*laughter*].
11	KPC:	'Cause it is true like there there's hardly any interruption in a Gaelic game.

---

91 The degree of Melchor's mastery of the local values within this community of practice is clear from the considerable furore created during the 2003 All-Ireland semi-final between Counties Kerry and Tyrone in which Peter Canavan (playing for Tyrone) was reported as having taken a dive that cost Kerry a penalty and eventually the game. The extent to which this remains a live issue at the time of my interview with Melchor can be seen from contemporaneous reports of 'feigning' in the *Irish Examiner* and *Irish Independent* https://www.irishexaminer.com/sport/other-sports/rule-makers-must-tackle-footballs-dark-arts-202029.html and https://www.independent.ie/sport/gaelic-games/gaelic-football/joe-brolly-column-peter-canavan-was-one-of-the-original-experts-in-feigning-31470670.html), last accessed 11 June 2019).

12	Melchor Nogoy:	Yeah, there isn't there like you're bleeding you're still get, you got to play on.
13	KPC:	You just walk you walk on, exactly ...
14	Melchor Nogoy:	But I don't know to be honest, I think you would get stick if you dive in Gaelic, that's why.
15	KPC:	Yeah, it's different culture, different traditions.

[MN (M); St.Benedict's; Armagh, Northern Ireland; 30 Jan. 2014]

Soccer, as an international sport, is less tied to local norms and values than Gaelic games are and it would not be surprising therefore if newcomers developed mutable linguistic patterns depending on the activity that is the focus of the various communities of practice in which they participate. In fact, there is evidence emerging that migrant speakers, in particular, walk a "sociolinguistic tightrope" (Dewaele 2004), as Melchor Nogoy does, between converging towards the majority language of the host society and diverging from it depending on their activity. Thus, Debaene and Harris (2013: 90–91) in a paper on L1 Polish speakers who are in the process of acquiring English in the Republic of Ireland remark that:

> ... contrary to the assimilative patterns adopted by immigrants in the past, current immigrants demand recognition and the right to disagree with the hegemonic ideology as they strive for the legitimacy of maintaining their differences. They may refuse therefore to acquire the host language (or local dialects or accents) and insist on maintaining their home languages ...

They base these views on case studies of participants who evidence both convergence and divergence as speakers negotiate different identities during the course of their daily lives amongst the host population and with fellow migrants. This includes interviewees who deliberately speak with a strong L2 accent, retain L1 transfers or might persist with "Type I Variation" (Howard, Mougeon and Dewaele 2013: 340) so as to express their ethnic identity and distinctiveness. In related research, Sachdev and Giles (2008: 358) claim that this is an important tactic by which bilinguals maintain intergroup distinctiveness, affirm their own ethnicity and enhance their self-esteem. Examples (51)–(54) from an interview with a triad of pre-teens at St. Peter's demonstrates this sort of convergence towards and divergence from L1 norms between two of the speakers, Jacek Burda and Mikolaj Wolak. Jacek, who was born in Northern Ireland of Polish migrant parents, is highly divergent and vacillates during the interview between Northern Irish and Polish accented varieties of English, using quite a few Type I variants which his "best friend" Mikolaj sometimes corrects for him (54):

(51) Extract from an interview with 'Jacek Burda', Armagh, 2014

    1 KPC: ... does your granny understand any English?
    2 Jacek Burda: Wee bit I **teached** her. I **teached** my granny for a tenner.

[JB (M); St. Peter's; Donaghmore, Northern Ireland; 29 April 2014]

(52) Extract from an interview with 'Jacek Burda', Armagh, 2014

    1 Jacek Burda: ... for my granny to see me after she **camed** with me.

[JB (M); St. Peter's; Donaghmore, Northern Ireland; 29 April 2014]

(53) Extract from an interview with 'Jacek Burda', Armagh, 2014

    1 Jacek Burda: ... my friend he's fourteen **age old** and he cannot drive a quad and he crashed.

[JB (M); St. Peter's; Donaghmore, Northern Ireland; 29 April 2014]

(54) Extract from an interview with 'Jacek Burda' and 'Mikolai Wolak', Armagh, 2014

    1 Jacek Burda: She crashed there with the wheel and the helmet **fall off**.
    2 Mikolaj Wolak: **Fell off** her.

[JB (M); St. Peter's; Donaghmore, Northern Ireland; 29 April 2014]

Despite only arriving in Northern Ireland at the age of three, the convergent variety which Mikolaj uses in his interview, by contrast, contains almost no inter-learner or L2 effects. In fact, it is practically indistinguishable from the local dialect with respect to accent, discourse-pragmatics, grammar and lexis to the extent that he could readily "pass" for a native speaker in Piller's (2002) terms. Ethnographic aspects of the interview are revealing in this respect too, in that the two boys have rather different opinions about the value of formally learning other languages in general and Polish in particular. This contrast is captured in (55), which demonstrates not only that Jacek has rather negative attitudes towards multilingualism but that he seems to resent the time his friend Mikolaj spends at Polish Saturday school when he could instead be engaging with him (see also § 4.2.1.2):

(55) Extract from an interview with 'Jacek Burda' and 'Mikolai Wolak', Armagh, 2014

1	KPC:	And do you think it's important to learn languages?
2	Jacek Burda:	Nope.
3	Mikolaj Wolak:	Yeah 'cause when you go to a different country or something then you know what to say.
4	KPC:	Mm-hm. And what about uh when you're ... when you're at home?
5	Mikolaj Wolak:	Sometimes on Saturdays we go to Polish school.
6	KPC:	Oh, okay tell me about Polish school.
7	Jacek Burda:	Sometimes? Each week. I don't. I don't want to.
8	Mikolaj Wolak:	Uh we [*him and his younger brother, Sylwester*] write to learn more Polish so we know Polish and English so we won't forget about Polish.
9	KPC:	Yes. And that is important to you?
10	Mikolaj Wolak:	Yeah 'cause when we go to Poland we uh we can't if we were talking to my granny or something ... then she wouldn't understand.
11	KPC:	And what about you Jacek, you say you don't want to go to Polish school so why is that now?
12	Jacek Burda:	Because it sounds like too because it's a wee bit hard for me like spelling ...
13	Mikolaj Wolak:	It's just like in P1 you do uh writing.
14	Jacek Burda:	Yeah, it's wee bit hard for me.
15	KPC:	And so, what happens if you forget your Polish though will you won't be able to talk to them will you?
16	Jacek Burda:	No I don't think. I'm going in nine weeks to Poland for a month.
17	Mikolaj Wolak:	He'll just say "Hello granny" and then she'll say "What did you say?" [*Laughter*]

[JB (M) and MW (M); St. Peter's; Donaghmore, Northern Ireland; 29 April 2014]

On the basis of this exchange, it seems reasonable to suggest that the retention of Polish in spoken and written form for Mikolaj is important for the pragmatic purpose of maintaining familial contacts. It also seems to some degree to be a means of expressing an intrinsic part of his outgroup identity which is concealed when he is conversing in Northern Irish English. Despite having been born in

Northern Ireland and thus lived in the country longer, Jacek, however, seems instead to harness entrenched L2 features in his English for this purpose. This may well be on account of the fact that his Polish is attriting (as described in §5.1.2) and his interest in learning to read and write in the language is not nearly so strong. Indeed, his lack of engagement becomes the butt of Mikolaj's joke in the last utterance here, which suggests that Jacek will have to resort to addressing his grandmother in English on his next visit to Poland which, of course, she will not understand despite him having "teached her" a "wee bit" for "a tenner" during his last trip, as he declares in (51). It may well be that Jacek's Polish has reached the "relexification" stage identified by Hill and Hill (1977) and discussed in §5.1.2 and this is what Mikolaj is noticing (see Demmans Epp 2017).

(x) Inter-learner variation effects such as those which obtain between Jacek and Micolaj have likewise been linked to cognitive or sociopsychological traits, since these have also been cited as promoting or inhibiting second language acquisition. They would include aptitude, attitude, intelligence and motivation in addition to whether or not the acquirer deals well with potentially anxious social situations or has the right kind of out-going personality to become a successful learner (Abrahamsson and Hyltenstam 2008; Bylund, Abrahamsson and Hyltenstam 2009; Carrell, Prince and Astika 1996; Dewaele and Furnham 1999; 2000; Gardner, Lalonde and Moorcraft 1985; Genesee, Lindholm-Leary, Saunders and Christian 2006; Hyltenstam 2016; Singleton 2017; Skehan 1989, 2014). Hence, Micolaj could just be more intelligent or motivated than Jacek or indeed may be more extroverted or have a greater capacity for learning additional languages. These endowments would presumably make him more metalinguistically aware (§5.1.2) as well as cognisant not only of the characteristics but also the status and contextual nuances of Northern Irish patterns of sociolinguistic variation in the first place.

(xi) Other types of exogenous constraint like dyad or triad effects and interlocutor social characteristics (native versus non-native speaker or class, gender and ethnic differences) have also been implicated in the scholarly literature (e.g. Dewaele 2004; Tarone 1988) as important for explaining the levels of L2 proficiency that speakers demonstrate in their interactions. An interesting case in point is Leung and Young-Scholten (2013) which explores the situation of Filipino domestic servants in Hong Kong who have acquired English as a second language. The L2 patterns of these caregivers are never adopted by the youngsters in the wealthy households to which they are attached because their charges are all too aware of the servants' low socio-economic status and hence show no signs of emulating them. Issues tied to these particular external constraints arising from the interview setting and protocols adopted within the *Múin Béarla* project will thus feature prominently in the next Chapter (§ 6.2.1), so as to weigh up their potential impact on the results presented subsequently.

The arguments and outcomes drawn from the sociolinguistics of L2 acquisition literature and summarised in (i)–(xi) will be central to the investigations in Chapters Seven to Nine, of how the L2 learners in the *Múin Béarla* corpus fare as they try to acquire the internal and external constraints on variation at different levels of the grammar that are typical of native speakers born and bred in the Mid-Ulster dialect region of Northern Ireland, whose interviews also form an integral part of this project, as detailed in Chapter Six, § 6.2.3.

5.2.2 Critical periods in second language acquisition and variationist linguistics

5.2.2.1 Early and late acquirers of additional language

The major finding to emerge from research in the field of second language acquisition since the earliest studies of the mid twentieth century is the disparity between adults and children when it comes to their potential for achieving competence in a second or third language. Youngsters like Mikolaj, whose high level of proficiency in Northern Irish English has already been noted, are considered capable of acquiring native-like ability in an L2, whereas older acquirers vary considerably in their levels of linguistic expertise and metalinguistic awareness. This has led to proposals for the existence of "critical" and "sensitive" pre-puberty nuero-cognitive phases beyond which native-like acquisition at all levels of the grammar becomes exponentially more difficult (Abrahamsson and Hyltenstam 2009; Asher and García 1969; Baum and Titone 2014; Birdsong 2018; Baume and Titone 2014; Bylund, Abrahamsson and Hyltenstam 2012; DeKeyser, 2000, 2013; DeKeyser, Alfi-Shabtay and Ravid 2010; Festman, Rodriguez-Fornells and Munte 2010; Hyltenstam 1992; Hurford 1991; Johnson and Newport 1989; Krashen 1973; 1981; Krashen, Long and Scarcella 1979; Lenneberg 1967; Rastelli 2014; Sorace 2008 *inter alia*).

That is not to say that there is universal agreement, of course, as Aitchison (2008) and Singleton (2005) point out regarding second language acquirers in hearing communities. Mayberry (1994) as well as Mayberry and Kluender (2018) report on children and adults learning American Sign Language as an L2, providing confirmation which also supports her more sceptical perspective. Similarly, research on early/late childhood and early adulthood bilinguals by Bak, Vega-Mendoza and Sorace (2014: 1) has produced excellent evidence which suggests that "the effects of bilingualism extend into the auditory domain and are not confined to childhood bilinguals, although their scope might be slightly different in early and late bilinguals", also reinforcing the perspective that the picture is more complex than it is often presented to be.

There is no consensus either on the specific mechanisms that generate these adult versus child disparities or the precise timing of their onset. As noted in the previous section, successful acquisition also appears to be influenced by sociopsychological and other individuated traits which are not strictly biological at all, as argued, for instance by early studies such as Snow and Hoefnagel-Höhle (1977) and (1979) as well as the later research reviewed in Birdsong (2016); Bylund, Abrahamsson and Hyltenstam (2012); Rastelli (2018) and Scovel (2000). Exponents of the "critical" or "sensitive" period hypothesis are, however, in the majority. Instead, they hold that age differences in acquisition potential are caused by those neural structures in the brain that impact upon how language is cognitively processed (Broca's and Wernicke's areas, for instance), decreasing in their malleability as children age beyond puberty (Ruben 1997; Uylings 2006) in a similar manner to other aspects of aging tied to cognition (Grady *et al.* 2006; Oberman and Pascual-Leone 2013). As a consequence, adult learners' lack of neuro-plasticity means that they struggle to attain the native-like competence ascribed to pre-pubescent acquirers (Gullberg and Indefrey 2006; Hyltenstam and Abrahamsson 2000, 2008; Lenneberg 1967; Long 2007, 2013; Paradis 2004; Pulvermüller 2003; Pulvermüller and Schumann, 1994). In a similar vein, there is a growing body of evidence in the Second Language Acquisition literature that supports what Bylund, Abrahamsson and Hyltenstam (2009: 216) have termed the "impediment account." Although there is less empirical substance for this perspective on nativelikeness in L2 speech, proponents of the model suggest that the "entrenchment" of L1 structures plays a greater role than a decrease in neural plasticity with age (as described in §5.2.1 above and MacWhinney 2017). Interestingly, the findings drawn from Bylund, Abrahamsson and Hyltenstam's (2012) own research on Spanish-Swedish bilinguals referred to earlier do not lend this theory much support, and it remains somewhat contentious (as observable by a review of Abrahamsson and Hyltenstam 2009; Asher and García 1969; Bylund, Abrahamsson and Hyltenstam 2012; DeKeyser, 2000, 2012; Hyltenstam 1992; Johnson and Newport 1989; Krashen, Long and Scarcella 1980; Lenneberg 1967; Oyama 1976; Patkowski 1980; Penfield and Roberts 1959; Snow and Hoefnagel-Höhle 1979).

5.2.2.2 Incrementation and stabilization

Given the fact that the *Múin Béarla* project focuses on investigating the extent to which young bilingual speakers successfully acquire the internal and external constraints on variation that typify their native-speaking peers, it can be assumed that this population is likely from a developmental perspective therefore to have a number of cognitive and other advantages over adult bilinguals in terms of its members' potential for acquiring additional languages. Anecdotal support for this view comes from ethnographic phases of the *Múin Béarla* interviews in one of the primary schools in the study (St. Peter's), in which children aged 5–8 are offered lessons in Irish as part of the curriculum while those in the upper school (aged 9–11) take classes in Chinese.[92] None of the pupils had encountered these languages prior to attending St. Peter's so they all started *ab initio*. Invariably, during interviews with these participants when asked who is the most proficient at these second or third languages in the school, the non-native speakers were singled out as especially skilled by comparison to their indigenous classmates.

This phenomenon is well-supported in the literature (Cape, Vega-Mendoza, Bak and Sorace 2018; Sanz 2000; Barac and Bialystok 2012). However, even native speakers who are uniquely placed to readily acquire the language of their local environment, are known not to learn precisely the input variety of their parents. In fact, the language of any speech community is thought to be subject to a process of "incrementation" during "transmission", as articulated in Labov (2007) *inter alia*. This phenomenon is rooted in what was referred to in the previous Chapter as the "social life of language" as Sankoff (1980b) defines it, and is largely divorced from the biological and cognitive domains just discussed (see also Meyerhoff and Nagy 2008). Incrementation functions to create maximal social distance from the caregiver generation (a phase intimately tied to adolescence) and is achieved in part by furthering linguistic diversity between parent and child (see Eckert 1997a, 2000, 2003, 2004, 2016; Kirkham and Moore 2013; Mendoza-Denton 2008). Since the explorations of variation and change in Northern Irish English presented in Chapters Seven to Nine focus on speakers at exactly this life stage, it is crucial to also consider the model of acquisition underpinning the manner in which this social group is implicated in motivating linguistic change within communities of speakers when they acquire their own native languages (Weinreich, Labov and Herzog 1968: 184–185). The divergences between primary caregivers and their offspring which ensue are at the core of "vernacular reorganisation" and are fundamental to the generation of competition between old and new forms (Smith and Durham 2019; Smith, Durham and Fortune 2007; Smith, Durham and Richards 2013); their frequency of use; and aspects of their functionality including what Labov (2007: 346) terms "scope and specificity". Kroch (1989) and Labov (2001:

---

92 There is no longer any statutory Key Stage 1 or 2 provision for languages in the Northern Ireland primary curriculum (Ayres-Bennett and Carruthers 2019) so this is an independent school-led initiative using local resources (such as free teaching from Ulster University's Confucius Institute established in 2012: https://www.ulster.ac.uk/confucius/about, accessed 6 July 2019).

448) have framed the phenomenon of historical and generational change, respectively, as being systematic, i.e. occurring at a "constant rate" and advancing in the same direction from parent to child. Socially motivated projection models of change such as that hypothesised in Labov (1994, 2001, 2007) in addition to Rutter (2014) and Tagliamonte (2016b) assume that there is also a critical period of sorts in this context. They place it between the ages of 5 and 17 (which is roughly coterminous with the age group which is the object of study here, as detailed in the next Chapter).[93] It is also worth noting in this regard that Roberts and Labov (1995) *inter alia* present persuasive arguments for placing the starting point for acquiring sociolinguistic variation as even earlier, i.e. from the age of 3 onwards (see also Corrigan 2010: 175; Kerswill and Williams 2005: 1030; Roberts 1994: 145–146; Smith and Durham 2019; Smith, Durham and Fortune 2007: 78–79, 87–88; Smith, Durham and Richards 2013: 307–308). Some studies have isolated the adolescent peak amongst certain speech communities as also occurring earlier than age 17 (Van Hofwegen and Wolfram 2010). However, a majority of apparent time studies focusing on adolescent speakers have found evidence for accelerated frequencies of vernacular features at some point during this life stage.

The oldest cohort of teenagers in the *Múin Béarla* corpus have experienced a longer period of "vernacular reorganization" than younger groups so their frequency of innovating forms will be incrementally higher. Moreover, individuals from the same community who are older than the 17-year-olds are likely to have stabilized their frequency of usage which is thus not as advanced. Furthermore, their grammars are now considered to be fixed at this life stage. It is hypothesised that such young adults have by then reached and passed the "peak" period for acquiring changes already in progress amongst their parents' generation and propelling them even further. Chambers (2009: 190) terms this phase "retrenchment" and Wagner (2012a: 181) describes it as "post-adolescent retreat." While the end result is essentially the same, teasing apart the competing hypotheses which underpin this phenomenon, i.e. "retrograde change", "vernacular reorganization", and, of course, "age-grading" is not straightforward and is well-nigh impossible without access to real time data, as the arguments in Ash (1982); Cedergren (1973, 1984); Chambers (2002); Corrigan (1997); Labov (2001); Sankoff

---

93 There was one newcomer participant in the Armagh adolescent sub-corpus of *Múin Béarla* aged 20, who was still attending secondary school, due to repeating examinations. The remainder of the participants in the youth sub-corpus of *Múin Béarla* were between the ages of 5 and 18. The dimensions and sub-divisions of the entire corpus and the rationale for confining the investigations of variation and change in Chapters Seven to Nine to participants attending post-primary school is articulated further in the next Chapter but is, naturally, informed by the socially motivated projection model of change introduced here.

(2013); Tagliamonte and D'Arcy (2009); Van Hofwegen and Wolfram (2010) and Wagner (2008, 2012a/b) *inter alia* confirm. For instance, what Ash (1982) defines as "retrograde change" is a scenario where – rather than the 17-year olds peaking and then retreating – the speech patterns of younger age groups instead capture the volte-face of an innovation across their entire community being led by them. The age-grading hypothesis, by contrast, typified by Cedergren (1988: 53) and Chambers (2002: 358–360), holds that "members of a speech community alter their vernacular at some juncture in their lives in such a way as to bring it into conformity with adult norms" (Chambers 2002: 358). It is important to bear in mind too that the generational change paradigm articulated in Labov (2001: 448) applies specifically to the dynamics of populations in the first world and particularly those which are urban (though see Corrigan 1997 on its application to real time morphosyntactic change in a rural community situated within a different dialect region of Northern Ireland to that which is the focus here). "Vernacular reorganization" in its original conception was also considered to apply to females only (to account for the degree to which women rather than men accelerate changes in progress towards community norms). This aspect of the concept has, however, been challenged in recent research by Denis *et al.* (2019) which reported the process as actually applying across both genders in their Toronto trend study of the innovative (BE LIKE) quotative, which is the focus of Chapter Nine. They argue that "the gender asymmetry of linguistic change should be conceived of as a matter of degree, not kind, and thus likely to be more apparent in some changes than others" (Denis *et al.* 2019: 61).[94]

5.2.3 Acquiring sociolinguistic variation

With regard to the acquisition of sociolinguistic variation and the manner in which change is propelled across generations and diachronically, it is also worth bearing in mind two further assumptions evidenced by the scholarly literature which will be returned to in subsequent Chapters. Firstly, not all sociolinguistic variables such as (BE LIKE) are subject to change in progress either synchronically or across time (and corroboration for both these aspects of its trajectory in Northern Irish English will be provided in Chapter Nine). In fact, there is good evidence to suggest that some variables have actually stabilized within Anglophone communities at the level of the adolescent peak introduced earlier (Cameron 2005; Wagner 2012a). The morphophonological (ING) variable

---

94 Also see Tagliamonte and D'Arcy (2009: 97) and D'Arcy (2015) for further suggested modifications of the paradigm in this regard.

to which Chapter Seven is devoted and the relative clause marker variable examined in Chapter Eight would both qualify here. This is on account of the fact that they pattern alike as regards their acknowledged status, such that there is one variant in each case that is considered to be the standard form and thus has overt prestige community-wide. Moreover, there are discernible correlations between their use and external social factors such as high socio-economic class and formal speech styles. Stable variables like these also show a curvilinear age-related pattern in which the frequency whereby adults use standard variants is higher than adolescents within the same community. Concomitantly, the latter favour non-standard variants prior to the post-adolescent retreat phase when they come to adopt adult norms (often considered to be motivated by linguistic marketplace forces coming into effect around that stage in the life-cycle and then retreating once more post-retirement (Bourdieu and Boltanski 1975; Chambers 2008: 189–190; Cheshire 2005a; Coupland, Coupland and Giles 1991; Rickford and Price 2013; Sankoff & Blondeau 2007; Wagner 2012a/b)). During the process of transmission, youngsters have been shown to have the capacity to observe lower frequencies of the standard variant in informal interactions and higher usage in formal contexts (Labov 2001; Smith and Durham 2019; Smith, Durham and Fortune 2007, 2009).[95] Specifically, they learn to reproduce these stylistic expectations in their own speech patterns. In addition, they become adept at correlating standard versus non-standard distinctions with diverse types of socio-economic status and degrees of social conformity such that they are then able to match these in their own production too depending on context, their own status socially, their aspirations and individual willingness to adhere to societal norms (Docherty, Foulkes, Tillotson and Watt 2006; Foulkes *et al.* 2010; Labov 2001; Rutter 2014; Smith and Durham 2019; Smith, Durham and Fortune, 2007, 2009; Smith, Durham and Richards 2013).

Secondly, mastery of the internal and external constraints on variation which apply to different variables is not necessarily simultaneous even amongst native speakers, just as there are developmental sequences associated with other aspects of typical child language acquisition (Levey 2016; Roberts 2004 *inter alia* and also see Goodluck, Guilfoyle and Harrington 2006 as well as Hoff and Shatz

---

95 With the proviso that very young children (<2 years of age) – taking their lead from the high frequency of standard forms in child directed speech towards them – have not yet acquired the wherewithal for style switching at this point (Smith and Durham 2019: 189). It is also the case that this ability seems to be variable-specific for those older children who have already acquired social constraints of this type. Indeed, this skill may, in fact, depend on the extent to which caregivers are aware of positive or negative evaluations within their local community towards the variants (Smith, Durham and Fortune 2007: 90–91).

2009).⁹⁶ Not surprisingly therefore, Levey (2016: 163) goes so far as to argue that "a central preoccupation in the developmental sociolinguistic literature concerns the sequence in which multiple constraints on variable usage are acquired." Findings from the literature on this issue differ, as de Vogelaer *et al.* (2017) as well as Smith and Durham (2019) also argue. Hence Labov (1989) reports children by the age of 7 having acquired constraints with respect to formal/informal style also found in the adult population in his study of (ING) amongst King of Prussia families. However, their grammars had not yet internalised certain categorical phonological and grammatical conditions on variation observed in the speech of the caregiver generation. Roberts (1994), by contrast, in an analysis of (T/D)-deletion word-finally in South Philadelphia, observed that although the children in her study were fully conversant with the phonological conditions on this variable, they had not completely mastered those which were grammatical nor had they learned any of the social ones at all, which echoes the findings of Cornips (2017) based on pre-pubescent speakers of Dutch and their acquisition of two-verb cluster word order. They were likewise comparatively late acquiring the nuances of extralinguistic conditioning. In this regard, Smith, Durham and Fortune (2007) show that their child participants in Buckie acquire adult-like linguistic constraints on (AU) and (VERBAL -S) before they reach school-going age. Interestingly, the rules for the former are internalised prior to those for the latter in spite of the fact that variation in the verbal-s paradigm might be conceived of as potentially more complex (see also Kerswill 1996: 199). In addition, Smith, Durham and Fortune (2007) demonstrate that the external stylistic conditioning associated with the caregiver population for [huːs] versus [haus] pronunciations of 'house' is acquired earlier than similar constraints on non-standard morphosyntactic forms like "My trouser**s is** falling doon" (Smith, Durham and Fortune 2007: 80). Other studies such as that reported in Foulkes, Docherty and Watt (2005) on the variation associated with /t/ glottalization that is typical of Tyneside English, have instead demonstrated that both the internal and external conditioning on the variable amongst their young acquirers were learned in lockstep.

A comparison of the research on diverse child and adolescent populations also reveals disparities between when the full complement of conditioning on

---

96 For discussions of the extent to which non-native speakers do or do not eventually master such constraint hierarchies, see subsequent chapters as well as Adamson and Regan (1991); Bayley (1994); Diskin (2017); Diskin and Levey (2019); Drummond (2012); Howley (2015); Major (2001); Meyerhoff and Schleef (2014); Ryan (2018); Sharma (2005); Sharma and Sankaran (2011); Schleef, Meyerhoff and Clark (2011); Schleef (2017); Verma, Corrigan and Firth (1992); Wolfram (1985); Young (1991) *inter alia*.

particular variables are acquired. A good case in point is the acquisition by Anglophones of the functions associated with the *like* DPM already noted. Hence, Miller and Weinert (1995: 366) conservatively estimate that they are learned "after age ten" based on evidence from the child data in their Scots corpus. Levey (2006, 2016), however, suggests that these constraints occur in the speech of British and Canadian pre-adolescent populations even before then. In a similar vein, D'Arcy (2017: 149) reports the fact that "discourse features and the strategies related to their use are in place before adolescence."

Although there will no doubt be mileage in future research investigating these and related issues within the pre-adolescent sub-corpus of *Múin Béarla*, it is for these reasons that the subsequent analyses presented in Chapters Seven to Nine are instead confined to the adolescent sub-corpus, so that issues of linguistic maturation do not also have to be considered. The preponderance of evidence suggests that the full cohort of linguistic and social constraints on (ING) and (BE LIKE), as well as those which apply to the system of relativisation in Northern Irish English, will already be in place amongst the *Múin Béarla* cohort of post-primary native speakers on the basis of previous research examining the developmental sequencing of sociolinguistic acquisition.[97] Now, while it is true that this population does not constitute the entire input for the L2 acquirers in the corpus who are also adolescents, there is robust evidence from the socio-psychological literature that the salience of the peer group at this life stage by comparison to caregivers or other adults is such that it is the dialectal norms of this particular speech community which is most likely to be those that the newcomers will be trying to emulate (Allen and Kern 2017; Andersen 2001; Brechwald and Prinstein 2011; Eckert 1997a, 2000, 2003, 2004, 2016; Fortman 2003; Kirkham and Moore 2013; Mendoza-Denton 2008; Quinn and Oldmeadow 2012; Tagliamonte 2016b). As such, triangulating the speech patterns across these two datasets should offer a window onto the emergence of structured variation in the inter-learner varieties of teenage L2 acquirers.

De Vogelaer *et al.* (2017) contend that "the acquisition of patterns of sociolinguistic variation has long been an under-investigated topic both in sociolinguistics and in language acquisition research". The findings reported in subsequent Chapters which compare these cohorts of adolescent speakers from an inter-disciplinary perspective will thus have important theoretical impacts that have relevance to both approaches to linguistic maturation. Key questions to be addressed include:

---

[97] In this regard, see Nardy, Chevrot and Barbu (2013) as well as Smith and Durham (2019) on (ING); Levey (2006) and Oetting and Newkirk (2011) on relativizing strategies; and D'Arcy (2017) as well as Denis *et al.* (2019) on (BE LIKE).

1. What is the nature of the process for acquiring sociolinguistic variation by migrant teenagers and does it differ in any respect from that which L1 learners also undergo during the critical period?

2. Do the linguistic and social constraint hierarchies of adolescent native-speakers become fully or partially internalized by their newcomer peers or do they reconstruct or indeed reject them altogether?

3. Is the acquisition of sociolinguistic competence dependent on some of the factors outlined in (i)–(xi) of §5.2 such as age of arrival, proficiency or length of residence?

4. Can any individual, ethnolectal or other pertinent social asymmetries be discerned across diverse sub-cohorts of immigrant and local adolescents?

6 Fieldwork, data collection methods and research tools

In general terms, this Chapter explores and evaluates the methodologies, protocols, fieldwork and investigative techniques underpinning the collection, digitisation, coding and analysis of the *Múin Béarla* corpus. The Chapter begins by examining the key historical and socio-cultural differences between the three fieldwork sites (Armagh, Belfast and Donaghmore) and explains why these areas and the participating schools within each region have been specifically targeted for the purposes of this project. There will be further discussion too of the participants and their social and demolinguistic characteristics as well as the context of their interviews (particularly the techniques used to delimit the "observer's paradox", as defined by Labov 2001: 36 and Milroy & Gordon 2003: 49, 52, 57, 68, 80). Also addressed here will be a review of the characteristics and dimensions of the resulting *Múin Béarla* database from both qualitative and quantitative perspectives. The Chapter will close with an evaluation of the methods used in language variation and change studies to determine the extent to which cohorts of speakers differ with respect to their operationalising of linguistic and social constraint hierarchies of the type already introduced in the previous Chapter.

6.1 Fieldwork sites

Armagh City, Northern Ireland's capital of Belfast, and the village of Donaghmore were chosen as the fieldwork sites for this project for a number of reasons. Key here is the fact that the overarching variety of Northern Irish English spoken in each location is similar. It is a dialect known as Mid-Ulster English, as illustrated in Chapter Two, Figure 9, reproduced as Figure 42 below, which also indicates the locations of the three areas relative to one another.[98]

Part of the rationale too is the fact that they are situated in regions which the previous Chapter demonstrated to be migrant-dense on the basis of where newcomer pupils are located across the diverse Local Government Districts (LGD) of Northern Ireland, i.e. the LGD of Armagh, Banbridge and Craigavon; that of Belfast; and, finally, Mid Ulster which is where the village of Donaghmore lies. Thus, migrant pupil numbers in each LGD were likely to be high enough even in the least populous of these to provide a robust judgement sample, allowing for the usual reductions as a result of absences, lack of consent and so on. Integral

---

98 The local base dialect therefore is the Mid-Ulster English type documented in §4.2 of Chapter 4.

https://doi.org/10.1515/9783110614190-006

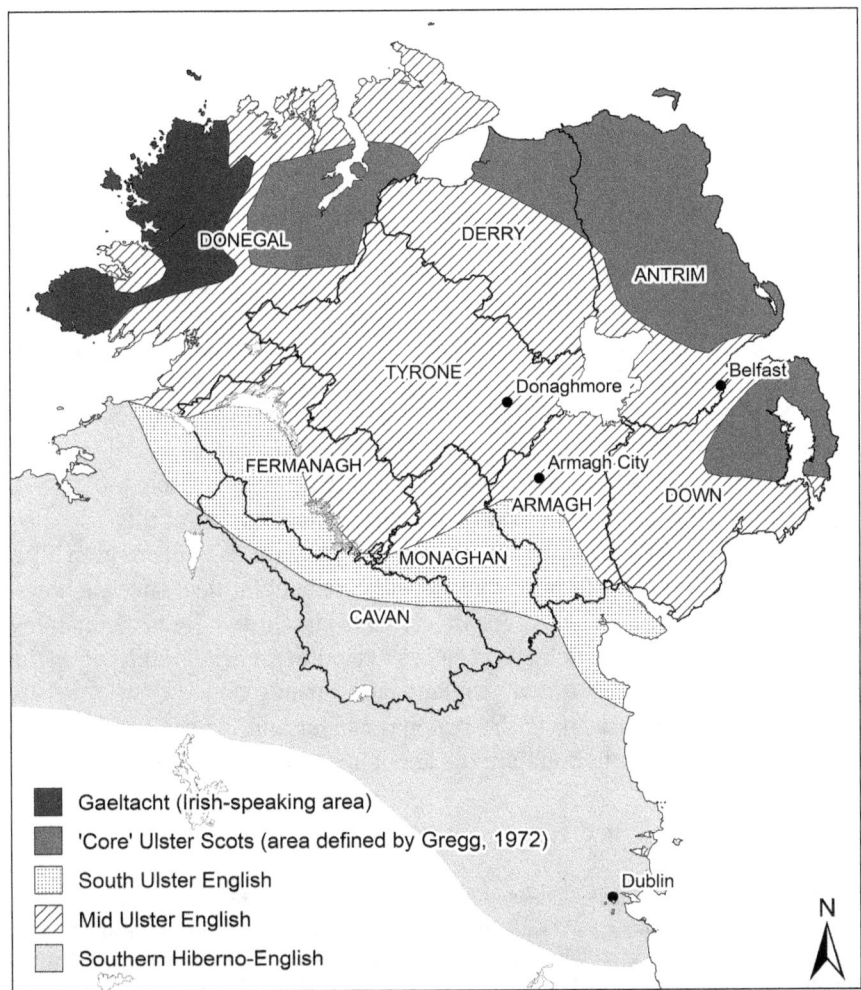

Figure 42 Spatial distribution of language and dialect zones in the original nine counties of Ulster

to the decision as well was the fact that I had personal contacts in each of the schools within these regions, anonymised here and elsewhere as St. Benedict's and St. Celine's, Armagh (both secondaries); St. Agnes's, Belfast and St. Peter's, Donagmore (primaries). This pre-existing connectivity allowed for ready access in an era when it is becoming increasingly difficult for researchers in the language sciences to study school-going populations on account of increased safeguarding measures (for good reason of course, as argued in Brevik 2013; Dalli & Te One 2012; DENI 2017b; Hammersley & Traianou 2012 and Rogers, Labadie & Pole 2016).

The fact that I was already embedded in each of the schools via multiple personal networks was also invaluable from the perspective of establishing trust with educators, parents and participants alike and the positive consequences of these pre-existing relationships will be discussed further in §6.1.2.[99]

6.1.1 History and socio-cultural context of Armagh, Donaghmore and Belfast

Armagh received its city status in 1994 though it remains the least populous settlement of this type on the whole island of Ireland (Beckett 2014) despite its 1.6% rise in population since 2001 as recorded in the 2011 Census (i.e. from 14,517 to 14,749) (Russell 2015: 9). In fact, this status arises largely from the fact that it is Ireland's ecclesiastical capital. Indeed, Armagh has been the home of both the Church of Ireland and Roman Catholic Primates for many centuries and supports not one but two Cathedrals –representing each denomination (Coote 1804/1984). Figure 43 illustrates their physical predominance on account of their elevated positions topographically within the city which, like Rome, is built on seven hills. The Lennox painting – timed to coincide with Armagh's new city designation – also represents the role which these architectural structures have in maintaining the socio-historical reputation of Armagh as a key site of religious faith within the Christian landscape of the island of Ireland more broadly.[100]

Belfast, by comparison, is the regional capital and, across the island of Ireland, is second only to Dublin in the Republic of Ireland in terms of its popu-

---

99 The project was undertaken following guidance for safeguarding and child protection laid out in DENI (2017b). This required me as the fieldworker undertaking a Disclosure and Barring Service check prior to entering any of the schools. Additionally, formal consent for participation was obtained from each school principal and parents. This included forms for signature as well as information in plain language about the purpose of the project. All of these were translated into the relevant home languages of allochthonous families to ensure sufficient understanding. Each post-primary youngster also had access to this material. Given the age of the post-primary pupils, while they also signed consent forms, there was an additional process involving a lengthy informal discussion prior to recording. This was so as to ensure that they understood what was being asked of them; what its purpose was; that there was no pressure on them to continue and that they could stop at any point. This conversation was conducted in a manner that was commensurate with their capacities and interests, following the good practice of Alderson & Morrow (2004) as well as the British Association of Applied Linguistics guidelines (https://baalweb.files.wordpress.com/2017/08/goodpractice_full.pdf, accessed 25th July 2019).
100 It was the Roman Catholic one that was adorned by the Italian migrants, Amici and Aureli, described in Chapter Four, §4.1. The site of the Church of Ireland building is traditionally linked with St. Patrick's first church on the hill from which Armagh City derives its name (see Chapter Two, §2.1.2).

Figure 43 *Buildings of Armagh* by Timothy Lennox 1994 (rights held by Friends of Armagh County Museum and reproduced with kind permission)

lation size, which stood at 280,962 residents in the 2011 Census.[101] Donaghmore is at the other end of the scale then from this so-called "Belfast Urban Metropolitan Area" since the Northern Ireland Statistics and Research Agency (NISRA) classify it instead as a "Small Village" on account of the fact that its population is only between 500 and 1000 people (NISRA 2005: 28–32).[102] One would expect the socio-cultural ambience of these three settlements not to be similar and that immigrants may well experience different lifestyle conventions while residing in each location that are worth exploring in future research. This is because the rural-urban distinction correlates with factors such as the manner in which health, social care and leisure facilities are situated and funded, how utilities and services are maintained and the range and types of education provided. Employment is also differentiated such that rural job opportunities are often distinct in character, less diverse or indeed scarcer than those in urban settings (NISRA 2005: 2). In fact, commuter journeys amongst members of these communities can be rather longer and induce weak-tie personal networks of communication and a more global perspective that are worth bearing in mind (NISRA 2005: 31). Exactly this scenario was identified for women in rural South Armagh between 1942 and 1974 by Corrigan (1997) on account of the fact that they were occasioned to travel out of their local communities for employment. These short-term migrations of the type also discussed in Chapter One, §1.3 in connection with the *Múin Béarla* participants, had a knock-on effect on their more rapid acquisition of standard morphosyntactic variables than their male peers, who instead worked close to home and had the type of close-knit networks that are more typical of small, peripheral communities (see also Cornips & de Rooij 2018; Dorian 1994; Douglas-Cowie 1975, 1978, 1984; Douglas-Cowie & Cowie 1979; Labov 1972; Milroy & Gordon 2003: 78; Kingsmore 1995; Omoniyi 2004: 33–34; Pitts 1982, 1985, 1986; Smith & Durham 2019: 26). In urban contexts, social structures in such spaces (at least in the western world) can engender personal communication networks that can be of the weak or strong type (Milroy 1992: 212; Milroy & Milroy 1992). This is due to the extent of social and other types of mobility as well as the degree of fragmentation between different domains that often accompanies city living (see Britain 2004, 2012, 2013, 2017; Milroy 1987a,b; Milroy 1992; Milroy & Gordon 2003; Milroy & Milroy 1985, 1992).

---

101 See Belfast Area Plan (2015) at https://www.planningni.gov.uk/downloads/volume_1_-_plan_strategy___framework-2.pdf (last accessed 19 July 2019).

102 The 2011 Census which superseded the NISRA classificatory document, records the population as now being marginally outside of that cut-off point but this descriptor remains more apt for this settlement than any other. See also Corrigan (2010: 12–14) and https://www.ninis2.nisra.gov.uk/public/documents/ur_report.pdf (last accessed 19 July 2019).

6.1.1.1 Armagh City

Corrigan (1997, Chapter Five, §2) explores the social history and settlement of Armagh where the County capital, Armagh City, is situated in more detail than is possible in this context. In sum, as the arguments in earlier Chapters contend, Armagh has been inhabited from as early as the Mesolithic period and became so successful as a Christian monastic centre that it fell prey to Viking raids in 832 AD (see Chapter Two, §§2.1.1–2.1.2.1). During this period the *Codex Armachanus* ('Book of Armagh') or Canon of Patrick was completed. It is a diglossic illuminated manuscript written in both Latin and Old Irish that contains early religious texts tied to St. Patrick (closely associated with the City, as already mentioned) as well as an almost complete copy of the New Testament.[103] By the Middle Ages, on account of its continued importance as the "Archbishoprick" where the Lord Primate of all Ireland had his seat (Coote 1804/1984: 18–21), the city will have supported speakers of Irish Gaelic, Latin, Norman French and Medieval English, as illustrated by the Armagh Diocesan Registry documents from 1428–1444 in Figure 4 of Chapter Two. The extent of top-notch agricultural land within the County boundaries made it a prime target for the plantation policies of successive Elizabethan and Jacobite schemes, and it was also subject to private colonising enterprises such as those of the Ayrshire Scot, James Hamilton, illustrated for the Fews barony in the south of the County in Figure 5 of the same Chapter. It is here that the distinctive dialect of South Ulster English is now spoken (see Figure 42 above). It is hardly surprising therefore that while Irish was maintained in the County's southernmost reaches until the twentieth century, because the mountainous land there was less favourable, the area in and around the County capital to the north and west was already predominantly English-speaking by the 1770s. This is indicated by the fact that only 6% of the population in the barony of Tiranny, where Armagh is situated, is estimated to have been Irish-speaking by this time (see Figure 17 of Chapter Three and §4.4.1 of Chapter Four).

The linguistic situation in twenty-first century Armagh City is, however, rather more diverse. Firstly, there is now excellent evidence of revival Irish associated with the County capital which boasts a post-primary Irish-Medium Unit ('*An Sruth Gaeilge*') at St. Celine's which took part in the *Múin Béarla* project. It opened in 2002, and, by the time of its most recent Education Inspection, the enrolment stood at 152.[104] Moreover, in 2018, the Chief Executive of the Department of Education for Northern Ireland ratified the establishment of a new grant-

---

[103] The manuscript is now housed in Trinity College, Dublin. See Casey (2014) for a full history.
[104] On-going industrial action over teachers' pay has thwarted this process ever since so the figure here refers to the 2013 report (see https://www.etini.gov.uk/news/chief-inspectors-report-2016-2018 – last accessed 27 April 2020).

aided co-educational other maintained Irish-Medium Primary School in the City to meet the growing demand for places.[105] Secondly, Armagh City, as with many urban and rural areas of the migrant dense Armagh, Bainbridge and Craigavon LGD referred to earlier, has benefitted greatly from the influx of newcomers since the EU expansion legislation documented in previous Chapters (the figure for the LGD as a whole in the 2011 Census was 5.4%).[106] Thus, while the overall population of Armagh City (those aged 3+) stood at 14,749 in the 2011 Census (Russell 2015: 7), 1,392 residents were born either elsewhere in the EU (though not in the Republic of Ireland or the United Kingdom)[107] or in another nation state. Moreover, the City's population has grown exponentially since the figures for the 1981 Census were released when it had just 12,700 residents. What is more, there were two wards in Armagh City in the 2011 Census (Callan Bridge and The Mall) where 10% or more of usual residents were born either in the EU 12 countries or outside of the EU (Russell 2013: 22–23). More than 40% of the city's population is now aged between 0 and 29 years old and the vast majority (9,407) declared their religious persuasion to be "Roman Catholic". As well as reflecting the faith background of Northern Ireland's autochthonous ethnic minority (see Corrigan 2010: 24–27 for definitions), this figure now also no doubt includes the numerous Lithuanian, Polish and Portuguese migrants who have recently taken up residence in Armagh.[108] In addition (and notwithstanding the issues associated with the "Main Language" question in population censuses referred to in Chapter Four, §4.2), 12,986 respondents in the 2011 equivalent declared this to be English (91.96%, when the Northern Ireland average was 96.86%). Gaelic was chosen by 56 individuals (0.4%) when the regional norm was 0.24%, but the numbers of Lithuanian and Polish speakers were considerably higher (2.97% and 1.83%, respectively). Indeed, the figures for residents whose "Main Language" was Lithuanian here are eight times greater than those across Northern Ireland (see also Krausova & Vargas-Silva 2014: 11 which likewise notes their concentration in Armagh and Dungannon). There are also noticeably more Polish, Latvian (0.69%), Russian (0.35%) and Malayalam (0.16%) speakers too than is typical for the region as a

---

105 The proposed case is set out at: https://www.education-ni.gov.uk/publications/dp-569-irish-medium-primary-school-armagh-city – last accessed 27 April 2020.
106 Armagh City, Banbridge and Craigavon Borough Communities Report, 2016 (https://www.armaghbanbridgecraigavon.gov.uk/download/125/communities-workshops/13650/communities-baseline-report.pdf – last accessed 27 April 2020).
107 These figures stand at 538 respondents for the Republic and 622 for elsewhere in the UK.
108 There were 3,273 members of "other Christian" religions (in the Armagh context this will be Church of Ireland or Presbyterian predominantly); 97 from other religious backgrounds and 799 who declared that they did not follow any religion at all.

whole.¹⁰⁹ The increased linguistic diversity of the latter is also reflected in Armagh City where 0.11% of the population are Slovak speakers and Chinese (0.2%), Portuguese (0.09%), Hungarian (0.06%) and Tagalog/Filipino (0.05%) are also recorded as "Main language". Figure 44 illustrates the entire range declared by residents over the age of 3 and it also captures the relative strengths of these communities within the City limits. These responses are set against the Northern Ireland averages, already introduced in Chapter Four, Figure 33 for comparative purposes. The graph clearly demonstrates the extent of linguistic diversity which recent migratory patterns have induced as well as the demolinguistic differences between Armagh and the region more broadly.

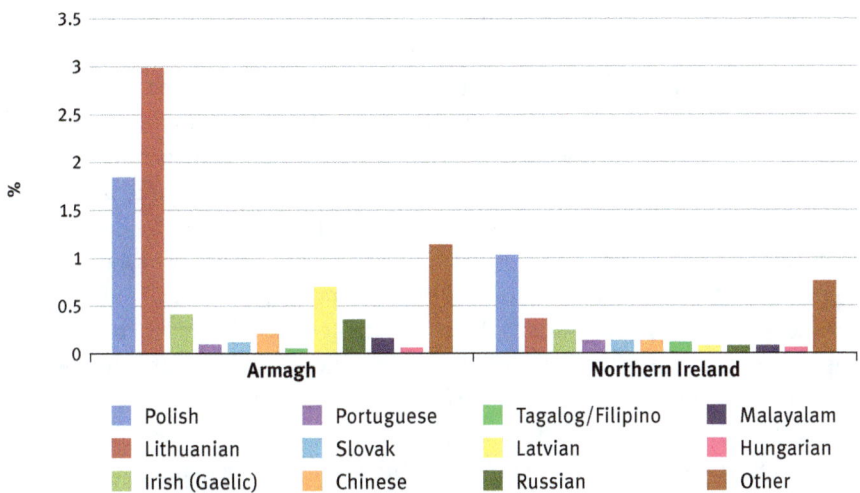

Figure 44 Main Languages other than English of those residing in Armagh City and Northern Ireland as a percentage of the population (aged 3+).¹¹⁰

It is obvious from this data that EU enlargement groups are particularly attracted to Armagh City and its environs but that there are also communities now settled there from further afield too. In fact, 9.4% of its entire population was born outside either the UK or Republic of Ireland according to the 2011 Census (Russell

---

109 See further: https://www.citypopulation.de/php/uk-northernireland.php?cityid=N11000051 and NINIS Main Language: KS2071 (Settlement 2015; https://www.ninis2.nisra.gov.uk/public/Theme.aspx?themeNumber=136&themeName=Census+2011 – last accessed 17 July 2019).
110 The languages included here are those with over 1,000 responses, as noted at https://www.ninis2.nisra.gov.uk/public/Metadata.aspx?ds=6653&lh=74&yn=2011&sk=136&sn=Census%202011&yearfilter= – last accessed 19 July 2019.

2015: 14). The pull factors will be similar to those already articulated for Northern Ireland more broadly in Chapter Four and indeed they are analogous to the reasons why autochthonous populations remain or return (and indeed to those forces that fuelled the colonisation of the region in the Early Modern period). In particular, while employment type is not especially diversified by comparison to a capital city such as Belfast discussed below, low waged jobs are plentiful in Agri-food businesses nearby such as Monaghan Mushrooms and Moy Park, previously examined in Chapters One and Four, as well as in the local restaurant/hotel and retail sectors. Indeed, a Department for the Economy recent report (2018: 20) notes that: "EU (26) born workers were underrepresented in high skilled occupations and overrepresented (28 %) in low skilled occupations" which would support this view. There are employment opportunities too for more skilled residents who undertake health care roles in Craigavon hospital, less than twenty minutes from the city centre, as well as in education. It is noteworthy though that almost 70 % of the occupations declared by Armagh's inhabitants in the 2011 Census are not amongst the highest earning roles (such as managerial or professional) but instead are in the lower earning bands (sales, machine operatives and other routine occupations of this sort) (Russell 2015: 27–28). Despite its city status, this lack of occupational diversity and the relative scarcity of manufacturing/construction industries or upper tier employment in either global financial, legal or other similar institutions, living in Armagh is probably much more like the experience one might have of residing in a modest urban settlement where there is a reasonably high degree of social cohesiveness. It remains to be seen, of course, whether this is reflected at all in the linguistic choices made by the young autochthonous and allochthonous *Múin Béarla* participants whose sociodemographic characteristics will be outlined further in § 6.2.1.

6.1.1.2 Donaghmore village

This area of County Tyrone, Northern Ireland has been inhabited since at least the Bronze Age (see Chapter Two, § 2.1.1), as evidenced by the presence of megalithic remains (stone circles and cairns) nearby such as that of the Beaghmore site illustrated in Figure 45 and analysed in Coyle (2014: 25) as well as various contributions to Ginn, Enlander & Crozier (2014).

The contemporary NISRA "Small Village" status of Donaghmore very much belies the origin of its Gaelic place-name *Domnach Mór* ('the great church')[111] which instead reflected its more exalted earlier prominence as the site of an

---

[111] See: McKay (2007: 58) and http://www.placenamesni.org/resultdetails.php?entry=10570, last accessed 19 July 2019.

Figure 45 Beaghmore Stone Circle, Co. Tyrone[112]

important abbey, also traditionally thought to have been founded by St. Patrick (Coyle 2014: 47). According to Lewis (1837), the settlement flourished, acquiring extensive lands, shrines and other costly material goods between the 9th century and the Middle Ages. It is situated in the south east of County Tyrone and belongs to the Mid Ulster LGD. Donaghmore is just two miles north west of the major urban settlement of Dungannon where the population has increased by 30% since the last Census in 2001 and 25% of its inhabitants were born outside either the UK or the Republic of Ireland (Russell 2015: 3, 9).

Donaghmore is also only 30 minutes' drive from Armagh City. In fact, from an ecclesiastical perspective, it too eventually came to belong to the Armagh "Archbishoprick" following the Henricine Reformation discussed in Chapter Two, §2.2.2. Coote (1804/1984: 20–21), for instance, reports the village to owe seventy pounds annually to the Archbishop of Armagh as documented in "the first fruits of the ecclesiastical benefices ... from the original record" (see also Lewis 1837, who by then puts the tithes at just over eight hundred and thirty pounds which reflects its growing prosperity in the early nineteenth century). Like Armagh itself,

---

[112] Image courtesy of Kevin Lagan and reproduced with permission.

Donaghmore, in fact, also has an important Christian heritage represented by a High Cross placed near the contemporary Roman Catholic Church but thought to date from as early as the tenth century (Coyle 2014: 28). Lewis (1837) notes that it was "mutilated" in the course of the 1641 rebellion, documented in Chapter Two, §2.4. This was likely on account of Donaghmore's indigenous Gaelic military connections during the Cromwellian wars, led by Hugh O'Neill, Earl of Tyrone and Rory O'Donnell, Earl of Tyrconnell.

The layout of the contemporary village dates back to the improvements of the enlightenment era documented in Chapter Three. Lewis (1837) describes the resulting settlement as "flourishing" once more supporting a major brewery producing an annual output of 10,500 barrels, a successful brick works and businesses manufacturing candles and soap. Farmers and weavers in the environs of Donaghmore also made key contributions to the burgeoning linen trade, detailed in Chapter Three. Unsurprisingly, therefore, the population of the settlement and surrounding parish at this time was more similar to that of contemporary Armagh since Lewis (1837) documents it to be "12,144 inhabitants." However, successive Censuses of Ireland from 1851 onwards testify to the devastating impact upon the area of the mortality and migration instigated by the Great Famine recounted in Chapter Three, §3.3. Donaghmore's population declined dramatically from its early nineteenth century heyday to a mere 430 people in 1851 and reduced again to only 234 in 1891 (see MacAfee 2000).[113] The 2011 Census records the fact that its population has now recovered somewhat, since the number of inhabitants was recorded as 1076, over 89% of whom declared themselves to be "Roman Catholic". A major component of the increase in residents with this background is the developments approved by the Planning Service of Northern Ireland's Department of the Environment both within the village limits and also across the greater Dungannon region in 2005, prior to the onset of the *Múin Béarla* project. It coincided with a greater demand for schools, housing and leisure facilities in the early 2000s prior to the global recession of 2007–2008 (see Chapter Four, Figure 25). This was generated by better employment opportunities in local businesses relating to an expanding service sector, alongside the buoyancy of longer-standing industries associated with engineering, food processing and mineral extraction. The timeframe of these changes, of course, also overlapped with the EU enlargement legislation already noted, which increased immigration to the region from predominantly Roman Catholic countries such as Poland. This initiative permitted the erection of new housing clusters and the expansion of educational opportunities within the greater Dungannon region, including the creation

---

[113] See: http://www.dippam.ac.uk/eppi/documents/13130/eppi_pages/336881 and http://www.dippam.ac.uk/eppi/documents/18814/eppi_pages/505464 (accessed on 19th July 2019).

of St. Peter's primary, Donaghmore, which became one of the project's participating schools.[114]

The changes in the demolinguistic profile of the village are clear from Figure 46 below which records the number of speakers over the age of 3 whose main languages were other than English.[115] What is especially striking here when compared to the previous set for Armagh, illustrated in Figure 44, is the reduction in the range of European languages spoken including Irish (Gaelic) and Hungarian but also those from the continent of Asia that featured in the Armagh data (i.e. Chinese, Malayalam and Tagalog/Filipino).[116] The number of speakers of Lithuanian as a "Main Language" is, by contrast, higher than the Northern Ireland average (0.93% versus 0.36%). However, the Armagh reversal for the pattern characterising Northern Ireland as a whole whereby speakers of Lithuanian greatly outnumber those who claimed Polish as their "Main Language" is not replicated here. Indeed, speakers of the latter are four times more prevalent in Donaghmore as a percentage of the population (4.28%) than they are on average for the region more broadly (1.02%).

It is also noteworthy that despite the fact that the main post-primary in Donaghmore, St. Joseph's, also has an Irish-Medium Unit (whose excellence was recognised as one of only seven such schools in 2016 by *Comhairle na Gaelscolaíochta*)[117] there is not a single individual in the village who declared Irish (Gaelic) to be their "Main Language" in the 2011 Census. This contrasts markedly with Armagh and, as we will see below, with Belfast where the language features much more prominently in this context. Another interesting difference between the demolinguistics of Donaghmore, the Northern Ireland average and the larger settlements that are the focus here is the number of inhabitants who claimed Portuguese as their "Main Language" (0.28%). Across the whole of Northern Ireland, this figure is less than half of that and in Armagh it is just 0.09%, as already noted, while it is even lower in Belfast (0.06%). The predominance of speakers whose heritage is Portuguese (and also Lithuanian and Polish) in Donaghmore

---
114 See: https://www.planningni.gov.uk/index/policy/development_plans/devplans_az/dungannon2010-adopted-plan.pdf, last accessed 19 July 2019.
115 These figures derive from: NINIS Main Language: KS2071 (Settlement 2015): https://www.ninis2.nisra.gov.uk/public/Theme.aspx?themeNumber=136&themeName=Census+2011, last accessed 17 July 2019.
116 Data for these languages is not represented in Figure 46 for either Donaghmore or Northern Ireland as the returns for the former are all 0%. See: NINIS Main Language: KS2071 (Settlement 2015): https://www.ninis2.nisra.gov.uk/public/Theme.aspx?themeNumber=136&themeName=Census+2011, last accessed 17 July 2019. Figures 45 and 47 show the figures for Northern Ireland.
117 This is the representative body for Irish-Medium Education set up by the Department of Education in 2000.

may well reflect the much narrower range of occupations available to migrant workers in this "Small Village" than there are elsewhere in Northern Ireland. As noted in Chapter Four, §4.2.1.2, large Agri-food businesses such as Dunbia (just 7 minutes outside of the village) attract employees who are either unskilled or who have arrived without qualifications in English (Department for the Economy 2018: 2, 20, 27). This situation has been exacerbated following the 2007–2008 recession where the type of small and medium enterprises that often employ more skilled migrant workers in this region have experienced a "sharp drop in 5-year survival rates for new firms" (Bailey 2015: 3). It is important to note too, of course, that recent analyses by the Department for the Economy (2018: 2) has shown unequivocally that since then: "Northern Ireland has been almost entirely reliant on employment from EU (26) migrants for the growth in employment levels particularly from 2013 to 2017", i.e. during the period of the *Múin Béarla* project. Unsurprisingly, therefore, the same report notes that economic activity across the whole of Northern Ireland is highest amongst those whose country of birth was either in the EU (26) (83%) or the rest of the world (74%) (Department for the Economy 2018: 19).

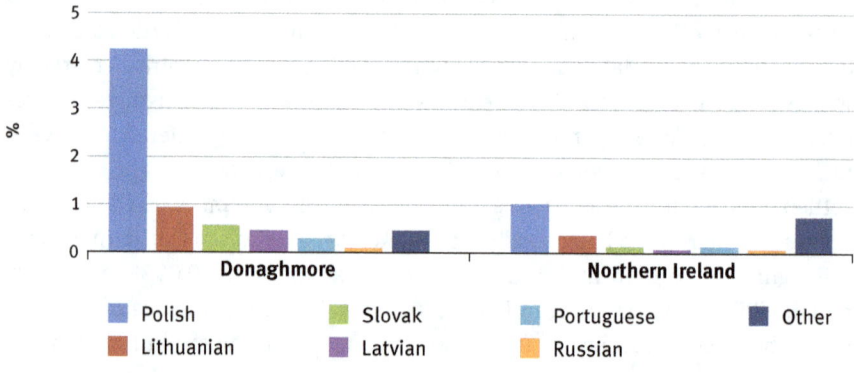

Figure 46 Main Languages other than English of those residing in Donaghmore and Northern Ireland as a percentage of the population (aged 3+)

6.1.1.3 Belfast City

Belfast has been synonymous with sociolinguistics ever since the *Speech Community and Language Variety in Belfast* and *Sociolinguistic Variation and Linguistic Change in Belfast* projects were undertaken by James and Lesley Milroy from the late 1970s onwards, at the height of the so-called "Troubles", discussed in some depth in Chapter Four, §4.1 (see Corrigan 1990, 1997; Harris 1984, 1985; Milroy 1987a,b; Milroy & Harris 1980; Milroy & Gordon 2003; Milroy & Milroy 1977, 1985,

1992, 1993; Pitts 1985, 1986 *inter alia*). This research explored socio-phonetic and socio-syntactic variables typical of this variety of Mid-Ulster English (including the system of relativisation detailed in Chapter Eight). It focused on speakers from inner and outer city Belfast as well as the suburban location of Lurgan, County Armagh with a particular focus on the function of personal network as an extralinguistic variable.

The external history of Belfast has already featured prominently in Chapters Three and Four so it does not require rehearsing further in any detail. In summary, the city played a crucial role as an internal migratory location for Famine victims seeking relief in the Victorian era as well as a focal point for emigrants with enough financial resources behind them to settle beyond Ireland's ravished shores. Its role as a major port was key in this respect. Indeed, Belfast's location at the confluence of the rivers Farset[118] and Lagan precipitated economic migratory movements in the industrial age as the city developed into a global powerhouse for the manufacture of linen and the construction of both ships and airplanes, captured in Figure 47.

In the post-industrial era, inward investment as a response to the cessation of violence has changed the economic base of Belfast from manufacturing and heavy industry to a city that offers employment opportunities within the service sector as well as in the creative/knowledge industries and technology (Belfast City Council 2018). However, as Hodson (2019: 232) also contends, as with many urban spaces in Northern Ireland, it remains "segregated, with eighty per cent of the population living in sectarian neighbourhoods." The divisions between the autochthonous ethnic minority and majority communities are thus important to observe from the perspective of language variation and change research. Although the Milroys' sociolinguistic analyses in the inner-city East Belfast community they targeted did not uncover linguistic features that indexed this very significant social attribution (Milroy & Milroy 1997: 210–211), this is not true of McCafferty (1998), (1999) and (2001) which explored Derry/Londonderry English. Instead, he found that the ethnic boundary actually had very important impacts on, for instance, the rapidity with which linguistic changes penetrated Roman Catholic versus Protestant cohorts of speakers in his study. As such, while the 2011 Census showed that the population of Belfast was much more evenly distributed from this perspective than the other fieldwork sites (where a majority of residents

---

118 Hence, the source of the original Irish place-name *Béal Feirste* 'mouth of the sand-bank ford (Farset)', according to McKay (1999: 21). It can be seen on the top left-hand side of the image inside the "hoop" of a famous landmark known as the Beacon of Hope sculpted by Andy Scott in 2007. The globe at her feet (not depicted here) has marked on its surface the cities where the people and industries of Belfast migrated and exported to.

Figure 47 Collage Image of Belfast taken by the author at arrivals, Belfast International Airport, 23rd June 2017[119]

---

[119] Original artwork by Melissa Houston and used with permission.

declared that they were Roman Catholic), the participants specifically targeted for this research in all three locations are being raised in the latter faith.[120] This is to ensure that any ethnic differences amongst population samples which emerge in the analyses that follow in subsequent Chapters are not, in fact, influenced by this potentially salient social factor. Post-industrial Belfast like elsewhere in Northern Ireland has witnessed increased ethnic and religious diversity beyond this autochthonous division arising from the arrival of new economic migrants. Indeed, Russell (2016: 6) reports that "[b]irths to non-UK born mothers have not been equally spread across Northern Ireland: the largest number of such births have occurred in Belfast" (alongside the south and west regions which are represented here by Armagh and Donaghmore, respectively). Moreover, while 96.69% of the population are "White", Belfast is the most "ethnically diverse council in Northern Ireland" (Belfast City Council 2018: 3). These recent population changes have had concomitant effects on the language ecology of the city, highlighted in Figure 48 to which I now turn.

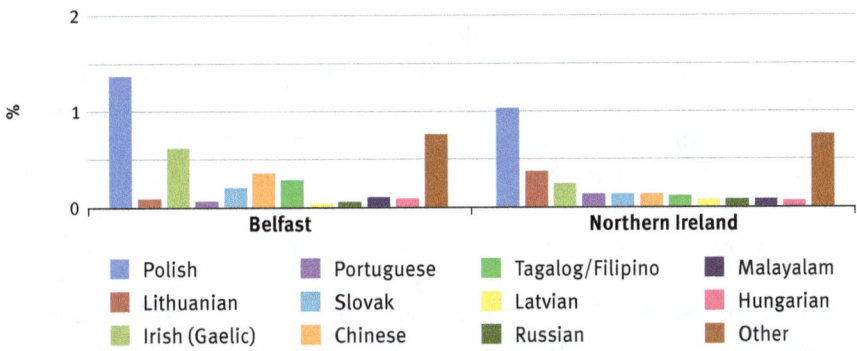

Figure 48 Main Languages other than English of those residing in Belfast and Northern Ireland as a percentage of the population (aged 3+)[121]

269,010 or 95.21% of respondents to the 2011 Census in the capital claimed that their main language was English so, unlike the figures for Armagh (91.96%) and Donaghmore (92.94%), the inhabitants of the metropolitan area have English

---

120 According to Russell 2015: 12, the figures for Belfast are: 48.6% Roman Catholic and 42.3% Protestant.
121 See Russell (2013) and NINIS Main Language: KS2071 (Settlement 2015): https://www.ninis2.nisra.gov.uk/public/Theme.aspx?themeNumber=136&themeName=Census+2011, last accessed 17 July 2019.

language skills which are rather more in line with the Northern Ireland average (96.86%) than those who reside in either of the two smaller settlements. Naturally, there may be any number of reasons for this. One might speculate, though, that the types of migrant attracted to opportunities in Belfast may well have a rather different socio-economic profile that includes English qualifications prior to arrival, by comparison to those who migrate to work in the Agri-food businesses that so typify the low-skilled work undertaken by migrant groups (principally the Lithuanians, Poles and Portuguese) in both Armagh and Donaghmore. As Figure 48 also demonstrates, other differences are discernible too, particularly the number of Lithuanian speakers in Belfast, which is noticeably closer in the capital to the Northern Ireland average than the higher figures for either Armagh or Donaghmore, which seem especially attractive to this allochthonous group. In addition, those who claimed Chinese to be their "Main Language" in Belfast (0.35%) is higher than the Northern Ireland average (0.13%) and more common than it is in either Armagh (0.2%) or Donaghmore (0%). These figures may well reflect a long-standing trend identified in Chapter Four, §4.2 for Chinese migrants to settle in eastern regions of Northern Ireland and in Belfast, in particular, i.e. following in the wake of bridgeheads who had already established themselves during migratory inflows of the previous century. The number of speakers of Tagalog/Filipino in Belfast (0.28%) is also comparatively high with respect not only to the Northern Ireland average (0.11%) but also to the small numbers from the Philippines who claim this to be their "Main Language" in Armagh (0.05%) and Donaghmore (0%). Hence, of the three participating schools across these two latter areas, only two Filipinos were located for interview in the *Múin Béarla* project (Melchor Nogoy whose community of practice is discussed in §5.2.1 of the previous Chapter and who attended St. Benedict's, Armagh as well as Rosejean Uy who was registered at St. Celine's, Armagh). By contrast, there were three Filipino children who volunteered in just the one school in Belfast. All of their mothers were nurses which is not surprising as this migrant group dominates in health and medical services. As such, they naturally tend to gravitate to larger settlements like Belfast where there are greater opportunities for this type of work and where there is already a long-standing Asian culture (see Chapter Four, §4.2.1.2 and Bell, Jarman & Lefebvre 2004: 5 as well as McElhinney 2009: 36).

Section 4.2.1.1 of Chapter Four records the history of language planning and revitalisation efforts associated with Irish Gaelic in twenty-first century Northern Ireland and Belfast has been at the heart of these movements, with the establishment there from the late twentieth century of a revival urban *Gaeltacht* in Shaw's Road, Belfast (known as *Pobal Feirste* 'People of the Farset') as well as numerous Irish-Medium schools from nursery to post-primary (see Antonini 2012; Antonini, Corrigan & Wei 2002; de Brún 2005). It is hardly surprising, therefore, that the capital boasted the highest figures of all the study sites for inhabitants claiming Irish (Gaelic) to be their "Main Language" in the 2011 Census (0.61 %).

Of interest too with respect to the capital, is the fact that while the figures for Polish speakers here is slightly higher than the Northern Ireland average, it is lower than either of the smaller settlements just discussed. Moreover, the number of Belfast's inhabitants claiming either Lithuanian or Portuguese as their "Main Language" in the 2011 Census is not only less than the Northern Ireland average but there are considerably fewer such communities here than there are in Armagh or Donaghmore. This may well be related to the nature of employment in the city which supports a higher number of residents (37.7 %) in professional and managerial occupations for which such newcomers may not be qualified. In support of this view, a recent Department for the Economy report on migration, labour and skills in Northern Ireland based on analyses of the 2011 Census and other similar data stated that:

> In terms of skill levels, and compared to Northern Ireland born residents, Census 2011 results indicate that Republic of Ireland and rest of the world born workers had much higher rates of level 4 and above qualifications.[122] Compared to Northern Ireland born residents, EU (26) born workers had much higher rates of 'other' qualifications which included work or vocational qualifications or qualifications gained outside the UK. This qualification level distinction to Northern Ireland born workers was reflected in the concentration of these workers at different occupational levels. Republic of Ireland and rest of the world born workers had higher rates of employment in professional occupations whilst EU (26) born workers had higher rates of employment in elementary occupations, process plant and machine operation occupations and also in skilled trades.

Finally, it is worth noting too that a very high proportion of Belfast's population (1.59 %) claimed "Other Languages" as their "Main Language" in the 2011 Census which likely reflects the attraction of rest of the world born workers to the higher tier employment types on offer within the capital. This figure is much greater than the Northern Ireland average of 0.75 % and while it is only slightly higher than that for Armagh (1.13 %), it is a considerable increase on the figure for Donaghmore (0.46 %), which has already been seen to be attractive to a much narrower range of allochthonous inhabitants on account of its size, rural location and available sectors of employment. It is for these reasons no doubt that the Belfast study site (St. Agnes's) generated participants whose home languages were as diverse as "Italian", "Telugu" and "Yoruba".

---

[122] This is a UK wide measure. In summary, Level 4 means at least a certificate of higher education or a higher apprenticeship or a higher national certificate. For further detail, see: https://www.gov.uk/what-different-qualification-levels-mean/list-of-qualification-levels, last accessed 20 July 2019.

6.1.2 Sociocultural context of participating schools

To preserve anonymity for the four schools which volunteered to participate in the project, this section focuses on details of their size and language ecologies that are exclusively relevant to the methodology and thus ignores other aspects of their educational environments such as achievements in state examinations which could lead to their being identified.[123]

All the schools which participated in this study are so-called "Catholic Maintained Schools". Educational providers within these are controlled by Boards of Governors nominated by trustees, along with parents, teachers and Education Authority representatives. The Council for Catholic Maintained Schools (CCMS) is responsible for the effective management of these schools and it is also the employing authority for all their teachers. It has been extremely useful in gaining access and permission to work in this sector that I am personally acquainted with members of the Educational Standards team at CCMS. In addition, my father acted on St. Benedict's Board of Governors for several years and was also a member of the CCMS Council. This association, alongside "linguistic gratuity" (Wolfram, Reaser & Vaughan 2008) outreach work that I had conducted in St. Benedict's, connected to an earlier UK research council funded project, greatly facilitated my involving the school in the new *Múin Béarla* initiative. As for St. Celine's, I am a former pupil and have undertaken sociolinguistic engagement projects there too, including continuing professional development events on multilingualism for teaching staff working within the Irish-Medium Unit. At the time of recording, I also had family members attending both this school and St. Peter's where I likewise offered outreach events including a whole school assembly for pupils and staff on language, migration and identity. Moreover, one of my siblings is not only a teacher but the Special Educational Needs coordinator at St. Agnes's and thus has considerable contact with newcomers and their families. Pupils, as well as members of the teaching team there, participated in interviews for an earlier UK research council funded project that also included a masterclass for pupils on local accents and dialects.

6.1.2.1 Post-primaries: St. Benedict's and St. Celine's, Armagh

Around the time when the *Múin Béarla* project began, St. Benedict's had an enrolment of just 218 pupils and they were drawn from various primary schools

---

[123] The schools data presented here is an amalgamation of information kindly provided by the principals; official reports from Northern Ireland's Education and Training Inspectorate on all four schools and statistics generated specifically for this project by Rachel Grumley, Paul Matthews and Leonie Robinson of the Department of Education for Northern Ireland to whom I am also grateful.

in Armagh City as well as its rural hinterland. It is a non-selective school for boys aged between 11 and 16.[124] The school identified 21% of its pupils as requiring additional learning support and in the region of 43% of attendees were entitled to free school meals (a socio-economic marker in a UK context associated with levels of deprivation, as Taylor (2017) also argues). There were thirty-one newcomer pupils attending the school altogether, and twenty-five of these consented to participate from a range of heritage backgrounds.[125] There were also twenty-four autochthonous individuals interviewed whose families had lived in Armagh for generations.

St. Celine's is a considerably larger non-selective school with an intake of over 1,100 pupils, almost all of whom are young women.[126] They are drawn from slightly further afield than those attending St. Benedict's (including larger urban centres such as Portadown which only has one Roman Catholic 11–16 post-primary and which does not offer state examinations).[127] 7% of the enrolment at the time when the interviews were conducted were newcomer pupils. 22.8% of its attendees were entitled to free school meals and over 15% were registered as having special educational needs. The newcomer intake was eighty-three pupils. Thirty-four of these young women were interviewed as part of the project alongside twenty-one local students who had long-standing family connections to the City. Two of the latter were young men who were attending the Irish-Medium Unit.

Apart from the relative sizes of the schools, coupled with the almost exclusively female intake at St. Celine's and the male-only enrolment at St. Benedict's, there are enough commonalities between these two schools as regards the age ranges of the pupils (12–20 years);[128] the level of special education support required

---

[124] Namely, pupils are not admitted on the basis of academic ability. Other Northern Irish schools are selective and entry to these (essentially grammar schools) depends on the outcome of a transfer test at age 11+. See: https://www.goodschoolsguide.co.uk/choosing-a-school/northern-ireland-education-system and https://www.nidirect.gov.uk/articles/types-school (last accessed on 24 July 2019).

[125] As a reminder, "Newcomer" is a term defined by the Department of Education for Northern Ireland as "a pupil who does not have satisfactory language skills to participate fully in the school curriculum and does not have a language in common with the teacher." See: Chapter Four, § 4.2.

[126] Most of the boys who attend (64 of them) are attached to the school's Irish-Medium Unit already discussed in § 6.1.1.1.

[127] This too is in the Mid-Ulster dialect region and is just fifteen minutes away by car.

[128] The 20-year old speaker is an aberration with respect to the norm for the post-primary sector including these two schools. She was a newcomer who struggled to pass state examinations on account of her competence levels in English and so was repeating her final year. The vast majority of participants in Armagh were actually aged 18 or younger and, on average across both schools, most speakers were in their mid to late teens.

for them; and the socio-economic and heritage backgrounds of their populations to make comparisons between participants possible. This would likewise include their Roman Catholic ethos and non-selective status, in particular, since grammar schools are more likely to attract middle class pupils who are not newcomers (Perry 2016) and this is not the profile of either St. Benedict's or St. Celine's, especially given their high rates of pupils qualifying for free school meals.[129] Indeed, a Transinfo report on newcomer pupil numbers in Northern Ireland post-primaries published in 2016 stated that 89% of the non-selective school intake across the region were designated as such. As noted in Chapter Four, §4.2, newcomers now constitute 4.7% of Northern Ireland's school-going population so the fact that St. Benedict's and St. Celine's have populations that vary from between 7% and 15% puts them both well above average in this respect. Across both schools, the heritage backgrounds of newcomer pupils are commensurate with the language ecology of Armagh City more broadly, as described in §6.1.1.1 and this is detailed further in §6.2.3.

6.1.2.2 Primaries: St. Agnes's, Belfast and St. Peter's, Donaghmore

The enrolment of St. Agnes's Primary School has remained steady, increasing slightly to 810 children around the time that the *Múin Béarla* project was conducted. 16% of the pupils were entitled to free school meals and 17% of them were identified as requiring extra support with aspects of their learning. Unsurprisingly, given the changes in the language ecology of Belfast considered here and in Chapter Four, §4.2, there has been an increase in the number of newcomer families enrolling in recent years. Thus, in the decade between the school years 2006/2007 and 2016/2017, the figures rose from just 5 to 89. At the time of the interviews for this study, the newcomer population was also higher than the Northern Ireland average, as was the case with the two post-primaries just discussed, and it represented over 7% of the entire cohort attending this school. Eighteen allochthonous and twenty-seven autochthonous pupils consented to be interviewed for the project.[130] Their home languages reflected the 2011 Census

---

129 This system mirrors a common trend in Northern Ireland towards single-gender post-primary education, as detailed in Smith (1995).
130 As before, consent for participants in the two primaries was also obtained from the school and parents using the same techniques used for the post-primaries (see §§6.1 and 6.2.1). Agreement was sought from the pupils formally too but, given their age, this process also involved a lengthy informal discussion prior to recording. This was so as to ensure that they understood what was being asked of them; what its purpose was; that there was no pressure on them to continue and that they could stop at any point. This conversation was conducted in a manner that was commensurate with their capacities and interests, following the good practice of Alderson

returns for the city already considered, including a wider range of "Other" languages than in any of the other schools (see §6.2.3).

St. Peter's Primary School pupil numbers have increased gradually in recent years and during the interview phase of the project there were 208. This change reflects the region's attractiveness to migrant populations already exemplified in §6.1.1.2 boosting newcomer numbers between 2006/2007 and 2017/2018 from 0 to 21. In fact, its newcomer population overall (11%) at the time of the study was also in line with those of the other three schools by being much higher than the regional average. Approximately 26% of the children here were entitled to free school meals and 13% of them were identified as requiring extra interventions with aspects of their learning. Eighteen youngsters with an indigenous heritage agreed to participate and nineteen newcomers took part. The latter had main languages in the rather narrow band already identified for this region by the 2011 Census and consisted exclusively of Lithuanian, Polish and Portuguese (see §6.2.3).

The age range of participants from St. Agnes's and St. Peter's is largely commensurate with that of the sector more broadly, i.e. 5–11 years old. As was the case with the post-primaries, these two schools do differ, however, in terms of their relative sizes and this will be an important factor to consider in future research examining the language, identity and the comparability of the migrant experience in small rural *versus* large urban settings. There is also another difference worth considering longer term and that is the largely single-gender character of the Armagh schools versus the mixed gender nature of the primaries. For present purposes, it is sufficient, however, to note the similarities between all the schools with respect to their CCMS statuses, their socio-economic and special educational needs profiles, their higher than average newcomer populations and the fact that the home languages of pupils in each school match the "Main Language" types identified in Armagh, Belfast and Donaghmore by the Census 2011 returns.

6.2 The *Múin Béarla* corpus

6.2.1 Context of the interviews

As already noted, my pre-existing personal relationships with the staff teams and pupils at each of these four schools was key to recruiting research participants. It was also important from the perspective of studying vernacular language, despite Eckert's (1997b: 58) misgivings that "conventional sociolinguistic wisdom tells us that schools and other normative institutions are highly

---

& Morrow (2004) as well as the British Association of Applied Linguistics guidelines (https://baalweb.files.wordpress.com/2017/08/goodpractice_full.pdf, accessed 25th July 2019).

problematic sites for the study of the vernacular." However, as she has also argued in support of her own choice of fieldwork site in the Belten High School study, in the Western world at least, educational establishments are central to the social lives of children. As such, they are not always the locus simply of standard speech. Moreover, Rampton's studies in the UK also support the view that the vernacular (and indeed crossing between different language practices) is not at all unusual in multi-ethnic school contexts such as those which are the focus here (Rampton 2006). The same is true of the research by Stenström (2014) which examines spontaneous teen talk in two other corpora collected in school settings (the *Bergen Corpus of London Teenage Language* (COLT) and *Corpus Oral de Lenguaje Adolescente de Madrid* (COLA)). I would argue that what Eckert (1997b) really intends here is that the rhythm and routine of certain aspects of school life exert pressure to conform to standard language. However, there are other domains in this same environment which encourage the opposite. As such, in each school, I set about constructing contexts for eliciting natural speech that were as non-normative as possible and ensured that my presence did not render the pupils "speechless", as Smith & Durham (2019: 30–31) report when they attempted to engage with another cohort of children in Buckie, Scotland. To that end, the schools were very obliging in allowing me to create quiet, relaxed interview spaces which were situated as far as possible from the main teaching and learning areas. A range of different types of seating were offered including bean bags, cushions, easy chairs and the like which could be rearranged by each interviewee to suit themselves (with the proviso that speakers remained close enough to the recording device).

In order to further delimit the observer's paradox, defined in §6, participants were generally interviewed in self-selected, ethnically homogeneous dyads or triads based on pre-existing friendship or kinship networks, since this has been shown to be very effective in previous research (Beal 1990; Docherty & Foulkes 1999; Watt & Milroy 1999).[131] For the bulk of the interview, the youngsters were encouraged to talk amongst themselves and pursue any topic that they were interested in without my intervening – unless certain speakers were not observing turn-taking rules and thus dominating the conversation (see 59 for an example and Levinson & Torreira 2015 for an overview). In order to ensure some overlap between interview topics (with respect to language practices (see

---

131 The demolinguistics of certain schools sometimes occasioned that individuals were interviewed alone. A good case in point is Gintaras Petkus from St. Agnes's whose interview features in (58) below and who was the only Lithuanian child in his age range in the school (which is unsurprising given the city's demolinguistic profile already discussed). This strategy is, however, extremely rare.

60), issues of integration and so on), I also led the conversations to a certain extent based on an interview protocol derived from question modules detailed in Tagliamonte (2006), though tailored to suit the ages and cultural backgrounds of these particular speakers (see also Labov 1972). I also availed of protocols used in the multi-ethnic sociolinguistic interviews which underpin Meyerhoff & Schleef (2012), (2014); Schleef, Meyerhoff & Clarke (2011); Diskin (2017); and Hoffman & Walker (2010).[132] It was useful too that I was an outsider in each study site from the perspective of teaching and learning so that I was not associated with the school's formal educational role in any way. This was reinforced by ensuring my appearance was as casual as possible in a similar manner to the mode adopted by Lesley Milroy when collecting vernacular speech during the Belfast studies already introduced:

> The fieldworker always dressed in a nondescript manner in rather shabby, dull-coloured clothes ... the object was to ensure that clothing did not mark the fieldworker by unambiguously signalling higher social status or identity with any specific social group (Milroy & Milroy 1977: 37).

It was also critical that I was of Northern Irish heritage myself and had a set of obvious personal connections that could be played upon to project an insider status when it came to local knowledge, communities of practice and other aspects of the youngsters' socio-cultural lives. The effectiveness of these strategies was reinforced by: (i) the very personal details which the participants revealed about themselves and their families that the schools were unaware of; (ii) the younger pupils often engaging in play during interview or becoming so boisterous that the interview had to be cut short and begun again on another occasion; (iii) the older pupils feeling relaxed enough to use swear words when especially animated, as in (56):

(56) Extract from an interview with 'Eamonn McKee' and 'Tommy McGee', Armagh, 2014

1	Eamonn McKee:	Yeah, he turned round and grabbed me and I turned round and just.
2	KPC:	Oh.
3	Tommy McGee:	Hit him=[133]
4	Eamonn McKee:	Hit him.
5	KPC:	[*Laughter*] So what happened? Did he fall?

---

132 I am grateful to these authors for sharing their unpublished versions with me.
133 This symbol indicates an interruption or overlap when another speaker is holding the floor.

	6	Eamonn McKee:	Well I turned around and he grabbed me like that and then I was like=
	7	Tommy McGee:	He used to do boxing though.
	8	Eamonn McKee:	He stunned me and then I couldn't like do you know I couldn't push him because there was a car behind him so but then I couldn't like sw-
	9	KPC:	Mm. Yeah.
	10	Eamonn McKee:	And then he just like stun back and then I just like started punching him again and then he turned around and goes "why the **fuck** did you hit me" and walked off.
	11	KPC:	So, he'd obviously had enough, then?
	12	Eamonn McKee:	Yeah.

[TMcG (M); EMcK (M); St. Benedict's; Armagh, Northern Ireland; 25 Feb. 2014]

(iv) the fact that newcomer pupils declared by their teacher "not to have spoken two words in class since they arrived" became extremely enthusiastic and loquacious during interview, as (57) demonstrates:

(57) Extract from an interview with 'Jasmyn Jiju', 'Raka Marar' and 'Aja Pandala', Belfast, 2014

	1	Jasmyn Jiju:	Can I tell you?=
	2	Aja Pandala:	Oh, can I tell you something?
	3	KPC:	It's Jasmyn's turn and then we'll come back to you Aja.
	4	Jasmyn Jiju:	Ehm there was this puppy was chasing me all around the house.
	5	KPC:	Yeah?
	6	Jasmyn Jiju:	'Cause I was only like I think four or three or five.
	7	KPC:	Was it the one that Aja had?
	8	Jasmyn Jiju:	No, it's a little puppy. It was keeping chasing me and then my cousins were chasing after it [*Laughter*] 'cause it was like chasing [*Laughter*]. I was so scared I was screaming all around and then I went up, there's this attic thing you can go up to the roof.
	9	KPC:	Yes?
	10	Jasmyn Jiju:	And I climbed over there and I was so scared. I didn't want to get down.
	11	KPC:	And what, and how did you get down in the end?

12	Jasmyn Jiju:	Ehm my dad. I was so scared. Now that dog is grown up. That's one of my big dogs.
13	KPC:	Okay.
14	Jasmyn Jiju:	And then the pup=
15	Raka Marar:	Her screams are really loud screams. [*Laughter*] It would just get down and she screamed once "what is this?" and then when I looked she was screaming her head off eh just=
16	Jasmyn Jiju:	To make us deaf=
17	Aja Pandala:	And why was she screaming?
18	Raka Marar:	She was just screaming for no reason and I was like "why are you screaming for? No reason, just no="
19	Jasmyn Jiju:	I actually don't know.

[JJ (F); AP (F); RM (F); St. Agnes's; Belfast, Northern Ireland; 26 March 2014]

In the very lively conversation exemplified here, the three young girls vie with each other to hold the floor and interrupt one another numerous times. Beal (1990: 32) describes a parallel scenario of "intense" competition generated using a similar interview method which seems to be extremely well suited for drawing youngsters out. Jasmyn, the protagonist of the puppy tale here, is actually the pupil who is so silent in class that her teacher expressed concerns to me about her suitability as a participant.

The interview phase of these interactions lasted approximately one hour in the case of the teenagers, though the entire session was considerably longer. This is because they also completed reading tasks of different types so as to eventually be able to monitor stylistic variation across the sample, though this will not be considered here. They were also invited to evaluate their own competence in English and other languages utilising the *Common European Framework of Reference for Languages* (CEFR) tool (Council of Europe 2001). This is an international standard for language proficiency used to assess L2 speakers' skills. All the bilingual participants were also assessed independently by the English as an Additional Language or Special Educational Needs coordinator in each primary/post-primary school using the same model. It is the latter which will be used to examine competence levels explored in subsequent Chapters on the basis that the school assessors have high levels of expertise in using the tool. Of course, it would be useful in future research to examine any dissonance between the youngsters' own subjective assessments and these more objective ones from educational professionals.

Although the primary school children were not required to undertake any reading tasks, their sessions overall were quite lengthy too on account of ensuring that they fully understood the consent process, as already discussed. Their interviews were also often longer than those of the teenagers and frequently occurred at different time periods rather than in a single sitting. This is because it can be hard to keep their undivided attention, as (58) shows, coupled with the fact that previous studies have demonstrated quite categorically that children are generally less loquacious than older speakers (Roberts 1994: 79–80; 2004: 336; Smith & Durham 2019: 31).[134]

(58)   Extract from an interview with 'Gintaras Petkus', Belfast, 2014

1	KPC:	And do you watch television in Lithuanian? Or is it always in English?
2	Gintaras Petkus:	Well, I talk differently. I talk differently, not in this language but I can talk this language.
3	KPC:	Yes, you talk this language very well.
4	Gintaras Petkus:	Yeah. Yeah, because my mum and dad and my ehm my baby also can talk as well.
5	KPC:	The other language?
6	Gintaras Petkus:	Not the other language, the same as our ones.
7	KPC:	Yes. And do you ever speak English at home?
8	Gintaras Petkus:	Well, um I have some invisible friends but they're sitting here.
9	KPC:	Oh, are they? OK, and are they speaking English or are they speaking the other language?
10	Gintaras Petkus:	They speak like us.
11	KPC:	So, they speak English like we=
12	Gintaras Petkus:	No, no! We- we ehm eh they speak like us so they they s- they always speak at night time with me.
13	KPC:	So, what do they say? Give me an example of what they say.
14	Gintaras Petkus:	Well, they say like, they they like loads of things to eat and me too. I r- even like sandwiches, they're my favourite stuff.

---

134 That said, not all youngsters are quite so recalcitrant, though. Gintaras Petkus in (60) really proved to be exceptional here and, despite being recorded alone for the reasons indicated already, he managed to produce a conversation of nearly 9,000 words and was extremely engaged and engaging despite his professions of "it's so boring". Moreover, some of the other primary school pupils produced interviews that were even longer. Narsa Dobis of St. Peter's, for example, had a total transcript of 11,000 words. As such, I am confident that the methods for offsetting observer impact were effective even amongst the youngest speakers in the sample.

15	KPC:	Are they your favourite stuff?
16	Gintaras Petkus:	Can I go now?
17	KPC:	No, you have to wait until twelve, 'til your lunch time.
18	Gintaras Petkus:	But ehm it's so boring.
19	KPC:	Oh, I thought we were having a good time.
20	Gintaras Petkus:	But ehm we but it's boring sitting uh down for me. It's always boring when I sit down.
21	KPC:	Oh, is it? Oh, I'm terribly sorry.

[GP (M); St. Agnes's; Belfast, Northern Ireland; 24 March 2014]

6.2.2 Recording and transcription

As already noted, participants could choose their own seating arrangements and, in many cases, they moved these around or changed positions during the course of the interview, but were restricted to remaining in close proximity to the recording device, as (59) demonstrates from the same interview with the three St. Agnes pupils who generated extract (57):

(59) Extract from an interview with 'Jasmyn Jiju', 'Raka Marar' and 'Aja Pandala', Belfast, 2014

1	Aja Pandala:	I want to stand up, it's uncomfortable, oh my legs.
2	KPC:	Have ehm have a wee cushion and make yourself more comfortable.
3	Aja Pandala:	Mm I don't really like cushions like sitting on cushions. I just like standing up. I would just probably just sit down on the carpet.
4	KPC:	Yeah sit on the carpet. As long as we can hear you it doesn't matter. Pop yourself down there in the middle.
5	Aja Pandala:	Okay.

[JJ (F); AP (F); RM (F); St. Agnes's; Belfast, Northern Ireland; 26 March 2014]

This was because I preferred to use the same equipment for all the interviews to ensure consistency. Since very young children are often overly curious about lapel microphones and the like and because I was not in a position to place it under clothing, for example, as one might if I were a caregiver (Smith & Durham 2019: 31), I chose instead a Roland Edirol R-09. This is a high resolution (24-bit/96kHz linear PCM), low-noise recording device. It has an in-built premium grade, high-sensitivity stereo condenser microphone which performs really well for the recording of group conversations like that illustrated here.

Across all study sites, 187 pupils were recorded to generate the *Múin Béarla* corpus between August 2012 and October 2014. In addition, 7 other individuals were also included and their data forms part of an adult sub-corpus. Two of these speakers were third party school staff who entered the recording sessions for short exchanges (to check on the whereabouts of students, for example). Speakers with the pseudonyms Ruairidh O'Connor, Enya O'Houlihan and Joe O'Houlihan were interviewed more formally. Their conversations ranged across topics such as the Irish revival movement, the participation of allochthonous children in Irish language classes and changes in local communities within their lifetimes (particularly with respect to education, since O'Connor is a representative of *Gael Linn*, one of the project's non-academic partners, and the O'Houlihans are retired teachers).[135] Nino O'Houlihan is their daughter-in-law who herself is a trilingual immigrant parent of three children with a Georgian/Russian heritage. Her conversation revolved around issues tied to her own experiences as a member of an ethnic minority in Northern Ireland as well as her struggles with passing her native languages on to her children. Menachem Bialystok is likewise from a migrant family but his ancestry is Jewish and so he belongs to a more established Northern Irish migrant community associated with the nineteenth century, as detailed in Chapter Three, §3.2. Leah Lonergan was the English as an Additional Language (EAL) coordinator at St. Celine's and was interviewed about CEFR practices, friendship groups, school procedures with regard to acculturation and integration of newcomers as well as the strategies that were in place for their acquisition of English and maintenance of home languages. These interviews will not be included in the multivariate analyses which follow but have informed other aspects of the research, as have more informal, unrecorded interviews with the four school principals, their deputies and teaching staff (particularly the EAL and Special Educational Needs teams).

As far as the pupil corpus is concerned, excluding my own input, it is in the region of 670,000 words in total. The speaker who contributed least (Aisling Donaldson of St. Celine's) has an interview that is just shy of 200 words, though this is exceptional and relates to the very particular context of that interview where she was called to a science class and never managed to return. The participant whose recording was the most substantial (Erelis Norkus, a young Lithuanian woman

---

[135] *Gael Linn* is a national organisation the principal aim of which is to foster and promote the Irish language and its heritage as a living language and as an expression of identity at policy and at community level. *Gael Linn* operates on an all-island basis, with offices in Dublin and Armagh.

also attending St. Celine's) supplied 14,165 words. The average contribution was, however, 3523 words per speaker and the median is 3116.

Time-aligned transcripts of all the recordings were created using the multimodal ELAN package detailed in Wittenburg *et al.* (2006) and demonstrated in Tacchetti (2013). As Nagy & Meyerhoff (2015) also observe, this software is ideally suited to transcribing within variationist linguistics since its functionality also readily permits the extraction and codification of variable tokens. In addition, ELAN offers options for preparing the data in advance of more complex statistical tasks such as those described in §6.3 below as well as the generation of concordances, which can be especially helpful when examining variants for which their functionality in context is key to an understanding of their variable use.

The sound files were rendered as text by adhering to a strict orthographic transcription protocol based on the gold standard practices outlined in Allen *et al.* (2007); Poplack (1989) and Tagliamonte (2007). Crucially, to allow for maximal digital manipulation and with long-term sustainability and potential new applications of the database in mind, this protocol for the most part applied standard British spelling conventions. This is perfectly reasonable given the fact that ELAN, as Figure 49 indicates, provides time-stamps so that any phonetic, morphophonological or similar details required (such as the token counting of variants of the (ING) variable, which will be examined in the next Chapter) are readily retrievable.

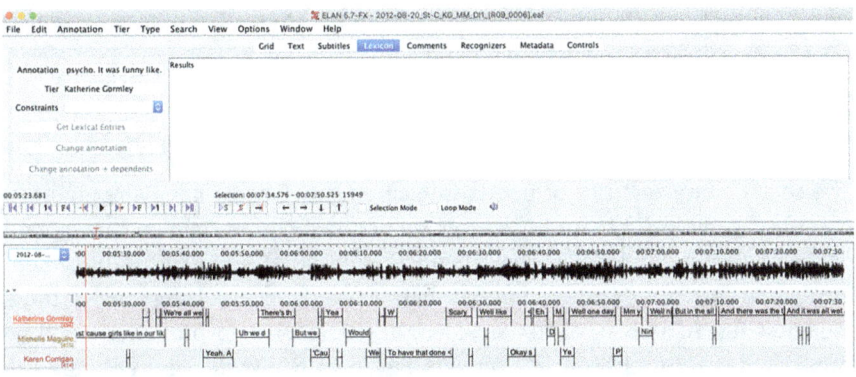

Figure 49 Screenshot of an ELAN transcription file

Occasionally, exchanges between me and pupils in St. Celine's Irish-Medium Unit were in Irish, but they tended to be openings and closings unless some aspect of the language was referred to in connection with modules on language learning and the like. Spellings and translations were supplied where required by a transcriber with a doctorate in Irish from Ulster University. Similarly, the newcomers introduced words or phrases from their first languages (such as *borscht,* which is a noun meaning a type of 'sour beetroot soup' common in Eastern Europe). These items were translated either by the participants themselves or by availing of Polish-English and similar reputable dictionaries like those published by Oxford University Press. Local dialect lexis (such as *cod* 'to kid someone', *mitch* 'to play truant', *prog* 'to steal') was spelled in accordance with forms found in either Dolan (2012), MacAfee (1996) or Robinson (1985) with some additions. These included, for example, distinguishing between *ach/och* spellings for the very particular Irish-English discourse marker that is a calque on the Irish interjection *ochón* 'alas' but which has evolved two different meanings expressing: (i) irritation or frustration; or (ii) sorrow (see Corrigan 2010: 98–99 and Corrigan 2015: 45–46). The former was rendered as *ach* in the protocol while the latter is spelled *och* so that this distinction is preserved for future research on wider aspects of discourse marking in the corpus than will be possible in Chapter Nine to follow.

As Poplack (1989) contends, any large-scale textual transcription exercise is subject to human error (see also Allen *et al.* 2007). To improve accuracy, therefore, each interview transcript was subject to a correction pass so that any inexactitudes in the base text could be improved. It was also to ensure that the transcription practices with respect to the protocol instructions could be made uniform across the entire corpus. This was a crucial process given the fact that such a megacorpus (in Poplack's 1989 terms) was the creation of many research associates over a protracted period of time.

6.2.3 Participants

The social characteristics of pupils in each of the schools have already been described generically in §6.1.2, so this section will concentrate on the method of their selection and broad demolinguistic and other socio-culturally salient attributes (particularly ethnolinguistic heritage and gender). More specific traits including age of arrival, birth dates, length of residency or proficiency will be considered where relevant in Chapters Seven to Nine when introducing the factor groups chosen for the multivariate analyses.

Participants were selected from school census data using a judgment sample method (Chambers 2003: 44–45 and 46; Milroy 1987b: 26–28 and 33). This technique maximised the possibility that the sample from each school would represent the range of languages spoken; that it would have roughly equal numbers of male and female participants; and so as to preclude the sample being unhelpfully disproportionate with regard to the sizes of either newcomer or native speaker populations. Efforts were also made to ensure that participants were grouped into gender and ethnically homogeneous cohorts, as noted earlier. The sampling method was employed in consultation with school staff and the participants themselves so that friendship and kinship networks would also be prioritised. Every effort was taken to explain that the sample derived from the census lists should exclude individuals who did not meet the following criteria:

(i)   No referrals for speech and language therapy.
(ii) No pupils with other special educational needs (such as Attention Deficit Disorder, that might impact upon attention span for example, or make this type of interaction uncomfortable for a participant should they be on the Autism Spectrum, for instance).
(iii) Autochthonous pupils and their parents must have been born and raised in the local community.
(iv) Allochthonous pupils ought not to have resided in another English-speaking country for an extended duration (i.e. no longer than a holiday or similar period prior to arrival in Northern Ireland).
(v)   Allochthonous pupils must not be of mixed heritage.

Nevertheless, some pupils slipped through the net for a variety of reasons. Pupils new to the school, for example, may not yet have met the criteria for the statementing of special educational needs. As such, there was one newcomer pupil who had a speech impediment and was named by the school as a participant. Another youngster (Ciarán Mookjai) was of mixed Thai/Northern Irish heritage and another two (one allochthonous (Sylwester Galat) and one autochthonous (Sarah Thomson)) were born and raised for part of their lives in the United States of America. In each case, while I carried on with their interviews when they presented themselves and their data forms part of the corpus in its entirety, their contributions will not be included in any of the multivariate analyses which follow so as not to introduce confounding factors that may impact negatively upon the results.[136]

Table 6 presents an overview of the original sample indicating study location, school, heritage and gender.

---

[136] In addition, there were three children whose interview content raised child protection issues that required further formal investigation, so their outputs are never referred to in any aspect of this work.

Table 6 Overview of school participants in the *Múin Béarla* corpus

Community	School	Heritage	Male	Female	Total
Armagh	Post-primary – St. Benedict's (N=49)	Northern Irish	24	0	24
		Newcomer	25	0	25
	Post-primary – St. Celine's (N=55)	Northern irish	2	19	21
		Newcomer	0	34	34
	TOTAL		51	53	104
Belfast	Primary – St. Agnes's (N=46)	Northern Irish	15	12	27
		Newcomer	9	10	19
	TOTAL		24	22	46
Donaghmore	Primary – St. Peter's (N=37)	Northern irish	10	8	18
		Newcomer	11	8	19
	TOTAL		21	16	37

Figures 50–53 present a demolinguistic breakdown of the sample per school, highlighting the sex of the speaker (female and male were the only gender options declared by participants). Also illustrated is their principal dialect and heritage languages. This strategy was chosen because while Mid-Ulster English (M-UE) is the dialect in all cases for the autochthonous cohorts, newcomers can be trilingual with some of their languages being restricted to certain domains, as argued and illustrated in Chapter 5, §5.1.1. This is the case for Jasmyn Jiju, for example, a participant in extract (57) above, who speaks English, Hindi and Malayalam though primarily uses the latter at home. All the Indian girls in this interview, in fact, are exposed to extensive translanguaging practices in this context, as (60) indicates:

(60) Extract from an interview with 'Jasmyn Jiju', 'Raka Marar' and 'Aja Pandala', Belfast, 2014

    1 Jasmyn Jiju: My mum knows lots of languages.
    2 KPC: So what does she know? What does she know, tell me=
    3 Aja Pandala: Same.
    4 Jasmyn Jiju: I don't know all of them, I think.
    5 KPC: Well give me some of the ones.
    6 Jasmyn Jiju: Ehm, Malayam,
    7 KPC: Mayalayam.

8	Jasmyn Jiju:	English, ehm, Tamil,
9	Aja Pandala:	Hindi?
10	Jasmyn Jiju:	Hindi ehm Arabic.
11	Jasmyn Jiju:	Ehm I don't know what is the other ones.
12	Jasmyn Jiju:	Telugu=
13	Raka Marar:	Telugu.
14	Jasmyn Jiju:	Yeah and another ... Eh there's some more I don't remember them.

[JJ (F); AP (F); RM (F); St. Agnes's; Belfast, Northern Ireland; 26 March 2014]

As such, the totals in Figures 50–53 are based on the languages declared by the school for these youngsters when submitted to the annual Department of Education for Northern Ireland census. There were some exceptions made in this regard when it became clear, during the interview module on home languages or in connection with the teenagers completing their CEFR forms, that the school information was actually incorrect. This was the case with Aja Pandala who features in (60) for whom the school registered Malayalam but who self-declared Telugu (and her preference for the latter was also supported by the other participants in Aja's interview).[137]

---

137 Such outcomes may be motivated by parents for prestige or similar reasons as is often the case with self-reported judgements of this type. An excellent case in point here arises from the responses by speakers of German to the 'Main Language' question in the 2011 Census in Northern Ireland. Although 3,908 individuals declared that their 'Country of Birth' was Germany (Krausova & Vargas-Silva 2014: 9), there are considerably fewer responses naming German as a primary language than there ought to be (just 728 individuals according to Northern Ireland Census 2011, NISRA (QS210NI) – 'Main Language'). One suspects therefore that these respondents actually declared their 'Main Language' to be English instead. Similar cases of underreporting have been documented for historical censuses in Ireland with respect to questions asking about knowledge of Irish where the number of returns for this category seriously underreport the facts on account of the language's low status at the time (see Chapter Four, § 4.2 for a discussion). Matras, Robertson & Jones (2016) provide some solutions to this issue in a school context and also see Little (2016).

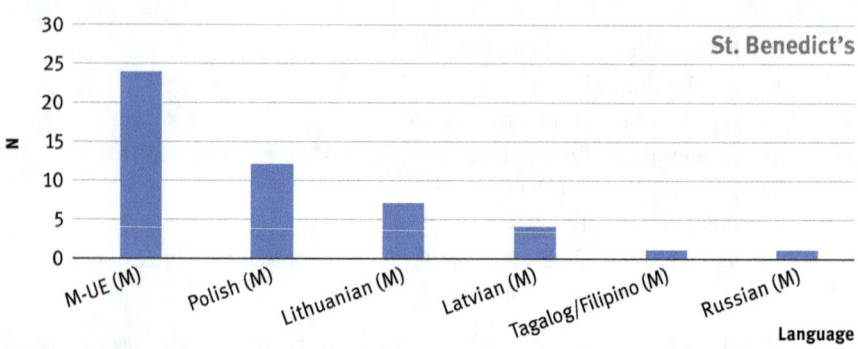

Figure 50 Main dialects and languages spoken at St. Benedict's, Armagh, 2012–2014[138]

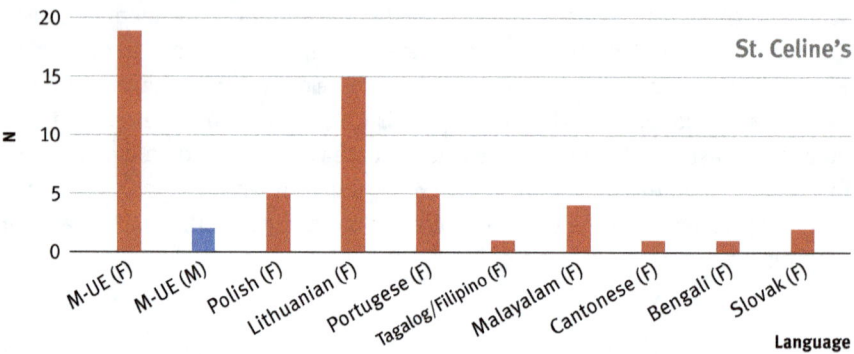

Figure 51 Main dialects and languages spoken at St. Celine's, Armagh, 2012–2014

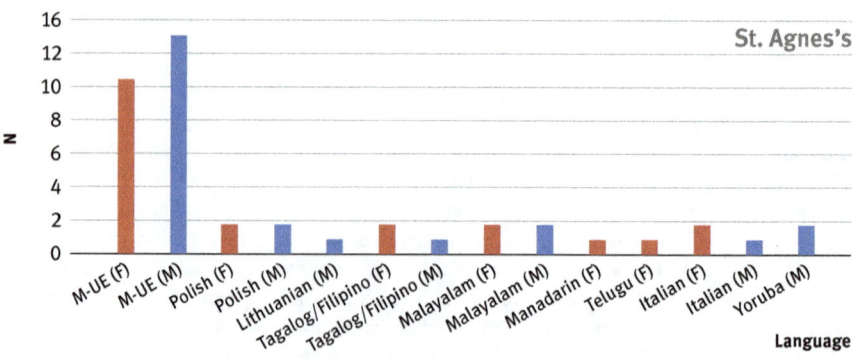

Figure 52 Main dialects and languages spoken at St. Agnes's, Belfast, 2012–2014

---

138 'Main Dialect' in each case is Mid-Ulster English (M-UE) and the graphs also show the gender breakdowns for males (M) and females (F) which will become relevant in forthcoming chapters.

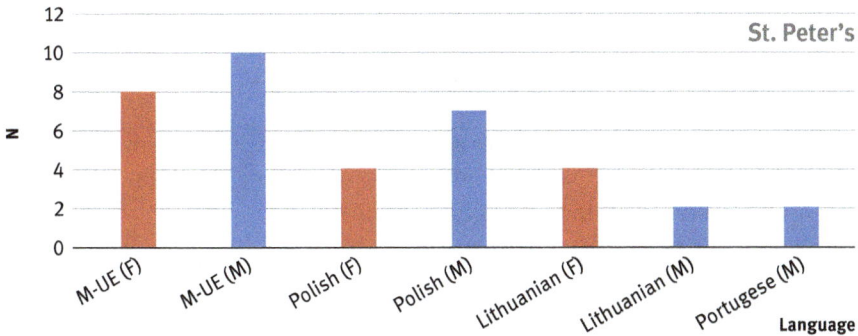

Figure 53 Main dialects and languages spoken at St. Peter's, Donaghmore, 2012–2014

6.3 Multivariate analysis

As noted elsewhere, three variables from different levels of the grammar will be analysed in subsequent chapters based on the data from these cohorts of speakers. For reasons that have already been alluded to and will become even more obvious later, these investigations will largely be restricted to comparisons between speakers of Lithuanian and Polish in the two Armagh schools alongside their peers who have extensive connections to the local community beyond their parents' generation. Suffice it to say at this point that what crucially informs this decision is the fact that while all three study sites belong to the Mid-Ulster English dialect zone illustrated in Figure 42, it should already be clear from previous discussion in § 6.1 that there are quite specific spatio-geographical factors which differentiate the communities. These might therefore have an impact on the processes associated with acquiring the variation that is typical of local sub-dialects of Mid-Ulster English since they govern the potential for newcomers to interact with native speakers. In this regard, Labov (2001: 19) contends that "a large part of the problem of explaining the diffusion of linguistic change" is simply the mechanical matter of ascertaining who speakers most regularly interact with (see also Fix 2013: 71). Taking this a step further, it is clear even from studies within a single superdiverse city such as those undertaken on London by Cheshire, Kerswill, Fox & Torgersen (2011) that – depending on the demographic composition of the borough (Hackney versus Havering in this case) – the extent to which dialect and language mixing is permitted to occur produces quite disparate feature pools. In Northern Irish contexts, the findings of Milroy & Milroy (1993) alongside Pitts (1982, 1985) also support this view. While exactly these factors are very much worth exploring from the perspective of the *Múin Béarla* corpus, to do so here would direct us away from the research questions that are our particular focus (repeated below for convenience).

1. What is the nature of the process for acquiring sociolinguistic variation by migrant teenagers and does it differ in any respect from that which L1 learners also undergo during the critical period?
2. Do the linguistic and social constraint hierarchies of adolescent native-speakers become fully or partially internalized by their newcomer peers or do they reconstruct or indeed reject them altogether?
3. Is the acquisition of sociolinguistic competence dependent on some of the factors outlined in (i)–(xi) of §5.2 such as age of arrival, proficiency or length of residence?
4. Can any individual, ethnolectal or other pertinent social asymmetries be discerned across diverse sub-cohorts of immigrant and local adolescents?

There is also the issue of speaker age to contend with in this regard. It would no doubt be fascinating to undertake apparent time analyses across the participant cohorts to address some of the critical period issues raised in Chapter Five, or to ascertain the extent to which changes in progress with respect to quotative usage, for example, have or have not infiltrated across both the 5–11 and 12–20-year old samples. Doing so, however, would also be beyond our present scope.

Finally, as will be discussed in more detail below and in subsequent Chapters, the variation and change framework adopted here relies on very strict parameters being observed. These include the size of population samples and therefore the potential frequency across the data set of occurrences and non-occurrences of the variants that are to be subjected to analysis. Thus, while this research has already offered original insights into communities of practice at St. Benedict's by referring to the interview material generated by Melchor Nogoy in §5.2.1, he is the sole speaker of Tagalog/Filipino across the entire Armagh sample. With an output of just 4,618 words associated with this linguistic heritage, it would be particularly difficult to generate enough tokens to examine all the dimensions of the morphosyntactic variable, in particular, discussed in Chapter Eight. This is a well-rehearsed problem in studies that orient towards a better understanding of variation "above and beyond phonology" (Sankoff 1980a), as detailed in Cheshire (2005a/b); Cornips & Corrigan (2005a: 6), Cornips & Corrigan (2005b: 100–105); Cornips & Gregersen (2016: 508–510); Henry (2004: 274–276); Labov (1991: 277) and Trousdale & Adger (2007) *inter alia*. Its source lies primarily in the open-ended nature of syntax so that systematic observations of linguistic and social variability of the type advocated here often result in only a small number of variant tokens which are thus inadequate for the statistical modelling techniques underpinning multivariate analysis.

Restricting the age range, community and heritage backgrounds of the speakers in these respects will thus permit comparative sociolinguistic analyses in the manner of Tagliamonte (2004a). It ought therefore to shed light on how and whether constraints are acquired by bilingual newcomers who are native speakers of first languages belonging to two different families (East Baltic and West Slavic). Moreover, the comparison will be able to extend further in that the relative sizes of the Lithuanian, Northern Irish and Polish populations in the Armagh schools indicated in Figures 50 and 51 are large enough to permit cross-variety investigations of three separate modules of sociolinguistic competence (phonetics-phonology; morphosyntax and discourse-pragmatics). This is key since, as Smith & Durham (2019: 44) argue, "much more can be uncovered in comparing and contrasting a number of different variables" (see also Tagliamonte & Molfenter 2007: 656). Undertaking cross-variable analyses of the *Múin Béarla* data will revisit theories proposed in the socio-acquisition literature focusing on young native speakers regarding the manner in which different types of variable and constraint are aquired as well as the developmental stages that youngsters pass through to eventually achieve sociolinguistic competence (Chambers 1992; Kerswill 1996; Smith & Durham 2019; Tagliamonte & Molfenter 2007). This will allow the testing, for instance, of whether or not migrant teenagers acquiring a new vernacular language follow these self-same trajectories. It will also evaluate the extent to which newcomers do or do not acquire variables from one level of the grammar more readily than they do those from other modules.

There is a further reason why Chapters Seven and Nine are dedicated to (ING) and (BE LIKE), respectively, that likewise falls out from this orientation. There are already studies of these variables in the context of migrant groups acquiring diverse British Isles' Englishes in rural Ireland, Dublin, Edinburgh, London and Manchester (Diskin 2015; Diskin & Levey 2019; Drummond 2012, 2015; Meyerhoff & Schleef 2012, 2014; Nestor 2013; Nestor, Ní Chasaide & Regan 2012; Nestor & Regan 2011; Schleef, Meyerhoff & Clark 2011; Truesdale & Meyerhoff 2015). Reference to these will therefore allow this new study to explore cross-geographical variation with respect to the autochthonous populations of these islands. In addition, the fact that each of the previous studies addresses the acquisition of an English dialect by Polish (and other heritage) speakers will permit the *Múin Béarla* data to be examined comparatively with respect to constraints on these variables from the perspective of exogenous communities too.

In terms of the quantificational techniques underpinning these comparisons, the approach is a multivariate or mixed-effects one which Labov (1994: 550) defines as an analytic procedure "that takes into account the operation of several

Table 7 Multivariate analysis of [θ] selection over all other realisations amongst Northern Irish, Lithuanian and Polish sub-samples of the *Múin Béarla* corpus. Predictors not selected as significant for the: (i) NI cohort: Following phon. environment, number of syllables, sex; (ii) Lithuanian cohort: Preceding phon. environment, following phon. environment, word/syllable position, number of syllables above 2, word class, sex, age; (iii) Polish cohort: Preceding phon. environment, following phon. environment, word/syllable position, number of syllables, word class, sex, age, age of arrival.[139]

	NI				Lithuanian				Polish			
Total N	225				278				231			
Deviance	154.027				174.127				243.035			
Df	7				6				3			
	Log Odds	N	%	FWs	Log Odds	N	%	FWs	Log Odds	N	%	FWs
Preceding Phon. Environment												
Consonant	1.097	82	0.561	0.750								
Vowel	0.176	128	0.656	0.544								
Pause	−1.273	15	0.600	0.219								
Following Phon. Environment												
Vowel					1.578	229	0.795	0.829				
Consonant					−0.424	44	0.614	0.395				
Pause					−1.154	5	0.600	0.240				
Word Class												
Lexical	1.611	157	0.752	0.833								
Functional	−1.611	68	0.309	0.167								
Age												
+1	0.610											
Lemma												
Random Std. Dev.	1.567				0.519				0.321			
Speaker												
Random Std. Dev.	0.597				2.126				1.221			
Number of Syllables												
1					0.600	122	0.828	0.646				
2+					−0.600	156	0.712	0.354				

---

139 For readers unfamiliar with these models, the term "deviance" is a measure of how well the model fits the data or the extent to which the actual data produced after running the computer programme deviates from the model's original predictions. The larger the deviance, the worse the fit. "Df" here refers to degrees of freedom which calculates the number of parameters in the model and thus assesses the model's complexity (i.e. the more factors that are added, the higher the df figure will become). "Log-odds" here gauges the effect size, reflecting the strength of the relationship between a factor or independent variable (such as preceding phonological environment or age) and a dependent variable (like TH). If log-odds are negative, there is a negative correlation between the variables (and of course above 0 means that they are positive). The

influences that jointly determine the end result." Table 7 presents an analysis of the *Múin Béarla* cohorts just described undertaken by Thorburn & Corrigan (2015) using this method to determine the selection of potential (TH) variants. They included the standard [θ] and non-standard variants such as TH-fronted forms [f], which Corrigan (2010: 41) and McCafferty (1999: 249), (2001: 184) note are often preferred by Northern Irish youngsters (as Foulkes & Docherty 1999 also report them to be amongst their peers in other parts of the UK).

As is customary with this analytic technique, a range of conditioning factors both internal (e.g. preceding phonological environment) and external (age) are examined simultaneously. The model expresses the fact that variation between the standard and non-standard variants is rule-governed which, in the terms of Weinreich, Labov and Herzog (1968: 100), implies that there are "linguistically and [socially] significant generalizations" that are quantifiable using this tool. In this particular case, it becomes clear that the constraints which are or are not significant across the three groups differ in certain respects. This finding may well imply that participants whose first languages are Lithuanian and Polish have not yet acquired the exact conditions governing this variable amongst their local peers. For example, although word class proved to be a significant factor for the conditioning of (TH) variation amongst the Northern Irish participants (i.e. the standard variant, [θ] is preferred in words which are lexical in function – hence the bold typeface), it was found not to be so for either of the Lithuanian or Polish cohorts.

The axiom of quantification in multivariate statistical analyses of this type requires controlled comparisons of reasonably frequently occurring tokens. These can only be achieved by ensuring that in any sample upon which calculations such as those in Table 7 are based: "every unit in the population has an equal chance of being represented" (Butler 1985: 2) (see also Rietveld & van Hout 2005; Speelman, Heylen & Geeraerts 2018; Tagliamonte & Baayen 2012). Hence, it is crucial, as indicated earlier, to consider in advance the number of participants

---

higher the value, the stronger the correlation. "Factor weight" basically reports exactly the same information but instead uses the range 0–1.00. If the correlation is 1.00, the outcome is known as a "knock out" (abbreviated as K.O. in subsequent models in Chapters Seven through Nine). This means that the distribution of tokens is categorical (i.e. either zero or 100%). If the result of these analyses has a log-odds that is close to 0 or a factor weight in the region of 0.50, then the result is a neutral one. Although the former probably demonstrate a more accurate fit of each category to the data, the latter can be useful for drawing overall comparisons between different sets of data and so will be regularly referred to in the comparative analyses which follow. For further details on the operation of the Rbrul software package used to generate these models, see Baayen (2008); Johnson (2009); Speelman, Heylen & Geeraerts 2018; Tagliamonte & Baayen (2012) as well as http://www.danielezrajohnson.com/Rbrul_manual.html, last accessed 31 July 2019.

and tokens of the variable that will be necessary in order to achieve representativeness in any social or linguistic factor group which features in the analysis. In early work in the paradigm, it was thought that since linguistic behaviour was relatively homogeneous, small samples would be sufficient to measure the correlations that occur:

> we found that from 10–20 instances of a given variable were sufficient to assign a value that fits into a complete matrix of stylistic variation ... numbers which might be totally inadequate for the study of attitudes, say towards racial segregation, with the associated reluctance to give straightforward personal response, are quite adequate for the study of phonological variables. (Labov 1966: 181).

However, the arguments summarised in Milroy (1987b) and Tagliamonte (2006) suggest that this view was overgeneralized. In addition, more complex variables require greater numbers of tokens implying that there appears to be no single criterion governing the representativeness of samples. Nevertheless, it certainly seems to be true, as Tagliamonte (2006: 85) also argues, that "variation analysis is best suited for a linguistic variable where at least some of the variants occur robustly." As such, the principle variants of the variables explored in Chapters Seven to Nine which follow are all frequently-occurring enough to make a mixed-effects approach possible.

There is also the issue of circumscribing the variable context to consider. This will involve systematically establishing inclusions and exclusions prior to counting tokens. In the case of (TH), which has no referential meaning, it is relatively straightforward to delimit the set of variants of the variable and exclude tokens where (TH) variants, for instance, occur in neutralization contexts such as <*I was with friends*>. However, analyses of variation at other levels of the grammar that likewise strictly adhere to criteria of functional, semantic and structural equivalence so as to determine a closed language set is more convoluted (D'Arcy 2017). The problem is neatly illustrated by structures such as the so-called Irish-English "Hot-news" perfect in <*She's **after** hitting our Áine*> (Corrigan 2010: 62). It is generally thought to be a calque on a type of Irish perfect with a similar form and function, as argued in Corrigan's (2010: 61–62) analysis of contemporary Mid-Ulster varieties and in Corrigan (1997), Hickey (2007: 198–199), Ó Corráin (2006), Ó Sé (2004), Ronan (2005) and elsewhere. The feature in Irish dialects of English is documented as having considerable longevity (McCafferty 2006) but there is simply no semantic/functional alternative in standard English. A variant such as <*she **has just hit** our Áine*> violates strict synonymy. Moreover, there is no functional equivalence either, since Kallen (1991: 62) has demonstrated that the structure can also be interpreted pragmatically as the universal perfect in examples like <*All the week **is after** being cold*>. As such, the three variables chosen for analysis not only have to be frequently occurring but there must also be no doubt as to the extent to which variants of each are synonymous with one another (Labov 1972: 118). The success of the aforementioned studies on (ING) and (BE LIKE) using similar quantificational techniques testifies to the value of further investigating variation and change with respect to these variables amongst the three cohorts of Armagh teenagers. While I am not aware of similar studies on the acquisition of relative clause marking patterns that typify any English dialect by exogenous groups, there have been various investigations of this variable within this framework on native speakers dating back to Cheshire (1982: 73), who successfully calculated the social and linguistic distribution of relative pronouns amongst Reading schoolchildren on the basis of just 82 tokens. In addition, this is one of the very few morphosyntactic variables included in the sociolinguistic studies undertaken by the Milroys and their associates in Belfast (Policansky 1982 *inter alia*). As such, there are already some preliminary findings as to how this variable might pattern amongst an indigenous population also speaking Mid-Ulster English (albeit many years hence).

I now turn to the variationist analyses of the three individual variables, beginning with (ING).

7 Hitt(ING) an Armagh Target

7.1 Setting the scene

Chapter Five, §5.2.3 introduced the idea that stable variables such as (ING) are acquired early by children and are in place before they reach school-going age. The foundation for this premise comes from research by Roberts (1997) *inter alia* which similarly explores the capacity for children to "hit" a "moving target", i.e. acquire changes in progress. This Chapter and the next will focus on the former while Chapter Nine is dedicated to the latter. On account of the comparative approach adopted, an important area of focus will be the extent to which Armagh adolescent newcomers are capable of likewise hitting local targets – moving or otherwise. This orientation will offer new insights into the extent to which their efforts match those of their peers elsewhere in the British Isles and also address theoretical questions regarding processes of first and second language acquisition (see: Diskin 2015; Diskin & Levey 2019; Drummond 2010, 2012, 2015; Elliott 2018; Howley 2015; Meyerhoff & Schleef 2012, 2014; Nestor 2013; Nestor, Ní Chasaide & Regan 2012; Nestor & Regan 2011; Schleef, Meyerhoff & Clark 2011 and Truesdale & Meyerhoff 2015 *inter alia*).

7.1.1 The origins of (ING) variability in Armagh English

The (ING) variable has been dubbed a "vernacular universal" by Chambers (2004: 129) on the basis that it is one of only a few phonological and grammatical variables that regularly occur in dialectal Englishes globally. The alternation is associated with final unstressed syllables with nominal or verbal function and the variants are an alveolar or apical/coronal [ɪn] and a velar nasal [ɪŋ]. The *Múin Béarla* examples in (61) and (62) (spoken within a few minutes of one another) clearly demonstrate that the Mid-Ulster English (M-UE) dialect of Armagh follows this universal tendency:

(61)   Extract from an interview with 'Michelle Maguire', Armagh, 2012
    1   Michelle Maguire: Don't think anyth**ing**'s [ŋ] hard
    [MM (F); M-UE; St. Celine's; Armagh, Northern Ireland; 20 AUG. 2012]

(62)   Extract from an interview with 'Michelle Maguire', Armagh, 2012
    1   Michelle Maguire: them two are always fight**ing** [ɪn]
    [MM (F); M-UE; St. Celine's; Armagh, Northern Ireland; 20 Aug. 2012]

As I will also argue with respect to the system of relative clause marking in Armagh English in the following Chapter, much contemporary variability is simply a by-product of diachronic linguistic change or, as Hazen (2006: 584) puts it in relation to (ING), the contemporary picture is a "synchronic echo" of the past. In fact, the mutability associated with this variable does indeed have its origins in changes between the Old and Middle English periods in particular. In this case, the synchronic apical (alveolar/coronal) *versus* velar realisations mirror the historical coalescence of once invariant and distinctive morphological forms (Houston 1985). As such, it preserves to some extent at least the grammatical functions which these once conveyed. In fact, there were three original Old English morphemes from which [ɪn]/[ɪŋ] descend: (i) The present participial inflectional suffix {-ind(e)/-end(e)} (63); (ii) The feminine derivational suffix {-ung(e)} (64); and (iii) Its masculine equivalent {-ing(e)} (65) (see Alexiadou 2013; Denison 1993; Elsness 1994; Houston 1985; Kastovsky 2006; Fischer & van der Wurff 2006; Fischer *et al.* 2000).

(63) Þæt hi   **wæron** genihtsume & on soþre lufe weall**ende**
      that they were   contented & in true love boiling
      'That they were contented and boiling in true love'
      (Denison 1993: 374 from *The Latin Hymns of the Anglo-Saxon Church*)

(64) Þænne faran   mid manegum scypum on hunt**unge** hranes
      then travelled with many   ships   on hunting whales
      'Then travelled whale hunting with many ships'
      (https://tapor.library.utoronto.ca/doecorpus/, last accessed 2nd August 2019 from Ælfric's, *Colloquy*)

(65) Þa se æþel**ing**   cwom
      then the son-of-a-noble came
      'Then the son of a nobleman came'
      (https://tapor.library.utoronto.ca/doecorpus/, last accessed 2 August 2019 from *The Exeter Book*)

As Lass (2006: 69) points out: "The story of English inflectional morphology from about 1100 is one of steady attrition". A key component driving this restructuring is the interaction between sound change and morphology which resulted, for example, in the loss of grammatical gender and case in the nominal category. The outcome was the production of what Lass (2006: 69) terms "prototypical" categories for the noun and verb. The masculine {-ing(e)} form of derived nouns thus coalesced with the {-ung(e)} form with which it was already rather close phonologically. Lass (2006: 80) admits that it is not fully understood how the merger between the participial {-ind(e)/-end(e)} and the {-ing(e)} of verbal nouns occurred (such as the new Middle English form for Old English *huntunge* in (66)).[140] However, as (67) testifies to, there is good evidence for extensive rivalry between these forms in different versions of *Laʒamon's Brut* which is a late twelfth or early thirteenth century manuscript (c. 1190–1215).

(66) *And when the Kinge had dyned, they wente a hunti**nge** agayne*
And when the King had dined they went a-hunting[141] again
'And when the king had dined they went hunting'
(https://quod.lib.umich.edu/m/middle-english-dictionary/dictionary – last accessed 2 August 2019, from *Rec. Bluemantle (Jul C. 6)*)

(67) Cotton Caligula A. lx. (*Laʒamon* A), Hand B
{-inde} x 1; {-ende} x 1; {-inge} x 1

Cotton Otho C. XIII (*Laʒamon* B)
{-inde} x 2; {-ende} x 2; {-ing(g)e} x 2
(Lass 2006: 81)

Even in the fourteenth century, a comparison of the contemporaneous works of Chaucer and Gower reveals competition between the writers since the former prefers the innovative {-inge} form whilst the latter favours {-ende} (Lass 2006: 81). Figure 54 from the Armagh Diocesan Registry materials already described in Chapter Two, §2.3, demonstrates that it is the Chaucerian type which dominates in fifteenth century Armagh. The text contains a variety of {-inge} forms including the progressive structure: *At the tyme I came to Cestere there **was** there mene of Lorde Grey abydynge* (bearing in mind that the graphemes <i> and <y> are interchangeable at this point).

On the basis that it is a long-established fact that there was considerable graphemic-phonemic correspondence in earlier forms of English (Stockwell & Barritt 1951), it is likely that *abydynge* here would have been pronounced with a final velar nasal. Wholesale simplification of consonant clusters containing nasal phonemes around the period when this original correspondence was written

---

140 Houston (1985: 273 ff.) does, however, provide several hypotheses some of which are very well supported by both diachronic and synchronic evidence.
141 The {a-} prefix here is generally viewed as a relic of the "on" preposition contained in (66) (see Elsness 1994: 8). It persists in some global Englishes including the South Armagh variety described in Corrigan (1997) which retains structures such as: *there was no turf **a-using** on it* [U504/L830-831/1970M/MS1784].

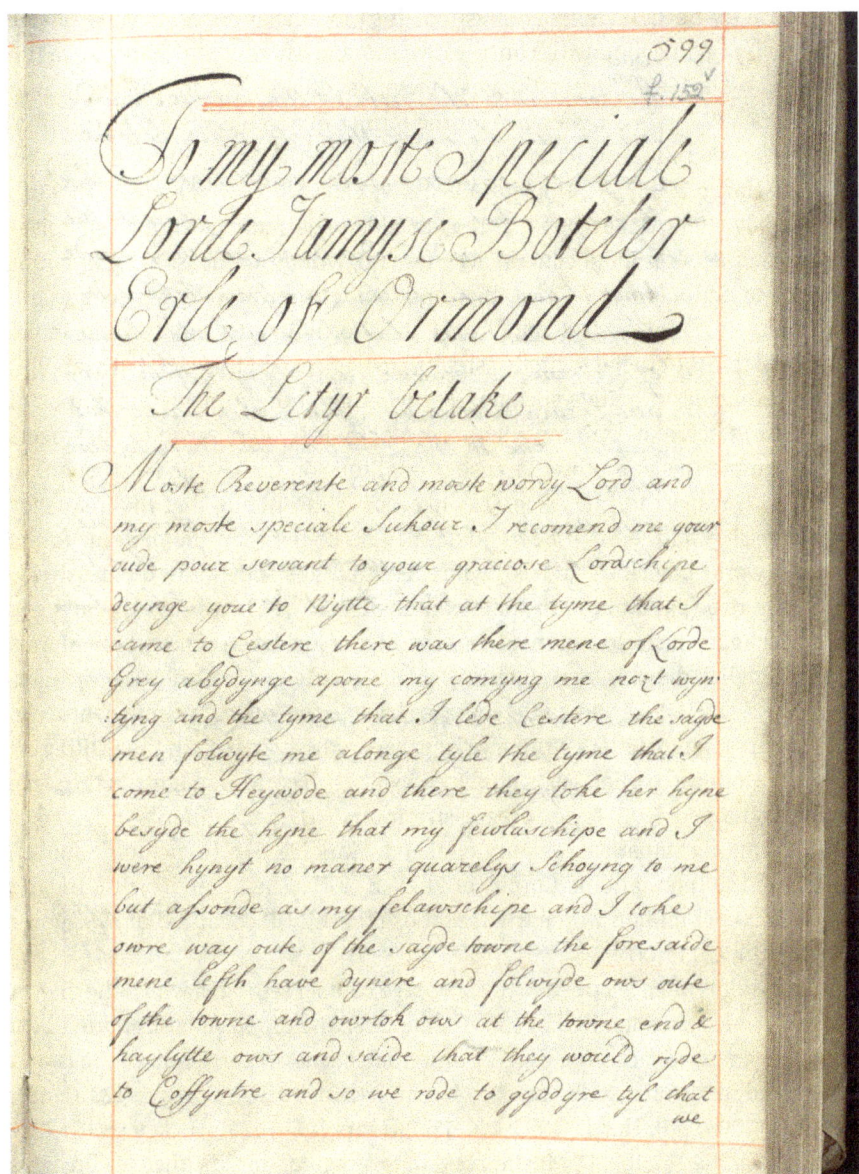

Figure 54 Sample page from a seventeenth century transcript of the original Armagh Diocesan Registry, 1428–1441[142]

---

[142] This facsimile is reproduced with the permission of the Deputy Keeper of the Records, the Public Record Office of Northern Ireland and the Registrar of the Diocese of Armagh (PRONI reference number DIO/4/2/4-599-P).

resulted in the development of new competing pronunciations for any morpheme spelled <i/yng>, i.e. one with conservative [ɪŋ] and another with innovative [ɪn] (Houston 1985: 26–27). Interestingly, as previous research has shown, vernacular grammars still retain a preference for the former in nominals (such as (61) from a native speaker in the *Múin Béarla* corpus) and for the latter in verbal elements (62) (see Hazen 2006: 583; Houston 1985: 389; Labov 1989: 87; Labov 2001: 88ff). Thus Labov (1989: 87) argues that the apical is preferred: "most in progressives and participles, less in adjectives, even less in gerunds and least of all in nouns like *ceiling* and *morning*." Since this condition on the variable has been established largely on the basis of data from either North America or elsewhere in the UK, it will thus be crucial to firstly establish to what extent this factor also applies to the vernacular of native-speaking participants in the Armagh sub-corpus of *Múin Béarla* before examining whether or not their Lithuanian and Polish peers have acquired this and other linguistic conditions on (ING) which are set out in §7.1.2. With respect to this issue, it is likewise worth noting that the frequency of progressives in the *Múin Béarla* data may be higher than the patterns found in other world Englishes. Indeed, while research has shown the progressive to be on the rise (particularly in American Englishes, as Elsness 1994: 9 argues), several scholars have documented the even higher incidence of progressive forms in Irish English dialects by comparison to other varieties. McCafferty & Amador-Moreno (2012a: 271–273) trace the increase back to the late eighteenth century in their comparison of letters written by speakers of Irish English in the CORIECOR corpus introduced earlier. Texts produced by English correspondents in the same period contained 50% fewer progressive forms (105 per million words *versus* 200). A similar comparison was undertaken by Kirk (2015) on synchronic spoken data from the International Corpus of English (ICE). The figures for ICE-Ireland were 10,620 per million words whereas those for ICE-GB consisted of 25% fewer tokens (Kirk 2015: 100).

This trait is often ascribed to the language contact setting in which the dialect evolved, which was detailed in earlier Chapters. The proposal is supported by a wide range of evidence from different sub-dialects north and south of the island articulated in McCafferty & Amador-Moreno (2012a, 2012b); Corrigan (2010: 68); Filppula (2004: 80); Harris (1993: 156–157); Henry (1957: 170); Hickey (2007: 222–224) and Kirk (2015: 87). For instance, (68) is a regular and distinctive construction in Irish English and varieties influenced by it (see Clarke 2010: 77–78). Progressive forms also occur in Irish negative imperatives and, indeed, pattern very similarly, as (69) demonstrates.

(68) don't **be** wander**ing** about!
(Corrigan 2010: 68)

(69) ná   bí   **ag caint**   liom!
don't   be   at+talking   with+me
'don't talk to me!'
(Corrigan 2010: 68)

There is also the possibility in Irish English which other global Englishes do not share of using a continuous form of the verb in stative contexts. This predilection may also change the frequency by which such forms (e.g. *believing, belonging, knowing, wanting, wishing* and the like) (and therefore the variable at issue here) may be found in *Múin Béarla* (see Harris 1993: 164 for synchronic examples and McCafferty & Amador-Moreno 2012a: 274–275 for diachronic ones).

7.1.2 The origins of (ING) variability in newcomer English

Language contact phenomena and (ING) variability is also an important consideration with respect to the English varieties spoken by the Lithuanian and Polish newcomer cohorts in the corpus. Chapter Five, §5.1.3 produced considerable evidence that the acquisition of a second language by non-native speakers can create patterns of interference from their first language at the segmental and other levels of the grammar. As the discussion in §5.2.1 elaborates, this process may persist in the L2 for a variety of reasons including external factors such as community of practice membership as well as the cognitive and sociopsychological characteristics of speakers. Although the latter will not be considered again in any detail here, the interview extracts captured in (70)–(73) demonstrate important differences between the realisations of the (ING) variable by two Lithuanian speakers attending St. Benedict's, Armagh. As can be seen from a summary of their social attributes in Table 8, the two teenagers are practically newcomer "twins". However, while Elada exhibits (ING) behaviour in (70)–(71) which reflects the local norms just described, Ramus does not (72)–(73). His variants include the L2 interference types [ɪŋk]/[ɪŋg] which are generated by his retention of aspects of Lithuanian phonology.

Table 8 Social and heritage attributes of Lithuanian newcomer "twins" at St. Benedict's

	Ramus Barcus	Elada Danis
Date of birth	03/03/2001	03/06/2001
Gender	M	M
Ethnicity	Lithuanian	Lithuanian
Length of residence (years)	2	2
Free School Meals	Yes	Yes
Time in other English speaking countries	None	England: two weeks
Birthplace of speaker and parents	Kaunas, Lithuania	Joniškis, Lithuania

(70) Extract from an interview with 'Elada Danis', Armagh, 2014
 Elada Danis: I went last year to my stepdad's dad's like wedd**ing** [ɪŋ]
 [ED (M); M-UE; St. Benedict's; Armagh, Northern Ireland; 27 Feb. 2014]

(71) Extract from an interview with 'Elada Danis', Armagh, 2014
 Elada Danis: his brother was play**ing** [ɪŋ] with loads of friends. Do you know what they were do**ing** [ɪŋ]? They were knock**ing** [ɪŋ] random doors.
 [ED (M); M-UE; St. Benedict's; Armagh, Northern Ireland; 27 Feb. 2014]

(72) Extract from an interview with 'Ramus Barcus', Armagh, 2014
 Ramus Barcus: Yeah like, we had shopp**ing** [ɪŋk] yesterday
 [RB (M); M-UE; St. Benedict's; Armagh, Northern Ireland; 29 Jan. 2014]

(73) Extract from an interview with 'Ramus Barcus', Armagh, 2014
 Ramus Barcus: I'm meet**ing** [ɪŋg] like Brazil people
 [RB (M); M-UE; St. Benedict's; Armagh, Northern Ireland; 29 Jan. 2014]

According to Girdenis (2014: 57) [ŋ] and [n] are in complementary distribution in this Baltic language. The former is reserved for following velar contexts and the latter for those that are alveolar, as illustrated by the contrasts in the words ra[ŋ]kà 'hand'/a[ŋ]gà 'hole' versus pì[n]davo 'braid-3PST'/pi[n]tà 'braided-NOM-SG.F' (see also Ambrazas 1997: 21). As such, Lithuanian norms do not permit the forms *ra[n]kà 'hand' or *a[n]gà 'hole'. It is hardly surprising therefore that when Lithuanian newcomers attempt to render nominal or verbal particles in Armagh English with final <-ing> spellings, they struggle not to persist with their Lithuanian positional variants [ɪŋg]/[ɪŋk] as Ramus regularly does. Examples (72) and

(73) contain an instance of each. This is likely connected to the place of articulation that Ramus uses for the following consonants which is also influenced to some extent by Lithuanian phonology (i.e. a palatal in the initial approximant of *yesterday*, generating [ɪɲk] in (72), and a velarized lateral approximant in *like* which thus precipitates the [ɪŋg] variant in (73)) (See Ambrazas 1997: 15, 35 and 36 as well as Girdenis 2014: 191).

A comparable assimilation regulation applies in South as well as West Slavic languages like Polish with respect to nasals, as Sussex & Cubberley (2009: 171) contends. Thus, the place of articulation of an obstruent following a nasal is also matched by the nasal itself, as the Polish word pairs in (74) from Gussmann (2002: 86) illustrate:

(74) **labial**   lampa   [lampa]   'lamp'
                  sępy   [sɛmpɨ]   'vulture, nom. pl.'
                  dębu   [dɛmbu]   'oak tree, gen. sg'
                  rąbać   [rɔmbatɕ]   'hew'
     dental   ręce   [rɛn̪tsɛ]   'hand, dat. sg'
                  wstędze   [fstɛn̪dzɛ]   'ribbon, dat. sg'
                  pętać   [pɛn̪tatɕ]   'to fetter'
                  nadęty   [nadɛn̪ti]   'pompus'
     palatal pędzi   [pɛɲdʑi]   '(s)he rushes'
                  rządzi   [ʒɔɲdʑi]   '(s)he governs'
                  sądzi   [sɔɲdʑi]   '(s)he thinks'
                  chęci   ['ɛɲtɕi]   'willingness, nom. pl'
     velar   księga   [kɕɛŋga]   'book'
                  urągać   [urɔŋga]   '(s)he abuses'
                  stęka   [stɛŋka]   '(s)he grumbles'
                  obłąkany [ɔbwɔŋkanɨ]   'crazy'

Hence, Paweł Pietras, a young Polish man also attending St. Benedict's, follows Ramus's patterns, producing [ɪŋg] in (75) and [ɪŋk] in (76).

(75) Extract from an interview with 'Paweł Pietras', Armagh, 2014
Paweł Pietras: once with our cousins, we were play**ing** [ɪŋg] there
[PP (M); M-UE; St. Benedict's; Armagh, Northern Ireland; 25 March 2014]

(76) Extract from an interview with 'Paweł Pietras', Armagh, 2014
Paweł Pietras: when we were rid**ing** [ɪŋk], he actually fell out of the little boat
[PP (M); M-UE; St. Benedict's; Armagh, Northern Ireland; 25 March 2014]

I view such realisations to also be transfer effects (as do Drummond 2012: 114–115 and Schleef, Meyerhoff & Clark 2011: 215–216, with regard to their Polish migrant speakers in Edinburgh, London and Manchester).

The analysis which follows will likewise therefore explore the frequency of these non-native variants since they too belong to the "envelope of variation" underpinning this particular study (Tagliamonte 2006: 86–87). There is one other variant ([zero]) which one of the non-native speakers generated on a single occasion when producing a verbal form with final {-ing} morphology, illustrated in (77). However, since they produce native-like [ɪn] variants for *slagging* and *coming* a few seconds before and after this utterance, I take this to simply be a hapax legomenon rather than a productive element of the newcomers' variable grammars, which [ɪŋk] and [ɪŋg] certainly are. These stopped variants have of course also been identified in autochthonous varieties of northern British English which Wells (1982: 365–366) terms "velar nasal plus" types. Hence, Newbrook (1999: 98) reports local West Wirrall (Cheshire/Merseyside) pronunciations of *something* with a final [ɪŋk] particularly amongst younger speakers (see also Braber & Robinson 2018: 57–58 on East Midlands dialects; Docherty & Foulkes 1999: 51 on Derbyshire and Tyneside; Drummond 2012: 113–114 on Mancunian and Mathisen 1999: 110–111 on the West Midlands). Neither of these are typical, however, of any variety of Irish English so they do not form part of the input dialect for Lithuanian or Polish newcomers to Armagh. This is useful since it does not confound the source of the variant in newcomer speech which proved to be an issue in Drummond's (2012: 113) study of migrants in Manchester where the local variety is typologically "velar nasal plus" in the sense of Wells (1982). In the same vein, Kingsmore (1995: 100–110) identified a syllabic nasal as a variant of /n/ in the speech of some participants in her study of Coleraine, Northern Ireland (see also Hickey 2007: 116). Furthermore, both Harris (1985: 58) and McCafferty (2007: 126) report dental [n̪] realisations in other urban centres there. However, neither of these pronunciations have been recorded either in this or in previous datasets of autochthonous varieties collected in Armagh by Corrigan (2010: 42 and 46) so they are not part of the closed set for (ING) examined here.

(77)   Extract from an interview with 'Patros Stain', Armagh, 2013
       Patros Stain: They were slagg**ing** [Ø] me like I'm a Dumbo
       [PS (M); M-UE; St. Benedict's; Armagh, Northern Ireland; 11 Oct. 2013]

7.1.3 Language-internal constraints

Previous research on unstressed {-ing} has examined a range of linguistic factors thought to condition the choice between [ɪŋ] and [ɪn]. They include the number of syllables in the lexical item, syllabic and lexical position of the variants as well as priming effects of various kinds (see Abramowicz 2007). For instance, Houston (1985: 22) discovered that velars were near categorical in *everything* but were not so in *nothing* – though this syllable length pattern was found only in her American corpus and not in her British one. Reference to a continuum of variation has already been made regarding the grammatical categories of the lexical item in which (ING) occurs. These, by contrast, have been demonstrated to almost universally condition the variation in native speaker varieties of English globally (Horvath 1985; Houston 1985; Labov 1989; Tagliamonte 2004b; Wagner 2012a/b; Watts 2005 *inter alia*). In Houston's early study of (ING) variation already referred to, she highlights another linguistic constraint in the form of a regressive homorganic assimilation effect comparable to that examined in the previous section with respect to Ramus Barcus's choices of [ɪŋk] *versus* [ɪŋg] in (72) and (73). Hence, [ɪŋ] was preferred with preceding velars whereas [ɪn] was favoured in cases where the place of articulation of the following consonant was also alveolar (Houston 1985: 45 ff.). A progressive homorganic dissimilation effect with respect to the place of articulation of consonants preceding [ɪŋ]/[ɪn] was also investigated (Houston 1985: 45 ff.). The analysis showed a dispreference in Houston's British corpus for the former when the preceding consonant was alveolar and *vice-versa* for the latter. Similarly, Tagliamonte's (2004b) study of York English revealed that both preceding and following phonological environments were significant priming factors. Despite the fact that these traits regularly occur in the L1 phonologies of speakers of English, Lithuanian and Polish (since such homorganic processes are arguably universal to some degree because they are phonetically motivated, as per Kroch 1978), these particular constraints are not, however, found across the board. Labov (2001: 87), for instance, declares progressive homorganic dissimilation not to be significant at all in his study. By contrast, Schleef, Meyerhoff & Clark (2011) report both regressive as well as progressive homorganic assimilation to also be productive amongst their sample of London indigenous teenagers. However, with respect to the speech of their Edinburgh peers, only the segment following {-ing} had any significant influence on the likelihood of [ɪŋ] or [ɪn] as speaker choices. Similarly, Wagner (2012a) in another study on a similar age group in Philadelphia generated conflicting results, in that while following alveolars did favour the likelihood that her participants would choose the [ɪn] form there was no progressive homorganic dissimilation effect either.

When the production of migrant speakers is added to the mix, the picture becomes rather more complex still. Thus, Meyerhoff & Schleef (2012: 402, 2014: 119) report that while grammatical category significantly conditions (ING) variation amongst both local Edinburgh teens as well as proficient Polish newcomers, the constraint rankings for each group differ. In addition, their sub-corpus generated by the latter cohort exhibits other conditions on the occurrence of [ɪn] including a frequency effect tied to particular lexical items. Such imperfect learning with respect to this and other aspects of the conditioning on this variable reported amongst native English speakers has also been found in an earlier (ING) study of Polish migrants documented in Schleef, Meyerhoff & Clark (2011: 226), in which they argue for the "re-ordering or non-replication of variable constraints", an idea which was already introduced in Chapter Five and will be elaborated on below. In a similar vein, Adamson & Regan (1991) investigated the extent to which native speaker linguistic constraints on (ING) in Philadelphia and Washington D.C. are acquired by L2 speakers whose first languages were Cambodian and Vietnamese. They found that even though grammatical category significantly predicted patterns of variation amongst all speakers in the two cities (Adamson & Regan 1991: 16), there were discrepancies regarding which grammatical categories were more likely to be associated with the alveolar variant in the L2 groups. Thus, while [ɪn] is rarely used by the local cohorts in nouns of the *nothing* type, as well as in prepositional forms like *during*, they are readily used in these contexts by non-native speakers. By contrast, the data from all three speaker groups included "evidence of regressive assimilation" (Adamson & Regan 1991: 14). Similarly, Drummond's (2012: 117) study of Polish migrants in Manchester reports that their linguistic behaviours with respect to (ING) usage and the constraints tied to grammatical category and preceding segment "largely reflect the patterns found in previous research" on indigenous English vernaculars. It will therefore be worth exploring these issues further in the analysis of *Múin Béarla* not least since I would expect it to shed light not only on processes of inter-language and L2 acquisition, but also on mechanisms of grammaticalization (particularly with respect to the nominal-verbal continuum) and the role which universal processes tied to the type of phonetic conditioning which Kroch (1978) argues for might play in facilitating or blocking acquisition.

7.1.4 Language-external constraints

Fischer (1958) was the first study of how (ING) was acquired in the speech of pre-adolescents in New England and the variable has gone on to become a "a staple of sociolinguists" (Hazen 2006: 581), as should already be apparent from the extensive research on its linguistic correlates detailed in the previous section. Fischer identified a range of external factors which seemed to condition the variation including age, class, gender and style and many of these patterns have been replicated across several studies on North American, Antipodean and UK vernaculars (Horvath 1985; Labov 1966; Mathisen 1999; Mechler & Buchstaller 2019; Shnukal 1982; Shuy, Wolfram and Riley 1968; Tagliamonte 2004b, 2012; Trudgill 1972; Wolfram & Christian 1976; Wagner 2012a/b).

As far as Northern Ireland is concerned, there have been three studies on the variable which sought to identify social factors that might condition (ING) variation locally. The first was on a rural community in Articlave, County Derry by Douglas-Cowie (1975, 1978, 1984), another was located in Coleraine (Kingsmore 1995) (both areas being within the Ulster Scots-speaking region referred to already in Chapter Four). A third (O'Neill 1987) is particularly relevant to this project since it was undertaken on Mid-Ulster English, specifically on the two majority ethnic groups residing in Armagh city at the time.[143] While there is not space here to discuss each of these in any detail, their findings evidence the type of social layering also ascribed to this variable in the previous research on other global Englishes already cited (and see Hazen 2006 and Tagliamonte 2012: 187–195 for overviews). In essence, they support Labov's (1972: 40) view that the variable is stable and "is a monotonic function of social class and contextual style", (i.e. regular social stratification is maintained in both monitored and unmonitored speech).

The orientation of the Articlave research, in particular, focuses on social perceptions of (ING) and other aspects of its variability. Kingsmore's (1995) study is rather more ambitious investigating as it does additional factors alongside class, gender and style that are not usually considered in research on this variable. They included rural/urban dimensions and network membership. Table 9 demonstrates sex and style conditioning *par excellence* since it shows the propensity for speakers to prefer [ɪn] when they are monitoring their speech less (i.e. in conversational style). Of particular interest here, is the finding that teenage, young adult and middle-aged adult male speakers in Coleraine in conversational style are comparatively low users of the non-standard variant when examined in relation to their female age mates. For example, young adult women categorically use [ɪn] in these contexts while young adult men employed this variant only 79 % of the time. The explanation which Kingsmore offers for this unusual outcome whereby the overall token count for the alveolar variant is "10 % higher" in females than it is in males is tied to the disparate personal communication networks in which

---

[143] I am grateful to Jeffrey Kallen for supplying me with a copy of this research which he supervised at Trinity College, Dublin.

the two genders are locally engaged (i.e. female networks are more likely to be characterised as "urban" and "working class" (Kingsmore 1995: 110)).

Table 9 Correlation of [ɪn] variant with age, sex and style (N.B. figures are given in percentages).[144]

	Word-list style		Conversational style	
	M	F	M	F
Teenagers	71	40	96	98
Young Adults	0	8	79	100
Middle-Aged Adults	5	4	65	74
Elderly Adults	63	33	89	89
All speakers	38	22	79	85

The more expected sex effect of the kind which typifies studies such as Trudgill (1972) and is documented for several global Englishes in Tagliamonte (2012: 189–190), was, however, replicated in O'Neill's (1987: 26) research on Armagh, as Table 10 indicates. The orientation was similar to that of McCafferty (1998, 2001) in that it primarily focused on uncovering potential ethnolinguistic differences in this city too that were tied to membership of either the Protestant or Roman Catholic faiths. In that regard, it would appear that across O'Neill's sample of twenty speakers aged 18–20 she has identified a pattern whereby Protestant females are the lowest users of the [ɪn] variant in formal contexts (only 6.6%). Roman Catholic women and Protestant men use it to the same degree and it is Roman Catholic males who are the most avid [ɪn] users. Even in this highly monitored style, 27% of their tokens of the variable are of this type and while their figure for casual style is not categorically the alveolar variant, as it was for this context amongst young adult females in Kingsmore's (1995) study of Coleraine, Roman Catholic males in Armagh do use many more tokens than their female peers. As before for formal style, it is the Protestant female group in O'Neill (1987) who are the most reluctant to utilise [ɪn] even in unmonitored speech contexts (just 35.5%).

---

[144] The age correlation which Kingsmore (1995) uncovers here regarding her findings for conversational style especially (compare the middle-aged rates with those for teens and the oldest cohort e.g.) is "rare", as Tagliamonte (2012: 190) also points out. I suspect therefore that they relate to some other changes which are constraining (ɪNG) in this dataset that there is not space to explore further at this juncture.

Table 10 Percentage of word final (ING) velar nasals which are realised as alveolar nasals amongst diverse ethnic and gender groups in casual and formal styles.

	Formal	Casual
Roman Catholic Males	27%	80.4%
Roman Catholic Females	13.3%	67.7%
Protestant Males	13.3%	61.1%
Protestant Females	6.6%	35.5%

Given the small-scale nature of O'Neill's (1987) study, she is rightly reluctant to offer far-reaching explanations for her findings. Nevertheless, the outcomes are important to the analysis presented in §7.3 in two key respects: (i) They reinforce the wisdom of my decision to focus entirely on Roman Catholic school-going populations so as not to potentially confound any results with additional ethnolinguistic considerations that might be operating across the samples; and (ii) They represent a useful baseline for investigating a gender constraint amongst the indigenous cohort of speakers which one would expect to remain apparent in the intervening quarter of a century between O'Neill's (1987) study and this one (given the stability of (ING) variation already argued for here and elsewhere). It will be interesting as well to explore the extent to which (ING) proves to likewise be stable for speakers in a language learning context, particularly on account of the re-ordering and non-replication tendencies of such migrant groups identified in previous research on this same variable (see Schleef, Meyerhoff & Clark 2011: 226).

As already noted in Chapter Four, §4.2, migrants often undertake roles in the host country that are rather different to those which they trained for or have experience of in the sending country (Bauder 2006; DEL 2009: 2, 42–43; Kobiałka 2014; Pietka, Clark and Canton 2013; Trevena 2013, 2014; Visintin, Tijdens and van Klaveren 2015). As such, analyses of their patterns of acquisition which have a class dimension can be problematic since the employment tier in which they currently work may not match their educational background, skills and social aspirations. In addition, the westernised class systems of reference (such as the UK's Registrar General's classification of occupations)[145] may be very far removed from the societal dynamics which operate within immigrant communities (particularly those tied to the developing world) whose members may well have rather diverse

---

[145] See https://www.ons.gov.uk/methodology/classificationsandstandards/otherclassifications/thenationalstatisticssocioeconomicclassificationnssecrebasedonsoc2010 (last accessed 28 April 2020) for the latest version and a history of its development.

experiences of class relations, as argued in Campling *et al.* (2016). Indeed, Milroy (1987b: 32–33) highlights the fact that standard UK-wide classification systems like these are not even necessarily compatible with the relationship between status and class within sub-regions of the UK. She notes, for example, the issues arising particularly for "investigators in Scotland and Northern Ireland" in this regard on account of their relative deprivation by comparison to England when attempting to apply such generic category distinctions locally (Milroy 1987b: 32).[146] It is for this reason that social class will not be examined here as a potential conditioning factor on (ING) behaviour. This will not be the case either for the variables analysed in Chapters Eight or Nine – even though an attempt has been made to control the population sample in this regard by restricting the study sites to two non-selective rather than selective schools where there are thus higher than average numbers of pupils qualifying for free school meals (see Chapter Six, §6.1.2.1). There is also the complexity of status and class to consider in the newcomer groups which is an important reason why Drummond (2012) in his study of (ING) amongst Polish speakers in Manchester does not address this issue either. The same is likely true for the other studies on this migrant group in Edinburgh and London already considered with respect to linguistic constraints by Schleef, Meyerhoff & Clark (2011) as well as Meyerhoff & Schleef (2012, 2014) though they suggest that this independent variable was also controlled for in sample selection (Meyerhoff & Schleef 2012: 400). Not surprisingly, given the orientations of these studies, other independent variables are considered that are not relevant to studies of (ING) in native-speaking contexts. Thus, Schleef, Meyerhoff and Clark (2011), for instance, used a verbal guise to investigate the newcomer teens' attitudes to the local Edinburgh or London accents which they were attempting to acquire. Also addressed were many of the factors introduced as relevant for L2 acquisition in §5.2.1 of Chapter Five, i.e. age, age of arrival, length of residence and proficiency. However, as already noted in Chapter Five, §5.1.3, Meyerhoff & Schleef (2014: 109) state that such external factors are generally not significant predictive factors for (ING) usage amongst their newcomer cohorts. Nonetheless, some of these independent variables may well still be worth exploring here, particularly since Drummond (2012: 120) reports length of residence as a significant factor influencing rates of alveolar use amongst the Polish migrants in his study.

---

146 See https://www.nisra.gov.uk/statistics/deprivation/northern-ireland-multiple-deprivation-measure-2017-nimdm2017 for the measures which apply to the study sites in Northern Ireland around the time of the data collection. Also see Abel, Barclay & Payne (2016: 1) whose study of deprivation revealed that: "Northern Ireland was the most deprived of all the UK countries. None of the areas in Northern Ireland were in the least deprived fifth of the UK, while 36.6% of the population of Northern Ireland were in the most deprived fifth of the UK."

He also comments that the male/female contrasts which invariably seem to be tied to (ING) usage across a range of global Englishes (including those already examined for indigenous communities in Northern Ireland) are confounded in a manner that is "quite striking" (2012: 118). Thus, the Polish female speakers in Manchester were "more likely to use the alveolar variant" (Drummond 2012: 125). The same reversal is also noted by Schleef, Meyerhoff & Clark (2011: 223–227). In their case, while gender proved not to be a significant conditioning factor on the linguistic behaviour of their Polish participants in London, the predicted native speaker pattern was again not replicated (i.e. the boys preferred the prestige variant while the young women favoured the alveolar one). Moreover, in Edinburgh while gender proved to be an important factor it could not be considered a significant constraint on [ɪŋ]/[ɪn] choice. Adamson & Regan whose 1991 study of Cambodian and Vietnamese learners of American English varieties was already discussed with respect to the linguistic constraints they uncovered, report instead that speaker sex actually proved to be a significant predictor of which variant was preferred by their L2 male and female speakers. Not only did they observe that the acquisition of the alveolar variant was acquired later (because [ɪŋ] is already part of their Asian L1 phonologies) but that the arrival of [ɪn] in their L2 English signified "integration into the speech community" (Adamson & Regan 1991: 4). The rationale here is based on their findings (*contra* Drummond 2012 and Schleef, Meyerhoff & Clark 2011) that in casual style, 15% of [ɪn] tokens were produced by non-native females which echoes the rate for their local peers of 20%. What is more, the alveolar variant featured in the speech of non-native men 23% of the time and while it is not nearly as frequent in this group as it is amongst the native male cohort (65%), Adamson & Regan (1991: 13) argue that the rates indicate that the L2 speakers are at least accommodating towards the norms of the indigenous male/female target groups.

Although the Cambodian and Vietnamese participants in this study are mainly older adults (only 5 out of 14 were in a similar age range to the sample populations in *Múin Béarla* and the Edinburgh and London studies already cited), it may well be worthwhile testing this gender constraint for the Armagh Lithuanian and Polish L1 teenagers too. This is especially so given Meyerhoff & Schleef's (2012: 407) proposal regarding adolescent migrants, in particular, who they argue:

> seem to acquire linguistic constraints more readily than non-linguistic constraints (e.g. attitudes, gender, etc.), and when non-linguistic constraints do emerge, there is a tendency for them to be associated with group categories, i.e. ones that already have a large degree of social meaning to teenagers, such as gender.

7.2 Research questions and methodology

This overview of previous research on the linguistic and social factors which have been demonstrated to constrain (ING) usage amongst native and non-native populations in the English-speaking world has suggested various lines of enquiry with respect to how this particular variable might pattern amongst the autochthonous and allochthonous teenagers in the Armagh *Múin Béarla* sample. Since the analysis in this context needs to be constrained in certain respects (to ensure replication, for instance, of the methods underpinning other studies with which the outcomes are to be compared), the discussion which follows will concentrate on the following research questions tailored to this particular variable. They are formulated on the basis of the outcomes of Houston (1985) *inter alia* reviewed in §§ 7.1.1–7.1.4 but hone in particularly on those described in Drummond (2012); Schleef, Meyerhoff & Clark (2011); Meyerhoff & Schleef (2012, 2014) on account of their relevance to another UK context as well as their focus on migrants whose first language is Polish. The research questions are accompanied by explanatory details from the coding protocol developed for the Armagh (ING) analysis which is largely based on those stipulated in these earlier works.

1. Are the constraint hierarchies associated with the linguistic factors (i)–(vii) below shared by adolescent L1 and L2 speakers of Armagh English?

   (i) Grammatical category
   adjective *(Irish is just so confus**ing** with the fadas)*
   discourse marker *(or someth**ing**)*
   gerund *(I hate danc**ing** in front of people)*
   noun (simple) *(he can say like "Good morn**ing**")*
   preposition *(and then we went to the match dur**ing** the night)*
   present participle *(Consider**ing** the cost is split three ways)*
   progressive verb *(why is he leav**ing**?)*
   pronoun *(I don't agree with anyth**ing**)*

   (ii) Preceding phonological context:
   apical
   glottal/velar
   other

   (iii) Following phonological context
   apical
   glottal/velar
   other vowel or consonant
   pause

(iv) Number of syllables in the lexical item with {-ing}
1–4 (e.g. *swimming, managing, entertaining*)

(v) Across-segment priming effects
preceding alveolar (e.g. *sinning*) or velar nasal (e.g. *singing*) within the same lexical item

(vi) Across-word priming effects
realization of preceding {-ing} variable as [ɪn]/[ɪŋ] etc. in preceding lexical items such as *I hate swimming and then cycling in the triathlon*

(vii) Lexical frequency
so as to test claims by Bybee (2007) *inter alia* which propose that this factor also has a potential impact on phonological variation

2. Are the constraint hierarchies associated with the social factors (i)–(ii) below shared by adolescent L1 and L2 speakers of Armagh English?

(i) Age
12 to 20 years of age

(ii) Sex
female/male

3. Are the constraint hierarchies associated with the social factors (i)–(ii) below shared by adolescent Lithuanian and Polish L2 speakers of Armagh English?

(i) Age of arrival
Pre-teen/post-teen

(ii) Length of residence
1.5 to 8+ years

4. Is there any correlation between ethnolinguistic heritage and (i) the variants associated with (ING) in this community (i.e. [ɪŋg]/[ɪŋk]/[ɪn]/[ɪŋ]) and (ii) their frequency of use?

Given the overarching comparative goal of the Armagh (ING) analysis, the coding protocol also mirrored certain decisions articulated in Drummond (2012) and Schleef, Meyerhoff & Clark (2011).[147] For instance, exclusions were applied

---

147 It is also important to note, of course, that Drummond (2012) as well as Schleef, Meyerhoff & Clark (2011) also coded for certain social variables such as attitudes towards local indigenous varieties amongst their migrant cohorts which will not be considered here.

Table 11 *Múin Béarla* sub-sample for (ING) analysis

Pseudonym	D.O.B	Sex	Ethnic Origin	Birthplace	L.O.R (years)
Katherine Gormley	02/12/1994	F	Northern Irish	South Tyrone	N/A
Sasha Grimley	22/06/1999	F	Northern Irish	Armagh	N/A
Ciara Hughes	26/09/1997	F	Northern Irish	Armagh	N/A
Michelle Maguire	01/03/1995	F	Northern Irish	Craigavon	N/A
Fergus Farrell	01/04/1999	M	Northern Irish	Armagh	N/A
Peter Logan	25/03/1999	M	Northern Irish	Armagh	N/A
Ciaran Maguire	17/06/1997	M	Northern Irish	Craigavon	N/A
Dara Maguire	17/06/1997	M	Northern Irish	Craigavon	N/A
Elzbieta Bayonaite	03/02/1997	F	Lithuanian	Kaunas, Lithuania	3
Roxy Bite	10/10/1999	F	Lithuanian	Kaunas, Lithuania	6
Laura Kažlauskaite	05/02/1996	F	Lithuanian	Vilkaviškis, Lithuania	5
Iera Simonis	11/11/1999	F	Lithuanian	Raseiniai, Lithuania	5
Ramus Barcus	03/03/2001	M	Lithuanian	Kaunas, Lithuania	2
Elada Danis	03/06/2001	M	Lithuanian	Joniškis, Lithuania	2
Daniellus Folkmanas	12/04/2002	M	Lithuanian	Joniškis, Lithuania	3
Leonas Lanka	04/10/2000	M	Lithuanian	Alytus, Lithuania	3
Ania Malek	01/09/1994	F	Polish	Kłodzko, Poland	5.5
Natasza Pasternak	17/10/1995	F	Polish	Bydgoszcz, Poland	8
Adrianna Wasko	17/05/2000	F	Polish	Wałbrzych, Poland	6
Polly Wiczorek	03/12/1994	F	Polish	Kraków, Poland	8+
Bolek Folta	01/01/2000	M	Polish	Morag, Poland	4
Andrzej Grzybowski	15/02/1998	M	Polish	Wałbrzych, Poland	2
Makary Mruk	10/04/2000	M	Polish	Gdańsk, Poland	1.5
Patros Stain	09/11/1997	M	Polish	Olsztyn, Poland	7

to tokens that were found in quoted or overlapping speech or were unclear due to phonetic reduction. In addition, in line with Schleef, Meyerhoff & Clark (2011: 216), particularly, "the first token of (ing) from every speaker was excluded" and only the first fifty were included giving a maximum token count of 1,146 which is roughly commensurate with that for the Schleef, Meyerhoff & Clark (2011: 216) Edinburgh corpus (1,556 tokens) based on a near identical protocol.[148] Attention was also paid to achieving a balanced sample of speakers from

---

148 The token count for Drummond (2012: 115) was also in the same ball park, i.e. 1,677.

the Armagh sub-corpus of *Múin Béarla* to include not only Polish speakers, as was the case for the previously cited studies of Edinburgh, London and Manchester, but which also incorporates a Lithuanian group. This was crucial so as to determine whether any diversity in (ING) usage arises as a result of social or linguistic differences between the East Baltic and West Slavic groups as well as amongst the autochthonous and allochthonous populations.[149] The demographics of the (ING) sub-sample of *Múin Béarla* are detailed in Table 11.

7.3 Results and discussion

7.3.1 Frequency distribution of (ING) variants

The data illustrated in Figure 55 indicate the distribution and token count of all (ING) variants among each teenage cohort in Armagh.

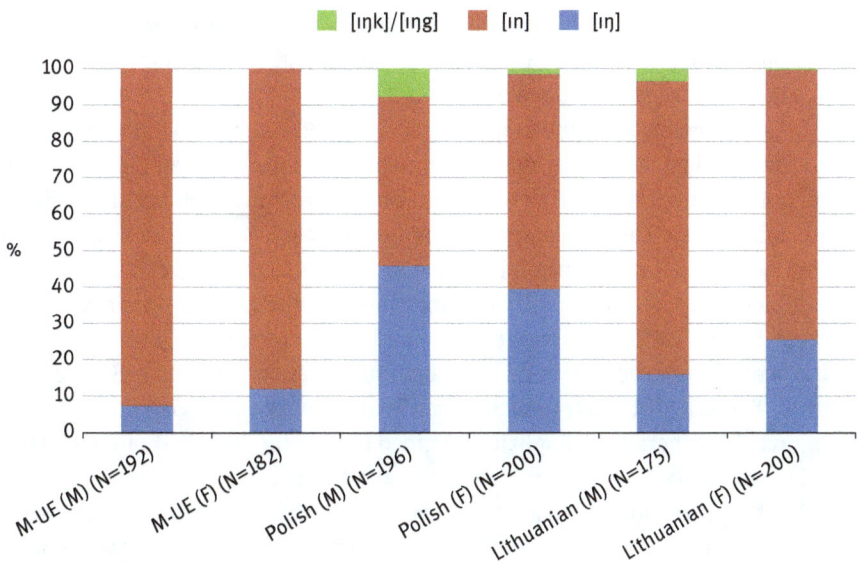

Figure 55 Percentage of (ING) variants by speaker group in Armagh[150]

---

149 That doing so might generate interesting differences is clear from the findings of Diskin (2015, 2017) which examined Chinese and Polish migrants' acquisition of Dublin English as well as Corrigan & Diskin (2020) which compares newcomer cohorts in both Armagh and Dublin (see Chapter Five, §5.2.1 for an overview of their results).
150 As usual, M-UE is an abbreviation of Mid-Ulster English and represents the dialect heritage of the local Armagh teens. F/M distinguishes males and females and N here indicates the number

As might be expected, given the relationship between [ɪŋk]/[ɪŋg] and transfer effects set out in §7.1.2, it is only the non-native speakers who use these variants in this data-set. Polish males produced the most tokens. Nevertheless, their production of this variant was extremely limited since it amounted to not quite 8% of their entire output. What is more, their Lithuanian peers produced less than half of that amount. There does seem to be some male/female distinction discernible though since the young Polish women in particular generated even fewer tokens than their male counterparts. In fact, their rates of use were much more similar to the Lithuanian females who were the lowest users of the variants amongst all four non-native speaker groups.

Gender differences also seem to be operating across all cohorts with respect to the usage of [ɪn] with the expected trend of local and Lithuanian females preferring this high-status variant over their male peers. The gender split is in the opposite direction, however, amongst the Polish cohorts. It is, in fact, men rather than women who favour velar realisations more which ties in with the constraints on this variable for speakers of the same heritage background in London and Manchester identified by Drummond (2012) and Schleef, Meyerhoff & Clark (2011), respectively, and noted earlier.

As predictable given the findings of O'Neill (1987) illustrated in Table 10 above, the male and female native speakers in this new Armagh Roman Catholic corpus are both high users of the alveolar variant in their conversational style. Indeed, this form is near categorical for the *Múin Béarla* teenage boys who use it almost 93% of the time (the figure for local girls is 88%). This suggests stability and reinforces the view that Mid-Ulster English shares the alveolar dominant pattern which Labov (2001: 90) identified for "Southern States English, northern English and Scots." It also obtains in the local Edinburgh variety reported in Schleef, Meyerhoff & Clark (2011: 217) (which is hardly surprising either given the historical origins of Northern Irish English, described in Chapter Two). Although the Lithuanian male cohort in Armagh does not reach these levels (their [ɪn] usage being 81% of all (ING) tokens), they do show a distinctive preference for this variant which clearly aligns with local patterns. Moreover, their female peers are not far behind since this is the dominant variant in their speech too (74%). What is very striking though is the dissonance again between the Lithuanian and local cohorts and those whose ethnolinguistic heritage is Polish. Fewer than half of the male

---

of (ING) tokens they each produced. The figures for [ɪŋg]/[ɪŋk] have been conflated since they represent such a small number of tokens overall (particularly amongst the young newcomer women of both Lithuanian and Polish descent). This finding is not especially surprising since low token counts for these variants in their Polish cohorts are also reported in Schleef, Meyerhoff & Clark (2011: 216) as well as Drummond (2012: 116–117).

tokens are alveolar and while 59 % of their female peers prefer this variant, they also do not come close to matching the rates for the young women who are born and raised in Armagh or Lithuania.

Figure 56 which collates the findings from the Armagh Polish male and female sub-corpora with those for Edinburgh, London & Manchester documented in Drummond (2012: 117) and Schleef, Meyerhoff & Clark (2011: 217) also proves thought-provoking in this respect.

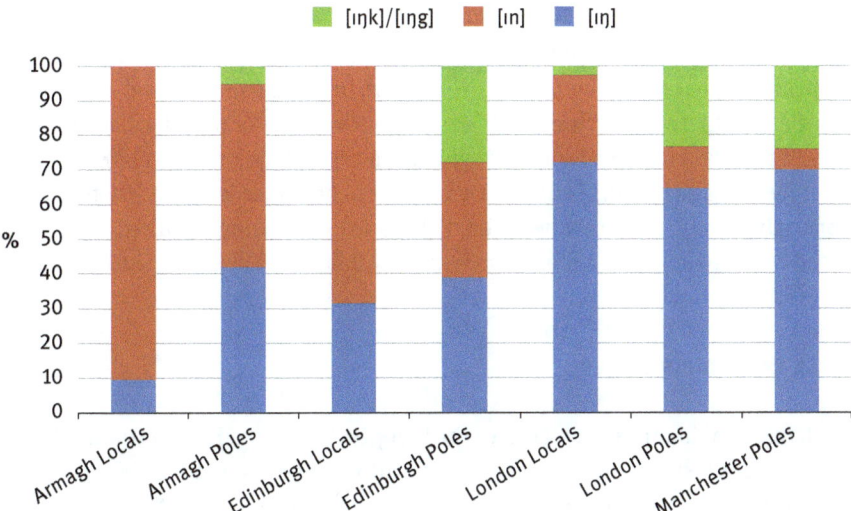

Figure 56 Percentage of (ING) variants amongst Polish L1 participants in Armagh, Edinburgh, London and Manchester[151]

Only 6 % of [ɪn] tokens were identified amongst the Polish L1 speakers participating in Drummond (2012: 117) who all preferred [ɪŋ] (70 % of their tokens).

---

[151] It is important to note that the data here is not exactly matched. For example, while the participants in Armagh, Edinburgh and London are all of school-going age, the Manchester sample comes from speakers aged between 18 and 40 (Drummond 2012: 113) so belong to a different life stage from an emic perspective (Eckert 1997a). In addition, while Drummond (2012: 112) also reports on data from "informal conversations", Schleef, Meyerhoff & Clark (2011: 216) conflate (ING) tokens for both conversational and reading tasks. That decision may suppress the levels of [ɪn] variation on account of the known stylistic constraint with respect to the alveolar *versus* velar patterns detailed in §7.1.4. Nevertheless, the figures across all four study sites offer interesting comparisons that would be worth taking further in analyses of the reading task data produced by the *Múin Béarla* teenage cohorts, for instance, and described in Chapter Six, §6.2.1 that there is not space here to consider.

The Armagh Polish male results are especially interesting therefore not only in the light of this outcome but also regarding the findings of Schleef, Meyerhoff & Clark (2011: 217). Their Polish cohorts are described as "sensitive to the overall rates of the apical variant", i.e. higher for Edinburgh native speakers than for those born and raised in London whose preference overall (like their Manchester peers) was for the velar variant. As already noted, this outcome better describes the sensitivity of the Lithuanian heritage cohorts in Armagh because the Polish migrant groups are rather more adrift from the community (ING) norms since they favour [ɪn] more than any of the others.

It is clear therefore that there may be interesting trends at work here with respect to speaker choice over [ɪn]/[ɪŋ]/[ɪŋk]/[ɪŋg] realisations and how these correlate with social factors such as gender and ethnolinguistic background. However, detailed analysis of the linguistic and social constraints on (ING) across all three Armagh cohorts is necessary in order to better understand whether local constraints (and their relative strength) are actually being acquired and replicated by these immigrant teenagers with East Baltic and West Slavic heritages.

7.3.2 Constraints on (ING)

With this goal in mind, all eleven of the independent or predictor variables listed in §7.2 were tested. I used the type of Rbrul mixed-effects multiple regression model characterised in §6.3 of Chapter Six and incorporated "speaker" as a random effect so as to improve confidence levels with respect to significant findings for any other factor, as advocated by Johnson (2009: 365). The most common Armagh variant [ɪn] was taken to be the application value and the results for the three ethnolinguistic groups are illustrated in Table 12.

It will already be apparent from the outcomes for certain predictors indicated immediately above that age, following phonological context and priming turned out to be not significant constraints typifying the hierarchies of the Armagh cohort and which both sets of migrant populations have arguably acquired. Of those applying to the non-native speakers alone, length of residence, for instance, did not prove to be a predictive factor either. This result is clearly of interest with respect to the findings in the opposite direction by Best & Tyler (2007), Diskin (2017), Drummond (2012), Flege (1995, 2009) and Saito & Brajot (2013) although it corroborates the evidence from Corrigan & Diskin (2020) as well as Meyerhoff & Schleef (2014) detailed in Chapter Five, §5.2.1.

Table 12 Significant constraints on (ING) among Armagh, Lithuanian and Polish cohorts. Factors favouring the application value of [ɪn] are indicated in bold. N.B. Predictors not selected as significant for the: (i) <u>M-UE cohort</u>: Grammatical category; Preceding phonological context; Following phonological context; Preceding variant; Priming; Speaker sex; Speaker age; (ii) <u>Lithuanian Newcomer cohort</u>: Following phonological context; Priming; Speaker age; Length of residence; (iii) <u>Polish Newcomer cohort</u>: Preceding phonological context; following phonological context; Priming; Speaker sex; Speaker age; Length of residence.

	M-UE				Lithuanian Newcomer				Polish Newcomer			
Total N				304				313				341
Deviance								169.269				199.775
Df								14				110
	Log Odds	N	%	FWs	Log Odds	N	%	FWs	Log Odds	N	%	FWs
Number of Syllables												
4+		5	1.000		0.504	9	0.889	0.623				
2	**0.839**	281	0.961	**0.698**	**1.131**	266	0.865	**0.756**				
3	−0.839	23	0.826	0.302	−1.635	38	0.316	0.163				
Preceding Nasal												
[ø]	**0.731**	248	0.968	**0.675**								
[n]	−0.731	56	0.875	0.325								
Grammatical Category												
Participle					**1.164**	50	0.920	**0.762**	**0.803**	44	0.682	**0.691**
Progressive					**0.968**	141	0.922	**0.725**	**1.224**	130	0.762	**0.773**
Adjective					**0.887**	17	0.765	**0.708**	−0.700	23	0.304	0.332
Gerund					**0.500**	20	0.750	**0.623**	0.410	48	0.458	**0.601**
Pronoun					−0.420	40	0.525	0.396	0.402	50	0.560	0.599
Discourse marker (−thing)					−0.724	26	0.462	0.327	**0.639**	28	0.679	**0.654**
Noun					−2.375	19	0.684	0.085	−2.779	18	0.111	0.058
Preceding Phon. Context												
Velar									**0.698**	57	0.807	**0.668**
Other									**0.501**	185	0.643	**0.623**
Alveolar									−1.200	99	0.424	0.232
Preceding Variant												
[ɪn]					**1.567**	218	0.876	**0.827**				
[ɪŋ]					**0.599**	89	0.629	**0.646**				
[ɪŋk]					−2.166	6	0.500	0.103				
Sex												
Male					**1.184**	147	0.932	**0.766**				
Female					−1.184	166	0.316	0.234				
Lexical Frequency												
Random Std. Dev.	9.067				0.001				1.170			
Speaker												
Random Std. Dev.	0.331				0.675				2.100			

There are also important disparities between the three cohorts with respect to how [ɪn] functions both linguistically and socially in their variable grammars. A really unusual result is the fact that grammatical category, known to be a near universal predictor of (ING) behaviour amongst English native speakers globally, has no significant effect on variant choice amongst the local Armagh cohort. This is especially noteworthy since Schleef, Meyerhoff & Clark (2011: 222) also report that this constraint was not significant either for the London-born teenagers in their sample. Moreover, they also remark that "For the Edinburgh-born adolescents, there is no evidence of a classic nominal-verbal continuum: common nouns behave no differently than verbs with respect to this variable" (Schleef, Meyerhoff & Clark 2011: 219). As they argue, this outcome may arise on account of the fact that their study systematically included all compounds with {-thing} (pronominal *anything* as well as discourse marker *or anything*) which were also considered here. Schleef, Meyerhoff & Clark (2011: 219–222) also suggest that the lack of a continuum "could be a local constraint." There may, in fact, be more mileage in this argument now that these Armagh findings have been added to the mix given the historical connections between the two dialects.[152] Moreover, in the Armagh case, there is also the fact alluded to in §7.1.1 that progressive forms in Irish English dialects occur at much higher rates by comparison to other varieties which might alter the constraint hierarchy in Armagh with respect to (ING) variability in interesting ways. In addition, Armagh progressives may well not be absolutely structurally and functionally identical anyway to those used in other vernaculars given the possibility of transfer effects from Irish that were also introduced in §7.1.1. As such, their inclusion within the same closed set as that used in other studies of (ING) in American, Antipodean and British varieties may well be somewhat moot given the arguments regarding the *after*-perfect in Armagh English rehearsed in Chapter Six, §6.3. Such matters would, however, be very worthwhile considering in future comparative research which pits the (ING) variability associated with the grammatical category constraint in Armagh English against hierarchies across the entire island of Ireland as well as elsewhere in the British Isles and beyond.

All that aside, as Table 12 demonstrates, the Lithuanian and Polish groups do have such a verbal>nominal continuum and would thus appear to have developed an (ING) variable system which is rather more like that of other English dialects reported in the literature. Although the constraint hierarchies for grammatical

---

[152] This is harder to argue for in a multicultural city such as London, though, despite the very significant numbers of Irish immigrants documented there from the Great Famine period onwards, detailed in Chapter Three. See Cheshire *et al.* (2011) for a discussion of the dialect's development and Delaney (2012) as well as MacRaild (2006, 2011) on Irish famine migration to Victorian British cities including London.

category amongst both cohorts are not perfectly matched by any means, it is undeniable that the alveolar variant is favoured in participles, progressives and gerunds by all the newcomers. However, when {-ing} is word final in nominal lexemes like *morning*, it becomes disfavoured, as indicated by the negative Log Odds for both Lithuanian and Polish participants in Table 12 (as per Labov 1989: 87 *inter alia)*. Their linguistic behaviour, therefore, is just as one might expect if these individuals had migrated instead to Manchester or York where Drummond (2012) and Tagliamonte (2004b), respectively, report a verbal>nominal continuum of exactly this type. As previously noted in Chapter Six, none of these newcomers had lived in another English-speaking country for longer than a holiday period, so it remains to be seen how exactly they have ended up with such a constraint hierarchy for grammatical category and whether it arises perhaps on account of the fact that their friendship networks are predominantly with each other rather than with the Armagh teenagers. Although the arguments in Cheshire *et al.* (2008: 1) suggest that this would indeed be a worthwhile exercise since such mechanisms can be the "motor of dialect change", addressing this issue would be well beyond the scope of the current analysis.[153] That said, there are no other factors which the migrant groups share with respect to (ING). Moreover, of the two predictors which proved to be significant for those born and raised locally (i.e. number of syllables and preceding nasal), it is only the Lithuanians who replicate one of these Armagh effects (i.e. the former). Thus, both groups disfavour the alveolar nasal in trisyllabic words and favour them in disyllables (though this is a much stronger effect in the Lithuanian data than it is for that produced by local speakers).

Unlike the Armagh group, the Lithuanian cohort show a very strong alveolar preference effect when the preceding nasal is also [ɪn] and a weaker one for [ɪŋ]. However, when the preceding nasal is the transfer-induced [ɪŋk] type, the alveolar variant is dispreferred since this factor actually produced negative Log Odds in the regression model.

While it was already noted that the distributional trend for sex differences amongst Armagh locals illustrated in Figure 56 was not found to be a significant conditioning factor in this model, it is very much in evidence in the conversational data from the Lithuanian cohort. Moreover, the constraint shows the classic pattern rather than that introduced earlier for the Polish participants in London and Manchester involved in the studies by Schleef, Meyerhoff & Clark (2011) and Drummond (2012: 125), respectively, i.e. the young Lithuanian women in Armagh disfavour the non-standard [ɪn] variant while their male peers favour it (as was already implicated in their distributional analysis also considered in Figure 55).

---

153 The mechanisms for doing so in future research on the *Múin Béarla* and emigrant correspondence corpora that have been the focus here will be explored in Chapter Ten.

The regression model captured in Table 12 clearly likewise shows that the Polish migrants have also acquired a rather different (ING) constraint hierarchy, since grammatical category (as noted earlier) and preceding segmental context (i.e. velar, other or alveolar) are the only two factors which influence their choice of [ɪn] over [ɪŋ]. As far as the phonological conditioning effect is concerned, [ɪn] is disfavoured when following another alveolar consonant but is preferred when preceding consonants are either velar or have some other place of articulation (with the strongest preference for velars).

The regression model presented in Table 12 thus permits a view of the acquisition process for L1 speakers of these East Baltic and West Slavic languages which goes well beyond the frequency effects described in Figures 55 and 56. It offers a window onto (ING) variation which describes how this variable operates for the first time in an Irish English context and of course goes further because it also provides insights into how two groups of migrant speakers with different L1s do or do not acquire the constraints impacting on this aspect of Armagh English morphophonology.[154] It should also be clear from these results that there is excellent evidence here to support the views articulated in the acquisition of sociolinguistic variation literature laid out in Chapter Five, §5.2.1 with regard to concepts such as "transformation under transfer" Meyerhoff (2003) and (2009: 312). In other words, even the Lithuanian migrants whose frequency distributions most closely matched those of the locals, rarely replicate the constraints which operate on local Armagh English. Even when they do so (as would seem to be the case for them with the independent variable "number of syllables") the strength of the effects is not identical between the autochthonous and allochthonous groups. It will therefore be very interesting to investigate in subsequent Chapters whether these Lithuanian and Polish L1 speakers more successfully acquire variables from other parts of the grammar.

---

154 This is crucial because it has already become apparent that each allochthonous group has developed quite unique patterns of (ING) conditioning. Such effects are rarely seen since most research in this vein compares native speaker English with the output of a single ethnolinguistic immigrant cohort (Drummond 2012; Meyerhoff & Schleef 2012, 2014; Schleef, Meyerhoff & Clark 2011). This prevents any observation of how migrants with different L1s might acquire local constraints given the diverse internal transfer effects which might be at play or indeed how constraint hierarchies might be transformed for indexical purposes tied to L1 heritage or other social affiliations. Corrigan & Diskin (2020) and Diskin (2017) are thus exceptional in this regard. As such, this issue will be returned to in Chapter Nine when the findings for the (BE LIKE) variable in the Armagh autochthonous and allochthonous groups are set against those of Diskin & Levey (2019) who examine native speakers in Dublin and Ottawa alongside output from Polish migrants in Dublin.

8 No taming the Armagh vernacular either

8.1 Setting the scene

In very general terms, the use of a relativization strategy of any kind is an attempt to either minimize or eliminate potential ambiguity between root and embedded clauses. Natural languages have individually solved this problem in a variety of ways, though there are arguments in the literature which suggest that there is a universality in the types of strategy available and in the ways in which specific strategies are constrained from a syntactic perspective, as already noted in Chapter Five, §5.1.3.

Cheshire (1999) in a paper on 'Taming the Vernacular' put the variability of relative clause strategies amongst adolescent speakers in three English towns under the spotlight. She found that a non-standard paradigm for the marking of relative clauses was well-established across England (even in more isolated urban centres such as Hull). The research by Tagliamonte, Smith & Lawrence (2005) entitled 'No Taming the Vernacular' took this research considerably further by providing systematic comparative analyses across a wide range of British dialects including the Ulster Scots variety spoken in the north east of Northern Ireland. Their findings suggest that relative marking using *who* (particularly in non-subject function) is much rarer here than it is in any other community that they studied (2005: 89). This outcome provides a useful baseline for an investigation along similar lines of the strategies employed almost a decade later by adolescent speakers of Mid-Ulster English and their Lithuanian and Polish peers who are in the process of acquiring the local Armagh variety.

It has already been noted in Chapter Five, §5.2.3 that despite its complexities, the relative clause paradigm and aspects of its variability amongst English-speaking children is in place before puberty (Levey 2006: 65; and also see Diessel & Tomasello 2005, Levey 2015, Oetting & Newkirk 2011, Romaine 1985).[155] Moreover, as §8.2.3 argues, the L1 relative systems of the Balto-Slavic populations of interest to this analysis have also been acquired long before then. What will be important to know therefore is whether newcomers are equally successful not only at learning the relevant Armagh English constructions and markers themselves but also at manipulating the constraints which have been identified on their operation in previous research.

---

[155] The complexity derives primarily from the fact that successful acquisition involves knowledge from different levels of the grammar, i.e. semantics and pragmatics as well as morphosyntax – a process which is documented as likely to incur "processing difficulties", according to Sorace (2005: 74) *inter alia*. See also Wiechman (2015) who details the types of processing issues tied to English relative clause formation specifically.

As already identified for (ING) variability in the previous chapter, that tied to the relative paradigm is likewise a reflex of longitudinal processes of change within English and these are articulated in the next section. This is then followed in §8.2 by a review of the systems documented in global Englishes (§8.2.1), Irish English (§8.2.2) and the strategies available in Balto-Slavic languages (§8.2.3). The chapter then closes in §§8.3 and 8.4 with analyses of the internal and external factors conditioning variation in the relative clause paradigm of L1 and L2 Armagh English in comparative perspective.

8.1.1 The origins of relative clause variability in Armagh English

There are aspects of relative clause variability in Armagh English which reflect its development as an L2 variety and thus do not exactly match those documented for the standard variety by Quirk *et al.* (1985, §13.10 and §13.14) or for other English vernaculars globally (Cheshire 1999; D'Arcy & Tagliamonte 2010; Levey 2006, 2015; Levey & Hill 2013; Tagliamonte, Smith & Lawrence 2005 *inter alia*). This is on account of the fact that certain variants used by local Armagh English speakers are considered to have been generated by convergence between Irish and conservative English patterns that were productive during the period when this region was colonized, as set out in Part I (Corrigan 1997, 2000, 2009, 2010; Filppula 1999; Hickey 2007; McCafferty 2007). This outcome is not unique, as Mesthrie (1991: 465–468) demonstrates with regard to the development of the relativisation system operating amongst speakers of South African Indian English, which is also influenced by substrate languages. Hence, varieties in both Armagh and South Africa incorporate ancillary relative strategies in English restrictive (RR) and non-restrictive (NRR) (or appositive) relative postmodification in addition to also employing the three principal relative marking types associated with the standard language (*WH-* relative pronoun *(WH-)*; *THAT-*complementizer *(TH-)* and omission (Ø)). By convention, RR and NRR are differentiated on the assumption that heads in the former can only be successfully identified by recourse to the given modification, (78) whereas an NRR head is either unique or has been identified independently in the preceding discourse (79) (Quirk *et al.* 1985: 858). In spoken language, these types are distinguished by intonation, and in writing by punctuation. Furthermore, it is apparent that their historical development, contemporary reflexes and syntactic functions are somewhat different.

(78) The clouds which are white are in that part of the sky

(79) The clouds, which are white, are in that part of the sky

8.1.2 Ancillary strategies in the history of English

It is not surprising that Old English would have made greater use of the ancillary relativizing strategies noted previously as it did not inherit any relative markers from Indo-European. Although subordinating relative constructions are by no means rare in Old English, most scholars agree that the English system of parataxis in this period was more fully developed (Strang 1970: 303–304). There are three specific types which are worthy of comment here, i.e. (i) "incipient hypotaxis" (Stockwell and Minkova 1991: 370; (ii) correlative and (iii) subordinating – Fischer, van Kemenade, Koopman & van der Wurff 2000: 88–91). As regards the first of these, research on child language, pidgins and creoles has identified certain linguistic categories (particularly, deictics such as demonstrative pronouns, interrogatives and place adverbials) which have the potential to perform the function of a relative marker in the absence of such a category in the grammar (Aitchison 1992; Levey 2000: 23–24; Romaine 1984a: 275, 1984b, 1988, 1992). This option was already available in Old English, as is apparent from (80) in which the demonstrative adverb *þær* seems to have an ambivalent function in the language as both adverb and conjunct:

(80) & þy   ilcan geare hie   fuhton   wiþ   Brettas   [156][*þær*   mon
     & that   same year   they   fight-PAST   against Britons   there-where   one
     nu   nemneþ   Cerdices ford]
     now   call-PRES.   Cerdicesford
     'and in that same year they fought against the Britons there-where it is now called Cerdicesford'
     [ChronA 16.1 (519), cited in Mitchell (1985: §2444)]

The use of 'copy-correlatives' with identical spelling at the head of both the root and subordinate clauses is another option available for the purpose of minimizing the ambiguity between the root and embedded clause (Stockwell & Minkova 1991). (81) and (82) illustrate the strategy in Old English and (83) suggests that it would seem to have persisted into the Early Modern period when Ireland was colonised:

(81) *þær* þæt gemynd biþ,   [*þær* biþ   þæt andgyt   and se wylla]
     there the mind   be-PRES. there be-PRES.   the understanding   and the will
     'where the mind is, there is the understanding and the will'
     [Thorpe, Anal, 65, cited in Stockwell and Minkova (1991: 370)]

---

[156] These brackets designate the phrase with relative clause function here and *passim*. The relative marker is in bold and the NP antecedent in italics.

(82) **þonne** hit dagian   wolde, [**þonne** toglad   hit]
      then   it dawning be-PAST then   glide-away-PAST it
      'when it was becoming dawn, then it glided away'
      [*Chronicle*, 979, cited in Stockwell and Minkova (1991: 370)]

(83) **Then** Gerames saw how the shipp was comynge to that porte, [**then** he sayd to his company, syrs, lett us go]
      [c. 16c, Berner's *Huon*, cited in Stockwell and Minkova (1991: 371)]

The third ancillary type, designated 'subordinating' above refers to the use of *and* without a coordinating function. Occurrences have been posited as far back as Old English, so that Denison (1986: §2.2); van Kemenade (1987: 177) and Mitchell (1964: 118) have remarked that conjoined sentences with clause-initial *ac/ond/ne* (*but/and/nor*) exhibit the SXV order associated with other Old English subordinates. This strategy persisted in Middle English (84) and became very frequent in the Early Modern period (85a), as Traugott (1972: 148) confirms, so that it too will have been an available target strategy for incipient Irish-English bilinguals to acquire (see Corrigan 1997, 2000, 2009; Filppula 1991). Moreover, the fact that examples like (85b) from the *Helsinki Corpus* are not attested may indicate that this strategy also relies on the presence of a resumptive pronoun (RP).

(84) Now, or   I fynde a man thus trewe and stable,
      Now before I find   a man thus true   and stable
      [**And** wol for love his deth so frely take]
      and   will for love his death so freely take
      'Now, before I find a man so true and loyal, **who** will so nobly accept death out of love!'
      [Chaucer *Legend* 703, cited in Fischer, van Kemenade, Koopman & van der Wurff 2000: 90)]

(85) a. [I] only found *five or six* in the said pond, [**and those** very sick and lean]
          'I only found five or six in the said pond each of which was very sick and lean' (Filppula (1991: 624))
      b. *[I] only found *five or six* in the said pond, [**and** __ very sick and lean]

8.1.3 Relative marking strategies in the history of English

There are two principal structures associated with relative clause marking in the history of English, i.e. (i) the zero, omission or contact relative type (Ø) linked to RRs and (ii) a relative marker category used for both the latter and NRRs which in contemporary mainstream English takes the forms *(WH-)* and *(TH-)*. From the Early Modern period onwards, Ball (1996) documents a paradigm shift whereby the *who* marker became favoured with personal subjects while *that* was more likely in other functions (see also D'Arcy & Tagliamonte (2010: 404) who describe this as "a divisional reorganization").

With respect to Ø, Jespersen (1933/1983: 360–361) used the term "contact" relative to define sentences which clearly participate in a matrix-embedding relationship in which a Noun Phrase (NP) is relativized without recourse to overt marking.[157] Fischer (1992: 17) states that "the employment of subjectless relatives in Middle English" has been attributed to post-Conquest borrowing from French although she notes that there is no "consensus of opinion on [this]." Indeed, some scholars believe that while it was rare and restricted to the subject position (Fischer, van Kemenade, Koopman & van der Wurff 2000: 93), the omission strategy originated in colloquial usage in Old English and continued into Middle English increasing in frequency during the Early Modern period (perhaps as a consequence of the parallel in French?) Amongst the latter, Fischer, van Kemenade, Koopman & van der Wurff (2000: 93); van der Auwera (1984); Lass (1987: 187); Nagucka (1980); Strang (1970: 303) and Visser (1963–1973: §538) all testify to the existence of Janus-like structures such as (86) in Old English:

(86) *Adam ben king and eue quuen of alle þe þinge* [ø *in werlde ben*]
  Adam are king and Eve queen of all the things in world are
  'Adam and Eve are king and queen of all the things **that** are in the world'
  [*Genesis and Exodus* 296–297, cited in Fischer, van Kemenade, Koopman & van der Wurff (2000: 93)]

By 970, the Old English indeclinable relative particle *þe* which has a clear relative and subordinating force, had become reasonably frequent in constructions which nowadays would be marked by *(WH-)* or *(TH-)* forms (see Table 13). Moreover, possibly as a reflex of the correlative type in §8.1.2, the 'doubly-filled COMP' or RP-type relative *se þe* 'he … etc. who' was common in emphatic contexts or where the marking of agreement was required. In Middle English, these two seem to

---

157 Siemund (2013: 265–266) identifies this type as "subject gapping" and remarks that the phenomenon is "widespread in non-standard varieties" (p. 266).

have coalesced into a weak form *þe* and a corresponding strong form *þæt* which eventually disambiguated their functions into article *versus* demonstrative and relative pronoun, respectively, as argued in Fischer, van Kemenade, Koopman & van der Wurff (2000: 91). A similar differentiation in status seems to have occurred with the ancestors of the modern *WH-* forms which are derived from the Old English interrogative class whose members included *hwā* 'who', *hwilc* 'which' and *hwǣr* 'where' (Fischer, van Kemenade, Koopman & van der Wurff 2000: 92–93; Lass 1987: 185–190; Nevalainen & Raumolin-Brunberg 2002: 112; Romaine 1984c: 447–452; and Strang 1970: 303–304).

Prior to the work of Romaine (1980, 1981) on Middle Scots, accounts of relativization in the history of English such as that of Mustanoja (1960: 190 ff.) (summarized in Table 13) could be described as monolithic. With no regard for social, regional or stylistic variation, the *WH-* relative pronouns are described as supplanting an earlier system in which *TH-* forms predominated and relative omission is extant in both Old and Middle English becoming confined in Modern English to object-contact positions.

Table 13 Relative clause marking in Old, Middle and Modern English (Mustanoja 1960: 190 ff.)

Marker Type	OE	ME	ModE
Demonstratives	se, sēo, þæt etc.	þat/that ⟶ the the	that
Indeclinable Relative Particle	þe	þe	N/A
Interrogatives	hwā, hwilc, hwǣr etc.	who, which, where etc.	who, which, where etc.
Omission (zero)	Ø	Ø	Ø (non-subject relatives only)

Although there is not space here to re-consider the arguments put forward in Chapter Five, §5.1.3 with respect to the relationship between relative clause marking strategies and the Case Accessibility Hierarchy, Romaine has argued that these relativization strategy changes between the Middle Ages and today are in some sense universally motivated and hence predictable via this mechanism (for summaries of the arguments, see Corrigan 1997; Hendery 2012, Herrmann 2005; Romaine 1984c and Siemund 2013). Suffice it to say at this point, that Romaine (1982, 1984c) proposes that the changes were incremental and that relative omission was the norm in the most complex positions (i.e. object of comparison, genitive and oblique) until *WH-* marking acquires its relativizing and subordinating functions. Gradually, subject relative omission became disfavoured to the extent that in the modern mainstream varieties globally, as already pointed out, *WH-* relative and *TH-* markers have become categorical in this function, though omission continues with objects and indefinites in certain registers. Hence, Quirk *et al.* (1985: 865) denotes (87) as ungrammatical, though it would be acceptable in a number of contemporary non-standard dialects, as we shall see.

(87)   *The table [ø stands in the corner has a broken leg]*

Genitive *of which* and oblique object *to which* are thought to have appeared first and to have become established in the period 1400–1500. The pronouns *whom* and *whose* which distinguish animacy of the antecedent as well as object and genitive functions surface in the fifteenth century while the nominative *who* only ousts the subject-contact unmarked type in the sixteenth (see also Ball 1996). Moreover, the adoption of the *WH-* strategy appears to have been sensitive to both stylistic stratification in the sense of Labov (1966) and RR *versus* NRR function. Hence it occurs first in more formal (particularly Latinate) styles and, again, the nominative type is confined to formal usage for longer than the object or genitive categories. Similarly, forms with co-referential *WH-* pronouns predominate in NRR post-modification and the *TH-* forms favour RR contexts.

Table 14 The expansion of relative markers in the history of English: a reconstruction (Romaine 1982: 53 ff.)

Strategy	c. 1100	c. 1400	c. 1500	c. 1600
TH-	þat	þat	that	that
WH-	þe	of which to which whose whom	of which to which which whose whom	of which to which which whose whom who
ø-	ø	ø	ø	ø

8.2 Relative formation strategies in L1 and L2 English vernaculars

There is considerably more research now available on relative formation strategies in contemporary spoken non-standard British and extra-territorial Englishes than there was when Tagliamonte, Smith & Lawrence (2005: 243) remarked that: "comparably little is known about relative markers" in vernacular Englishes. Findings overall suggest that the scenario presented in Table 13 cannot be generalized, as § 8.2.1 will demonstrate. The system in Irish English outlined in § 8.2.2 also warrants special attention partly because Armagh English is one of its dialects but also on account of the fact that its ancillary strategies may originate in a convergence process arising from the language shift scenario detailed in Part I. § 8.2.3 examines relative clause marking paradigms in the L1s of migrant participants in the *Múin Béarla* corpus in case there might also be interlanguage issues here to address that may have some impact on the analyses which follow in §§ 8.3. and 8.4.

8.2.1 Relative formation strategies in global Englishes

Contemporary non-standard Englishes globally have recourse to complex relative marking types (including *WH*-forms) such as those outlined immediately above as well as versions of the ancillary strategies mentioned in § 8.1.2 (especially 'Subordinating *And*' (88) and the RP/correlative type (89)–(94) which are relics from earlier stages of English). In many of these varieties, as the sample from a wide range of global Englishes in (88)–(104) reveals, the typical ratio of relative pronouns lags behind the Modern English column of Table 13 and they appear instead to be at various points along the reconstructed continuum of Table 14. While there is certainly evidence for *WH*-marking too (95)–(98), these varieties can readily be characterized as necessitating greater reliance by their speakers on Ø and *TH*- strategies in order to relativize heads in both subject position (101) as well as in more complex ones such as genitive – particularly where RRs are concerned (Tagliamonte, Smith & Lawrence 2005: 94). Moreover, the *WH*- strategy has much in common with the velar nasal [ŋ] variant discussed in the previous chapter since it is likewise often reserved for formal contexts and is generally associated with speakers who are well-educated and of high social status (Beal & Corrigan (2002: 126, 2007: 110–112); Buchstaller & Corrigan (2015: 90); Cheshire, Adger & Fox 2013: 56; D'Arcy & Tagliamonte 2010: 384; Levey (2006: 57); Nevalainen & Raumolin-Brunberg (2002: 119–120); Romaine (1982: 206); Sigley (1997: 230); Tagliamonte, Smith & Lawrence (2005: 92) *inter alia*).[158]

---

[158] Though Hinrichs, Szmrescsanyi & Bohman (2015) note new trends even in written discourse towards *that* in place of *which* that is worth mentioning.

Regional Englishes globally also boast a wider range of relative markers than those found in mainstream varieties. They include *what* (105), *as* (106), *at* (107) and have been documented as being present in English since the Middle English period (Mustanoja 1960: 202 and Poussa 2002 for *what*). Indeed, they may have arisen through contact with Scandinavian peoples even earlier (Beal & Corrigan 2005: 224 regarding *at*). As Hermann (2005: 24–28), Levey (2006: 49–51), Beal & Corrigan (2005: 225) and Buchstaller & Corrigan (2015: 88–90) all remark, these are dialect specific and tend, for example, to be more closely associated with urban centres (Cheshire 1999: 67; Tagliamonte 2002: 164), particularly those in southern Britain (Poussa 1988 and Cheshire, Adger & Fox 2013). Moreover, Cheshire, Edwards & Whittle (1993: 69), Levey (2006: 57) as well as Tagliamonte (2002: 148) all report on the infrequency of these types by comparison to relatives marked by WH-, TH- and Ø. All of these marked and unmarked forms will of course need to be considered further, however, in connection with the target Armagh dialect which the allochthonous participants in *Múin Béarla* are acquiring to which I now turn. They will also be relevant when deciding on the envelope of variation in §8.3, particularly given their frequency of occurrence in the sample.

(88)   She had *a child* [**and the child** died in the ship]
        (South African Indian English; cited in Mesthrie (1992: 78)

(89)   *The girl* [**that her** eighteenth birthday was on that day was stoned – coudnae stand up]
        (Scots; cited in Miller 1993: 111)

(90)   This is *the man* [**ø his** horse was stolen]
        (Somerset English; cited in Ihalainen 1985: 66)

(91)   *The spikes* [**that** you stick in the ground and throw rings over **them**]
        (Scots: cited in Miller 1993: 111–112)

(92)   Starter is *a thing* [**that it** gets hot quickly]
        (South African Indian English: cited in Mesthrie 1991: 467)

(93)   **which one** *principal* came here [**she**'s strict just like the other faller]
        (South African Indian English; cited in Mesthrie 1991: 466)

(94)   in New York on Manhattan Island **there** is *a theatre* **there** [**that**...]
        (Scots; cited in Miller 1993: 113)

(95)   Beside me was *the lady* [**who** presented the queen]
        (Scots; cited in Tagliamonte, Smith & Lawrence 2005: 76)

(96)   We used to have *the snowstorms* [**which** we don't get now]
        (Quebec English; cited in Levey & Hill 2013: 33)

(97) The attitude of many Europeans to *things* [**which** were sacred] caused a further area of separation
(New Zealand English; cited in Sigley 1997: 207)

(98) You know *my cousin* [**whose** husband died]
(Tyneside English; cited in Beal & Corrigan 2005: 219)

(99) Leck is *a young boy* [ø was coming home from school]
(Tyneside and Northumbrian; cited in Beal 1993: 208)

(100) He's got *one boy* [ø is twelve, and the other is nine]
(South African Indian English; cited in Mesthrie 1991: 466)

(101) *The man* [**that** went]
(Southern British English; cited in Edwards 1993: 228)

(102) It's double *(-T)*[159] *money* [**what** you're getting at home]
(Sheffield English; cited in Beal & Corrigan 2005: 222)

(103) *The food* [**as** I bought]
(Southern British English; cited in Edwards 1993: 229)

(104) *Kelvin* [**at** my first husband]
(Sheffield English; cited in Beal & Corrigan 2005: 224)

8.2.2 Relative formation strategies in Irish English

On the basis that other contemporary vernaculars retain a variety of conservative relativizing strategies, we might hypothesize that the relative pronoun ratio incorporated in the grammar of Armagh English will, likewise, not concur with that of the standard and may contain gaps so that certain categories (especially complex types such as the genitive in (90), for instance) might be unrelativizeable without recourse to alternative RP strategies and the like.

Corrigan (2010); Herrmann (2005); Finlay (1994); Finlay & McTear (1986); Harris (1993); Geisler (2002); McCafferty (2007); Montgomery (2006); Policansky (1976, 1982) and Robinson (2006b) offer general descriptions of the linguistic and social distribution of relativisation in contemporary varieties of Northern Irish English. Tagliamonte, Smith & Lawrence (2005) provides a similar but more

---

[159] This abbreviation represents a common lower northern English phenomenon known as 'Definite Article Reduction.' See Beal, Burbano-Elizondo & Llamas (2012: 50) and the summary in Buchstaller & Corrigan (2015: 82).

focused and nuanced treatment of Ulster Scots communities and it also has a diachronic dimension. Moreover, this research diverges from the others because it recognises the importance of using formal models to account for relativising processes, an approach that is also typified by Henry (1995) and Corrigan (1997, 2009) though the latter differ from one another in certain respects. Firstly, Henry (1995) focuses exclusively on Ø- marking in the Belfast variety of Mid-Ulster English while Corrigan's research is centred on South Ulster English but includes all the marked and unmarked forms which are documented in this dialect. Secondly, Corrigan's investigations (1997, 2009) address both diachronic as well as language contact issues whereas Henry (1995) takes a purely synchronic approach.

In sum, the research to date suggests that the *as, at* and *what* forms noted earlier are generally not reported to be productive in any contemporary variety except Ulster Scots which has *at* (108) and for which Tagliamonte, Smith & Lawrence (2005: 76) also report *what* (see also Filppula 1999: 185; Herrmann 2005: 27; Hickey 2007: 260; Montgomery 2006: 78–80; Robinson 2006b: 104–105). Instead, as examples (105)–(110) from Corrigan (2010: 71) indicate, relative marking is principally achieved using zero (106) alongside *TH-* forms like *that* (107) and *WH-* pronouns such as *who* (108). However, as already mentioned, the latter relative marking type is reported to be very infrequent in Northern Irish English dialects (especially in non-subjects). Thus, Tagliamonte, Smith & Lawrence (2005: 89) record a figure of just 5 % for Ulster Scots when the relative is in subject function (i.e. where it would be expected most) by comparison to other peripheral areas of the UK including those which contributed the region's founder populations, i.e. Scotland and North West England where the rates were 10 % and 14 %, respectively.[160] By comparison, there is better evidence of the two ancillary strategies detailed in §8.1.2, namely, resumptive pronoun marking as in (109) where *she* here is an RP referring back to *cousin* as well as 'Subordinating *And*' (110) (which would be glossed as 'You'll see *a wee clock* in the window [**which** is still going]').

(105)   *The girl* [**at** saw me]

(106)   because of all *the paedophilia* [ø went on in the church]

(107)   most of *the working class* [**that** lived on the street] was like that

---

160 See also Levey & Pichler (2020) which uncovers interesting cross-dialectal distinctions tied to the peripherality or otherwise of the diverse transatlantic communities in their study. This will be worth bearing in mind for the next phase of *Múin Béarla* research which will examine the relative paradigm in Donaghmore and Belfast to ascertain whether type of community is also a relevant factor governing variant choice in a Northern Irish context.

(108) there was *a very domineering lady* on it [**who** called herself 'a Professor']

(109) I've *a cousin* [ø a nurse, **she** lives in Ederney]

(110) You'll see *a wee clock* in the window [**and** it goin' yet]

In fact, all of the research to date notes that, in line with the situation cross-dialectally in the vernacular Anglophone world (as evidenced by Herrmann 2005, Kortmann, Lunkenheimer & Ehret 2020, as well as Siemund 2013 *inter alia*) WH- forms are the least favoured strategy in all Northern Irish English vernaculars. There are, however, interesting local differences suggesting that the distribution of the marking in (105)–(110) is both internally and externally constrained. Thus, although Geisler (2002) in his investigation of the *Northern Ireland Transcribed Corpus of Speech* (NITCS) finds that the grammatical function of the relative marker was not critical in determining speaker choice, some linguistic constraints were observable. Of particular note were the RR/NRR nature of the relative clause and the type of antecedent (subject, object and so on) that the relative marker was correlated with. Corrigan (1997), (2009) as well as Henry (1995) and Tagliamonte, Smith & Lawrence (2005), by contrast, find more pronounced internal factors influencing relative marking alongside these. Thus, Henry (1995: 124–125) notes that zero marking of subject relatives is only possible in relative clauses that contain in their matrix clause either *there* existentials (108) above or a limited set of verbs including stative possessives (109). The phenomenon is also restricted to quite specific discourse contexts (the matrix clause must introduce a new individual as topic and the relative clause must comment on them).

In a similar vein, Tagliamonte, Smith & Lawrence (2005) find that zero in Ulster Scots, which is their focus, is favoured in the subject relatives of simple clauses but disfavoured elsewhere. Likewise, Corrigan (2009) demonstrates that while speakers agree that zero marking is very acceptable when it occurs in existential constructions like (111) below, it is less acceptable in other types of relative clause.

(111) there was *a lot of us* [ø went to South Africa]
(Derry English; cited in Corrigan 2010: 72)

External factors have also been implicated in variable choice including regional differences. Hence, Geisler (2002) reports *WH-* forms being more frequent in Down (52%) (which includes the capital, Belfast) than they are in either Armagh or Derry (31% and 4%, respectively). Moreover, he finds an ethnic link between high use of *WH-* forms and Protestantism and there were gender correlations too, so that Protestant men were more likely to use the variant than their female peers in certain contexts. Interestingly, the distribution amongst males and females based on this data is rather different to that observed by Corrigan (2009) in which the more usual gender pattern, namely, that women take the lead in innovating towards standard norms (i.e. Labov's Principle 2) was observed.

Corrigan (2009) also explores the origins of relative marking strategies in South Ulster English arguing that zero, *WH-* and *TH-* forms derive from the original founder populations. The resumptive pronoun strategy (109) as well as the 'Subordinating *And*' type (110) which are generally used in the more complex relative clauses where zero is dispreferred have certain parallels in both Irish and Planter English (see also Adger & Ramchand (2006); Filppula (1999); McCloskey (1985, 1990, 2001, 2002, 2017); Ó Siadhail (1984, 1989); Ramat & Roma (2007) *inter alia)*. However, as (88), (92) and (93) demonstrate, these forms are not exclusive to Northern Irish English dialects so the most likely explanation is one of possible convergence between the L1 (Irish) and earlier forms of English (L2) from the plantation period onwards (see also Sieumund 2013: 262).

8.2.3 The origins of relative clause variability in newcomer English

Given the earlier discussion of linguistic contact, coupled with the arguments in Chapter Five and in §7.1.2 with respect to (ING) variability and the transfer of L1 phonological conditioning to L2 Armagh English, there is the possibility that such inter-language phenomena might also have an impact on the migrant participants' output regarding their acquisition of relative clause marking strategies. Reviewing the facts here at the very least could make an important contribution to the debate in this area typified by Cheshire, Adger & Fox (2013), Lealess & Smith (2011), Mesthrie (1991), Poplack, Zentz & Dion (2012) as well as Poplack & Levey (2010). They explore the degree to which relative clause marking can indeed be viewed as: "a vulnerable area for language contact" (Poplack, Zentz & Dion 2012: 247) in English-French bilingual contexts in Quebec, Canada as well as in South Africa and superdiverse London.

In this regard, as (112)–(118) indicate, both Lithuanian and Polish have recourse to relative clause strategies which share similarities with those recorded in regional Englishes, in Irish and indeed in other European languages, as Fiorentino (2007), Hendery (2012), Murelli (2011), Ramat & Roma (2007) and Siemund (2013) make clear. Polish *którzy* in (112) is a *WH-* marked inflected pronoun contrasting with the uninflected form *co* 'that' which is more typical of conversational Polish (Guz 2017: 3, 2018: 17). When the latter is used in object function, it is often combined with a RP (*go* 'he' in (113)), particularly in the following contexts: (i) animate human antecedents (which is why the absence of *go* would be ungrammatical here, as shown); (ii) non-accusative objects and (iii) non-matching case forms between the head and object. There is evidence too of copy-type relative clauses in which identificatory material from the head is repeated in the relative clause headed by *co* (114) and (115), which is reminiscent of the ancillary strategies illustrated for English in examples like (89). In addition, both RR and NRR options are possible with the *co* marker in complementiser function being restricted to the former type (see Bondaruk 1995, Citko 2016, Guz 2017, Hladnik 2015 and Szczegielniak 2005, for more nuanced treatments).

(112) Ci   ludzie   [**którzy/co** tu   przychodzą]
      These people **who/that** here   come-3PL
      'These people who/that come here'
      (Polish *WH-/TH-* marked relative clause in subject function; cited in Guz 2017: 3)

(113) Ten nauczyciel [**co**   *(go)   spotkałeś]
      this teacher   that he-ACC met-2SG
      'This teacher that he met'
      (Polish *TH-* marked relative clause in object function with human antecedent; cited in Guz 2017: 3)

(114) jakieś mi się   **robaki** wdały   nie wiem
      some me REFL   bugs   came.round-3PL I   don't know
      [**co tak skakały**   te robaczki   po tych listkach]
      that so jumped-3PL   these worms-DIM over these leaves
      'some bugs came round, I don't know, that jumped about these little bugs all over the leaves'
      (Polish *TH-* marked relative clause where the head noun *robaki* is resumed in *robaczki*; cited in Guz 2017: 14)

(115) Marysia zna   chłopców, [**co ich** Ania lubi]
      Mary   knows   boys   that them Anne likes
      'Mary knows some boys that Ann likes'
      (Polish *TH-* marked relative clause where the head noun *chłopców* is resumed in the pronoun *ich*; cited in Szczegielniak 2005: 166)

On account of Lithuanian's equally complex morphology, there are a range of relative pronouns available including the Polish cognate forms *kàs; katràs, katrà; kóks, kokià* and *kurìs, kurì* (Ambrazas 1997: 200; Holvoet 2016: 232). This is because they agree with the head noun in gender and number. Pronominal case is then determined by its function in the embedded clause (Mathiassen 1996: 79). The principal subordinating markers are *kàd, jóg* and *tàs/tà* (all meaning 'that') (Ambrazas (1997: 429, 732); Holvoet (2016: 227–232). Although the scholarship on relative clause formation in Lithuanian is not as plentiful as it is with respect to either English or Polish, a review of major grammars such as Ambrazas (1997), Mathiassen (1996) and Ramonienė & Pribušauskaitė (2008) captures a system which is actually rather like that of its sister Balto-Slavic language just described as well as that which applies to the regional English vernaculars detailed in §§ 8.2.1 and 8.2.2. Hence, *kuriuõs* in (116) has a similar function to that of *which* in (96) and (97) above whereas *kuriẽ* in (119) is best translated as 'who' which is equivalent to *którzy* in Polish (112). There is the usual division between RR and NRR types as well as the unintegrated strategies (in the terms of Guz 2017, and Miller 2006) which are more common in the spoken varieties that have featured prominently already, including correlative types like (118).

(116)   *grybùs   [**kuriuõs** geresniùs] dė́k į̃   krẽpš į̃*
        the mushrooms-ACC which   better-ACC   put in basket
        'Put the mushrooms which are the better into the basket'
        (Lithuanian *WH*- marked relative; cited in Ambrazas 1997: 702)

(117)   *Nemė́gstu žmoniǫ̃ [**kuriẽ** nemóka laikýti liežùvio už   dantų̃]*
        Not-like-me people who   cannot hold   tongues behind teeth
        'I don't like people who cannot hold their tongues'
        (Lithuanian *WH*- marked relative; cited in Ambrazas 1997: 732)

(118)   *Taĩ **tas** pàts žmogùs [**kurìs** padė́jo   jíems pabė́gti]*
        It-is that same man   who   had-helped them escape
        'It is the (very) same man who helped them to escape'
        (Lithuanian *TH*-marked and *WH*- marked correlative; cited in Ambrazas 1997: 732)

Maciukaite (2004) takes a more experimental rather than traditional grammatical approach and focuses on children's' acquisition of RR strategies in Lithuanian. Her findings show that youngsters with this L1 seem to have acquired the relative pronoun *kurìs* by the age of three which is half the time it is reported to take for speakers of other languages including English, as noted in § 8.1. Moreover, they produce a variety of relative clauses just as their adult caregivers do but there are some key differences. For instance, adult Lithuanian requires the head noun to precede the relative pronoun whereas L1 acquirers of the language are more flexible in this respect, permitting it not just in this position but also following the relative pronoun (and indeed in several other positions in the clause). Although this issue will not be addressed here since there is no evidence that the Lithuanian cohort in the *Múin Béarla* sample likewise observe this tendency, it would be useful to repeat Maciukaite's (2004) experiments on teenage L1 speakers of Lithuanian acquiring English and other languages to see whether this trend is indeed replicated in other contexts.

In sum, both Lithuanian and Polish have relative paradigms that are similar in many respects to those outlined in §§ 8.2.1 and 8.2.2. This finding is not unexpected given the arguments already introduced in Fiorentino (2007), Hendery (2012), Murelli (2011), Ramat & Roma (2007) and Siemund (2013) regarding relativisation across the "European *Sprachbund*" (Fiorentino 2007: 263). Where the two Balto-Slavic languages differ from English of course is in the regularity and transparency of inflectional marking that is embedded within their relative systems (Arkadiev, Holvoet & Wiemer 2015) which was once true too of earlier stages of English, as I showed in §§ 8.1.1 and 8.1.3. So, the question is, how will L1 speakers of these languages fare when faced with learning a paradigm which resembles their own in much of its operation but which has considerably diminished possibilities for overt case marking? That this may be relevant is apparent from another relative acquisition study by Peeters-Podgaevskaja, Janssen & Baker (2018) in the same vein as Maciukaite (2004) though this time involving Russian and Polish monolingual and bilingual children between the ages of 3 and 7. Although both languages incorporate case marking in their relative paradigms, the Russian system is more akin to the Anglo type in that the options are irregular and more opaque. As a consequence, the L1 Russian participants produced a significantly worse performance than their Polish peers when it came to successfully reproducing object *versus* subject relatives. Such issues will therefore be worth revisiting when the relative paradigm variability of the Lithuanian and Polish participants in *Múin Béarla* is considered in the next section (if indeed language convergence is possible in the acquisition of relativisation by L2 speakers *contra* Poplack, Zentz & Dion (2012) *inter alia*).

8.3 Research questions, methodology and constraints

This research overview has generated various lines of enquiry with respect to how this particular variable might pattern amongst the autochthonous and allochthonous teenagers in the Armagh *Múin Béarla* sample detailed in § 7.2. For the reasons documented in Chapter Six, § 6.3 concerning the issue of token infrequency and morphosyntactic variation, this will likely lead to a reduced number of variants for consideration by comparison to those available for (ING). While this decision will narrow the scope of the analysis regarding the making of direct comparisons with certain aspects of the previous studies just cited, it was considered crucial to achieving the overarching goal of this work, i.e. to track variation at different levels of the grammar within a discrete and balanced sample of the Armagh adolescent population. This preliminary study will thus be expanded in future research to pursue analyses of relative clause marking that generated significant outcomes in other studies for which higher numbers of tokens per variant is a must.

Since the analysis needs to be constrained (to ensure replication, for instance, of the methods underpinning other studies with which the outcomes are readily comparable), the research questions listed in (1) to (4) will be addressed. They are posed on the basis of the results for investigations on RR and NRR constructions detailed in Beal & Corrigan (2002), (2005), (2007); Cheshire, Adger & Fox (2013); D'Arcy & Tagliamonte (2010); Geisler (2002); Levey (2006); Levey & Hill (2013); Tagliamonte (2002) and Tottie & Rey (1997). In all instances these two types will never be conflated in the Armagh analyses for the reasons detailed in Tagliamonte, Smith & Lawrence (2005: 85). There will, naturally, be a particular focus on the findings of Geisler (2002) alongside Tagliamonte, Smith & Lawrence (2005) since both of these stand out as being the only variationist research that I am aware of that has been conducted on relativisation in Northern Irish English vernaculars to date. There do not appear to have been any investigations of variability in the relative clause paradigm from the perspective of new migrants to the British Isles previously so the analyses that follow will be breaking entirely new ground in this respect.

As before for (ING), the research questions below are accompanied by examples from the *Múin Béarla* corpus where required to aid the reader. Explanatory details for the internal and external linguistic constraints investigated are also provided. These are abstracted from the coding protocol developed for the Armagh analysis which is largely based on those stipulated in these earlier works.[161]

1. What is the system of relative marking in Armagh English and is it as resistant to *WH*-infiltration – as Romaine (1982: 212) puts it – as the Northern Irish varieties examined by Geisler (2002) and Tagliamonte, Smith & Lawrence (2005) over a decade ago?

2. To what extent do the newcomer cohorts share the variants and distributional patterning of the relative paradigm of the indigenous community?

---

[161] I am particularly indebted to Stephen Levey in this regard who shared a version of the protocol he has been developing for investigating variability in the relative paradigm at Ottawa which has been revised in certain respects to accommodate my rather particular orientation and sample.

3. Of the linguistic determinants listed in (i) and (ii) below, which one(s) condition the choice of relative marker by allochthonous and autochthonous participants?[162]

   (i) Syntactic function of the relative marker (subject (S) or non-subject (Non-S)):
   – *the teacher* (S) [**that** takes us up the mountain]
   – you don't say *anything* (Non-S) [**that** you prepared]
   [MM (F); M-UE; St. Celine's; Armagh, Northern Ireland; 20 Aug. 2012]

   (ii) Animacy of the antecedent head NP (human, animal or inanimate)

4. Is the choice of relative marker socially evaluated with respect to either ethnolinguistic background (Lithuanian, Mid-Ulster English or Polish) or gender (male *versus* female)?

Given the importance to the Armagh relative clause analysis of drawing comparisons where they are possible between the local and newcomer systems for Mid-Ulster English with those identified for Ulster Scots and other global Englishes recorded in previous research, the coding protocol circumscribed the variable context in such a way that it aligned with those earlier studies. Hence, the following exclusions were applied: (i) relativisers which had antecedents that took the form of either a full clause or proper noun or where the NP was in some other respect referentially unique; (ii) adverbial relative clauses; (iii) relativisers in prefabricated expressions and reported speech; (iii) false starts and repeated syntactic structures (though when these were lists, the first relative marker was included while the rest were not); (iv) cases where neither the semantics nor the intonation contour permitted a clear reading of whether a relative clause was RR or NRR and, finally, (v) so-called *WHIZ* deletion contexts in which the copula and relative marker are both optionally deleted. Also notable in this regard is the decision for this study at least to exclude the unmarked ancillary or unintegrated strategies identified in §§ 8.1.2 and 8.2.2 which also occur in the *Múin Béarla* corpus and

---

[162] A number of other internal linguistic factors have been explored in the literature (including type of antecedent; lexical specificity of the antecedent; adjacency of the relative marker to its antecedent head NP; relative clause length and structure of the matrix clause (existential, stative possessive or cleft)). These will not be considered here since the number of tokens of *WH-/TH-/Ø* is so small that many of the cells required for such analyses would remain empty and thus any conclusions drawn on the basis of them would be spurious. They will instead be explored in a future analysis drawn from a larger speaker sample so that issues constraining the internal linguistic variation raised particularly in Henry (1995) and Corrigan (2009) can be examined using variationist models.

are distributed between the local and newcomer participants in a manner which is worthy of further investigation using a more qualitative approach. There are three reasons for this, firstly, on account of their infrequency which makes them unsuited to multivariate analysis, secondly because they are structurally so different from the marked type and thirdly, so as to strictly comply with the stipulations of previous studies with which comparisons are being drawn in which they were also excluded.

8.4 Results and discussion

8.4.1 Relativizing strategy variants in the *Múin Béarla* corpus

A distributional analysis of marked relative tokens in the *Múin Béarla* sample reveals that Armagh English shares with those other Northern Irish English varieties documented in the research detailed in § 8.2.2 a reluctance to avail of both the *whom* variant more readily associated with formal writing (compare the findings of Hinrichs, Szmrescsanyi & Bohmann (2015: 810); Hillberg (2015: 126, 132) and Sigley (1997), for instance) and the *what* type so typical of the southern British and urban varieties discussed in § 8.2.1. In fact, just a handful of *what* tokens occurred amongst local participants. There is some evidence that newcomers also have recourse to this strategy but it is even rarer amongst this group. (119) is an example from Polly Wiczorek, a young woman of Polish heritage attending St. Celine's but she has resided longer in Armagh than any other newcomer in this sample (more than eight years). As such, she is more likely to have encountered this structure perhaps than any of her peers whose average length of residence is considerably shorter (50 % less in fact).

(119) I couldn't understand *anything* [**what** Patrick was saying now]
       [PW; (F); M-UE; St. Celine's; Armagh, Northern Ireland; 05 Aug. 2013]

Moreover, neither *at* nor *as* featured as relative markers in the speech of any participant despite Tagliamonte, Smith & Lawrence (2005: 76) reporting the former in one of their Ulster Scots communities, as noted earlier. This finding fits very well, though, with the views of Buchstaller & Corrigan (2015: 89) that they are actually "rare across the English-speaking world" (see also Kortmann & Wolk 2012).

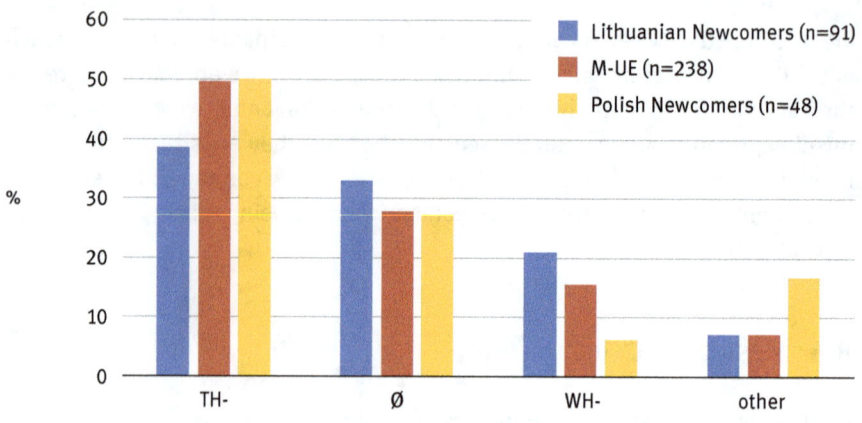

Figure 57 Overall distribution of relative markers amongst ethnolinguistic groups in Armagh

8.4.2 Distribution of relativizing variants in *Múin Béarla*

Figure 57 displays the results for the diverse relative marked and unmarked strategies in restrictive relative clauses coded within the *Múin Béarla* corpus as recorded from all three ethnolinguistic cohorts of speakers in Armagh.

When the data from Mid-Ulster English speakers is considered as a group, the pattern of usage is remarkably similar to that reported for other indigenous varieties, as Figure 58 will show. Hence, *that* relatives dominate with a frequency of 44.8%, Ø is not as common (29.5%) and *who* (at just 17.2%) is not the preferred variant of any single native (or indeed non-native-speaking group). What is even more striking from our perspective is the degree to which the strategies employed by the Polish group pattern more closely with the system employed by the local teenagers (especially as regards *TH-* and zero) than the paradigm which seems to have been adopted by the Lithuanian newcomers. The latter favour *WH-* much more than the Mid-Ulster English speakers do and, indeed, use it over three times more than their Polish peers do. This is particularly curious with respect to the distributional analysis of (ING) provided in §7.3.1 of the previous chapter. In that case, it was the Lithuanian group which more closely matched the frequencies of the indigenous speakers' preferences for the non-standard [ɪn] variant than did the Polish teens (who were also higher users of the language transfer [ɪŋk]/[ɪŋg] variants). When it came to the multivariate regression analysis of course, it was clear that both the allochthonous cohorts had reanalyzed several of the constraints operating on (ING) variability in Armagh English so it remains to be seen

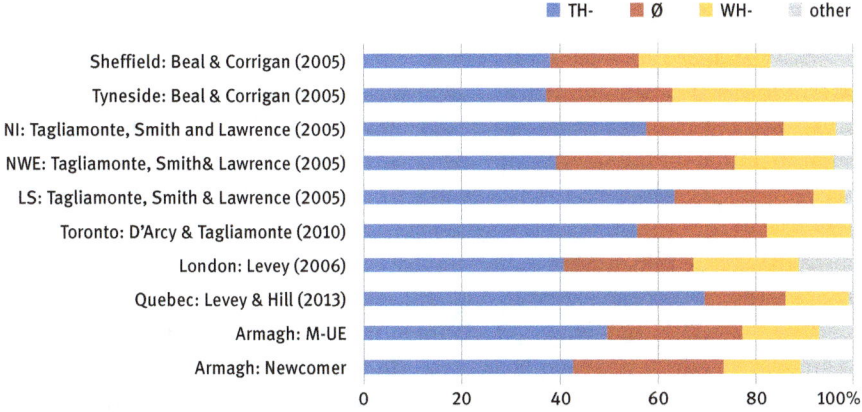

Figure 58 Percentage distribution of relative clause markers in diverse English vernaculars

whether these superficial distributional differences with respect to relative clause marking are also as important as they might seem to be at first blush. Prior to that though, it is worth expanding the comparison to likewise include data from the corpus of Toronto English examined in D'Arcy & Tagliamonte (2010: 389) and that for Quebec reported in Levey and Hill (2013: 47). Closer to home, Figure 58 also records the results from Levey (2006: 58) for London pre-adolescents. Included too are findings from Tagliamonte, Smith & Lawrence (2005: 88), divided into their Lowland Scots (LS), North Western English (NWE) and Northern Irish (NI) dialect regions. The North East and Midlands of England are represented by data from historical twentieth century corpora of Tyneside and Sheffield, respectively, analysed in Beal & Corrigan (2005: 217).[163] For the moment, the figures for both sets of

---

[163] Namely, the *Diachronic Electronic Corpus of Tyneside English* (DECTE) and the *Survey of Sheffield Usage* (SSU) from 1981. See https://research.ncl.ac.uk/decte/, last accessed 19 Aug. 2019 and Beal & Corrigan (2002), (2005). The sub-corpus of DECTE referred to here is the 1990's one (https://research.ncl.ac.uk/decte/pvc.htm), last accessed 19 Aug. 2019. Every effort has been made to ensure that the coding protocols underpinning all of these studies do not vary markedly so that such comparisons truly are genuine. However, the reader should note that it is impossible to control for other aspects of these studies which had rather different research goals and protocols (one-to-one interviews as in the SSU *versus* dyadic interviews in *Múin Béarla*, as described in Chapter Six e.g.). They also occurred during different time periods (late twentieth to early twenty-first century). This is important since, while variability in the relative pronoun system is considered stable, as already noted, D'Arcy & Tagliamonte (2010: 402) report accommodation effects regarding relative pronoun choice in their Toronto corpus which arose from gender diversity in dyadic contexts.

Armagh L2 speakers have been combined in Figure 58 though it has already been noted that there are potential differences in their systems that require further exploration. Although the relative frequencies across these studies are, naturally, not absolutely identical, it is indeed remarkable that the predominant pattern (including that for the L2 Armagh variety) is *TH>Ø>WH*.[164] As such, none of these vernaculars seem 'tamed' towards Standard English norms and *WH-* avoidance seems to be the order of the day whether you grow up in Canada or indeed almost anywhere in the British Isles.

In order to test the extent to which these cross-dialectal distributional differences map onto significant effects upon the dynamics of how relative paradigms operate in a sub-sample of these studies, a Pearson's Chi-Squared *(X^2)* test was undertaken on the data from *Múin Béarla* set against that from D'Arcy & Tagliamonte (2010), Levey & Hill (2013) and the various UK sub-corpora cited in Tagliamonte, Smith and Lawrence (2005). In this case, the distributional data for the Lithuanian, Polish and Mid-Ulster English *Múin Béarla* (MB) participants isolated in Figure 59 are also kept separate with a view to uncovering whether the apparent dissimilarities between ethnolinguistic cohorts already reviewed are actually significant or not. In order to ensure that the results are not declared as such when this is not so, a Bonferroni correction factor of 10 was applied *post-hoc* (making the critical value the more conservative *p*=0.005) (see Rietveld & van Hout (2005: 65) for a rationale). What this means, in effect, is that results are not declared as statistically significant unless their *p*-values are less than this new, more conservative number. Any row in Table 15 that is marked with * is significant at the usual $p = 0.05$ level while (*) indicates where significance has been lost once Bonferroni's adjustment was made.

Even using this cautionary approach, however, a range of interesting findings emerged. Firstly, the distributions of relative clause markers used by Polish and Lithuanian newcomers are significantly different from one another using the usual X^2 measure (though this is lost after the *post-hoc* test). Secondly, neither subgroup (either individually or when combined) actually diverges significantly from the local Mid-Ulster English cohort. As such, while there is indeed some inter-ethnolinguistic diversity amongst the Lithuanian and Polish participants which needs to be considered in a more wide-ranging analysis than is possible in this context, there is robust distributional support for treating L2 English speakers as a coherent analytic group. This will prove very useful in our subsequent multivariate analyses from the perspective of the low token counts for this

---

[164] The PVC corpus is somewhat anomalous in this respect since there are equal numbers of both marked forms. However, this is likely due to the preponderance of subject relatives in this very small data-set, an issue which will be teased apart later in this discussion.

Table 15 X^2 statistics from pairwise comparisons (df = 3) with Bonferroni's adjustment

		X^2	p	
Lithuanian	M-UE	3.50	0.321	
Polish	M-UE	6.62	0.085	
Lithuanian	Polish	7.93	0.047	(*)
MB newcomers	M-UE	2.64	0.450	
M-UE	Levey & Hill (2013)	66.48	0.000	*
M-UE	D'Arcy & Tagliamonte (2010)	100.53	0.000	*
M-UE	Tagliamonte, Smith & Lawrence (2005) LS	41.79	0.000	*
M-UE	Tagliamonte, Smith & Lawrence (2005) NWE	10.82	0.013	(*)
M-UE	Tagliamonte, Smith & Lawrence (2005) NI	5.17	0.160	
MB newcomers	Tagliamonte, Smith & Lawrence (2005) NI	10.97	0.012	(*)

variable mentioned earlier. Indeed, a decision on similar grounds was made by Tagliamonte, Smith & Lawrence (2005: 86) which elected to consider data from Cullybackey and Portavogie together on the basis that "separate analyses showed that their patterns of use for relative markers" were likewise close enough to justify doing so.

Where do the patterns uncovered for *Múin Béarla* then fit when compared to the Canadian and other corpora from the British Isles? The stand out finding here is that the distribution of patterns amongst the Mid-Ulster English speakers is significantly different from all other data sets tested with the exception of the NI subgroup documented in Tagliamonte, Smith & Lawrence (2005). This appears to provide strong support for the existence and indeed persistence of robust patterns of relative pronoun usage in rural and suburban vernaculars in this dialectologically unique region. In fact, one might go so far as to assert that it demonstrates evidence for a distance effect in Armagh, Cullybackey and Portavogie vis`a vis mainstream British and North American varieties (Toronto, for example, is considered to be "a standard dialect, representative of General (standard) Canadian English", according to D'Arcy & Tagliamonte 2010: 387). It remains to be seen of course in further research whether the pre-adolescents in the Belfast sub-corpus of *Múin Béarla* can also be categorised in these terms given their residence in the regional capital where other conservative Mid-Ulster English patterns have already been documented as having disappeared as early as the 1980s (Milroy 1981: 94; Pitts 1986: 209).

Of interest with respect to the results reported in Table 15 too is the fact that the *Múin Béarla* combined newcomer subgroup does actually diverge significantly from the Tagliamonte, Smith & Lawrence (2005) NI cohort. This is especially interesting since the same tests reveal that the Armagh local and Lithuanian/Polish newcomer subgroups do not significantly diverge from one another. While this finding is worth exploring further, the low token counts available for this particular analysis again preclude any definitive statement as to why this might be the case at this juncture (particularly because the X^2 significance for this pairwise comparison is lost when Bonferroni's *post-hoc* adjustment is applied).

8.4.3 Internal linguistic constraints on Armagh relativizing strategies

However, in addition to these suggestive diatopic and ethnolinguistic patterns revealed in the comparisons between Figures 57, 58 and Table 15, attending to internal linguistic constraints may take us further here especially as they have proved fruitful when examined in previous research. The first of these concerns the grammatical role played by the gap in the relative clause, i.e. as subject or as non-subject (the latter including both object and oblique forms, as is also the case in studies such as D'Arcy & Tagliamonte (2010) and Cheshire, Adger & Fox (2013)). Figure 59 provides another cross-dialectal distributional analysis which this time hones in on markers used in subject functioning relative clauses, where *WH-* pronouns are supposed to predominate, comparing the Armagh results with those from D'Arcy & Tagliamonte (2010: 391); Levey (2006: 59); Levey & Hill (2013: 48); Tagliamonte, Smith & Lawrence (2005: 89)).[165] Instead, there is not a single community in which the *TH-* pronoun is not favoured and both the allochthonous and autochthonous groups in *Múin Béarla* follow suit in this respect. In fact, another X^2 test with a Bonferroni *post hoc* adjustment demonstrates no significant difference between them for this constraint. There are some interesting cross-varietal differences, though, with respect to the reversal of fortunes of Ø and *WH-* in some communities by comparison to the pattern revealed in Figure 58. It would appear that the *TH>Ø>WH-* system is maintained in subject relative clauses in all three peripheral communities featured in Tagliamonte, Smith & Lawrence (2005). However, *WH-* is ousting Ø in Armagh (newcomers and Mid-Ulster English locals alike) as well as in London, Toronto and Quebec so that *who* is now more frequent in this context while Ø is avoided in each location (possibly as a result of ambiguity avoidance and the additional processing effort required when zero is used in

---

[165] Some slight but principled adjustments were made to the original data in order to make this possible, e.g. incorporating the *what* results from Levey (2006: 59) in 'other' so as to align the findings from all the studies as displayed.

these contexts, as Levey & Hill (2013: 33) also point out).[166] It would appear therefore that although *TH-* is still favoured over *WH-* (for *Múin Béarla* locals the figures are 61.79 % *versus* 29.27 %, respectively), there are clear signs that the latter has indeed infiltrated the relative paradigm – at least when the grammatical role of the gap is subject. This is true even of the Armagh sample whose relative paradigm originally seemed rather closer to that of the Cullybackey and Portavogie participants in earlier stages of the analysis.

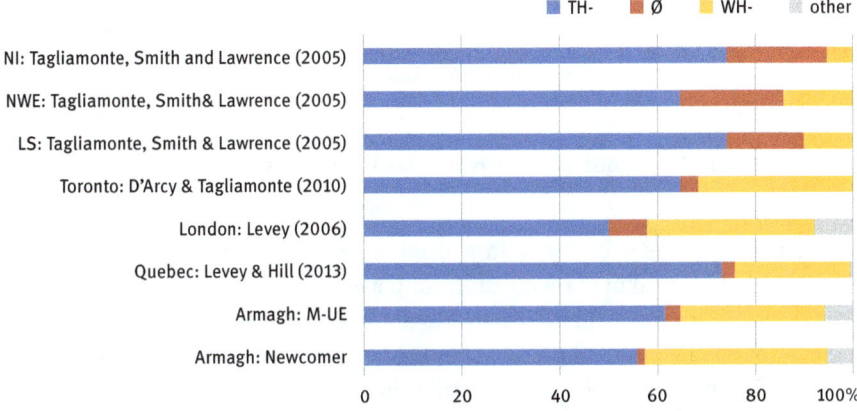

Figure 59 Cross-dialectal distribution of relative markers in subject function

The results presented in Figure 60 for non-subject in Armagh by comparison to the findings of D'Arcy & Tagliamonte (2010: 391); Levey (2006: 59), Levey & Hill (2013: 48), Tagliamonte, Smith & Lawrence (2005: 89) demonstrate a rather different scenario for the *Múin Béarla* participants.[167] It helps explain the seeming incongruence between Figures 58 and 59 since their pattern now shifts to Ø>*TH*>*WH-*. The same is true of D'Arcy & Tagliamonte's (2010) study of Toronto and Levey's (2006) findings for London though not that of Levey & Hill (2013) on the Quebec variety. It now patterns more similarly to Tagliamonte, Smith & Lawrence's (2005) results for their conservative Northern Irish cohort (so that both of these communities prefer the order (*TH*>Ø)). Of interest too, is the fact that both allochthonous

---

166 Though see Romaine (1982: 78) who argues against this view on the basis that "tonic placement would probably disambiguate most doubtful choices" in speech (which could be worth exploring further in a different type of analysis of the *Múin Béarla* data involving experimental speech perception tasks and the like).
167 Once more, slight adjustments where required such as the collapsing of Levey's (2006: 59) categories of 'object' and 'oblique' as 'non-subject' in line with the other analyses.

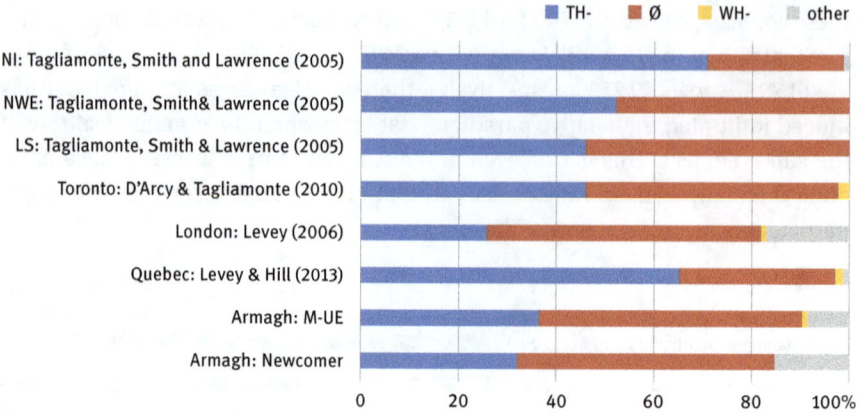

Figure 60 Cross-dialectal distribution of relative markers in non-subject function

and autochthonous sub-groups in Armagh share a non-subject relative system that is rather more akin to their results for Lowland rather than Ulster Scots with higher frequencies of Ø than *TH-*. Once again, a X^2 test with a Bonferroni *post-hoc* adjustment bears out the lack of a significant difference between the newcomer and Mid-Ulster English teenagers' distributions.

In sum, marked forms (*TH-/WH-*) are preferred by all the Armagh cohorts and they vie with each other as subject relativisers. The unmarked (Ø) form is, by contrast, far out of favour in this context. With respect to cases where the gap instead has object or oblique function, however, it is the unmarked variant which is much preferred. This outcome fits very well with the cross-dialectal comparisons, particularly when the age groups are also younger speakers (Levey 2006) or where the study is sited in a major urban centre that is very much associated with a mainstream variety (London (Levey 2006)/Toronto (D'Arcy & Tagliamonte 2010)). This finding is also useful of course since it runs counter to Geisler's (2002: 137) assertion based on NITCS that "the grammatical function of the relative marker in the relative clause is not an essential variable in the data". This outcome may of course be linked to the fact that his data-set patterns more closely to Tagliamonte, Smith & Lawrence's (2005) conservative Northern Ireland corpus because it was originally collected in the 1970s–1980s as an off-shoot of the *Survey of English Dialects* (see Barry (1981) for a description of their methodology).[168]

---

[168] That is not to say of course that such historical corpora have no value. Indeed, the *Tape-Recorded Survey of Hiberno-English Speech* from which NITCS is derived is considered to be so important that the author along with Joan Rahilly of Queen's University, Belfast and staff from the Sound Archive of the Ulster Folk and Transport Museum and the British Library are currently col-

Most studies of variability in relative pronoun choice also rightly consider the relationship between animacy of the antecedent and optionality between marked and unmarked forms because humans (often expected in these contexts to require *who)* ought to pattern independently of 'animals', for instance, which are more likely to be unmarked or designated with a *TH*-form. As I argued in § 8.2.3, the Polish newcomers in the *Múin Béarla* study are already familiar with a system in which animacy combines with the choice of relativiser and the type of construction required to ensure grammaticality such that *co* 'that' (the unmarked form) must be combined with a RP in the relative clause when used to express animate human antecedents as subjects. There is also the general dominance in both newcomers' L1s of high levels of morphological complexity which assists in the semantic interpretation of relative clauses and might also predispose them to favour *who* in this context given the fact that it incorporates relevant morphosyntactic and semantic information. In a similar vein, Cheshire, Adger & Fox (2013) have examined the L1s of their bilingual Hackney participants to explain innovative animacy and subjecthood discourse features of *who* in the relative paradigms favoured by non-Anglos in their study of Multicultural London English. As such, it will be interesting to observe how the allochthonous groups deal with pronoun choice in subject relatives when the antecedents are 'human'; non-human but animate ('animals') or inanimate ('things'). In such cases, when RP and other ancillary strategies are ruled out of the equation, one would expect *who* to correlate with human subjects (particularly for the bilingual speakers whose L1 systems might predispose them in this direction). The results for both newcomer and local Armagh populations are presented in Table 16, which also features the findings for this same constraint from D'Arcy & Tagliamonte (2010: 392) as well as Tagliamonte, Smith & Lawrence's results for Cullybackey and Portavogie (2005: 91). These were chosen, in particular, since the former proved to be reasonably close to the distributions of the Armagh relative paradigm for subjects while that of Tagliamonte, Smith & Lawrence was furthest away (despite including these Northern Irish communities).[169]

---

laborating on a major digitisation project to preserve this unique material as part of the *Save Our Sounds* programme (https://www.bl.uk/projects/save-our-sounds), last accessed 21 Aug. 2019.
169 On account of the paucity of tokens representing some of these categories in this *Múin Béarla* sample, this set is less nuanced than that developed in D'Arcy & Tagliamonte (2010) and Tagliamonte, Smith & Lawrence (2005) occasioning the collapsing of some of their categories here but in a principled fashion (e.g. combining "human", "people" and "collective nouns that represented people" as per Tagliamonte, Smith & Lawrence (2005: 90)). It will serve for present purposes but would need to be examined more closely in future research on the *Múin Béarla* corpus with respect to this particular constraint on the variation.

Table 16 Cross-dialectal distribution of relative markers in subject function by animacy of the antecedent

Community	Animacy	that		zero		who		other		Total N
		N	%	N	%	N	%	N	%	
Múin Béarla: M-UE	Human	58	59	4	4	35	36	1	1	98
Múin Béarla: Newcomer		17	41	1	2	22	54	1	2	41
Toronto: D'Arcy & Tagliamonte (2010)		478	46	38	4	520	50	N/A		1036
NI: Tagliamonte, Smith & Lawrence (2005)		163	73	48	21	13	6	N/A		224
Múin Béarla: M-UE	Thing	17	74	0	0	0	0	6	26	23
Múin Béarla: Newcomer		15	88	0	0	0	0	2	12	17
Toronto: D'Arcy & Tagliamonte (2010)		583	97	21	4	0	0	N/A		603
NI: Tagliamonte, Smith & Lawrence (2005)		68	78	17	20	2	2	N/A		87
Múin Béarla: M-UE	Animal	1	50	0	0	1	50	0	0	2
Múin Béarla: Newcomer		1	100	0	0	0	0	0	0	1
Toronto: D'Arcy & Tagliamonte (2010)		27	87	2	6.5	2	6.5	0	0	31
NI: Tagliamonte, Smith & Lawrence (2005)		11	73	2	13.5	2	13.5	0	0	15

In the first place, it is clear that human subjects dominate across not only the Armagh data (69% of it, in fact) but also in the Toronto and Cullybackey/Portavogie corpora which is no doubt due to the nature of the speech event in some respect (as discussed in §6.2.1 of Chapter Six). Unsurprisingly perhaps it is *that* which is the most frequent choice for all communities cross-dialectally (and inter-ethnically) when it comes to marking inanimates when used in subject position within RRs. As regards other correlations between relative pronoun type and head noun animacy, it is the newcomers to Armagh who actually prefer *who* with human subjects (54% of their tokens) and this finding will thus be examined further in §8.4.4 which is dedicated to social constraints. The rest of these are expressed using *that* (41%). The zero variant – not unexpectedly given the conditioning one might expect here – is opted for very infrequently indeed. Their local peers, by comparison, persist with the *TH-* relative pronoun (59%) and while there are a few more tokens of Ø used by them, it is also very much the dispreferred variant in this context. As for how these patterns fit with the outcomes of D'Arcy & Tagliamonte (2010) and Tagliamonte, Smith and Lawrence (2005), it is the Armagh newcomers now whose output most closely matches the mainstream variety in Toronto, which does indeed pattern more like educated and prestigious varieties that are more susceptible to prescriptive tendencies of this sort (though the differences in each case between the choice of *who* or *that* is rather more minimal than what one might expect in writing, for instance (see Hinrichs, Szmrescsanyi & Bohmann 2015: 810). What is interesting of course is the extent to which the Mid-Ulster English speakers in *Múin Béarla* also differ from the Ulster Scots group studied by Tagliamonte, Smith & Lawrence (2005). In particular, the dissonance between them with respect to permitting human subject antecedents to remain unmarked is rather striking. The indigenous Armagh group pattern more like their newcomer peers as well as the Canadian participants of D'Arcy & Tagliamonte (2010) in this regard. They much prefer a relative pronoun in these contexts even if it isn't the expected *WH-* form. The low token counts for restrictive subject relatives in which the antecedent head noun is an 'animal' is not robust enough in the Armagh data from either cohort to be taken further at this point and, indeed, even in the Toronto corpus which is much larger all told (3,220, according to D'Arcy & Tagliamonte 2010: 388), the number of tokens is really rather too small to attempt further explanation which would not be spurious.

8.4.4 External social constraints on Armagh relativizing strategies

The facts first documented in Romaine (1982) and reviewed in § 8.2.1 suggest that in vernacular Englishes *who*, *that* and zero forms (particularly with respect to subject relatives) are available to express social meaning. That said, scholars have also claimed the opposite, i.e. that the relative paradigm is actually impenetrable to social indexing since it is a "covert variable" (Tottie & Rey 1997: 245). It will thus be useful at this point to further explore some of the key findings here with respect to the allochthonous *versus* autochthonous preferences in subject relatives with human antecedents which were argued earlier to perhaps reflect the rich morphological agreement systems which the L2 speakers are accustomed to from both Lithuanian and Polish. Table 17 reports the results for the independent binary variable 'native' (i.e. Mid-Ulster English speaker born and bred in Armagh versus 'non-native' or newcomer) and also compares the preponderance of relativizer variants by syntactic function across the sample (*who ~that* being the application value for 'subject' and *that~zero*, the value for non-subject on the basis of the earlier findings).

Table 17 Multivariate regression model comparing relative markers by syntactic function for human antecedents and nativeness

Subject				Non-subject			
Application value = *who~that*				Application value = *that~zero*			
Total N = 132				Total N = 31			
Log likelihood = −88.3				Log likelihood = −21.342			
p = 0.0475				p = 0.69			
Nativeness	FW	N	%	**Nativeness**	FW	N	%
Newcomer	0.606	39	56.4	Newcomer	[0.544]	10	54.4
M-UE	0.394	93	37.6	MU-E	[0.456]	21	45.6
Range 21				Range 9			

There is a slight tendency for non-native speakers to favour a marked *that* form in non-subject relatives of this type over Ø whereas this is not the case for the locals (though the effect is not a strong one and it is not significant). What is especially noteworthy though is the factor weight of 0.606 which is generated by the regression model with respect to newcomer preferences for *who* over *that* with human subject antecedents. This result clearly demonstrates that 'nativeness' does indeed significantly condition variable relativizer use in these scenarios. The local Armagh cohort by comparison do not favour the *WH-* variant here and indeed, the range between the two groups (21) is high, indicating a low probability of occurrence of *who* amongst indigenous speakers of Mid-Ulster English by comparison to their newcomer peers who are learning the variety as a second or third language. While caution is needed here in the light of the findings introduced in §8.2.3 of Lealess & Smith (2011), Poplack, Zentz & Dion (2012) as well as Poplack & Levey (2010) regarding whether or not the relative paradigm is indeed susceptible to transfer effects, this is definitely an avenue worthy of further investigation from cross-linguistic contact and variationist perspectives (just as Cheshire, Adger & Fox (2013: 68–71) have done with respect to innovative uses of *who* as a topic introducer in Multicultural London English which seems to have parallels in aspects of their participants' L1s.)

As a stable variable one might also predict that relativizing strategies in the Armagh vernacular would adhere to Labov's Principle 2, i.e. females are more likely to use the prestige variant than males. However, Levey (2006: 65) finds that: "none of the relativization strategies is sensitive to speaker sex" in his investigation of the variable amongst pre-adolescents in London. By contrast, Beal & Corrigan (2002: 128) do record sex differences in North East England with respect to the choice of relative pronoun variants. While females showed a balanced distribution of the three variants, 50% of the male data was actually represented by the zero form. Tagliamonte, Smith & Lawrence (2005: 92) as well as Tottie & Rey (1997: 242) both likewise report such a connection between this variant and male speech. Indeed, D'Arcy & Tagliamonte (2010: 392) in their more recent and wide-ranging study that has already been extensively examined here argue that "both the *wh-* relatives and the null form (especially in subject position) are socially and stylistically diagnostic" (see also Levey & Hill 2013: 48–49). In support of this claim, they provide evidence that the factors of age, education and occupation turn out to be statistically significant predictors of relative pronoun choice in restrictive subject relatives (D'Arcy & Tagliamonte 2010: 392).

Since the nature of the *Múin Béarla* dataset is such that it precludes any investigation of education or occupation and as the age range does not conform to the 10–92 year interval of D'Arcy & Tagliamonte's (2010) Toronto study, I will confine the next stage of this investigation to another of the factors which they found to significantly condition variation in this area of the grammar, i.e. sex. A key reason for the choice is to further explore the apparently contradictory findings reported in Geisler (2002) and Corrigan (2009) regarding whether it is males or females who prefer the *WH-* variant in this region. Doing so will be a valuable contribution to our understanding of the phenomenon in a Northern Irish context, particularly since Geisler (2002: 141 and 145) reveals that sex differentiation in his data seems motivated as much by idiolect as it is by social indexing at the group level which obfuscates the picture somewhat (see also Chapter Five, §5.2.1 for more on this phenomenon in monolingual and bilingual contexts). Focusing on sex as an external variable is also dictated by the findings for this constraint with respect to (ING) in §7.3.1 of the previous chapter so that comparisons can be drawn across different levels of the grammar. It will likewise be important in the context of the goals of this research to evaluate whether ethnolinguistic differences between the allochthonous and autochthonous cohorts interact at all with social conditioning that is tied to gender. This is potentially important since nativeness appeared to be relevant in the distributional analyses of internal linguistic effects in §8.4.3 and it has already been shown to be a strong predictor in the multivariate regression presented in Table 17. As per D'Arcy & Tagliamonte's (2010) model, I will next explore these two factors from a distributional perspective and then also using multivariate regression analyses which the reader will recall are more suited to testing the significance or otherwise of potentially conditioning factors.

Figure 61 presents the findings for a combined distributional analysis of the social attributes 'sex' and 'nativeness' when the relative gap is in either subject or non-subject position.

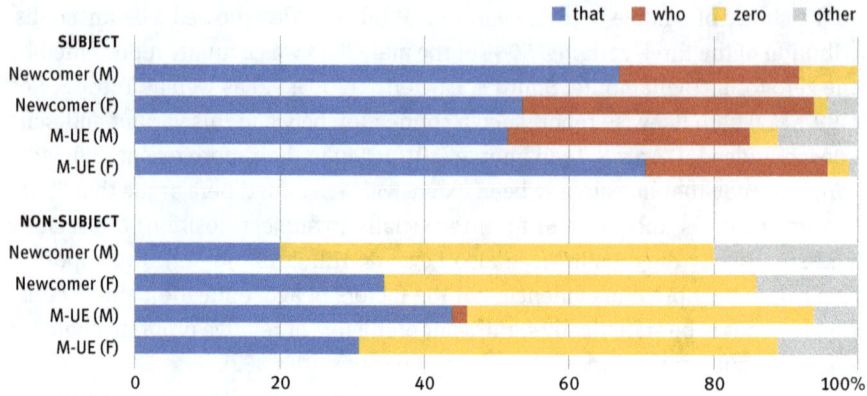

Figure 61 Distribution of subject and non-subject relative markers in restrictives by sex and nativeness

In the first place, these new data-sets reinforce the trend already identified with respect to marked forms being favoured in subject relatives (especially *TH-*) while zero is more likely to be tolerated in non-subjects across both genders. Interestingly, focusing on findings for the former type of relative clause first, it is the L2 female group which shows the highest frequency of *WH-* while the Mid-Ulster English-speaking local girls lag considerably behind them. This is especially noteworthy given Geisler's (2002: 139) results introduced in §8.2.2 which demonstrated that *NITCS* speakers in County Armagh produced the second highest proportion of *WH-* forms of all six counties in Northern Ireland. What is even more striking though is the fact that local boys are more avid users of *who* than their female peers, who actually show the highest frequency for *that* of all speaker groups. Their usage levels are closely followed by those of the newcomer males, who pattern more like them with respect to rates of *TH-/WH-* than any other group (including the Armagh-born boys). So far then, there is a gender pattern which, for native speakers at least runs counter to what one might have expected. The situation regarding the young newcomer women, by contrast *versus* their male peers is rather more like the type of social indexing reported elsewhere in which the prestige variant is more likely to be the preserve of females.

As far as the results presented for non-subjects is concerned, while the dominant relative pronoun for all participants turns out this time to be the unmarked variant, there is only one set of speakers (i.e. Mid-Ulster English-speaking males) who produce any tokens of *who* at all. Again, the same trends identified earlier are at work here too with respect to the *TH-* and zero variants, i.e. while the former dominates in subject relativizing contexts, it is the latter which is favoured most when the gap is object or oblique case in function. In this context, the two cohorts of female speakers, however, pattern rather more alike than they did when the relative pronoun was acting as subject but the male speakers (particularly the local boys and their frequency of *TH-* at the expense of Ø) continue to observe rather different trends from one another. The newcomers record the highest frequencies of the latter while their Armagh-born peers surprisingly use this variant least frequently of all the cohorts.

On the basis that both sets of L1 and L2 speakers attend predominantly single-sex schools, these results confound expectations given the usual dynamics of gender and peer group social order within school-based communities of practice which have been asserted in several studies of adolescents within this framework (Eckert 2003). The distributions reflected in Figure 61 would, in fact, seem to suggest that, to some extent at least, language is being appropriated by the allochthonous/autochthonous sub-groups to create boundaries between them. Such decisions may be motivated by any number of reasons of course but in this context it might include whether the reason for the female newcomers' high frequency of *who* relativisers in subject position is tied to their desire to identify themselves as 'global' rather than 'local', an idea which is pursued further in subsequent chapters.

The next stage in the analysis is to explore whether factors such as 'nativeness' and 'sex' actually do turn out to significantly constrain the variation between these cohorts of Armagh teenagers. The results of multivariate regression analyses to determine the interaction of these factor groups to the probability of *TH-*/Ø occurring in subject/non-subject relatives, respectively, is shown in Tables 18 and 19.

Table 18 Regression table for subject relative markers by nativeness and sex (application value = *that*)

	Total N = 182	Log likelihood = –122.569	Significance = 0.245		
			FW	N	%
Nativeness: Sex		Newcomer: M	[0.583]	12	58
		M-UE: F	[0.583]	67	58
		Newcomer: F	[0.417]	47	42
		M-UE: M	[0.417]	56	42
	Range 17				
Nativeness		M-UE	[0.507]	123	62
		Newcomer	[0.493]	59	56
	Range 1				
Sex		F	[0.514]	114	63
		M	[0.486]	68	55
	Range 3				

Table 19 Regression table for non-subject relative markers by nativeness and sex (application value = *zero*)

Total N = 195   Log likelihood = –133.958   Significance = 0.545

		FW	N	%
Nativeness: Sex	Newcomer: M	[0.548]	10	60
	M-UE: F	[0.548]	65	59
	Newcomer: F	[0.452]	70	51
	M-UE: M	[0.452]	50	48
Range 10				
Nativeness	Newcomer	[0.513]	80	53
	M-UE	[0.487]	115	54
Range 3				
Sex	F	[0.505]	135	55
	M	[0.495]	60	50
Range 1				

Both tables show similar segregations to those identified in the distributional analyses displayed in Figure 61. Thus, they indicate that newcomer males and native females both slightly favour the use of *that* in subject positions while newcomer females and the local boys slightly disfavour this variant in this context (Table 18). This outcome is further supported by the results for non-subjects in Table 19 where the newcomer males and Mid-Ulster English-speaking females both slightly favour Ø in non-subject positions whereas the migrant females and Armagh-born boys both slightly disfavour it here. In each regression, however, the factor weights conditioning the use of the variants indicate that neither the interaction nor the effects of sex and nativeness in isolation achieve statistical significance. This suggest that, as it turns out and in contravention of what the distributional frequencies may have suggested, neither is actually sensitive enough to be performing social indexing functions within the communities of practice of St. Benedict's or St. Celine's. As such, the findings here, with respect to sex at least, map onto those reported in Levey (2006: 65) when examining his pre-adolescent London data as well as those of D'Arcy & Tagliamonte (2010: 396) who also find this "anomalous result" for this ostensibly stable sociolinguistic variable. They did, however, uncover interaction effects with education and sex i.e. *who* usage is actually an important social marker for "middle-aged, more educated, professional women" which is of course not possible to test for here. Such gender differences will be worthwhile pursuing further of course in connection with the (BE LIKE) variable to be examined next, particularly given the strong evidence in the available scholarship that it would seem to be appropriated for gender marking purposes amongst a wide range of teenage communities globally (Tagliamonte & Hudson 1999: 148, 160–161; Tagliamonte 2012: 249, 2016: 44).

The absence of strong social constraints on much of the variability observable in the Armagh relative clause paradigm (and indeed on (ING) in the previous chapter) are likewise worthwhile reflecting on in the light of Meyerhoff & Schleef's (2012: 407) proposal that external independent variables are more readily acquired than internal ones by teenage migrants (given their life stage from an emic perspective in which gender plays a key role in the formation of identity). In fact, the derogation of the newcomer groups from this hypothesis may have another source. It could instead be linked to the fact that relativizing strategies (alongside (ING)) are both "unobtrusive" which may well render them "unlikely to be subject to conscious alteration on the part of speakers" (Tottie & Rey 1997: 245). This is reported not to be the case for (BE LIKE), so it will be interesting to explore how this dependent variable patterns with respect to the internal and external factors that might instead constrain its use amongst the allochthonous and autochthonous cohorts in Armagh, which will be the central aim of the next chapter.

9 Going global and sounding hyperlocal in Armagh

Cross-linguistically, as we will discover in §9.3, quotation is a discourse device used in conversation that allows hearers to vicariously share actions, attitudes, dialogue, emotions and thoughts that only the speaker was party to when they first occurred.[170]

The (BE LIKE) quotative serves just this reconstructed dialogue purpose and has seen a meteoric rise in its popularity across the Anglophone world, leading William Labov to liken its spread to the effects of a tsunami (see also Kortmann, Lunkenheimer & Ehret 2020; as well as Tagliamonte 2012: 248; and Tagliamonte, D'Arcy & Rodríguez Louro 2016: 824, 825).[171] One of the earliest multi-local, multivariate analyses of the conditioning on (BE LIKE) was Tagliamonte & Hudson (1999) which was followed a decade later by Buchstaller & D'Arcy (2009) charting its passage ever further across the globe. Their research discovered that certain intralinguistic constraints on the variable identified previously patterned consistently throughout varieties in the British Isles, North America and the Antipodes. Other conditions on the global patterning of (BE LIKE) variability (including social constraints) appear instead to arise from the dynamics of local systems of quotation. Moreover, parity between varieties depends upon the type and frequency of contact between speakers who are spearheading this innovation (often adolescents, as already noted) and other generations within their communities. In this sense then, quotative systems have been shown to be restructured upon (BE LIKE's) arrival in the classic 'transformation under transfer' sense of Meyerhoff (2009), (2012). This model has already been used successfully elsewhere in this work in the context of migrants' abilities to acquire (successfully or otherwise) the local internal and external constraints on variation in their L2 when the variable was a stable one. I now turn to an application of this heuristic regarding their acquisition of this innovative discourse-pragmatic marker[172] and once more

---

170 "Hyperlocal" is a term used in journalism and marketing to refer to communities (or even groups of individual residents) on a very modest geographical scale. It will be used here to characterise particularly local or idiosyncratic aspects of the quotative system identified in Armagh English. The chapter title echoes that of Diskin & Levey (2019) which will be referred to frequently *passim*.

171 That said, an e-WAVE search reveals several English varieties in which the feature is actually attested as absent, including Appalachian English as well as various English based pidgins and creoles (see: https://ewave-atlas.org/parameters/235#2/7.0/7.9, last accessed 8 April 2020).

172 D'Arcy (2017: 2–3) makes a distinction with respect to *like* in the following terms, i.e. when in discourse-pragmatic function, it encodes textual relations such as connecting a new utterance to discourse that has already been uttered. As a discourse-particle, by contrast, *like* signals interpersonal connections and thus conveys subjectivity beyond the text. Buchstaller (2014) and

take a comparative approach by mapping the local system of quotation in the Mid-Ulster English dialect not only to the newcomers' varieties but also to others on the island of Ireland as well as beyond its shores. §9.1 outlines the development of the quotative system of which (BE LIKE) is a relative newcomer before moving on in §9.2 to explore how it patterns in vernacular Englishes locally and globally as well as in L2 varieties of these. §9.3 will focus on what Labov (2008) terms the "mysteries of the substrate", i.e. if quotative systems are also prone to contact effects of the type considered in previous chapters. In order to ascertain whether *Múin Béarla* allochthonous participants share the frequency patterns and internal/external constraints on quotative variation identified for the local Armagh dialect alongside those previously isolated in translocal vernaculars, §9.5 is devoted to distributional and multivariate regression analyses of the key conditioning factors.

9.1 'Blow-ins', relics and the like: How quotation developed in Mid-Ulster English

Research such as Buchstaller (2014); Cichosz (2018); D'Arcy (2012), (2017); Ferrara & Bell (1995); Meehan (1991); Romaine & Lange (1991); as well as Tagliamonte & Hudson (1999) *inter alia* reveals that quotative systems in the Anglophone world have been engaged in processes of change (including decategorization, grammaticalization and lexicalization) for many centuries. Romaine & Lange (1991), for instance, argue that the syntagm (BE LIKE) is prototypical in this respect in that *like* was once solely prepositional in function and was subsequently recategorized so that it could perform complementiser roles thus extending its semantic and syntactic domains. By contrast, Buchstaller (2014) proposed that originally *like* performed a discourse marker (i.e. a textual) function historically and was later coupled with the verb *be* which already pre-existed in the system of quotation in English (120) so as to form the modern Noun Phrase + Copula + (Discourse Marker) + Quote construction.

(120) From then on it **was,** "Oh did you know Brian plays da da?..."
        NP + Copula + Quote

(Historical New Zealand English (1939); cited in D'Arcy 2017: 18)

D'Arcy (2017) both argue that the *like* of (BE LIKE) developed from the original marker function and that is what will be assumed here.

Either way, what is uncontested is that this quotative now boasts the typical syntactic and prosodic characteristics of this part of speech including stress shift from *like* to the reported clause which follows, coupled with a high likelihood that the /aɪ/ of the form itself will be unaccented and monophthongal (Turton & Schleef 2016: 26, 29).

Crucially, (BE LIKE) in (121) is indeed a 'blow-in' (to use a well-known Armagh phrase meaning 'interloper') (Romaine & Lange 1991). It followed *go* in this respect diachronically (122) and jostles for position in vernacular Englishes alongside zero (123) (a comparatively early quotative); *goes, going, went* etc. and *thinking* (124) (both of which arrived later). There are more traditional variants too including verbs of saying (125) (*say* itself being the first such marker, as we will see below). (BE LIKE) similarly competes with other innovative local forms such as *be+all* (126) (California (Rickford et al. 2007)); *here+be+speaker* (127) (Belfast (Milroy & Milroy 1977; Finlay & McTear 1986)); *okay (fine)* (128) (Indian English (Davydova 2017)) and *this+be+speaker* (129) (London (Cheshire et al. 2011; Fox 2012)).[173] These have established themselves within a productive system of quotation that has been extant since the Old English period, as (130) and (131) demonstrate. *Cwæþ(ð)* 'said'/*sey* 'say' in (130)/(131) act as the verb in the reporting clause, the function of which is to introduce reconstructed dialogue as direct speech, just as (BE LIKE) has been appropriated for in contemporary vernacular Englishes (and as *be* does in (120)).

(121) I **was like**, "What reunion?"
       (Rural AAVE, cited in Cukor-Avila 2012: 616)

(122) And **she goes** {*sound of intake of breath*}, "did you hear that Peter ... he's going with a girl?'
       (West Australian vernacular English, cited in Rodríguez Louro 2016: 145)

(123) And then she rings up **Ø**, "I've been cut off"
       (New Zealand English, cited in Buchstaller and D'Arcy 2009: 297)

(124) And I **thought**, "Well we need some more popcorn"
       (American English, cited in Buchstaller 2014: 34)

---

173 Buchstaller (2006), (2014); Butters (1980), (1982); D'Arcy (2012); Höhn (2011), (2012) and Rodríguez Louro (2013) document the diachrony of these quotative markers in different varieties of English (and see Buchstaller (2014: 2) for a more comprehensive list of innovative discourse markers (which she terms "non-canonical" cross-linguistically)).

(125) I **said**, "Is your dad gonna sell it?"
(Canadian English (Victoria), cited in D'Arcy 2015: 44)

(126) I'**m all**, "Dude, you're not helping your cause!"
(Californian English, cited in Buchstaller et al. 2010: 192)

(127) **here's me**, "No, it's not me"
(Belfast pre-adolescents, cited in Finlay & McTear 1986: 182)

(128) so that used to be **okay (,) fine**, "We are sitting in an English class"
(Indian English, cited in Davydova 2016: 185)

(129) **this is them**, "what area are you from?"
(Multicultural London English, cited in Fox 2012: 232)

(130) Ða   **cwæð** Eadweard, "hit is wyrse ðe   uncer naðor
      Then said   Edward   it is worse that us   neither
      hit næbbe"
      it should-not-have
      'Then Edward said "it is worse that neither of us should have it"'
      (Carlton 1970: 36 from *The Old English Charters*)

(131) But ȝit I **sey**, "Mery whoos childe is this?"
      But yet I say   "Mary whose child is this?"
      (Mazzon 2009: 85 from *N-Town Plays*)

As Ogura (1981) and (1996: 59–60) note, the form *cweðan* in (130) (from which the Modern English word 'quote' derives), was once the most frequent quotative in Old English. It then gave way to *secgan* 'to say' at the end of the Middle English period (131). Originally, the two had specialist syntactic functions with the former being used in direct speech contexts and taking the dative of person with a *to* prepositional phrase as its direct object while the latter was preferred for indicating indirect speech as well as in interrogatives. *Secgan* was also accompanied by the dative of person but without a *to* prepositional phrase. Eventually though, *secgan* absorbed *cweðan*'s "major syntactic features" (Ogura 1996: 60). Subsequently, *tellan* 'to tell' which was originally polysemous, also moved into this same syntactic-semantic space in a typical "layering" scenario such as that described by Romaine & Lang (1991) (see also Tagliamonte & Hudson 1999: 149–151). This trajectory accounts of course for the variation in Modern vernacular Englishes (including Mid-Ulster) between a wide range of quotative verbs in their systems which still retain 'tell' and 'say' but also include other reporting verbs used for reconstructing dialogue such as 'admit', 'ask', 'bid', 'cry', 'shout' and so on.

It was noted in §9 that inner monologues tied to attitudes, opinions and viewpoints can also be expressed as reported speech and 'think'/'thought' are the preferred discourse markers for serving this function in mainstream Modern English. Old English once had two verbs of thinking, i.e. *þyncan* 'to think' or 'consider' and the impersonal verb *þencan* 'methinks'. Eventually, they merged in Middle English once the system of inflectional morphology became eroded which has already been shown to be relevant for the development of (ING) and the system of relativisation in vernacular Englishes (Bromhead 2009: 184). Indeed, by the time that Ireland was colonised in the Early Modern period, it has been argued that the two had become synonymous (Bromhead 2009: 178; Ogura 2016: 33–34, 42; Palander-Colin 1998: 425 ff.). Although *þyncan/þencan* were once used exclusively for introducing indirect speech (Ogura 1996: 67; Ogura 1986), eventually 'think' became acceptable in the late nineteenth and early twentieth centuries as a discourse marker for reporting self-revelations directly as if they were re-enacted speech ((124) above and the historical (132) below) (see also Bromhead 2009: 180; D'Arcy 2012: 357, 360–361; D'Arcy 2017: 20–21; and Palander-Colin 1998).

(132) It's really disappointing now that, you know, you **think,** "Oh I'd like to ask them."
(Historical New Zealand English (1945); cited in D'Arcy 2017: 207)

There is another aspect of the historical development of quotative clauses that is worth pausing on here and that is the fact that they can be accompanied by a process known as 'quotative-inversion' in which the subject and verb instead of preceding the constructed dialogue, as they are in (120)–(132) are actually postposed and inverted. This option was also possible in Old English (133) and example (134) shows this so-called "parenthetical reporting construction" type (Cichosz 2018) drawn from the historical speech corpus of South Armagh English developed for Corrigan (1997: Appendix) and referred to in previous chapters.[174] In (134), the subject (*the chile [child]*) and verb (*sez [says]*) come after the reporting clause and take V>S order. Cichosz (2018: 184) argues that this construction in mainstream English is favoured in writing and, as here, when the subject is

---

[174] This material is reproduced courtesy of the National Folklore Collection, University College, Dublin, Ireland where the Michael J. Murphy manuscripts, which is the original source, is housed. At their request, the actual personal names of the individuals referred to in the narratives have been substituted for pseudonyms.

not a pronoun and 'say' is the verb, citing Quirk *et al.* (1985: 1024, fn.c) (see also Buchstaller 2014: 39; D'Arcy 2012: 349; Rodríguez Louro 2016: 147).

Although D'Arcy (2015: 47) remarks upon the rarity of these constructions in the global English speech samples examined by her (as does Rodríguez Louro (2016: 147) who declares them "obsolete" in Western Australian English corpora), this South Armagh database is actually replete with examples in which pronominals appear in these postposed inverted constructions (135). They also occur with a much wider range of verbs in this database than one might expect given the arguments in Cichosz (2018) *inter alia*.

(133)   Ic   eom   se þe   eom,   cwæð   he
        I   am   who   am   said   he
        'I am who I am, he said'
        (Cichosz 2018: 189, from *Exodus: 3.14.2367*)

(134)   Extract from an interview with Turlough Doran, Dromintee, 1942

   Manuscript: 974
   Date: 1942
   Informant: Mr. Turlough Doran
   Location: Dromintee
   Topic: Strange child/fairies

   U3259/L4675–4676
   "Me hammer an' anvil!", **sez   the chile**, gatherin' itself an' scootin' out ...
                            V   S

(135)   Extract from an interview with Mr. Barry McKinney, Dromintee, 1965

   Manuscript: 1693
   Date: 1965
   Informant: Mr. Barry McKinney
   Location: Dromintee
   Topic: Fairies

   U854/L1471
   "What happened Peggy Maguire's cow?", **says he.**
                                          V   S

Los (2009) suggests that structures such as (133) may be derivable from the Old English (and indeed wider Germanic) pattern of verb second (V2) (another feature which disappeared from the late Middle English period onwards in the standard language (though see Corrigan (1997) for examples of its survival in South Ulster English)). However, Los (2009: 110) concludes (*contra* D'Arcy 2015: 47) that parenthetical reporting clauses really ought not to be considered as engendererd by V2 on the basis of their distinctive discourse properties. Cichosz (2018: 211) goes further, suggesting that rather than being a vestige of the verb second pattern, the contemporary variation in quotatives between S>V and V>S is, in fact, a more "recent development" from the Late Modern English period onwards, i.e. long after Ireland was first colonised. As such, the frequency and presence of a wider than expected range of parenthetical reporting constructions which are inverted in this historical South Ulster English corpus produced in a region where there were still Irish speakers at the time some of the interviews were conducted (Chapter Four, §4.1.1) may, instead, be due to language transfer. This is because Irish has a very particular syntactic frame for parenthetical reporting clauses in which the order is invariably V>S, as in both *arsa* 'says' > *seisean* 'he+emphatic' in (136a) below and *a dúirt* 'said' > *sé* 'he' (137a). This rule derives from the verb-initial nature of the language typologically, which is why the S>V orders in (136b/137b) are ungrammatical. Although issues of this sort will be considered again in §9.3 when the quotative systems of Balto-Slavic and other languages are also reviewed from a contact linguistics perspective, this hypothesis will not be taken any further here since the teenagers in *Múin Béarla* rarely use parenthetical reporting clauses.[175] It would, however, be worthwhile investigating these constructions in Irish and in Early/Late Modern English alongside comparisons of relative frequencies and verb type found in contemporary spoken corpora from the island of Ireland such as SPICE-Ireland and ICE corpora associated with other regions globally (including Great Britain) which were not in contact with a Celtic language historically.[176]

(136) a. "*Cuma liom*" **arsa** **seisean**...
         Equal with-me say-PAST 3P-S-EMPH
         "I don't care" he said

       b. *"*Cuma liom*" **seisean** **arsa**...
          Equal with-me 3P-S-EMPH say-PAST
          "I don't care" he said...

---

175 There is, however, evidence of these in the speech of older generations from Armagh collected during fieldwork for another AHRC-funded project: *The Empire Speaks Back: Northern Irish English as a Post-Colonial Dialect* (AH/F001878/1) which will be examined further in §9.2. This *Empire* corpus was analysed with respect to quotative usage in Corrigan (2010: 101–102) and it contains examples such as: "I'd have to go home and think about that" **says** I. [Ollie Corr: Male, aged 72, *Empire Corpus*, 2008–2009].
176 These acronyms stand for 'Systems of Pragmatic Annotation in the Spoken Component of ICE-Ireland' and International Corpus of English, respectively. Details of the former can be viewed at: http://www.johnmkirk.co.uk/cgi-bin/generic?instanceID=11 and for the latter, see: http://ice-corpora.net/ice/index.html, last accessed 26 August 2019.

(137) a. *"Agus ... bhuel"*, ***a dúirt sé** ...*
 And well say-PAST 3P-S-M
 "And well", he said ...

 b. **"Agus ... bhuel"*, **sé** *a dúirt*
 And well 3P-S-M say-PAST
 "And well", he said ...

(Native Ulster Irish speech samples from *Raidió na Gaeltachta, Tamalt Comhrá*, 2002: *Nua-Chorpas na hÉireann:* https://focloir.sketchengineco.uk/auth/run.cgi/simple_search?home=1, last accessed 26 August 2019)

9.2 The quotative systems of Mid-Ulster and other vernacular Englishes

9.2.1 (BE LIKE) *et al.* beyond Armagh

As Buchstaller (2014: 1) remarks: "quotation is an extraordinarily dynamic domain". She refers, in particular, to the number of innovations which have arisen in the systems of diverse vernacular Englishes since sociolinguists such as Milroy & Milroy (1977: 3) first commented on what they described as "the social and situational constraints [on the use of] direct speech markers" in their Belfast community studies of the early 1970s (see Chapter Six, § 6.1.1.3 and § 9.2.2 below). Since then, research even on those 'blow-in' types listed in § 9.1 has come such a long way since Tagliamonte & Hudson (1999: 148) declared that relatively little was known about how innovations like this are positioned "within the quotative system as a whole". The review which follows does not therefore attempt a comprehensive account of all the literature in this area of research. It will instead hone in on specific aspects of the internal and external constraints that have been shown to condition variation in Irish English and other global vernaculars which will be especially relevant for the analyses presented in § 9.4–9.5.

With that in mind, there are four intra-linguistic conditioning factors which have been identified as constraining the variable grammar of vernacular quotative systems from both diachronic and synchronic perspectives, namely: (i) content of the quote (internal monologue/inner states often favour (BE LIKE) as well as *think* quotative markers (124) above); (ii) grammatical person of the matrix subject (first person preferred over third, e.g. when (BE LIKE) is the quotative (121) but not when it is *say* (125) or *go* (122)); (iii) mimesis (whether or not the quotation is accompanied by nonlexicalized sounds or gesturing effects, as in (122) above, in which case *go*, (BE LIKE) and zero are often found to be the preferred options) and (iv) temporal reference (past tense is favoured with *say* (125) but disfavoured when the quotative introducer is (BE LIKE) which is more often associated with present and particularly historic present contexts so that utterances like (121) are rather unusual). In general, the distributional and statistical models examined in a range of studies focusing on the quotative systems of diverse vernacular Englishes thus far have shown that communities globally by and large conform with respect to these grammatical constraints on quotative choice. Nevertheless, there is also good evidence to suggest that (BE LIKE) and other more recent variants may not be at exactly the same developmental stage in each locale and so are confined in some respect to niche positions within the grammar while older variants (especially *say*) are considerably more flexible with respect to contexts of use (see §9.4 as well as Blyth *et al.* (1990); Buchstaller (2014); Buchstaller & D'Arcy (2009); Cheshire *et al.* (2011); Cukor-Avila (2002); D'Arcy (2004), (2012), (2017); Durham *et al.* 2012; Ferrara & Bell (1995); Mathis & Yule (1994); Romaine & Lange (1991); Tagliamonte & D'Arcy (2004), (2007), (2009); Tagliamonte, D'Arcy & Rodríguez Louro (2016); Tagliamonte & Denis (2014); Tagliamonte & Hudson (1999) *inter alia*).[177]

The effects of speaker age, diachrony, ethnicity, gender and region have all been investigated in relation to systems of quotation in global English vernaculars (see Buchstaller (2014); Buchstaller & D'Arcy (2009); Cukor-Avila (2002); D'Arcy (2012), (2017); Rodríguez Louro (2013), (2016); Tagliamonte & Hudson (1999); Tagliamonte, D'Arcy & Rodríguez Louro (2016) amongst others). In this regard, for instance, Tagliamonte, D'Arcy & Rodríguez Louro (2016) find parallels globally regarding the actuation of (BE LIKE) by diverse regional populations born in the 1960s. Subsequent generations have increased usage exponentially and they argue that this has been fostered by changes in patterns of social networking which have moved beyond the local to become supralocal or global.[178] What is more, they propose that the rise of (BE LIKE) is also linked to the new nature of storytelling practices in the Western world because they too have been altered in the latter half of the twentieth century so that narratives – as well as being driven by events tied to personal experience – now regularly also encompass the

---

[177] There are two other system-internal constraining factors that have also been investigated in the relevant literature, i.e. specification of an addressee and verb placement (particularly postposition as discussed in §9.1) though they will not be considered here (see D'Arcy (2012) for an analysis that does include these).

[178] Though see Buchstaller & D'Arcy (2009) as well as Davydova & Buchstaller (2015) which propose that youngsters in Britain and New Zealand are actually not as readily able to engage in face-to-face exposure with American vernacular English speakers as this hypothesis suggests.

expression of the storyteller's mental and emotional state (the conversational turn where (BE LIKE) is generally reported to reign supreme).[179]

As far as gender is concerned, while in the popular imagination the (BE LIKE) quotative variant is strongly associated with young teenage women,[180] this factor has, in fact, been shown not to be a durable constraint on variation in the quotative system at all, as Buchstaller (2014: 99) and Davydova & Buchstaller 2015: 448–449) also point out. Either the innovative variant patterns, as expected, just as it did in Macaulay's (2001) analysis of adolescent Scottish data where females led the change, or the sex effect is actually in the opposite direction (i.e. favoured instead by males (Dailey-O'Cain 2000; Höhn 2011, 2012; Diskin & Levey 2019)). Moreover, some researchers have found that gender does not significantly condition the variation at all (Tagliamonte & Hudson 1999) or that it does constrain usage but that the patterns are dissimilar across regional space perhaps indicating highly localised differences in the social evaluation of the variant (Buchstaller & D'Arcy 2009). Hence, even within the same city, Fox (2012) finds that females lead (BE LIKE) innovation in Hackney (inner London) while males do so in Havering (outer). This discontinuity across communities also characterises some other innovative quotative variants such as go and be all (Buchstaller 2014). As such, it will be interesting to see what, if any, gender effects apply in *Múin Béarla*.

As Cukor-Avila (2012: 617) contends, investigations of ethnic differences and quotative usage within communities are not as plentiful as those examining other extralinguistic factors. The issue has though been considered in Buchstaller *et al.* (2010) as well as Cukor-Avila (2002), (2012); D'Arcy (2010) and Kohn & Askin Franz (2009) *inter alia*. The first of these examined quotative *all* usage amongst ethnically 'White' and 'Chicano/Mexican' Americans in California. Buchstaller *et al.* (2010) found that while the former ethnic group favoured the innovation in their early data sample (1990–1994), the effect was neutralised a decade later when this once novel but short-lived variant had declined amongst all speakers.

D'Arcy's (2010) study is based in New Zealand and examines contrasts between the English vernaculars of participants who are of Māori or Pākehā descent.[181] She finds that the systems of quotation which the two groups use are

---

179 This is another avenue that could be explored with regard to the twentieth century folklore corpus already considered with respect to quotative usage in §9.1 alongside the *Empire* and *Múin Béarla* corpora which were also gathered in County Armagh but from 2008 onwards.
180 See, for instance, the poem by Joseph O'Connor performed in 2012 on Ireland's *Late Late Show* which imagines a conversation between two teenage girls who use phrases like: "I'm like "Talk to the hand"" (https://www.youtube.com/watch?v=fKEdV93qcQY0, last accessed 27 Aug. 2019).
181 'Māori' are descended from a migrant Eastern Polynesian population which settled in New Zealand in the Middle Ages. The term 'Pākehā ' is a Māori-language term for New Zealanders of European descent who arrived in the nineteenth century.

actually rather dissimilar, i.e. (BE LIKE) is more readily employed by the cohort who are of European stock while it is the zero variant which the Māori prefer. These results led D'Arcy (2010: 82) to argue that, in contrast to the findings of Buchstaller *et al.* (2010) on the other side of the world, in New Zealand at least: "speakers quote their ethnicity by creatively using the resources available for the construction of dialogue as acts of identity."

There are several studies of AAVE and Chicano English in the United States which have also come to a similar conclusion with respect to a wide range of variables from different levels of the grammar (see Bloomquist, Green & Lanehart (2015) and Fought (2006) for overviews). Not surprisingly, therefore, Cukor-Avila (2002), (2012) alongside Kohn & Askin Franz (2009) all focus on whether the quotative system has been appropriated for the purposes of this type of ethnically-driven social indexing too. In particular, they have examined how (BE LIKE) has diffused into communities of AAVE and Chicano speakers. Interestingly (and in contrast to D'Arcy's (2010) findings with respect to her Māori population) they demonstrate that this variant has become not only productive in these ethnolects but is, in fact, favoured by these groups (particularly amongst adolescent speakers). Cukor-Avila (2012) also finds that there is a rural-urban divide regarding the transmission of this variant amongst AAVE speakers more broadly whereby city dwellers have incorporated it into their quotative system a generation before it diffuses to more rural settings. This finding will be worth exploring in future research which pits the pre-adolescent speakers in the Belfast sub-corpus of *Múin Béarla* against their peers growing up in the village of Donaghmore. For the moment, though, it would appear that taking cognisance of ethnolinguistic distinctions in the distributional and statistical analyses which follow may well generate divergent patterns of use underpinning the variability in the quotative systems of the three cohorts of speakers in the Armagh sample.[182]

There have been even fewer studies on the acquisition of English quotative systems by speakers of other languages and they too have addressed these external factors. Thus, Corrigan (2016) as well as Diskin & Levey (2019) investigated age, diachrony, regional and sex differences between native and non-native populations in different regions of the world. Their findings also indicate that communities cross-dialectally and with respect to L1 /L2 distinctions can "sound

---

[182] Although there is not space here to discuss the issue at length, it is important to note that the research on ethnically diverse communities in New Zealand and the United States is based on clear racial divisions. However, while there is no doubt that the Armagh, Lithuanian and Polish cohorts in this study are ethnolinguistically distinctive, all these participants are of European descent so that any social indexing which is uncovered cannot be considered to be racially motivated as such.

local" even when they are "going global" (Diskin & Levey 2019: 53). Naturally, given their orientation, the scope of such studies also extends to: (i) Ethnolinguistic background (Corrigan 2016; Diskin 2015); (ii) Exposure to native speaker varieties (Davydova & Buchstaller 2015; Davydova 2017) and (iii) Proficiency (Corrigan 2016; Diskin 2015; Diskin & Levey 2019; Meyerhoff & Schleef 2014). For the most part, this research reveals that both proficiency in English as well as length and types of exposure (in the form of time spent abroad for EFL students, age of arrival in the case of migrants and high or low exposure to mass media) "has a measurable impact" (Diskin & Levey 2019: 58–59) on the usage rates of (BE LIKE) as well as other innovative variants such as *go*. Indeed, Meyerhoff & Schleef (2014: 120) report that their low proficiency cohort produced just a single (BE LIKE) token. Similarly, Davydova (2017: 44) in her study of University students in New Delhi notes gaps between not only the number of quotations used by Hindi *versus* English dominant bilinguals but also their preferences for (BE LIKE). It is the former who disfavour this variant (0.4 *versus* 7.7 tokens per speaker on average) and indeed they also produce fewer quotatives overall than their peers who interact more regularly in English than in Hindi. This factor therefore will also be worth bearing in mind when considering the potential external constraints on the quotative systems of the *Múin Béarla* bilinguals in §9.5.

9.2.2 The quotative systems of Irish English vernaculars

Previous work describing the quotative systems identified in Ulster Englishes is presented in Corrigan (2010), (2016); Höhn (2011), (2012); Milroy & Milroy (1977) and Finlay & McTear (1986). Quotation strategies in the Irish English vernaculars of the Republic of Ireland have also been documented in scholarship typified by Diskin (2015); Diskin & Levey (2019); Diskin & Regan (2015); Höhn (2011), (2012); Nestor (2013); Nestor, Ní Chasaide & Regan (2012) and Schweinberger (2012). That said, the paucity of accountable, comparative studies of quotative variation and change across these regions which extends Corrigan (2016) has recently led Diskin & Levey (2019: 75) to call for new research. Its aim would be to ascertain whether the results which they report for autochthonous and allochthonous participants in their Dublin study are simply hyperlocal or can instead be considered pan-Hiberno and thus shared across the island of Ireland. A key objective of the analyses reported in §§9.4–9.5 is to do exactly that. Thus, they will compare how the quotative system used by native and non-native speakers operates in a major capital where the base dialect is Southern Hiberno-English (see Chapter 6, Figure 42) with that which is typical of the Mid-Ulster dialect spoken in the much smaller suburb of Armagh over a hundred kilometers further north across the

Irish border. The results will also of course be considered in the light of the internal and external constraints identified in other global Englishes summarized in §9.2.1. Prior to that, though, it will be important to establish whether quotative devices in Irish English share the same developmental pathways which they have taken in other vernaculars. They may not of course since varieties on the island of Ireland are often reported as being late adopters of innovations diffusing from major centres of influence beyond its shores. Thus TH-fronting, which is discussed in Chapter Six, §6.3, has not, to my knowledge, infiltrated Southern Hiberno-English yet and did not do so in Northern Irish varieties until the early twenty-first century (McCafferty 2001: 184). Even then, it is confined there to teenagers when Kerswill (2003: 234) deems it to already be a "widespread majority" form elsewhere in the UK.

We are fortunate in this regard that Höhn (2011), (2012) and Diskin & Levey (2019) have all used spontaneous speech data from (SP)ICE-Ireland to track the development of the quotative system in Irish English between 1990–1994 and 2002–2005. Their findings suggest that the trajectory of change follows the expected patterns reported elsewhere (Tagliamonte, D'Arcy, and Rodríguez Louro 2016: 831; 2006: 8), i.e. the 'blow-in' *be like* variant was first adopted by speakers with birth dates in the 1970s and then rises rapidly in popularity. Its position within the quotative system *vis à vis* other variants is obvious from the summary in Diskin & Levey (2019: 63) reproduced in Table 20. Also noteworthy is the absence of *go* and *think* amongst the older generation in the 1990–1994 sample which also seem to have been first introduced into Irish English by speakers born in the 1970s. In all periods and irrespective of age cohort, *say* remains the most popular quotative marker with older speakers largely fluctuating between it and zero, thus they continue to eschew (BE LIKE) even in the twenty-first century materials. While *go*, which has already been demonstrated to also be an innovation in the history of English, appears to be competing with *be like* amongst the youngest generation in this more recent dataset, it is holding its ground. However, *think* remains a bit player amongst all cohorts and irrespective of time period.

The research by Höhn (2011), (2012) as well as Diskin & Levey (2019) arrives at these findings by collating data collected from speakers of the entire gamut of Irish English dialects. It is possible, as Diskin & Levey (2019: 56) themselves report, that doing so "precludes any detailed examination of locally specific constraints on quotative variation and change" and this may be crucial given the findings of Corrigan & Diskin (2020) which uncovered diatopic distinctions with respect to the discourse-pragmatic feature *like* in Armagh and Dublin, already referred to in Chapter Five, §5.2.1. In order to hone in on the developmental trajectory of the very particular quotative system that typifies Mid-Ulster English, therefore, it will be worth exploring the choices of speakers born solely in this region in the *Empire*

Table 20 Distribution of quotatives in SPICE-Ireland (spontaneous speech only) according to time period sampled (1990–1994 versus 2002–2005) and speaker age (19–33 versus 34–50+). Note: Percentages have been rounded to the nearest whole number.

	1990–1994				2002–2005			
	19–33		34–50+		19–33		34–50+	
Variant	N	%	N	%	N	%	N	%
Say	187	55	48	70	61	33	113	81
Go	71	21	0	0	41	22	3	2
Zero	41	12	21	30	15	8	14	10
Be like	16	5	0	0	37	20	0	0
Think	10	3	0	0	15	8	7	5
Other[183]	16	5	0	0	14	8	3	2
Total	**341**		**69**		**183**		**140**	

Table 21 Speaker demographics of the *Empire Corpus* sub-sample

Name	Initials	Age	Location
Heather Patten	HP	90	Belfast
Jenny Taylor	JT	46	Belfast
Kate Prince	KP	21	Belfast
Sarah McConville	SMcC	19	Lurgan
Declan McCreevy	DMcC	12	Armagh

Corpus, detailed in §9.1 from two different perspectives. In the first place, it will be useful to examine the patterning of variants synchronically across different generations. Secondly, although models of how innovations diffuse spatially such as those referred to earlier in Kerswill (2003) are not without their critics (Britain 2013: 606–611), there nevertheless may be mileage too in reflecting upon this aspect of the *Empire Corpus*. Doing so might uncover synchronic differences between Mid-Ulster English speakers residing in the capital, Belfast *versus* those in Armagh and other suburban areas like Lurgan, previously examined from this

---

[183] These would include variants already introduced in §9.1 such as 'ask', 'tell', 'shout' and so on.

perspective by Pitts (1982), (1985), (1986) with respect to the spread of socio-phonetic change westwards from Belfast along the Lagan corridor (Corrigan 2010: 8). Table 21 presents a summary of the relevant demographic characteristics of the *Empire* sub-sample chosen for these purposes.

As can be seen, these participants represent three generations of women from Belfast so as to perhaps catch a glimpse in apparent time of the diachrony of quotatives in this single Mid-Ulster English-speaking location. There are also two speakers from Armagh (DMcC) and Lurgan (SMcC) who are similar in age to those in the *Múin Béarla* sample and who have been chosen to exemplify two smaller urban areas.[184] Under the 'cascade' or 'gravity' model whereby large urban centres are taken to be the epicentres of linguistic change (Trudgill 1974), one would expect innovations in the quotative system to diffuse from Belfast to Lurgan first, followed by Armagh given its more peripheral location with respect to the urban hierarchy. Table 22 presents the results of an analysis which quantified the relative frequency per 1000 words per speaker of the predominant quotative variants documented in Höhn (2011), (2012) as well as Diskin & Levey (2019), namely *be like, go, say, think* and zero. It also incorporates the 'non-canonical', hyperlocal *here+be*+speaker variant initially documented amongst Mid-Ulster English speakers by Milroy & Milroy (1977) and exemplified in (127) of §9.1.

Table 22 Relative frequency (N) per 1,000 words per speaker of traditional and innovative quotative variants in the *Empire Corpus*

	DMcC	SMcC	KP	JT	HP
Say	78	38.6	44.4	68.1	78.6
Go	0	0	2.2	4.4	0
Zero	9.8	12.9	2.2	5.5	21.4
Be Like	0	20.0	15.6	0	0
Think	2.5	5.7	24.4	12.0	0
Here+Be+Speaker	0	0	0	4.4	0

The results indicate that the hyperlocal variant is still productive in Mid-Ulster English although it is not used frequently enough by any speaker other than the middle-aged Belfast participant for it to register in this analysis. Unsurprisingly, the other variant also documented in Milroy & Milroy (1977) which turned out to

---

184 As usual, these are pseudonyms to preserve the anonymity of participants. See Corrigan (2010: 19–23) for more detail regarding their demographics than is warranted here.

likewise dominate in (SP)ICE-Ireland, i.e. *say,* is similarly the most frequent quotative marker irrespective of location or generation. Indeed, the youngest speaker (DMcC) from the most peripheral urban area (Armagh) shows a preference for this variant which is a near exact match for that of the oldest participant (HP) in the capital. Her quotative system likewise has much in common with that which characterises the 34–50+ cohort exemplified in Diskin & Levey (2019) for the whole island in real time. Thus, she also favours the zero quotative, another long-standing vernacular variant. Moreover, it is striking that despite their youth, the two most regionally peripheral speakers, i.e. SMcC from Lurgan and DMcC from Armagh have higher token counts for this variant than either the youngest (KP) or middle-aged (JT) Belfast women do. As previously noted, reported thought and attitude are often conveyed in quotative contexts nowadays by some form of *think*, which, by contrast, is a relative newcomer to the system. In this case, the highest frequency users are, as one might therefore expect, concentrated in the young and middle-aged cohorts with the Belfast speakers producing the most tokens followed by the Lurgan participant and then the Armagh pre-teen. The youngest Belfast speaker (KP) produces the highest number of *think* tokens overall and she is also a regular user of the *go* 'blow-in', though it is the middle-aged Belfast woman (JT), who is the most avid user overall. The oldest speaker (HP) has no tokens of this variant in her interview. What is even more interesting is that both of the participants outside of the capital (SMcC/DMcC) also avoid quotative *go*. Table 22 likewise captures the fact that the situation is radically different for the newest variant on the block, i.e. *be like*. No tokens are recorded from the two older Belfast women (JT) and (HP) but the younger females, i.e. KP, who was also born and bred in Belfast, as well as SMcC from Lurgan have relative frequencies which demonstrate that this variant undoubtedly belongs to their quotative repertoires. It is also striking to observe that DMcC, who is from the most peripheral location as far as influence from Belfast is concerned, has no tokens of (BE LIKE) at all. It will be interesting therefore to see in §§9.4–9.5 whether his peers attending the same school in Armagh have begun to adopt this innovation in the intervening period between my interview with him and theirs.

While the small scale of this analysis precludes any definitive answers with respect to either the diachrony of quotative usage in Mid-Ulster English or its diffusion across geographical space, the patterns of variation and change which it uncovers suggest that there is some evidence for innovation in apparent time and for a delay in the diffusion of certain novel forms from the capital to more peripheral suburbs. At the very least, the re-organisation of the quotative system captured in the apparent time and diatopic data in Table 22 is reassuringly similar to the longitudinal trends identified in Höhn (2011), (2012) as well as Diskin & Levey (2019) using undifferentiated dialectal spoken data for the whole island.

This outcome thus makes an excellent starting point for the *Múin Béarla* analyses which follow in §§ 9.4 and 9.5.

9.3 Quotative systems and contact

In the discussion of how English quotative variants evolved in § 9.1, the possibility that the post-posed quotative structure favoured by some older Armagh English speakers was mooted to be a consequence of an earlier phase of bilingualism. Such opportunities occur on account of the presence cross-linguistically of similar mechanisms for signalling reported thought and speech, as Buchstaller and van Alphen (2012a); Buchstaller (2014); D'Arcy (2017); Guz (2019a); Güldemann (2008) and Haddican & Zweig (2012) also argue in their reviews of quotative forms cross-linguistically. Hence, Buchstaller (2014: 20–24) reports that innovative quotatives (in both Indo-European as well as in other unrelated language families) stem from a restrictive set of linguistic resources. These include demonstrative deictics such as *here* (which operates in the hyperlocal *here+be+speaker* Mid-Ulster English quotative already considered) as well as lexis that conveys approximation (e.g. English *like* and Irish *mar* 'like' which has, in fact, been transferred to become the Irish-English discourse-pragmatic marker *mar-yah/moryah/moya* detailed in Corrigan (2015: 39, 42)).[185]

As early as Poplack (1980), it was suggested that the lack of complexity associated with discourse markers more broadly alongside their peripherality in the clause, made them vulnerable to borrowing. This was argued to be an especially noticeable trait amongst low proficiency bilinguals in immigrant contexts who used them to signal their knowledge of the prestigious majority language. Matras and Reershemius (2016) goes even further by suggesting that discourse markers are singularly prone to transfer effects. Moreover, there have been several studies which demonstrate the fact that bilinguals frequently code-switch when using them and that various aspects of the minority language's quotative system can be subject to interference from the L2 (see also De Fina 2000; Matras 1998, 2000; Maschler 2017; Maschler & Schiffrin 2015; Sánchez-Muñoz 2007; Sankoff *et al.* 1997). It will be important therefore to consider the possibility that the quotative systems of the Lithuanian and Polish bilingual participants in the *Múin Béarla* sample may also be subject to similar contact processes. Prior to doing so, it will be worthwhile exploring how traditional discourse-pragmatic markers operate

---

[185] Quantifiers such as English *all* have also been recorded performing these functions cross-linguistically. See also Guz (2019a: 196–198) for a very comprehensive list of the main source constructions which have this function in Polish and other languages.

in these Balto-Slavic languages. Similarly, it will be useful to determine whether there is any sign of non-canonical quotatives of the types identified in previous research which may thus facilitate the acquisition of innovative speech introducers that may likewise be present amongst the indigenous population such as *here+be*+speaker or (BE LIKE).

Adamczyk (2017: 370) remarks on the dearth of scholarship on discourse markers in Slavic Linguistics, attributing this to the rather prescriptive research tradition associated with these languages (including Polish) which has focused on grammar and the written word at the expense of spoken interaction which is at the heart of how discourse-pragmatics operates in any language. Although the very recent publication of Guz (2018), (2019a), (2019b) has ameliorated this situation somewhat with respect to Polish especially, this area of Baltic linguistics has been similarly hampered. Indeed, there are even fewer scholarly works on this language family all told, as already noted in the previous chapter (see also Arkadiev, Holvoet & Wiemer (2015: 47) who state that "Apart from sociolinguistics and syntax, semantics and pragmatics have remained the worst investigated parts in the description of all Baltic languages").[186] As such, this introduction to quotation in Polish and Lithuanian is necessarily brief but should suffice for present purposes.

Lithuanian and Polish share with English and other languages cross-linguistically a range of what Güldemann (2008) first termed 'canonical' quotative introducers. Lithuanian relies on reporting verbs such as *kalbė́ti* 'speak', *klausti* 'ask', *sakýti* 'say', *pãsakoti* 'tell' and so on (Ambrazas 1997: 256; Holvoet 2016: 228) which are regularly used in the oblique mood to introduce constructed dialogue, as (138) demonstrates.[187]

(138) *Tà **sãkanti**, "Dukté̇ tesiẽ, bet sàvo sū́nus sudègink..."*
she said+OBL (your)daughter may stay but your sons must burn
'She said: "your daughter may stay but you must burn all your sons"'
(Cited in Ambrazas 1997: 265)

---

186 The further development and analysis of the Lithuanian spoken corpora documented in Kamandulytė-Merfeldienė (2017) will thus be crucial here.
187 Oblique as opposed to indicative mood is required in these contexts on account of the fact that the quotative is conveying information that the speaker wishes to leave open to interpretation as to its veracity (Ambrazas 1997: 262). As such, (141), which is extracted from a fairy tale, operates in a similar manner to that ascribed by Buchstaller (2014: 8, 22) to certain uses of *be like* in English, i.e. the epistemic stance can remain unspecified thus allowing speakers to be non-committal so as to avoid "potential objections".

Polish similarly employs *mówić* 'speak'/'say'; *powiedzieć* 'tell'/'say' and others such as *pytać* 'ask' in this function. When the reporting verb is *mówić*, Guz (2019a: 204–205) contends that it is the historic present form that is favoured, as (139) confirms.

(139)   no   to   **mówię,**   "okej fajnie już teraz   nic   nie widzę"
         well   then   say+I   okay great now at present nothing no see+I
         'So I say: "okay, great, now I can't see anything"'
         (Cited in Guz 2019a: 204)

Speakers of both languages can also avail of the English strategy already considered, i.e. the use of cognition verbs (*manýti* in Lithuanian and in Polish *myśleć* 'think') to convey reported thought (Ambrasaz (1997: 256) and Guz (2019a: 204), respectively).

     Non-canonical quotative introducers have also been recorded for these Balto-Slavic languages. For instance, Holvoet (2016: 247–250) reports on the new developments in Lithuanian exemplified in (140) and (141) whereby the complementiser particles *asteit* and *neva* 'that' (i.e. QUOT.COMP.), which previously only functioned to convey epistemic or evidential (hearsay) meaning, have evolved so that they can now also introduce quoted utterances in which a "free interpretation" of the reported speech is given (2016: 247).[188]

(140)   *Jis*   *tik*   *papurtė*   *galv-ą,*   "***atseit***   *ne-trauk*",
        3.NOM.SG.M only shake.PST.3 head-ACC.SG **QUOT.COMP** NEG-pull.IMP.2SG
        o   *poto*   *apsižiūri,*   *kad*   *danči-o*   *nėra.*
        but after.that realize.PRS.3 COMP tooth-GEN.SG be.PRS.3.NEG
        'He only shook his head {atseit} "Don't pull", but a moment later he realized the tooth was out already.' ('.. as if to say "Don't pull"')

(141)   *gydytoj-as*   ***sakė,***   "*kad*[189] ***neva***
        doctor-NOM.SG say.PST.3 COMP **QUOT.COMP**
        neram-us   *vaik-as ...*"
        nervous-NOM.SG.M child-NOM.SG
        'the doctor said that {neva} "it's an excitable child ..."'

---

188 Although this strategy is not reported in reviews such as Buchstaller (2014) or Buchstaller & van Alphen (2012b), it is not uncommon cross-linguistically for reporting verbs and those conveying comparison to grammaticalize into complementisers. As such, it is not wholly surprising that the latter can, in turn, serve a quotative function in certain languages, as reported in various contributions to Boye & Kehayov (2016) and in Klamer (2000).

189 These particles when in quotative function can be preceded by the usual complementiser marker *kad* 'that', as here, or can occur alone (Holvoet 2016: 247).

In a similar vein, Guz (2018), (2019a,b) documents the existence of quotatives in Polish that are also not introduced by reporting verbs but by a much wider range of discourse pragmatic particles serving this function (including the zero type which is often used in mimetic contexts in this language as it is similarly reported to be in English vernaculars). Other novel forms which serve this function include: (i) a self-standing nominal type (often a pronoun) which may or may not be preceded by conjunctions such as *a* 'and' or *ale* 'but' (Conj.P); (ii) demonstrative deictics of the *here+be*+speaker Mid-Ulster English category which can also incorporate a comparative element (similar to *like* in English), i.e. the adverbial *tak* 'thus'/'like so' and the adjectival form *tak-{i/-a/-ie etc.}* meaning 'like this'; (iii) generic verbs of action such as *zrobić* ('make') which are often reserved to introduce sound effects alongside paralinguistic verbs that are likewise associated with non-verbal communication cross-linguistically by Buchstaller (2014: 27) (e.g. Polish *śmieją* 'laughs'); (iv) a quotative complementizer featuring *że* 'that' (142) which operates rather similarly to Lithuanian *atseit* and *neva* in (140)/(141) and finally (v) amalgam types which can combine elements of the quotative markers already described in the manner of (143) in which the deictic comparative *taki* 'like this' binds with the quotative marker *że* in a quotative frame which has much in common with the *be+all/be+like* syntagms which are frequently reported for English vernaculars too, as noted in §9.2.1.

(142) miałam na przykład dwa tygodnie **że**   "o będę
      had-1SG for example two weeks **QUOT.COMP** oh AUX-FUT.1SG
      mało jadła   i   ćwiczyła"
      little ate-3SG and exercised-3SG
      'I had this period of two weeks like, "right, I will eat little and I will exercise"'
      (Cited in Guz 2018: 80)

(143) i   w ogóle ta   koleżanka **taka**   **że**   "no spoko spoko
      and at all this friend   **(is) like this QUOT. COMP** oh great great
      będziecie sobie   tam   mieszkać"
      you are   welcome there live
      'and this friend (is) like this, "oh, great, great, you are welcome to live there"'
      (Cited in Guz 2019a: 219)

This summary of the quotative systems in the two daughter languages of Balto-Slavic which are of prime concern here underlines two key aspects of their linguistic behaviour that may be relevant to the acquisition of the quotative introducers that typify Mid-Ulster English which have already been presented but will be explored further in subsequent sections. In the first place, canonical discourse markers such as verbs of saying abound in both languages so one would predict these to be readily acquired in English by speakers of Lithuanian and Polish. Indeed, Guz (2019a: 204) reports from his analysis of a sub-sample of the *Spokes Corpus*[190] that *mówić* 'speak'/'say' accounted for 86% of the quotative introducers in his data, followed by *powiedzieć* 'tell'/'say' which was the next most frequent marker (although it accounts for a mere 9% of the sample). While there is no similar benchmark that I am aware of for Lithuanian (for the reasons recounted above), it will be interesting to observe whether this propensity in Polish has any impact on the relative distribution of quotatives in their systems more broadly and, what is more, whether their frequencies for *say* as an introducer match either those of the autochthonous cohort or their Lithuanian migrant peers. There will also be issues worth examining further in the multivariate regression analysis regarding linguistic constraints on the variable. Polish speakers, for instance, may well significantly prefer to use the historic present with Mid-Ulster English *say* because this is the preferred temporal arena for *mówić* 'say' in Polish. Secondly, it should now be obvious that despite the other congruences identified above between canonical and non-canonical strategies for discourse marking between Balto-Slavic and English (which is not surprising given the trends previously identified both within and outwith Indo-European), there are dissonances too. Thus, while Polish (and other languages) permit generic action verbs such as *make* to act as a quotative, this marker has not so far been identified with this function in English dialects. Moreover, the scholarly literature that I have consulted makes no mention that verbs of motion such as the innovative Mid-Ulster English *go* marker favoured by younger speakers in the Belfast sample of the *Empire Corpus* undertake this discourse-pragmatic role in either Lithuanian or Polish. The behaviour of both allochthonous groups will therefore be worth exploring in these respects too. Moreover, each Balto-Slavic language permits a non-canonical quotative introducer option which has not yet been reported for English vernaculars, i.e. the marking of constructed dialogue by the complementisers *atseit, neva* and *że*. Will this trait, therefore, be replicated amongst the L2 acquirers of Armagh English, in which case language transfer might be also implicated? Such an outcome is certainly possible in the abstract given the arguments made earlier that of all the levels of the grammar that have been considered in this work thus far, it is the area of discourse-pragmatics which seems to be most vulnerable to contact effects. These issues will be examined in the analyses following an outline of the research questions, methods and constraints on variability to which I now turn.

---

190 This is a freely available 2-million-word corpus of spoken Polish detailed at: http://spokes.clarin-pl.eu., last accessed 6 Sept. 2019.

9.4 Research questions, methodology and constraints

The review thus far which has catalogued the evolution of various quotative introducers in the history of English more broadly as well as in varieties of Irish English specifically raises queries that are worth exploring regarding how closely the quotative system of Armagh English matches those of global vernaculars documented in previous research. Possible differences may arise on account of the particular hyperlocal context of this dialect. It has been influenced to some degree by contact with the Irish language and may also lag behind mainstream varieties on account of its peripherality on the stage of world Englishes (as it appears to do in relation to aspects of its system of relative clause formation, for instance). The discussion of quotative introducer types, their distributions and the constraints on their operation in Lithuanian and Polish are also worthy of further consideration. With that in mind, the same *Múin Béarla* sub-sample that has already been interrogated with respect to (ING) and relative marking will be examined next.[191]

Research questions 1–5 will be considered here and they arise from the hypotheses, methods and outcomes underpinning the scholarship reviewed in previous sections.

1. What is the system of quotation in Armagh English and does it match the findings from the *Empire Corpus* and from Höhn (2011), (2012) as well as Diskin & Levey (2019) regarding the evolution of Irish English quotative introducers?

2. To what extent do the newcomer cohorts share the variants and distributional patterning of the quotative system favoured by the indigenous community and is there any evidence for contact effects?

3. Of the linguistic determinants explicated in §9.2.1 and listed/exemplified in (i)–(iv) below, which one(s) condition the choice of *be like, say* or zero by allochthonous and autochthonous participants?

   (i) TENSE
   This factor has been implicated as constraining variant choice in a number of studies and appears to generate fine-grained distinctions cross-dialectally

---

191 Notwithstanding the possibility outlined in the previous Chapter that quantifying a restricted data sample may present issues in this regard, I view a consistent analytical approach across all three variables within an identical sub-corpus as paramount given the orientation of this project. It is certainly possible, of course, to uncover findings that have implications for improving our knowledge of discourse-pragmatics and for evaluating models of acquisition and the like with rather modest data-sets, as Corrigan (2016), Meyerhoff & Schleef (2014) and Diskin & Levey (2019) have already shown. See also Davydova (2019: 4).

(Buchstaller 2014: 110). As already noted, the results of research by Tagliamonte & D'Arcy (2007: 209) *inter alia* contend that *be like* is favoured in the conversational historical present (HP) particularly amongst younger speakers whereas *say* is more often found in simple past contexts. As such, tokens within the *Múin Béarla* sub-sample were divided so as to determine whether tense and its associated verb morphology influenced quotative selection. Three specific types were extracted, i.e. past temporal reference when combined with past tense morphology (144); present temporal reference when combined with non-past tense morphology (145) and past temporal reference but also combined with non-past tense morphology, i.e. the HP (146).

(144) I **was,** "You can trust me on that one"
[CH; (F); M-UE; St. Celine's; Armagh, NI; 28 Jan. 2014]

(145) That's what I call him and it**'s like,** "What's up, Paddy?"
[LL; (M); Lithuanian; St. Benedict's; Armagh, NI; 29 Jan. 2014]

(146) Then he put the music on and he**'s like,** "Louder!"
[LL; (M); Lithuanian; St. Benedict's; Armagh, NI; 29 Jan. 2014]

(ii) GRAMMATICAL PERSON

This independent variable was explored to examine whether the trends identified in the scholarship summarised in §9.2.1 also played out in Armagh English. Of particular concern was the tendency for the non-canonical *be like* introducer to be favoured in first person (147) while third person is more likely to occur when canonical quotatives such as *say* are used (148).

(147) I**'m like,** "She's not in."
[MM; (F) M-UE; St. Celine's; Armagh, NI; 20 Aug. 2012]

(148) She **said,** "Yeah, you'll be you'll be a godmother."
[PW; (F) Polish; St. Celine's; Armagh, NI; 5 Aug. 2013]

(iii) MIMESIS

This factor refers to utterances representing reported discourse that are best thought of as a re-enactment or dramatic performance of some sort. Mimetic contexts can thus often include constructed dialogue which is not conventional speech as such but is conveyed by means of gestures, suprasegmental phonology, ideophones and so on, as in (149). Such expressions are reported to favour (BE LIKE) and zero quotative introducers rather than more traditional variants like *say*. This effect has, in fact, been described cross-dialectally as: "probably the most consistent of the host of conditioning factors that have been investigated for quotative *be like* and the only one where no conflicting information has been reported across the English-speaking world" (Buchstaller 2014: 102). As such, it will be interesting to observe whether this distinction also applies to Armagh English and similarly if identical constraints are found in the recordings from both sets of newcomer speakers.

(149) Whenever they came back we **were like**,"WAAAH".
[DF; (M); Lithuanian; St. Benedict's; Armagh, NI; 27 Feb. 2014]

(iv) CONTENT OF THE QUOTE

This condition on quotative variation, as its name suggests, differentiates between constructed dialogue that conveys internal monologue or the inner state of a speaker with that which instead captures external verbal actions (i.e. the gestures and sounds associated with mimesis as well as non-mimetic speech). As already reported in §9.2.1, the reporting of verbal actions is more closely associated with *say* (150) than it is with *be like* (151) which, by contrast, favours contexts where the constructed dialogue expresses thoughts and emotions.

(150) He came over to him and **said**, "How do you do?"
[DF; (M); Lithuanian; St. Benedict's; Armagh, NI; 27 Feb. 2014]

(151) The next minute the horse took off and I **was like**,
"Right, okay"
[CH; (F); M-UE; St. Celine's; Armagh, NI; 28 Jan. 2014]

4. Is the choice of *be like* socially evaluated with respect to either ethnolinguistic background (Lithuanian, Mid-Ulster English or Polish) or gender (male *versus* female)?

5. Does the proficiency of L2 speakers have a role to play in the competent acquisition of the linguistic determinants outlined in (3i–iv) above?

In keeping with previous studies, the protocol determining the closed set of quotative variants included the recording of any strategy for reporting the speech, sounds or thoughts of oneself or another (Buchstaller 2006: 5; Diskin 2015: 48; Tagliamonte & Denis 2014: 121, *inter alia*). Exclusions were applied to rule out incomplete or inaudible quotations as well as tokens of *think* or *say* that introduce indirect speech, as recommended by Tagliamonte & Denis (2014: 121) and others. In addition, constructed dialogue in which there was code-switching between the introducer (in English) and any quotation rendered partially or wholly in Irish, Lithuanian or Polish (as in (152)) were also omitted from the analyses just in case this somehow also impacted upon speaker choices.

(152) somebody at the other side of me would ask me something and **I would say**, "Co?" which means 'What?' in Polish
[NP; (F); Polish; St. Celine's; Armagh, NI; 24 Jan. 2014]

Although Durham *et al.* (2012: 322) as well as Tagliamonte and D'Arcy (2004: 504) excluded tokens where the quotative introducer was *it's like* (as in (145) above) on account of their exceptionality (i.e. they are restricted to animate subjects), they were coded for here and will be included in the frequency analysis in §9.5.2 so as to map the *Múin Béarla* results as closely as possible to those reported in Diskin & Levey (2019) who did not exclude them either. However, as per Tagliamonte & Denis (2014: 121) and Tagliamonte & Hudson (1999: 169, n. 10), which follow this same practice, they are not included in the multivariate analyses since such structures are not entirely variable.

9.5 Results and discussion

9.5.1 Quotative introducers in the *Múin Béarla* corpus

The procedures outlined in §9.4 resulted in the extraction of 1,697 tokens altogether including zero introducers (example (123) above) as well as tokens of the predominant quotative verbs in Englishes globally, as outlined in §9.2.1, i.e. *be like, go, say* and *think*. Verbs such as *ask* (153), *shout, tell* and the like were also searched for during this process as were non-canonical quotatives found in other varieties including *be all* as in (154) and discourse *like* (155). None of these occurred especially often in this sub-sample, so all such infrequent tokens within the variable context have been collapsed into the OTHER category visible in Figure 62 in §9.5.2.

(153) He found them and my dad **asks**, "Oh my God why do you have so many beers?"
[PW; (F) Polish; St. Celine's; Armagh, NI; 5 Aug. 2013]

(154) And she was **all**, "Ah, I'll know it'll never be you burning cars anyway"
[CH; (F); M-UE; St. Celine's; Armagh, NI; 28 Jan. 2014]

(155) I just keep on talking and she **like**, "Would you just shut up and talk Polish", you know. She doesn't like it, but
[NP; (F); Polish; St. Celine's; Armagh, NI; 24 Jan. 2014]

What Güldemann (2012: 124) terms "speaker-instantiating quotative indexes" of the hyperlocal *here+be*+speaker category in (127), already discussed, were also coded for. However, there were no tokens of this type in the *Múin Béarla* subsample nor were there any instances of the related *this+be+speaker* construction (129) identified in Multicultural London English by Cheshire *et al.* (2011) and Fox (2012) (nor indeed were any other similar introducers found). The absence of the hyperlocal variant, in particular, which was recorded by Milroy & Milroy (1977: 54) and then was still extant nearly a decade later amongst Finlay & McTear's (1986: 182) sample of Belfast school children appears to indicate that it is now moribund in Mid-Ulster English – at least among adolescents. This is exactly what the results from the frequency analysis of the *Empire Corpus* in §9.2.2 would likewise predict since the pre-adolescent Armagh local has no *here's me* tokens in this 2008 data-set either. In fact, it is only the middle-aged Belfast speaker who retains the variant and she would herself have been of school-going age when Finlay & McTear conducted their research there more than two decades before.[192]

On account of the presence in Lithuanian and Polish of quotatives which are essentially complementisers in form but can function as introducers (i.e. *atseit*, *neva* and *że* detailed in §9.3), it was also considered crucial to code for any English complementisers being used in constructed dialogue contexts. Similarly, generic action verbs such as *make* which can have quotative function in Polish, for instance, were also added to the coding protocol. However, neither of these potential transfer-induced types were located in either the allochthonous or autochthonous samples. Although there were some examples of what Diskin & Levey (2019: 69) term "speaker-nominal" variants (156), they are both rare (N=7) and restricted to the newcomers. Since Diskin & Levey (2019: 69) state that they not only appeared in their L1 Polish sample (N=13) but also in the speech of their indigenous Dublin English cohort too (N=2), I would not wish to draw any further conclusions about this variant *vis à vis* L2 transfer, interlanguage or otherwise at this juncture but it is interesting to note that Guz (2018), (2019a,b) documents this same quotative type as regularly occurring in Polish (see §9.3).

---

[192] That is not to say, of course, that the form is no longer in use since I have overheard it many times from speakers of Mid-Ulster English. However, they too are all middle-aged or older, so it is clearly receding in the vernacular grammar and was possibly another "short-lived innovation", as Buchstaller *et al.* (2012) report *be all* to have been in California. *Here+be*+speaker therefore seems to be an excellent example of the type of innovative variant isolated in Chapter Five, §5.2.2.2, in that young Armagh speakers by 2008 had already passed the "peak" period for acquiring this change already in progress amongst their parents' generation and propelling it even further (see Chambers 2009: 190, and Wagner 2012a: 181).

(156)   No, but sometimes like in class when I'm talking with my friend **Polish people** turn around, "Are you talking about me?"
[AW; (F); Polish; St. Celine's; Armagh, NI; 24 Jan. 2014]

In fact, by and large, when viewed as a holistic system, both newcomer groups have a similar complement of quotative markers in their conversations to that which obtains for the Armagh local speakers and there is no compelling evidence for transfer or interlanguage effects – from this perspective at any rate.[193] As 9.5.2 will demonstrate, however, the relative frequencies of quotative introducers amongst all three groups is dissimilar in certain key respects that will be addressed next.

9.5.2   Distribution of quotative introducers

9.5.2.1   Local English varieties

Figure 62 itemises the quotative variants found in the sample and provides a comparison across each Armagh cohort. As far as the innovative *be like* variant is concerned, while the form is absent from the conversation with the St. Benedict's speaker interviewed in 2008, it has seen a meteoric rise amongst Armagh locals to the point where *be like* actually now dominates, introducing nearly 38% of the constructed dialogues found in the entire sub-sample. This 'blow-in' has thus turned the tables on *say* (20.4%) which still held the lead in the (S)PICE-Ireland analyses by Höhn (2011), (2012); Diskin & Levey (2019) as well as in the *Empire Corpus* (even amongst the youngest speaker from Armagh). The zero variant for local speakers is the next most prevalent in their quotative systems (17.1%) followed by *go* which appeared to be holding its own in (S)PICE-Ireland and gaining ground in the *Empire Corpus* as an innovative feature of Belfast-born middle-aged and younger speakers but not of participants outside of the capital. This included Armagh where it has undoubtedly arrived since it now comprises 12.8% of the quotative sample amongst local born teens. It is noticeable, too, that the traditional zero quotative type which was used with very high frequencies by the oldest Belfast speaker in the *Empire Corpus* but also remained buoyant in the quotative systems of the younger speakers in Armagh and Lurgan continues to prevail nearly a decade later amongst a teenage sample in one of these peripheral suburbs. This finding is particularly striking when zero only constituted 8% of the 19–33 year olds' output in the 2002–2005 data-set from SPICE-Ireland which

---

[193] New research on a larger *Múin Béarla* sample which, for instance, follows Diskin & Levey (2019) by unpacking the OTHER category with respect to native *versus* non-native speakers could well prove fruitful in this regard, though.

included adult data for the island as a whole (Diskin & Levey (2019: 62). *Think*, a less conservative variant, actually proved to be rather inconsequential to the discourse system more broadly in all the historical Irish English data-sets considered in §9.2.2, as it remains amongst the *Múin Béarla* adolescents (just 1.7 % of their quotative tokens). The same is true for *it's like* which barely registers in the system at all (1 %). Variants in the OTHER category in Diskin & Levey's (2019) analysis of SPICE-Ireland were also quite trivial diachronically. Although they included discourse *like* as well as infrequent verbal introducers such as *tell*, their classification also features *it's like* (only 3 tokens, according to Diskin & Levey (2019: 63, n. 7), which is considered as a separate category here. As such, while the result of 8 % for the 19–33 year olds in 2002–2005 from SPICE-Ireland is not directly comparable with the 9.5 % figure generated by the *Múin Béarla* local teens, they are in the same ball park suggesting that the number of miscellaneous variants has not changed either to any degree in the intervening years.

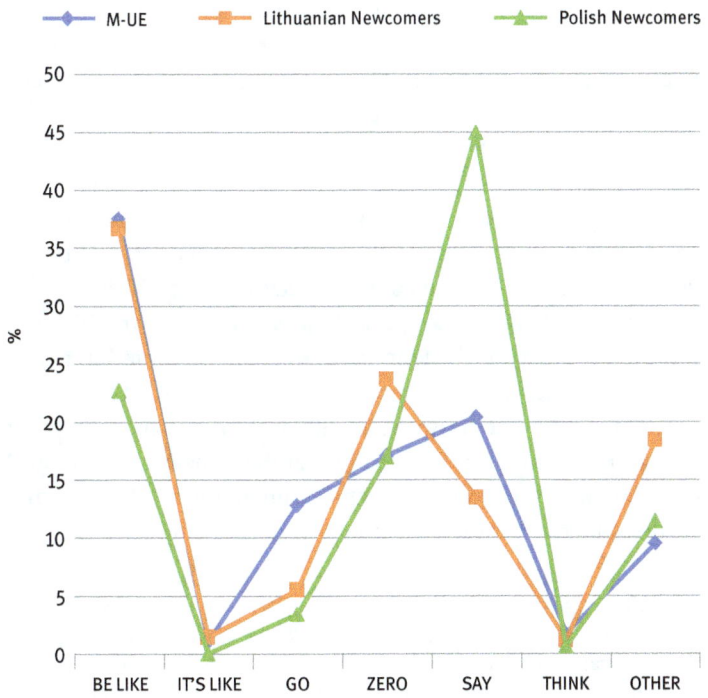

Figure 62 Distribution of quotatives amongst autochthonous and allochthonous cohorts in Armagh

How does the local Armagh quotative system fare though when compared to those for contemporary indigenous Dublin and Ottawa Englishes outlined by Diskin & Levey (2019: 66) and Meyerhoff & Schleef's (2014: 111) analysis of local Edinburgh-born adolescents? Although the judgments underpinning their distributional analyses are not exact replicas either of each other or of the analysis presented in Figure 62, they are worth considering, particularly since some interesting parallels occurred between the Armagh and Edinburgh teens when examining variability across the two cities with respect to (ING) in Chapter Seven.[194] Moreover, Diskin & Levey (2019) is the first comprehensive, comparative study of the quotative system within a Southern Hiberno-English-speaking city which will form a crucial bridge to examining that of a more peripheral suburb in which Mid-Ulster English is the base dialect.

The caveats already stated notwithstanding, the continuum for Edinburgh is *be like* (47.0%) > *say* (21.1%) > zero (16.7%) > *go* (11.8%) > OTHER (3.4%) (Meyerhoff & Schleef 2014: 111). The proportion of variants in each category thus matches the Armagh local teenage system just described remarkably well (although the figure for *be like* in *Múin Béarla* is roughly 10% adrift showing that this innovation is not yet as prominent here as it is in the Scottish capital). As for the larger principal cities of the Irish Republic and Canada, the continua are: (i) Dublin: *be like* (25%) > *say* (21%) > zero (14%) > OTHER (12%) > *it's like* (10%) > *go* (8%) > discourse *like* (6%) > *think* (4%) and (ii) Ottawa: *be like* (64%) > discourse *like* (10%); > *say* (9%) > zero (6%) > OTHER (5%) > *it's like* (4%) > *go* (2%) > *think* (1%) (Diskin & Levey 2019: 66). On this basis, local adult Dubliners have a quotative system which is closer to those of Armagh and Edinburgh teenagers than that of their transatlantic neighbour where *be like* is preeminent amongst even adult speakers so that it presents a "more homogenized system in which no other competing variant accounts for more than 10% of the variable context" (Diskin & Levey 2019: 66). Indeed, when considered in terms of the incrementation model introduced in §5.2.2.2 of Chapter Five, in Ottawa the *be like* innovation is heading towards what Nevalainen & Raumolin-Brunberg (2003: 55) view to be a "nearing completion" phase while in Dublin it remains within their "new and vigorous" category. Despite the relative proximity between Dublin and Armagh, there are, however, curious dissonances between the quotative systems in both samples.

---

194 For instance, Meyerhoff & Schleef (2014: 111) report on variability within a narrower range of quotative introducers (only *be like, say, zero, go* and OTHER) and it is not readily apparent what constitutes the latter category for them. Diskin & Levey's (2019: 66) decision-making is more similar to that used here since they include all the types in Figure 61, the only difference being that they foreground the discourse *like* variant (chiefly it would appear on the basis of its prominence in Ottawa (10%)) while I included it in the OTHER category on account of its rarity in the Armagh data (just the single token exemplified in (155) above).

Unexpectedly perhaps, *be like* turns out to be rather more prominent in Mid-Ulster English (37.5%) (i.e. a "mid-range" innovation as Nevalainen & Raumolin-Brunberg (2003: 55) would define it) than this variant is in the dialect associated with the arguably more global capital city, which Corrigan & Diskin (2020) contend it to be with respect to the behaviour of *like* as a discourse pragmatic marker (see §5.2.2.1). This disparity regarding the *be like* 'blow-in' may well arise from the age differences between the two samples since models of change across the lifespan such as those also discussed in §5.2.2.2 would predict that when changes are rapidly advancing, the "usage patterns of young adults (late adolescence, early 20s) will reflect the leading edge of change, at least in rapidly advancing changes" (Tagliamonte 2016b: 259) of the type which this variant certainly appears to be. Of interest too from a comparative perspective, is the fact that while the conservative *say* and zero quotatives continue to compete as introducers in the systems outlined for Armagh, Dublin and Edinburgh, they are being eclipsed in Ottawa not only by *be like* but also by discourse *like* which, it has already been noted, is extremely rare in the *Múin Béarla* data sample (though it is the fifth most dominant quotative marker in Dublin which is another respect in which the cities north and south of the border differ). Moreover, while *go* in Armagh and Edinburgh both remain amongst the top four variants used by local speakers when constructing dialogue, it has been ousted in Dublin by both the OTHER and *it's like* categories. Although Meyerhoff & Schleef (2014) do not calculate the proportion of quotative *think* tokens used by their local sample, it remains a marginal variant in both cities on the island of Ireland as well as in the Canadian capital.

9.5.2.2 Newcomer varieties

Turning now to the distributions of the quotative systems that typify the Lithuanian and Polish newcomers in the *Múin Béarla* sample depicted in Figure 62 and comparing them with each other as well as to that of the system documented in the previous section for the local teens, there are really rather marked differences all round. In the first place, it is only the Lithuanian sub-sample which shares the Armagh preference for *be like* as the majority quotative (36.6%). Moreover, even they do not favour *say* as their second most frequent variant which is more typically the position it occupies locally. Instead, they prefer zero (23.6%) while *say* for them only reaches fourth place in the continuum (13.4%) being preceded by OTHER (18.4%). In stark contrast, *say* happens to be the most prevalent option amongst their Polish peers (and this disparity between the three cohorts regarding *be like* will be explored further in §9.5.4). In fact, *say* constitutes almost half of their quotative tokens (44.9%) while the remainder consists primarily of *be like* (22.7%) > zero (17.0%) > OTHER (11.4%). In fact, it is only the local infrequent patterns for the bit-player *it's like* and *think* variants which both sets of newcomers seem to have collectively unequivocally acquired (though they have reversed their order of magnitude, i.e. *it's like* > *think* versus Armagh local *think* > *it's like*). What is more, neither of these allochthonous cohorts avail of the *go* variant to the same degree that the local Armagh teens do, producing over twice as many tokens as the Lithuanian sample (5.5%) and over three times the number recorded amongst the Polish participants (just 3.4%).

The review in §9.3 of the quotative systems in Lithuanian and Polish may illuminate these findings somewhat. In the first place, to my knowledge, there is no evidence that motion verbs in either of these languages can act as quotative introducers which may account for this difference between the autochthonous and allochthonous cohorts since the use of *go* as a quotative marker will entail newcomers acquiring lexico-semantic and functional properties for motion verbs which do not obtain in their L1s.[195] Moreover, it was also noted that the form *mówić* meaning 'say' in Polish dominated in Guz's (2019a: 204) analysis of the *Spokes* corpus to the point where the variable context of the quotative system was rather homogeneous (and thus similar to that which Diskin & Levey (2019: 66) have found in Ottawa which is governed in just this manner by *be like*). In the same vein, Guz's analysis of *Spokes* also finds that *powiedzieć*, meaning 'tell' or indeed 'say' is the next most frequent discourse introducer after *mówić*. This result may also account for the unusually high proportion of the Polish newcomers' sample being *say* and it may likewise explain the frequency of their OTHER category by comparison to the local speakers since this included quite a few tokens of the English *tell* variant (N=17).[196] Attending to frequency distributions in the L1 is crucial, as Sankoff *et al.* (1997: 205, 209) found in their analysis of English *like* and French *comme* 'like' amongst bilinguals in Montréal. They are used at rather different rates in each language and this influenced the English dominant bilinguals to use the latter in French with a frequency which matched Anglophone rather than Francophone norms indicating that transfer effects were "highly likely" (p. 209). If this is indeed a plausible explanation here too, then one would expect a similar finding to show up in the distributional analyses of Polish English acquirers by Meyerhoff & Schleef (2014: 111) as well as Diskin & Levey (2019: 66). As regards the latter, they do indeed report

---

195 The grammaticalization of motion verbs into quotative introducers is actually very rare cross-linguistically, as Buchstaller (2014: 23) also contends.

196 Ideally, one would also like to have similar figures showing the frequencies of different quotative introducers in conversational Lithuanian so as to determine whether their reluctance to use *say* here, which is of course a perfectly viable option in their system too (i.e. *sakýti* n §9.3), is tied to having a rather divergent quotative marking hierarchy. Meyerhoff (2000) reports facing a similar issue regarding a distinctive type of pro-drop which characterises Bislama and which she suspects may be a calque on the substrate but which cannot be proven because there are no references to this type of variation in traditional grammars.

a continuum amongst their high proficiency newcomer West Slavic group as being of the order: *say* (26%) > *be like* (20%) > zero (18%) > OTHER (17%) > *think* (12%) > *it's like* (5%) > Discourse *like* (2%) > *go* (1%).[197] As far as the first four categories are concerned, while there is considerably less difference between the frequencies of *say* and *be like* in the Dublin data than there is for the Armagh Poles, the pattern is identical to that of their peers north of the border. Thus, *say* is, as predicted, the most preferred variant. What is more, there is a similar reluctance amongst the Dublin newcomers of Polish descent to utilise *go* as an introducer lending further support to the proposal that this may be because there is no L1 equivalent.

Reviewing Meyerhoff & Schleef (2014), however, presents a somewhat different pattern that is worth pausing over. The hierarchy they identify is: zero (39.5%) > *say* (25.6%) > *be like* (23.3%) > OTHER (9.3%) > *go* (2.3%). As such, while this group is also less likely to use a motion verb to introduce a quotative and *say* is indeed preferred over the *be like* quotative, it does not take pole position as it did in either Armagh or Dublin amongst speakers of this same ethnolinguistic heritage. In the Edinburgh scenario, this place is instead held by zero which is considerably more highly favoured here than it is either by the Polish cohorts north or south of the Irish border nor indeed by the L1 control populations (Armagh (17.1%), Dublin (14%) and Edinburgh (16.7%), respectively). Diskin & Levey (2019: 69) commenting on this disparity amongst the Edinburgh Polish and local samples alongside the high rates of zero quotative use in their lower proficiency Dublin Polish cohort (27%) suggest that the zero quotative might be preferred because it: "is an ideal context-dependent strategy that less advanced learners can exploit to pragmatically encode their own speech as well as that of others." This may indeed be an interesting hypothesis worth pursuing in future research particularly since it echoes the findings of D'Arcy (2010: 69) concerning the dominance of null quotatives amongst speakers of Māori English which, after all, is also an L2 historically. It might similarly account for the relatively high rates of zero quotatives (23.6%) preferred by Armagh speakers of Lithuanian heritage too who, unlike the Polish sub-sample, are more variable with respect to proficiency levels, as will be demonstrated in §9.5.4. However, I would argue that the idea is not straightforward to evaluate across these investigations at the present time. In particular, because proficiency levels were self-reported in the studies by Diskin & Levey (2019: 57) and Meyerhoff & Schleef (2014: 110) (whose results seem to combine the output from speakers of lower and higher proficiencies anyway on

---

197 I report these figures here, since their proficiency rates most closely match the Armagh Polish sample and that of the data presented for Edinburgh. Additionally, Meyerhoff & Schleef (2014: 121) and Diskin & Levey (2019: 66) both record very few tokens of *be like* amongst lower proficiency speakers which would also make the comparisons more problematic.

account of the low overall token count (i.e. just 43 quotatives)). In addition, the Dublin and Edinburgh studies do not appear to have used the same benchmarking systems. What is more, while both Diskin & Levey (2019) and the present study each relied on the Common European Framework of Reference for Language (see §6.2.1 of Chapter Six) to assess this independent factor there are important dissonances to consider. In the case of the *Múin Béarla* participants, for instance, competence levels were evaluated by teachers who have considerably more experience of the process than the adult consultants in Diskin & Levey (2019) who were permitted to self-evaluate their proficiency. Such issues could lead to the type of confounding factors which can make such comparisons unreliable.

It remains to be seen of course to what extent the remarkable distributional contrasts which this section has uncovered between local benchmark groups as well as newcomers of Balto-Slavic extraction across the British Isles remain relevant when a more fine-grained approach is taken to the variability between *be like*, *say* and zero in the multivariate analyses that follow.

9.5.3 Internal linguistic constraints on quotative introducers

The predominant factor groups identified as operating on the quotative systems of vernacular Englishes are four-fold (see §§9.2.1 and 9.4). Table 23 below based on independent multivariate analyses shows the relative contributions made by each of these linguistic constraints on the selection of *be like*, *say* and zero by the allochthonous and autochthonous groups in Armagh. Since proficiency has been argued to significantly influence the linguistic conditioning of quotative variant choice in Diskin & Levey's (2019) analysis of L1 Dublin and L2 Polish migrant Englishes, which will also be reported on in §9.5.4, these results are confined to newcomers who have each been assigned an identical CEFR rating, i.e. "Independent User." This means that they have a median level of proficiency and are no longer a "Basic User" but have not yet reached the level of "Proficient User."

As regards the Armagh benchmark group, tense proves to be a significant constraining factor across all three variants. Comparing their results for *be like* in the first instance, the constraint hierarchy is Past>Present>HP. This outcome is remarkably different not only to the findings for the Edinburgh-born population in Meyerhoff & Schleef (2014: 116) but also to those in Diskin & Levey (2019: 66–67) for Ottawa English. What is more, it similarly runs counter to results for Pākehā New Zealanders and many other studies of Canadian English (Buchstaller & D'Arcy 2009; Tagliamonte & D'Arcy 2007) as well as those on American vernaculars examined in Buchstaller & D'Arcy (2009). In these varieties, it is the HP which favours *be like* and it disfavours past temporal reference. In fact, the strong favouring effect for the latter in *be like* contexts amongst Armagh-born speakers instead patterns rather similarly to the constraints reported for Māori English in D'Arcy (2010) and for those of certain historical dialects in Northern England by Buchstaller & D'Arcy (2009) as well as in contemporary Multicultural London English (Fox 2012: 39) in which, like here, it is the simple past especially which favours *be like*. In fact, it is quotative *say* in Armagh local speech where there are favouring effects for the present and HP though that for the latter is weaker. Of interest in this regard too, is the fact that Diskin & Levey (2019: 67) report a "moderately" favouring effect for *be like* in past temporal contexts in their synchronic Dublin English sample (.58) as well as a "weak association" between this variant and past tense in SPICE-Ireland ((.51) in the 2002–2005 sample of 19–33 year olds, p. 64). This has led them to propose that the "temporal constraint may pattern differently in Irish English varieties *vis à vis* Northern American ones" (2019: 67). This suggestion is also congruent with Buchstaller & D'Arcy's (2009: 309) earlier assertion that this constraint on the variation is "subject to local re-organization as *be like* finds its niche in the respective quotative systems." When the hyperlocal grammatical person findings for the *Múin Béarla* sample are added to the mix therefore, they lend considerable further support to their hypothesis and this constraint should be examined in comparative studies that rely on the same methodologies across the entire island of Ireland to test it more comprehensively.

As far as the newcomers are concerned, the effects for temporality are no longer significant (hence the use of [ ] here). Moreover, despite their median levels of proficiency, there is a real mismatch between the order of effects as well as their magnitude. For instance, the Lithuanian newcomers have rather different patterns for *be like*, i.e. Past>HP> Present, despite the fact that in the distributional analysis their variant choices for *be like*, *say* and zero were most similar to those made by the indigenous group. In fact, it is the Polish L2 speakers whose system more closely resembles that testified to in many of the other global investigations of this variant just discussed since participants with this heritage also prefer HP with *be like*. Interestingly, Diskin & Levey (2019: 70–71) do not report the same effect for their upper proficiency Polish cohort in the Irish Republic who actually did not produce "a single occurrence of *be like* with the historical present." This grammatical distinction has, however, been acquired since they do avail of it in *say* contexts where it is actually the most favoured of all possible environments (though again, this is not so amongst either the independent Lithuanian or Polish cohorts in *Múin Béarla* who thus pattern rather differently to their migrant peers in Dublin).[198]

---

[198] Interestingly, the Dublin result is exactly what a transfer model might predict since *say* is reported by Guz (2018), (2019a,b) to likewise favour the HP in Polish. As such, it is their Armagh peers who are out of kilter with what one might have expected on this basis.

Table 23 Independent multivariate analyses of the contribution made by linguistic factors to the selection of *be like, say* and *zero* in the speech of (i) L1 speakers of Armagh (Mid-Ulster) English; (ii) Lithuanian newcomer L2 English speakers (Independent Users) and (iii) Polish newcomer L2 English speakers (Independent Users)

		M-UE			Lithuanian (independent)			Polish (independent)		
		be like	say	zero	be like	say	zero	be like	say	zero
		FW	FW	FW	FW	FW	FW	FW	FW	FW
Tense	Present	0.452	0.607	0.998	0.424	0.624	0.997	0.289	0.577	0.995
	HP	0.278	0.559	<0.001	0.512	0.415	<0.001	0.808	0.360	<0.001
	Past	0.759	0.338	0.989	0.564	0.459	0.995	0.368	0.566	0.996
	Range	0.481	0.269	0.997	0.140	0.209	0.996	0.519	0.217	0.995
Grammatical person	1	[0.584]	[0.470]	[0.481]	0.577	[0.417]	[0.479]	[0.585]	[0.437]	[<0.999]
	3	[0.452]	[0.530]	[0.519]	0.423	[0.583]	[0.521]	[0.415]	[0.536]	[>0.001]
	Range	0.132	0.060	0.038	0.154	0.166	0.042	0.170	0.099	0.998
Mimesis	Mimetic	0.594	0.305	[0.556]	0.572	0.318	[0.543]	0.670	0.382	[<0.001]
	Non-Mimetic	0.406	0.695	[0.444]	0.423	0.682	[0.457]	0.330	0.618	[>0.999]
	Range	0.188	0.390	0.112	0.149	0.364	0.086	0.340	0.236	0.998
Content of quote	Reported Thought	[0.573]	0.958	[0.540]	[0.474]	<0.001	[0.404]	[<0.001]	[<0.001]	[0.817]
	Reported Speech	[0.427]	0.997	[0.460]	[0.526]	>0.999	[0.596]	[>0.999]	[>0.999]	[0.183]
	Range	0.146	0.039	0.080	0.052	0.998	0.192	0.998	0.998	0.634

Continuing with *be like* amongst the local cohort then and switching now to constraints on grammatical person, the results show that there is no significant effect here for any of the variants, although *be like* marginally favours first person over third while the opposite is true for *say* and zero (though in each case the effects are similarly weak). This has been demonstrated to be a consistent conditioning factor on *be like* usage, as argued in Buchstaller & D'Arcy (2009: 296), citing studies ranging from Ferrara & Bell (1995) to Tagliamonte & Hudson's (1999) comparative analyses of dialects on both sides of the Atlantic. It is also reported more recently for Ottawa English in Diskin & Levey (2019: 67) and likewise applies to both their autochthonous and upper proficiency Polish cohorts in Dublin (though the effects in each case are rather stronger than they are for the Armagh locals and the difference between the association with first and third person in their case is significant). As for *say* and zero amongst the indigenous *Múin Béarla* cohort, the opposite scenario prevails, i.e. they each moderately favour third person and disfavour first. Turning now to the L2 speakers, once more the effects which prevail are not significant for the Polish participants but, in this respect, they have actually acquired the local conditioning constraints for all three variants with the distinction for zero being particularly acute. As for their Lithuanian peers, they do show a significant conditioning effect for *be like* and, yet again, they follow both the order of effect and its relative magnitude associated with the L1 controls. The same is true for *say* and zero though in these cases the effects within this group are no longer significant. These outcomes are critical to bolstering the rather bold assertions made in Buchstaller & D'Arcy (2009: 306); Tagliamonte & D'Arcy (2004); Tagliamonte, D'Arcy & Rodríguez Louro (2016) that the grammatical person constraint is "universal" (particularly when *be like* is in the early stages of diffusion into a dialect which it may well be for Armagh English since its frequency has not yet reached Nevalainen & Raumolin-Brunberg's (2003: 55) "nearing completion" stage, as argued in §9.5.2.1.).

The possibility that there are global conditioning factors associated with the choice of *be like* over its nearest rivals *say* and zero, has also been mooted to explain the proclivity for the 'blow-in' to appear in mimetic contexts (see the cross-dialectal reviews demonstrating these parallels in Buchstaller (2014: 110), Buchstaller & D'Arcy (2009), D'Arcy (2010)). It is not perhaps remarkable therefore that the Armagh locals in Table 23 follow this exact pattern nor indeed that the magnitude of effects is quite as strong as it is. There is little doubt that when re-enactments occur in Mid-Ulster English conversations, *say* is avoided and both zero and *be like* especially have the highest probabilities of occurring. What is more noteworthy given our orientation is that both the Lithuanian and Polish newcomers also observe the same Mimetic>Non-Mimetic hierarchy for *be like* and zero (though these effects are not always significant and there is some inter-group variance in this respect as well as in the magnitude of the effects). Indeed, the results for the Polish cohort indicate a knock out for zero in this context. This finding may be connected to the fact noted in §9.3 that the zero type is reported by Guz (2018), (2019a,b) to similarly be frequent in mimetic contexts in their L1 (no doubt on account of its universal link cross-linguistically with prosodic cues that are "space builders" isolating the reported clause from preceding material in Buchstaller's (2014: 45) terms). There may also be a transfer connection here with the direction and strength of the constraint for zero in mimetic environments in Diskin & Levey's (2019: 71) results for both their upper (.59) and lower ([.54]) proficiency Polish participants.

The Armagh Polish cohort is not alone either with respect to the favouring of *be like* in mimetic contexts since Diskin & Levey (2019: 71–72) also report that this variant is preferred here by their upper proficiency Polish participants (though the mimetic effect is weaker for their group than it is in the hierarchy of their Armagh peers i.e. (.53) (Dublin) *versus* (.67)). They also note that while their Ottawa sample likewise conforms to global patterns ((.54) for mimetic contexts and (.47) for non-mimetic), their local Dublin native speakers reverse the expected order ((.47) *versus* (.53)). This calls into question the "universality" of this conditioning factor and provides useful evidence for Buchstaller & D'Arcy's (2009: 315) suggestion that this effect can become "attenuated in receptor varieties." It also demonstrates an interesting dissonance between the linguistic behaviour of indigenous and migrant groups north and south of the Irish border that needs further research.

The pragmatic content of the quotation which these three variants introduce is also considered to be a significant constraining factor cross-dialectally. *Be like* (particularly in the earliest studies of its variable dynamics) has been found to be the prototypical marker of internal thought (Buchstaller & D'Arcy (2009); Cukor-Avila (2002); Tagliamonte & D'Arcy 2007); Tagliamonte & Hudson 1999). It is perhaps reassuring therefore to uncover in Table 23 that the probability of *be like* being similarly favoured in this context amongst Armagh locals is very high indeed and that the effect is significant (just as it proved to be for the American English, British English and New Zealand English varieties analysed in Buchstaller & D'Arcy (2009: 306) as well as the Scottish vernacular examined in Meyerhoff & Schleef (2014: 116) and the Ottawa English data interrogated in Diskin & Levey (2019: 67)). The result for Mid-Ulster English is also interesting because it runs counter to the finding of Diskin & Levey (2019: 67) regarding the preferences of speakers in the 2002–2005 component of SPICE-Ireland for whom *be like* was actually significantly favoured in the reported speech context. In their contemporary Dublin corpus, the effect is now neutralized which they speculate may fall out from a historical state of Irish English in which *be like* was first favoured in this context. In order to pursue this line of argument for Northern Irish vernaculars, in particular, one could scrutinize the diachronic data from the *Tape-Recorded Survey of Hiberno-English Speech* once the digitisation and transcription process for that corpus is complete (see § 8.4.3 of the previous Chapter). For now, the question still remains an open one though the result for the local-born Armagh teenagers in which the balance has now been tipped in the global direction may arise on account of the difference in age range between the adult Dublin native-speaking cohort in Diskin & Levey (2019) and that of *Múin Béarla*.

As for the zero variant amongst the Mid-Ulster English-speaking youngsters, it also shows a slight favouring effect for internal dialogue contexts but it is not significant as it was with respect to *be like*. Moreover, *say* shows the opposite effect but this result is indeed significant. How then have the newcomers fared with respect to their acquisition of this constraint across all three variants? As Table 23 indicates, bar the result for *say* amongst the Lithuanian sample, none of the effects amongst either group for any of the variants proved to be significant and there are several knock-out results indicating categoricity. Moreover, the local Reported Thought>Reported Speech hierarchy for this condition on *be like* is not maintained by the Lithuanian teens who seem yet to acquire it. Furthermore, there is no evidence for their Polish peers having learned this constraint either since they actually show a knock-out effect indicating that for them at least *be like* is nearly categorical in reported speech which is the opposite of what one might expect given local preferences. It is, in fact, zero which has the highest probability of occurring in reported thought contexts for this cohort. While this outcome matches local norms somewhat better, again, the magnitude of effects is anything but similar between the two groups being much stronger for the Polish cohort than is the local norm. Additionally, this is another indigenous constraint which the Lithuanian newcomers have yet to master since the hierarchical order is reversed and they instead show a preference for this variant in reported speech. Regarding *say* then, the Lithuanian cohort has a knock-out effect for this variant in direct speech contexts as do their Polish peers (though they differ in the significance of the effects, as already noted).

Taking the results for the distributional and multivariate analyses as a whole then, it is clear that in some aspects of their operation within the local Armagh teenagers' quotative systems there is robust evidence for the existence of worldwide constraints which this L1 benchmark cohort also shares. More importantly, the results also indicate hyperlocal effects which seem in some respects to parallel findings from investigations of other varieties on the island of Ireland but not in all cases. The inclusion of data from two sets of migrant speakers adds a novel dimension here too. Since there is good evidence that these newcomers will not have been introduced to discourse markers formally at school (Sankoff *et al.* 1997: 193), it is probable that the properties of quotative introducers appear to be acquired on a case by case basis via exposure to the system utilised by age-mates born and reared in Armagh. Hence, while there are aspects of the L2 speakers' variable grammars which match local norms (grammatical person/mimesis), there is also support for proposing that there may be inter-language/transfer effects alongside re-ordering and reallocation at this level of the grammar just as the previous analyses of (ING) and the system of relativisation has likewise revealed. Since external constraints have also been implicated as impacting upon quotative variability in previous research, the next section takes a closer look at whether these factors are also at play in this *Múin Béarla* sample.

9.5.4 External linguistic constraints on quotative introducers

Three extralinguistic effects will be examined here, in particular, ethnolinguistic heritage, gender and proficiency. To that end, a multivariate regression analysis was undertaken which used *be like* as the application value and male *versus* female alongside home language as independent conditioning factors. The results are presented in Table 24.

Reviewing the figures for gender first, previous research on the association between this factor and *be like* was scrutinized in §9.2.1 so will not be rehearsed again here. Suffice it to say that it has not been found to be a globally transferable constraint (as is indeed fairly typical for social conditioning on variation more broadly). In this regard, Diskin & Levey (2019: 67) report a male-female differential with respect to *be like* in both their Ottawa sample and in their Dublin L1 benchmark cohort leading to particularly robust effects in the latter capital for its prevalence amongst men (though based on a rather modest sample). The opposite effect was, however, found amongst their Polish upper proficiency participants. Does gender have a similar constraining effect on the *Múin Béarla* teenage sub-sample which is of interest here and is its direction the same or different to local Southern Hiberno-English norms in this Mid-Ulster English dialect region north of the border? Certainly, in terms of distribution, it is the case that the young Armagh women rather than their male peers produce the lion's share of tokens (70.42%). Moreover, the factor weights reinforce this finding since the probability that *be like* is favoured by the former is rather strong (and indeed the difference between male and female behaviour is significant).

The analyses presented in previous sections underlined certain key differences between the L1 cohort and their L2 peer groups with respect to the frequencies of *be like* and the constraints on its use. Table 24 takes this issue a step further by examining the extent to which a participant's home language explicitly conditions the role which *be like* plays in their quotative system. Comparing the log odds for all 3 groups, it is obvious that there is a negative correlation between the Polish participants and *be like* which is not matched by either of the other cohorts. Turning to the factor weights, this finding is repeated such that having a home language which is Polish considerably reduces the probability of *be like* being preferred as a quotative introducer. For those whose L1 is instead Lithuanian, this factor exerts a weak positive effect whereas for those whose L1 is English there is a much stronger correlation both with respect to the log-odds and the factor weight.

Table 24 Independent multivariate analyses of the contribution made by the social factors 'sex' and 'home language' to the selection of *be like* in the speech of (i) L1 speakers of Armagh English; (ii) Lithuanian newcomer L2 English speakers and (iii) Polish newcomer L2 English speakers

Home language (p = 0.0408)				
Factor	Log Odds	N	%	FW
English	0.57	702	0.38	0.64
Lithuanian	0.26	819	0.37	0.56
Polish	−0.84	176	0.22	0.30
Sex (p = 3.22e-05)				
Factor	Log Odds	N	%	FW
F	0.79	1195	0.41	0.68
M	−0.79	502	0.23	0.31

Diskin & Levey (2019: 74) on the basis of similar results to those presented in the previous section regarding differences between L1 constraint norms and an L2 speaker's acquisition of their order and magnitude of effects, contend that "incomplete mastery" is a trademark feature of even the most proficient second language users. They also record marked differences between their upper and lower proficiency Polish participants which highlight the fact that this type of nuanced multivariate analysis can also reveal that language competence can be an important external variable to consider in its own right. Table 25 does just that for *Múin Béarla*. It provides the results from a stratified sample which has been subjected to another multivariate analysis of internal conditioning factors but which this time compares local Armagh norms regarding what proved to be their most diametrically opposed quotative introducers, i.e. *be like* and *say* with the constraint hierarchies for these same variants from two sets of Lithuanian participants (independent *versus* basic).

Table 25 Independent multivariate analyses of the contribution made by linguistic factors to the selection of *be like* and *say* in the speech of (i) L1 speakers of Armagh (Mid-Ulster) English; (ii) Lithuanian newcomer L2 English speakers (Independent Users) and (iii) Lithuanian newcomer L2 English speakers (Basic Users)

	M-UE		Lithuanian (independent)		Lithuanian (basic)	
	be like	*say*	*be like*	*say*	*be like*	*say*
	FW	FW	FW	FW	FW	FW
Tense						
Present	0.452	0.607	0.424	[0.624]	0.303	[0.508]
HP	0.278	0.559	0.512	[0.415]	0.484	[0.451]
Past	0.759	0.338	0.564	[0.459]	0.711	[0.542]
Range	*0.481*	*0.269*	*0.140*	*0.209*	*0.408*	*0.091*
Grammatical person						
1	[0.584]	[0.470]	0.577	[0.417]	[0.587]	[0.378]
3	[0.452]	[0.530]	0.423	[0.583]	[0.413]	[0.622]
Range	*0.132*	*0.060*	*0.154*	*0.166*	*0.174*	*0.244*
Mimesis						
Mimetic	0.594	0.305	0.572	0.318	0.614	0.325
Non-Mimetic	0.406	0.695	0.423	0.682	0.386	0.675
Range	*0.188*	*0.390*	*0.149*	*0.364*	*0.228*	*0.350*
Content of quote						
Reported Thought	[0.573]	0.958	[0.474]	<0.001	[0.515]	[<0.001]
Reported Speech	[0.427]	0.997	[0.526]	>0.999	[0.485]	[>0.999]
Range	*0.146*	*0.039*	*0.052*	*0.998*	*0.030*	*0.998*

Leaving the local norms aside, as their dimensions have already been established and honing in on the contrasts between the two sets of speakers with the same home language but whose grasp of English is not commensurate, there are congruences and disparities which are worth highlighting. Notwithstanding the significance levels, ranges and the relative strengths of the constraints associated with each L2 cohort, both the Lithuanian independent and basic users share the same conditioning factors with respect to grammatical person and mimesis. As already noted, these represent local Armagh norms, are also typical for the independent Polish L2 speakers and appear in some sense to be universal across English vernaculars globally. This achievement for a group of basic users is all the more remarkable when Sankoff *et al.* (1997: 213) have previously argued that:

"the more successful L2 speakers were those who could control native discourse markers in a nativelike fashion."

Noteworthy too is the fact that both sets of Lithuanian participants, irrespective of competence levels, share the same sensitivities to the pragmatic content of the quote which are near identical bar the fact that the categorical probability of *say* occurring with reported speech is significant for the independent users but not for those whose usage was classified as basic. In fact, the only key difference between these cohorts of different ability levels is with respect to tense. Focusing on *be like* first (and again ignoring differences in the ranges and strengths of the constraint hierarchy for present purposes), the two groups show parallel conditioning in the same Past>HP>Present direction which is not matched by either the local-born speakers or the system adopted by the Polish migrant group detailed earlier. When it comes to the *say* variant, however, their two constraint hierarchies differ. For the basic users, the order is Past>Present>HP whereas for their peers who were assessed as being more competent in English, the pattern is Present>Past>HP which, as has already been observed, differs from the local target variety were the constraint is Present>HP>Past as well as from that typified by the independent Polish users, i.e. Present>Past>HP. Sorace (2005: 56) argues that "the developmental paths and outcomes of L2 acquisition present similarities" with those that obtain in L1 contexts. As such, it may be worthwhile considering Diskin & Levey's (2019: 74) observation regarding the failure of their L2 Polish speakers to also fully acquire the temporal constraints which apply in local Dublin English that this instability may similarly be present when native English speakers first acquire the discourse marker system. Levey (2016) reports that the acquisition of the diverse constraint categories associated with this variable is indeed sequential in children (though this is not so for other types, as Smith & Durham (2019) contend). It has the order grammatical conditioning first followed by pragmatic because the latter is more complex in Kerswill's (1996: 199) terms, involving as it does an interface level between the syntax and discourse/pragmatic knowledge. Sorace (2005: 55) terms these "soft constraints" and argues that such constructions can present "processing difficulties" in L2 acquisition contexts too (2005: 74) (see also Meyerhoff & Schleef 2014: 120). However, what is interesting about the second language learners in this Armagh analysis of constructed dialogue marking – irrespective of their competence in English – is that there are certain local grammatical constraints which they readily acquire (i.e. those associated with personhood) while there are others that they continue to struggle with even when their L2 competence levels are high (temporal reference). Moreover, far from there being a sequential delay in their acquisition of soft constraints after purely structural "hard" ones, in the sense of Sorace (2005: 55), as there is when children acquire the English discourse marking system, this is not necessarily so since the L2 cohorts exhibit exactly the constraints which obtain in mimetic environments amongst local-born speakers. This conundrum is beyond the scope of the present work to resolve but it underlines the importance of not assuming that L2 acquisition will necessarily follow an identical developmental path as that undertaken by first language acquirers of the same language. It is a reminder too that when it comes to learning the system of discourse marking in a hyperlocal English variety, the degree of variability amongst L2 speakers is such that some account needs to be taken of other factors too which may be generating the constraint rankings but which in this type of multivariate analysis remain entirely invisible. In addition to proficiency, they may include, for instance, the "mysteries of the substrate" (Labov 2008) which has been addressed here to some extent and, as Corrigan (2016), Davydova (2019), Diskin & Levey (2019), Meyerhoff (2009) and Sankoff *et al.* (1997) all argue, is a critical line of enquiry in language contact settings such as these. There are other potentially confounding issues too that are entirely socio-psychological or individuated in origin including those which were reviewed in § 5.2.1 of Chapter Five but which have not been considered yet at all here. This issue, in particular, will thus be an important starting point for the discussion of issues tied to belonging, identity and integration that is an important theme in the next chapter which further problematises the findings reviewed so far for (ING), relativization and quotation.

10 Population movements: sociolinguistic consequences

"*þa gelomp for sumum intingan, þæt he semninga gewat in Hibernia Scotta eloond, þonon he ær cwom*" ['Then it happened for some reason that he departed to Ireland, the island of the Scots, from where he had come' (Bede 4.26.352.2, cited in Thomas Miller (ed.) 1890–1898. *The Old English Version of Bede's Ecclesiastical History of the English People*. London: Tübner)].

10.1 Superdiversity then and now

The *Ecclesiastical History of the English People* penned by the Venerable Bede in AD 731 centres on the conflict between the pre-Schism Roman church and Celtic Christianity which echoes the contemporary religio-cultural and socio-economic struggles that have been fundamental in propelling the refugee crisis in the Global North from 2015 onwards, detailed in Chapter Four, §4.2. Bede's *History* also brings to the fore the multicultural composition of the entire British Isles during his lifetime as a result of various population movements in the region's history. The text is replete too with references to translation between Anglo-Saxon, Old Irish and of course Latin, the *lingua franca* of the era which was a significant outcome of these migrations. The opening quotation captures the *peregrinus* nature of monastic life in this period which was not dissimilar to the stepwise migration patterns charted in Chapter One, §1.4 and applied not only to nineteenth century Irish famine emigration to the United States documented in Chapter Three but also to the experiences of the Sinha family who immigrated to Armagh from Kerala two centuries later. Part I of this work was dedicated to detailing the economic and socio-cultural motivations for and linguistic consequences of these ancient and modern 'wanderings' in and out of "Hibernia Scotta." In answer to the issues raised in the preface regarding the potential consequences of the changing nature of migration on language ecologies, Chapters One to Four argued that while the process is far from new, the advent of better transport infrastructures and social media has enhanced opportunities not only for contact between languages but for the maintenance of socio-cultural and linguistic links with friends and family in sending and receiving countries alike. From this perspective, the relatively moderate diversity of communities in Anglo-Saxon Britain has given way to the development of multicultural, plurilingual cities such as Belfast, London and Manchester which are 'superdiverse' in Vertovec's (2007, 2014) terms. Even modest urban centres like Armagh, which would once have been an epicentre of cultural and religious life in Anglo-Saxon times and then waned, as many peripheral regions on the island of Ireland did during the Great Famine and then The Troubles, have yet again become attractive settlement destinations for migrants from far and wide. Just as Latin was a *lingua franca* when Armagh was sacked by the Vikings in AD 832, so Mid-Ulster English acts in the same capacity for the diverse array of newcomers who have arrived in this dialect region of Northern Ireland more recently.

Chapters Five to Nine in Part II of this work then focused on issues first raised in the preface, namely, how and whether these newcomers acquire this dialect, what effect it has on their first language and if there is evidence of language transfer from it into their L2 (see §10.2). Chapter Five, in particular, examined models of language acquisition, contact, shift and transfer in the light of data from *Múin Béarla*, finding that there is ample proof in this data-set that speakers' control of the L2 is constrained in a manner which established formal and variationist models of acquisition do indeed predict. The same is true for the support which this corpus offers regarding the tendency for home languages to attrite in these contexts especially where younger speakers are concerned (particularly with respect to monostylism (Dressler and Wodak-Leodolter 1977); relexification (Hill & Hill 1977) and morphological simplification (Dorian 1981, 1989)). That said, the *Múin Béarla* interviews also provided examples of individuals who bucked these trends, likely due to a range of socio-psychological issues that were beyond the scope of this project to explore more fully at this stage but are certainly worthy of further consideration.

Another key research question established in the preface was whether L2 varieties of Armagh English differed from local norms. Three linguistic domains that were likely to be diagnostic of internal and external conditioning were thus put under the microscope, i.e. morphophonology (Chapter Seven), syntax (Chapter Eight) and discourse-pragmatics (Chapter Nine), adopting the comparative sociolinguistic method originally developed to examine the origins of African-American Vernacular English (Tagliamonte 2004a: 730). The results presented here are the first to uncover what the patterns of local speakers are in the twenty-first century for (ING), relative clause formation and quotation. They were then used as benchmarks to evaluate the extent to which variation and change in Mid-Ulster English equates to the patterns of variability for these same features documented in other vernaculars in the British Isles and beyond. These chapters also established how variability in the grammar of newcomers compares not only with that which obtains in hyperlocal and global Englishes but also whether differences can be discerned which reflect the diverse Balto-Slavic heritages of these "new speakers" (Bermingham 2018, and Ó Murchadha *et al.* 2018: 4). This theme will also be addressed in this final chapter (§10.2). It will likewise be devoted to collating the findings in Part II with a view to answering other research questions posed in the preface including: (i) Are variables from different linguistic modules acquired more or less readily by learners? and (ii) Does it matter whether the dependent variable being learned is stable or not? (§10.3). The chapter will then close with a discussion of the ways in which transnational newcomers both historically and today use language as a symbol to express their sense of belonging or otherwise to the receiving communities where their migratory journeys have brought them (§10.4), which is another aspect of this project that deserves more attention but which there was not space here to more fully explore.[199]

10.2 Substrate effects

Labov (2008: 315) comments that: "There can be little doubt about the existence of substrate effects in many cases when a whole population abandons their original language and adopts another." Attention was drawn to several aspects of Mid-Ulster English which bear the hallmarks of the large-scale language shift processes (charted for the island of Ireland in Part I) to which Labov refers. It would include: (i) TH-stopping in contexts where dental fricatives would be expected in other global Englishes (Chapter Five, §5.1.3); (ii) The high incidence of progressives and their use in stative contexts detailed in Chapter Seven, §7.1.1 and (iii) The frequency and verbal range of post-posed quotations documented in South Ulster English, which are arguably calques from similar constructions in the substrate converging on a related option available in the early English target grammar (Chapter Nine, §9.1).

Labov (2008: 2015) goes on to propose that: "there are situations in which the direction of linguistic influence remains unexplained, the causal connections are obscure, or the expected effect does not occur." A key aim of the attention paid in Part II to the operation of (ING), relative clause formation and the system of quotation, therefore, was to tackle more systematically than is usually the case in variation and change studies of newcomer Englishes whether any such calques from Balto-Slavic were discernible. Also considered was the possibility that the direction of such effects was predictable from some aspect or other of their L1 and care was likewise taken to accommodate these facts when determining the envelope of variation for each variable. Although this *modus operandi* was sometimes hampered by the lack of appropriate comparable evidence in the L1s (particularly Lithuanian), the method did uncover some intriguing differences between the distributions and constraint hierarchies of both sets of newcomers *vis à vis*

---

199 See for instance Blackledge & Creese (2009), (2017), (2019); Legaudaite (2009); Drummond & Schleef (2016); Kerswill (2018).

the linguistic behaviours of the local benchmark group, which are potentially attributable to their substrate languages. For example, despite the fact that Mid-Ulster English is not a "velar nasal plus" type (Wells 1982: 365–366), the Lithuanian and Polish teenagers living in Armagh were prone to introducing [ŋk] and [ŋg] for lexemes such as *playing* in phonological contexts where it would also be expected in their first languages (Chapter Seven, §7.1.2.). There is also the finding that *who* relativisers had a statistically higher probability of occurring in relative clauses containing human subjects uttered by the bilingual speakers than they did in the interviews with the local control cohort. This was argued to be what one might expect of newcomers with morphologically rich L1s in which making such distinctions was crucial too (Chapter Eight §8.4.3). Transfer was also invoked to explain the predilection amongst both sets of newcomers for zero quotatives and for the infrequency of the *go* variant (which were matched amongst migrant cohorts of similar heritages in research on these populations in Dublin and Edinburgh). Influence from the distribution of quotative introducers in Polish, where *powiedzieć* 'tell' and particularly *mówić* 'say' induce a quotative system which is significantly more homogeneous than the hyperlocal Armagh English norm was also uncovered. As expected, therefore, the Polish *Múin Béarla* participants also replicated high frequencies for these reporting verbs (as did newcomers of the same heritage in Diskin & Levey's (2019) analysis of their acquisition of Southern Hiberno-English). This particular finding proved, however, to be a good case in point with respect to Labov's cautionary note that the transfer effect is not always as predicted since this feature turned out not to be universal in the L2 English of Polish teens. That is because *say* was attested as only the second most frequent variant amongst this cohort in Meyerhoff & Schleef's (2014) rather similar study of quotative introducers in Edinburgh (§9.5.2.2).

We likewise should be mindful of convergence arguments more broadly considering the views expressed in Poplack & Levey (2010: 409) that "differences between cohorts or overall rates may be masking other effects that are independent of the contact situation." There is also the issue highlighted in Corrigan (1997), (2000); Cornips & Corrigan (2005a,b); Filppula, Klemola & Paulasto (2009); Kortmann (2003); Meyerhoff (2009); Sankoff (2001); Thomason & Kaufmann (1988) *inter alia* and in all three preceding chapters that it can be difficult to separate, for instance, constraints on relativisation processes in Armagh English, Lithuanian or Polish which are distinctive from those which simply apply across the entire 'European Sprachbund' (§8.2.3). The existence of cross-linguistic universal processes (such as homorganic assimilation (§7.1.3)) should give pause for thought too as does the emergence of robust evidence that canonical quotation marking strategies have been readily identified cross-linguistically (Buchstaller and van Alphen (2012a); Buchstaller (2014); D'Arcy (2017); Guz (2019a);

Güldemann (2008); Haddican & Zweig (2012). What I would argue, though, is that triangulating evidence from comparative analyses of variables from at least two source languages alongside the target vernacular, as has been the model introduced here, is imperative to determine what exactly might have been calqued and by whom. This endeavour must be accompanied by detailed examination of frequency distributions and the conditioning effects uncovered by multivariate regression analyses so as to determine whether L2 and L1 vernaculars really are "sisters under the skin" (Tagliamonte 2004a: 132). This principled comparative process is by far the most suitable method for determining whether newcomers' acquisition is impacted upon in some way or other by L1 transfer (see also Poplack, Zentz & Dion 2012, and Meyerhoff 2009).[200] When more studies of immigrant L2 varieties using this model become available, only then will sociolinguists be in a significantly better position to provide the answers which Labov (2008) is desperately seeking.

10.3 Constraints, complexity and acquisition

There is considerable research on which domains of linguistic behaviour are more or less learnable in bilingual contact scenarios such as those being played out in the *Múin Béarla* interviews. It has also become clear that a basic principle of L2 and second dialect acquisition arising from language contact, variation and change models involves what Meyerhoff (2009: 313) terms "transformation under transfer." In other words, new contact varieties are regularly discovered not to necessarily be slavish replicas of the target vernacular but to be a novel, creative variety of it in which constraint hierarchies are restructured, differentially weighted or altogether rebuffed. The findings revealed here further our understanding of these proposals in several respects. In the first place, there is evidence presented from each linguistic domain that not only is Armagh English novel or hyperlocal in some respect or other *vis à vis* global Englishes but the L2 varieties of it spoken by the Lithuanian and Polish teenagers can likewise be

---

200 Meyerhoff (2009) recognises three different types of contact-induced transfer, i.e. 'weak transfer' or 'replication', 'strong transfer' and 'calqueing' which are differentiated using considerations such as significance and the hierarchical ordering of constraints in the source and target languages. While the relevant facts about the variable grammars of Lithuanian and Polish quotation marking e.g. are not yet available so as to test these types in this context, these are exactly the kinds of benchmark that I would advocate for discriminating between contact proper and what might be dismissed as simply seeking "pattern replication" when undertaking this type of exercise (Matras & Sakel 2007). See also Buchstaller & D'Arcy (2009), D'Arcy (2010), and Tagliamonte (2004a) in connection with the efficacy of this model in dialect contact scenarios.

characterised in this way. Thus, while this Mid-Ulster English dialect conforms to certain constraints also reported elsewhere (such as the favouring effect for the *be like* variant in quotative contexts where mimesis is involved (§ 9.5.3)), there are other 'classic' constraints with which it does not comply. This would include its rejection of the nominal-verbal continuum for the (ING) variable reported in § 7.3.2 which may fall out from having a progressive system that is marked in some respects by the language shift process already noted. Moreover, in that regard, it shares its hyper-apical nature for (ING) with varieties that are 'sisters under the skin' on account of the contact opportunities brought about by migration and documented in Part I, i.e. Scots in Scotland and Scotch-Irish American English. It is similarly marginal in other aspects of its grammar (particularly with respect to the stable variables (ING) and relative marking strategies) that are congruent with the patterns observed in studies on the northern English and Scottish founding dialects which gave rise to it. This proved to be especially so with regard to certain aspects of its relativisation system. New evidence was discovered, for instance, when comparing Mid-Ulster English to the Ulster Scots relative marking preferences identified in Tagliamonte, Smith & Lawrence (2005) that clearly demonstrates a peripherality effect applying to the whole region which cuts it off in certain respects from on-going developments in mainstream global Englishes (§§ 8.4.2–8.4.3). There is confirmation too, of course, that local teenagers born and raised in Armagh are not wholly detached from innovations happening elsewhere. That proved to be especially so with respect to aspects of their system of quotation which has been argued here and elsewhere to be in a state of flux by comparison to either {-ing} or relative marking strategies, which often prove to be more stable cross-dialectally. The analysis in Chapter Nine documented how the local participants have adopted the *be like* 'blow-in' to be their most favoured variant a mere decade after it appears to have been entirely absent from the dialect (§§ 9.2.2 and 9.5.2). Moreover, other Mid-Ulster English non-canonical quotative introducers which were thought to be prototypical for the region, such as the *here+be+*speaker type, have been abandoned by this generation altogether.

One of the stand out findings from this research has, of course, also been the extent to which the Lithuanian and Polish *Múin Béarla* cohorts do or do not participate in such new trends either from a distributional or a constraint hierarchy perspective. Thus, the Baltic group similarly favour innovative *be like* but their Slavic peers do not. Even with respect to stable variables, their patterns of linguistic behaviour uncovered in the corpus typify the transformation under transfer model. For example, while the Lithuanian heritage L2 participants share one of the local Armagh predictor factors for [ɪn] (i.e. number of syllables in lexemes such as *swimming, managing, entertaining*), the relative strengths of the effect across both cohorts was markedly different. Moreover, what was particularly useful about simultaneously comparing speakers from two different heritage backgrounds, which is an all too rare strategy in research within this framework, was to observe the extent to which their behaviours also differed from one another. Hence, far from re-organising the number of syllables constraint on (ING), speakers whose home language was Polish, simply had not acquired it at all. Indeed, there were many internal conditioning factors on Armagh English with which the newcomers did not comply either by rejection of this type or restructuring. These findings robustly demonstrate the manner in which issues of identity and integration in migrant contexts are indeed negotiated through linguistic means.

As regards social predictors, as one might have expected given their well-recognised idiosyncratic behaviour from community to community, this research has also uncovered a high degree of variability with respect to the social indexing of the three features investigated. As far as relative pronoun choice was concerned, for instance, while the distributional analyses presented in §8.4.4 did seem to implicate gender as a predictive factor in the operation of WH-TH-Ø variants, when the results of the regression analyses were also reviewed, social constraints on much of the variability rates observed across all three cohorts of male and female speakers seemed not to be a significant predictor of behaviour in the end. This finding ties rather well with Tottie & Rey's (1997: 245) characterisation of relativiser variants as being in Milroy's (2007) terms "under the counter" for social indexing purposes (though the idea was originally used to refer to sound changes). This proved to by and large be true too for the other stable variable examined here, i.e. (ING). While the young men of Lithuanian descent significantly favoured the low prestige [ɪn] variant in {-ing} contexts, they did not acquire this from their local peers for whom sex is not a predictor (nor is it for the Polish boys who match the local constraint here). By contrast, sex differentiation proved to be a distinctly overt aspect of the quotative systems of all these adolescents since females across the three cohorts significantly favoured the innovative *be like* variant whereas males did not. This finding reinforces the view put forward by Milroy (2007) that such changes are instead "off the shelf" or at the discretion of the speaker. She associates them with youth norms (which of course this variant is regularly perceived to be) and, as such, widely accessible beyond hyperlocal networks (though see the alternative view proposed by Buchstaller & D'Arcy (2009)).

Two other external variables were examined which honed in particularly on the behaviour of the newcomer groups relative to one another. They tested hypotheses regarding factors which are often considered proxies for amount of face-to-face contact between migrant groups and the local communities in which they now reside. They include length of residence or proficiency, for instance, which are regularly implicated in L2 speakers' abilities to match local constraint hierarchies, as has been argued in previous research (§ 5.2.1). As with other investigations of these independent variables, however, the extent to which they exert influence on newcomer speech is far from straightforward (compare Meyerhoff & Schleef's (2014: 109) lack of correlation here with Saito and Brajot's (2013: 857) finding that length of residence was indeed a "predictive" factor in L2 acquisition contexts). Hence, when length of residence was considered as a potential conditioning factor on (ING) preferences amongst the two allochthonous groups in *Múin Béarla*, it was not found to significantly condition the variation, as per Meyerhoff & Schleef (2014). The issue of L2 proficiency was also instructive from this perspective. Diskin & Levey (2019) record marked differences in the mastery of constraints on the Dublin English quotative system between their upper and lower proficiency Polish participants. The results for this same variable in Armagh were therefore very interesting in that there was no difference between Lithuanian users whose CEFR scores characterised them as either basic or independent regarding their ability to match local preferences for certain internal constraints on the system of quotation (i.e. grammatical person and mimesis). There was, however, inter-group variation between the two sets of L2 speakers of Lithuanian heritage with respect to other conditioning factors on this variable. Hence, neither the basic nor the independent group had acquired the constraints on variation with respect to reported speech/thought that were typical of local norms. Moreover, as far as the tense factor was concerned, there was inter-group variation between not only the basic and independent users but also with respect to their preferences and those of native speakers. What is more, none of the variation observed between users with different competence levels seems to have been the result of what Meyerhoff (2009) refers to as cognitive demand. This concept is allied to the notion of 'markedness' introduced in § 5.1.3 and ties in with the rarity of features cross-linguistically as well as the domains of language which must be mastered in order to acquire a form. The standard view is that language learning is more straightforward when a feature's specifications are confined to a single linguistic domain. As such, acquiring the local grammatical category constraints on (ING) may have proved problematic for the Lithuanian and Polish L2 English speakers because it requires knowledge of both morphology and phonology. Similarly, learning the connection between the *who* relativiser and animacy in subjective relatives needs comprehension which is syntactic-semantic in nature. It is remarkable, therefore, that it was actually the non-native speakers in this study who outperformed the local teenagers in their control of this condition (§ 8.4.3). This result echoes the findings of Maciukaite (2004) as well as Peeters-Podgaevskaja, Janssen & Baker (2018) that Balto-Slavic pre-adolescents are also very adept at making such distinctions very early in the acquisition process by comparison to control groups on account of the transparency of the morphological marking in their L1s (§ 8.2.3). By the same token, the constraint system for quotative introducers expects learners to master not only syntactic knowledge but also that which is lexical and discourse-pragmatic. In this case, there is some evidence from *Múin Béarla* that L2 speakers can actually learn complex syntactic-pragmatic constraints (those that are 'hard' in Sorace's (2005) terms such as mimesis) while simultaneously being unable to understand those which are reportedly 'soft' (temporal referencing). This project has been key therefore to discovering new evidence that cognitive demand as it is currently understood needs to be reconsidered, particularly since one would expect it to universally constrain the variable grammars of L2 speakers which it does not, in fact, appear to. The results presented in Chapter Nine, in particular, with respect to the sequential ordering of the hard and soft and external/internal constraints that apply to L1 *versus* L2 acquisition also demonstrate that the processes are not necessarily mirror images of one another. This is another research area for which the outcomes of this investigation will act as an impetus to new empirical studies that combine models drawn from language variation and change as well as language development (see also Foulkes, Docherty & Watt 2005; Kerswill 1996; Smith & Durham 2019; Smith, Duham & Fortune 2007).

10.4 Language as a social symbol

From the 'Fourth Wave' perspective articulated in § 5.2.1, acquiring sociolinguistic competence is of course not simply reducible to aspects of development or models of learnability since doing so discounts the important cognitive and socio-psychological traits of individual speakers. These include their all-important attitudinal dispositions to heritage and L2 vernaculars and cultures which can diverge widely across speakers even those who, in many other respects, might at first blush appear to be 'newcomer twins', as the extracts from allochthonous participants in §§ 5.2.1 and 7.1.2. testify to. This is because language is a powerful emblematic tool for indexing social messages about how speakers identify themselves, what their socio-cultural backgrounds are and which personal social networks or communities of practice they engage with. Ethnographic aspects of the *Múin Béarla* corpus which have been referred to in Chapters Four and Five, in particular, have also demonstrated that just as the identities of monolinguals have repeatedly been shown in sociolinguistic research to be mutable, so it is with these young bilingual migrants who, in certain respects, have a wider sociolinguistic apparatus at their disposal for crossing between identities to express their affiliation to one group or another dependent on the circumstances of the interaction. Thus, as Cornips & De Rooij (2018: 2) argue, "feelings of belonging are best seen not as simply enduring through time and space, but as changing and variable across situations and stages of life." Engaging in this essentially ideological process will, on occasion, include passing as a native speaker in Piller's (2002) terms, which is argued to be an important option for some of the newcomer project participants on account of their linguistic behaviours illustrated in § 5.2.1. Further interrogation of the *CORIECOR* database, which was frequently referred to in Part I when examining the congruences between how Irish emigrants historically and recent immigrants to Northern Ireland negotiate their diasporic identities, is instructive in this respect too, as the testimony in (157) demonstrates.

(157) Extract from Moses Paul letter, Virginia, 1840

Title:	From Moses Paul, Va to John Graham, Co Londonderry
Source:	Document T 2850/1/5 Presented by Gr G. Gillespie
Achive:	Public Record Office of Northern Ireland
Doc.No.:	9406154
Date:	29/12/1840
Doc.Type:	EMG
Log:	Document added by LT, 07:06:1994

I am now nearly two years in this republic, and have not recd. the first scrape of your pen – not even on the back of a newspaper. Why is this? am I beneath your notice because **I am turned American** ... From what I have often heard sister saying, I presume she is still as prejudiced as ever against America & Americans [...] this is wrong – persons living in Europe cannot have any idea of this country & should not condemn it so unmercifully without judge or jury – certainly **we differ from you** in some points very materially, but it is not worth talking of. It is more than likely, if I tell you that Americans are a LITTLE better than savages that you will not believe me, for I recollret [recollect?] sisters expression is – "AMERICANS ARE WORSE THAN SAVAGES" – ... **we** have our niggers by the thousands, and a very useful part of the creation they are – I know **we** are blamed for slavery, but **we** cannot help it – **we** are obliged to have niggers ...

This extract is an excellent example of Piller's "temporary, context-, audience- and medium-specific performance" (2002: 179). The letter writer's pique at not hearing from his family is expressed by his declaring in this belonging routine that he has changed his affiliation from a European of Irish heritage to "I am turned American." He sustains this novel identification with locals in the receiving country throughout by linguistic choices such as the strategic uses he makes of pronominals, i.e. "we" Americans *versus* "you" Europeans. Moreover, he professes to uphold local,

Anti-Abolitionist values which were becoming unpopular in pre-Famine Ireland, as indicated by Daniel O'Connell's prominent role in the World Anti-Slavery Convention held in London earlier in the same year that this letter was penned. In fact, as Murphy (2010: 122) contends, O'Connell was driven to admonish Irish-Americans for taking the same stance as Moses Paul does in statements he made in 1843 including: "Over the broad Atlantic I pour forth my voice saying 'Come out of such a land, you Irishmen; or, if you remain, and dare countenance the system of slavery that is supported there, we will recognize you as Irishmen no longer.'" As Murphy (2010: 149) goes on to argue when describing how events unfolded subsequently, O'Connell "addressed the American repealers as Irish men. They had responded as Americans". This appears to be exactly the perspective captured in Moses Paul's letter. His tactic here underlines what Bucholtz and Hall (2004: 383) would refer to as "adequation", i.e. an attempt to pursue socially recognised similarity with local peers and to reinforce his "distinction" from other suppressed groups such as African-American slaves. Although the circumstances are somewhat different, the gesture is very much on a par with the strategies employed by the young Filipino, Melchor Nogoy, and described in § 5.2.1 to erase "distinction" between himself and his local peers when engaging in a school-based Gaelic football community of practice (see Bucholtz and Hall 2004: 384). Just as it was all too easy to come by evidence elsewhere in *Múin Béarla* as to what motivates Melchor here, *CORIECOR* is also replete with descriptions such as those conveyed in (158) as to why members of the Irish diaspora (particularly Roman Catholics) often felt occasioned to practice such manoeuvres too thereby passing themselves off as "adopted citizens" so as not to be singled out as "foreign" in their host communities either.

(158) Extract from P. Kennedy letter, Strasburg, Virginia, 1855

Title: P. Kennedy, Strasburg, Virginia to Vere Foster
Source: D 3618/D/8/9a: Deposited by the Late Mrs A. C. May
Archive: Archive: The Public Record Office, Northern Ireland
Doc.No.:   9102033
Date: 19/03/1855
Doc.Type: EMG
Log: Document added by JM, 16:11:1993.

Scoundrels will go into the parts of cities, inhabited by the Irish, and will commence a crusade against their religion, then a fight will commence, a person will be killed, directly there is a cry raised against **foreigners**, and it has turned out now against Protestant as well as Papist, although it was first got up to upset the Catholics ... The Editor of The New York Herald, owned and edited by Bennett, the Scotchman, has commenced a tirade against **adopted citizins [citizens?]**, worse than a native American, and it is really a fact ... it has turned against all **foreigners** no matter what creed they belong to.

Interestingly, as I also argued in previous chapters, similar negative attitudes prevail at the present time. Indeed, the rise in hate crimes of a racial nature being reported in the local media has led Northern Ireland to be dubbed the "race hate capital of Europe", according to Doebler, McAreavey, Shortall and Shuttleworth (2016–2017: 1).[201] Nevertheless, there are some allochthonous participants in the *Múin Béarla* corpus for whom the persistent expression of their ethnolinguistic identity is an enduring commitment irrespective of powerful societal forces of this type. The attitude of two Russian-speaking boys attending St. Benedict's alongside Melchor Nogoy, captured in their interview with me in (159), demonstrate that convergence to hegemonic imperatives is not always a necessary goal for newcomers. Hence, Nestor dismisses the castigation "foreigner" as simply "like a word in English in the dictionary", i.e. for him devoid of the "distinction" (Bucholtz & Hall 2005: 600) attributed to the notion in (158) which he reports his anti-immigrant local peers of course to "think it is".

(159) Extract from an interview with 'Nestor Antonovich' and 'Nikolay Danshov', Armagh, 2014

1	KPC:	So what do they say what kind of things do they say?
2	Nestor Antonovich:	Bad words
3	KPC:	*[whispers]* Tell me
4	Nestor Antonovich:	Should I even tell them like just bad words eh well well I don't know see like there's a the thing like Irish people that they if they're someone from different countries they say **"foreigner" but that's actually I don't think so it's really bad but like because it's actually like a word like English word it's not a slag or something so when someone say to me "foreigner"**
5	Nikolay Danshov:	Same thing, like
6	Nestor Antonovich:	I'm saying "Yes it's that's yes I know"

---

201 See: http://www.niassembly.gov.uk/globalassets/documents/raise/knowledge_exchange/briefing_papers/series6/doebler141216.pdf, last accessed 16 Sept. 2019). The most recent official figures can be found at: https://www.psni.police.uk/inside-psni/Statistics/hate-motivation-statistics/, last accessed 16 Sept. 2019.

7	KPC:	So it feels bad when they say you're a foreigner?
8	Nestor Antonovich:	Yeah **they think it is** but it for me **it's like it's like a word in English in the dictionary** like yeah
9	KPC:	So what?

[NA/MA (M); St. Benedict's; Armagh, Northern Ireland; 20 Jan. 2014]

Such agnostic 'so what?' views from transnational migrants in contemporary Northern Ireland have the power to fundamentally change the fabric of its society, to create the right conditions for fuelling variation and change not just in the L2 varieties but in the L1 target. This possibility is argued for by Cheshire *et al.* (2011) when explaining divergence in adolescent use in the London boroughs of Hackney and Havering which are differentiated by the type of rapid population changes also considered here, i.e. involving large numbers of non-native speakers settling in the former but not in the latter. It is possible therefore that aspects of the novel constraint hierarchies identified in Chapters Seven, Eight and Nine, also remarked upon in §10.3, could represent the beginning of a longer-term language change process for Armagh English which, of course, was itself engendered by language shift historically due to population movements propelled by the self-same macro-, meso- and micro-structural drivers explicated in Chapter One which likewise motivated the families of Nestor and Nikolay to make Northern Ireland their new home.

10.5 Concluding remarks

This wide-ranging study of Northern Irish communities which have recently been rapidly and intensively settled by diverse migrant groups offers insights not only into how their linguistic environments have been fundamentally altered by these population movements but also into the social and linguistic processes promoting or inhibiting patterns of variation and change in local dialects. The advances presented in Part I of the volume provide excellent evidence too for the benefit of taking an inter-disciplinary perspective since it has relied in no small part on applying models and theories stemming from historical studies, geography and sociology, in particular, so as to improve our interpretation of Ulster's language ecologies in the present as well as the past. The very promising results arising from the comparative investigation of local and newcomer teenagers now residing in Armagh shown in Part II sets the stage for new research on contact dialects within the region and beyond which will delve ever further into issues of second language acquisition in migrant contexts that assume the novel 'Fourth

Wave' approach advocated here. I have likewise demonstrated that gaining a fuller understanding of the language learning process in these circumstances can only be achieved by viewing it through a lens that is also attuned to various sub-disciplines of linguistics (formal and variationist as well as functional, historical and typological).

Although this type of holistic orientation to linguistic communities and their migratory processes is so far the road 'less travelled by',[202] I very much hope that it will not be so for long.

---

[202] I refer here to a well-known poem by Robert Frost called *The Road Not Taken*.

References

Aaron, Jessi E. & José Esteban Hernández. 2007. Quantitative evidence for contact-induced accommodation: Shifts in /s/ reduction patterns in Salvadoran Spanish in Houston. In Kim Potowski & Richard Cameron (eds.), *Spanish in contact: Policy, social and linguistic inquiries*, 329–344. Amsterdam: John Benjamins.

Abel, Gary A., Matthew E. Barclay & Rupert A. Payne. 2016. Adjusted indices of multiple deprivation to enable comparisons within and between constituent countries of the UK including an illustration using mortality rates. *British Medical Journal Open* 6 (11). 1–6. https://bmjopen.bmj.com/content/bmjopen/6/11/e012750.full.pdf (accessed 8 August 19).

Abrahamsson, Niclas & Kenneth Hyltenstam. 2008. The robustness of aptitude effects in near-native second language acquisition. *Studies in Second Language Acquisition* 30 (4). 481–509.

Abrahamsson, Niclas & Kenneth Hyltenstam. 2009. Age of onset and nativelikeness in a second language: Listener perception versus linguistic scrutiny. *Language Learning* 59 (2). 249–306.

Abramowicz, Łukasz. 2007. Sociolinguistics meets exemplar theory: Frequency and recency effects in (ing). *University of Pennsylvania Working Papers in Linguistics* 13. 27–37.

Adamczyk, Magdalena. 2017. On the pragmatic expansion of Polish *gdzieś tam* 'somewhere (there)/about'. In Chiara Fedriani & Andrea Sansó (eds.), *Pragmatic markers, discourse markers and modal particles: New perspectives*, 369–397. Amsterdam: John Benjamins.

Adams, George Brendan. 1958. The emergence of Ulster as a distinct dialect area. *Ulster Folklife* 4. 61–73.

Adams, George Brendan. 1964. The last language census in Northern Ireland. In George Brendan Adams (ed.), *Ulster dialects: An introductory symposium*, 111–145. Cultra: Ulster Folk and Transport Museum.

Adams, George Brendan. 1967. Phonemic systems in collision in Ulster English. In Ludwig Erich Schmitt (ed.), *Verhandlungen des weiten internationalen Dialektologenkongresses*, 1–6. Wiesbaden: Franz Steiner Verlag.

Adams, George Brendan. 1975. Language census problems. *Ulster Folklife* 21. 68–72.

Adams, George Brendan. 1976. Aspects of monoglottism in Ulster. *Ulster Folklife* 22. 76–87.

Adams, George Brendan. 1979. The validity of language census figures in Ulster, 1851–1911. *Ulster Folklife* 25. 113–122.

Adamson, Hugh Douglas. 1989. Variable rules as prototype schemas. In Susan Gass, Carolyn Preston, Dennis Preston & Larry Selinker (eds.), *Variation in second language acquisition: Psycholinguistic issues*, 219–232. Clevedon: Multilingual Matters.

Adamson, Hugh Douglas & Vera Regan. 1991. The acquisition of community speech norms by Asian immigrants learning English as a second language. *Studies in Second Language Acquisition* 13 (1). 1–22.

Adger, David & Gillian Ramchand. 2006. Dialect variation in Gaelic relative clauses. *Rannsachadh na Gàidhlig* 3. 179–192.

Aitchison, Jean. 1992. Relative clauses in Tok Pisin. In Marinel Gerritsen & Dieter Stein (eds.), *Internal and external factors in syntactic change*, 295–316. Berlin & New York: Mouton de Gruyter.

Aitchison, Jean. 2008. *The articulate mammal*, 5th edn. London: Routledge.

Aitken, A. J. 1981. The Scottish vowel-length rule. In Michael Benskin & Michael Louis Samuels (eds.), *So meny people longages and tonges: Philological essays in Scots and mediaeval English, presented to Angus McIntosh*, 131–157. Edinburgh: M. Benskin & M. L. Samuels.

Akenson, Donald Harman. 1970. *The Irish education experiment: The national system of education in the nineteenth century*. London: Routledge & Kegan Paul.

Akenson, Donald Harman. 1989. Pre-university education, 1782–1870. In William Edward Vaughan (ed.), *A new history of Ireland – Vol. V: Ireland under the Union, I: 1801–1870*, 523–537. Oxford: Oxford University Press.

Akenson, Donald Harman. 1992. The historiography of the Irish in the United States of America. In Patrick O'Sullivan (ed.), *The Irish world wide – Vol. 2: The Irish in the new communities*, 99–127. Leicester: Leicester University Press.

Alderson, Priscilla & Virginia Morrow. 2004. *Ethics, social research and consulting with children and young people*. Ilford, Essex: Barnado's.

Alexiadou, Artemis. 2013. Nominal vs. Verbal -ing constructions and the development of the English progressive. *English Linguistics Research* 2 (2). 26–140.

Allard, Réal & Rodrigue Landry. 1994. Subjective ethnolinguistic vitality: A comparison of two measures. *International Journal of the Sociology of Language* 108. 117–144.

Allen, Kelly-Ann & Margaret L. Kern. 2017. *School belonging in adolescents*. New York: Springer.

Allen, Will, Joan C. Beal, Karen P. Corrigan, Warren Maguire & Hermann L. Moisl. 2007. A 'linguistic time-capsule': The Newcastle Electronic Corpus of Tyneside English. In Joan C. Beal, Karen P. Corrigan & Hermann L. Moisl (eds.), *Creating and digitizing language corpora – Vol. 2: Diachronic databases*, 16–48. Houndmills, Basingstoke: Palgrave Macmillan.

Amador-Moreno, Carolina P. 2012. The Irish in Argentina: Irish English transported. In Bettina Migge & Máire Ní Chiosáin (eds.), *New perspectives on Irish English*, 289–309. Amsterdam: John Benjamins.

Amador-Moreno, Carolina P. 2019. *Orality in written texts: Using historical corpora to investigate Irish English (1700–1900)*. London & New York: Routledge.

Amador-Moreno, Carolina P. 2020. 'Matt & Mrs Connor is with me now. They are only beginning to learn the work of the camp': Irish emigrants writing from Argentina. In Raymond Hickey (ed.), *Keeping in touch: Familiar letters across the English-speaking world*, 139–162. Amsterdam: John Benjamins.

Amador-Moreno, Carolina P., Karen P. Corrigan, Kevin McCafferty & Emma Moreton. 2016. Migration databases as impact tools in the education and heritage sectors. In Karen P. Corrigan & Adam J. Mearns (eds.), *Creating and digitizing language corpora – Vol. 3: Databases for public engagement*, 25–67. Basingstoke: Palgrave Macmillan.

Ambrazas, Vytautas (ed.). 1997. *Lithuanian grammar*. Lithuania: Institute of the Lithuanian Language.

Ammerlaan, Ton. 1996. *You get a bit wobbly: Exploring bilingual retrieval processes in the context of first language attrition*. Nijmegen: University of Nijmegen dissertation.

Andersen, Gisela. 2001. *Pragmatic markers and sociolinguistic variation: A relevance-theoretic approach to the language of adolescents*. Amsterdam: John Benjamins.

Andrews, John. 2000. Plantation Ireland: A review of settlement history. In Terry Barry (ed.), *A history of settlement in Ireland*, 140–157. London: Routledge.

Androutsopoulos, Jannis. 2006a. Introduction: Sociolinguistics and computer mediated communication. *Journal of Sociolinguistics* 10 (4). 419–438.

Androutsopoulos, Jannis. 2006b. Multilingualism, diaspora, and the internet: Codes and identities on German-based diaspora websites. *Journal of Sociolinguistics* 10 (4). 520–547.

Antonini, Rachele. 2012. *Language attitudes in old and new Gaeltacht communities*. Newcastle: Newcastle University dissertation.

Antonini, Rachele. 2016. Caught in the middle: Child language brokering as a form of unrecognised language service. *Journal of Multilingual and Multicultural Development* 37 (7). 710–725.
Antonini, Rachele, Karen P. Corrigan & Li Wei. 2002. The Irish language in the Republic of Ireland and in Northern Ireland. In Ammon Ulrich, Klaus J. Mattheie & Peter H. Nelde (eds.), *Language policy and small languages*. [Special issue]. *Sociolinguistica: International Yearbook of European Sociolinguistics* 16. 118–128. Tübingen: Max Niemeyer Verlag.
Appadurai, Arjun. 1996. *Modernity at large: Cultural dimensions of globalization*. Minneapolis, Minnesota: University of Minnesota Press.
Appleton, Ronnie, Michael Black, Dennis Coppel, Tom Hartley, Steven Jaffe, Susan Kelly, Ben Maier & Grace Radford. 2014. *The Jewish community in Belfast: The Wolfson Centre*. Belfast: Institute for Conflict Research.
Arkadiev, Peter, Axel Holvoet & Björn Wiemer. 2015. Introduction. In Peter Arkadiev, Axel Holvoet & Björn Wiemer (eds.), *Contemporary approaches to Baltic linguistics*, 1–110. Berlin & Boston: De Gruyter Mouton.
Ash, Sherry. 1982. *The vocalisation of /l/ in Philadelphia*. Philadelphia: University of Pennsylvania dissertation.
Asher, James J. & Ramiro García. 1969. The optimal age to learn a foreign language. *Modern Language Journal* 53 (5). 334–341.
Auer, Peter & Li Wei (eds.). 2007. *Handbook of multilingualism and multilingual communication*. Berlin & New York: Mouton de Gruyter.
Auwera, Johan van der. 1984. More on the history of subject contact clauses in English. *Folia Linguistica Historica* 5. 171–184.
Ávila-Ledesma, Nancy E. & Carolina P. Amador-Moreno. 2016. "The more please [Places] I see the more I think of ome": On gendered discourse of Irishness and migration experiences. In Jesús Romero-Trillo (ed.), *Yearbook of corpus linguistics and pragmatics 2016: Global implications for society and education in the networked age*, 85–106. Switzerland: Springer International.
Ayres-Bennett, Wendy & Janice Carruthers. 2019. *Enhancing policy and improving the uptake of provision of modern languages teaching*. http://qpol.qub.ac.uk/enhancing-policy-improving-uptake-and-quality-of-provision-of-modern-languages-teaching (accessed 5 July 2019).
Baayen, R. Harald. 2008. *Analyzing linguistic data: A practical introduction to statistics using R*. Cambridge: Cambridge University Press.
Baetens-Beardsmore, Hugo. 1982. *Bilingualism: Basic principles*. Clevedon: Multilingual Matters.
Bailey, Mark. 2015. *The contribution of small businesses to Northern Ireland*. Belfast: Ulster University SME Centre and Federation of Small Businesses. https://www.fsb.org.uk/docs/default-source/Publications/the-contribution-of-small-businesses-to-northern-ireland.pdf?sfvrsn=1 (accessed 19 July 2019).
Bak, Thomas H. & Dina Mehmedbegovic. 2017. Healthy linguistic diet: the value of linguistic diversity and language learning across the lifespan. *Languages, Society and Policy*. http://www.meits.org/policy-papers/paper/healthy-linguistic-diet (accessed 6 March 2018).
Bak, Thomas H., Mariana Vega-Mendoza & Antonella Sorace. 2014. Never too late? An advantage on tests of auditory attention extends to late bilinguals. *Frontiers in Psychology* 5 (1). https://www.ncbi.nlm.nih.gov/pmc/articles/PMC4033267/ (accessed 5 July 2019).
Baker, Colin. 2006. *Foundations of bilingual education and bilingualism*. Clevedon: Multilingual Matters.

Bakewell, Oliver & Hein de Haas. 2007. African migrations: Continuities, discontinuities and recent transformations. In Leo de Haan, Ulf Engel & Patrick Chabal (eds.), *African alternatives,* 95–118. Leiden: Brill.

Ball, Catherine N. 1996. A diachronic study of relative markers in spoken and written English. *Language Variation and Change* 8. 227–258.

Barac, Raulaca & Ellen Bialystok. 2012. Bilingual effects on cognitive and linguistic development: Role of language, cultural background, and education. *Child Development* 83 (2). 413–422.

Barrett, Rusty 1997. The homo-genius speech community. In Anna Livia & Kira Hall (eds.), *Queerly phrased,* 181–201. New York: Oxford University Press.

Barry, Michael V. 1981. The methodology of the tape-recorded survey of Hiberno-English speech. In Michael V. Barry (ed.), *Aspects of English dialects in Ireland,* 18–46. Belfast: Institute of Irish Studies, QUB.

Barry, Terry. 2000. Rural settlement in medieval Ireland. In Terry Barry (ed.), *A history of settlement in Ireland,* 110–123. London & New York: Routledge.

Barton, Brian. 1995. *Northern Ireland in the Second World War.* Belfast: Ulster Historical Foundation.

Barton, Brian. 2010. Northern Ireland, 1939–45. In J. R. Hill (ed.), *A new history of Ireland – Vol. VII: Ireland 1921–84,* 235–260. Oxford: Oxford University Press.

Bates, Elizabeth & Brian MacWhinney. 1989. Functionalism and the competition model. *The Crosslinguistic Study of Sentence Processing* 3. 73–112.

Bates, Jessica & Lee Komito. 2012. Migration, community and social media. In Gerard Boucher, Annette Grindsted & Trinidad L. Vicente (eds.), *Transnationalism in the global city,* 97–112. Bilbao: University of Deusto.

Bauder, Harald. 2006. *Labor movement: How migration regulates labor markets.* Oxford: Oxford University Press.

Bauere, Viktorija, Paul J. Densham, Jane Millar & John Salt. 2007. Migrants from Central and Eastern Europe: Local geographies. *Population Trends* 129. 7–19.

Baum, Shari & Debra Titone. 2014. Moving toward a neuroplasticity view of bilingualism, executive control and aging. *Applied Psycholinguistics* 35 (5). 857–894.

Bayley, Robert. 1994. Interlanguage variation and the quantitative paradigm: Past tense marking in Chinese-English. In Elaine Tarone, Susan Gass & Andrew D. Cohen (eds.), *Research methodology in second language acquisition,* 157–181. Hillsdale: Lawrence Erlbaum.

Bayley, Robert. 2004. Linguistic diversity and English language acquisition. In Edward Finegan & John R. Rickford (eds.), *Language in the USA: Themes for the 21st century,* 268–286. Cambridge: Cambridge University Press.

Bayley, Robert. 2005. Second language acquisition and sociolinguistic variation. *Intercultural Communication Studies* 14 (2). 1–15.

Bayley, Robert & Vera Regan. 2004. Introduction: The acquisition of sociolinguistic competence. *Journal of Sociolinguistics* 8 (3). 323–338.

Beal, Joan C. 1990. 'A real fright': Adolescents' narratives of vicarious experience. *Language and Style* 21 (4). 16–34.

Beal, Joan C. 1993. The grammar of Tyneside and Northumbrian English. In James Milroy & Lesley Milroy (eds.), *Real English: The grammar of English dialects in the British Isles,* 187–213. London: Longman.

Beal, Joan C., Lourdes Burbano-Elizondo & Carmen Llamas. 2012. *Urban North-Eastern English: Tyneside to Teeside.* Edinburgh: Edinburgh University Press.

Beal, Joan C. & Karen P. Corrigan. 2002. Relativization in Tyneside and Northumbrian English. In Patricia Poussa (ed.), *Relativisation on the North Sea Littoral*, 125–134. Munich: Lincom Europa.

Beal, Joan C. & Karen P. Corrigan. 2005. A tale of two dialects: Relativisation in Newcastle and Sheffield. In Markku Filppula, Juhani Klemola, Marjatta Palander & Esa Pentillä (eds.), *Dialects across borders*, 211–230. Amsterdam: John Benjamins.

Beal, Joan C. & Karen P. Corrigan. 2007. Time and Tyne: A corpus-based study of variation and change in relativization strategies in Tyneside English. In Stephen Elspaß, Nils Langer, Joachin Scharloth & Wim Venadenbussche (eds.), *Germanic language histories 'from below', (1700–2000)*, 99–114. Berlin & New York: Mouton de Gruyter.

Beal, Joan C. & Karen P. Corrigan. 2009. The impact of nineteenth century Irish-English migrations on contemporary northern Englishes: Tyneside and Sheffield compared. In Esa Penttilä & Heli Paulasto (eds.), *Language contacts meet English dialects: Studies in honour of Markku Filppula*, 231–258. Newcastle upon Tyne: Cambridge Scholars Publishing.

Beckett, John. 2014. Inventing and reinventing the modern city: The 2012 city status competition in the United Kingdom. *Urban History* 41 (4). 705–720.

Beebe, Leslie M. 1980. Sociolinguistic variation and style-shifting in second language acquisition. *Language Learning* 30. 433–437.

Belfast City Council. 2017. *Policy on linguistic diversity: draft for consultation*. https://yoursay.belfastcity.gov.uk/chief-executives/draft-policy-on-linguisic-diversity/supporting_documents/2017.04.21%20Draft%20Policy%20on%20Linguistic%20Diversity%20Version%20Approved%20at%20SPR%2021.4.17%20FINAL%20FOR%20WEB.pdf (accessed 6 April 2018).

Belfast City Council. 2018. *Belfast local development plan: Technical supplement 3. Employment and economy*. https://www.google.com/search?client=firefgox-b-d&q=Local+Economic+Factors+Social+appraisal+-+Belfast+City+Council (accessed 24 July 2019).

Bell, Kathryn, Neil Jarman & Thomas Lefebvre. 2004. *Migrant workers in Northern Ireland*. Belfast: Institute for Conflict Research.

Benor, Sarah Bunin. 2010. Ethnolinguistic repertoire: Shifting the analytic focus in language and ethnicity. *Journal of Sociolinguistics* 14 (2). 159–183.

Benor, Sarah Bunin. 2012. *Becoming frum: How newcomers learn the language and culture of Orthodox Judaism*. New Brunswick: Rutgers University Press.

Ben-Zeev, Sandra. 1977. The influence of bilingualism on cognitive strategy and cognitive development. *Child Development* 48 (3). 1009–1018.

Bermingham, Nicola. 2018. Double new speakers? Language ideologies of immigrant students in Galicia. In Cassie Smith-Christmas, Noel P. Ó Murchadha, Michael Hornsby & Máiréad Moriarty (eds.), *New speakers of minority languages: Linguistic ideologies and practices*, 111–130. Basingstoke: Palgrave Macmillan.

Berwald, Olaf (ed.). 2013. *A Companion to the works of Max Frisch*. New York: Boydell & Brewer.

Besley, Timothy & Hannes Mueller. 2009. *Estimating the peace dividend*. http://eprints.lse.ac.uk/25427/1/estimating_the_peace_dividend.pdf (accessed 6 March 2018).

Best, Catherine T. & Michael D. Tyler. 2007. Non-native and second-language speech perception. In Ocke-Schwen Bohn & Murray J. Munro (eds.), *Language experience in second language speech learning: In honour of James Emil Flege*, 13–34. Amsterdam: John Benjamins.

Betz, Emma M. 2011. Word choice, turn construction, and topic management in German conversation: Adverbs that are sensitive to interactional positioning. In Michael T. Putnam (ed.), *Studies on German language islands*, 415–454. Amsterdam: John Benjamins.

Bhatia, Tej K. & William C. Ritchie (eds.). 2008. *The handbook of bilingualism and multilingualism.* Oxford: Blackwell Publishing.

Bialystok, Ellen. 1993. Metalinguistic awareness: The development of children's representations of language. In Chris Pratt & Alison Garton (eds.), *Systems of representation in children: Development and use,* 211–233. London: Wiley & Sons.

Bialystok, Ellen, Kathleen F. Peets & Sylvain Moreno. 2014. Producing bilinguals through immersion education: Development of metalinguistic awareness. *Applied Psycholinguistics* 35 (1). 177–191.

Biberauer, Theresa & Ian Roberts. 2017. Conditional inversion and types of parametric change. In Bettelou Los & Pieter de Haan (eds.), *Word order change in acquisition and language contact: Essays in honour of Ans van Kemenade,* 57–77. Amsterdam: John Benjamins.

Birdsong, David. 2016. Age and second language acquisition and processing: A selective overview. *Language Learning* 56. 9–49.

Birdsong, David. 2018. Plasticity, variability and age in second language acquisition and bilingualism. *Frontiers in Psychology* 9. https://www.frontiersin.org/articles/10.3389/fpsyg.2018.00081/full (accessed 5 July 2019).

Bisagni, Jacopo. 2014. Prolegomena to the study of code-switching in the old Irish glosses. *Peritia* 24/25. 1–58.

Blackledge, Adrian & Angela Creese. 2009. A linguistic ethnography of identity: adopting a heteroglossic frame. In Siân Preece (ed.), *The Routledge handbook of language and identity,* 272–288. London: Taylor and Francis.

Blackledge, Adrian & Angela Creese. 2017. Translanguaging in mobility. In Suresh Canagarajah (ed.), *The Routledge handbook of migration and language,* 31–46. London: Routledge.

Blackledge, Adrian & Angela Creese. 2019. *Voices of a city market: An ethnography.* Bristol: Multilingual Matters.

Blaney, Roger. 1996. *Presbyterians and the Irish language.* Belfast: Ulster Historical Foundation/The Ultach Trust.

Blee, Emma. 2011. *From Vietnam to Northern Ireland.* Moira, County Down: Agenda NI Magazine.

Bliss, Alan J. 1979. *Spoken English in Ireland, 1600–1740.* Dublin: Dolmen Press.

Bliss, Alan J. 1991. The English language in early modern Ireland. In Theodore William Moody, Francis Xavier Martin & Francis John Byrne (eds.), *A new history of Ireland, Vol. III: Early modern Ireland 1534–1691,* 546–559. Oxford: Oxford University Press.

Block, David. 2007. *Second language identities.* London: Continuum.

Blommaert, Jan. 2010. *The sociolinguistics of globalisation.* Cambridge: Cambridge University Press.

Blondeau, Hélène & Naomi Nagy. 2008. Subordinate clause marking in Montreal Anglophone French and English. In Miriam Meyerhoff & Naomi Nagy (eds.), *Social lives in language – sociolinguistics and multilingual speech communities: Celebrating the work of Gillian Sankoff,* 273–313. Amsterdam: John Benjamins.

Bloomquist, Jennifer, Lisa J. Green & Sonja L. Lanehart (eds.). 2015. *The Oxford handbook of African American language.* Oxford: Oxford University Press.

Blyth, Carl, Sigrid Recktenwald & Jenny Wang. 1990. I'm like, "Say what ?!": A new quotative in American oral narrative. *American Speech* 65. 215–227.

Boal, Frederick W. 1999. From undivided cities to undivided cities: Assimilation to ethnic cleansing. *Housing Studies* 14 (5). 585–600.

Boal, Frederick W. & Stephen Royle. 2006. *Enduring city: Belfast in the twentieth century.* Belfast: Blackstaff Press.

Bogusz, Barbara. 2004. *Irregular migration and human rights: Theoretical, European and international.* Leiden & Boston: Martinus Nijhoff Publishers.

Bondaruk, Anna. 1995. Resumptive pronouns in English and Polish. In Edmund Gussmann (ed.), *Licensing in syntax and phonology,* 27–55. PASE Studies and Monographs 1. Lublin: Folium.

Bonness, Dania. 2016. *"There is a great many Irish Settlers here". Exploring Irish English diachronically using emigrant letters in the Corpus of Irish English Correspondence (CORIECOR).* Bergen: University of Bergen dissertation.

Booker, Sparky. 2018. *Cultural exchange and identity in late medieval Ireland: The English and Irish of the four obedient shires.* Cambridge: Cambridge University Press.

Bot, Kees de, Paul Gommans & Carola Rossing. 1991. L1 loss in an L2 environment: Dutch immigrants in France. In Herbert W. Seliger & Robert M. Vago (eds.), *First language attrition,* 87–99. Cambridge: Cambridge University Press.

Bourdieu, Pierre. 1986. The forms of capital. In Richardson, John G. (ed.), *Handbook of theory and research for the sociology of education,* 241–258. New York: Greenwood Press.

Bourdieu, Pierre & Luc Boltanski. 1975. 'Le fétichisme de la langue'. *Actes de la Recherche en Sciences Sociales* 4. 2–32

Boye, Kasper & Petar Kehayov (eds.), 2016. *Complementizer semantics in European languages.* Berlin & Boston: De Gruyter Mouton.

Boylan, Ciara. 2016. Economy in independent Ireland. In Richard Bourke & Ian McBride (eds.), *The Princeton history of modern Ireland,* 403–421. Oxford & Princeton: Princeton University Press.

Bozdag, Cigdem, Andreas Hepp & Laura Suna. 2012. Diasporic media as the 'focus' of communicative networking among migrants. In Isabelle Rigoni & Eugenie Saitta (eds.), *Mediating cultural diversity in a globalized public space,* 96–115. London: Palgrave Macmillan.

Braber, Natalie & Jonnie Robinson. 2018. *East Midlands English.* Berlin & Boston: De Gruyter Mouton.

Braidwood, John. 1964. Ulster and Elizabethan English. In George Brendan Adams (ed.), *Ulster dialects. An introductory symposium,* 5–109. Cultra, County Down: Ulster Folk and Transport Museum.

Bratt Paulston, Christina. 1994. *Linguistic minorities in multilingual settings.* Amsterdam: John Benjamins.

Bray, Gerald (ed.). 2006. *Records of convocation XVI, Ireland 1101–1690.* Suffolk: The Boydell Press.

Braziel, Jane Evans & Anita Mannur. 2003. *Theorizing diaspora: A reader.* Oxford: Wiley.

Brechwald, Whitney A. & Mitchell J. Prinstein. 2011. Beyond homophily: A decade of advances in understanding peer influence processes. *Journal of Research on Adolescence* 21 (1). 166–179.

Brevik, Lisbeth M. 2013. Research ethics: An investigation into why school leaders agree or refuse to participate in educational research. *Problems of Education in the 21st Century* 52 (1). 7–20.

Britain, David. 2002. Diffusion, levelling, simplification and reallocation in past tense BE in the English Fens. *Journal of Sociolinguistics* 6(1). 16–43.

Britain, David. 2003. Exploring the importance of the outlier in sociolinguistic dialectology. In David Britain & Jenny Cheshire (eds.), *Social dialectology: In honour of Peter Trudgill,* 191–208. Amsterdam: John Benjamins.

Britain, David. 2004. Space and spatial diffusion. In Jack K. Chambers, Peter Trudgill & Natalie Schilling-Estes (eds.), *The handbook of language variation and change,* 603–637. Oxford: Blackwell Publishing.

Britain, David. 2012. Countering the urbanist agenda in variationist sociolinguistics: Dialect contact, demographic change and the rural-urban dichotomy. In Sandra Hansen, Christian

Schwarz, Philipp Stoeckle & Tobias Streck (eds.), *Dialectological and folk dialectological concepts of space*, 12–30. Berlin & Boston: De Gruyter Mouton.
Britain, David. 2013. Space, diffusion and mobility. In Jack K. Chambers & Natalie Schilling (eds.), *Handbook of language variation and change* (2nd edn.), 471–500. Oxford: Wiley-Blackwell.
Britain, David. 2017. Which way to look?: Perspectives on "urban" and "rural" in dialectology. In Emma Moore & Chris Montgomery (eds.), *A sense of place: Studies in language and region*, 171–188. Cambridge: Cambridge University Press.
Britain, David & Peter Trudgill. 1999. Migration, new-dialect formation and sociolinguistic refunctionalisation: Reallocation as an outcome of dialect contact. *Transactions of the Philological Society* 97 (2). 245–256.
Britain, David & Peter Trudgill. 2005. New dialect formation and contact-induced reallocation: Three case studies from the Fens. *International Journal of English Studies* 5 (1). 183–209.
Bromhead, Helen. 2009. *The reign of truth and faith*. Berlin & New York: Mouton de Gruyter.
Browder, Laura. 1999. 'One hundred percent American': How a slave, a janitor and a former Klansman escaped racial categories by becoming Indians. In Timothy B. Powell (ed.), *Beyond the binary: Reconstructing cultural identity in a multicultural context*, 107–138. New Jersey & London: Rutgers University Press.
Brown, Cynthia A. 1998. The role of L1 grammar in the L2 acquisition of segmental structure. *Second Language Research* 14 (2). 136–193.
Brún, Fionntán de. 2005. *Belfast and the Irish language*. Dublin: Four Courts Press.
Bucholtz, Mary. 1995. From mulatta to mestiza: Passing and the linguistic reshaping of ethnic identity. In Kira Hall & Mary Bucholtz (eds.), *Gender articulated: Language and the socially constructed self*, 351–373. New York: Routledge.
Bucholtz, Mary. 1999. You da man: Narrating the racial other in the production of white masculinity. *Journal of Sociolinguistics* 3 (4). 443–460.
Bucholtz, Mary & Kira Hall. 2004. Language and identity. In Alessandro Duranti (ed.), *A companion to linguistic anthropology*, 369–394. Malden: Blackwell.
Bucholtz, Mary & Kira Hall. 2005. Identity and social interaction: A sociocultural linguistic approach. *Discourse Studies* 7 (4–5). 585–614.
Burrell, Kathy. 2010. Staying, returning, working and living: Key themes in current academic research undertaken in the UK on migration movements from Eastern Europe. *Social Identities* 16 (3). 297–308.
Buchstaller, Isabelle. 2006. Diagnostics of age graded linguistic behavior. *Journal of Sociolinguistics* 10 (1). 3–30.
Buchstaller, Isabelle. 2014. *Quotatives: New trends and sociolinguistic implications*. Oxford: Wiley-Blackwell.
Buchstaller, Isabelle & Karen P. Corrigan. 2015. Morphosyntactic features of Northern English. In Raymond Hickey (ed.), *Researching Northern English*, 71–98. Amsterdam: John Benjamins.
Buchstaller, Isabelle & Alexandra D'Arcy. 2009. Localized globalization: A multilocal, multivariate investigation of quotative *like*. *Journal of Sociolinguistics* 13 (3). 291–331.
Buchstaller, Isabelle, John R. Rickford, Elizabeth Closs-Traugott, Thomas Wasow & Arnold Zwicky. 2010. The sociolinguistics of a short-lived innovation: Tracing the development of quotative *all* across spoken and internet newsgroup data. *Language Variation and Change* 22. 191–219.
Buchstaller, Isabelle & Ingrid van Alphen (eds.). 2012a. *Quotatives. Cross-linguistic and cross-disciplinary perspectives*. Amsterdam: John Benjamins.
Buchstaller, Isabelle & Ingrid van Alphen. 2012b. Preface: Introductory remarks on new and old quotatives. In Isabelle Buchstaller & Ingrid Van Alphen (eds.), *Quotatives. Cross-linguistic and cross-disciplinary perspectives*, xi–xxx. Amsterdam: John Benjamins.

Busch, Brigitta. 2016. Categorizing languages and speakers: Why linguists should mistrust census data and statistics. *Urban Language & Literacies* 189. https://www.academia.edu/20770728/WP189_Busch_2016._Categorizing_languages_and_speakers_Why_linguists_should_mistrust_census_data_and_statistics (accessed 12 March 2018).
Butler, Christopher. 1985. *Statistics in linguistics*. Oxford: Basil Blackwell.
Butler, Judith. 1990. *Gender trouble: Feminism and the subversion of identity*. New York: Routledge.
Butters, Ronald R. 1980. Narrative *go* "say". *American Speech* 55. 304–307.
Butters, Ronald R. 1982. Editor's note [on 'be + like']. *American Speech* 57 (2). 149.
Bybee, Joan. 2007. *Frequency of use and the organization of language*. Oxford: Oxford University Press.
Buysse, Lieven. 2010. Discourse markers in the English of Flemish university students. In Iwona Witczak-Plisiecka (ed.), *Speech actions in theory and applied studies*, 461–484. Newcastle: Cambridge Scholars Publishing.
Bylund, Emanuel. Niclas Abrahamsson & Kenneth Hyltenstam. 2009. The role of language aptitude in first language attrition: The case of pre-pubescent attriters. *Applied Linguistics* 31 (3). 443–464.
Bylund, Emanuel, Niclas Abrahamsson & Kenneth Hyltenstam. 2012. Does L1 maintenance hamper L2 nativelikeness? A study of L2 ultimate attainment in early bilinguals. *Studies in Second Language Acquisition* 34 (2). 215–241.
Byrne, Francis John. 2005. The Viking age. In Dáibhí Ó Cróinín (ed.), *A new history of Ireland – Vol. I: Prehistoric and early Ireland*, 609–631. Oxford: Oxford University Press.
Byrne, Ross P., Rui Martiniano, Lara M. Cassidy, Matthew Carrigan, Garrett Hellenthal, Orla Hardiman, Daniel G. Bradley & Russell McLaughlin. 2018. Insular Celtic population structure and genomic footprints of migration. *PLOS Genetics* 14 (1). https://doi.org/10.1371/journal.pgen.1007152 (accessed 18 June 2019).
Callame, Jon & Esther Charlesworth. 2009. *Divided Cities: Belfast, Beirut, Jerusalem, Mostar and Nicosia*. Philadelphia: University of Pennsylvania Press.
Campbell, Lyle & Martha C. Muntzel. 1989. The structural consequences of language death. In Nancy Dorian (ed.), *Investigating obsolescence: Studies in language contraction and death*, 181–196. Cambridge: Cambridge University Press.
Cameron, Richard. 2005. Aging and gendering. *Language in Society* 34. 23–61.
Campling, Liam, Satoshi Miyamura, Jonathan Pattenden & Benjamin Selwyn. 2016. Class dynamics of development: A methodological note. *Third World Quarterly* 37 (10). 1745–1767.
Canagarajah, Suresh. 2007. The ecology of global English. *International Multilingual Research Journal* 1 (2). 89–100.
Canagarajah, Suresh 2017. Introduction. In Suresh Canagarajah (ed.), *The Routledge handbook of migration and language*, 1–27. Abingdon, Oxon: Routledge.
Cancino, Herlinda, Ellen J. Rosansky & John H. Schumann. 1978. The acquisition of English negatives and interrogatives by native Spanish speakers. In Evelyn Hatch (ed.), *Second language acquisition*, 207–230. Rowley: Newbury House.
Canny, Nicholas. 2001. *Making Ireland British 1580–1650*. Oxford: Oxford University Press
Cape, Ruth, Mariana Vega-Mendoza, Thomas H. Bak & Antonella Sorace. 2018. Cognitive effects of Gaelic-medium education on primary school children in Scotland. *International Journal of Bilingual Education and Bilingualism*. https://doi.org/10.1080/13670050.2018.1543648 (accessed 6 July 2019).
Carlton, Charles. 1970. *Descriptive syntax of the Old English charters*. The Hague: Mouton.

Carrell, Patricia L., Moneta Speaker Prince & Gusti Gede Astika. 1996. Personality types and language learning in an EFL Context. *Language Learning* 46 (1). 75–99.
Carruthers Janice & Micheál B. Ó Mainnín. 2018. Languages in Northern Ireland: Policy and practice. In Michael Kelly (ed.), *Languages after Brexit: How the UK speaks to the world*, 159–172. Houndmills, Basingstoke: Palgrave Macmillan.
Casey, Denis. 2014. Brian Boru and the Book of Armagh. *History Ireland* 22 (2). https://www.historyireland.com/volume-22/brian-boru-book-armagh/ (accessed 17 July 2019).
Castles, Stephen. 2010. Understanding global migration: A social transformation perspective. *Journal of Ethnic and Migration Studies* 36 (10). 1565–1586.
Castles, Stephen, Heine de Haas & Mark J. Miller. 2014. *The age of migration: International population movements in the modern world* (5th edn.). Houndmills, Basingstoke: Palgrave Macmillan.
Cavanagh, Matt & Alex Glennie. 2012. International students and net migration in the UK. https://www.ippr.org/files/images/media/files/publication/2012/04/international-students-net-migration_Apr2012_8997.pdf (accessed 5 April 2018).
Cedergren, Henrietta. 1973. *The interplay of social and linguistic factors in Panama*. New York: Cornell University dissertation.
Cedergren, Henrietta. 1984. Panama revisited: Sound change in real-time. Paper presented at NWAVE X, University of Pennsylvania, Philadelphia, 7–10 October.
Cedergren, Henrietta. 1988. The spread of language change: Verifying inferences of linguistic diffusion. In Peter Lowenberg (eds.), *Language spread and language policy: Issues, implications and case studies*, 45–60. Washington, DC: Georgetown University Press.
Census of Ireland. 1913. *Census of Ireland, 1911: General report*. London: Her Majesty's Stationery Office.
Chambers, Jack K. 1992. Dialect acquisition. *Language* 68. 673–705.
Chambers, Jack K. 2002. Patterns of variation including change. In Jack K. Chambers, Peter Trudgill & Natalie Schilling-Estes (eds.), *The handbook of language variation and change*, 349–372. Oxford: Blackwell.
Chambers, Jack K. 2003. *Sociolinguistic theory* (2nd edn.). Oxford: Blackwell.
Chambers, Jack K. 2004. Dynamic typology and vernacular universals. In Bernd Kortmann (ed.), *Dialectology meets typology*, 127–145. Berlin & New York: Mouton de Gruyter.
Chambers, Jack K. 2009. *Sociolinguistic theory* (3rd edn.). Oxford: Blackwell.
Chambers Jack K. & Peter Trudgill. 1998. *Dialectology* (2nd edn.). Cambridge: Cambridge University Press.
Chambers, Jack K. & Natalie Schilling (eds.). 2013. *The handbook of language variation and change* (2nd edn.). Oxford: Wiley-Blackwell.
Chapelle, Carol A. 2003. *English language learning and technology: Lectures on applied linguistics in the age of information and communication technology*. Amsterdam: John Benjamins.
Chart, David Arthur (ed.). 1935. *The register of John Swayne, Archbishop of Armagh and Primate of Ireland, 1418–1439, with some entries of earlier and later bishops*. Belfast: Her Majesty's Stationery Office.
Chen, Baoguo, Aihua Ning, Aihua Hongyan Bi & Susan Dunlap. 2008. Chinese subject-relative clauses are more difficult to process than the object-relative clauses. *Acta Psychologica* 129 (1). 61–65.
Cheshire, Jenny. 1982. *Variation in an English Dialect*. Cambridge: Cambridge University Press.
Cheshire, Jenny 1999. Taming the vernacular: Some repercussions for the study of syntactic variation and spoken grammar. *Cuadernos de Filologia Inglesa* 8. 59–80.

Cheshire, Jenny. 2005a. Age and generation-specific use of language. In Ulrich Ammon, Norbert Dittmar, Klaus J. Mattheier & Peter Trudgill (eds.), *Sociolinguistics: An introductory handbook of the science of language and society* (2nd edn.), 1552–1563. Berlin & New York: Mouton de Gruyter.

Cheshire, Jenny. 2005b. Syntactic variation and spoken language. In Leonie Cornips & Karen P. Corrigan (eds.), *Syntax and variation: Reconciling the biological and the social*, 81–108. Amsterdam: John Benjamins.

Cheshire, Jenny, David Adger & Sue Fox. 2013. Relative who and the actuation problem. *Lingua* 126. 51–77.

Cheshire, Jenny, Viv Edwards & Pamela Whittle. 1993. Non-standard English and dialect levelling. In James Milroy & Lesley Milroy (eds.), *Real English: The Grammar of English Dialects in the British Isles,* 53–96. London: Longman.

Cheshire, Jenny, Sue Fox, Paul Kerswill & Eivind Torgersen. 2008. Ethnicity, friendship network and social practices as the motor of dialect change: Linguistic innovation in London. *Sociolinguistica* 22 (1). 1–23. http://eprints.whiterose.ac.uk/75066/1/Cheshire_u.a._pdf.pdf (accessed 11 August 2019).

Cheshire, Jenny, Paul Kerswill, Sue Fox & Eivind Torgersen. 2011. Contact, the feature pool, and the speech community: The emergence of multicultural London English. *Journal of Sociolinguistics* 15. 151–196.

Cichosz, Anna. 2018. Parenthetical reporting clauses in the history of English: The development of quotative inversion. *English Language and Linguistics* 23 (1). 183–214.

Citko, Barbara. 2016. Types of appositive relative clauses in Polish. *Studies in Polish Linguistics* 11 (3). 85–110.

Clahsen, Harald. 1984. The acquisition of German word order: A test case for cognitive approaches to L2 development. In Roger Andersen (ed.), *Second languages: A crosslinguistic perspective*, 219–242. Rowley, MA: Newbury House.

Clahsen, Harald & Pieter Muysken. 1986. The availability of universal grammar to adult and child learners: A study of the acquisition of German word order. *Second Language Research* 2 (2). 93–119.

Clarke, Aidan with Robert Dudley Edwards. 1991. Pacification, plantation and the Catholic question, 1603–1623. In Theodore William Moody, Francis Xavier Martin & Francis John Byrne (eds.), *A new history of Ireland – Vol. III: Early modern Ireland, 1534–1691,* 187–231. Oxford: Oxford University Press.

Clarke, Sandra. 2010. *Newfoundland and Labrador English*. Edinburgh: Edinburgh University Press.

Clyne, Michael. 1967. *Transference and triggering*. The Hague: Martinus Nijhoff.

Clyne, Michael. 1982. *Multilingual Australia*. Melbourne: River Seine.

Clyne, Michael. 1992. Linguistic and sociolinguistic aspects of language contact, maintenance and loss: Towards a multi-facet theory. In Willem Fase, Koen Jaspert & Sjaak Kroon (eds.), *Maintenance and loss of minority languages,* 17–36. Amsterdam: John Benjamins.

Clyne, Michael. 1997. Multilingualism. In Florian Coulmas (ed.), *The handbook of sociolinguistics*, 301–314. Malden: Wiley-Blackwell.

Clyne, Michael. 2005. *Australia's language potential*. Sydney: University of New South Wales Press.

Coakley, John. 2004. *Ethnic conflict and the two-state solution: The Irish experience of partition.* https://www.qub.ac.uk/research-centres/CentreforInternationalBordersResearch/Publications/WorkingPapers/MappingFrontiersworkingpapers/Filetoupload,175435,en.pdf (accessed 12 March 2018).

Coetsem, Frans van. 1988. *Loan phonology and the two transfer types in language contact.* Dordrecht: Foris.
Cohen, Marilyn. 1997. *Linen, family and community in Tullylish, County Down, 1690–1914.* Dublin: Four Courts Press.
Cohen, Robin. 1996. Introduction. In Robin Cohen (ed.), *Theories of migration*, xi–xvii. Cheltenham: Edward Elgar.
Cohen, Robin. 2008. *Global diasporas: An introduction* (2nd edn.). London: Routledge.
Collin, Simon, Thierry Karsenti & Oliver Calonne. 2015. Migrants' use of technologies: An overview of research objects in the field. *Journal of Technologies and Human Usability* 10 (3/4). 1–30.
Collyer, Michael. 2007. In-between places: Trans-Saharan transit migrants in Morocco and the fragmented journey to Europe. *Antipode* 39 (4). 620–635.
Collyer, Michael. 2010. Stranded migrants and the fragmented journey. *Journal of Refugee Studies* 23 (3). 273–293.
Comas-Quinn, Anna & Racquel Mardomingo. 2009. Mobile blogs in language learning: Making the most of informal and situated learning opportunities. *ReCALL* 21 (1). 96–112.
Connolly, Paul & Michaela Keenan. 2000. *Opportunities for all: Minority ethnic people's experiences of education, training and employment in Northern Ireland.* Belfast: Northern Ireland Statistics and Research Agency (NISRA).
Connolly, Sean J. 2007. *Contested Island: Ireland 1460–1630.* Oxford: Oxford University.
Cook, Vivian J. 2009. Language user groups and language teaching. In Vivian J. Cook & Li Wei (eds.), *Contemporary applied linguistics – Vol. 1: Language teaching and learning*, 54–74. London: Continuum.
Coote, Sir Charles. 1984 [1804]. *Statistical survey of the County of Armagh,* 2nd edn. Ballynahinch, County Down, NI: Davidson Books.
Cornips, Leonie. 2017. Child acquisition of sociolinguistic variation: Adults, children and (regional) standard Dutch two-verb clusters in one community. In Gunther de Vogelaer & Matthias Katerbow (eds.), *Acquiring sociolinguistic variation*, 91–116. Amsterdam: John Benjamins.
Cornips Leonie & Karen P. Corrigan. 2005a. Toward an integrated approach to syntactic variation. In Leonie Cornips & Karen P. Corrigan (eds.), *Syntax and variation: Reconciling the biological and the social*, 1–30. Amsterdam: John Benjamins.
Cornips, Leonie & Karen P. Corrigan. 2005b. Convergence and divergence in grammar. In Peter Auer, Frans Hinskens & Paul Kerswill (eds.), *Dialect change: Convergence and divergence in European languages*, 96–134. Cambridge: Cambridge University Press.
Cornips, Leonie & Vincent de Rooij (eds.). 2018. *The sociolinguistics of place and belonging: Perspectives from the margins.* Amsterdam: John Benjamins.
Cornips, Leonie & Frans Gregersen. 2016. The impact of Labov's contribution to general linguistic theory. *Journal of Sociolinguistics* 20 (4). 498–524.
Correa-Velez, Ignacio & Sandra M. Gifford. 2007. When the right to be counted doesn't count: The politics and challenges of researching the health of asylum seekers. *Critical Public Health* 17 (3). 273–281.
Corrigan, Karen P. 1990. Northern Hiberno-English: The state of the art. *Irish University Review* 20. 91–119.
Corrigan, Karen P. 1992. "I gcuntas Dé múin Béarla do na leanbhain": Eismirce agus an Ghaeilge sa naoú aois deag ("In the name of God teach the children English": Emigration and the Irish language in the nineteenth century). In P. O'Sullivan (ed.), *The Irish world wide – Vol. 2:*

The Irish in the new communities, 143–161. Leicester & New York: Leicester University Press & St. Martin's Press.

Corrigan, Karen P. 1996. Language attrition in nineteenth century Ireland: Emigration as murder machine? *Belfast Working Papers in Language and Linguistics* 13. 43–84.

Corrigan, Karen P. 1997. *The syntax of South Armagh English in its socio-historical perspective.* Dublin: University College Dublin dissertation.

Corrigan, Karen P. 1999. Language contact and language shift in County Armagh, 1178–1659. In J. P. Mallory (ed.), *Linguistic diversity in Ulster*, 54–69. Holywood, County Down: Museums & Galleries of Northern Ireland.

Corrigan, Karen P. 2000. What are small clauses doing in South Armagh English, Irish and Planter English? In Hildegard L. C. Tristram (ed.), *Celtic Englishes II*, 75–96. Heidelberg: Carl Winter Universitätsverlag.

Corrigan, Karen P. 2003a. The ideology of nationalism and its impact on accounts of language shift in nineteenth century Ireland. [Special issue]. *Arbeiten aus Anglistik und Amerikanistik]. Acts of Identity* 28 (2). 201–229.

Corrigan, Karen P. 2003b. The Irish diaspora and language. In Brian Lalor (ed.), *Encyclopaedia of Ireland*, 546. New Haven & London: Yale University Press.

Corrigan, Karen P. 2009. Irish daughters of northern British relatives: Internal and external constraints on the system of relativisation in South Armagh English. In Markku Filppula, Juhani Klemola & Heli Paulasto (eds.), *Vernacular universals and language contacts*, 133–162. London: Routledge.

Corrigan, Karen P. 2010. *Irish English – Vol. 1: Northern Ireland.* Edinburgh: Edinburgh University Press.

Corrigan, Karen P. 2015. 'I always think of people here, you now, saying *like* after every sentence': The dynamics of discourse-pragmatic markers in Irish-English. In Carolina Amador-Moreno, Kevin McCafferty & Elaine Vaughan (eds.), *Pragmatic markers in Irish English*, 37–64. Amsterdam: John Benjamins.

Corrigan, Karen P. 2016. "When I was a kid no one came...the only black men here had uniforms on them". Paper presented at NWAV45, University of Vancouver, 3–6 November. https://linguistics.arts.sfu.ca/nwav45/wp-content/uploads/2017/02/Corrigan2016-WhenIWasKidNooneCame-plenary-NWAV45.pdf (accessed 2 August 2019).

Corrigan, Karen P. & Chloé Diskin 2020. 'Northmen, southmen, comrades all?': The adoption of discourse *like* by migrants North and South of the Irish border. *Language in Society* 49 (2): 1–29.

Corrigan, Karen P. 2020. From Killycomain to Melbourne: Historical contact and the feature pool. In Karen V. Beaman, Isabelle Buchstaller, Susan Fox & James A. Walker (eds.), *Advancing socio-grammatical variation and change in honour of Jenny Cheshire*, 319–340. London: Routledge.

Cosgrove, Art (ed.). 1976. *A new history of Ireland – Vol. II: Medieval Ireland 1169–1534.* Oxford: Clarendon Press.

Council of Europe. 2001. *Common European framework of reference for languages.* Strasbourg, France: Language Policy Unit.

Coupland, Nikolas, Justine Coupland & Howard Giles. 1991. *Language, society and the elderly: Discourse, identity and ageing.* Oxford: Basil Blackwell.

Cousens, S. H. 1960. The regional pattern of emigration during the great Irish famine, 1846–51. *Transactions and Papers of the Institute of British Geographers* 28 (1). 119–134.

Coyle, Cathal. 2014. *The little book of Tyrone.* Dublin: The History Press.

Craig, Colette Grinevald. 1997. Language contact and degeneration. In Florian Coulmas (ed.), *The handbook of sociolinguistics*, 257–270. Oxford: Basil Blackwell.

Craig, Colette Grinevald & Michel Bert. 2011. Speakers and communities. In Peter K. Austin & Julia Sallabank (eds.), *The Cambridge handbook of endangered languages*, 45–65. Cambridge: Cambridge University Press.

Craig, David H. 1974. A history of the Belfast city hospital. *The Ulster Medical Journal* 43 (1). 1–14.

Crowley, Tony. 2005. *Wars of words: The politics of language in Ireland 1537–2004*. Oxford: Oxford University Press.

Crowley, Tony. 2006. The political production of a language: The case of Ulster-Scots. *Journal of Linguistic Anthropology* 16 (1). 23–35.

Crowley, Tony. 2012. *Scouse: A social and cultural history*. Liverpool: University of Liverpool Press.

Cummins, James. 1978. Bilingualism and the development of metalinguistic awareness. *Journal of Cross-Cultural Psychology* 9 (2). 131–149.

Cutler, Cecilia A. 1999. Yorkville crossing: White teens, hip hop and African American English. *Journal of Sociolinguistics* 3 (4). 428–442.

Cukor-Avila, Patricia. 2002. *She say, she go, she be like*: Verbs of quotation over time in African American Vernacular English. *American Speech* 77 (1). 3–31.

Cukor-Avila, Patricia. 2012. Some structural consequences of diffusion. *Language in Society* 41 (5). 615–640.

Czaika, Mathias & Hein de Haas. 2015. The globalization of migration: Has the world become more migratory? *International Migration Review* 48 (2). 283–323.

Dailey-O'Cain, Jennifer. 2000. The sociolinguistic distribution of and attitudes toward focuser *like* and quotative *like*. *Journal of Sociolinguistics* 4 (1). 60–80

Dalli, Carmen & Sarah Te One. 2012. Involving children in educational research: Researcher reflections on challenges. *International Journal of Early Years Education* 20 (3). 224–233.

Daly, Mary & David Dickson (eds.). 1990. *The origins of popular literacy in Ireland: Language change and educational development 1700–1920*. Dublin: Anna Livia Ltd.

Daniels, Roger. 1991. *Coming to America: A history of immigration and ethnicity in American life*. New York: Harper.

Darby, John & Geoffrey Morris. 1974. *Intimidation in housing*. http://cain.ulst.ac.uk/issues/housing/docs/nicrc.htm (accessed 28 February 2018).

Darby, John & Roger MacGinty. 2000. Northern Ireland: Long, cold peace. In John Darby & Roger MacGinty (eds.), *The management of peace processes*, 61–106. Houndmills, Basingstoke: Palgrave Macmillan.

Davis, Graham. 1992. The historiography of the Irish famine. In Patrick O'Sullivan (ed.), *The Irish world wide – Vol. 6: The meaning of the famine*, 15–39. Leicester & London: Leicester University Press.

Davies, Norman. 1997. *Europe: A history*. Oxford: Oxford University Press.

Davydova, Julia. 2015. Linguistic change in a multilingual setting: A case study of quotatives in Indian English. In Peter Collins (ed.), *Grammatical change in English world-wide*, 297–334. Amsterdam: John Benjamins.

Davydova, Julia. 2017. *Quotation in indigenised and learner English: A sociolinguistic account of variation*. Berlin & Boston: De Gruyter Mouton.

Davydova, Julia. 2019. Quotative *like* in the Englishes of the Outer and Expanding Circles. *World Englishes* 38 (4). 578–592.

Davydova, Julia & Isabelle Buchstaller. 2015. Investigating quotative marking in a German student community. *American Speech* 90 (4). 441–478

D'Arcy, Alexandra. 2004. Contextualizing St. John's youth English within the Canadian quotative system. *Journal of English Linguistics* 32 (4). 323–345.
D'Arcy, Alexandra. 2010. Quoting ethnicity: Constructing dialogue in Aotearoa/New Zealand. *Journal of Sociolinguistics* 14 (1). 60–88.
D'Arcy, Alexandra. 2012. The diachrony of quotation: Evidence from New Zealand English. *Language Variation and Change* 24. 343–369.
D'Arcy, Alexandra. 2015. Quotation and advances in understanding syntactic systems. *Annual Review of Linguistics* 1 (1). 43–61.
D'Arcy, Alexandra. 2017. *Discourse-pragmatic variation in context: Eight hundred years of LIKE*. Amsterdam: John Benjamins.
D'Arcy, Alexandra & Sali A. Tagliamonte. 2010. Prestige, accommodation and the legacy of relative *who*. *Language in Society* 39. 383–410.
Debaene, Ewelina & John Harris. 2013. Divergence, convergence and passing for a native speaker: Variations in the use of English by Polish migrations in Ireland. In David Singleton & Vera Regan (eds.), *Linguistic and cultural acquisition in a migrant community*, 85–105. Bristol: Multilingual Matters.
Debski, Robert. 2012. The Internet in support of community languages: Websites created by Poles living abroad. *Information Technology, Education and Society* 13 (1). 5–20.
DeKeyser, Robert M. 2000. The robustness of critical period effects in second language acquisition. *Studies in Second Language Acquisition* 22. 499–533.
DeKeyser, Robert M. 2012. Age effects in second language learning. In Susan M. Gass & Alison Mackey (eds.), *Handbook of second language acquisition*, 442–460. London: Routledge.
DeKeyser, Robert M. 2013. Age effects in second language learning. *Language Learning* 63 (S1). 52–67.
DeKeyser, Robert M., Iris Alfi-Shabtay & Dorit Ravid. 2010. Cross-linguistic evidence for the nature of age effects in second language acquisition. *Applied Psycholinguistics* 31. 413–438.
Delaney, Enda. 2012. *The curse of reason: The great Irish famine*. Dublin: Gill & Macmillan.
Delaney, Enda. 2014. *The great Irish famine: A history in four lives*. Dublin: Gill & Macmillan.
Delaney, Enda. 2016. Diaspora. In Richard Bourke & Ian McBride (eds.), *The Princeton history of modern Ireland*, 490–508. Oxford & Princeton: Princeton University Press.
Delargy, Mary. 2007. Language, culture and identity: The Chinese community in Northern Ireland. In Mairéad Nic Craith (ed.), *Language, power and identity politics*, 123–145. Basingstoke: Palgrave.
Demmans Epp, Carrie. 2017. Migrants and mobile technology use: Gaps in the support provided by current tools. *Journal of Interactive Media in Education* 1 (2). 1–13. https://www-jime.open.ac.uk/articles/10.5334/jime.432/ (accessed 30 May 2018).
Denis, Derek, Matt Hunt Gardner, Marisa Brook & Sali A. Tagliamonte. 2019. Peaks and arrowheads of vernacular reorganisation. *Language Variation and Change* 31 (1). 43–67.
Department for Employment and Learning (DEL). 2009. *The economic, labour market and skills: Impacts of migrant workers in Northern Ireland*. https://www.oxfordeconomics.com/publication/open/222535 (accessed 8 March 2018).
Department for the Economy. 2018. *Northern Ireland, migration, labour and skills*. https://www.economy-ni.gov.uk/sites/default/files/publications/economy/Northern-Ireland-migration-labour-and-skills-Final.pdf (accessed 21 July 2019).
Department of Education Northern Ireland (DENI). 2009. *Every school a good school: Supporting newcomer pupils*. https://www.education-ni.gov.uk/sites/default/files/publications/de/newcomer-policy.pdf (accessed 16 April 2018).

Department of Education Northern Ireland (DENI). 2017a. *Statistical bulletin 2/17: Annual enrolments at schools and in funded pre-school education in Northern Ireland, 2016/17*. https://www.education-ni.gov.uk/sites/default/files/publications/education/Statistical%20Bulletin%20combined..Census%20statistical%20bulletin%20-%20Feb%2017%20FINAL%20revised.pdf (accessed 8 March 2018).
Department of Education Northern Ireland (DENI). 2017b. *Safeguarding and child protection in schools*. https://www.education-ni.gov.uk/publications/safeguarding-and-child-protection-schools-guide-schools (accessed 25 July 2019).
Department of Education Northern Ireland (DENI). 2019a. *Statistical bulletin 2/19: Annual enrolments at schools and in pre-school education in Northern Ireland, 2018/19*. https://www.education-ni.gov.uk/publications/school-enrolments-201819-statistical-bulletins (accessed 3 July 2019).
Department of Education Northern Ireland (DENI). 2019b. *School enrolments in Northern Ireland, 2018/19: Key statistics*. https://www.education-ni.gov.uk/publications/school-enrolments-201819-statistical-bulletins (accessed 3 July 2019).
Denison, David. 1986. On word order in Old English. *Dutch Quarterly Review* 16. 277–295.
Denison, David. 1993. *English historical syntax*. London: Longman.
Devine, Thomas M. 2006. *Clearance and improvement: Land, power and people in Scotland, 1700–1900*. Edinburgh: John Donald Publishers.
Devlin Trew, Johanne. 2013. *Leaving the north: Migration and memory, Northern Ireland 1921–2011*. Liverpool: Liverpool University Press.
Dewaele, Jean-Marc. 2004. 'Vous' or 'tu'? Native and non-native speakers of French on a sociolinguistic tightrope. *International Review of Applied Linguistics* 42. 383–4002.
Dewaele, Jean-Marc & Adrian Furnham. 1999. Extraversion: The unloved variable in applied linguistic research. *Language Learning* 19 (3). 509–544.
Dewaele, Jean-Marc & Adrian Furnham. 2000. Personality and speech production: A pilot study of second language learners. *Personality and Individual Differences* 28. 355–365.
Diessel, Holger & Michael Tomasello. 2005. A new look at the acquisition of relative clauses. *Language* 81 (4). 882–906.
Dietz, Angelika. 2011. *Dimensions of belonging and migrants by choice: Contemporary movements between Italy and Northern Ireland*. Berlin: Waxmann.
Diskin, Chloé. 2015. *Discourse-pragmatic variation and language ideologies among native and non-native speakers of English: A case study of Chinese and Polish migrants in Ireland*. Dublin: University College Dublin dissertation.
Diskin, Chloé. 2017. The use of the discourse-pragmatic marker *like* by native and non-native speakers of English in Ireland. *Journal of Pragmatics* 120. 144–157.
Diskin, Chloé & Stephen Levey. 2019. Going global and sounding local: Quotative variation and change in L1 and L2 speakers of Irish (Dublin) English. *English World-Wide* 40 (1). 53–78.
Diskin, Chloé & Vera Regan. 2015. Migratory experience and second language acquisition among Polish and Chinese migrants in Dublin, Ireland. In Fanny Forsberg Lundell & Inge Bartning (eds.), *Cultural migrants and optimal language acquisition*, 137–177. Bristol: Multilingual Matters.
Docherty, Gerard J. 1992. *The timing of voicing in British English obstruents*. Berlin: Foris Publications.
Docherty, Gerard J. & Paul Foulkes. 1999. Derby and Newcastle: Instrumental phonetics and variationist studies. In Paul Foulkes & Gerard J. Docherty (eds.), *Urban voices*, 47–73. London: Arnold.

Docherty, Gerard J., Paul Foulkes, Jennifer Tillotson & Dominic James Landon Watt. 2006. On the scope of phonological learning: Issues arising from socially structured variation. In Louis Goldstein, Douglas Harry Whalen & Catherine T. Best (eds.), *Laboratory Phonology* 8, 393–421. Berlin & New York: Mouton de Gruyter.

Doebler Stefanie, Ruth McAreavey, Sally Shortall & Ian Shuttleworth. 2016–2017. *Negativity toward immigrant out-groups among Northern Ireland's Youth – are younger cohorts becoming more tolerant?* Northern Ireland Assembly, Knowledge Exchange Seminars. http://www.niassembly.gov.uk/globalassets/documents/raise/knowledge_exchange/briefing_papers/series6/doebler141216.pdf (accessed 16 September 2019).

Doherty, Charles. 2000. Settlement in early Ireland: A review. In Terry Barry (ed.), *A history of settlement in Ireland*, 50–80. London: Routledge.

Dolan, Terence Patrick. 2012. *A dictionary of Hiberno-English* (3rd edn.). Dublin: Gill and Macmillan.

Donnelly, James S. 1981. Hearts of oak, hearts of steel. *Studia Hibernica* 21. 7–73.

Dorian, Nancy C. 1973. Grammatical change in a dying dialect. *Language* 49 (2). 413–438.

Dorian, Nancy C. 1977. The problem of the semi-speaker in language death. *International Journal of the Sociology of Language* 12. 23–32.

Dorian, Nancy C. 1980. Language shift in community and individual: The phenomenon of the laggard semi-speaker. *International Journal of the Sociology of Language* 25. 85–94.

Dorian, Nancy C. 1981. *Language death: The lifecycle of a Scottish Gaelic dialect*. Philadelphia: University of Pennsylvania Press.

Dorian, Nancy C. (ed.). 1989. *Investigating obsolescence: Studies in language contraction and death*. Cambridge: Cambridge University Press.

Dorian, Nancy C. 1994. Varieties of variation in a very small place: Social homogeneity, prestige norms and linguistic variation. *Language* 70. 631–696.

Dorian, Nancy C. 2010. *Investigating variation: The effects of social organisation and social setting*. New York: Oxford University Press.

Doughty, Catherine J. & Michael H. Long (eds.). 2006. *The handbook of second language acquisition*. Oxford: Blackwell.

Douglas-Cowie, Ellen. 1975. A sociolinguistic study of Articlave, Co. Londonderry – a preliminary report. *Ulster Folklife* 21. 55–67.

Douglas-Cowie, Ellen. 1978. Linguistic code-switching in a Northern Irish village: Social interaction and social ambition. In Peter Trudgill (ed.), *Sociolinguistic patterns in British English*, 37–51. London: Edward Arnold.

Douglas-Cowie, Ellen. 1984. The sociolinguistic situation in Northern Ireland. In Peter Trudgill (ed.), *Language in the British Isles*, 533–545. Cambridge: Cambridge University Press.

Douglas-Cowie, Ellen & Roddy Cowie. 1979. Speaking without hearing. *Journal of the Northern Ireland Speech and Language Forum* 5. 54–70.

Dowling, Patrick H. 1935. *The hedge schools in Ireland*. Dublin: Talbot Press.

Doyle, Carey & Ruth McAreavey. 2016. Patterns and processes of recent migration in Northern Ireland. *Irish Geography* 49 (1). 47–72.

Dressler, Wolfgang U. 1988. Language death. In Frederick J. Newmeyer (ed.), *Linguistics: Volume IV*, 184–192. Cambridge: Cambridge University Press.

Dressler, Wolfgang U. & Ruth Wodak-Leodolter. 1977. Language preservation and language death in Brittany. *International Journal of the Sociology of Language* 12. 33–44.

Drummond, Rob. 2010. *Sociolinguistic variation in a second language: The influence of local accent on the pronunciation of non-native English speakers living in Manchester*. Manchester: University of Manchester dissertation.

Drummond, Rob. 2011. Glottal variation in /t/ in non-native English speech: Patterns of acquisition. *English World-Wide* 32 (3). 280–308.
Drummond, Rob. 2012. Aspects of identity in a second language: ING variation in the speech of Polish migrants living in Manchester, UK. *Language Variation and Change* 24. 107–133.
Drummond, Rob. 2015. Non-native Northern English. In Raymond Hickey (ed.), *Researching Northern Englishes*, 459–477. Amsterdam and Philadelphia: John Benjamins.
Drummond, Rob. & Erik Schleef. 2016. Identity in variationist sociolinguistics. In Siân Preece (ed.), *The Routledge handbook of language and identity*, 50–65. London: Taylor and Francis.
Dubois, Sylvie & Barbara Horvath. 1998. Let's tink about dat: Interdental fricatives in Cajun English. *Language Variation and Change* 10 (1). 245–261.
Dubois, Sylvie & Barbara Horvath. 2000. When the music changes, you change too: Gender and language change in Cajun English. *Language Variation and Change* 11 (1). 287–313.
Dudley Edwards, Robert with Bridget Hourican. 2005. *An atlas of Irish history* (3rd edn.). London: Routledge.
Duffield, Nigel. 1995. *Particles and projections in Irish syntax*. Dordrecht: Kluwer.
Duffy, Patrick J. 2000. Trends in nineteenth and twentieth century settlement. In Terry Barry (ed.), *A history of settlement in Ireland*, 206–227. London: Routledge.
Dunbar, Robert. 2002/2003. Language legislation and language rights in the United Kingdom. *European Yearbook of Minority Issues* 2 (1). 95–126.
Dustmann, Christian & Tommaso Frattini. 2013. *The fiscal effects of immigration to the UK, CDP 22/13*. http://www.cream-migration.org/publ_uploads/CDP_22_13.pdf (accessed 8 March 2018).
Durham, Mercedes, Bill Haddican, Eytan Zweig, Daniel E. Johnson, Zipporah Baker, David Cockeram, Esther Danks & Louise Tyler. 2012. Constant linguistic effects in the diffusion of be like. *Journal of English Linguistics* 40 (4). 316–337.
Eaton, Martin. 2007. From Porto to Portadown: Portuguese workers in Northern Ireland's labour market. *Portuguese Journal of Social Science* 6 (3). 171–191.
Eaton, Martin. 2010. Portuguese migrant worker experiences in Northern Ireland's market town economy. *Portuguese Studies* 26 (1). 10–26.
Eckert, Penelope. 1997a. Age as a sociolinguistic variable. In Florian Coulmas (ed.), *The handbook of sociolinguistics*, 151–167. Malden, MA: Wiley-Blackwell.
Eckert, Penelope. 1997b. Why ethnography? In Ulla-Brit Kotsinas, Anna-Brita Stenström & Anna-Malin Karlsson (eds.), *Ungdomspråk I Norden*, 52–62. Stockholm: Stockholm University.
Eckert, Penelope. 2000. *Linguistic variation as social practice*. Oxford: Blackwell.
Eckert, Penelope. 2003. Language and adolescent peer groups. *Journal of Language and Social Psychology* 22 (1). 112–118
Eckert, Penelope. 2004. Adolescent language. In Edward Finegan & John R. Rickford (eds.), *Language in the USA*, 361–374. Cambridge: Cambridge University Press.
Eckert, Penelope. 2008. Variation and the indexical field. *Journal of Sociolinguistics* 12 (4). 453–476.
Eckert, Penelope. 2012. Three waves of variation study: The emergence of meaning in the study of sociolinguistic variation. *Annual Review of Anthropology* 41. 87–100.
Eckert, Penelope. 2016. *Third wave variationism*. http://www.oxfordhandbooks.com/view/10.1093/oxfordhb/9780199935345.001.0001/oxfordhb-9780199935345-e-27?print=pdf (accessed 1 June 2018).
Eckman, Fred R. 2004. Optimality theory, markedness and second language syntax: The case of resumptive pronouns in relative clauses. *Studies in Phonetics, Phonology and Morphology* 10 (1). 89–110.

Eckman, Fred R. 2007. Hypotheses and methods in second language acquisition: Testing the noun phrase accessibility hierarchy on relative clauses. *Studies in Second Language Acquisition* 29 (2). 321–327.

Eckman, Fred R., Lawrence Bell & Diane Nelson. 1988. On the generalisation of relative clause instruction in the acquisition of English as a second language. *Applied Linguistics* 9 (1). 1–20.

Edwards, Viv. 1993. The grammar of Southern British English. In James Milroy & Lesley Milroy (eds.), *Real English: The grammar of English dialects in the British Isles,* 214–238. London: Longman.

Ehala, Martin. 2010. Refining the notion of ethnolinguistic vitality. *International Journal of Multilingualism* 7 (4). 363–378.

Ehrensberger-Dow, Maureen & Chris Ricketts. 2010. Language attrition: Measuring how 'wobbly' people become in their L1. *Across Languages and Cultures* 2 (1). 1–20.

Elliott, Mariann. 2000. *The Catholics of Ulster.* London: Penguin Press.

Elliott, Zuzana. 2018. *Sociolinguistic variation among Slovak immigrants in Edinburgh, Scotland.* Edinburgh: University of Edinburgh dissertation.

Ellis, Steven G. 2011. The English pale: A failed entity? *History Ireland* 19 (2). 14–17.

Elsness, Johan. 1994. On the progression of the progressive in Early Modern English. *International Computer Archive of Modern English* 18. 5–26.

Eubank, Lynn. 1987. The acquisition of German negation by formal language learners. In Bill Van Patten, Trisha R. Dvorak & James F. Lee (eds.), *Foreign language learning,* 33–51. Cambridge, MA: Newbury House.

Evans, E. Estyn. 1981. *The personality of Ireland: Habitat, heritage and history.* Belfast: Blackstaff Press.

Fasold, Ralph. 1984. *The sociolinguistics of society.* Oxford: Blackwell.

Feng-Bing, Monica. 2006. *Deconstructing ethnic identity of Chinese children in Northern Ireland.* http://www.qualitative-research.net/index.php/fqs/article/view/174/389 (accessed 28 February 2018).

Fenton, James. 2006a. *The hamely tongue: A personal record of Ulster-Scots in County Antrim* (3rd edn.). Belfast: The Ullans Press.

Fenton, James. 2006b. Ulster-Scots in the twenty-first century. In Anne Smyth, Michael Montgomery & Phillip Robinson (eds.), *The academic study of Ulster-Scots: Essays for and by Robert J. Gregg,* 39–44. Cultra, County Down: Ulster Folk and Transport Museum.

Ferguson, Frank. 2008. *Ulster-Scots writing: An anthology.* Dublin: Four Courts Press.

Ferrara, Kathleen & Barbara Bell. 1995. Sociolinguistic variation and discourse function of constructed dialogue introducers: The case of Be+like. *American Speech* 70 (3). 265–290.

Festman, Julia, Antoni Rodriguez-Fornells & Thomas F. Münte. 2010. Individual differences in control of language interference in late bilinguals are mainly related to general executive abilities. *Behavioural and Brain Functions* 6 (5). 1–12.

Filppula, Markku. 1986. *Some aspects of Hiberno-English in a functional sentence perspective.* Joensuu: Joensuu Publications in the Humanities.

Filppula, Markku. 1991. Subordinating *and* in Hiberno-English syntax: Irish or English origin? In Per Sture Ureland & George Broderick (eds.), *Language contact in the British Isles,* 617–631. Berlin & New York: Mouton de Gruyter.

Filppula, Markku. 1999. *The grammar of Irish English: Language in Hibernian style.* London: Routledge.

Filppula, Markku. 2004. Irish English: Morphology and syntax. In Bernd Kortmann & Edgar W. Schneider (eds.), *A handbook of varieties of English: A multimedia reference tool – Vol. 2: Morphology and syntax,* 73–101. Berlin & New York: Mouton de Gruyter.

Filppula, Markku, Juhani Klemola & Heli Paulasto (eds.). 2009. *Vernacular universals and language contacts: Evidence from varieties of English and beyond*. New York: Routledge.

Fina, Anna de. 2000. Orientation in immigrant narratives/the role of ethnicity in the identification of characters. *Discourse Studies* 2 (2). 131–157.

Finlay, Cathy. 1994. Syntactic variation in Belfast English. *Belfast Working Papers in Language and Linguistics* 12: 69–97.

Finlay, Cathy & Michael F. McTear 1986. Syntactic variation in the speech of Belfast schoolchildren. In John Harris, David Little & David Singleton (eds.), *Perspectives on the English Language in Ireland*, 175–186. Dublin: CLCS/TCD.

Fiorentino Giuliana. 2007. European relative clauses and the uniqueness of the relative pronoun type. *Rivista di Linguistica* 19 (2). 263–291.

Fischer, David Hackett. 1991. *Albion's seed: Four British folkways in America*. Oxford: Oxford University Press.

Fischer, John L. 1958. Social influences on the choice of a linguistic variant. *Word* 14. 47–56.

Fischer, Olga. 1992. Syntactic change and borrowing: The case of the accusative and infinitive construction in English. In Marinel Gerritsen & Dieter Stein (eds.), *Internal and external factors in syntactic change*, 17–88. Berlin & New York: Mouton de Gruyter.

Fischer, Olga & William van der Wurff. 2006. *Syntax*. Cambridge: Cambridge University Press.

Fischer, Olga, Ans van Kemenade, Willem Koopman & William van der Wurff (eds.). 2000. *The syntax of early English*. Cambridge: Cambridge University Press.

Fishman, Joshua A. 2003 [1967]. Bilingualism with and without diglossia; Diglossia with and without bilingualism. In Christina Bratt Paulston & G. Richard Tucker (eds.), *Sociolinguistics: The essential readings*, 359–366. Oxford: Blackwell Publishing.

Fishman, Joshua A. 1976. *Bilingual education: An international sociological perspective*. Rowley, MA: Newbury House.

Fishman, Joshua A. 1991. *Reversing language shift*. Clevedon: Multilingual Matters.

Fishman, Joshua A. 2000. *Can threatened languages be saved?* Clevedon: Multilingual Matters.

Fitzgerald, Garrett. 1984. Estimates for baronies of minimum level of Irish-speaking amongst successive decennial cohorts: 1771 to 1861–1871. *Royal Irish Academy* 84 (Section C). 117–155.

Fitzgerald, Garrett. 2003. Irish-speaking in the pre-famine period: A study based on the 1911 census data for people born before 1851 and still alive in 1911. *The Royal Irish Academy* 103 (Section C[5]). 191–283.

Fitzgerald, Patrick. 2006. Mapping the Ulster diaspora 1607–1960. *Familia* 22 (1). 1–17.

Fitzgerald, Patrick & Brian Lambkin. 2008. *Migration in Irish history, 1607–2007*. Houndmills: Palgrave.

Fitzpatrick, David. 1994. *Oceans of consolation: Personal accounts of Irish migration to Australia*. New York: Cornell University Press.

Fix, Sonya. 2013. *Age of second dialect acquisition and linguistic practice across ethno-racial boundaries in the Urban Midwest*. http://repository.upenn.edu/pwpl/vol19/iss2/9 (accessed 6 April 2018).

Flaherty, Eoin. 2014. Assessing the distribution of social-ecological resilience and risk: Ireland as a case study of the uneven impact of famine. *Ecological Complexity* 19 (1). 35–45.

Flege, James Emil. 1995. Second language speech learning: Theory, findings and problems. In Winifred Strange (ed.), *Speech perception and linguistic experience: Issues in cross-language research*, 233–272. Baltimore: York Press.

Flege, James Emil. 2007. Language contact in bilingualism: Phonetic system interactions. In Jennifer Cole & José Ignacio Hualde (eds.), *Laboratory phonology* 9, 353–380. Berlin & New York: Mouton de Gruyter.

Flege, James Emil. 2009. Give input a chance! In Thorsten Piske & Martha Young-Scholten (eds.), *Input matters in SLA*, 175–190. Clevedon: Multilingual Matters.
Flege, James Emil & William Samuel Brown. 1982. The voicing contrast between English /p/ and /b/ as a function of stress and position-in-utterance. *Journal of Phonetics* 10 (1). 335–345.
Flege, James Emil & Wieke Eefting. 1987. The production and perception of English stops by Spanish speakers of English. *Journal of Phonetics* 15 (1). 67–83.
Flege, James Emil, Elaina M. Frieda & Takeshi Nozawa. 1997. Amount of native-language (L1) use affects the pronunciation of an L2. *Journal of Phonetics* 25 (2). 169–186.
Flege, James Emil, Grace H. Yeni-Komshian & Serena Liu. 1999. Age constraints on second language acquisition. *Journal of Memory and Language* 41 (1). 78–104.
Flynn, Suzanne. 1987. *A parameter-setting model of L2 acquisition*. Dordrecht: Reidel.
Flynn, Suzanne. 1989. Spanish, Japanese and Chinese speakers' acquisition of English relative clauses: New evidence for the head-direction parameter. In Kenneth Hyltenstam & Loraine K. Obler (eds.), *Bilingualism across the lifespan*, 116–131. Cambridge: Cambridge University Press.
Fortman, Jennifer. 2003. Adolescent language and communication from an intergroup perspective. *Journal of Language and Social Psychology* 22 (1). 104–111.
Fortunati, Leopoldina, Raul Pertierra & Jane Vincent (eds.). 2012. *Migration, diaspora and information technology in global societies*. London: Routledge.
Foster, Gavin Maxwell. 2015. *The Irish civil war and society: Politics, class and conflict*. Basingstoke: Palgrave Macmillan.
Fought, Carmen. 2002. Ethnicity. In Jack K. Chambers, Peter Trudgill & Natalie Schilling-Estes (eds.), *The handbook of language variation and change*, 444–472. Oxford: Blackwell.
Fought, Carmen. 2006. *Language and ethnicity*. Cambridge: Cambridge University Press.
Foulkes, Paul. 2010. Exploring social-indexical variation: a long past but a short history. *Laboratory Phonology* 1 (1). 5–39.
Foulkes, Paul & Gerard J. Docherty (eds.). 1999. *Urban voices*. London: Arnold.
Foulkes, Paul, Gerard J. Docherty & Dominic Watt. 2005. Phonological variation in child-directed speech. *Language* 81 (1). 177–206.
Foulkes, Paul, Gerard J. Docherty, Ghada Khattab & Malcah Yaeger-Dror. 2010. Sound judgments: perceptions of indexical features in children's speech. In Denis Preston & Nancy Niedzielski (eds.), *A reader in sociophonetics*, 327–356. Berlin & New York: Mouton de Gruyter.
Fox, Susan. 2012. Performed narrative: The pragmatic function of *this is*+ speaker and other quotatives in London adolescent speech. In Isabelle Buchstaller & Ingrid van Alphen (eds.), *Quotatives: Cross-linguistic and cross-disciplinary perspectives*, 231–258. Amsterdam: John Benjamins.
Froggatt, Peter. 1989. The response of the medical profession to the Great Famine. In Margaret Crawford (ed.), *Famine: The Irish experience 900–1900*, 134–156. Edinburgh: John Donald.
Gal, Susan. 1979. *Language shift: Social determinants of linguistic change in bilingual Austria*. New York: Academic Press.
Galambos, Sylvia Joseph & Susan Goldin-Meadow. 1990. The effects of learning two languages on levels of metalinguistic awareness. *Cognition* 34 (1). 1–56.
Gallois, Cynthia, Julie Cretchley & Bernadette M. Watson. 2012. Approaches and methods in intergroup communication. In Howard Giles (ed.), *The handbook of intergroup communication*, 31–43. London: Routledge.
García, Ofelia. 2009. *Bilingual education in the twenty-first century*. Oxford: Wiley-Blackwell.
Gardner, Peter Robert. 2016. Ethnicizing Ulster's protestants?: Ulster-Scots education in Northern Ireland. *Identities* 45 (1). 1–20.

Gardner, Robert C., Richard N. Lalonde & R. Moorcraft. 1985. The role of attitudes and motivation in second language learning: Correlational and experimental considerations. *Language Learning* 35 (2). 207–227.

Garicano, Luis & Esteban Rossi-Hansberg. 2006. The knowledge economy at the turn of the twentieth century: The emergence of hierarchies. *Journal of the European Economic Association* 4 (2/3). 396–403.

Garner, Steven & Chris Gilligan. 2015. The ethnic demography of Ireland. In Rogelio Sáenz, David G. Embrick & Néstor P. Rodríguez (eds.), *The international handbook of the demography of race and identity*, 503–536. London: Springer.

Gass, Susan. 1979. Language transfer and universal grammatical relations. *Language Learning* 29. 327–344.

Gass, Susan M. & Junkyu Lee. 2007. Second language acquisition of relative clauses. *Studies in Second Language Acquisition* 29 (2). 329–335.

Geary, F. & W. Johnson. 1989. Shipbuilding in Belfast. *Irish Economic Social History* XVI. 42–64.

Geisler, Christer. 2002. Relativization in Ulster English. In Patricia Poussa (ed.), *Relativization on the North Sea Littoral*, 135–146. Munich: Lincom Europa.

Genesee, Fred, Kathryn Lindholm-Leary, Bill Saunders & Donna Christian (eds.). 2006. *Educating English language learners*. Cambridge: Cambridge University Press.

Genova, Nicholas de. 2017. The "migrant crisis" as racial crisis: Do Black Lives Matter in Europe? https://www.tandfonline.com/doi/full/10.1080/01419870.2017.1361543 (accessed 6 March 2018).

Gibbon, Peter. 1975. *The origins of Ulster unionism: The formation of popular Protestant politics*. Manchester: Manchester University Press.

Gil, Kook-Hee, Heather Marsden & Melinda Whong. 2017. *The meaning of negation in the second language classroom: Evidence from 'any'*. http://journals.sagepub.com/doi/abs/10.1177/1362168817740144 (accessed 23 May 2018).

Giles, Howard, Richard Y. Bourhis & Donald M. Taylor. 1977. Towards a theory of language in ethnic group relations. In Howard Giles (ed.), *Language, ethnicity and intergroup relations*, 307–348. London: Academic Press.

Gillam, Richard. 2003. *Unicode demystified: A practical programmer's guide to the encoding standard*. Boston & London: Addison-Wesley.

Gillen, Ultán. 2016. Ascendency Ireland, 1660–1800. In Richard Bourke & Ian McBride (eds.), *The Princeton history of modern Ireland*, 48–73. Oxford & Princeton: Princeton University Press.

Gilmartin, Mary. 2015. *Ireland and migration in the twenty-first century*. Manchester: Manchester University Press.

Gilmartin, Mary & Bettina Migge. 2015. European migrants in Ireland: Pathways to integration. *European Urban and Regional Studies* 22 (3). 285–299.

Ginn, Victoria, Rebecca Enlander & Rebecca Crozier (eds.). 2014. *Exploring prehistoric identity in Europe: Our construct or theirs?* Oxford & Philadelphia: Oxbow Books.

Girdenis, Aleksas. 2014. *Theoretical foundations of Lithuanian phonology* (2nd edn. Revised). Vilinius: Universitetas Vilnensis.

Gnevsheva, Ksenia. 2015. Style-shifting and intra-speaker variation in the vowel production of non-native speakers of New Zealand English. *Journal of Second Language Pronunciation* 1 (2). 135–156.

Gnevsheva, Ksenia. 2017. Within-speaker variation in passing for a native speaker. *International Journal of Bilingualism* 21 (2). 213–227.

Goldstein, Tara. 1997. *Two languages at work: Bilingual life on the production floor.* Berlin & New York: Mouton de Gruyter.

Golonka, Ewa M., Anita R. Bowles, Victor M. Frank, Dorna L. Richardson & Suzanne Freynik. 2014. Technologies for foreign language learning: a review of technology types and their effectiveness. *Computer Assisted Language Learning* 27 (1). 70–105.

Goodluck, Helen, Eithne Guilfoyle & Síle Harrington. 2006. Merge and binding in child relative clauses: the case of Irish. *Journal of Linguistics* 42 (3). 629–661.

Gopal, Deepthi & Yaron Matras. 2013. *What languages are spoken in England and Wales? Briefing paper in the dynamics of diversity: Evidence from the 2011 census series.* http://hummedia.manchester.ac.uk/institutes/code/briefingsupdated/what-languages-are-spoken-in-england-and-wales.pdf (accessed 6 March 2018).

Görlach, Manfred. 2000. Ulster Scots – A language? In John M. Kirk & Dónall P. Ó Baoill (eds.), *Language and politics: Northern Ireland, the Republic of Ireland, and Scotland* (Belfast studies in language, culture and politics), 13–32. Belfast: Queen's University Belfast.

Gorter, Durk. 2006. Introduction: The study of the linguistic landscape as a new approach to multilingualism. In Durk Gorter (ed.), *Linguistic landscape: A new approach to multilingualism,* 1–6. Clevedon: Multilingual Matters.

Grady, Cheryl L., Melanie V. Springer, Donaya Hongwanishkul, Anthony R. McIntosh & Gordon Winocur. 2006. Age-related changes in brain activity across the adult life span. *Journal of Cognitive Neuroscience* 18 (2). 227–241.

Graham, Brian J. 2000. Urbanisation in Ireland in the high middle ages. In Terry Barry (ed.), *A history of settlement in Ireland,* 124–139. London: Routledge.

Graham, J. M. 1952. Settlement and population. *British Association for the Advancement of Science* 1952 (1). 167–178.

Grant, James. 1990. The great famine and the poor law in Ulster: The rate-in-aid issue of 1849. *Irish Historical Studies* 27 (105). 30–47.

Green, David W. & Li Wei. 2016. Code-switching and language control. *Bilingualism: Language and Cognition* 19 (5). 883–884.

Grenoble, Lenore A. 2003. *Language policy in the Soviet Union.* Dordrecht & New York: Kluwer.

Grosjean, François. 1982. *Life with two languages: An introduction to bilingualism.* Cambridge, MA: Harvard University Press.

Gross, Eva. 2016. Personal reflections on a new life in Northern Ireland. In Gisela Holfter (ed.), *German-speaking Exiles in Ireland 1933–1945,* 275–288. Amsterdam & Leiden: Brill & Rodopi.

Grigonis, Simas. 2016. EU in the face of migrant crisis: Reasons for ineffective human rights protection. *International Comparative Jurisprudence* 2 (1). 93–98.

Güldemann, Thomas. 2008. *Quotative indexes in African languages.* Berlin & New York: Mouton de Gruyter.

Gullberg, Marianne & Peter Indefrey (eds.). 2006. *The cognitive neuroscience of second language acquisition.* Michigan: Blackwell.

Gussmann, Edmund. 2002. *Phonology: Analysis and theory.* Cambridge: Cambridge University Press.

Gut, Ulrike, Robert Fuchs & Eva-Marie Wunder (eds.). 2015. *Universal or diverse paths to English phonology.* Berlin & Boston: De Gruyter Mouton.

Guy, Gregory R. 1980. Variation in the group and the individual: The case of final stop deletion. In William Labov (ed.), *Locating language in time and space,* 1–36. London: Academic Press.

Guz, Wojciech. 2017. Wh-pronoun and complementizer relative clauses: Unintegration features in conversational Polish. *Studies in Polish Linguistics* 12 (1). 1–26.

Guz, Wojciech. 2018. Unintegration and polyfunctionality in Polish 'co' relative clauses. *Journal of Slavic Linguistics*. 26 (1). 17–54.
Guz, Wojciech. 2019a. Direct quotation strategies in conversational Polish. In Anna Bondaruk & Krzysztof Jaskuła (eds.), *All around the word. Papers in honour of Bogdan Szymanek on his 65th birthday*, 193–222. Lublin: Wydawnictwo KUL.
Guz, Wojciech. 2019b. *Quotative uses of Polish że*. Lublin: Wydawnictwo KUL.
Haan, de Pieter. 2017. The EFL teacher's nightmare: Information structure transfer from L2 English to L1 Dutch. In Bettelou Los & Pieter de Haan (eds.), *Word order change in acquisition and language contact: Essays in honour of Ans van Kemenade*, 337–352. Amsterdam: John Benjamins.
Haddican, William & Eytan Zweig. 2012. The syntax of manner quotative constructions in English and Dutch. *Linguistic Variation* 12 (1). 1–26.
Hainsworth, Paul (ed.). 1998. *Divided society: Ethnic minorities and racism in Northern Ireland*. London: Pluto Press.
Håkansson, Gisela. 1995. Syntax and morphology in language attrition: A study of five bilingual expatriate Swedes. *International Journal of Applied Linguistics* 5 (2). 153–171.
Hall, Kira. 1995. Lip service on the fantasy lines. In Kira Hall and Mary Bucholtz (eds.), *Gender articulated*, 183–216. New York: Routledge.
Hammersley, Martyn & Anna Traianou. 2012. *Ethics and educational research*. https://www.bera.ac.uk/publication/ethics-and-educational-research (accessed 13 July 2019).
Hanna, Rachel. 2019. *Reader and listener responses to asylum-seekers' life narratives: Language and empathy*. Belfast: Queen's University Belfast dissertation.
Harris, John. 1984. English in the North of Ireland. In Peter Trudgill (ed.), *Language in the British Isles*, 115–134. Cambridge: Cambridge University Press.
Harris, John. 1985. *Phonological variation and change: Studies in Hiberno-English*. Cambridge: Cambridge University Press.
Harris, John. 1993. The grammar of Irish English. In James Milroy & Lesley Milroy (eds.), *Real English: The grammar of English dialects in the British Isles*, 139–184. London: Longman.
Harris, Ruth-Ann M. 1998. The warp of Ulster's past: Interdisciplinary perspectives on the Irish linen industry, 1700–1920. *Journal of Interdisciplinary History* 29 (1). 106–108.
Harrison Taylor, William. 2017. *Unity in Christ and country: American Presbyterians in the revolutionary era 1758–1801*. Alabama: The University of Alabama Press.
Harzallah, Mohamed Salah. 2009. The great Irish famine: Public works relief during the liberal administration. *Nordic Irish Studies* 8 (1). 83–96.
Harwood, Jake, Howard Giles & Richard Y. Bourhis. 1994. The genesis of vitality theory: Historical patterns and discoursal dimensions. *International Journal of the Sociology of Language* 108 (1). 167–206.
Hawkins, Roger. 1989. Do second language learners acquire restrictive relative clauses on the basis of relational or configurational information? The acquisition of French subject, direct object and genitive restrictive relative clauses by second language learners. *Second Language Research* 5 (1). 158–188.
Hayes-McCoy, Gerard A. 1996. *Scots mercenary forces in Ireland (1565–1603)*. Dublin: Éamonn de Búrca publishing.
Hazen, Kirk. 2006. IN/ING variable. In Keith Brown (ed.), *Encyclopaedia of language and linguistics: Volume 5* (2nd edn.), 581–584. Oxford: Elsevier.
Health and Social Care (HSC). 2014. *Health intelligence briefing: Minority ethnic groups – population update from the 2011 Census*. http://www.hscbusiness.hscni.net/pdf/ME_2011_Census_HIB_April_2014.pdf (accessed 21 March 2018).

Hellermann, John & Andrea Vergun 2007. Language which is not taught: The discourse marker use of beginning adult learners of English. *Journal of Pragmatics* 39 (1). 157–179.

Hendery, Rachel. 2012. *Relative clauses in time and space*. Amsterdam: John Benjamins.

Henry, Alison. 1995. *Belfast English and Standard English: Dialect variation and parameter setting*. Oxford: Oxford University Press.

Henry, Alison. 2004. Variation and syntactic theory. In Jack K. Chambers, Natalie Schilling-Estes & Peter Trudgill (eds.), *The handbook of language variation and change*, 267–282. Oxford: Blackwell.

Henry, Patrick Leo. 1957. *An Anglo-Irish dialect of north Roscommon*. Dublin: University College Dublin.

Hepp, Andreas, Cigdem Bozdag & Laura Suna. 2012. Mediatized migrants: Media cultures and communicative networking in the diaspora. In Leopoldina Fortunati, Raul Pertierra & Jane Vincent (eds.), *Migration, diaspora and information technology in global societies*, 168–185. London: Routledge.

Herbison, Ivan, Phillip Robinson & Anne Smyth (eds.). 2012. *Spelling and pronunciation guide: The Ulster-Scots academy implementation proposals*. Belfast: Ullans Press.

Hermann, Tanja. 2005. Relative clauses in English dialects of the British Isles. In Bernd Kortmann, Tanja Herrmann, Lukas Pietsch & Susanne Wagner, *A comparative grammar of English dialects: Agreement, gender, relative clauses*, 21–124. Berlin & New York: Mouton de Gruyter.

Herity, Michael & George Eogan. 1996. *Ireland in prehistory*. London: Routledge.

Hickey, Raymond. 1997. Assessing the relative status of languages in medieval Ireland. In Jacek Fisiak (ed.), *Studies in Middle English linguistics*, 181–205. Berlin & New York: Mouton de Gruyter.

Hickey, Raymond. 2002. *A source book for Irish English*. Amsterdam: John Benjamins.

Hickey, Raymond (ed.). 2004a. *Legacies of colonial Englishes: Studies in transported dialects*. Cambridge: Cambridge University Press.

Hickey, Raymond. 2004b. Development and diffusion of Irish English. In Raymond Hickey (ed.), *Legacies of colonial Englishes: Studies in transported dialects*, 82–120. Cambridge: Cambridge University Press.

Hickey, Raymond. 2007. *Irish English: History and present-day forms*. Cambridge: Cambridge University Press.

Hill, Jane 1973. Subordinate clause density and language function. In Claudia Corum, T. Cedric Smith-Stark & Ann Weiser (eds.), *You take the high node and I'll take the low node: Papers from the Comparative Syntax Festival*, 33–52. Chicago: Chicago Linguistic Society.

Hill, Jane & Kenneth Hill. 1977. Language death and relexification in Tlaxcalan Nahuatl. *International Journal of the Sociology of Language* 12. 55–69.

Hillberg, Sanna. 2015. *Relativization in Scottish Standard English*. Joenssu: University of Eastern Finland dissertation.

Hindley, Reginald. 1990. *The death of the Irish language: A qualified obituary*. London: Routledge.

Hinrichs, Lars, Benedikt Szmrecsanyi & Axel Bohmann. 2015. *WHICH*-hunting and the standard English relative. *Language* 91 (4). 806–836.

Hinterhölzl, Roland. 2017. From OV to VO in English: How to kroch the nut. In Bettelou Los & Pieter de Haan (eds.), *Word order change in acquisition and language contact: Essays in honour of Ans van Kemenade*, 9–34. Amsterdam: John Benjamins.

Hinterhölzl, Roland & Ans van Kemenade. 2012. The interaction between syntax, information structure and prosody in word order change. In Terttu Nevalainen & Elizabeth Closs Traugott (eds.), *The Oxford handbook of the history of English*, 803–821. Oxford: Oxford University Press.

Hladnik Marko. 2015. *Mind the gap. Resumption in Slavic relative clauses*. Utrecht: Utrecht University dissertation.
Hodson, Pete. 2019. Titanic struggle: Memory, heritage and shipyard deindustrialisation in Belfast. *History Workshop Journal* 87. 224–249.
Hoff, Erika & Marilyn Shatz (eds.). 2009. *Blackwell handbook of language development*. Oxford: Blackwell.
Hoffman, Michol F. & James A. Walker. 2010. Ethnolects and the city: Ethnic orientation and linguistic variation in Toronto English. *Language Variation and Change* 22. 37–67.
Hofstra, Warren R. 2011a. Searching for peace and prosperity: Opequon settlement, Virginia, 1730s–1760s. In Warren R. Hofstra (ed.), *Ulster to America: The Scots-Irish experience 1680–1830*, 105–122. Tennessee: The University of Tennessee Press.
Hofstra, Warren R. (ed.). 2011b. *Ulster to America: The Scots-Irish experience 1680–1830*. Tennessee: The University of Tennessee Press.
Hofwegen, Janneke van & Walt Wolfram. 2010. Coming of age in African American English: A longitudinal study. *Journal of Sociolinguistics* 14 (4). 427–455.
Hogan-Brun, Gabrielle. 2018. This post-Brexit linguanomics. In Michael Kelly (ed.), *Languages after Brexit*, 49–59. Houndmills: Palgrave-Macmillan.
Höhn, Nicole. 2011. *Quotatives in the Jamaican acrolect*. Freiburg: University of Freiburg, Inaugural dissertation.
Höhn, Nicole. 2012. "They were all like, 'What's Going on?'": New quotatives in Jamaican and Irish English. In Marianne Hundt & Ulrike Gut (eds.), *Mapping unity and diversity worldwide*, 263–290. Amsterdam: John Benjamins.
Holder, Daniel. 2001. *30 years seen but not heard: A listening session with the Bangladeshi (Sylheti) community in Northern Ireland*. Belfast: Multicultural Resource Centre.
Holder, Daniel & Charo Lanao. 2001. *Latinoamérica Está: A study on the Latin American community in Northern Ireland: Experiences with public bodies and at work*. Belfast: Multicultural Resource Centre.
Holfter, Gisela (ed.). 2014. *The Irish context of Kristallnacht: Refugees and helpers*. Trier: Wissenschaftlicher Verlag.
Holfter, Gisela (ed.). 2016. *German-speaking exiles in Ireland 1933–1945*. Amsterdam & Leiden: Brill & Rodopi.
Holland, Dorothy. 1988. Culture sharing across gender lines: An interactionist corrective to the status-centered model of culture sharing. *American Behavioral Scientist* 31 (2). 219–234.
Holmberg, Anders. 2015. Verb-second. In Tibor Kiss & Artemis Alexiadou (eds.), *Syntax – theory and analysis: An international handbook*, 342–382. Berlin & Boston: De Gruyter Mouton.
Holmer, Nils Magnus. 1940. *On some relics of the Irish language spoken in the Glens of Antrim*. Uppsala: Universitets Aarskrift.
Holvoet, Axel. 2016. Semantic functions of complementizers in Baltic. In Boye Kasper & Petar Kehayov (eds.), *Complementizer semantics in European languages*, 225–264. Berlin & Boston: De Gruyter Mouton.
Horvath, Barbara. 1985. *Variation in Australian English*. Cambridge: Cambridge University Press.
Houston, Anne C. 1985. *Continuity and change in English morphology: The variable (ING)*. Pennsylvania: University of Pennsylvania dissertation.
Howard, Martin, Isabelle Lemée & Vera Regan. 2006. The L2 acquisition of a phonological variable: The case of /l/ deletion in French. *Journal of French Language Studies* 16 (1). 1–24.
Howard, Martin, Raymond Mougeon & Jean-Marc Dewaele. 2013. Sociolinguistics and second language acquisition. In Robert Bayley, Richard Cameron & Ceil Lucas (eds.), *The Oxford handbook of sociolinguistics*, 340–359. Oxford: Oxford University Press.

Howley, Gerry. 2015. *The acquisition of Manchester dialect variants by adolescent Roma migrants.* Salford: University of Salford dissertation.
Hudson, Richard. 1997. The rise of auxiliary DO: Verb-non-raising of category-strengthening. *Transactions of the Philological Society* 95. 41–72.
Hughes, James. 2014. Reconstruction without reconciliation: Is Northern Ireland a "model"? In Bill Kissane (ed.), *After Civil War: Division, reconstruction and reconciliation in contemporary Europe. National and ethnic conflict in the 21st Century,* 245–272. Philadelphia: University of Pennsylvania Press.
Hughes, Kathleen. 2005a. The Church in Irish society: 400–800. In Dáibhí Ó Cróinín (ed.), *A new history of Ireland – Vol. I: Prehistoric and early Ireland,* 301–329. Oxford: Oxford University Press.
Hughes, Kathleen. 2005b. The Irish Church: 800-c.1050. In Dáibhí Ó Cróinín (ed.), *A new history of Ireland – Vol. I: Prehistoric and early Ireland,* 635–654. Oxford: Oxford University Press.
Hurford, James R. 1991. The evolution of the critical period for language acquisition. *Cognition* 40 (3). 159–201.
Hyltenstam, Kenneth. 1977. Implicational patterns in interlanguage syntax variation. *Language Learning* 27 (2). 383–410.
Hyltenstam, Kenneth. 1992. Non-native features of near-native speakers: On the ultimate attainment of childhood L2 learners. In Richard Jackson Harris (ed.), *Cognitive processing in bilinguals.* [Special issue]. *Advances in Psychology,* 351–368. Amsterdam: Elsevier.
Hyltenstam, Kenneth (ed.). 2016. *Advanced proficiency and exceptional ability in second languages.* Berlin & Boston: De Gruyter Mouton.
Hyltenstam, Kenneth & Niclas Abrahamsson. 2000. Who can become native-like in a second language, all, none or some? *Studia Linguistica* 54 (2). 150–166.
Hyltenstam, Kenneth & Niclas Abrahamsson. 2008. The robustness of aptitude effects in near-native second language acquisition. *Studies in Second Language Acquisition* 30 (4). 481–509.
Ihde, Thomas W. 1993. *The Irish language in the United States.* Westport, CT: Bergin & Garvey
Ionesco, Dina, Daria Mokhnacheva & François Gemenne. 2016. *Atlas des migrations environnementales.* Paris: Sciences Po Les Presses.
Ioup, Georgette & Anna Kruse. 1977. Interference versus structural complexity as a predictor of second language relative clause acquisition. In H. Douglas Brown, Carlos A. Yorio & Ruth H. Crymes (eds.), *On TESOL '77 – teaching and learning English as a second language: Trends in research and practice,* 159–171. Washington, DC: TESOL.
Irwin, Gregory & Seamus Dunn. 1997. *Ethnic minorities in Northern Ireland.* Belfast: University of Ulster.
Ivković, Dejan & Heather Lotherington. 2009. Multilingualism in cyberspace: Conceptualising the virtual linguistic landscape. *International Journal of Multilingualism* 6 (1). 17–36.
Jake, Janice L. & Carol Myers-Scotton. 2017. The 4-M model revisited: Codeswitching and morpheme election at the abstract level. *International Journal of Bilingualism* 21 (1). 340–366.
Jarman, Neil. 2005. *Changing patterns and future planning: Migration and Northern Ireland.* Belfast: Institute for Conflict Research.
Jeon, K. Seon & Kim Hae-Young. 2007. Development of relativization in Korean as a foreign language: The noun phrase accessibility hierarchy in head-internal and head-external relative clauses. *Studies in Second Language Acquisition* 29 (2). 253–276.
Jespersen, Otto H. 1933/1983. *Essentials of English grammar,* (2nd edn.). New York: Holt & Company.

Johnson, Daniel E. 2009. Getting off the GoldVarb standard: Introducing Rbrul for mixed-effects variable rule analysis. *Language and Linguistics Compass* 3 (1). 359–383.

Johnson, Jacqueline S. & Elissa L. Newport. 1989. Critical period effects in second language learning: The influence of maturational state on the acquisition of English as a second language. *Cognitive Psychology* 21. 60–99.

Johnstone, Barbara. 1996. *The linguistic individual: Self-expression in language and linguistics*. New York: Oxford University Press.

Jones, Iestyn. 2013. Ulster's early medieval houses. *Medieval Archaeology* 57 (1). 212–222.

Jones, Maldwyn Allen. 1960. *American immigration*. Chicago: University of Chicago Press.

Jones, Mari C. (ed.). 2014. *Endangered languages and new technologies*. Cambridge: Cambridge University Press.

Kallen, Jeffrey L. 1986. *Linguistic fundamentals for Hiberno-English syntax*. Dublin: Trinity College Dublin dissertation.

Kallen, Jeffrey L. 1991. Sociolinguistic variation and methodology: *After* as a Dublin variable. In Jenny Cheshire (ed.), *English around the world*, 61–74. Cambridge: Cambridge University Press.

Kallen, Jeffrey L. 1994. English in Ireland. In Robert Burchfield (ed.), *The Cambridge history of the English language (volume V), English in Britain and overseas: Origins and development*, 148–196. Cambridge: Cambridge University Press.

Kallen, Jeffrey L. (ed.). 1997. *Focus on Ireland*. Amsterdam: John Benjamins.

Kallen, Jeffrey, L. 2010a. The political border and linguistic identities in Ireland: What can the linguistic landscape tell us? In Carmen Llamas & Dominic Watt (eds.), *Language, borders and identity*, 154–168. Edinburgh: Edinburgh University Press.

Kallen, Jeffrey L. 2010b. Changing landscapes: Language, space, and policy in the Dublin linguistic landscape. In Adam Jaworski & Crispin Thurlow (eds.), *Semiotic landscapes: Language, image, space*, 41–59. London: Continuum.

Kallen, Jeffrey, L. 2013. *Irish English – Vol. 2: The Republic of Ireland*. Berlin & Boston: De Gruyter Mouton.

Kamandulytė-Merfeldienė, Laura. 2017. Grammatically coded corpus of spoken Lithuanian: Methodology and development. *World Academy of Science, Engineering and Technology International Journal of Cognitive and Language Sciences* 11 (4). 874–878.

Kamusella, Tomasz. 2009. *The politics of language and nationalism in modern central Europe*. Basingstoke: Palgrave.

Kapur, Narinder. 1997. *The Irish Raj: Illustrated stories about Irish in India and Indians in Ireland*. Antrim: Greystone Books Ltd.

Kasper, Gabriele & Eric Kellerman (eds.). 1997. *Communication strategies: psycholinguistic and sociolinguistic perspectives*. London: Longman.

Kastovsky, Dieter. 2006. Vocabulary. In Richard Hogg & David Denison (eds.), *A history of the English language*, 199–270. Cambridge: Cambridge University Press.

Kavanagh, Seamus. 2001. *A lexicon of the old Irish glosses in the Würzburg manuscript of the epistles of St. Paul*. Austria: Österreichische Akademie der Wissenschaften.

Keenan, Edward L. 1972. Relative clause formation in Malagasy (and some related and not so related languages). In Paul M. Peranteau, Judith N. Levi & Gloria C. Phares (eds.), *The Chicago witch hunt*, 169–189. Chicago: Chicago Linguistics Society.

Keenan, Edward L. 1975. Variation in universal grammar. In Ralph W. Fasold & Roger W. Shuy (eds.), *Analyzing variation in language*, 136–148. Washington, DC: Georgetown University Press.

Keenan, Edward L. 1985. Relative clauses. *Relative Typology and Syntactic Description* 2 (1). 141–170.

Keenan, Edward L. 1987. Multiply-headed noun phrases. *Linguistic Inquiry* 18 (3). 481–490.
Kemenade, Ans van. 1987. *Syntactic case and morphological case in the history of English.* Dordrecht: Foris.
Kemenade, Ans van. 2012. Rethinking the loss of verb second. In Terttu Nevalainen & Elizabeth Closs Traugott (eds.), *The Oxford handbook of the history of English,* 822–834. Oxford: Oxford University Press.
Kempny, Marta. 2010. *Polish migrants in Belfast: Border crossing and identity construction.* Newcastle: Cambridge Scholars Publishing.
Kempny, Marta. 2013. Tales from the borderlands: Polish migrants' representations of the Northern Irish conflict in Belfast. *Space and Culture* 16 (4). 435–446.
Kennedy, Liam, Paul S. Ell, E. Margaret Crawford & Leslie A. Clarkson. 1999. *Mapping the great Irish famine.* Dublin: Four Courts Press.
Kerswill, Paul. 1996. Children, adolescents and language change. *Language Variation and Change* 8 (2). 177–202.
Kerswill, Paul. 2003. Dialect levelling and geographical diffusion in British English. In David Britain & Jenny L. Cheshire (eds.), *Social dialectology in honour of Peter Trudgill,* 223–243. Amsterdam: John Benjamins.
Kerswill, Paul. 2018. Dialect formation and dialect change in the industrial revolution: British vernacular English in the nineteenth century. In Laura Wright (ed.), *Southern English varieties then and now,* 8–38. Berlin & Boston: De Gruyter Mouton.
Kerswill, Paul & Ann Williams. 2005. New towns and koinéization: Linguistic and social correlates. *Linguistics* 43 (5). 1023–1048.
Kessler, Greg & Dawn Bikowski. 2010. Developing collaborative autonomous learning abilities in computer mediated language learning: Attention to meaning among students in wiki space. *Computer Assisted Language Learning* 25 (1). 41–58.
Kibbee, Douglas A. 1991. *For to speke Frenche trewely: The French language in England, 1000–1600: Its status, description and instruction.* Amsterdam & Philadelphia: John Benjamins.
Killen, James. 1997. Communications. In F. H. A. Aalen, Kevin Whelan & Matthew Stout (eds.), *Atlas of the rural Irish landscape,* 206–219. Cork & Toronto: Cork University Press & Toronto University Press.
Kinealy, Christine. 1995. *The great calamity: The Irish famine, 1845–52.* London: Gill & Macmillan.
Kinealy, Christine & Gerard MacAtasney. 2000. *The hidden famine: Hunger, poverty and sectarianism in Belfast 1840–50.* London: Pluto Press.
Kinealy, Christine & Trevor Parkhill. 2014. *The famine in Ulster.* Belfast: Ulster Historical Foundation.
King, Russell. 2002. Towards a new map of European migration. *International Journal of Population Geography* 8 (2). 89–106.
King, Russell. 2012a. *Theories and typologies of migration: An overview and a primer.* https://www.researchgate.net/publication/260096281_Theories_and_Typologies_of_Migration_An_Overview_and_A_Primer (accessed 4 April 2018).
King, Russell. 2012b. Geography and migration studies: Retrospect and prospect. *Population, space and place* 18 (2). 134–153.
King, Russell & Ronald Skeldon. 2010. 'Mind the gap!': Integrating approaches to internal and international migration. *Journal of Ethnic and Migration Studies* 36 (10). 1619–1646.
Kingsley, Leilarna. 2013. Language choice in multilingual encounters in transnational workplaces. *Journal of Multilingual and Multicultural Development* 34 (6). 533–548.
Kingsmore, Rona K. 1995. *Ulster Scots speech: A sociolinguistic study.* Tuscaloosa: University of Alabama Press.

Kirk, John M. 2015. The progressive in Irish-English: Looking both ways? In Peter Collins (ed.), *Grammatical change in English world-wide*, 87–118. Amsterdam: John Benjamins.
Kirk, John M. & Dónall P. Ó Baoill (eds.). 2002. *Travellers and their language*. Belfast: Cló Ollscoil na Banríona.
Kirkham, Sam & Emma Moore. 2013. Adolescence. In Jack K. Chambers & Natalie Schilling (eds.), *The handbook of language variation and change* (2nd edn.), 277–298. Oxford: Wiley-Blackwell.
Klamer, Marian. 2000. How report verbs become quote markers and complementisers. *Lingua* 110. 69–98.
Kobiałka, Ewa. 2014. *Language variation, identity and social class: The case of Polish migrants in Ireland*. Dublin: University College Dublin dissertation.
Kohn, Mary Elizabeth & Hannah Askin Franz 2009. Localized patterns for global variants: The case of quotative systems of African American and Latino speakers. *American Speech* 84. 259–297.
Komito, Lee. 2011. Social media and migration: Virtual community 2.0. *Journal of the American Society for Information Science and Technology* 62 (6). 1075–1086.
Komito, Lee & Jessica Bates. 2009. Virtually local: Social media and community amongst Polish nationals in Dublin. *Aslib Proceedings: New Information Perspectives* 61 (3). 232–244.
Komito, Lee & Jessica Bates. 2011. *Migrants' information practices and use of social media in Ireland: Networks and community*. https://dl.acm.org/citation.cfm?id=1940761 (accessed 30 May 2018).
Kortmann, Bernd (ed.). 2003. *Dialectology meets typology: Dialect grammar from a cross-linguistic perspective*. Berlin & New York: Mouton de Gruyter.
Kortmann, Bernd, Kerstin Lunkenheimer & Katharina Ehret (eds.). 2020. *The electronic world atlas of varieties of English 3.0*. [eWAVE 3.0]. Leipzig: Max Planck Institute for Evolutionary Anthropology. https://ewave-atlas.org/ (accessed 4 April 2020).
Kortmann, Bernd & Benedikt Szmrecsanyi. 2004. Global synopsis: Morphological and syntactic variation in English. In Bernd Kortmann, Edgar Schneider, Kate Burridge, Richard Mesthrie & Clive Upton (eds.), *A handbook of varieties of English: Volume 2*, 1142–1202. Berlin & New York: Mouton de Gruyter.
Kortmann, Bernd & Benedikt Szmrecsanyi. 2009. World Englishes between simplification and complexification. In Thomas Hoffman & Lucia Siebers (eds.), *World Englishes – Problems, properties and prospects*, 263–286. Amsterdam: John Benjamins.
Kortmann, Bernd & Christoph Wolk. 2012. Morphosyntactic variation in the Anglophone world. In Bernd Kortmann & Kerstin Lunkenheimer (eds.), *The Mouton world atlas of variation in English*, 906–935. Berlin & Boston: De Gruyter Mouton.
Krashen, Stephen D. 1973. Lateralization, language learning and the critical period: Some new evidence. *Language and Learning* 23. 63–74.
Krashen, Stephen D. 1981. *Second language acquisition and second language learning*. Oxford: Pergamon Press.
Krashen, Stephen D., Michael A. Long & Robin C. Scarcella. 1979. Age, rate and eventual attainment in second language acquisition. *TESOL Quarterly* 13. 573–582.
Kroch, Anthony S. 1978. Toward a theory of social dialect variation. *Language in Society* 7 (1). 17–36.
Kroch, Anthony, S. 1989. Reflexes of grammar in patterns of language change. *Language Variation and Change* 1. 199–244.

Krausova, Anna & Carlos Vargas-Silva. 2014. *Briefing census profile: Northern Ireland.* http://www.migrationobservatory.ox.ac.uk/wp-content/uploads/2016/04/CensusProfile-Northern_Ireland.pdf (accessed 9 March 2018).

Kytö, Merja. 2004. The emergence of American English: Evidence from seventeenth-century records in New England. In Raymond Hickey (ed.), *Legacies of colonial English: Studies in transported dialects*, 121–157. Cambridge: Cambridge University Press.

Labov, William. 1966. *The social stratification of English in New York City.* Washington, DC: Center for Applied Linguistics.

Labov, William. 1972. *Sociolinguistic patterns.* Philadelphia: University of Pennsylvania Press.

Labov, William. 1989. The child as linguistic historian. *Language Variation and Change* 1 (1). 85–97.

Labov, William. 1991. The boundaries of a grammar: Inter-dialectal reactions to positive *anymore*. In Peter Trudgill & Jack K. Chambers (eds.), *Dialects of English: Studies in grammatical variation*, 273–288. London: Longman.

Labov, William. 1994. *Principles of linguistic change – Vol. 1: Internal factors.* Oxford: Blackwell.

Labov, William. 2001. *Principles of linguistic change – Vol. 2: Social factors.* Oxford: Blackwell.

Labov, William. 2007. Transmission and diffusion. *Language* 83. 344–387.

Labov, William. 2008. Mysteries of the substrate. In Miriam Meyerhoff & Naomi Nagy (eds.), *Social lives in language – sociolinguistics and multilingual speech communities: Celebrating the work of Gillian Sankoff*, 315–326. Amsterdam: John Benjamins.

Labov, William, Sharon Ash & Charles Boberg. 2006. *The atlas of North American English: Phonetics, phonology and sound change.* Berlin & New York: Mouton de Gruyter.

Lambrecht, Knud. 1987. On the status of SVO sentences in French discourse. In Russell Tomlin (ed.), *Coherence and grounding in discourse*, 217–262. Amsterdam: John Benjamins.

Lan, Yu Ju, Yao Ting Sung & Kuo En Chang. 2007. A mobile device supported peer assisted learning system for collaborative early EFL reading. *Language Learning and Technology* 11 (1). 130–151.

Landry, Rodrigue & Richard Y. Bourhis. 1997. Linguistic landscape and ethnolinguistic vitality: An empirical study. *Journal of Language and Social Psychology* 16 (1). 23–49.

Lass, Roger. 1987. *The shape of English.* London: J. M. Dent & Son.

Lass, Roger. 2006. Phonology and morphology. In Richard Hogg & David Denison (eds.), *A history of the English language*, 43–108. Cambridge: Cambridge University Press.

Latonero, Mark, Danielle Poole & Jos Berens. 2018. *Refugee connectivity: A survey of mobile phones, mental health, and privacy at a Syrian refugee camp in Greece.* https://datasociety.net/output/refugee-connectivity (accessed 30 May 2018).

Laufer, Batia & Tamar Levitsky-Aviad. 2006. Examining the effectiveness of "Bilingual Dictionary Plus": A dictionary for production in a foreign language. *International Journal of Lexicography* 19 (1). 135–155.

Lealess, Allison V. & Chelsea T. Smith. 2011. Assessing contact induced language change: The use of subject relative markers in Quebec English. *Cahiers Linguistiques d'Ottawa* 36. 20–38.

Legaudaite, Jolanta. 2009. Similarities and differences between slang in Kaunas and London teenagers' speech. In Anna-Brita Stenström & Annette Myre Jørgensen (eds.), *Young speak in a multilingual perspective,* 177–202. Amsterdam: John Benjamins.

Lenihan, Pádraig. 2007. *Consolidating conquest: Ireland 1603–1727.* Abingdon, Oxford: Routledge.

Lenneberg, Eric. 1967. *Biological foundations of language.* New York: Wiley & Sons.

Lennon, Joseph. 2004. *Irish orientalism.* New York: Syracuse University Press.

Leung, Alex & Martha Young-Scholten. 2013. Reaching out to the other side: Formal-linguistics-based SLA and socio-SLA. *Applied Linguistics Review* 4 (2). 259–290.

Levey, Stephen. 2000. Language change and adaptation in a Tok Pisin newspaper. *English Today* 16 (2). 20–25.

Levey, Stephen. 2006. The sociolinguistic distribution of discourse marker *like* in preadolescent speech. *Multilingua* 25 (4). 413–441.

Levey, Stephen. 2015. A comparative variationist perspective on relative clauses in child and adult speech. In Rena Torres Cacoullos, Nathalie Dion & André Lapierre (eds.), *Linguistic variation: Confronting fact and theory*, 22–37. London: Routledge.

Levey, Stephen. 2016. The role of children in the propagation of discourse-pragmatic change: Insights from the acquisition of quotative variation. In Heike Pichler (ed.), *Discourse-pragmatic variation and change in English*, 160–182. Cambridge: Cambridge University Press.

Levey, Stephen & Caroline Hill. 2013. Social and linguistic constraints on relativizer omission in Canadian English. *American Speech* 88 (1). 32–62.

Levey, Stephen & Heike Pichler. 2020. Revisiting transatlantic relatives: Evidence from British and Canadian English. In Yoshiyuki Asahi (ed.), *Proceedings from Methods XVI*, 239–247. Frankfurt: Peter Lang.

Levinson, Stephen C. & Francisco Torreira. 2015. Timing in turn-taking and its implications for processing models of language. *Frontiers of Psychology* 6. 731. https://www.frontiersin.org/articles/10.3389/fpsyg.2015.00731/full (accessed 26 July 2019).

Lewis, Samuel. 1837. *A topographical dictionary of Ireland*. https://www.libraryireland.com/topog/D/Donaghmore-Dungannon-Tyrone.php (accessed 19 July 2019).

Leyburn, James G. 1989. *The Scotch-Irish: A social history*. Chapel Hill: University of North Carolina Press.

Liempt, Ilse van. 2011a. 'And then one day they all moved to Leicester': The relocation of Somalis from the Netherlands to the UK explained. *Population, Space and Place* 17 (3). 254–266.

Liempt, Ilse van. 2011b. Young Dutch Somalis in the UK: Citizenship, identities and belonging in a transnational triangle. *Mobilities* 6 (4). 569–583.

Lightfoot, David W. 1991. *How to set parameters: Arguments from language change*. Cambridge, MA: The MIT Press.

Little, David. 2016. Languages at school: A challenge for multilingual cities. In Lid King & Lorna Carson (eds.), *The multilingual city: Vitality, conflict, change*, 149–176. Bristol: Multilingual Matters.

Lo, Adrienne. 1999. Codeswitching, speech community membership and the construction of ethnic identity. *Journal of Sociolinguistics* 3 (1). 461–479.

Lombardi, Linda. 2003. Second language data and constraints on manner: Explaining substitutions for the English interdentals. *Second Language Research* 19 (1). 225–250.

Long, Mike. 2007. *Problems in SLA*. Mahwah, NJ: Lawrence Erlbaum Associates.

Long, Mike. 2013. Maturational constraints on child and adult SLA. In Gisela Granena & Mike Long (eds.), *Sensitive periods, language aptitude and ultimate L2 attainment*, 3–41. Amsterdam: John Benjamins.

Los, Bettelou. 2009. The consequences of the loss of verb-second in English: Information structure and syntax in interaction. *English Language and Linguistics* 13 (1). 97–125.

Los, Bettelou & Pieter de Haan (eds.). 2017. *Word order change in acquisition and language contact: Essays in honour of Ans van Kemenade*. Amsterdam: John Benjamins.

Lucas, Angela. 2005. Hiberno-English literature. In Sean Duffy, Ailbhe MacShamráin & James Moynes (eds.), *Medieval Ireland: An Encyclopaedia*, 213–214. London: Routledge.

Lynn, Sara. 2013. *Mapping the deployment of migrant labor in Northern Ireland*. Belfast: Northern Ireland Strategic Migration Partnership.

Luthra, Renee, Lucinda Platt & Justyna Salamońska. 2014. *Migrant diversity, migration motivations and early integration: The case of Poles in Germany, the Netherlands, London and Dublin*. Essex: Institute for Social and Economic Research, University of Essex.

Lyons, Marian & Thomas O'Connor. 2008. *Strangers to citizens: The Irish in Europe, 1600–1800*. Bray: Wordwell Press.

MacAfee, Caroline. 1996. *Concise Ulster dictionary*. Oxford: Oxford University Press.

MacAfee, William. 2000. The population of County Tyrone 1600–1991. In Charles Dillon & Henry A. Jeffers (eds.), *Tyrone: History and society*, 443–461. Dublin: Geography Publications.

Mac an Bhreithiún, Bharain & Anne Burke. 2014. Language, typography, and place-making: Walking the Irish and Ulster-Scots linguistic landscape. *The Canadian Journal of Irish Studies* 38 (1/2). 84–125.

Macaulay, Ronald K. S. 1978. Variation and consistency in Glaswegian English. In Peter Trudgill (ed.), *Sociolinguistic variation in speech communities*, 132–143. London: Arnold.

Macaulay, Ronald K. 2001. You're like 'why not?': The quotative expression of Glasgow adolescents. *Journal of Sociolinguistics* 5 (1). 3–21.

MacGhabhann, Fiachra. 1997. *Place names of Northern Ireland: County Antrim: Volume 7*. Belfast: The Institute of Irish Studies, Queen's University Belfast.

MacGiolla Chríost, Diarmait. 2005. *The Irish language in Ireland: From Goídel to globalisation*. London: Routledge.

MacGiolla Easpaig, Dónall. 2009. Ireland's heritage of geographical names. *Wiener Schriften zur Geographie und Kartographie* 18 (1). 79–85.

Maciukaite, Simona. 2004. *Acquisition of relative clauses in Lithuanian*. Washington, DC: Georgetown University dissertation.

Mac Póilin, Aodán (ed.). 1997. *The Irish language in Northern Ireland*. Belfast: Iontaobhas Ultach.

MacRaild, Donald M. 2006. *The Irish in Britain*. Dundalk: Dundalgan Press.

MacRaild, Donald M. 2011. *The Irish diaspora in Britain, 1750–1939*. Basingstoke: Palgrave Macmillan.

MacWhinney, Brian. 2017. Exposure is not enough. *Bilingualism: Language and Cognition* 20 (1). 25–26.

Maginn, Christopher & Steven G. Ellis. 2015. *The Tudor discovery of Ireland*. Dublin: Four Courts Press.

Maguire, Warren, Lynn Clark & Kevn Watson. 2013. Introduction. What are mergers and can they be reversed? *English Language and Linguistics* 17 (2). 229–239.

Maher, Julianne. 1991. A cross-linguistic study of language contact and attrition. In Herbert W. Seliger & Robert M. Vago (eds.), *First language attrition*, 67–84. Cambridge: Cambridge University Press.

Major, Roy C. 2001. *Foreign accent: The ontogeny and phylogeny of second language phonology*. London: Lawrence Erlbaum.

Major, Roy C. 2004. Gender and stylistic variation in second language phonology. *Language Variation and Change* 16 (3). 169–188.

Major, Roy C. 2008. Transfer in second language phonology. In Jette G. Hansen Edwards & Mary L. Zampini (eds.), *Phonology and second language acquisition*, 63–94. Amsterdam: John Benjamins.

Malischewski, Charlotte-Anne. 2013. *Integrated in a divided society?: Refugees and asylum seekers in Northern Ireland*. https://www.rsc.ox.ac.uk/files/files-1/wp91-integration-divided-society-northern-ireland-2013.pdf (accessed 6 March 2018).

Manning, Patrick with Tiffany Trimmer. 2013. *Migration in world history* (2nd edn.). London: Routledge.

Mar-Molinero, Clare & Darren Paffey. 2018. Transnational migration and language practices: The impact on Spanish-speaking migrants. In Wendy Ayres-Bennett & Janice Carruthers (eds.), *Manual of romance sociolinguistics*, 745–768. Berlin & Boston: De Gruyter Mouton.

Maschler, Yael. 2017. The emergence of Hebrew *loydea / loydat* ('I dunno m/f') from interaction: Blurring the boundaries between discourse marker, pragmatic marker, and modal particle. In Andrea Sansò & Chiara Fedriani (eds.), *Pragmatic markers, discourse markers and modal particles: New perspectives,* 37–69. Amsterdam/Philadelphia: John Benjamins.

Maschler, Yael & Deborah Schiffrin. 2015. Discourse markers: Language, meaning, and context. In Deborah Tannen, Heidi E. Hamilton & Deborah Schiffrin (eds.), *The handbook of discourse analysis* (2nd edn.), 189–221. Chichester, UK: John Wiley & Sons, Ltd.

Mathiassen, Terje. 1996. *A short grammar of Lithuanian.* Columbus, Ohio: Slavica Publishers Inc.

Mathis, Terrie & George Yule. 1994. Zero quotatives. *Discourse Processes* 18. 63–76.

Mathisen, Anne. 1999. Sandwell, West Midlands: Ambiguous perspectives on gender patterns and models of change. In Paul Foulkes & Gerard J. Docherty (eds.), *Urban voices: Accent studies in the British Isles,* 107–123. London: Arnold.

Matras, Yaron. 1998. Utterance modifiers and universals of grammatical borrowing. *Linguistics* 36 (2). 281–331.

Matras, Yaron. 2000. Fusion and the cognitive basis for bilingual discourse markers. *International Journal of Bilingualism* 4 (4). 505–528.

Matras, Yaron & Gertrud Reershemius. 2016. Functions of a particle in two minority languages: *Nu/no* in Yiddish and Romani. In Peter Auer & Yael Maschler (eds.), *NU/NÅ: A family of discourse markers across the languages of Europe and beyond,* 132–161. Berlin & Boston: De Gruyter Mouton.

Matras, Yaron & Alex Robertson. 2015. Multilingualism in a post-industrial city: Policy and practice in Manchester. *Current Issues in Language Planning* 16 (3). 296–314.

Matras, Yaron, Alex Robertson & Charlotte Jones. 2016. Using the school setting to map community languages: A pilot study in Manchester, England. *International Journal of Multilingualism* 13 (3). 353–366.

Matras, Yaron & Jeanette Sakel. 2007. Investigating the mechanisms of pattern replication in language convergence. *Studies in Language* 31 (4). 829–865.

Matthews, Paul. 2014. *Enrolments at schools and in funded pre-school education in Northern Ireland 2013/2014 (revised).* https://www.gov.uk/government/statistics/enrolments-at-schools-and-in-funded-pre-school-education-in-northern-ireland-2014-to-2015 (accessed 12 March 2018).

Matthews, Paul. 2016. *Statistical bulletin 3/2016: Annual enrolments at schools and in funded pre-school education in Northern Ireland, 2015–2016.* http://dera.ioe.ac.uk/25593/1/statistical-bulletin-annual-enrolments-at-schools-and-in-funded-pre-school-education-in-northern-ireland-2015-16-final.pdf (accessed 12 March 2018).

Maurais, Jacques. 2003. Towards a new global linguistic order? In Jacques Maurais & Michael A. Morris (eds.), *Languages in a globalising world*, 13–36. Cambridge: Cambridge University Press.

Mayberry, Rachel I. 1994. First-language acquisition after childhood differs from second language acquisition: The case of American Sign Language. *Journal of Speech and Hearing Research* 36 (6). 1258–1270.

Mayberry, Rachel I. & Robert Kluender. 2018. Rethinking the critical period for language: New insights into an old question from American Sign Language. *Bilingualism: Language and Cognition* 21 (5). 866–905.

Mazzon, Gabriela. 2009. *Interactive dialogue sequences in Middle English drama*. Amsterdam: John Benjamins.

McAreavey, Ruth. 2010. Transcending cultural differences: The role of language in social integration. *Translocations: Migration and Social Change* 6 (2). 596–601.

McCafferty, Kevin. 1998. Barriers to change: Ethnic division and phonological innovation in Northern Hiberno-English. *English World-Wide* 19 (1). 7–32.

McCafferty, Kevin. 1999. (London)Derry: Class, ethnicity and change. In Paul Foulkes & Gerard J. Docherty (eds.), *Urban voices: Accent studies in the British Isles,* 246–264. London: Arnold.

McCafferty, Kevin. 2001. *Ethnicity and language change: English in (London)Derry, Northern Ireland*. Amsterdam: John Benjamins.

McCafferty, Kevin. 2006. Be after V-ing on the past grammaticalisation path: How far is it after coming? In Hildegard L. C. Tristram (ed.), *The Celtic Englishes IV*, 130–151. Potsdam: Universitätsverlag.

McCafferty, Kevin. 2007. Northern Irish English. In David Britain (ed.), *Language in the British Isles,* 122–134. Cambridge: Cambridge University Press.

McCafferty, Kevin & Carolina P. Amador-Moreno. 2012a. CORIECOR: A corpus of Irish English correspondence. Compiling and using a diachronic corpus to study the evolution of Irish English. In Bettina Migge & Máire Ní Chiosáin (eds.), *New perspectives on Irish English*, 265–287. Amsterdam: John Benjamins.

McCafferty, Kevin & Carolina P. Amador-Moreno. 2012b. 'I will be expecting a letter from you before this reaches you': Studying the evolution of a new dialect using a corpus of Irish English correspondence (CORIECOR). In Marina Dossena & Gabriella Del Lungo Camiciotti (eds.), *Letter writing in late modern Europe*, 179–204. Amsterdam: John Benjamins.

McCarthy, Daniel P. 2004. The original compilation of the annals of Ulster. *Studia Celtica* XXXVIII. 69–95.

McCavitt, John. 2005. *The flight of the Earls*. Dublin: Gill & Macmillan.

McColl Millar, R. 2007. *Northern and insular Scots*. Edinburgh: Edinburgh University Press.

McCone, Kim R. 1985. The Würzburg and Milan glosses: Our earliest sources of middle Irish. *Ériu* 36 (1). 85–106.

McCoy, Gordon. 1997. Protestant learners of Irish in Northern Ireland. In Aodán Mac Póilin (ed.), *The Irish language in Northern Ireland*, 131–169. Belfast: The Ultach Trust.

McCoy, Gordon. 2001. From cause to quango?: The peace process and the transformation of the Irish language movement. In John M. Kirk & Dónall P. Ó Baoill (eds.), *Linguistic politics: Language policies for Northern Ireland, the Republic of Ireland and Scotland*, 205–218. Belfast: Queen's University Belfast.

McCloskey, James. 1985. The modern Irish double relative and syntactic binding. *Ériu* 36. 45–84.

McCloskey, James. 1990. Resumptive pronouns, A-bar binding and levels of representation in Irish. In Randall A. Hendrick (ed.), *The syntax of the modern Celtic languages*, 199–248. San Diego: Academic Press.

McCloskey, James. 1996. On the scope of verb movement in Irish. *Natural Language and Linguistic Theory* 14 (1). 47–104.

McCloskey, James. 2001. The morphosyntax of WH-extraction in Irish. *Journal of Linguistics* 37 (1). 67–100.

McCloskey, James. 2002. Resumption, successive cyclicity and the locality of operations. In Samuel David Epstein & T. Daniel Seeley (eds.), *Derivation and explanation in the minimalist program*, 184–226. Oxford: Blackwell.

McCloskey, James. 2017. Resumption. In Martin Everaert & Henk van Riemsdijk (eds.), *The Wiley-Blackwell companion to syntax* (2nd edn.), 94–117. Oxford: Blackwell.

McCutcheon, William Alan. 1965. *The canals of the north of Ireland*. London: David & Charles.

McCutcheon, William Alan. 1984. *The industrial archaeology of Northern Ireland*. Rutherford, New Jersey: Fairleigh Dickinson University Press.

McElhinney, Dympna. 2009. *Filipino nurses in Altnagelvin area hospital: A pilot case-study*. https://www.community-relations.org.uk/sites/crc/files/media-files/Filipino%20Nurses%20in%20Altnagelvin%20Area%20Hospital.pdf (accessed 19 July 2019).

McDermott, Philip. 2008. Towards linguistic diversity? Community languages in Northern Ireland. *Shared Space: A Research Journal on Peace, Conflict and Community Relations in Northern Ireland* 5 (1). 5–20.

McDermott, Philip. 2011. *Migrant languages in the public space: A case study from Northern Ireland*. Münster: Lit Verlag.

McDermott, Philip. 2012. Cohesion, sharing and integration? Migrant languages and cultural spaces in Northern Ireland's urban environment. *Current Issues in Language Planning* 13 (3). 187–205.

McDermott, Philip. 2018. From ridicule to legitimacy? 'Contested languages' and devolved language planning. *Current Issues in Language Planning Online*, 121–139. https://doi.org/10.1080/14664208.2018.1468961 (accessed 23 August 2019).

McIntosh, Angus M. & Michael L. Samuels. 1968. Prolegomena to a study of medieval Anglo-Irish. *Medium Aevum* 37 (1). 1–11.

McKay, Patrick. 1999. *A dictionary of Ulster place-names* (1st edn.). Belfast: Cló Ollscoil na Banríona.

McKay, Patrick. 2007. *A dictionary of Ulster place-names* (2nd edn.). Belfast: Cló Ollscoil na Banríona.

McKendry, Eugene. 2017. Irish and Polish in a new context of diversity in Northern Ireland's schools. *Studia Celtica Posnaniensia* 2 (1). 143–161.

McKenna, Patrick. 1992. Irish migration to Argentina. In Patrick O'Sullivan (ed.), *The Irish world wide: History, heritage, identity – Vol. 1: Patterns of migration*, 63–82. Leicester: Leicester University Press.

McKittrick, David & David McVea. 2000/2012. *Making sense of the Troubles: The story of conflict in Northern Ireland*. London: Penguin.

McLaughlin, Jim. 1994. *Ireland: The emigrant nursery and the world economy*. Cork: Cork University Press.

McMonagle, Sarah. 2010. Deliberating the Irish language in Northern Ireland: From conflict to multiculturalism? *Journal of Multilingual and Multicultural Development* 31 (3). 253–270.

McMonagle, Sarah & Phillip McDermott. 2014. Transitional politics and language rights in a multi-ethnic Northern Ireland: Towards a true linguistic pluralism? *Ethnopolitics* 13 (3). 45–266.

McNulty, Margaret. 2014. *Embracing diversity: Information update, 2014*. https://www.embraceni.org/wp-content/uploads/2012/09/2014-Information-Update-FINAL.pdf (accessed 7 March 2018).

McNulty, Margaret. 2017. *Refugees in Northern Ireland: Some basic facts*. https://www.embraceni.org/wp-content/uploads/2012/09/Refugee-booklet-January-2017-F.pdf (accessed 7 March 2018).

McVeigh, Robbie. 2002. *A place of refuge? Asylum seekers and refugees in Northern Ireland: A needs assessment*. Belfast: Refugee Action Group.

Mechler, Johanna & Isabelle Buchstaller. 2019. [In]stability in the use of a stable variable. *Linguistics Vanguard* 5 (2). https://doi.org/10.1515/lingvan-2018-0024 (accessed 10 June 2020).

Mede, Enisa. 2011. The acquisition of word order (verb placement) in an adult Serbo-Croatian-Turkish bilingual. *Procedia Behavioral and Brain Sciences* 15 (1). 134–137.

Meehan, Teresa. 1991. It's like 'what's happening in the evolution of like'?: A theory of grammaticalization. *Kansas Working Papers in Linguistics* 16. 37–51.

Mehmedbegovic, Dina & Thomas H. Bak. 2017. Towards an interdisciplinary lifetime approach to multilingualism: From implicit assumptions to current evidence. *European Journal of Language Policy* 9 (2). 149–167.

Meinhof, Ulrike Hanna (ed.). 2002. *Living with borders: Identity discourses on East-West borders in Europe*. Aldershot: Ashgate.

Meisel, Jürgen M., Harald Clahsen & Manfred Pienemann. 1981. On determining developmental stages in natural second language acquisition. *Studies in Second Language Acquisition* 3 (2). 109–135.

Mendoza-Denton, Norma. 2008. *Homegirls: Language and cultural practice among Latina youth gangs*. Oxford: Wiley-Blackwell.

Mesthrie, Rajend. 1991. Syntactic variation in South African Indian English: The relative clause. In Jenny Cheshire (ed.), *English around the world: Sociolinguistic perspectives*, 462–473. Cambridge: Cambridge University Press.

Mesthrie, Rajend. 1992. *English in language shift*. Cambridge: Cambridge University Press.

Meyerhoff, Miriam. 2000. The emergence of creole subject-verb agreement and the licensing of null subjects. *Language Variation and Change* 12 (2). 203–230.

Meyerhoff, Miriam. 2003. Formal and cultural constraints on optional objects in Bislama. *Language Variation and Change* 14 (3). 323–346.

Meyerhoff, Miriam. 2009. Replication, transfer and calquing: Using variation as a tool in the study of language contact. *Language Variation and Change* 21 (3). 297–317.

Meyerhoff, Miriam. 2012. Uncovering hidden constraints in micro-corpora of contact Englishes. In Joybrato Mukerhjee & Magnus Huber (eds.), *Corpus linguistics and variation in English*, 109–130. Amsterdam: Rodopi.

Meyerhoff, Miriam & Naomi Nagy (eds.). 2008. *Social lives in language: Sociolinguistics and multilingual speech communities*. Amsterdam: John Benjamins.

Meyerhoff, Miriam & Erik Schleef. 2012. Variation, contact and social indexicality in the acquisition of (ing) by teenage migrants. *Journal of Sociolinguistics* 16 (3). 398–416.

Meyerhoff, Miriam & Erik Schleef. 2014. Hitting an Edinburgh target: Immigrant adolescents' acquisition of variation in Edinburgh English. In Robert Lawson (ed.), *Sociolinguistics in Scotland*, 103–128. Houndmills, Basingstoke: Palgrave Macmillan.

Migge, Bettina. 2012. Irish English and recent immigrants to Ireland. In Bettina Migge & Máire Ní Chiosáin (eds.), *New perspectives on Irish English*, 311–326. Amsterdam: John Benjamins.

Migge, Bettina. 2015. *Now* in the speech of newcomers to Ireland. In Carolina P. Amador-Moreno, Kevin McCafferty & Elaine Vaughan (eds.), *Pragmatic markers in Irish English*, 390–407. Amsterdam: John Benjamins.

Miller, David W. 1983. The Armagh troubles, 1784–1795. In Samuel Clark & James S. Donnelly (eds.), *Irish peasants: Violence & political unrest*, 155–191. Manchester: Manchester University Press.

Miller, David W. (ed.). 1990. *Peep o' day boys and defenders: Selected documents on the disturbances in County Armagh, 1784–1796*. Belfast: Public Record Office of Northern Ireland.

Miller, Jim. 1993. The grammar of Scottish English. In James Milroy & Lesley Milroy (eds.), *Real English: The grammar of English dialects in the British Isles*, 99–138. London: Longman.

Miller Jim. 2006. Spoken and written English. In Bas Aarts & April McMahon (eds.), *The handbook of English linguistics*, 670–691. Oxford: Blackwell.

Miller, Jim & Regina Weinert. 1995. The function of LIKE in dialogue. *Journal of Pragmatics* 23 (4). 365–393.

Miller, Kerby A. 1985. *Emigrants and exiles: Ireland and the Irish exodus to North America*. New York: Oxford University Press.

Miller, Thomas (ed.). 1890–1898. *The Old English version of Bede's ecclesiastical history of the British people*. London: Tübner.

Milroy, James. 1981. *Regional accents of English: Belfast*. Belfast: Blackstaff Press.

Milroy, James. 1992. *Linguistic variation and change: On the historical sociolinguistics of English*. Oxford: Blackwell.

Milroy, James & John Harris. 1980. When is a merger not a merger? The MEAT/MATE problem in a present-day English vernacular. *English World-Wide* 1 (1). 199–210.

Milroy, James & Lesley Milroy. 1977. Speech and context in an urban setting. *Belfast Working Papers in Language and Linguistics* 2. 1–85.

Milroy, James & Lesley Milroy. 1985. Linguistic change, social network and speaker innovation. *Journal of Linguistics* 21. 339–384.

Milroy, James & Lesley Milroy. 1992. Social network and social class: Towards an integrated sociolinguistic model. *Language in Society* 21. 1–26.

Milroy, James & Lesley Milroy. 1993. Mechanisms of change in urban dialects: The role of class, social network and gender. *International Journal of Applied Linguistics* 3. 57–77.

Milroy, James & Lesley Milroy. 1997. Network structure and linguistic change. In Nikolas Coupland & Adam Jaworski (eds.), *Sociolinguistics: A reader and coursebook*, 199–211. Houndmills, Basingstoke: Macmillan.

Milroy, Lesley. 1980. Social network and language maintenance. In Barbara Mayor & Anthony Kendrick Pugh (eds.), *Language, communication and education*, 70–81. Kent: The Open University.

Milroy, Lesley. 1987a. *Language and social networks*. Oxford: Basil Blackwell.

Milroy, Lesley. 1987b. *Observing and analysing natural language*. Oxford: Basil Blackwell.

Milroy, Lesley. 2007. Off the shelf or under the counter? On the social dynamics of sound changes. In Christopher M. Cain & Geoffrey Russom (eds.), *Studies in the history of the English language III: Managing chaos*, 149–172. Berlin & New York: Mouton de Gruyter.

Milroy, Lesley & Matthew Gordon. 2003. *Sociolinguistics: Method and interpretation*. Oxford: Blackwell.

Mitchell, Bruce. 1964. Syntax and word order in *The Peterborough Chronicle*, 1122–1154. *Neuphilologische Mitteilungen* 65. 113–144.

Mitchell, Bruce. 1985. *Old English syntax*, 2 Vols., Oxford: Clarendon.

Montague, Richard & Peter Shirlow. 2014. *Challenging racism: Ending hate*. http://democracyandpeace.org/wp-content/uploads/2015/12/Challenging_Racism_Ending_Hate.pdf (accessed 8 March 2018).

Montgomery, Michael B. & Robert J. Gregg. 1997. The Scots language in Ulster. In Charles Jones (ed.), *The Edinburgh history of the Scots language*, 569–622. Edinburgh: Edinburgh University Press.

Montgomery, Michael B. 2006. Aspects of the morphology and syntax of Ulster-Scots. In Anne Smyth, Michael Montgomery & Philip Robinson (eds.), *The academic study of Ulster-Scots: Essays for and by Robert J. Gregg*, 75–86. Belfast: National Museums and Galleries of Northern Ireland, Ulster Folk and Transport Museum.

Montgomery, Michael B. 2017. *From Ulster to America: The Scotch-Irish heritage of American English*. Belfast: Ullans Press.

Montrul, Silvina. 2009. Incomplete acquisition of tense-aspect and mood in Spanish heritage speakers. *The International Journal of Bilingualism* 13 (3). 239–269.

Moriarty, Mairéad. 2015. *Globalizing language policy and planning: An Irish language perspective*. Basingstoke: Palgrave Macmillan.

Morley, Vincent. 2009. Catholic disaffection and the oath of allegiance of 1774. In James Kelly, John McCafferty & Charles Ivar McGrath (eds.), *People, politics and power: Essays on Irish history, 1660–1850, in Honour of James I. McGuire*, 122–143. Dublin: University College Dublin Press.

Morley, Vincent. 2016. The Irish language. In Richard Bourke & Ian McBride (eds.), *The Princeton history of modern Ireland*, 320–342. Oxford & Princeton: Princeton University Press.

Morris, Robert J. 2013. Urban Ulster since 1600. In Liam Kennedy & Phillip Ollerenshaw (eds.), *Ulster since 1600: Politics, economy and society*, 121–139. Oxford: Oxford University Press.

Mougeon, Raymond & Katherine Rehner. 2001. Acquisition of sociolinguistic variants by French immersion students: The case of restrictive expressions, and more. *The Modern Language Journal* 85 (3). 398–415.

Mougeon, Raymond, Katherine Rehner & Terry Nadasdi. 2004. The learning of spoken French variation by immersion students from Toronto, Canada. *Journal of Sociolinguistics* 8 (3). 408–432.

Mougeon, Raymond, Terry Nadasdi & Katherine Rehner. 2010. *The sociolinguistic competence of immersion students*. Bristol: Multilingual Matters.

Mufwene, Salikoko. 2001. *The ecology of language evolution*. Cambridge: Cambridge University Press.

Müller, Simone 2005. *Discourse markers in native and non-native English discourse*. Amsterdam: John Benjamins.

Murelli, Adriano. 2011. *Relative constructions in European non-standard varieties*. Berlin & New York: Mouton de Gruyter.

Murphy, Angela F. 2010. *American slavery, Irish freedom: Abolition, immigrant citizenship, and the Transatlantic movement for Irish repeal*. Baton Rouge: Louisiana State University Press.

Murray, Edmundo. 2006. *Becoming Irlandés: Private narratives of the Irish emigration to Argentina (1844–1912)*. Buenos Aires: Literature of Latin America.

Murray, L. P., Reverend. 1934. The history of the parish of Creggan in the seventeenth and eighteenth centuries. *Louth Archaeological Society Journal* 8 (1). 117–129.

Mustanoja, Tauno F. 1960. *A Middle English syntax, part I: Parts of speech*. Helsinki: Mémoires de la Société Néophilologique, 23.

Muysken, Pieter. 2000. *Bilingual speech: A typology of codemixing*. Cambridge: Cambridge University Press.

Myers-Scotton, Carol. 1997. *Duelling languages: Grammatical structure in codeswitching*. Oxford: Clarendon Press.

Myers-Scotton, Carol. 2009. Codeswitching. In Nikolas Coupland & Adam Jaworski (eds.), *The new sociolinguistics reader*, 473–448. New York: St. Martin's Press & Palgrave Macmillan.

Nagucka, Ruta. 1980. Grammatical peculiarities of the contact clause in Early Modern English. *Folia Linguistica Historica* 1. 171–184.

Nagy, Naomi & Alexei Kochetov. 2013. Voice onset time across the generations: A cross-linguistic study of contact-induced change. In Pieter Siemund, Ingrid Gogolin, Minka Edith Schulz & Julia Davydova (eds.), *Multilingualism and language contact in urban areas: Acquisition, identities, space, education*, 19–38. Amsterdam: John Benjamins.

Nagy, Naomi & Miriam Meyerhoff. 2015. Extending ELAN into variationist sociolinguistics. *Linguistics Vanguard* 1 (1). 271–281.

Nardy, Aurélie, Jean-Pierre Chevrot & Stéphanie Barbu. 2013. The acquisition of sociolinguistic variation: Looking back and thinking ahead. *Linguistics* 51 (2). 255–284.

Neal, Frank. 1988. *Sectarian violence: The Liverpool experience, 1819–1894*. Manchester: Manchester University Press.

Neal, Frank. 1997. Black '47: Britain and the famine Irish. In Brendan Ó Conaire (ed.), *The Famine Lectures*, 329–356. Roscommon: Herald Boyle.

Neal, Frank. 1998. *Black '47: Britain and the famine Irish*. Basingstoke: Palgrave Macmillan.

Neal, Frank. 1999. The foundations of Irish settlement in Newcastle-upon-Tyne: The evidence in the 1851 Census. *Immigrants and Minorities* 18 (2.3). 71–93.

Neary-Sundquist, Colleen. 2014. The use of pragmatic markers across proficiency levels in second language speech. *Second Language Learning and Teaching* 4 (4). 637–663.

Neilson, William. 1990 [1908]. *An introduction to the Irish language in three parts* (2nd edn.). Belfast: Ultach Trust.

Nestor, Niamh. 2013. The positional distribution of discourse *like*: A case study of young Poles in Ireland. In David Singleton, Vera Regan & Ewelina Debaene (eds.), *Linguistic and cultural acquisition in a migrant community*, 49–74. Bristol: Multilingual Matters.

Nestor, Niamh, Caitríona Ní Chasaide & Vera Regan. 2012. Discourse *like* and social identity: A case study of Poles in Ireland. In Bettina Migge & Máire Ní Chiosáin (eds.), *New perspectives on Irish English*, 327–353. Amsterdam: John Benjamins.

Nestor, Niamh & Vera Regan. 2011. The new kid on the block: A case study of young Poles, language and identity. In Merike Darmody, Naomi Tyrrell & Steve Song (eds.), *The changing faces of Ireland*, 35–52. Rotterdam: Sense Publishers.

Neve, de Geert. 2005. *The everyday politics of labour*. Delhi: Social Science Press.

Nevalainen, Terttu & Helena Raumolin-Brunberg. 2002. The rise of relative *who* in Early Modern English. In Patricia Poussa (ed.), *Relativisation on the North Sea Littoral*, 109–121. Munich: Lincom Europa.

Nevalainen, Terttu & Helena Raumolin-Brunberg. 2003. *Historical sociolinguistics*. Amsterdam: John Benjamins.

Newbrook, Mark. 1999. West Wirral: Norms, self-reports and usage. In Paul Foulkes & Gerard J. Docherty (eds.), *Urban voices: Accent studies in the British Isles*, 90–106. London: Arnold.

Newlin-Łuckowicz, Luiza. 2013. TH-stopping in New York City: Substrate effect turned ethnic marker? *University of Pennsylvania Working Papers in Linguistics* 19 (1). 151–160.

Newlin-Łuckowicz, Luiza. 2014. From interference to transfer in language contact: Variation in voice onset time. *Language Variation and Change* 26 (1). 359–385.

Newmeyer, Frederick J. 2003. 'Basic word order' in formal and functional linguistics and the typological status of 'canonical' sentence types. In Dominique Willems, Bart Defrancq, Timothy Colleman & Dirk Noël (eds.), *Contrastive analysis in language: Identifying linguistic units of comparison*, 69–88. London: Palgrave Macmillan.

Ní Bhaoill, Róise. 2010. *Ulster Gaelic voices: Bailiúchan Doegen 1931*. Belfast: Iontaobhas Ultach & Ultach Trust.

Ní Chiosáin, Máire. 1999. Syllables and phonotactics in Irish. In Harry van der Hulst & Nancy Ritter (eds.), *The syllable: Views and facts*, 551–576. Berlin & New York: Mouton de Gruyter.

NicCraith, Mairéad. 2001. Politicised linguistic consciousness: The case of Ulster-Scots. *Nations and Nationalism* 7 (1). 21–37.

NISRA. 2005. *Report of the inter-departmental urban-rural definition group: Statistical classification and delineation of settlements.* Belfast: NISRA.

NISRA 2008. *Population and migration estimates Northern Ireland 2007 – Statistical Report.* http://ubdc.gla.ac.uk/dataset/northern-ireland-small-area-population-estimates-census-2001-basis (accessed 28 April 2018).

NISRA. 2011. *Top 5 countries of birth (excl. UK and ROI) as share of local residents born outside UK and ROI: Northern Ireland 2011.* https://public.tableau.com/profile/migobs#!/vizhome/NorthernIreland/COBdistributionD (accessed 6 March 2018).

NISRA. 2012. *Statistics bulletin: Census 2011: Key statistics for Northern Ireland.* https://www.nisra.gov.uk/sites/nisra.gov.uk/files/publications/2011-census-results-key-statistics-northern-ireland-report-11-december-2012.pdf (accessed 7 March 2018).

NISRA. 2013a. *Census of population, 2011: Table QS208NIa.* http://www.ninis2.nisra.gov.uk/Download/Census%202011/QS208NI%20(a).ods (accessed 9 March 2018).

NISRA. 2013b. *Statistics bulletin: Census 2011: Detailed characteristics for Northern Ireland on ethnicity, country of birth and language.* https://www.nisra.gov.uk/sites/nisra.gov.uk/files/publications/2011-census-results-detailed-characteristics-statistics-bulletin-28-june-2013.pdf (accessed 21 March 2018).

NISRA. 2016a. *Long-term international migration (2015): Administrative data relating to Northern Ireland, 15 December 2016.* https://www.nisra.gov.uk/sites/nisra.gov.uk/files/publications/Mig1415-Stock.xls (accessed 8 March 2018).

NISRA. 2016b. *Migration 1871–2016.* https://www.nisra.gov.uk/sites/nisra.gov.uk/files/publications/Migration-1871-2016.XLS (accessed 17 May 2018).

NISRA 2016c. *Medical card registrations from non-UK Nationals.* https://www.nisra.gov.uk/sites/nisra.gov.uk/files/publications/Mig1415-Table2.xls (accessed 15 March 218).

NISRA. 2017. *Long-term international migration statistics for Northern Ireland (2016).* https://www.nisra.gov.uk/news/2016-mid-year-population-estimates-northern-ireland (accessed 3 July 2019).

NISRA. 2019. *Mid-year population estimates for Northern Ireland: Statistical bulletin.* https://www.nisra.gov.uk/sites/nisra.gov.uk/files/publications/MYE18-Bulletin.pdf (accessed 3 July 2019).

Nolan, Bobbie. 2014. *Inimircigh agus an Ghaeilge: The Irish language and identity in Ireland's North American and British diasporas, 1850–90.* Edinburgh: University of Edinburgh MSc thesis.

Nolan, Bobbie. In preparation. *Language and identity among Irish migrants in San Francisco, Philadelphia and London, 1850–1920.* Edinburgh: University of Edinburgh dissertation.

Norton, Bonny & Carolyn McKinney. 2011. An identity approach to second language acquisition. In Dwight Atkinson (ed.), *Alternative approaches to second language acquisition*, 73–94. New York: Routledge.

Oberman, Lindsay & Alvaro Pascual-Leone. 2013. Changes in plasticity across the lifespan: Cause of disease and target for intervention. *Progress in Brain Research* 207. 91–120.

Odlin, Terence. 1989. *Language transfer: Cross-linguistic influence in language learning.* Cambridge: Cambridge University Press.

Odlin, Terence (ed.). 1994. *Perspectives on pedagogical grammar.* Cambridge: Cambridge University Press.

Oetting, Janna B. & Brandi L. Newkirk. 2011. Children's relative clause markers in two non-mainstream dialects of English. *Clinical Linguistics and Phonetics* 25 (8). 725–740.

Ogura, Michiko. 1981. *The syntactic and semantic rivalry of QUOTH, SAY and TELL in Medieval English*. Osaka: Kansai University of Foreign Studies.
Ogura, Michiko. 1986. Old English verbs of thinking. *Neuphilologische Mitteilungen* 87 (3). 325–341.
Ogura, Michiko. 1996. *Verbs in Medieval English*. Berlin & New York: Mouton de Gruyter.
Ogura, Michiko. 2016. Some peculiar forms of Old English verbs. *Studia Anglica Posnaniensia* 51 (2). 31–43.
Ohlmeyer, Jane H. 2006. A laboratory for empire: Early modern Ireland and English imperialism. In Kevin Kenny (ed.), *Ireland and the British Empire*, 26–60. Oxford: Oxford University Press.
Ohlmeyer, Jane H. 2016. Conquest, civilization, colonization: Ireland, 1540–1660. In Richard Bourke & Ian McBride (eds.), *The Princeton history of modern Ireland*, 21–47. Oxford & Princeton: Princeton University Press.
Okólski, Marek & John Salt. 2014. Polish emigration to the UK after 2004: Why did so many come? *Central and Eastern European Migration Review* 3 (2). 11–37.
Omoniyi, Tope. 2004. *The sociolinguistics of borderlands: Two nations, one community*. Asmara, Eritrea: Africa World Press.
Otheguy, Ricardo, Ana Celia Zentella & David Livert. 2007. Language and dialect contact in Spanish in New York: Toward the formation of a speech community. *Language* 83 (4). 770–802.
Otway-Ruthven, Annette Jocelyn. 1968. *History of medieval Ireland*. London: Ernest Benn Ltd.
Ouakrime, Mohamed. 2001. Promoting the maintenance of endangered languages through the Internet: The case of Tamazight. In Chris Moseley, Nicholas Ostler & Hassan Ouzzate (eds.), *Endangered languages and the media: Proceedings of the Fifth FEL Conference (Agadir, Morocco, 20–23 September 2001)*, 61–67. Bath, United Kingdom: Foundation for Endangered Languages.
Oyama, Susan. 1976. A sensitive period for the acquisition of a non-native phonological system. *Journal of Psycholinguistic Research* 5 (3). 261–283.
Ozeki, Hiromi & Yasuhiro Shirai. 2007. Does the noun phrase accessibility hierarchy predict the difficulty order in the acquisition of Japanese relative clauses? *Studies in Second Language Acquisition* 29 (2). 169–196.
Ó Baoill, Dónall P. 1991. Contact phenomena in the phonology of Irish and English in Ireland. In P. Sture Ureland & George Broderick (eds.), *Language contact in the British Isles*, 581–595. Tübingen: Max Niemeyer.
Ó Corráin, Ailbhe. 2006. On the 'after perfect' in Irish and Hiberno-English. In Hildegard L. C. Tristram (ed.), *The Celtic Englishes II*, 153–173. Heidelberg: Carl Winter.
Ó Cróinín, Dáibhí. 2005. Hiberno-Latin literature to 1169. In Dáibhí Ó Cróinín (ed.), *A new history of Ireland – Vol. I: Prehistoric and early Ireland*, 371–403. Oxford: Oxford University Press.
Ó Cuív, Brian. 1991. The Irish language in the early modern period. In Theodore William Moody, Francis Xavier Martin & Francis John Byrne (eds.), *A new history of Ireland – Vol. III: Early modern Ireland, 1534–1691*, 509–542. Oxford: Oxford University Press.
Ó Dochartaigh, Cathair. 1987. *Dialects of Ulster Irish*. Belfast: Institute of Irish Studies, Queen's University Belfast.
Ó Dochartaigh, Niall. 2016. Northern Ireland since 1920. In Richard Bourke & Ian McBride (eds.), *The Princeton history of modern Ireland*, 141–167. Oxford & Princeton: Princeton University Press.
O'Donaghue, Tom A. 2000. *Bilingual education in Ireland, 1904–1922*. Perth: Centre for Irish Studies, Murdoch University.

Ó Duibhín, C. 2007. *Irish in County Down Since 1750* (2nd edn.). Downpatrick: Cumann Gaelach Leath Chathail.
Ó Gráda, Cormac. 2000. *Black '47 and beyond: The great Irish famine in history, economy, and memory*. Princeton: Princeton University Press.
O'Hearn, Denis. 2000. Peace dividend, foreign investment, and economic regeneration: The Northern Irish case. *Social Problems* 47 (2). 180–200.
O'Kelly, M. J. 2005a. Ireland before 3000 B.C. In Dáibhi Ó Cróinín (ed.), *A new history of Ireland – Vol. I: Prehistoric and early Ireland*, 49–68. Oxford: Oxford University Press.
O'Kelly, M. J. 2005b. Neolithic Ireland. In Dáibhi Ó Cróinín (ed.), *A new history of Ireland – Vol. I: Prehistoric and early Ireland*, 69–97. Oxford: Oxford University Press.
Ó Mainnín, Mícheál. 1992. *Place-names of Northern Ireland: County Down: Volume 3*. Belfast: The Institute of Irish Studies, Queen's University Belfast.
Ó Murchadha, Noel P., Michael Hornsby, Cassie Smith-Christmas & Máiréad Moriarty. 2018. New speakers: Familiar concepts. In Cassie Smith-Christmas, Noel P. Ó Murchadha, Michael Hornsby & Máiréad Moriarty (eds.), *New speakers of minority languages: Linguistic ideologies and practices*, 1–22. Basingstoke: Palgrave Macmillan.
O'Neill, Dervilla M. 1987. *Ethnolinguistic differences within a Northern Irish community*. Dublin: Trinity College Dublin MPhil dissertation.
O'Neill, T. E. 1980. *Anglo-Norman Ulster: The history & archaeology of an Irish barony 1177–1400*. Edinburgh: John Donald.
O'Reilly, Camille C. 1999. *The Irish language in Northern Ireland*. Basingstoke: Macmillan.
O'Reilly, Karen. 2015. Migration theories: A critical overview. In Anna Triandafyllidou (ed.), *Routledge handbook of immigration and refugee studies*, 25–33. London: Routledge.
Ó Riagáin, Donall. 2003. *Language and law in Northern Ireland*, Belfast: Cló Ollscoil na Banríona.
Ó Riagáin, Pádraig. 1997. *Language policy and social reproduction: Ireland 1893–1993*. Oxford: Oxford University Press.
Ó Sé, Diarmuid. 2004. The 'after' perfect and related constructions in Gaelic dialects. *Ériu* 54. 179–248.
Ó Searcaigh, Seamus. 1925. *Foghraidheacht Ghaedhilge an Tuaiscirt*. Belfast: Brown & Nolan.
Ó Siadhail, Mícheál. 1984. *Agus/(is)/and*: A shared syntactic feature. *Celtica* 16 (1). 125–137.
Ó Siadhail, Mícheál. 1989. *Modern Irish: Grammatical structure and dialectal variation*. Cambridge: Cambridge University Press.
Ó Snodaigh, Padraig. 1995. *Hidden Ulster: The other hidden Ireland* (revised edn.). Belfast: Lagan Press.
O'Sullivan, Tony, Gillian Young, Kenneth Gibb & Patrice Reilly. 2014. *Migrant workers and the housing market: A report to the Northern Ireland housing executive*. https://www.nihe.gov.uk/getmedia/47957b8e-cd67-4332-a243-991c7d9dbacc/Final-Migrant-Workers-Report-Jan-2015.pdf.aspx?ext=.pdf (accessed 8 March 2018).
Palander-Colin, Minna. 1998. Grammaticalization of I THINK and METHINKS in Late Middle and Early Modern English. *Neuphilologische Mitteilungen*. 99 (4). 419–442.
Palmer, Patricia. 2001. *Language and conquest in early Modern Ireland: English renaissance literature and Elizabethan imperial expansion*. Cambridge: Cambridge University Press.
Paradis, Michel. 2004. *A neurolinguistic theory of bilingualism*. Amsterdam: John Benjamins.
Pargas, Damian Alan. 2014. *Slavery and forced migration in the Antebellum South*. Cambridge: Cambridge University Press.
Parkinson, Alan F. & Éamon Phoenix (eds.). 2010. *Conflicts in the north of Ireland, 1900–2000: Flashpoints and fracture zones*. Dublin: Four Courts Press.

Patkowski, Mark S. 1980. The sensitive period for the acquisition of syntax in a second language. *Language Learning* 30 (2). 449–468.
Paul, Anju Mary. 2011. Stepwise international migration: A multistage migration pattern for the aspiring migrant. *American Journal of Sociology* 116 (6): 1842–1886.
Paul, Anju Mary. 2017. *Multinational maids*. Cambridge: Cambridge University Press.
Pauwels. Anna. 2016. *Language maintenance and shift*. Cambridge: Cambridge University Press.
Peeters-Podgaevskaja, Alla V., Bibi E. Janssen & Anne E. Baker. 2018. The acquisition of relative clauses in Russian and Polish in monolingual and bilingual children. *Linguistic Approaches to Bilingualism* 10 (2): 216–248.
Penfield, Wilder & Lamar Roberts. 1959. *Speech and brain mechanisms*. Princeton, NJ: Princeton University Press.
Pennycook, Alastair & Emi Otsuji. 2015. *Metrolingualism: Language in the city*. Abingdon: Routledge.
Perry, Caroline. 2016. *Academic selection: A brief overview*. http://www.niassembly.gov.uk/globalassets/documents/raise/publications/2016-2021/2016/education/4816.pdf (accessed 25 July 2019).
Phoocharoensil, Supakorn & Nirada Simargool. 2010. English relativization and learners' problems. *Pan-Pacific Association of Applied Linguistics* 14 (1). 109–129.
Pienemann, Manfred. 1989. Is Language Teachable? Psycholinguistic Experiments and Hypotheses. *Applied Linguistics* 10 (1). 52–79.
Pietka, Emilia, Colin Clark & Noah Canton. 2013. 'I know that I have a university diploma and I'm working as a driver': Explaining the EU post-enlargement movement of highly skilled Polish migrant workers to Glasgow. In Birgit Glorius, Izabela Grabowska-Lusinska & Aimee Kuvik (eds.), *Mobility in transition: Migration patterns after EU enlargement*, 133–154. Amsterdam: IMISCOE Research, Amsterdam University Press.
Piller, Ingrid. 2002. Passing for a native speaker: Identity and success in second language learning. *Journal of Sociolinguistics* 6 (2). 179–208.
Pingali, Sailaja. 2009. *Indian English*. Edinburgh: Edinburgh University Press.
Pintzuk, Susan. 1993. Verb-seconding in Old English: Verb movement to Infl. *The Linguistic Review* 10. 5–35.
Pintzuk, Susan. 1996. Old English verb-complement word order and the change from OV to VO. *York Papers in Linguistics* 17. 241–264.
Pitts, Ann H. 1982. *Urban influence in Northern Irish English: A comparison of variation in two communities*. Michigan: University of Michigan dissertation.
Pitts, Ann H. 1985. Urban influence on phonological variation in a northern Irish speech community. *English World-Wide* 6. 59–85.
Pitts, Ann H. 1986. Differing prestige values for the (ky) variable in Lurgan. In John Harris, David Little & David Singleton (eds.), *Perspectives on the English language in Ireland*, 209–221. Dublin: CLCS/TCD.
Policansky, Linda. 1976. Syntactic variation in Belfast English. *Belfast Working Papers in Language and Linguistics* 5. 217–231.
Policansky, Linda. 1982. Grammatical variation in Belfast English. *Belfast Working Papers in Language and Linguistics* 6 (1). 37–66.
Poplack, Shana. 1980. 'Sometimes I'll start a sentence in Spanish y termino en Español': Toward a typology of code-switching. *Linguistics* 18 (7–8). 581–618.
Poplack, Shana. 1989. The care and handling of a mega-corpus: The Ottawa-Hull French project. In Ralph W. Fasold & Deborah Schiffrin (eds.), *Language change and variation*, 411–451. Amsterdam: John Benjamins.

Poplack, Shana, Lauren Zentz & Nathalie Dion. 2012. What counts as (contact-induced) change. *Bilingualism: Language and Cognition* 15 (2). 247–254.
Poplack, Shana & Stephen Levey. 2010. Contact-induced grammatical change: A cautionary tale. In Peter Auer & Jürgen Erich Schmidt (eds.), *Language and space*, 391–419. Berlin & New York: Mouton de Gruyter.
Potter, Michael. 2014. *Refugees and asylum seekers in Northern Ireland: NIAR 348-14*. http://www.niassembly.gov.uk/globalassets/Documents/RaISe/Publications/2014/ofmdfm/6314.pdf (accessed 6 March 2019).
Potter, Michael & Jennifer Hamilton. 2014. Picking on vulnerable migrants: Precarity and the mushroom industry in Northern Ireland. *Work, Employment and Society* 28 (3). 390–406.
Poussa, Patricia. 1988. The relative WHAT: two kinds of evidence. In Jacek Fisiak (ed.), *Dialectology. Regional and social*, 443–474. Berlin & New York: Mouton de Gruyter.
Poussa, Patricia (ed.). 2002. *Relativisation on the North Sea Littoral*. Munich: Lincom Europa.
Preston, Dennis R. 1989. *Sociolinguistics and second language acquisition*. Oxford: Basil Blackwell.
Pulvermüller, Friedemann. 2003. Sequence detectors as a basis of grammar in the brain. *Theory of Biosciences* 122 (1). 87–103.
Pulvermüller, Friedemann & John H. Schumann. 1994. Neurobiological mechanisms of language acquisition. *Language Learning* 44. 681–734.
Py, Bernard. 1986. Native language attrition amongst migrant workers: Towards extension of the concept of interlanguage. In Eric E. Kellerman & Michael Sharwood Smith (eds.), *Crosslinguistic influence in second language acquisition*, 163–172. New York: Pergamon Institute of English.
Quinn, Sally V. & Julian A. Oldmeadow. 2012. Is the i-generation a 'we' generation? Social networking use and belonging in 9- to 13- year olds. *British Journal of Developmental Psychology* 31 (1). 136–142.
Quirk, Joel & Darshan Vigneswaran. 2012. *Slavery, migration and contemporary bondage in Africa*. Trenton, NJ: Africa World Press.
Quirk, Randolph, Sidney Greenbaum, Geoffrey Leech & Jan Svartvik (eds.). 1985. *A grammar of contemporary English*. London: Longman.
Raftery, Barry. 2005. Iron-age Ireland. In Dáibhí Ó Cróinín (ed.), *A new history of Ireland – Vol. I: Prehistoric and early Ireland*, 134–180. Oxford: Oxford University Press.
Ramat Paolo & Elisa Roma (eds.). 2007. *Europe and the Mediterranean as linguistic areas: Convergences from a historical and typological perspective*. Amsterdam: John Benjamins.
Ramonienė, Meilutė & Joana Pribušauskaitė. 2008. *Practical grammar of Lithuanian*. Vilnius, Lithuania: Baltu lanku leidyba.
Rampton, Ben. 1995. Crossing: Language and ethnicity among adolescents. London: Longman.
Rampton, Ben. 1999a. Styling the other: Introduction. *Journal of Sociolinguistics* 3 (1). 421–427.
Rampton, Ben. 1999b. Deutsch in inner London and the animation of instructed language. *Journal of Sociolinguistics* 3 (1). 480–504.
Rampton, Ben. 2001. Crossing. In Alessandro Duranti (ed.), *Key terms in language and culture*, 49–51. Oxford: Blackwell.
Rampton, Ben. 2005. *Language and ethnicity among adolescents*. Manchester: St. Jerome.
Rampton, Ben. 2006. Language and ethnicity at school: Some implications from theoretical developments in sociolinguistics. *Language in Society* 116 (2). 51–71.
Rampton, Ben. 2013. Styling in a language learned later in life. *Modern Language Journal* 97 (2). 360–382.

Rampton, Ben. 2016. Styling and identity in a second language. In Siân Preece (ed.), *The Routledge handbook of language and identity*, 458–475. London: Taylor and Francis.
Rampton, Ben. 2018. Stylisation and the dynamics of migration, ethnicity and class. In Natalie Braber & Sandra Jansen (eds.), *Sociolinguistics in England*, 97–125. Houndmills, Basingstoke: Palgrave Macmillan.
Rankin, Kathleen. 2002. *Linen houses of the Lagan Valley and their families*. Belfast: Ulster Historical Society.
Rastelli, Stefano. 2014. *Discontinuity in second language acquisition: The switch between statistical and grammatical learning*. Bristol: Multilingual Matters.
Rastelli, Stefano. 2018. Neurolinguistics and second language teaching: A view from the crossroads. *Second Language Research* 34 (1). 103 –123.
Ravenstein, Ernest G. 1885. The laws of migration. *Journal of the Royal Statistical Society* 48 (2). 167–235.
Ravenstein, Ernest G. 1889. The laws of migration. *Journal of the Royal Statistical Society* 52 (2). 214–305.
Reeves-Smyth, Terence. 1997. Demesnes. In F. H. A. Aalen, Kevin Whelan & Matthew Stout (eds.), *Atlas of the Irish rural Landscape*, 197–205. Toronto: University of Toronto Press.
Refugee Action Group. 2007. *Forced to flee: Frequently asked questions about asylum seekers and refugees in Northern Ireland* (3rd edn.). http://www.mcrc-ni.org/publications.html (accessed 6 March 2018).
Regan, Vera. 1996. Variation in French interlanguage: A longitudinal study of sociolinguistic competence. In Robert Bayley & Dennis R. Preston (eds.), *Second language acquisition and linguistic variation*, 177–202. Amsterdam: John Benjamins.
Regan, Vera. 2004. The relationship between the group and the individual and the acquisition of native speaker variation patterns: A preliminary study. *International Review of Applied Linguistics in Language Teaching* 42 (4). 335–348.
Regan, Vera. 2005. From speech community back to classroom: What variation analysis can tell us about the role of context in the acquisition of French as a foreign language. In Jean-Marc Dewaele (ed.), *Focus on French as a foreign language: Multi-disciplinary approaches*, 191–209. Clevedon: Multilingual Matters.
Regan, Vera. 2010. Sociolinguistic competence, variation patterns and identity construction in L2 and multilingual speakers. *EUROSLA Yearbook* 10 (1). 21–37.
Rickford, John R., Isabelle Buchstaller, Thomas Wasow, Arnold Zwicky & Elizabeth Traugott. 2007. Intensive and quotative ALL. Something old, something new. *American Speech* 82 (1). 3–31.
Rickford, John R. & Mackenzie Price. 2013. Girlz II women: Age-grading, language change and stylistic variation. *Journal of Sociolinguistics* 17 (2). 143–179.
Ridner, Judith A. 2018. *The Scots Irish of early Pennsylvania*. Philadelphia: Philadelphia University Press.
Rietveld, Toni & Roeland van Hout. 2005. *Statistics in language research: Analysis of variance*. Berlin & New York: Mouton de Gruyter.
Rijke, Persijn M. de. 2016. *'[S]ince we came across the Atalantic': An empirical diachronic study of Northern Irish English phonology*. Bergen: University of Bergen dissertation.
Roberts, Julie. 1994. *Acquisition of variable rules: (-t,d) deletion and (ing) production in preschool children*. Philadelphia, PA: Institute for Research in Cognitive Science, IRCS Report 96–09.
Roberts, Julie. 1997. Hitting a moving target: Acquisition of sound change in progress by Philadelphia children. *Language Variation and Change* 9 (2). 249–266.

Roberts, Julie. 2004. Child language variation. In Jack K. Chambers, Peter Trudgill & Natalie Schilling-Estes (eds.), *The handbook of language variation and change*, 333–348. Oxford: Blackwell.
Roberts, Julie & William Labov. 1995. Learning to talk Philadelphian. *Language Variation and Change* 7. 101–122.
Roberts, Ian G. 1985. Agreement praramters and the development of English modal auxiliaries. *Natural Language and Linguistic Theory* 3. 21–57.
Roberts, Ian G. 1993. *Verbs and diachronic syntax*. Dordrecht: Kluwer.
Roberts, Ian G. 1995. Directionality and word order change in the history of English. In Ans van Kemenade & Nigel Vincent (eds.), *Parameters of morphosyntactic change*, 397–258. Cambridge: Cambridge University Press.
Robinson, Mairi (ed.). 1985. *The concise Scots dictionary (CSD)*. Edinburgh: Polygon.
Robinson, Philip. 1991. The use of the term 'clachan' in Ulster. *Ulster Folklife* 27 (1). 30–35.
Robinson, Philip. 1994. *The plantation of Ulster: British settlement in an Irish landscape, 1600–1670*. Belfast: Ulster Historical Foundation.
Robinson, Philip. 2006a. The mapping of Ulster-Scots. In Anne Smyth, Michael Montgomery & Philip Robinson (eds.), *The academic study of Ulster-Scots: Essays for and by Robert J. Gregg*, 3–18. Holywood, County Down: Ulster Folk & Transport Museum.
Robinson, Philip. 2006b. *Ulster-Scots: A grammar of the traditional written and spoken language*. Belfast: The Ullans Press.
Rodríguez Louro, Celeste. 2013. Quotatives down under: be like in cross-generational Australian English speech. *English World-Wide* 34. 48–76.
Rodríguez Louro, Celeste. 2016. Quotatives across time: Western Australian English then and now. In Heike Pichler (ed.), *Discourse-pragmatic variation and change in English: New methods and insights*, 139–159. Cambridge: Cambridge University Press.
Rogers, Rebecca, Meredith Labadie & Kathryn Pole. 2016. Balancing voice and protection in literacy studies with young children. *Journal of Childhood Literacy* 16 (1). 34–59.
Romaine, Suzanne. 1978. Post-vocalic /r/ in Scottish English: Sound change in progress. In Peter Trudgill (ed.), *Sociolinguistic patterns in British English*, 144–157. Baltimore: University Park Press.
Romaine, Suzanne. 1980. The relative clause marker in Scots English: Diffusion, complexity and style as dimensions of syntactic change. *Language in Society* 9. 221–249.
Romaine, Suzanne. 1981. Syntactic complexity, relativization and stylistic levels in Middle Scots. *Folia Linguistica Historica* 2. 56–77.
Romaine, Suzanne. 1982. *Socio-historical linguistics: Its status and methodology*. Cambridge: Cambridge University Press.
Romaine, Suzanne. 1984a. *The language of children and adolescents: The acquisition of communicative competence*. Oxford: Basil Blackwell.
Romaine, Suzanne. 1984b. Relative clauses in child language, pidgins and creoles. *Australian Journal of Linguistics* 4. 257–281.
Romaine, Suzanne. 1984c. Towards a typology of relative-clause formation strategies in Germanic. In Jacek Fisiak (ed.), *Historical syntax*, 437–470. Berlin & New York: Mouton de Gruyter.
Romaine, Suzanne. 1985. Syntactic variation and the acquisition of strategies of relativization in the language of Edinburgh school children. In Sven Jacobsen (ed.), *Papers from the third Scandinavian symposium on syntactic variation*, 19–33. Stockholm: Almqvist & Wiksell.
Romaine, Suzanne. 1988. *Pidgin and Creole languages*. London: Longman.
Romaine, Suzanne. 1989. *Bilingualism*. Oxford: Basil Blackwell.

Romaine, Suzanne. 1992. The evolution of complexity in a creole language: Acquisition of relative clauses in Tok Pisin. *Studies in Language* 16. 139–182.
Romaine, Suzanne. 1995. *Bilingualism* (2nd edn.). Oxford: Basil Blackwell.
Romaine, Suzanne & Deborah Lange 1991. The use of *like* as a marker of reported speech and thought: A case of grammaticalization in progress. *American Speech* 66 (3). 227–279.
Ronan, Patricia. 2005. The *after*-perfect in Irish English. In Markku Filppula, Juhani Klemola, Marjatta Palander & Esa Penttilä (eds.), *Dialects across borders: Selected papers from the 11th International Conference on methods in dialectology (Methods XI), Joensuu, August 2002*, 253–270. Amsterdam: John Benjamins.
Rossiter, Phyllis. 2006. *A living history of the Ozarks.* Gretna: Pelican Publishing Company.
Rothwell, William. 1998. Anglo-Norman at the (green)grocer's. *French Studies* LII (1). 1–16.
Ruben, Robert J. 1997. A time frame of critical/sensitive periods of language development. *Acta Oto-Laryngologica* 117 (2). 202–205.
Rusciano, Frank Louis. 2016. *World opinion and the Northern Ireland peace process.* Basingstoke: Palgrave Macmillan.
Russell, Bethany R., Alejandro Morales & Russell D. Ravert. 2015. Using children as informal interpreters in paediatric consultations. *International Journal of Human Rights in Healthcare* 8 (3). 132–143.
Russell, Paul. 1995. *An introduction to the Celtic languages.* London: Longman.
Russell, Paul. 2005. 'What was best of every language': The early history of the Irish language. In Dáibhí Ó Cróinín (ed.), *A new history of Ireland – Vol. I: Prehistoric and early Ireland*, 405–448. Oxford: Oxford University Press.
Russell, Raymond. 2011. *Migration in Northern Ireland: A demographic perspective (NIAR 246-11).* Belfast: Northern Ireland Assembly, Research and Information Service.
Russell, Raymond. 2012. *Migration in Northern Ireland: An update (NIAR 10-12).* Belfast: Northern Ireland Assembly, Research and Information Service.
Russell, Raymond. 2013. *Census 2011: Key statistics at assembly area level (NIAR 161-13).* Belfast: Northern Ireland Assembly, Research and Information Service.
Russell, Raymond. 2014. *Census 2011: Key statistics at LGD 2014 level (NIAR 296-14).* http://www.niassembly.gov.uk/globalassets/Documents/RaISe/Publications/2014/general/6014.pdf (accessed 12 March 2018).
Russell, Raymond. 2015. *Key statistics for settlements: Census 2011 (NIAR 99-15).* Belfast: Northern Ireland Assembly, Research and Information Service.
Russell, Raymond. 2016. *International migration in Northern Ireland: An update (NIAR 35-15).* Belfast: Northern Ireland Assembly, Research and Information Service.
Russell, Raymond. 2017. *International migration in Northern Ireland: An update (NIAR 56-17).* Belfast: Northern Ireland Assembly, Research and Information Service.
Rutter, Ben. 2014. The acquisition of newly emerging phonetic variation: /str-/ in American English. *Journal of Child Language* 41. 1166–1178.
Ryan, Sadie Durkacz. 2018. *Language, migration and identity at school: A sociolinguistic study with Polish adolescents in Glasgow.* Glasgow: University of Glasgow dissertation.
Sachdev, Itesh & Howard Giles. 2008. Bilingual accommodation. In Tej. K. Bhatia & William C. Ritchie (eds.), *The handbook of bilingualism*, 353–378. Oxford: Blackwell.
Saito, Kazuya & François-Xavier Brajot. 2013. Scrutinizing the role of length of residence and age of acquisition in the interlanguage pronunciation development of English /ɹ/ by late Japanese bilinguals. *Bilingualism: Language and Cognition* 16 (4). 847–863.
Salaberry, M. Rafael. 2001. The use of technology for second language learning and teaching: A retrospective. *The Modern Language Journal* 85 (1). 39–56.

Sanchez-Castro, Olga & Jeffrey Gil. 2009. Two perspectives on language maintenance: The Salvadorian community in Queensland and the Spanish community in South Australia. *International Journal of Language Society and Culture* 6 (3–5). 36–47.

Sánchez-Muñoz, Ana. 2007. Style variation in Spanish as a heritage language: A study of discourse particles in academic and non-academic registers. In Kim Potowski & Richard Cameron (eds.), *Spanish in contact: Policy, social and linguistic inquiries*, 153–172. Amsterdam: John Benjamins.

Sankoff, Gillian. 1980a. Above and beyond phonology in variable rules. In Gillian Sankoff (ed.), *The social life of language*, 81–94. Philadelphia: University of Pennsylvania Press.

Sankoff, Gillian (ed.). 1980b. *The social life of language*. Philadelphia: University of Pennsylvania Press.

Sankoff, Gillian. 1997. Deux champs sémantiques chez les anglophones et les francophones de Montréal [Two semantic fields among Anglophones and Francophones from Montreal]. In Julie Auger & Yvan Rose (eds.), *Exploration du lexique*, 133–146. Québec, Canada: CIRAL.

Sankoff, Gillian. 2001. Linguistic outcomes of language contact. In Jack K. Chambers, Peter Trudgill & Natalie Schilling-Estes (eds.), *The handbook of language variation and change*, 638–668. Oxford: Blackwell.

Sankoff, Gillian. 2013. Longitudinal studies. In Robert Bayley, Richard Cameron & Ceil Lucas (eds.), *The Oxford handbook of sociolinguistics*, 261–279. Oxford: Oxford University Press.

Sankoff, Gillian, Pierrette Thibault & Naomi Nagy [with Hélène Blondeau, Marie-Odile Fonollosa & Lucie Gagnon]. 1997. Variation in the use of discourse markers in a language contact situation. *Language Variation and Change* 9. 191–217.

Sankoff, Gillian & Hélène Blondeau. 2007. Language change across the lifespan: /r/ in Montreal French. *Language* 83. 560–588.

Sanz, Cristina. 2000. Bilingual education enhances third language acquisition: Evidence from Catalan. *Applied Psycholinguistics* 21. 23–44.

Sayers, Dave. 2012. Standardising Cornish: The politics of a new minority language. *Language Problems and Language Planning* 36 (2). 99–119.

Schaffer, Patricia. 2000. *Laws in Ireland for the suppression of Popery commonly known as the Penal Laws*. https://www.law.umn.edu/library/irishlaw (accessed 6 March 2018).

Schleef, Erik. 2017. Developmental sociolinguistics and the acquisition of t-glotalling by immigrant teenagers in London. In Gunter de Vogelaer & Matthias Katerbow (eds.), *Acquiring sociolinguistic variation*, 305–341. Amsterdam: John Benjamins.

Schleef, Erik, Miriam Meyerhoff & Lynn Clark. 2011. Teenagers' acquisition of variation: A comparison of locally born and migrant teens' realisation of English (ing). *English World-Wide* 32. 206–236.

Schmid, Monika S. 2002. *First language attrition, use and maintenance: The case of German Jews in Anglophone countries*. Amsterdam: John Benjamins.

Schmid, Monika S. 2013. First language attrition. Wiley Interdisciplinary Reviews. *Cognitive Science* 4 (2). 117–123

Schmid, Monika S. & Kees de Bot. 2008. Language attrition. In Alan Davies & Catherine Elder (eds.), *The handbook of applied linguistics*, 210–234. Oxford: Blackwell.

Schmid, Monika S., Kees de Bot & Barbara Köpke. 2013. Language attrition as a complex, nonlinear development. *International Journal of Bilingualism* 17 (6). 675–682.

Schmidt, Annette. 1985. *Young people's Dyirbal: An example of language death from Australia*. Cambridge: Cambridge University Press.

Schweinberger, Martin. 2012. The discourse marker *like* in Irish English. In Bettina Migge & Máire Ní Chiosáin (eds.), *New perspectives on Irish English*, 179–202. Amsterdam: John Benjamins.

Scontras, Gregory, Zuzanna Fuchs & Maria Polinsky. 2015. *Heritage language and linguistic theory*. https://www.frontiersin.org/articles/10.3389/fpsyg.2015.01545/full (accessed 23 May 2018).

Scott, Sheila. 2003. Second language acquisition of relative clauses in Irish. In Juana M. Liceras, Helmut Zobl & Helen Goodluck (eds.), *Sixth generative approaches to second language acquisition conference (GASLA 2002): L2 Links*, 260–268. Sommerville, MA: Cascadilla Proceedings Project.

Scovel, Thomas. 2000. A critical review of the critical period hypothesis. *Annual Review of Applied Linguistics* 20. 213–223.

Sebba, Mark. 2010. Discourses in transit. In Adam Jaworski & Crispin Thurlow (eds.), *Semiotic landscapes: Language, image, space*, 59–76. London: Continuum.

Sebba, Mark. 2018. Awkward questions: Language issues in the 2011 census. *Journal of Multilingual and Multicultural Development* 39 (2). 181–193.

Sebba, Mark. 2019. Named into being? Language questions and the politics of Scots in the 2011 census in Scotland. *Language Policy* 18. 339–362.

Seedhouse Paul (ed.). 2017. *Task-based language learning in a real-world digital environment: The European digital kitchen*. London: Bloomsbury.

Seliger, Herbert, W. 1989. Deterioration and creativity in childhood bilingualism. In Kenneth Hyltenstam & Loraine K. Obler (eds.), *Bilingualism across the lifespan*, 173–184. Cambridge: Cambridge University Press.

Seliger, Herbert W. & Robert M. Vago. 1991. The study of first language attrition: An overview. In Herbert W. Seliger & Robert M. Vago (eds.), *First language attrition*, 3–16. Cambridge: Cambridge University Press.

Selinker, Larry. 1992. *Rediscovering inter-language*. London: Longman.

Sharma, Devyani. 2005. Language transfer and discourse universals in Indian English article use. *Studies in Second Language Acquisition* 27 (4). 535–566.

Sharma, Devyani. 2014. Transnational flows, language variation, and ideology. In Marianne Hundt & Devyani Sharma (eds.), *English in the Indian diaspora*, 215–242. Amsterdam: John Benjamins.

Sharma, Devyani & Lavanya Sankaran. 2011. Cognitive and social forces in dialect shift: Gradual change in London Asian speech. *Language Variation and Change* 23 (1). 399–428.

Sharpe, Richard. 2000. The thriving of Dalriada. In Simon Taylor (ed.), *Kings, clerics and chronicles in Scotland 500-1297*, 47–61. Dublin: Four Courts Press.

Sharwood Smith, Michael. 1989. Crosslinguistic influence in language loss. In Kenneth Hyltenstam & Loraine K. Obler (eds.), *Bilingualism across the lifespan*, 185–201. Cambridge: Cambridge University Press.

Sharwood Smith, Michael & Eric E. Kellerman. 1986. *Crosslinguistic influence in second language acquisition*. New York: Pergamon Press.

Sharwood Smith, Michael & Paul van Buren. 1991. First language attrition and the parameter-setting model. In Herbert W. Seliger & Robert M. Vago (eds.), *First language attrition*, 17–30. Cambridge: Cambridge University Press.

Shnukal, Anna. 1982. You're getting somethink for nothing: Two phonological variables of Australian English. *Australian Journal of Linguistics* 2 (2). 197–212.

Shuy Roger, Walt Wolfram & William K. Riley. 1968. *Linguistic correlates of social stratification in Detroit speech*. Final report, Cooperative Research Project Number 6-1347. US Office of Education.

Siemund, Peter. 2013. *Varieties of English: A typological approach*. Cambridge: Cambridge University Press.

Sigley, Robert. 1997. The influence of formality and channel on relative pronoun choice in New Zealand English. *English Language and Linguistics* 1 (2). 207–232.
Simms-Williams, Patrick. 1998. The Celtic languages. In Anna Giacalone Ramat & Paolo Ramat (eds.), *The Indo-European languages*, 345–379. London: Routledge.
Silverstein, Michael. 2003. Indexical order and the dialectics of sociolinguistic life. *Language and Communication* 23 (1). 193–229.
Singler, John V. 1988. The homogeneity of the substrate as a factor in pidgin/creole genesis. *Language* 64 (1). 27–51.
Singleton, David. 2005. The critical period hypothesis: A coat of many colours. *International Review of Applied Linguistics in Language Teaching* 43 (4): 11–18.
Singleton, David. 2017. Language aptitude: Desirable trait or acquirable attribute? *Studies in Second Language Learning and Teaching* 7 (1). 89–103.
Skaaden, Hanne. 2005. First language attrition and linguistic creativity. *International Journal of Bilingualism* 9 (3–4). 435–452.
Skehan, Peter. 1989. *Individual differences in second language learning*. London: Routledge.
Skehan, Peter (ed.). 2014. *Processing perspectives on task performance*. Amsterdam: John Benjamins.
Smith, Alan. 1995. Education and the conflict in Northern Ireland. In Séamus Dunn (ed.), *Facets of the conflict in Northern Ireland*, 168–186. London: Palgrave Macmillan.
Smith, Brendan. 2013. *Crisis and survival in late medieval Ireland: The English of Louth and their neighbours, 1330–1450*. Oxford: Oxford University Press.
Smith, Jennifer & Mercedes Durham. 2019. *Sociolinguistic variation in children's language*. Cambridge: Cambridge University Press.
Smith, Jennifer, Mercedes Durham & Liane Fortune. 2007. "Mam, my trousers is fa'in doon!": Community, caregiver, and child in the acquisition of variation in a Scottish dialect. *Language Variation and Change* 19. 63–99.
Smith, Jennifer, Mercedes Durham & Liane Fortune. 2009. Universal and dialect-specific pathways of acquisition: Caregivers, children and t/d deletion. *Language Variation and Change* 21 (1). 69–95.
Smith, Jennifer, Mercedes Durham & Hazel Richards. 2013. The social and linguistic in the acquisition of sociolinguistic norms: Caregivers, children and variation. *Linguistics* 51 (2). 285–324.
Smith, Peter. 1995. *Oidhreacht Oirghiall: A bibliography of Irish literature and philology relating to the south-east of Ulster – north Leinster region*. Printed sources. Belfast: Iontaobhas Ultach.
Smith-Christmas, Cassie & Tadhg Ó hIfearnáin. 2015. Gaelic Scotland and Ireland: Issues of class and diglossia in an evolving social landscape. In Dick Smakman & Patrick Heinreich (eds.), *Globalising sociolinguistics: Challenging and expanding theory*, 256–269. London: Routledge.
Smyth, William J. 2000. Ireland a colony: Settlement implications of the revolution in military-administrative, urban and ecclesiastical structures, c.1550–1730. In Terry Barry (ed.), *A history of settlement in Ireland*, 158–186. London & New York: Routledge.
Smyth, William J. 2006. *Map-making, landscapes and memory: A geography of colonial and early modern Ireland c.1530–1750*. Cork: Cork University Press.
Snow, Catherine E. & Marian Hoefnagel-Höhle. 1977. Age differences in the pronunciation of foreign sounds. *Language and Speech* 20 (4). 357–365.
Snow, Catherine E. & Marian Hoefnagel-Höhle. 1979. Individual differences in second-language ability: A factor-analytic study. *Language and Speech* 22 (2). 151–162.

Soares, Anthony. 2002. *Relatório sobre trabalhadores portugueses na Irlanda do Norte*. Belfast: Multicultural Resource Centre.
Sommerfelt, Anders. 1929. South Armagh Irish. *Norsk Tidsskrift for Sprogvidenskap* 2 (1). 107–194.
Sorace, Antonella. 2005. Selective optionality in language development. In Leonie Cornips & Karen P. Corrigan (eds.), *Syntax and variation: Reconciling the biological and the social*, 55–80. Amsterdam: John Benjamins.
Sorace, Antonella. 2008. Near-nativeness. In Catherine J. Doughty & Michael H. Long (eds.), *The handbook of second language acquisition*, 130–151. Oxford: Blackwell Publishing.
Speelman, Dirk, Kris Heylen & Dirk Geeraerts (eds.). 2018. *Mixed-effects regression models in linguistics*. Berlin: Springer.
Spencer, Mark G. & David A. Wilson (eds.). 2006. *Ulster Presbyterians in the Atlantic world*. Dublin: Four Courts Press.
Spolsky, Bernard. 1988. Bilingualism. In Frederick J. Newmeyer (ed.), *Linguistics: Volume IV*, 100–118. Cambridge: Cambridge University Press.
Stack, Eddie. 2015. *Doolin: People, place and culture*. Galway: Tintaun Media.
Stam, Nike. 2017. A typology of code-switching in the commentary to the Félire Óengusso. Utrecht: Landelijke Onderzoekschool Taalwetenschap.
Stenson, Nancy. 1982. On short-term language change: Developments in Irish morphology. In Anders Ahlqvist (ed.), *Fifth international conference on historical linguistics*, 324–331. Amsterdam: John Benjamins.
Stenson, Nancy. 1990. Phrase structure congruence, government and Irish-English code-switching. In Randall Hendrick (ed.), *The syntax of the modern Celtic languages*, 167–200 (*Syntax and semantics* 23). San Diego: Academic Press.
Stenström, Anna-Brita. 2014. *Teenage talk: From general characteristics to the use of pragmatic markers in a contrastive perspective*. Houndmills, Basingstoke: Palgrave Macmillan.
Stockwell, Robert P. & C. Westbrook Barritt. 1951. *Some Old English graphemic-phonemic correspondences – aa, ea and a*. Washington, DC: Battenburg Press.
Stockwell, Robert P. & Donka Minkova. 1991. Subordination and word order change in the history of English. In Dieter Kastovsky (ed.), *Historical English syntax*, 367–408. Berlin & New York: Mouton de Gruyter.
Stout, Geraldine & Matthew Stout. 1997. Early landscapes: From prehistory to plantation. In F. H. A. Aalen, Kevin Whelan & Matthew Stout (eds.), *Atlas of the rural Irish landscape*, 31–63. Cork: Cork University Press, and Toronto: Toronto University Press.
Stout, Matthew. 2000. Early Christian Ireland: Settlement and environment. In Terry Barry (ed.), *A history of settlement in Ireland*, 81–109. London: Routledge.
Strang, Barbara. 1970. *A history of English*. London: Routledge.
Sussex, Roland & Paul Cubberley. 2009. *The Slavic languages*. Cambridge: Cambridge University Press.
Svašek, Maruška. 2009. Shared history? Polish migrant experiences and the politics of display in Northern Ireland. In Kathy Burrell (ed.), *Polish migration to the UK in the 'new' European Union*, 129–148. Farnham, Surrey: Ashgate Publishing Ltd.
Sweeney, Kevin. 1988. *The Irish language in Northern Ireland 1987: Preliminary report of a survey of knowledge, interest and ability*. Belfast: Department of Finance.
Swift, Roger. 1992. The historiography of the Irish in nineteenth-century Britain. In Patrick O'Sullivan (ed.), *The Irish world wide – Vol. 2: The Irish in the new communities*, 52–81. Leicester & London: Leicester University Press.
Szczegielniak, Adam. 2005. Two types of resumptove pronouns in Polish relative clauses. *Linguistic Variation Yearbook* 5. 165–185. Amsterdam: John Benjamins.

Tacchetti, Maddalena. 2013. *User guide for ELAN Linguistic Annotator version 4.1.0.* http://www.mpi.nl/corpus/manuals/manual-elan_ug.pdf (accessed 27 July 2019).
Tagliamonte, Sali A. 2002. Variation and change in the British relativizer system. In Patricia Poussa (ed.), *Relativisation on the North Sea Littoral*, 147–165. Munich: Lincom Europa.
Tagliamonte, Sali A. 2004a. Comparative sociolinguistics. In Jack K. Chambers, Peter Trudgill & Natalie Schilling-Estes (eds.), *The handbook of language variation and change*, 729–763. Oxford: Wiley-Blackwell.
Tagliamonte, Sali A. 2004b. Someth[in]'s go[ing] on! Variable -*ing* at ground zero. In Britt-Louise Gunnarsson, Lena Bergström, Gerd Eklund, Staffan Fidell, Lise H. Hansen, Angela Karstadt, Bengt Nordberg, Eva Sundergren & Mats Thelander (eds.), *Language variation in Europe: Papers from the Second International Conference on language variation in Europe: ICLAVE 2 Uppsala, Sweden, June 12–14, 2003*, 390–403. Uppsala: Uppsala University Department of Scandinavian Languages.
Tagliamonte, Sali A. 2006. *Analysing sociolinguistic variation*. Cambridge: Cambridge University Press.
Tagliamonte, Sali A. 2007. Representing real language: Consistency, trade-offs and thinking ahead! In Joan C. Beal, Karen P. Corrigan & Hermann L. Moisl (eds.), *Creating and digitising language corpora – Vol. 1: Synchronic databases*, 205–240. Houndmills, Basingstoke: Palgrave Macmillan.
Tagliamonte, Sali A. 2012. *Variationist sociolinguistics: Change, observation, interpretation*. Oxford: Wiley-Blackwell.
Tagliamonte, Sali A. 2016a. *Making waves: The story of variationist sociolinguistics*. Oxford: Wiley-Blackwell.
Tagliamonte, Sali A. 2016b. *Teen talk: The language of adolescents*. Cambridge: Cambridge University Press.
Tagliamonte, Sali A. 2018. Comparative sociolinguistics. In Jack K. Chambers & Natalie Schilling-Estes (eds.), *The handbook of language variation and change* (2nd edn.), 128–156. Oxford: Wiley-Blackwell.
Tagliamonte, Sali A. & R. Harald Baayen. 2012. Models, forests and trees of York English: *Was/were* variation as a case study for statistical practice. *Language Variation and Change* 24. 135–178.
Tagliamonte, Sali A. & Alexandra D'Arcy. 2004. *He's like, she's like*: The quotative system in Canadian youth. *Journal of Sociolinguistics* 8 (4). 493–514.
Tagliamonte, Sali A. & Alexandra D'Arcy. 2007. Frequency and variation in the community grammar: Tracking a new change through the generations. *Language Variation and Change* 19 (2). 199–217.
Tagliamonte, Sali A. & Alexandra D'Arcy. 2009. Peaks beyond phonology: Adolescence, incrementation and language change. *Language* 85 (1). 58–108.
Tagliamonte, Sali A., Alexandra D'Arcy & Celeste Rodríguez Louro. 2016. Outliers, impact, and rationalization in linguistic change. *Language* 92 (4). 824–849.
Tagliamonte, Sali A. & Derek Denis. 2014. Expanding the transmission/diffusion dichotomy: Evidence from Canada. *Language* 90 (1). 90–136.
Tagliamonte, Sali A. & Rachel Hudson. 1999. *Be like et al.* beyond America: the quotative system in British and Canadian youth. *Journal of Sociolinguistics* 3 (2). 147–172.
Tagliamonte, Sali A. & Sonja Molfenter. 2007. How'd you get that accent? Acquiring a second dialect of the same language. *Language in Society* 36 (5). 649–675.
Tagliamonte, Sali A., Jennifer Smith & Helen Lawrence. 2005. No taming the vernacular: Insights from the relatives in Northern Britain. *Language Variation and Change* 17. 75–112.

Tarallo, Fernando & John Myhill. 1983. Interference and natural language processing. *Language Learning* 33 (1). 55–76.
Tarone, Elaine. 1988. *Variation in interlanguage*. London: Edward Arnold.
Tarone, Elaine. 2007. Sociolinguistic approaches to second language acquisition research: 1997–2007. *The Modern Language Journal* 91. 837–848.
Taylor, Alan M. 2009. CALL-based versus paper-based glosses: Is there a difference in reading comprehension? *CALICO Journal* 27 (1). 147–160.
Taylor, Anne & Susan Pintzuk. 2012. Rethinking the OV/VO alternation in Old English: The effect of complexity, grammatical weight, and information status. In Terttu Nevalainen & Elizabeth Closs Traugott (eds.), *The Oxford handbook of the history of English*, 835–845. Oxford: Oxford University Press.
Taylor, Chris. 2017. The reliability of free school meal eligibility as a marker of socio-economic disadvantage: Evidence from the millennium cohort study in Wales. *British Journal of Educational Studies* 66 (1). 29–51.
Tennant, Victoria. 2000. *Sanctuary in a cell: The detention of asylum seekers in Northern Ireland*. Belfast: Law Centre (NI).
Ter Horst, Tom. 2017. *Code-switching in the Irish-Latin Leabhar Breac*. Utrecht: Landelijke Onderzoekschool Taalwetenschap.
The Portland Trust. 2007. *Economics in peacemaking: Lessons from Northern Ireland*. http://www.portlandtrust.org/sites/default/files/pubs/epm_northern_ireland.pdf (accessed 6 March 2018).
Thomas, Morgan D. 2005. Manufacturing industry in Belfast, Northern Ireland. *Annals of the Association of American Geographers* 46 (2). 175–196.
Thomason, Sarah Grey. 2001. *Language contact: An introduction*. Edinburgh: Edinburgh University Press.
Thomason, Sarah Grey. 2003. Contact as a source of language change. In Brian D. Joseph & Richard Janda (eds.), *The handbook of historical linguistics*, 687–712. Malden: Wiley-Blackwell.
Thomason, Sarah Grey. 2010. Contact explanations in linguistics. In Raymond Hickey (ed.), *The handbook of language contact,* 31–47. Malden: Wiley-Blackwell.
Thomason, Sarah Grey & Terrence Kaufman. 1988. *Language contact, creolization, and genetic linguistics*. Berkley, CA: University of California Press.
Thorburn, Jennifer & Karen P. Corrigan. 2015. "I sound Irish, like": Investigating the acquisition of local phonology by new migrants in Northern Ireland. Paper presented at NWAV 44, University of Toronto, 22–25 October.
Tier, Skate. 2014a. *Irish: Map showing the percentage of people aged 3+ who spoke Irish (Gaelic) in the 2011 census*. https://upload.wikimedia.org/wikipedia/commons/f/f6/Irish_speakers_in_2011.png (accessed 4 May 2018).
Tier, Skate. 2014b. *Ulster Scots: Map showing the percentage of people aged 3+ who spoke Ulster Scots in the 2011 census*. https://upload.wikimedia.org/wikipedia/commons/archive/d/de/20160228183144%21Ulster-Scots_speakers_in_the_2011_census_in_Northern_Ireland.png (accessed 15 March 2018).
Tier, Skate. 2014c. *Foreign languages: Map showing the percentage of people aged 3+ whose main language was other than English or Irish (Gaelic) in the 2011 census*. https://commons.wikimedia.org/wiki/File:Foreign_languages_in_northern_ireland.png (accessed 13 March 2018).
Tóth, Gergely. 2007. *Linguistic interference and first language attrition: German and Hungarian in the San Francisco Bay Area*. New York & Berlin: Peter Lang.

Tottie, Gunnel & Michel Rey. 1997. Relativization strategies in Earlier African American English. *Language Variation and Change* 9. 219–247.

Transinfo. 2016. *Newcomer pupils: Post-primary, Northern Ireland.* http://www.transinfo.co.uk/uploads/3/4/9/4/34947008/transinfo_pp_newcomer_2015_16.pdf (accessed 25 July 2019).

Traugott, Elizabeth Closs. 1972. *History of English syntax: A transformational approach to the history of English sentence structure.* New York: Holt, Rinehart and Winston.

Trevena, Paulina. 2013. Why do highly educated migrants go for low-skilled jobs? A case study of Polish graduates working in London. In Birgit Glorius, Izabela Grabowska-Lusinska & Aimee Kuvik (eds.), *Mobility in transition: Migration patterns after EU enlargement*, 169–191. IMISCOE Research, Rotterdam: Amsterdam University Press.

Trevena, Paulina. 2014. *Brain waste as threat to identity: Highly educated migrants in low-skilled jobs.* https://cream.conference-services.net/resources/952/2371/pdf/MECSC2011_0303_paper.pdf (accessed 8 March 2018).

Trousdale, Graham & David Adger (eds.). 2007. Theoretical accounts of dialect variation. [Special issue]. *Journal of English Language and Linguistics* 11 (2).

Trudgill, Peter. 1972. Sex, covert prestige and linguistic change in the urban British English of Norwich. *Language in Society* 1 (2). 179–195.

Trudgill, Peter. 1974. Linguistic change and diffusion: Description and explanation in sociolinguistic dialect geography. *Language in Society* 3 (2). 215–246.

Trudgill, Peter. 2006. *New dialect formation: The inevitability of colonial Englishes.* Edinburgh: Edinburgh University Press.

Truesdale, Sarah & Miriam Meyerhoff. 2015. Acquiring some *like*-ness to others. *Te Reo* 58. 3–28.

Turton, Danielle & Erik Schleef. 2016. Sociophonetic variation of *like* in British dialects: effects of function, context and predictability. *English Language and Linguistics* 22 (1). 35–75.

UNESCO. 2017. *Migration as a development challenge: Root causes and policy Implications.* http://unesdoc.unesco.org/images/0024/002470/247089E.pdf (accessed 11 May 2018)

UNESCO. 2018. *A lifeline to learning: Leveraging technology to support education for refugees.* http://unesdoc.unesco.org/images/0026/002612/261278e.pdf (accessed 31 May 2018).

UNHCR. 2016. *Connecting refugees.* http://www.unhcr.org/5770d43c4.pdf (accessed 30 May 2018).

Uylings, Harry B. M. 2006. Development of the human cortex and the concept of 'critical' or 'sensitive' periods. *Language Learning* 56. 59–90.

Vago, Robert M. 1991. Paradigmatic regularity in first language attrition. In Herbert W. Seliger & Robert M. Vago (eds.), *First language attrition*, 241–251. Cambridge: Cambridge University Press.

Vaughan, William E. & André Jude Fitzpatrick. 1978. *Irish historical statistics: Population, 1821–1971.* Dublin: Royal Irish Academy.

Verma, Mahendra K., Karen P. Corrigan & Sally Firth. 1992. The developing phonological system of Panjabi/Urdu speaking children learning English as a second language in Britain. In Jonathan Leather & James Allan (eds.), *New Sounds: Proceedings of the 1992 Symposium on the acquisition of second-language speech*, 174–199. Amsterdam: University of Amsterdam.

Vertovec, Steven. 2007. Super-diversity and its implications. *Ethnic and Racial Studies* 30 (6). 1024–1054.

Vertovec, Steven. 2014. *Superdiversity.* London: Routledge.

Visintin, Stefano, Kea Tijdens & Maarten van Klaveren. 2015. Skill mismatch among migrant workers: Evidence from a large multi-country dataset. *IZA Journal of Migration* 4 (1). 1–34.

Visser, Frederik Theodor. 1963–1973. *An historical syntax of the English language*, 4 Vols. Leiden: Brill.

Vogelaer, Gunther de, Jean-Pierre Chevrot, Matthias Katerbow & Aurélie Nardy. 2017. Bridging the gap between language acquisition and sociolinguistics. In Gunther de Vogelaer & Matthia Katerbow (eds.), *Acquiring sociolinguistic variation*, 1–42. Amsterdam: John Benjamins.

Vuuren, Sanne van & Rina de Vries. 2017. Common framework, local context, local anchors: How information-structural transfer can help to distinguish within CEFRC2. In Bettelou Los & Pieter de Haan (eds.), *Word order change in acquisition and language contact: Essays in honour of Ans van Kemenade,* 353–370. Amsterdam: John Benjamins.

Wagner, Heinrich. 1958. A linguistic atlas and survey of Irish dialects. *Lochlann* 1 (1). 9–48.

Wagner, Suzanne Evans. 2008. *Linguistic change and stabilisation in the transition from adolescence to adulthood*. Philadelphia: University of Pennsylvania dissertation.

Wagner, Suzanne Evans. 2012a. Real-time evidence for age grad(ing) in late adolescence. *Language Variation and Change* 24. 179–202.

Wagner, Suzanne Evans. 2012b. Age grading in sociolinguistic theory. *Language and Linguistics Compass* 6 (6). 371–382.

Warden, Alex J. 2013. *The linen trade: Ancient and modern*. London: Routledge.

Warm, David D. 1998. The Jews of Northern Ireland. In Paul Hainsworth (ed.), *Divided society: Ethnic minorities and racism in Northern Ireland,* 222–239. London: Pluto Press.

Warner, Anthony. 1993. *English auxiliaries: Structure and history*. Cambridge: Cambridge University Press.

Warschauer, Mark. 2002. Languages.com: The internet and linguistic pluralism. In Ilana Snyder (ed.), *Silicon literacies*, 62–74. London & New York: Routledge.

Watt, Dominic & Lesley Milroy. 1999. Patterns of variation and change in three Newcastle vowels: Is this dialect levelling? In Paul Foulkes & Gerard J. Docherty (eds.), *Urban voices: Accent studies in the British Isles*, 25–46. London: Arnold.

Watts, Emma L. 2005. *Mobility-induced dialect contact: A sociolinguistic investigation of speech variation in Wilmslow, Cheshire*. Essex: University of Essex dissertation.

Webb, James. 2009. *Born fighting: How the Scotch-Irish shaped America*. Edinburgh: Mainstream Publishing.

Wei, Li. 2013. Codeswitching. In Robert Bayley, Richard Cameron & Ceil Lucas (eds.), *Oxford handbook of sociolinguistics,* 360–378. Oxford: Oxford University Press.

Wei, Li. 2018. Translanguaging as a practical theory of language. *Applied Linguistics* 39 (1). 9–30.

Weinreich, Uriel. 1953. *Languages in contact*. The Hague: Mouton.

Weinreich, Uriel, William Labov & Marvin Herzog. 1968. Empirical foundations for a theory of language change. In Winfred P. Lehmann & Yakov Malkiel (eds.), *Directions for historical linguistics: A symposium*, 97–195. Austin: University of Texas Press.

Wells, John C. 1982. *Accents of English 2: The British Isles*. Cambridge: Cambridge University Press.

Wheeler, James Scott. 1999. *Cromwell in Ireland*. Dublin: Gill & Macmillan.

Whelan, Kevin. 1996. *The tree of Liberty*. Cork: Mercier Press.

Whelan, Kevin. 1997. Towns and villages. In F. H. A. Aalen, Kevin Whelan & Matthew Stout (eds.), *Atlas of the rural Irish landscape*, 180–196. Cork & Toronto: Cork University Press & Toronto University Press.

Whelan, Kevin. 2000. Settlement and society in eighteenth century Ireland. In Terry Barry (ed.), *A history of settlement in Ireland,* 187–205. London: Routledge.

Williams, Jane (ed.). 2006. *Our lives: The second world war and its legacy in the Northwest and Causeway regions*. Coleraine: Causeway Museum Service & Derry City Council Heritage and Museum Service.

White, Timothy J. (ed.). 2013. *Lessons from the Northern Ireland peace process*. Madison, WI: University of Wisconsin Press.

Wiechman, Daniel. 2015. *Understanding relative clauses*. Berlin & Boston: De Gruyter Mouton.
Wihtol de Wenden, Catherine. 2016. New migrations. *SUR 23: International Journal on Human Rights* 13 (23): 17–28.
Wittenburg, Peter, Hennie Brugman, Albert Russel, Alex Klassmann & Han Sloetjes. 2006. *ELAN: A professional framework for mutlimodality research*. Paper presented at the *Fifth International Conference on Language Resources and Evaluation,* University of Genoa, 22–28 May. http://www.lrec-conf.org/proceedings/lrec2006/ (accessed 27 July 2019).
Wode, Henning. 1977. Four early stages in the development of L1 negation. *Journal of Child Language* 4 (1). 87–102.
Wode, Henning. 1980. Grammatical intonation in child language. In Linda R. Waugh & Dwight Le Morton Bolinger (eds.), *The melody of language*, 331–345. Pennsylvania: University Park Press.
Wode, Henning. 1981. Language-acquisitional universals. *Native Language and Foreign Language Acquisition* 379 (1). 218–234.
Wölck, Wolfgang. 2004. Universals of language maintenance, shift and change. *Collegium Antropologicum* 28 (1). 5–12.
Wolf, Hans-Georg. 2012. A cognitive sociolinguistic approach to the lexicon of Cameroon English and other World Englishes. In Eric A. Anchimbe (ed.), *Language contact in a postcolonial setting,* 63–76. *Language Contact and Bilingualism* 4. Berlin & Boston: De Gruyter Mouton.
Wolfram, Walt. 1985. Variability in tense marking: A case for the obvious. *Language Learning* 35. 229–253.
Wolfram, Walt. 2013. The contact dynamics of socio-ethnic varieties in North America. In Daniel Schreier & Marianne Hundt (eds.), *English as a contact language,* 131–148. Cambridge: Cambridge University Press.
Wolfram, Walt & Donna Christian. 1976. *Appalachian speech*. Washington, DC: Centre for Applied Linguistics.
Wolfram, Walt, Jeffrey Reaser & Charlotte Vaughan. 2008. Operationalising linguistic gratuity: From principle to practice. *Language and Linguistics Compass* 2 (6). 1109–1134.
Wright, Sue (ed.). 2004. Multilingualism on the Internet. *International Journal on Multicultural Societies* 6 (1). https://wayback.archive-it.org/10611/20171126024258/http://www.unesco.org/new/en/social-and-human-sciences/resources/periodicals/diversities/past-issues/vol-6-no-1-2004/ (accessed 30 May 2018).
Xu, Yi. 2014. Evidence of the accessibility hierarchy in relative clauses in Chinese as a second language. *Language and Linguistics* 15 (3). 435–564.
Yang, Guobin. 2003. The Internet and the rise of a transnational Chinese cultural sphere. *Media, Culture and Society* 25 (1). 469–549.
Yelland, Gregory W., Jacinta Pollard & Anthony Mercuri. 1993. The metalinguistic benefits of limited contact with a second language. *Applied Psycholinguistics* 14 (4). 423–444.
Young, Richard. 1991. *Variation in inter-language morphology*. New York: Peter Lang.
Zwickl, Simone. 2002. *Language attitudes, ethnic identity and dialect use across the Northern Ireland border: Armagh and Monaghan*. Belfast: Cló Ollscoil na Banríona.

Language index

Albanian 88
Anglo-Norman 25–31, 34
Arabic 12, 88, 126, 201

Baltic (see also Lithuanian) 216, 289, 320
    East ~ 205, 229, 232, 236
Balto-Slavic (see also Lithuanian, Polish) 237, 238, 251, 252, 278, 289–292, 304, 316, 317, 322
Bengali 88, 202
Brythonic 22
    Breton 22, 138
    Cornish 22
    Welsh 22, 31
Bulgarian 88

Cambodian 220, 225
Cantonese 75, 87, 88, 129, 202
Celtiberian 21
Celtic (see also Brythonic, Celtiberian, Gaelic, Galatian, Goedelic, Irish, Lepontic, Manx Gaelic, Old Irish, Ulster Irish) 21–23, 27, 278
    ~ varieties 21–23
Chiltiupan Pipil 133
Chinese (see also Cantonese, Haka, Hokkien, Mandarin, Teochew) 88, 112, 126, 139, 142, 143, 161, 175, 179, 183, 184
Czech 88

Dutch (see also West Germanic) 12, 13, 131, 138, 142, 165
Dyirbal 133

English (see also West Germanic)
    African-American Vernacular ~ (AAVE) 274, 282, 316
    American ~ 9, 15, 214, 225, 274, 280, 308, 320
        Scotch-Irish American ~ 320
    Appalachian ~ 272
    Armagh ~ 10, 211, 216, 226, 227, 234, 236–238, 244, 246, 249, 253, 255, 256, 272, 276, 288, 292–295, 307, 311, 316, 318, 319, 321, 327
        South ~ 144, 276

Belfast ~ 144, 247, 274
British ~ 205, 218, 237, 244, 246, 255, 259, 308
Californian ~ 133, 274, 275
Canadian ~ 259, 275, 304
Derry ~ 181, 248
Early Modern English (EModE) 44, 239–241, 278
Indian ~ (see also South African Indian English) 12, 238, 245, 246, 274, 275
Italian ~ 138
Irish English (IE) (see also Northern Irish English, Southern Irish-English/Hiberno-English) VII, 7, 12, 31, 51, 100, 105, 109, 120, 124, 131, 137–139, 143, 144, 147, 157, 159, 161, 163, 166, 168, 214, 215, 218, 230, 234, 236, 238, 244, 246–249, 253, 262, 278, 279, 283, 284, 293, 299, 305, 308
Lingua Franca ~ 128
London ~ 263, 266, 275, 297, 305
    Multicultural ~ (MLE) 234, 263, 266, 275, 297, 305, 315
Manchester ~ 205
Middle (Medieval) ~ 173, 211, 212, 240–242, 245, 275–277
Newcomer ~ 215, 249, 253, 301, 311, 312, 317
New Zealand ~ 246, 273, 274, 276, 308
Northern Irish ~ (NIE) 3, 7, 12, 100, 105, 109, 120, 124, 144, 147, 157, 159, 161, 163, 166, 168, 230, 246–249, 253, 278
    Mid-Ulster English (M-UE) VII, VIII, 42, 79, 159, 168, 181, 187, 200, 202, 203, 208, 209, 210, 221, 229, 230, 233, 237, 247, 254, 256, 258–262, 265–266, 268, 270, 273, 275, 279, 283–288, 291, 292, 294–297, 300, 301, 306–310, 312, 316–318, 320
South Ulster English 41, 79, 173, 247, 249, 277, 278, 317
Ulster English 15

https://doi.org/10.1515/9783110614190-012

Ulster Scots 41, 79–81, 90, 91, 95–101, 111, 112, 221, 237, 247, 248, 254, 255, 262, 265, 320
North Western (NWE) ~ 257, 259, 261, 262
Old ~ (Anglo-Saxon) 100, 211, 212, 239–242, 275–277, 315
Ottawa ~ 300, 304, 307, 308
Quebec ~ 245 257, 261, 262
Scottish (Scots) ~ 9, 36, 42, 47, 60, 124, 166, 230, 242, 245, 308, 320
    Edinburgh English 205, 218–220, 230, 300–304, 318
    Lowland Scots 257, 262
    Older Scots 41, 44
Sheffield ~ 246, 257
Somerset ~ 245
South African Indian ~ (*see also* Indian English) 238, 245, 246
Southern Irish/Hiberno- ~ 75, 173, 262, 283, 284, 300, 309, 310, 318
    Dublin English 143, 205, 229, 284, 297, 300–310, 313, 322
    Western Irish English 143, 144
Standard ~ 148, 164, 165, 172, 190, 207, 208, 221, 238, 244, 246, 249, 258
Swahili ~ 131
Toronto ~ 138, 257, 259, 260, 261, 262, 264, 265
Tyneside (and Northumbrian) ~ 165, 218, 246, 257
(West) Australian (Vernacular) ~ 51, 133, 274, 277

Farsi 88
Finnish 142
French 31, 32, 34, 88, 137, 142, 143, 173, 241, 249, 302
    Norman ~ 31, 32, 34, 173

Gaelic (*see also* Celtic, Irish, Manx Gaelic, Old Irish, Scots/Scottish Gaelic, Ulster Irish) 31, 32, 47, 48, 76, 124, 173–176, 179, 183–185
Galatian 21
Gaulish 21
Georgian 196
German (*see also* West Germanic) 125, 140, 141, 142, 201

Goedelic (*see also* Celtic, Irish, Manx Gaelic, Old Irish, Scottish Gaelic, Ulster Irish) 22

Haka 88
Hebrew 132, 142
Hindi 12, 87, 88, 200, 201, 283
Hokkien 129
Hungarian 88, 101, 125, 175, 179, 183

Irish (*see also* Celtic, Manx Gaelic, Old Irish, Scottish Gaelic, Ulster Irish) 6, 9, 22–25, 31, 40, 43, 46, 48, 60–62, 75–78, 80, 81, 84, 90–101, 104, 108, 111, 112, 118, 123, 124, 136–139, 142–144, 161, 173, 174, 175, 179, 181, 183–187, 196–198, 201, 208, 214, 215, 234, 238, 240, 249, 278
Italian 141, 185, 202

Japanese 139, 142, 143

Korean 139, 143

Latin 22–24, 30–32, 124, 132, 173, 211, 315, 316
    Hiberno-~ 24
Latvian 85, 88, 101, 114, 174, 175
Lepontic 21
Lithuanian (*see also* Baltic, Balto-Slavic) VIII, X, 88, 101, 105, 110–112, 114, 116, 127, 134, 135, 152, 174, 179, 180, 183, 184, 185, 189, 194, 202, 203, 206, 207, 215–217, 219, 227–230, 232–237, 249–252, 254, 256, 258–260, 265, 282, 288–295, 297, 299, 301–303, 305–307, 309, 311–313, 317–322

Malay 112, 129
Malayalam 12, 85, 101, 111, 174, 175, 179, 183, 200, 201, 202
Mandarin 88, 129
Manx Gaelic (*see also* Celtic, Gaelic, Goedelic) 22

Old Irish (*see also* Celtic, Gaelic, Goedelic) 22–25, 31, 124, 173, 315
Old Norse 24, 25

Polish (*see also* Balto-Slavic, Slavic) VIII, X, 88, 91, 101, 105–108, 112–115, 117, 126,

127, 134, 139, 144, 147, 148, 153, 155–158, 174, 175, 179, 180, 183, 185, 189, 198, 202, 203, 205–207, 214, 215, 217–220, 224–237, 249–252, 254–256, 258–260, 263, 265, 282, 288–298, 301–313, 318–322
Portuguese 86, 88, 101, 104, 105, 112, 114, 116, 117, 174, 175, 179, 180, 183–185, 189

Romanian 88, 101
Russian 85, 88, 101, 106, 107, 112, 138, 141, 174, 175, 180, 183, 196, 202, 252, 326

Scottish Gaelic (*see also* Celtic, Goedelic, Irish, Manx Gaelic, Old Irish, Ulster Irish) 22, 32
 East Sutherland ~ 132, 133
Sign Language
 American ~ 159
 British ~ 101
 Irish ~ 101
Singlish 129
Slavic (*see also* Polish) 205, 217, 229, 232, 236, 289, 303, 320
 South ~ 217
 West ~ 205, 217, 229, 232, 236, 303
Slovak 88, 101, 112, 134, 175, 180, 183, 202

Somali 12, 13, 88
Spanish 88, 118, 132, 133, 140–142, 150, 151, 160,
Swedish 140, 142, 151, 160

Tagalog/Filipino 10, 101, 111, 112, 153, 154, 158, 175, 179, 183, 184, 202, 204, 325
Tamil 201
Telugu 85, 185, 201, 202
Teochew 129
Tetum 88, 114
Thai 88, 126, 199
Turkish 141

Ukrainian 88, 138
Ullans 80
Ulster Irish/Gaelic (*see also* Celtic, Gaelic, Goedelic, Irish) 31, 32, 61, 75, 77, 279
Urdu 88

Vietnamese 220, 225

West Germanic (*see also* Dutch, English, German) 41, 43

Yoruba 185, 202

Subject index

A8/A2
    ~ countries 83, 86, 87, 90, 101, 128
    ~ populations 90, 102
accent 11, 110, 155, 156, 186, 224
    (Northern) Irish ~ 11, 155
adequation 153, 154, 325
adolescent (*see also* teenager) 128, 162–167, 190, 204, 210, 220, 225–227, 237, 253, 269, 281, 282, 297, 299, 300, 327
    post-~ 162, 164
    pre-~ 151, 166, 220, 257, 259, 266, 270, 275, 282, 297, 322
age of arrival (AoA) 125, 150, 151, 167, 198, 204, 206, 224, 227, 283
Age of Enlightenment 20, 49, 50, 60, 178
Aitken's Law 42
allochthonous 17, 19, 29, 31, 35, 51, 53, 60, 64, 70, 80, 82, 84, 89, 91, 107, 114, 120, 124, 144, 170, 176, 184, 185, 188, 196, 199, 226, 229, 236, 245, 252, 254, 256, 260, 261, 263, 265, 267, 269, 271, 273, 283, 292, 293, 297, 299, 302, 304, 322, 323, 326
America(n) IX, 9, 44, 67, 324, 325
    Chicano/Mexican ~ 281
    Irish ~ (*see also* Scotch-Irish) 67
    Latin ~ 82
    Polish ~ 139
    North ~ 7, 9, 18, 49, 54, 58, 59, 68, 70, 214, 221, 272
    South ~ 7
Anglophone 125, 138, 147, 163, 166, 248, 272, 273, 302
Antipodes 7, 272
Armagh/*Ard Mhacha* 4–6, 10–12, 22–24, 30–33, 35, 36, 40, 42–44, 46, 47, 49–51, 53, 55, 57, 60–62, 71, 73, 75–78, 87, 89, 94, 101, 103, 104, 106–109, 111, 113, 116, 117, 126, 127, 135, 136, 147–150, 152–157, 162, 168–179, 181, 183–192, 196, 200, 202
Armenian 16
asylum 4, 71, 72, 75, 83, 84, 86, 102
autochthonous 17, 29–31, 38, 47 , 49, 51, 53, 64–66, 80, 83, 91, 101, 107, 109, 112, 118, 120, 123, 144, 153, 174, 176, 181, 183, 187, 188, 199, 200, 205, 218, 226, 229, 236, 252, 254, 260, 262, 265, 267, 269, 271, 283, 292, 293, 297, 299, 302, 304, 307

Bangladesh(i) 71, 82
Belfast 18, 42, 51, 52, 54, 55, 57, 61, 66, 67, 70–74, 78, 80, 82, 87, 89, 91, 92, 97, 100, 103, 104, 111, 113, 117, 168–170, 172, 176, 179–185, 188, 189, 191–195, 200–202, 209, 248, 259, 275, 279, 282, 285–287, 292, 297, 298, 315
    ~/Good Friday Agreement 79, 83, 90–92, 112
bilingual(ism) (*see also* monoglot, monolingual(ism), multilingual(ism) plurilingual(ism), translanguaging) 13, 23, 34, 48, 60, 76, 77, 85, 94, 113, 119, 123–125, 128–134, 136–139, 142, 143, 145, 149, 151, 155, 159–161, 193, 205, 240, 249, 252, 263, 267, 283, 288, 302, 318, 319, 323
Black African 82, 83
blow-in 273, 274, 279, 284, 287, 298, 301, 307, 320
Britain (*see also* United Kingdom) 12, 13, 15, 50, 58, 59, 70, 245, 278, 280, 315
British 12, 17, 29, 34, 36, 37, 39, 40, 44–46, 48, 50, 51, 53, 54, 58–60, 64, 70, 166, 197, 219
    ~ Isles 23, 25, 102, 205, 210, 234, 253, 258, 259, 272, 304, 315, 316
Bronze Age 21, 22, 176
Bulgaria(n) 83, 88, 101, 103

Case Accessibility Hierarchy (CAH) 143, 242
Celtic 21–23, 27, 315
change
    discourse-pragmatic 138, 148, 156, 205, 272, 284, 288, 289, 292, 293, 316, 323
    external 49, 119
    generational ~ 162, 163
    grammatical ~ VIII, 132, 136, 210, 273, 316
    ~ in progress 162, 163, 204, 210, 297

internal 49, 119, 120, 238, 316
linguistic ~ X, 9, 19, 31, 35, 40, 49, 60,
    101, 119, 161–163, 179–181, 203, 211,
    286, 317
morpho-syntactic ~ 133, 136, 163, 204,
    209
phonological ~ 132, 138, 210
retrograde ~ 162, 163
social ~ 3, 49, 55, 146, 161, 162, 280, 327
variation and ~ VIII, 119, 128, 161, 162,
    168, 181, 204, 209, 283, 284, 287,
    316, 317, 319, 323, 327
China 75, 84, 85, 103
Chinese IX, 74, 75, 81–84, 105, 108, 112, 113,
    129, 151, 184, 229
colonial 15, 19, 26, 29, 30, 51, 52, 86
    post-~ 12, 278
colonisation 19, 28, 31, 32, 34, 37, 39, 176
Common European Framework of Reference
    for Languages (CEFR) 117, 193, 196, 201,
    304, 322
community of practice 151, 152, 153, 154, 155,
    184, 191, 204, 215, 269, 270, 323, 325
Conradh na Gaeilge 'the Gaelic League' 92
constraint 131, 137, 147–150, 158–160, 164–
    168, 204, 205, 207, 219, 220, 223–227,
    230–237, 248, 252, 253, 256, 260–265,
    267, 271–273, 279–281, 283, 284, 292,
    293, 295, 304–314, 317–323, 327
    external ~ VIII, 148, 150, 158–160, 164,
        220, 248, 254, 272, 273, 279, 283,
        284, 310
    ~ hierarchy 234–236, 302, 303, 304, 307,
        308, 309, 313, 320
    internal ~ VIII, 148, 150, 159, 160, 164,
        219, 248, 253, 254, 260, 267, 271,
        272, 273, 279, 280, 304, 322, 323
    ~ ranking 149, 220, 314
conditioning 165, 207, 220, 221, 224, 225,
    235, 236, 238, 249, 264, 267, 270, 272,
    273, 279, 294, 304, 307, 308, 310–313,
    316, 319, 321, 322
Corpora VII, IX, 20, 41, 43, 91, 125, 131, 143,
    144, 151, 229, 231, 232, 235, 238, 246,
    252, 257–260, 262–264, 277, 278, 281,
    282, 286, 289, 291
    Bergen Corpus of London Teenage Lan-
        guage (COLT) 190

Corpus of Irish-English Correspondence
    (CORIECOR) VII, 7, 64, 68, 72
Corpus Oral de Lenguaje Adolescente de
    Madrid (COLA) 190
Diachronic Electronic Corpus of Tyneside
    English 257
Phonological Variation and Change Corpus
    (PVC) 257, 258
Empire Corpus 278, 281, 285, 286, 292,
    293, 297, 298
Helsinki Corpus 240
International Corpus of English 214, 278
    (SP)ICE-Ireland 278, 284, 287
Michael J. Murphy Corpus 43, 76
Múin Béarla Corpus 106, 107, 120, 138,
    140, 145, 159, 162, 168, 189, 191, 193,
    195–197, 199–203, 206, 214, 244,
    253–256, 263, 281, 296, 323, 326
Northern Ireland Transcribed Corpus of
    Speech (NITCS) 248, 262, 268
Nua-Chorpus na hÉireann 279
Spokes Corpus 292, 302
Survey of English Dialects 262
Survey of Sheffield Usage 257
Tape-Recorded Survey of Hiberno-English
    Speech 262, 309
Toronto English Corpus 211, 257, 265
Critical Period (Hypothesis) 159–162, 167, 204
crossing (see also passing) 128, 190, 323
Czech Republic 101, 103

Dál Riada 32
demolinguistic(s) X, 101, 119, 125, 168, 175,
    179, 190, 198, 200
Department of Education for Northern Ireland
    (DENI) 84, 85, 87, 89, 91, 101, 118, 169,
    170, 173, 186, 187, 201
dialect
    ~ acquisition 9, 124, 136, 144, 159, 203,
        205, 209, 229, 282, 216, 319
    ~ contact/mixing (see also linguistic
        contact) 38, 48
    eye ~ 139
    regional ~ 9, 28, 80, 81, 89, 97, 144, 170,
        174, 189, 242, 245, 248, 249, 251,
        259, 280–282
    ~ shift 9, 13, 137, 244, 261

~ zone/region 41–47, 159, 163, 169, 188, 203, 311, 316
diaspora/diasporic VII, 16, 20, 86, 118, 126, 324, 325
diglossia 23, 31, 125
discourse 96, 129, 131, 136, 138, 141, 142, 147, 148, 156, 158, 166, 198, 205, 226, 233, 234, 238, 244, 248, 263, 272–274, 276, 278, 284, 288, 289, 291–294, 296, 299–303, 309, 313, 314, 316, 323
  ~ features 166, 263, 284, 299
  ~ (pragmatic) marker (DPM) 147, 198, 226, 233, 234, 272, 273, 275, 276, 288, 289, 301, 309, 313
  ~ (pragmatic) particle 129, 272, 291
  ~ pragmatic(s) 136, 138, 149, 156, 205, 289, 292, 293, 316, 323
distinction 153, 325, 326
Donaghmore XI, 43, 134, 135, 156, 157, 168, 170, 172, 176–180, 183–185, 188, 189, 200, 203, 247, 282
Dublin 24, 25, 36, 50, 65, 143, 149, 150, 170, 196, 205, 229, 236, 283, 284, 297, 300, 301, 303–305, 307–310, 318
Dutch-Somali/Somali-Dutch 9, 12, 19, 44
dyad(ic) (*see also* triad) 4, 107, 158, 190, 257

Edinburgh 149, 150, 205, 218–220, 224, 225, 228–232, 234, 300, 301, 303, 304, 318
Emain Macha/eo-muin Macha 22, 23
emigrant (*see also* immigrant, migrant) 4, 7, 58, 64, 70, 324
  ~ correspondence (*see also* CORIECOR) 235
  ~ nursery 118
emigration (*see also* immigration, migration) IX, 17, 20, 35, 52, 54, 57, 58, 61–63, 67, 73, 84, 86, 118, 119, 315
entrenchment/entrenched 151, 158, 160
Estonia 101
ethnic(ity) 9, 13, 16, 17, 25, 30, 35, 36, 38, 45, 46, 49, 53, 72–74, 80–83, 86, 87, 89, 101, 102, 104, 105, 112, 118, 120, 124, 128, 151, 153–155, 158, 174, 181, 183, 190, 191, 196, 199, 216, 221, 223, 228, 248, 264, 280–282
  ~ cleansing 16, 17, 25, 30, 38, 49, 73
  ~ differences 158, 183, 281

~ discrimination 72, 112
~ groups 9, 13, 16, 35, 36, 53, 73, 74, 81–83, 105, 112, 155, 221, 223, 281
~ identification/identities 81, 82, 151, 154, 223
~ majority 80–83, 101, 105, 112, 181, 221
~ minority 72, 73, 80–83, 86, 87, 89, 101, 102, 105, 174, 181, 196
ethno
  ~graphic 146, 147, 152, 156, 161, 323
  ~linguistic VIII, IX, 5, 19, 40, 44, 49, 60, 100, 105–107, 112, 120, 128, 137, 147, 198, 222, 223, 227, 230, 232, 236, 254, 256, 258, 260, 267, 282, 283, 295, 303, 310, 326
    ~ groups 44, 49, 105, 107, 112, 128, 147, 232, 256
  ~religious 16
Europe(an) 3–5, 12, 21, 23, 24, 58, 59, 70, 71, 80, 81, 83, 84, 100–102, 126, 179, 193, 198, 246, 249, 252, 281, 282, 304, 318, 324, 326
  Central ~ 83
  Continental ~ 12, 21, 23, 59
  Eastern ~ 71, 83, 102, 198
  ~ Union (EU) 6, 83, 84, 86, 88, 114, 119, 174–176, 178, 180, 185

Foras na Gaeilge 'Foundation for Irish' 91, 95
founder 31, 247, 249
  ~ population 31, 247, 249
  ~ principle 31

Gael Linn IX, 196
Gaeltacht(aí) 46, 60, 61, 75, 77–79, 81, 184, 279
Gender (*see also* sex) 5, 102, 111, 128, 133, 151, 158, 163, 188, 189, 198–200, 202, 211, 216, 221–223, 225, 230, 232, 248–250, 254, 257, 267–271, 280, 281, 295, 310, 321
Georgian 15, 196
German(y) 11, 51, 70, 72, 85, 87, 103, 141, 142, 201
Glasgow 7, 59
global VIII, 4, 17, 50, 56, 84, 90, 118, 147, 172, 176, 178, 181, 212, 215, 221, 222, 225, 238,

244, 254, 269, 272, 277, 279, 280, 283, 301, 305, 307–309, 315
globalisation 64, 118, 120
Great
~ Depression 68
~ Famine 4, 7, 12, 16, 20, 28, 49, 55, 56, 57, 58, 59, 61, 62, 66, 178, 181, 234, 315, 316, 325
~ War 67
Hungary 101, 103
hyperlocal (*see also* local) 272, 283, 286, 288, 293, 297, 305, 309, 314, 316, 318, 319, 321

identity 9, 40, 51, 80, 118–120, 128, 129, 146, 151, 152, 155, 157, 186, 189, 191, 196, 271, 282, 314, 321, 323, 324, 326
immigrant (*see also* emigrant, migrant) 5, 16, 19, 51, 72, 7883, 105, 119, 123, 133, 150, 155, 167, 172, 196, 204, 223, 232, 234, 236, 238, 319, 324
anti-~ 326
immigration (*see also* emigration, migration) VII, 16, 19, 20, 70, 78, 81, 83, 84, 102, 178
~ kindergarten 119
incrementation 160, 161, 300
indexical 147, 236
India(n) 10–12, 71, 81–83, 85, 87, 200, 238, 245, 246, 274, 275
indigenous (*see also* native) 3, 19–21, 25, 26, 44, 60, 65, 81–83, 104, 105, 107, 133, 161, 178, 189, 209, 219, 220, 223, 225, 227, 253, 256, 265, 266, 289, 293, 297, 300, 305, 307–309
ING-variable VIII, 139, 144, 148, 163, 165, 166, 197, 205, 209–236, 238, 249, 252, 256, 271, 276, 316, 320–322
Iran 84
Irish
~ monoglot(tism) 60, 62, 75, 77, 123
~ nationalism 54, 80
~ Raj 72
~ settlements 5, 14, 15, 19–23, 25, 27, 34, 35, 38, 39, 41, 42, 44, 46, 47, 50, 51, 55, 59, 78, 87, 89, 170, 172, 173, 175–179, 183–185, 316
~ speakers 9, 61, 75, 78, 111, 278
~ traveller population 81, 82
Iron Age 21, 22

Jew(ish) 16, 17, 51, 70–72, 74, 81, 82, 102, 125, 133, 196

language
~ acquisition VII, X, 118, 123–128, 137, 140–146, 149–151, 158–160, 164, 166, 210, 215, 220, 252, 311–314, 316, 319, 323, 327
~ attrition 123–125, 130–136
~ contact VII, 3, 9, 31, 60, 120, 123, 125, 132, 133, 136–138, 214, 215, 247, 249, 314, 319
~ ecology X, 20, 21, 31, 32, 35, 49–51, 61, 64, 75, 90, 183, 188
first ~ (L1) VII, VIII, 12, 91, 118, 123–125, 130–134, 136–142, 144–146, 148, 149, 151, 153, 155, 160, 167, 198, 204, 205, 207, 215, 219, 220, 225–227, 231, 236–238, 244, 249, 251, 252, 263, 269, 282, 297, 302–304, 306–314, 316–319, 323, 327
~ groups 3, 16, 61, 112, 147, 207, 220, 256, 266, 269, 310–313
heritage ~ 88, 100, 114, 115, 123, 124, 126, 132, 134, 138, 147, 152, 200
~ interference 136–139, 142, 144, 145, 215, 288
~ maintenance 13, 104, 105, 114, 118, 126, 196, 315
native ~ 124, 136, 142, 143, 161, 196
~ practices 3, 126, 128, 190
~ revitalisation 90, 91–99
second ~ (L2) VII, VIII, 22, 77, 78, 104, 123–125, 129–132, 136–143, 145, 147–152, 155, 156, 158–160, 166, 193, 210, 215, 220, 224–227, 238, 244, 249, 252, 258, 265, 268, 269, 272, 273, 282, 288, 292, 295, 297, 303–307, 310–314, 316, 318–323, 327
~ shift VII, 22, 62, 125, 133, 136–139, 145, 244, 317, 320, 327
~ switching 32, 131, 134, 288
~ transfer 139, 140, 256, 278, 292, 316
~ variation 119, 128, 168, 181, 323
Latvia 85, 88, 101, 107, 112, 114, 128, 174, 175, 180, 183, 202
Length of residence (LoR) 150, 167, 204, 216, 224, 227, 232, 233, 255, 321, 322
Lingua Franca(e) 31, 105, 123, 315, 316

Subject index — **393**

linguistic
~ consequences VII, 3, 20, 31, 53, 58, 94, 104, 153, 170, 315
~ contact (*see also* dialect contact) 20, 29, 249, 266
~ diversity 19, 60, 95, 112, 119, 161, 175, 258
~ ecology 20, 31, 35
~ effects 16, 125, 267, 310
~ environment 31, 100, 124, 130, 145, 150, 161, 190, 219, 308, 327
~ gratuity 186
~ heterogeneity 16, 31, 75
~ landscape 91, 100, 112
Lithuania(n) 5, 71, 85, 87, 101, 103, 106, 108, 112, 114, 116, 127, 128, 139, 147–149, 184, 190, 196, 205, 214, 215, 218, 225, 228, 229, 230–236, 256, 258–260, 282, 288, 292, 294, 295, 299, 301–303, 305–307, 309, 311–313, 319, 320–322
Liverpool 7–9, 59
local(s) (*see also* hyperlocal) VII, VIII, 15, 23, 39, 43, 51, 57, 73, 74, 75, 81, 84, 87, 89, 95, 100, 101, 103, 104, 105, 114, 116, 128, 146–151, 153–156, 161, 164, 167, 168, 172, 176, 178, 186, 187, 191, 196, 198, 199, 203, 204, 207, 210, 215, 218, 220, 224, 225, 227, 229, 230–232, 234–238, 248, 254–256, 258–261, 263, 264, 266, 268–270, 272–274, 280, 283, 297–305, 307–313, 316, 318, 320–322, 324–327
Local Government District (LGD) 87, 89, 101, 103, 104, 168, 174, 177
London XI, 11, 14, 37, 59, 66, 67, 181, 190, 203, 205, 218, 219, 224, 225, 229–232, 234, 235, 249, 257, 260–263, 266, 270, 274, 275, 281, 297, 305, 315, 324, 325, 327

Manchester 12, 56, 59, 205, 218, 220, 224, 225, 229–232, 235, 315
Māori 281, 282, 303, 305
Mellon Centre for Migration Studies (MCMS) IX
Mesolithic period VII, 19, 21, 173
metalinguistic awareness 133, 158, 159
migrant (*see also* emigrant, immigrant) VII, VIII, XI, 3–7, 9, 10, 12, 13, 15, 16, 19, 25, 31, 35, 44, 51, 58, 59, 64, 68, 70–73, 75, 78, 81–87, 89, 100, 102–107, 109, 114, 115, 117–120, 123, 125, 126, 128–130, 133, 134, 140, 144, 147–151, 155, 167, 168, 170, 172, 174, 180, 181, 183, 184, 189, 196, 204, 205, 218, 220, 223–227, 229, 232, 234–236, 244, 249, 253, 270–272, 281, 283, 288, 292, 304, 305, 308, 309, 313, 316, 318, 319, 321, 323, 324, 326, 327
mediatized ~ 126
migration (*see also* emigration, immigration) VII, IX, 1, 3–5, 7, 9, 11–13, 15–24, 28, 29, 35, 38, 44, 49–55, 57–59, 61–64, 67, 70–75, 78, 81–84, 86, 87, 90, 91, 102, 103, 118–121, 125, 128, 172, 178, 185, 186, 234, 315, 320
bridgehead 13, 15, 16, 58, 82, 184
chain ~ 12–15, 19, 44, 58, 103
economic ~ 3, 16–19, 72, 73, 83, 86, 103, 119, 181, 183, 315
external ~ 4–7, 20, 31, 44, 49, 50, 55, 61, 119, 271
forced ~ 16–18, 38, 50, 51, 53, 57, 72
internal ~ 4–7, 10, 20, 44, 49, 50, 55, 60, 61, 64–81, 119, 181, 271
international ~ 4, 5, 82, 85, 119
linear ~ 7–11
permanent ~ 5, 19
return ~ 5, 70, 80–83, 117, 118, 189
seasonal ~ 5
stepwise ~ 7–12, 86, 128, 315
transnational ~ 3, 4, 7, 10, 64–80, 105, 119, 327
voluntary ~ 4, 16–18, 35
monoglot (*see also* bilingual(ism), monolingual(ism), multilingual(ism), plurilingual(ism), translanguaging) 60, 62, 75, 77, 123, 149
monolingual(ism) (*see also* bilingual(ism), monoglot, multilingual(ism), plurilingual(ism), translanguaging) 40, 76, 123–125, 136, 138, 145, 146, 151, 252, 267, 323
morphophonology 236, 316
mother tongue 12, 53, 104, 105, 125, 126, 151
multilingual(ism) (*see also* bilingual(ism), monoglot, monolingual(ism), plurilingual(ism), translanguaging) IX, 86, 105, 114, 123, 124, 126, 128, 146, 152, 156, 186

multivariate 196, 198, 199, 203, 205–207, 255, 256, 258, 266, 267, 269, 272, 273, 292, 296, 304, 306, 309–312, 314, 319
~ analyses 196, 198, 199, 203, 205, 206, 255, 258, 272, 296, 304, 306, 309, 311, 312, 314
independent ~ 304, 306, 311, 312

native(ness) (*see also* indigenous) 9, 22, 44, 47, 49, 76, 80, 82, 97, 99, 109, 124, 132, 136, 138–140, 142, 143, 146–150, 152, 156, 158, 159, 161, 164, 166, 196, 198, 203, 205, 209, 214, 219, 220, 225, 226, 230, 232, 234, 236, 256, 266–270, 279, 282, 283, 298, 308, 313, 322, 324, 325
Newcastle 59
newcomer 13, 71, 75, 84, 85, 88, 89, 91, 107, 118, 120, 128, 145, 152, 153, 155, 162, 166–168, 174, 185–189, 192, 196–200, 203–205, 210, 215, 216, 218, 220, 224, 229, 230, 233, 235, 237, 249, 253–266, 268–271, 273, 287, 293, 295, 297–299, 301–307, 309, 311, 312, 316–319, 321–324, 326, 327
new speaker 3, 78, 100, 137, 138, 316
Nigeria 84
North America 7, 9, 15, 18, 49, 54, 58, 59, 67, 68, 70, 214, 221, 259, 272
North East England 266
Northern Ireland (NI) VII, IX–XI, 3, 5–7, 11, 20, 27, 32, 35, 39, 41, 44–47, 56, 61, 62, 66, 70, 72–75, 78, 80–84, 86–88, 90–96, 98–109, 111–119, 124, 127, 128, 135, 136, 145, 151–153, 155–159, 161, 163, 168, 172–176, 178–181, 183–188, 192, 193, 195, 196, 199, 201, 210, 213, 216–218, 221, 224, 225, 237, 248, 254, 255, 262, 268, 316, 324–327
~ Assembly IX, 92, 94, 96, 100, 326
~ census 45–47, 71, 74, 75, 78–84, 87, 91–95, 98–104, 111, 119, 174–185, 188, 201
~ Council for Ethnic Minorities (NICEM) 87
~ population VII, 3, 45, 56, 73, 74, 78–87, 90, 92, 101, 102, 112, 118, 124, 172–183, 188, 205, 224, 327
~ Statistics and Research Agency (NISRA) 55, 81–84, 87, 89, 90, 92, 95, 98, 99, 101, 103, 112, 172, 176, 201

North West England 247, 257

observer's paradox 168, 190
Orior/Orrier 30, 60–62, 75
Ottawa 66, 236, 253, 300–302, 304, 307, 308, 310

Pākehā 281, 304
Pakistan(i) 71, 82
passing (*see also* crossing) 129, 152, 196, 324, 325
Peace (process) 78, 83, 95
Penal Law(s) 17, 18, 52, 65
plantation 19, 21, 28–30, 34–40, 43–45, 173, 249
~ schemes 34–48, 173
~ settlement 19, 29, 35, 38, 39, 44
plurilingual(ism) (*see also* bilingual(ism), monoglot, monolingual(ism), multilingual(ism), translanguaging) 3, 11, 106, 128, 131, 315
pogrom 16, 102
Poland 71, 84, 85, 87, 101, 103, 117, 128, 139, 157, 158, 178, 228
Polish 17, 83, 87, 88, 105, 107, 108, 112, 113, 117, 126, 127, 139, 147, 148, 149, 153, 174, 205–207, 214, 215, 218, 220, 225, 228, 229, 230, 231–237, 252, 254, 255, 256, 258–260, 263, 282, 288, 294, 295, 296, 297, 298, 299, 301–311, 313, 318–322
Portugal 86, 103
Portuguese 82, 88, 104, 105, 112, 174, 179, 184
pre-pubescent 160, 165
Presbyterian 17, 19, 44, 50, 53, 54, 60, 80, 174
prestige 112, 164, 201, 225, 266, 268, 321
overt ~ 164
proficiency 112, 124, 125, 151, 158, 159, 167, 193, 198, 204, 224, 283, 288, 295, 303–305, 307, 308, 310, 311, 314, 321, 322
progressive 147, 151, 212, 214, 219, 226, 233–235, 317, 320
Protestant(ism) 18, 29, 40, 41, 45, 46, 53, 55, 65, 70, 72, 73, 80, 181, 183, 222, 223, 248, 325

Quebec 245, 249, 257, 260–262
quotation VIII, 29, 129, 272–274, 279–281, 283, 289, 293, 295, 308, 314–320, 322

quotative 163, 204, 272–276, 278–305, 309–311, 318, 320–323
~ introducer 280, 289–294, 296, 298, 300, 302, 304, 310, 311, 318, 320, 323
~ marker 274, 279, 284, 287, 291, 298, 301, 302
~ system 272, 273, 278–284, 286–288, 291, 293, 298, 300–302, 304, 305, 309, 311, 318, 321, 322
BE LIKE 163, 166, 205, 209, 236, 270–274, 279–289, 293–313, 320
go 274, 278–287, 296–303, 318
here+be+speaker 274, 286, 288, 289, 291, 297, 320
non-canoncial ~ 289, 290, 292, 296, 320
particle 290, 291
say 274–280, 284–287, 290–305, 309, 311, 318
think/thought 274, 276, 284, 286, 287, 299, 301–303
zero 274, 279, 284–287, 293–305, 309, 318

re-allocation 137, 149, 310
re-analysis 137
recession 84, 90, 178, 180
refugee 9, 17, 40, 72, 75, 83, 84, 86, 90, 102, 125, 126, 128, 133, 315
register (see also style) 99, 128, 132, 243
relative VIII, 143, 144, 164, 209, 211, 237–239, 241–271, 293, 316–318, 320–322
contact ~ 241
copy ~ 239, 250
indeclinable ~ 241, 242
~ marker VIII, 239, 241, 243–245, 248, 254–256, 259, 261, 262, 264, 266, 268–270
non-restrictive ~ (NRR) 238, 243, 248, 250, 251, 253, 254
~ omission 238, 241–243
~ paradigm 237, 238, 241, 244, 247, 252, 253, 258, 261, 263, 265, 266, 271
~ particle 241, 242
~ pronoun 143, 209, 238, 242, 244, 246, 250–252, 257, 259, 263–265, 267–269, 321

restrictive ~ (RR) 238, 243, 248, 250, 251, 253, 254, 265, 267, 268
subject ~ 243, 247, 248, 252, 254, 258, 260–269
subjectless ~ 241, 242, 254, 262, 265–270
subordinating ~ 239, 241, 243, 244, 247, 249, 251
TH- 238, 241–245, 247, 249, 250, 254, 256, 257, 260–262, 264, 268, 269
WH- 238, 241–245, 247–251, 254, 256–258, 260–262, 265–268
zero/Ø 207, 233, 218, 238, 241–249, 254, 256, 258, 260–262, 264–270, 274, 279, 282, 284–287, 291, 293, 294, 296, 298, 300, 301, 303–309, 318
relativisation 140, 166, 181, 237, 238, 242, 246, 252, 253, 266, 276, 310, 314, 318, 320
~ strategy 140, 237, 242, 266
~ system 238, 320
relativiser 254, 262, 263, 265, 266, 269, 318, 321, 322
relic(t) 75, 78, 211, 244, 273
re-ordering 149, 220, 223, 310
Republic of Ireland 5, 24, 25, 41, 49, 83, 91–93, 102, 103, 119, 155, 170, 174, 175, 177, 185, 283
restructuring 211, 272, 319, 321
resumptive pronoun 143, 144, 240, 244, 246, 247, 249, 263
(Roman) Catholic 17–19, 23, 29, 31, 34, 35, 40, 47, 49–55, 60, 64–66, 70–73, 80, 81, 116, 132, 170, 174, 178, 181, 183, 186–188, 222, 223, 230, 325
Romania(n) 83, 84, 88, 101, 103, 140
Russia(n) 16, 71, 85, 88, 101, 106, 107, 112, 138, 141, 165, 174, 175, 180, 183, 196, 202, 252, 326

school 5, 6, 14, 65, 68, 82, 84, 85, 87, 89, 91, 101, 107, 118, 129, 135, 145, 153, 154, 156, 161, 162, 165, 168–170, 178, 179, 184, 186–191, 193, 194, 196, 198–201, 203, 205, 209, 210, 216, 223, 224, 231, 246, 269, 287, 297, 309, 325
Bunscoil 78

  Catholic maintained ~ 116, 186
  hedge ~ 65
  Irish Medium (Unit) 78, 91, 92, 108, 173,
   174, 179, 184, 186, 187, 197
  Meánscoil 78
  non-selective ~ 187, 188, 224
  post-primary ~ 91, 116, 162, 170, 173,
   179, 184, 186–189, 193, 200
  primary ~ 78, 84, 89, 161, 162, 174, 179,
   186–189, 193, 194, 200
  Saturday ~ 115–117, 156, 157
Scotch-Irish (*see also* Irish American) 54, 58,
 61, 320
Scotland IX, 23, 25, 27, 28, 32, 34, 35, 53, 69,
 81, 150, 190, 224, 247, 320
Scottish Vowel Length Rule (SVLR) 42, 43
sex (*see also* gender) 133, 146, 200, 206, 221,
 222, 225, 227, 228, 233, 235, 266–270,
 281, 282, 311, 321
Sheffield 246, 257
Slovakia 85, 101, 112, 134
Slovenia 101
social
  ~ class 146, 158, 164, 221, 224
  ~ groups 9, 17, 36, 81, 161, 191
  ~ networks 19, 53, 60, 115, 125, 151, 172,
   190, 221, 280, 323
sociolinguistic competence 145–147, 167, 204,
 205, 323
Somalia 12, 13, 84
stabilization 160
stable variable 164, 210, 266, 320, 321
status 9, 17, 18, 31, 34, 51, 60, 80–82, 96, 97,
 101, 102, 105, 125, 158, 164, 170, 176, 188,
 189, 191, 201, 224, 230, 242, 244
  socio-economic 17, 18, 51, 52, 55, 56, 82,
   83, 158, 164, 184, 187–189, 315
Statutes of Kilkenny 29
Stormont X
stress 41, 148, 210, 219, 274
style (*see also* register) 9, 11, 29, 34, 51, 75,
 128, 132, 164, 165, 172, 221–223, 225,
 230, 243
substrate/substratal 144, 151, 238, 273, 302,
 314, 317, 318
Sudan 84
superdiverse/superdiversity 3, 20, 81, 91, 100,
 102, 203, 249, 315

syntax 139, 204, 205, 237, 289, 313, 316
Syria 84
teenager (*see also* adolescent) 74, 117, 144,
 149, 150, 152, 153, 162, 167, 193, 194, 201,
 204, 205, 209, 215, 219, 222, 225, 226,
 232, 234, 235, 252, 256, 262, 269, 278,
 284, 300, 309, 318–320, 322, 327
Thai IX, 62, 88, 99, 100, 126, 199
The Pale 16, 25, 26, 29, 34, 144
The Troubles 67, 73, 74, 78, 83, 90, 316
Toronto 64, 138, 163, 211, 257, 259–262, 264,
 265, 267
transformation under transfer 149, 236, 272,
 319, 320
translanguaging IX, 3, 123, 128, 129, 200
triad (*see also* dyad) 155, 158, 190
Tyneside 165, 218, 246, 257
Tyrone 15, 18, 34, 36, 40, 43, 46, 48, 52, 60,
 68, 75, 114, 154, 176–178, 228

Ulaid 22, 25
Ulster VII, 4, 6, 15–43, 46, 49–64, 70, 72,
 75–81, 87–91, 95–101, 111, 112, 118, 123–
 125, 132, 136, 161, 168, 169, 173, 177, 197,
 221, 237, 247–249, 254, 255, 262, 265,
 277–279, 283, 317, 320, 327
Ulster-Scots Academy 99
Unionism 73
Unionist 68, 70, 94, 97
United Kingdom (UK) (*see also* Britain) X, 5, 6,
 9–13, 83, 72, 75, 80, 83, 84, 86, 102, 119,
 128, 174, 175, 185–187, 224, 247, 258
United States (of America) (USA) (*see also*
 America) 7, 13, 56, 57, 85, 87, 103, 125,
 132, 150, 199, 282, 315

variable VIII, 124, 146, 148, 150, 163–166, 172,
 181, 197, 203–211, 214, 215, 218, 220–224,
 226, 227, 230, 232, 234, 236, 248, 252,
 254, 259, 262, 265–267, 270–272, 279,
 282, 292–294, 296, 300, 302, 303, 308,
 310, 311, 313, 317, 319–324
  ~ context 208, 254, 300, 302
  ~ grammar 218, 234, 279, 318
  dependent ~ VII, XIII, 206, 224, 236, 271,
   294, 317, 322
  independent ~ 206, 224, 232, 236, 271,
   294, 322
  linguistic ~ 146, 163, 208

morphosyntactic ~ 148, 165, 172, 204,
      209, 252
  social ~ 124
  sociolinguistic ~ 270
  socio-phonetic ~ 181
  socio-syntactic ~ 181
  stable ~ VIII, 164, 209, 210, 221, 223,
      257, 266, 270, 272, 317, 320, 321
variation(ist) X, 31, 32, 119, 128, 139, 144–
    146, 148–150, 155, 158–168, 180, 181, 193,
    197, 203–205, 207–209, 218–221, 223,
    227, 231, 236, 238, 242, 245, 252–254,
    263, 266, 267, 269, 272, 273, 275, 278,
    279, 281, 283, 284, 287, 295, 302, 305,
    310, 316, 317, 319, 322, 323, 327, 328
  ~ and change VIII, 119, 128, 161, 162, 168,
      181, 204, 209, 283, 284, 287, 316,
      317, 319, 323, 327
  discourse-pragmatic ~ 136, 138, 148,
      156, 205, 272, 284, 288, 289, 292,
      293, 316, 323
  morphosyntactic ~ 165, 204, 209, 252

phonological ~ 139, 148, 163, 165, 206–
    208, 210, 227, 233, 236, 249, 316
sociolinguistic ~ 148, 150, 158, 162, 163,
    166, 167, 180, 204, 236
vernacular 9, 15, 23, 31, 32, 97, 98, 100, 146–
    149, 161–163, 189–191, 205, 210, 214,
    220, 221, 234, 237, 238, 244, 246, 248,
    251, 253, 257–259, 265, 266, 273–276,
    279–281, 283, 284, 287, 291–293, 297,
    304, 308, 309, 312, 316, 319, 323
  ~ universal 148, 210, 312
Vietnamese Boat People 74
Viking 24, 173, 316

War of Independence 54, 66, 67
Wave 82, 118, 120, 128, 145, 146, 151, 272,
    323, 328
  Fourth ~ 145, 146, 323, 327
  Second ~ 146
  Third ~ 128, 146, 151

Zimbabwe 84

www.ingramcontent.com/pod-product-compliance
Lightning Source LLC
Chambersburg PA
CBHW052042220426
43663CB00012B/2412